The Litigation Paralegal

A Systems Approach

The Litigation Paralegal

A Systems Approach

Second Edition

James W. H. McCord, J.D.
Eastern Kentucky University

West Publishing Company
St. Paul   New York   Los Angeles   San Francisco

Copyedit: Joan Torkildson
Design: John Rokusek
Cover: Kristen M. Weber
Art: Rolin Graphics
Composition: The Clarinda Company
Production, prepress, printing, and binding by West Publishing Company

WEST'S COMMITMENT TO THE ENVIRONMENT
In 1906, West Publishing Company began recycling materials left over from the production of books. This began a tradition of efficient and responsible use of resources. Today, up to 95 percent of our legal books and 70 percent of our college texts are printed on recycled, acid-free stock. West also recycles nearly 22 million pounds of scrap paper annually—the equivalent of 181,717 trees. Since the 1960s, West has devised ways to capture and recycle waste inks, solvents, oils, and vapors created in the printing process. We also recycle plastics of all kinds, wood, glass, corrugated cardboard, and batteries, and have eliminated the use of styrofoam book packaging. We at West are proud of the longevity and the scope of our commitment to the environment.

Photo credits
Pages **1, 72, 113** Richard Anderson; **48** Stock Boston, © John Coletti; **191** © 1984 James Mansfield; **323, 360, 393** Richard Anderson; **464** Stock Boston, © Jim Pickerell.

COPYRIGHT ©1988   By WEST PUBLISHING COMPANY
COPYRIGHT ©1992   By WEST PUBLISHING COMPANY
                    610 Opperman Drive
                    P.O. Box 64526
                    St. Paul, MN   55164-0526

Printed in the United States of America

99 98 97 96 95 94 93   8 7 6 5 4 3 2

Library of Congress Cataloging-in-Publication Data

McCord, James W. H.
    The litigation paralegal : a systems approach / James W.H. McCord.
  —2nd ed.
      p.   cm.   — (West's paralegal series)
    ISBN 0-314-93370-0 (hard)
    1. Civil procedure—United States.   I. Title.   II. Series.
  KF8841.M39 1992
  347.73′5—dc20
  [347.3075]   91-35789
                                                                CIP

To my parents
Marks W. and Hazel C. McCord
with love and admiration

Contents

Preface

The Litigation Paralegal: A Systems Approach, 2nd Edition is guided by the same idea as the first edition: that paralegal students and faculty need a learning resource written specifically for them, a resource combining the theories and principles of law with practical paralegal skills, paralegal ethics, and a sensitivity toward the goals and needs of the paralegal profession, all in the context of the law office.

I have made a sincere effort to improve on the usefulness and quality of the first edition by implementing numerous suggestions from educators and students. Some changes have been made simply to reflect changes in the law or in legal procedures. Others incorporate things that I was not able to include in the first edition. This second edition contains expanded discussions on jurisdiction and venue, ethics, and alternative dispute resolution. The appendices on torts, contracts, and the Model Rules of Professional Conduct are new. This edition includes more reference tables and more tips from experienced paralegals; many assignments have been added or revised as experience and suggestions dictated.

It is also exciting to be able to provide a substantially expanded instructor's manual and a thorough and challenging student workbook to accompany this second edition of the text. These supplementary materials have been coauthored with my wife, Sandy, and it is our hope that they will greatly enhance the teaching and learning of litigation skills.

A Course Plan

The text, instructor's manual, and student workbook form a course plan consisting of substantive text, exercises in paralegal skills (competencies), a variety of classroom activities, assignments, review questions, tests, and answer keys. The approach of the text places the student in a law office setting where the instructor assumes the role of the paralegal's supervising attorney. This office training procedure uses a systems approach in which the student develops a litigation system folder complete with forms, documents, checklists, rules, and practice tips. The system will be complete by the end of the course and should provide the student with a valuable resource.

The text, instructor's manual, and workbook are flexible and have been designed to accommodate approaches other than a systems approach.

The System Folder

Use of the system can be a valuable process in both teaching and learning litigation paralegal skills. Because a good system folder will help the student on the job and maybe even in securing a job, the system folder should provide an extra incentive to do the assignments thoroughly and accurately. It will help the student learn the benefits of being organized and develop the confidence to create a system in any area of law. Utilization of the systems approach will also reinforce the skills presented in the text.

The Text

The Litigation Paralegal: A Systems Approach introduces students to the law office and takes them through the steps and tasks involved in litigation chronologically, from the facts of the cases they will be working on to judgment enforcement. Chapter by chapter they will build proficiency in the specific tasks or competencies that will be required of them as paralegals.

In each chapter the student will be given the following:

1. One or more specific litigation tasks,
2. Substantive and procedural background on the task,
3. Guidelines and directions on how to perform the task,
4. Examples from a sample case on how to perform the task,
5. Assignments, to develop an understanding of procedures and to perform the task in the context of one or more of the other provided cases, and
6. Study guide questions to review and reinforce learning.

The Workbook

The workbook supplements the text by providing the following for each chapter:

1. Chapter objectives
2. Chapter outline
3. Key terms to define
4. Learning exercises that mix text assignments with additional problems and practice tasks in a chronological development of the chapter and its objectives. Space and format are provided to facilitate the completion of assignments.
5. Review questions and answers that provide students with the means to test their understanding of the material in the chapter. This section includes fill-in-the-blank, true/false, multiple-choice, and short answer questions.

The Expanded Instructor's Manual

For each chapter this manual provides:

1. Chapter objectives
2. Suggestions for instructional supplements
3. Suggestions for class activities
4. Chapter outline
5. Key terms to define (definitions appear within the chapters as well as in the glossary)
6. Learning exercises and suggested answers or approaches
7. Chapter tests and answers. These are a combination of objective questions, short-answer questions, essay questions, and take-home projects.

In addition, test material can easily be drawn from the study guide questions at the end of each text chapter and from the review questions in the workbook.

Computer Assignments, Computerized System Folder, and WESTEST

A number of assignments in the text and workbook are either specifically labelled computer assignments or can be easily performed as computer assignments. Assignments such as document drafting, form creation, research, deposition summaries, timekeeping, billing, data storage, and damage calculations can be computerized. The entire system folder could be done on computer, allowing students to leave the course with their own system diskettes.

The test bank for this text is now computerized on the time-saving WESTEST, available from West Publishing free of charge to instructors using this text.

Acknowledgments

The following persons deserve considerable credit for making this second edition possible: above all my wife Sandra Lee McCord who worked tirelessly on this edition as well as the first, my son Quinten for his patience and his help, all those educators and students who shared their ideas and concerns, those who kindly allowed us to reprint needed material, and West's editors including Elizabeth Hannan, Laura Evans, and Patricia Bryant. I continue to be ever grateful to those whose influence on the first edition carries over into the second edition: William Statsky, Susan Tubb, Christian Bryant Clark, Janice Warm, Carol Wilson, Leslie Whitmer, Allyn Gilespie, Michael Eubanks and his litigation students, Eastern Kentucky University and my colleagues and secretaries in the Department of Government, The National Association of Legal Assistants, The National Federation of Paralegal Associations, and the members of the original advisory committee for this text including Jill Brown Burton, Patrick R. Hugg, Joel Schuler, and Lea Nordlicht-Shedd.

I also want to express my appreciation to those attorneys and educators who carefully reviewed the first edition and commented on how it could be improved: David Dye, Missouri Western State; Allen Gordon, Oakland University in Michigan; Jill E. Martin, Quinnipiac College; Margaret T. Stopp, University of West Florida; and those reviewers who chose to remain unnamed.

James W. H. McCord

The Litigation Paralegal

A Systems Approach

1

Prologue

- ■ Introduction
  - ■ Case I
  - ■ Case II
  - ■ Case III
  - ■ Case IV
  - ■ Case V

■ Introduction

The following cases are typical of the kinds of circumstances that spawn litigation. They are real in the sense that there are hundreds of cases just like these, involving human pain and deeply felt emotions.

In the chapters to come, paralegal tasks will be presented in the context of one or more of these cases. Case I, the *Forrester* case, will be the text's

What are the likely sources of litigation in a fast-paced world?

main reference. Some of the other cases will be used for task assignments. The remaining cases are included to give you a feel for other kinds of litigation and to provide your instructor with some flexibility in choosing a case for instructional purposes. The cases will also be used to place you in as realistic a law office setting as a textbook can create.

In each chapter you will be given:

1. One or more specific litigation tasks,
2. Substantive and procedural background on each task,
3. Guidelines and directions on how to perform the task,
4. Examples from a sample case on how to perform the task, and
5. Assignments to do the task in the context of the provided case or an alternative case.

Should your instructor choose to use the system development approach to this course, one of your continuous assignments will be to construct a paralegal's litigation system folder. A system folder is a detailed procedure manual that provides direction, forms, and checklists for tasks regularly performed by a paralegal. As a personal resource it provides advantages in efficiency, uniformity, accuracy, and quality. It can also be easily updated. Use of the system can be a valuable process for learning paralegal skills. Because a good system folder will help you on the job, and perhaps in securing a job, the system folder should provide an extra incentive to do the assignments thoroughly and accurately. It will help you learn the benefits of being organized and develop the confidence to create a system in any area of law. Regular use of the system approach will help reinforce the individual litigation skills presented in the text.

■ Case I

Forrester v. Hart and Mercury Parcel Service, Inc.

On her way to work Tuesday, February 26, Ann Forrester ducked her head against the cold wind and stepped gingerly across the ice patches on Highway 328 to put a letter in the mailbox. Her husband, William Forrester, and children, Sara, age four, and Michael, age eight, waited in the car in the Forrester driveway, ready to be dropped off at work, day care, and school.

Michael yawned and drew pictures on the frosty car window with his fingernail. Sara banged her new pink snowboots against the seat. "Cut that out, Sara!" William warned, then opened the car door to yell, "Hurry up, Ann, or we'll be late!" She didn't seem to hear.

Richard Hart, married and father of three teenage children, sang along with the radio as he drove his Mercury Parcel Service van the morning of February 26. After delivering this express package, he would take a breakfast break. It hadn't been fun driving in the wind and patchy ice from Ohio into the state of Columbia.

As the van topped a sharp crest in the road, Mr. Hart saw a woman on the right side of the road stepping out onto the highway. He pressed down on the brake pedal, but the van didn't stop.

The woman, Ann Forrester, looked up at the approaching van. Richard Hart hit the brake hard. The van skidded. Ann Forrester scrambled frantically, in vain. Mr. Hart could not bring the vehicle under control and it struck Ms. Forrester, then smashed into a tree.

◼ Case II

Ameche v. Congden

Margie and Leroy Congden, owners of Maple Meadows Campground, were told that electrical outlets at some of the campsites weren't working. The Congdens groaned. It was the middle of the busiest season of the year.

Leroy confirmed that the problem included all sites from 30 to 39, and found that repair would necessitate digging a trench across the ten campsites to excavate the faulty wiring.

"We have to keep those sites available, at least until after Labor Day," Margie told Leroy. "There's no way we can notify all the people who have made reservations that we won't have a place for them, and there isn't another campground within one hundred miles."

Leroy made an appointment with an electrician to do the repairs after September 7, then ran a connecting line of extension cords from the outlet at site 40 to the affected sites. He was careful to string the cords along the gravel edge of the campsites away from traffic areas. The rubber casing on one of the cords was broken in several places, he noticed, but concluded it would not be a problem.

On the afternoon of August 21, Carl and Zoe Ameche set up their camper on site 36 of Maple Meadows Campground. Meanwhile, their six-year-old son, Zach, playfully collected bugs and sticks and gathered gravel into piles.

When Carl finished with the camper, he noticed an extension cord connection lying on the ground near where his son was playing. He pulled the cord away from the campsite into a grassy area.

Mr. and Mrs. Ameche unpacked and relaxed in their camper, occasionally noticing a flickering of the camper light. Emerging later, they found the grassy area behind their campsite in flames. Carl found Zachary unharmed, trapped on the other side of the fire, and was able to carry him to safety, but received severe burns on his own arms and legs in the process. Since most campers had not yet checked in, there were no other injuries, but several campsites, some recreation facilities, and many of the venerable maple trees for which the camp was named, were destroyed.

◼ Case III

Coleman v. Make Tracks, Inc.

Harold James, an executive in Make Tracks, Inc., propped his feet on his desk and looked out over the skyline of Legalville. He had finally brought his successful bicycle company into the motor age with the new three-wheeled all-terrain vehicle, Big Track, now being shipped to markets across the region.

James had pushed diversification to capture a more modern image for the company in a speed-conscious society. The positive reaction to TV ads featuring the Big Track over bold computer graphics and rock music seemed to bear him out.

His friends had urged him to take the safer route, to stay with bicycles. After all, he had three kids to educate. He was glad he had not listened.

At the Coleman farm on Labor Day, September 4, laughter and wisecracks focused on Sean Coleman, the only child of Sam and Emma Coleman. His effervescent personality and athletic skills had made him a leader at Lafayette County High. His intelligence and academic record convinced adults in the community that he would go far. In two years he would be off to Columbia State

University, where he planned to major in agriculture in preparation for managing the family farm.

Now Sean was celebrating with his friends—trading stories, eating hot dogs, and taking turns riding the new Big Track three-wheeled all-terrain vehicle that he had received for his recent sixteenth birthday.

"So, Hotshot," called Sean's best friend, Jason Hackett, "let's see you ride that thing like they do on TV!"

Sean gave him a thumbs-up signal, and was off, riding up a nearby hill. Rapidly increasing speed, he hit full throttle at the steepest incline before the crest of the hill. The front wheel lifted off the ground, flipping the vehicle backward onto Sean. The country rescue squad rushed him to the hospital, unconscious.

■ Case IV

Briar Patch Dolls, Inc. v. Teeny Tiny Manufacturing Co.

Pandemonium broke out in the aisles of toy departments across the country. There were less than forty shopping days until Christmas and the stock of popular Briar Patch Dolls was 30 to 60 percent short.

Briar Patch Dolls seemed to be an overnight craze, but it had taken Paul and Judy Heinz twelve years to build up from the cottage industry production of a few hand-sewn rag dolls for a local gift shop. The business had grown slowly and gradually until last year, when the Heinzes decided on a major expansion. They invested their last dollars in new equipment, employees, and a national advertising campaign that produced Christmas orders for 100,000 dolls—ten times last year's number. Production of the dolls proceeded on schedule.

Paul and Judy Heinz obtained clothing for the dolls from the Teeny Tiny Clothing Manufacturing Company, Inc., which made the trademark denim overalls worn by all Briar Patch Dolls. Three friends owned and operated Teeny Tiny Clothing and had expanded it to keep pace with Briar Patch. Although not all past contracts for the denim overalls had been filled on time, sales of the dolls had not been substantially hurt.

The general manager and primary force in the enterprise was Ethel Meyers, an energetic, creative woman. Her partners, Harriet Smith and Alice McGinnis, were mostly interested in supplementing their families' incomes while their children were in college.

In January of the prior year, a contract had been signed between Briar Patch Dolls and Teeny Tiny Manufacturing for 100,000 pairs of doll overalls, sewn to specification, to be delivered in increments of 25,000 on March 15, May 15, July 15, and September 15. Within thirty days of delivery, Briar Patch was to pay one dollar for each pair of overalls delivered in satisfactory condition.

On March 11, Ethel Meyers died. Teeny Tiny Manufacturing tried to meet the contract anyway. On March 15, 24,000 overalls were delivered, of which 5,000 were unsatisfactory. The other delivery dates were met as follows:

May 15:	15,000 pieces, 5,000 unsatisfactory
July 15:	10,000 pieces, 5,000 unsatisfactory
September 15:	7,000 pieces, 3,000 unsatisfactory
October 15:	3,000 pieces, 2,000 unsatisfactory

As a result of the delays, inadequate shipments, and defects, Briar Patch was able to fill only 40 percent of its orders. At a profit of ten dollars per doll, Briar Patch lost $600,000.

This year children's television programming is saturated with colorful ads for Jolly Lolly clown dolls, which have replaced Briar Patch Dolls as number one on children's Christmas lists.

■ Case V

Rakowski v. Montez Construction Co.

Darlene Rakowski stares out the city bus window, not even trying to hide her tears from the other passengers.

Was it only two years ago she had begun work on the Willow River Dam, proud to be the first woman to be hired for a nonsecretarial position by Montez Construction Company? Adam Stroud, the foreman who hired her, said he really didn't think a woman was tough enough for the job, but she was determined to try.

As she arrived the first day, catcalls and whistles erupted from the crew. A couple of the men followed her, doing an exaggerated bump and grind, a practice that was to continue.

Ms. Rakowski was assigned menial tasks, primarily fetch and carry orders on the ground. Rarely was she allowed to work with equipment on actual construction, although her vocational school training had prepared her to do so.

Soon after her arrival on the construction site, photos of nude women with her name written on them were taped on equipment and supplies where she would see them. Lewd jokes about her were circulated loudly in her presence. Obscene articles and pornographic magazines were frequently hidden in her lunch pail.

Ms. Rakowski complained from time to time to Adam Stroud, who responded by saying, "The boys are just having a little fun. You're taking this all too seriously."

As the incidents continued, Ms. Rakowski became more distraught, occasionally bursting into tears, which only intensified the mocking and jeering from her fellow workers. In desperation she went to Carlos Montez, owner of the company. He promised to look into the problem, and advised her to "loosen up."

The crew's behavior did not change. Complaints about the quality of her work and her inability to lift certain items, follow directions, and operate tools safely were filed in her personnel record. She was not given the normal opportunity to rebut such charges. Very upset, Ms. Rakowski missed more and more work.

Having made her decision to look for another job, Ms. Rakowski travels from employment agency to employment agency with no success. She feels trapped, wondering, "What am I going to do?"

In the upcoming weeks, you will be given numerous paralegal assignments. The text contains many such assignments from which your instructor or you may choose. They will help you apply and learn the material you have read. When doing the assignments, assume that you are in the state of Columbia, whose laws are the same as the laws of your state. Because most of your future work will be in your state, pay particular attention to the applications of this text and assignments to the practice of law in your state.

2

Welcome to the Law Office: A Paralegal Handbook

- Introduction
- Structure and Personnel of the Law Office
- Important Office Procedures
- Techniques for Thriving in the Law Office
- The Training Procedure
- Ethical and Other Professional Responsibilities
- Your Professional Development
- The Court Systems
- A Case Roadmap
- Concluding Comments

■ Introduction

Your orientation to the law firm is our first priority. This manual describes the structure and personnel of the law office and some of the essential procedures, such as timekeeping and billing, employed by most law firms. Thriving in a law office environment is crucial to your well-being and is addressed here as well. Learning processes employed in your training are introduced in the manual, as are the ethical and professional responsibilities that you must assume from your first day forward. In addition, the manual reviews our court system and the somewhat complex issues of jurisdiction, venue, and related concepts. In short, the *Paralegal Handbook* addresses fundamentals essential to becoming an effective litigation paralegal.

WHITE, WILSON & McDUFF

ATTORNEYS AT LAW
FEDERAL PLAZA BUILDING, SUITE 700
THIRD AND MARKET STREETS
LEGALVILLE, COLUMBIA 00000
(111) 555-0000

Memo to: Terry Salyer
From: Isadora Pearlman

Welcome to our law office. We are pleased that you have accepted employment with our firm and look forward to what we hope will be a mutually beneficial relationship. Today, I will be introducing you to the people who make this firm a success.

After your brief office orientation, please read the following paralegal handbook that we have put together for you. The handbook is written with the assumption that you have no prior litigation experience. I will then be working closely with you on several of our current cases. We will take our time so that you will learn the fundamentals well and gain confidence as you become a litigation paralegal.

Meanwhile, relax and enjoy getting acquainted. We know you will be an important addition to our firm.

Isadora Pearlman

A PARALEGAL HANDBOOK

WHITE, WILSON & MCDUFF
ATTORNEYS AT LAW
FEDERAL PLAZA BUILDING, SUITE 700
THIRD AND MARKET STREETS
LEGALVILLE, COLUMBIA 00000
(111) 555-0000

■ Structure and Personnel of the Law Office

Titles

This firm is structured like many other law firms in the United States. *Partners* are the attorney-owners of the law firm and share in its profits. *Senior partners* are the partners who have been with the firm the longest and often have the greatest ownership share. Attorneys who have not yet become partners and are salaried are *associates. Staff attorneys,* the newest breed of attorney, are hired for economic reasons and, unlike associates, have no expectation of becoming partners. Some attorneys may have the designation *of counsel,* which means they maintain an advisory capacity or refer clients to the law firm (or do both).

Personnel other than lawyers include paralegals, law clerks, and legal secretaries. *Paralegals* are educated in legal skills and provide legal services under the supervision of an attorney, or as otherwise permitted by law. *Law clerks* work in the law office while completing their law degrees. Clerical and word processing services for the office are provided by *legal secretaries.* Although large firms can have legal administrators, paralegal managers, investigators, and receptionists, the structure in our office is typical of the small or medium-size firm. The office organization chart in figure 2:1 may be helpful.

Figure 2:1 White, Wilson, and McDuff Office Organization Chart

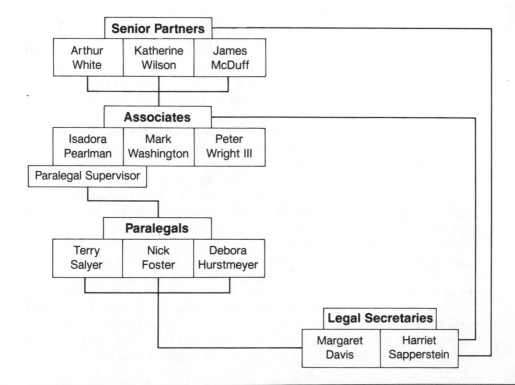

The Work of the Firm

This firm is primarily involved in **litigation.*** Litigation is a lawsuit—the process whereby one person sues another in a court of law to enforce a right or to seek a remedy such as financial compensation. Our firm handles the following types of cases:

Personal injury cases arise when an individual has been physically injured from the negligence (carelessness) of another—for example, an automobile accident or a slip and fall case. This type of case accounts for most of the litigation work we do.

Products liability cases belong to a special type of personal injury case in which the individual has been physically injured by a defective product, such as an exploding beverage bottle, adulterated food, or unsafe machinery.

Contracts cases involve one party having suffered a loss from the failure of another party to meet the terms of an agreement between them. A typical contract case could involve the failure to complete construction of a house, or the failure to pay once construction is complete.

Corporation cases are brought by one corporation against another, such as trademark violation or industrial espionage.

Antitrust cases deal with individuals, government, or a business suing another business for harmful trade practices, such as price discrimination, unfair competition, or monopolization of a market.

Civil rights cases involve an individual or the government suing another party for violation of rights guaranteed by federal law. A typical civil rights litigation might involve race, sex, or age discrimination.

The Role of the Paralegal

The paralegal has become an important component in our delivery of legal services. You will spend the largest share of your time gathering and organizing factual information and drafting legal documents. You will also conduct legal research and investigation, assist at hearings and trials, oversee the timely filing of matters, and help the office keep our clients informed as to the status of their cases.

In addition, the firm will bill clients directly for your services in the same manner we bill for the time of our attorneys. We are not allowed to bill for the time of a legal secretary or clerk. The paralegal, therefore, is an important source of income and profit for the firm. Because you will be performing tasks formerly done by an attorney, but billed to the client at a lower rate, the client, too, will benefit from your work. As long as you work efficiently, you will help this firm provide legal services to more people at a more reasonable cost. Therein lies the heart of the paralegal profession.

Isadora Pearlman, one of the firm's associates, serves as the coordinator of our paralegal staff and the liaison between the partners and the paralegals. She will allocate tasks to the paralegals. Should you have any questions or concerns about your position, please direct them to her. Any questions concerning a particular task should be directed to the attorney for whom the task is being completed. Any work you have that must be typed should be given to Margaret Davis, one of the legal secretaries.

*Bold-faced terms are defined in the glossary.

The law office is an important extension of our legal system. What contribution can your work here make to our system of justice?

Important Office Procedures

Every office will have a variety of established procedures that each new employee must learn. Procedures are necessary for the sake of efficiency, uniformity, and quality. Learning the required procedures will save you time and embarrassment and help you to survive and thrive in the law office. One of the first things you should do, therefore, is to locate and read the office procedures manual. It will provide you with information ranging from pay periods and sick leave to cash receipts and long-distance calls. Three procedures of particular importance are timekeeping, disbursement entry, and deadline control.

Timekeeping

Timekeeping is a procedure whereby attorneys and paralegals regularly record how much time they spend on a client's case or on other matters. A law firm is compensated for its work and analyzes its productivity on the basis of such records. The time spent on a client's case that can be billed to the client is called **billable hours.** The lawyer's fee, and hence the firm's income, is based on billable hours. It is essential, therefore, to keep accurate time records from the start. The timekeeping form used in our office is seen in figure 2:2.

Figure 2:2   Permanent Time Log

White, Wilson & McDuff
Permanent Time Log

Service Codes

CT Court
C   Conference
DD Document
    Drafting
I   Investigation

L Letter
M Memorandum
P Preparation
R Research

T   Telephone
TR Travel
O   Other

No Charge Items

NC No Charge
B   Bar Function
CE Continuing
    Education
CR Client Relations
PS Public Service

Date	File No.	Client	Atty/ Plgl	Service Code	Hours	Tenths	By Billing Department	
							Rate/Hr	Amount
9/11-	PI-309	*Roberts, J.*	T.S.	I	2	3		
9/11-	PI-106	*Samuels, S. J.*	T.S.	D.D.	1	7		

Date	File No.	Client	Atty/ Plgl	Service Code	Hours			

Carboned Time Slip
(Tear off when completed)

Comments: _____

_____

_____

_____

Out of Pocket Expense (enter also on disbursement form)

_____

_____

No. 1003
No. 1004
No. 1005
No. 1006

Guidelines for Recording Your Time

1. Enter the client's name and file number and the date.
2. Place your initials under paralegal (Plgl).
3. Enter the service code for the service provided. Write NC if time was spent on nonbillable time such as a professional meeting.
4. Record the number of complete hours worked on service.
5. Record the number of incomplete hours worked on service in tenths of an hour (six minutes equals one-tenth of an hour).

6. Record the hourly rate charged for your service and amount to be added to bill (usually done by secretary or bookkeeper).
7. Add comments to specify service.
8. Enter information on any out-of-pocket expenses incurred that are to be reimbursed by client, such as long-distance phone calls, mileage traveled, meals, and so on.
9. Remove the time slip from the permanent log.
10. Collect all the slips for the day and turn them in to the secretary or bookkeeper.

Time logs are designed so that when you fill out the time slip, a permanent record of the entry is carboned onto the permanent log below the time slip. This permanent log becomes a record of your activities (both billable and nonbillable) for the day, week, month, and so on. The time slip will go to the client's billing file.

ASSIGNMENT 2:1

To develop a timekeeping habit during this training period, keep track of your time spent on assignments. Use the log in figure 2:3 (since time slips may not be available) with abbreviations from the time slip, figure 2:2. Use a separate notebook or loose-leaf paper that can be placed at the back of your system folder. (The system folder will be discussed later in this chapter.)

Disbursement Entry

Disbursements are those expenses that are incurred on behalf of the client and can be directly attributed to that client's case. Disbursements include such things as phone calls, postage, and filing fees. Figure 2:4 is an example of a disbursement form.

Guidelines for Recording Disbursements

1. Enter the client's name, file number, the date, and your initials under paralegal (Plgl).
2. Enter the expense code.
3. Record the amount of the expense.
4. Enter comments to provide specific information.
5. Remove the disbursement slip from the permanent log.
6. Collect all slips at the end of the day and give them to the secretary or bookkeeper.

Figure 2:3   Time Log

Name _____

Case No.	Service*	Comment	Date	Hr & 10ths
1	R	Review file	9-1	.1
1	C	Conference with client	9-1	1.5
2	DD	Draft medical authorization	9-2	.5

*Use service codes from time slip.

Figure 2:4   Permanent Disbursement Record

<table>
<tr><td colspan="6">White, Wilson & McDuff
Permanent Disbursement Record</td></tr>
<tr><td colspan="6">Expense Codes:</td></tr>
<tr>
<td>C Photocopies
CT On-Line Computer
    Time
F Filing and Other Fees</td>
<td>L Lodging
M Meals
ON Overnight
    Express</td>
<td>P Postage
$ Cash
TG Telegrams</td>
<td>T Telephone
TR Travel
O Other</td>
</tr>
</table>

Date	File No.	Client	Atty/Plgl	Expense Code	Amount

Date	File No.	Client	Atty/Plgl	Expense Code	Amount

Carboned Disbursement Slip
(Tear off when completed)

Comments: _____

_____

_____

_____

No. 2230
No. 2231
No. 2232

The disbursement slips will go to the client's billing file. The time and disbursement slips are then totaled by the secretary or bookkeeper to make up the client's bill. This kind of record keeping leads to well-documented bills and reduces disputes over fees.

Deadline (Docket) Control

Hovering over every attorney and paralegal is the fear of making a mistake costing the client a significant sum of money or, even worse, the client's one lifetime opportunity to sue for just compensation or to challenge an unjust suit. Mistakes lead to malpractice (errors and omissions) claims that, if not settled, lead to costly malpractice lawsuits. Such claims raise the firm's insurance costs, damage reputations, and can result in disciplinary action by the state bar. One misconception, however, is that good attorneys and good paralegals do not make mistakes. The reality is that even the best make mistakes—and the longer you provide legal services, the more likely you will make such an error. Keep in mind, however, that a good paralegal knows that errors are likely and takes every precaution.

Studies tell us that some of the errors most often leading to malpractice claims include missed dates when an action must be filed (statute of limitations), missed procedural deadlines, failure to know or properly apply the law, failure to do adequate research and investigation, faulty drafting of

Figure 2:5   Deadline Slip

White, Wilson, & McDuff								
Client			DEADLINE SLIP			File No.		
Atty	Start	Deadline	Plgl	Start	Deadline	Staff	Start	Deadline
Task:			Task:			Task:		
Remarks:			Remarks:			Remarks:		
Reminder: 1 2 Final Done:			Reminder: 1 2 Final Done:			Reminder: 1 2 Final Done:		

legal documents, failure to inform client, incorrect or inadequate advice, conflicts of interest, and acts and omissions of associates and employees.[1] One of these studies found personal injury practice (tort cases for plaintiffs) and commercial law practice (two primary areas of practice for this firm) to be two of the three areas of practice most subject to malpractice claims.[2]

Systems methods (to be described later) reduce errors. Another important method is deadline control. Missed deadlines are the primary reason law offices are sued for professional malpractice. Every office must have a system whereby important deadlines are met. These systems, often called tickler systems, involve a regular calendaring (docketing) process. When the attorney or a paralegal in the office becomes aware that a deadline must be met, a deadline control slip is filled out. Figure 2:5 is an example.

The attorney is ultimately responsible for meeting deadlines and therefore should be the one responsible for filling out the deadline slip. It is conceivable, however, that the task may fall to the paralegal. In any case, be aware of how to fill out the form.

Guidelines for Filling Out a Deadline Slip

1. Enter the name of the client and the file number of the case to which the deadline applies.
2. Enter the task that must be completed. Some tasks will require that other related tasks must also be done by other people in the firm. Hence, the slip is divided into three sections: the task needing to be done by the attorney is listed in the left section; that needing completion by the paralegal appears in the middle section; and that needing to be done by the secretary or other staff member is listed in the right section.
3. Enter the deadline date for the particular task in the designated box in the appropriate section.

4. Enter the start date (the day the task should be started) in the designated box for the appropriate section. (Notice how the dates of the various related tasks are logically sequenced on the form.)
5. Enter under "Remarks" any specific direction to assist in completing the task.
6. Do not complete the lower boxes.
7. Remove one copy of the multicopy form for your calendar and send the remaining copies to the secretary in charge of the deadline control system.

On each start date, the person responsible for the designated task will receive a reminder and will receive increasingly urgent reminders until the task is done. The person charged with the task indicates its completion by initialing after "Done" at the bottom of the appropriate section. The deadline system should also include a post-deadline reminder that the target date was missed, and some corrective action should be taken.

ASSIGNMENT 2:2
Set up a simple deadline calendar for this training period. Use any type of standard calendar. Enter all important deadlines such as assignment due dates and exam dates. Use a system of advance reminder dates prior to the actual deadline and post-deadline reminders for necessary corrective action.

■ Techniques for Thriving in the Law Office

In addition to learning office procedures and following them closely, practicing the following techniques will help you thrive in the law office.

■ Become acquainted with your fellow employees. Let them know you are interested in them and enjoy their company. Respect for others and a sincere smile foster good working relationships.
■ Know how to assign work. Decide to whom the work should be assigned and submitted, how much advance notice is normally required before the expected completion date, what procedure is appropriate in last-minute rushes, whether completion dates should be given, and whether special forms for delegating tasks are used. Compliance with these procedures will enhance your relationship with those to whom you assign work and will contribute to office efficiency.
■ Submit work as error-free as possible. Take the time to check grammar, spelling, citations, form, brevity, accuracy, and clarity. When time permits, study the rules of good writing to improve your communications skills.
■ Keep careful track of client files. Misplaced case files lead to frustration and can adversely affect our representation of a client. Follow strictly the office policy on checking out and returning files.
■ When addressing clients, use Mr., Ms., Dr., or other appropriate titles. Avoid first names unless there is no doubt the situation makes it acceptable.
■ Be sensible when using the telephone. How you conduct yourself when using the phone is a direct reflection on this firm. Exercise good common sense and be polite, businesslike, and brief. It is important that everyone you speak with on the phone understand that you are not an

attorney. Make this clear at the outset of the conversation whenever there might be any doubt. Plan ahead for phone calls; knowing what information you need helps keep conversations brief. Incomplete messages and misunderstandings on the phone can be a problem; it is a good idea to have people repeat addresses and phone numbers that you have given them and for you to repeat information that you receive.

- In addition, some phone conversations are important enough to confirm in writing the terms, dates, or arrangements discussed on the phone. If possible, this should be done immediately following the phone call. The letter serves as an important record of the conversation. In some instances where a letter of confirmation seems inappropriate, a brief memo to the file may be useful.

- Learn to complete assignments efficiently. Each time you receive an assignment during the training period or otherwise, be sure you thoroughly understand it and the time frame in which it must be completed. Obtain the facts underlying the task—know why you are doing the task. Ask questions to determine exactly what is required of you, especially if you have never done such an assignment before.

- Once you have the assignment in mind, decide the best way to complete the task. Use the guides and examples provided during your training. Ask the attorney for additional guidance. Do not try to reinvent the wheel on each assignment. If the information supplied to you is insufficient, you should seek examples in our legal form files, in numerous form books, in the statutes, and in the state and federal rules. Ask the advice of others who have done similar work and would be glad to give you some suggestions. Keep a log of each of your assignments, indicating when the task was given and when it was completed. Such a log will help you build a system folder, described later in this handbook. It will also help you list specific skills on your resume should you decide to apply for an advanced position in this firm or elsewhere. It will be used in an annual evaluation of your work.

- Remember the importance of your work to our clients. On any job there will be times when you are tired or simply bored. These are times rife with the potential for error. It is important to remind yourself that our clients rely heavily on us, and what we do has considerable impact on their lives and businesses.

- Keep a sense of humor. While you need to regard your work seriously, it is equally important to be able to laugh, to see the humor in your own follies as well as in the situations in which you find yourself. Of all creatures, it is said, we alone have the gift for laughter; maybe that is why we have thrived.

■ The Training Procedure

Procedure, Task Information, Assignments

You will begin your training with several cases currently being handled by this firm. You will work through the cases at a relatively slow pace, concentrating on the paralegal tasks one step at a time as they arise chronologically. For each assigned task you will be given the following:

1. Information on the nature and purpose of the task to be performed
2. Directions or guidelines as to how to perform the task
3. Examples of the completed tasks
4. Opportunities to perform the task yourself
5. Evaluation of your work

During this training period you will be performing the following duties:

1. Researching
2. Investigating
3. Interviewing
4. Organizing materials
5. Summarizing materials
6. Drafting documents, forms, and correspondence
7. Responding to questions on concepts, principles, and procedures

Developing a Litigation System

One of the most important tasks during your training period will be developing a litigation system. This system will be a chronological collection of the guidelines, forms, correspondence, checklists, procedures, pertinent law, and so on, for all steps in the litigation process. Such a system will help you produce work that is efficient, uniform, and complete. Your training assignments will include the building of this litigation system. A 1½- to 2-inch three-ring binder will serve as a convenient system folder. It should have sufficient tabbed dividers to accommodate the divisions listed in the system folder contents in the appendix to this text. The folder should have the following divisions:

1. Quick reference information
   a. Office structure and procedure
   b. General information (courts, names, addresses, deadlines, and so on)
2. Interview
3. Investigation
4. Pleadings and service of process
5. Discovery
6. Settlement
7. Pretrial
8. Trial
9. Post-trial
10. Appeal

As you are asked to do certain tasks, place the necessary information (making copies when needed) into the appropriate section of the system in chronological order. Your system will gradually take shape and should be complete by the conclusion of the training period.

Learn to create efficient legal systems by doing the best job you can on this system. Not only will you have a reliable litigation system for future use, but also you will have learned a valuable organizational skill that can be applied to numerous areas of law while enhancing your value to the law firm.

ASSIGNMENT 2:3
Set up a 1½- to 2-inch three-ring binder with the tab dividers arranged as described earlier. Copies of the office structure and forms previously discussed should be placed in the system folder as indicated in the appendix. Begin a table of contents for your system folder and add to it as you add to your folder.

▪ Ethical and Other Professional Responsibilities

Soon you will be working with cases and the people involved in those cases. In dealing with others, be ever mindful of the high standard of professional ethics to which your actions must conform. **Professional ethics,** as applied to attorneys, are the rules of conduct that govern the practice of law. It is the responsibility of each person working for this firm to know what is expected and to act accordingly. A breach of ethical standards will reflect badly upon this firm and may also lead to the disbarment of one or more of our attorneys. It may cost you your job and subject you to prosecution for the unauthorized practice of law.

What a Paralegal May Not Do

Except as specifically permitted by law, paralegals *may not* perform any of the following functions:

1. Provide legal services directly to the public without the supervision of an attorney.
2. Give legal advice or counsel a client. Legal advice is independent professional judgment based on knowledge of the law and given for the benefit of a particular client.
3. Represent a client in court or other tribunal or otherwise act as an advocate for a client.
4. Accept or reject cases for the firm.
5. Set any fee for representation of a client.
6. Split legal fees with an attorney (bonuses and profit sharing plans not tied to a specific case are permissible).
7. Be a partner with a lawyer when any of the activities of the partnership include the practice of law (exception: the District of Columbia).
8. Have their names printed on the firm's letterhead (this is permitted in Columbia and some other states).
9. Solicit cases for a lawyer.

What a Paralegal May Do

Paralegals may perform a wide array of tasks and be confident their work will not create a breach of ethics if it meets certain criteria.[3]

Paralegals may represent clients at federal administrative hearings. This includes hearings of matters such as supplemental Social Security or black lung benefits. Some states have passed administrative procedure acts similar to that of the federal government permitting paralegal representation without attorney supervision.

Recent American Bar Association studies and one in California have underscored the unmet legal needs of millions of U.S. citizens. Based on the California study, a committee of the California Bar has recommended that paralegals be licensed to practice law in limited instances. Paralegal licensure will continue to be hotly debated in the 1990s. In the meantime, paralegal services are circumscribed by the following conditions:

1. The task must be delegated by an attorney.
2. It must be performed under an attorney's supervision.

3. Paralegals must clearly designate their status as a paralegal.
4. The lawyer must retain a direct relationship with the client (the attorney must retain control over the relationship).
5. The task must involve information gathering or be ministerial and cannot involve the rendering of legal advice or judgment (unless the legal advice or judgment is provided by the paralegal directly to the attorney).
6. The work must be given final approval or be examined by the attorney.
7. The work must not have a separate identity but merge with the attorney's final work product.

In addition, a paralegal may have a business card with the firm's name on it so long as the paralegal is designated a paralegal.

Confidentiality, Honesty, Conflict of Interest, and Other Ethical Considerations

Paralegal ethical standards, for all practical purposes, are the same as those for attorneys. Attorneys, not paralegals, are going to be disciplined by the bar for ethical breaches. Paralegals, however, are bound by the nature of their jobs to uphold each rule as if they were the attorney.

Attorneys are bound by the ethical standards set by their state's highest court. Most states have adopted the American Bar Association's *Model Rules of Professional Conduct* with some local amendments. Studying the *Model Rules of Professional Conduct* provides a paralegal with an understanding of most of the ethical standards in effect in any particular state. A copy of the *Model Rules* is provided for you in the appendix. Because some states have deleted or amended some of the ABA's rules, however, you should obtain a copy of your state's version of the ethical standards. These are available through state bar associations. Place these in the ethics section of your system folder. The following discussions highlight the portions of the *Model Rules* most important for you to learn at this point. Other sections of the rules will be presented as they arise in the context of a particular paralegal task.

A paralegal shall hold inviolate the confidences of a client. Except with written permission, nothing the client tells you or that you learn about the client may be revealed to anyone outside the office, not even to a spouse or parent. In addition, to preserve confidentiality, a client's statement to you or other employees of the firm should not be made in the presence of outsiders (Rule 1.6). The duty to preserve confidentiality extends beyond the conclusion of the case [Rule 1.6(a)].

A paralegal must maintain the highest standards of professional integrity and avoid any dishonesty, fraud, deceit, or misrepresentation. This rule applies to all dealings with the client, judges, court employees, opposing attorneys, and the public. (See Rules 3.3, 3.4, 3.5, 3.6, 4.1, 4.3, 4.4, and 8.1–8.4.)

A paralegal should avoid and reveal any conflicts of interest. A lawyer is required to represent the client zealously and to avoid interests or conflicts that would dilute allegiance to the client. A paralegal must also be loyal to the client and avoid such conflicts (Rules 1.7–1.13).

A conflict of interest would occur if this firm accepted a case to sue Mr. Hart, and then was hired by Mr. Hart to sue someone else. In this situation, confidential information learned from Mr. Hart in the second case could be used against him in the first case. In such circumstances, the second case should not be accepted.

In another example, if a client represented by the firm sued the O.K. Manufacturing Company, a conflict of interest would arise if the paralegal assigned to the case owned stock in the company. It is obvious that the paralegal may hesitate to do the best job possible when the outcome of the case could have an adverse effect on the paralegal's income. In such a situation, the paralegal should inform the supervising attorney of the conflict. A remedy for the conflict would be to take the paralegal off that case.

A third type of conflict of interest can occur when a paralegal changes jobs from one law firm to another. If the paralegal worked on behalf of Mr. Hart at the first firm, but now must handle cases against Mr. Hart at the second firm, it is likely that confidential information gained from Mr. Hart while working for the first firm would be used against him at the second firm. Again, the paralegal should inform the supervising attorney and be removed from any involvement in any cases against Mr. Hart.

Courts have not been consistent in addressing the issue of whether a newly hired paralegal with confidential information gained at a former law firm disqualifies the new firm from handling any cases where a conflict might exist. In *Williams v. Trans World Airlines*, 588 F. Supp. 1037 (W.D. Mo. 1984) and *Glover Bottled Gas Corp. v. Circle M Beverage Barn, Inc.*, 129 A.D.2d 678, 514 N.Y.S.2d 440 (1987), the court ruled that disqualification of the firm was necessary. In *Schiessle v. Stephens*, 717 F.2d 417 (7th Cir. 1983) and *Kapco Manufacturing Co, Inc. v. C & O Enterprises, Inc.*, 637 F. Supp. 1231 (N.D. Ill. 1985), the ruling said disqualification was not necessary if the paralegal was screened out of the cases in question (a "Chinese wall"); to do otherwise was an unfair restraint on freedom of employment.[4] Why is this such an important issue? Economics. No firm likes to give up a good client or a profitable case. If at any time paralegals feel unable to give clients their best work, they should discuss it with the attorneys on the cases.

Firms also appreciate assistance in efforts to provide free legal services to the poor, called **pro-bono cases.** Paralegals and local paralegal associations have accepted as their own the attorney's obligation to provide legal services. Doing pro-bono work with the bar is beneficial to the law firm, the paralegal, and the person served.

Other Professional Considerations

Some professional ethics are not found in the codes but are nevertheless quite important. It is especially important in professional working relationships to have mutual respect and loyalty between employer and employees. Publicly criticizing one's fellow workers is not consistent with professional loyalty. That is also true regarding clients, who deserve the utmost courtesy, respect, and every effort on our part to preserve their dignity.

Professional loyalty to the firm extends to the practice of law, which supercedes loyalty to any specific individual. Attorneys are expected to call attention to the unethical practices of other attorneys (Rule 8.3—not adopted in some states) or in some instances, of their own clients [Rule

1.6(b)(1)—to prevent serious crimes, and Rule 3.3, perjury]. Similarly, a paralegal must be prepared to report unethical behavior to the appropriate person within the firm.

It is helpful for each of us to be mindful that our actions reflect upon this firm and the professions we each represent. We encourage you to go beyond this brief word of caution on ethics. Study ethics in more detail as you learn other litigation tasks. The more you know about the ethical responsibilities of the attorney and paralegal, the more likely you will be able to spot and avoid trouble. Additional ethical considerations will be specially highlighted as they arise in the chapters ahead.

ASSIGNMENT 2:4

Draft an outline of the significant ethical considerations highlighted in this section of the handbook. Consult the ABA *Model Rules of Professional Conduct* in the appendix or a copy of your state's ethical standards. Include sections on what a paralegal may or may not do, what is necessary to avoid the unauthorized practice of law, and other ethical considerations. Place these in the ethics section of your system folder. As you read further in this text and in other sources, insert in your folder the citations for key ethical rules and guidelines.

ASSIGNMENT 2:5

Using the ethical standards and rules cited in this section, answer the following questions on ethics.

1. One of our clients asks you what judge will be hearing the client's case. You answer, "Judge Arnow." Are you guilty of the unauthorized practice of law?
2. (a) You have just researched an issue and have found that inattentive driving is a breach of the duty of care that a driver owes to others. In a phone conversation the client asks you, "If the driver of the vehicle that struck me was inattentive, is he in the wrong?" You answer yes. Is this the unauthorized practice of law?
   (b) What if the paralegal can honestly say, "I just spoke with Mr. White [client's attorney] and he said, 'Yes, the driver would be in the wrong' "?
3. Ms. Pearlman asks you to draft a release of medical information form for a client. This form is drafted and signed by the client and given to the hospital. Under what conditions can you do this and avoid the unauthorized practice of law?
4. You are working on a client's case for Ms. Pearlman. She is gone, so you want to consult with Mr. White, another attorney in our firm. To do so, however, you must reveal to Mr. White some confidential information about the client. Would this be a breach of confidentiality?
5. Is leaving an open file on your desk in the presence of another client a breach of confidentiality?
6. In interviewing a client, you and your attorney are convinced that some information provided by the client is false. What consequences can result from the presentation of such information to the court? What model rule of professional conduct applies?
7. Your supervising attorney asks you to release to the press a letter from a third party. The attorney says, "I'll finally get even by truly embarrassing the s.o.b." What should you do?

■ Your Professional Development

White, Wilson, and McDuff has always encouraged its employees to improve themselves professionally. For that reason, our firm will support you in your efforts toward personal professional development. Keep informed of what is going on in your field; attend continuing education seminars; participate in paralegal associations; and subscribe to literature that will benefit your career. Here is a brief list of some organizations, their addresses, and pertinent literature. Seek information as well from the local affiliates of these national organizations and from your city, regional, and state associations.

National Association of Legal Assistants, Inc.
1420 South Utica
P.O. Box 7587
Tulsa, OK 74105
(918) 587-6828
Publication: *Facts and Findings*

National Federation of Paralegal Associations
Administrative Offices
104 Wilmot Road
Suite 201
Deerfield, IL 60015-5195
(312) 940-8800
Publication: *National Paralegal Reporter*

Professional Legal Assistants, Inc.
250 Bell Plaza, Room 1610
Salt Lake City, UT 84111-2013

American Bar Association Standing Committee on Legal Assistants

ABA Center
750 North Lake Shore Drive
Chicago, IL, 60611
(312) 988-5618
Publication: *Legal Assistants: Update*

American Association for Paralegal Education
P.O. Box 40244
Overland Park, KS 66204
(913) 381-4458
Publications: The AAfPE Newsletter
The Journal of Paralegal Education

Other Publication:

Legal Assistant Today
James Publishing, Inc.
3520 Cadillac Avenue
Suite E
Costa Mesa, CA 92629

ASSIGNMENT 2:6
Locate the names, addresses, and phone numbers of your local and state paralegal associations. If you need help obtaining this information, try the director of a local paralegal program or any experienced paralegal in our firm or elsewhere in the state. The headquarters of the state bar association might also have such information. For future reference, you may choose to place your expanded lists of sources for professional development in your system folder.

■ The Court Systems

This section discusses the function, structure, and jurisdiction of both the federal and state courts. Then it explains the relationship between jurisdiction and venue, and how these distinct concepts determine the choice of a proper court for a lawsuit.

Basic Components of a Court System

The federal and state court systems have at least two types of courts in common: the trial court and the appellate court.

The Trial Court

The trial court is the real workhorse of the court system. This is where most lawsuits are filed. Trial courts decide questions of law and questions of fact. Questions of fact focus on what happened: How fast was Mr. Hart driving? Was the floor wet? Was the traffic light red? The jury, if there is one, or judge decides the questions of fact. Questions of law focus on the law or proper procedure to be applied to a particular case: Is the evidence admissible? Was the hearing conducted in a fair and impartial manner? Is the statute constitutional? Questions of law are always decided by the judge. The great majority of cases are resolved in the trial court. Trial courts have a variety of names: county, district, superior, common pleas, traffic, circuit, city, justice of the peace, or even supreme court in New York state. The trial courts may also be divided into branches or specialized courts: criminal, juvenile, probate, or family court.

The Apellate Court

When the losing party feels that questions of law were erroneously decided by the trial court judge, it has the right to appeal the case to an appellate court. The appellate court considers questions of law only and does not retry the facts of the case. The federal and state court systems each have a final court of appeal. This court is called the supreme court in most systems. Others call it the court of appeals, supreme judicial court, or supreme court of appeals. The published opinion of an appellate court becomes the rule of law (precedent) in the particular geographical jurisdiction of that court.

The Intermediate Appellate Court

Approximately half the states and the federal system have an intermediate appellate court. Where it exists, this court stands between the trial court and the court of final review. Most appeals from the trial courts must go to the intermediate appellate court and are resolved there. Some cases, usually of considerable significance, are appealed from the intermediate appellate court and are accepted by the supreme court or court of final appeal for review.

Jurisdiction

Jurisdiction is the power or authority of a court to hear and decide the questions of law or fact (or both) presented by a lawsuit. Most courts have a **geographical jurisdiction,** meaning that they hear cases that arise within specific geographical boundaries. The boundaries may encompass the city limits for municipal courts or the entire nation for the U.S. Supreme Court. Court decisions become law only within the specific geographical boundaries in which the court has jurisdiction.

The court also has **personal jurisdiction.** This means the court must have the power over the particular person named in the lawsuit to enter a judgment against that person. This is usually accomplished by serving a summons and a copy of the complaint on the person being sued (the defendant). Traditionally, state courts can get personal jurisdiction over defendants located in the state. Today more states are passing long-arm statutes that permit service in other states under prescribed circumstances. In federal courts, personal jurisdiction is gained by serving the necessary documents within the geographical district of the court. Personal jurisdiction is discussed further in chapter 6.

Each court has some form of **subject matter jurisdiction.** This jurisdiction is defined by the nature or subject of the lawsuits handled by that court—for example, criminal, juvenile, civil, or appellate cases.

When a court has **general jurisdiction,** it can hear all types of cases. Most states have trial courts of general jurisdiction where subject matter jurisdiction is assumed unless one party can demonstrate that the court does not have the necessary subject matter jurisdiction.

Original jurisdiction indicates that cases first enter the system at this court level—they "originate" here. Therefore, a court having original jurisdiction over criminal cases is the first to hear and try criminal cases. Most trial courts are courts of original jurisdiction.

A court has **limited jurisdiction** when its authority to hear and decide cases is limited to specific types of cases. A court specifically labeled a traffic court can hear only traffic cases; criminal court, only criminal cases; and so forth. Limited jurisdiction becomes **exclusive jurisdiction** when a court is the only court permitted to handle a specific type of case.

Frequently the jurisdiction of a court is limited by the amount of money claimed in the lawsuit. For example, a state's lower court may have jurisdiction over all civil cases up to $5,000, with the higher trial court having jurisdiction over all civil cases involving more than that amount. Frequently this monetary value is referred to as the **jurisdictional amount.**

Pendent jurisdiction is discretionary and permits a federal court already having jurisdiction over a matter of federal law to hear a state claim if that claim is based on essentially the same facts as the federal claim. The federal court could not hear the state law issue on its own. Pendent jurisdiction is possible only when the issue is coupled with a claim the federal court can hear.

A similar concept is **ancillary jurisdiction,** which is frequently called pendent party jurisdiction. Ancillary jurisdiction permits a court to add claims, counterclaims, parties, and so on, that it would not have jurisdiction over to a matter it does have jurisdiction over so that all claims between the parties can be finalized at one time.

Another type of jurisdiction is **removal jurisdiction.** Most often this refers to the ability of federal district courts to remove cases from state courts to federal court if the federal court has jurisdiction to hear the case.

When two courts have jurisdiction on the same type of case, the courts are said to have **concurrent jurisdiction.**

The jurisdiction of each court is legally defined by the constitution and statutes of the governmental entity that creates the court. There are other aspects of jurisdiction, such as property (in rem) jurisdiction, which will be addressed later in this text.

Federal Courts and Their Jurisdiction

Article III of the Constitution establishes the main federal courts and their jurisdictions. These courts are called constitutional courts and their judges are tenured for life. The constitutional courts consist of the United States

Supreme Court, the United States Court of Appeals, and the United States District Court.

Legislative courts are established by act of Congress under Article I of the Constitution. Their judges have set terms. These are the specialized courts such as the United States Claims Court and the United States Tax Court.

All federal courts have limited subject matter jurisdiction and can exercise their power only with specific authorization. This authorization requires a constitutional source (Article III or Article I) and an act of Congress (found as United States Code provisions).

The *United States Supreme Court* is the highest-level appellate court in the federal system. Its one chief justice and eight associate justices function as the authority on the Constitution and ensure the supremacy of federal law. Supreme Court jurisdiction is defined in Article III of the Constitution and cannot be increased or decreased by Congress. It has appellate jurisdiction over appeals from the United States Court of Appeals (28 U.S.C. § 1254) and from the highest-level appellate courts in each state if the appeal raises a question of federal law (28 U.S.C. § 1257). Since 1988, cases reach the Supreme Court almost exclusively by **writ of certiorari.**[5] This is a discretionary procedure that allows the Court to take only the cases that, in its opinion, have sufficient national significance to warrant its attention. The Court also uses the writ to resolve issues in which the courts of appeals are in serious conflict. Some constitutional matters come to the Court through a certification process distinct from the writ of certiorari.

The Supreme Court also has original jurisdiction in the following matters.

1. Controversies between two or more states (exclusive);
2. All actions or proceedings to which ambassadors, public ministers, and consuls of foreign states are a party;
3. All controversies between the United States and a state; and
4. All actions or proceedings by a state against citizens of another state or against aliens.

Items 2–4 are subject matter jurisdictions held concurrently with lower federal courts.

The *United States Court of Appeals* is the intermediate appellate court in the federal system. It is divided into thirteen courts consisting of eleven regional circuits, a Court of Appeals for the District of Columbia, and the U.S. Court of Appeals for the Federal Circuit. The courts of appeals have appellate jurisdiction over all appeals taken from final decisions of the United States District Court (28 U.S.C. § 1291). The relatively new Court of Appeals for the Federal Circuit has exclusive subject matter jurisdiction over appeals in patent, trademark, and plant variety protection cases, plus appeals from the U.S. Claims Court and those involving government employment and international trade (28 U.S.C. § 1295). It reviews decisions of the U.S. Court of International Trade, the U.S. Claims Court, the U.S. Court of Veterans Appeals, and the decisions of the Board of Appeals or the Board of Patent Interferences of the Patent and Trademark Office, the Commission of Patents and Trademarks, and the Trademark Trial and Appeals Board.

The map in figure 2:6 shows the geographical arrangement of the circuits for the U.S. Court of Appeals and their respective federal district courts. One

Figure 2:6 U.S. Courts of Apeals and U.S. District Courts

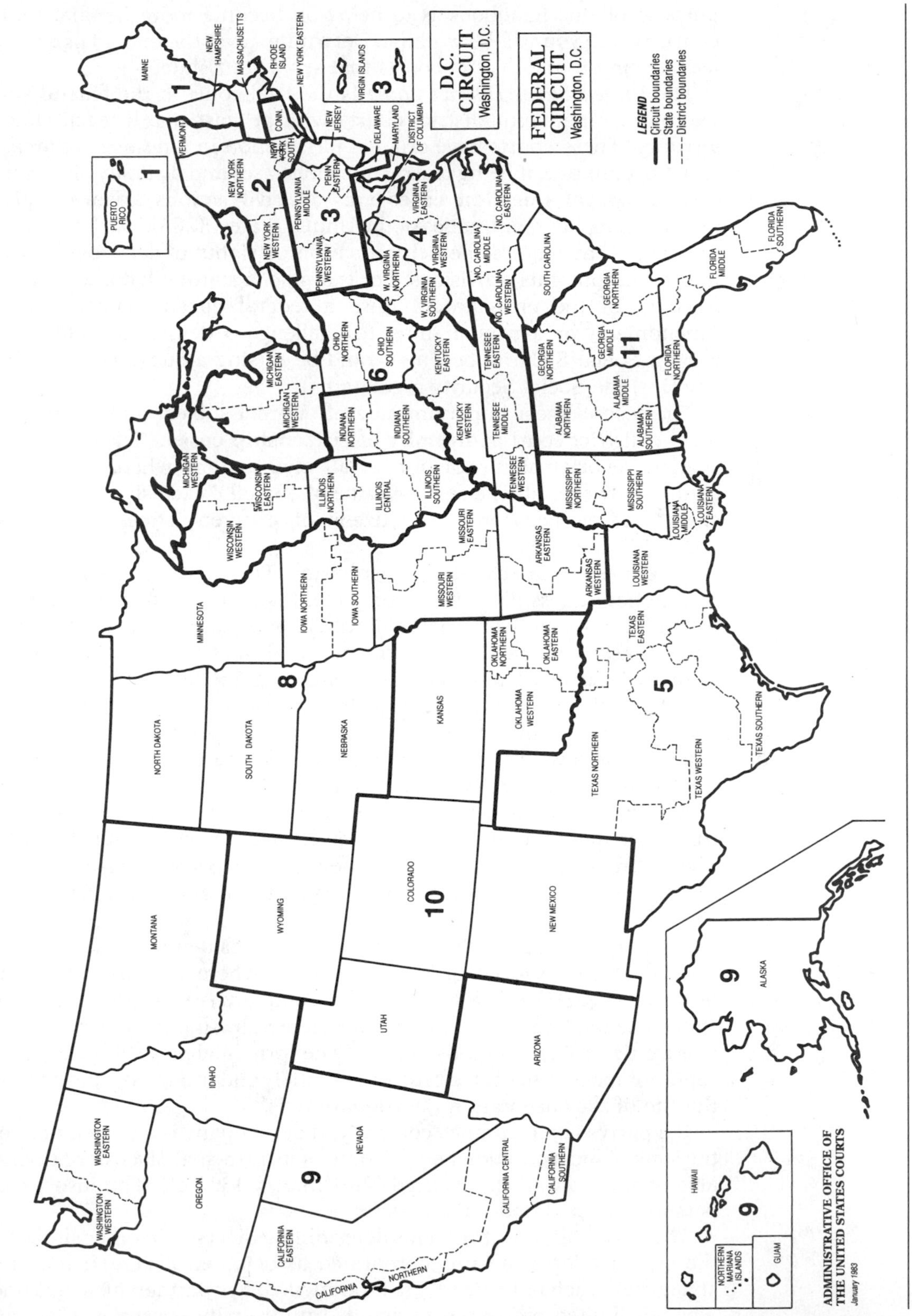

ADMINISTRATIVE OFFICE OF
THE UNITED STATES COURTS
January 1983

A PARALEGAL
HANDBOOK

purpose of this handbook is to help you become more familiar with the courts where you will be working. Determine from the map in figure 2:6 the federal circuit and district courts that serve your state.

The *United States District Court* is the trial court in the federal system. There are ninety-four district courts with at least one in each state and territory. These courts have original jurisdiction in a number of areas, the two most important being federal question cases and diversity of citizenship cases. **Federal question cases** are "all civil actions arising under the Constitution, laws, or treaties of the United States" (28 U.S.C. § 1331). These are cases that require the determination of rights under federal law and interpretation of its provisions. For example, a statute that unduly restricts freedom of the press would raise a federal question under the First Amendment, or a person suing to challenge a denial to that person of certain Social Security benefits would be raising a question about federal law (i.e., the Social Security regulations).

The second most important area of original subject matter jurisdiction for the district court is **diversity of citizenship cases.** "The district courts shall have original jurisdiction of all civil actions where the matter in controversy exceeds the sum or value of $50,000, exclusive of interest and costs, and is between . . . citizens of different states" [28 U.S.C. § 1332(a)(2)].

Several issues arise under this provision. The district court does not have jurisdiction unless diversity is complete. Each defendant must be a citizen of a different state from each plaintiff.[6] For example, three plaintiffs, two from Kansas and one from Wisconsin, could sue four defendants, two from Missouri and two from Nebraska, assuming $50,000 in dispute; but the same plaintiffs could not sue in federal district court if just one defendant was from the same state as any of the plaintiffs. For the purpose of determining diversity jurisdiction, citizens of the District of Columbia are treated as if they were citizens of a state.[7]

A citizen's state is defined as the state of domicile. The **domicile** is the true permanent home—the place one intends to return after being away. This is frequently determined by looking at a person's place of employment, site of voting or automobile registration, site of property, and the like.[8]

For purposes of diversity, a corporation is considered a citizen of both the state in which it is incorporated and the state where it has its principal place of business [28 U.S.C. § 1332(c)]. If a company is incorporated in several states, the modern view (though not accepted in all jurisdictions) is to treat it as a citizen of each of those states.[9] The "principal place of business" is the center of most of the corporation's activities, and if that isn't determinative, the site of the corporation's headquarters is.[10]

If a party is an insurance company, that company is a citizen not only of the state of incorporation and the state of its principal place of business, but also of the state of the insured [28 U.S.C. § 1332(c)]. The insured is the person protected under the policy.

There are still some problems determining diversity in other situations. If the organization is an unincorporated association, it is a citizen of each state where each of its members is domiciled. For partnerships, it is unclear whether limited partners are included in diversity questions. Class action (numerous individuals with a common legal interest, i.e., all users of a certain product) citizenship is generally in the state of the named representative.[11]

Here are other points on diversity jurisdiction. Diversity of citizenship must be alleged in the complaint (the document that states the claim) (28 U.S.C. § 1653). Once it is established, it cannot be altered by the parties' moving from state to state. It must exist, however, at the time a case is removed to federal court. Diversity does not give federal district courts jurisdiction in domestic relations or probate matters.[12]

In addition to diversity being complete, the "amount in controversy" must meet the $50,000 requirement. Normally the district court will accept jurisdiction based on the allegation of amount in the complaint unless it is legally clear that the plaintiff cannot recover the required amount.[13] Federal jurisdiction is not lost if recovery is eventually less than the requirement, but costs may be assessed [28 U.S.C. § 1332(b)].

Here is how the "amount in controversy" is determined in several contexts:

1. If the suit is for a declaratory judgment or an injunction, it is the value of the object in controversy.
2. In most actions, it is the amount of plaintiff's harm or the defendant's costs to comply.
3. If suing under a federal statute that permits recovery of attorney's fees, that amount can be added to make $50,000.
4. If the case is an installment contract case and it is the entire contract that is in dispute, it is the value of the entire contract; otherwise it is just the amount that has accrued in the installments to date.
5. If the case involves one plaintiff against one defendant, it is the value of all claims against defendant (i.e., a combination of tort and contract claims).
6. If there are multiple plaintiffs, each plaintiff's claim must be $50,000 or more. The claims cannot be combined to make the amount.
7. If multiple parties own property in common, it is the value of the property that is determinative (for three plaintiffs owning property in common, the value would not have to be $150,000).
8. In a class action, each person's claim must be in excess of the $50,000 amount.
9. If there is a counterclaim, determination under current law is not clear.[14]

In addition to the federal question cases and diversity cases involving more than $50,000, federal district courts have original subject matter jurisdiction over the following:

1. Exclusive jurisdiction over all admiralty, maritime, and prize cases (28 U.S.C. § 1333);
2. All suits brought by the United States, its agencies, or officers (28 U.S.C. § 1345);
3. Suits against the United States or its officers (concurrent with U.S. Claims Court up to $10,000)(28 U.S.C. § 1346);

4. Suits to compel officers of United States to perform their duty (28 U.S.C. § 1361);
5. Removal of suits against federal officers in state courts (28 U.S.C. § 1442):
6. Suits in Bankruptcy (28 U.S.C. § 1334);
7. Suits in patents, plant variety protection, copyrights, trademarks, and unfair competition (28 U.S.C. § 1338);
8. Suits involving Internal Revenue and customs duties (28 U.S.C. § 1340);
9. Suits in civil rights (28 U.S.C. § 1343); and
10. Suits affecting ambassadors and other public ministers and consuls (28 U.S.C. § 1351).

State courts have concurrent jurisdiction with federal courts in all matters within federal jurisdiction, except if federal jurisdiction is exclusive as in the case of copyright and patent law.

The district courts have subject matter, diversity jurisdiction over suits between citizens of a state and citizens or subjects of a foreign state [28 U.S.C. § 1332(a)(2)], and where citizens or subjects of foreign states are "additional parties" on either side of the suit, and where a foreign state sues "citizens of a state or of different states" [28 U.S.C. § 1332(a)(3) and (4)]. This type of diversity jurisdiction involving foreign states and their citizens or subjects is called **alienage jurisdiction.**

Specialized federal courts are established as Article I legislative courts. Their judges have specified terms, usually fifteen years, and their salaries are not protected from congressional decreases as are those of the constitutional courts. The most important specialized courts are as follows:

1. The *United States Court of International Trade* decides disputes between citizens and the government on issues arising from import transactions (28 U.S.C. § 1581–85).
2. The *United States Claims Court* decides claims of U.S. citizens against the government based on federal law or contracts [28 U.S.C. § 1491(a)(1)] (some of this jurisdiction is concurrent with U.S. district courts, especially in Internal Revenue Service taxes improperly collected).
3. The *United States Tax Court* has original (trial) jurisdiction over taxpayer challenges to deficiency determinations of the Internal Revenue Service (26 U.S.C. § 6213).
4. The courts and magistrate courts adjunct to the United States District Courts (28 U.S.C. §§ 7441–87) include:
   a. *Federal magistrate courts* (whose judges are now called magistrate judges),
   b. *Bankruptcy courts,*
   c. Hearing of some private civil disputes and criminal matters.
5. The *United States Court of Military Appeals* hears appeals from the Courts of Military Review (civil judges) (10 U.S.C. § 867).
6. The *United States Court of Veterans Appeals* reviews decisions of the Board of Veterans Appeals (38 U.S.C. § 4052).

See the diagram of the federal court system in figure 2:7. Note the flow of appeals in the system.

Figure 2:7   The Federal Court System

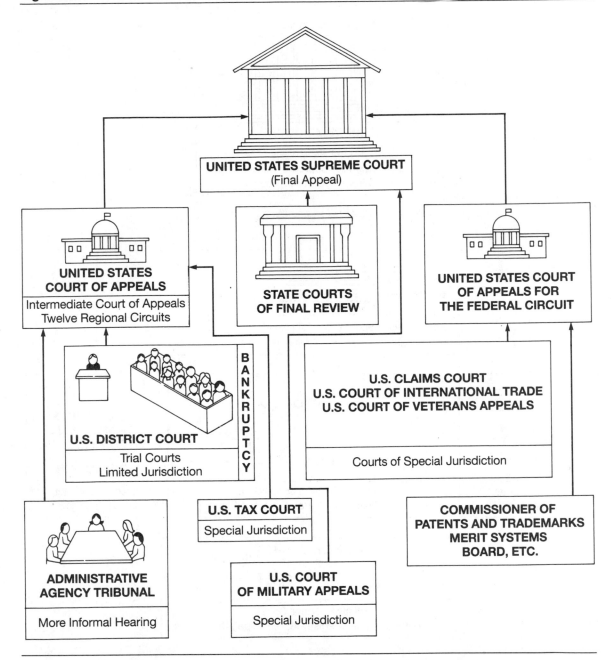

State Courts and Their Jurisdiction

The diagram in figure 2:8 is illustrative of the structure of many state court systems. Note the flow of appeals in this diagram. Obtain or create a diagram of your state system noting which courts function as trial courts (original jurisdiction) and as intermediate or final level courts of appeal (appellate jurisdiction). Be able to identify the subject matter jurisdiction of

Figure 2:8   The State Court System

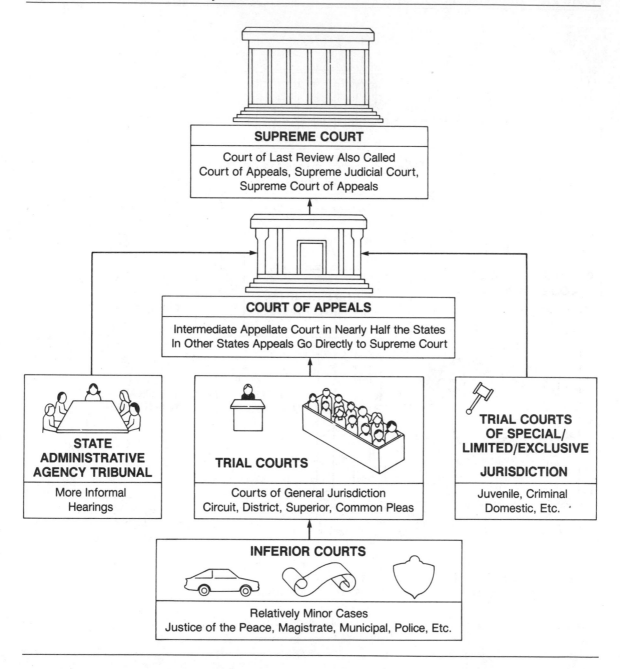

each of your state courts. This is important because most of your work will be done in state court.

State courts are considered courts of general jurisdiction. All legitimate claims, including most of those that can go into the federal courts, can be filed in the state courts of original jurisdiction.

ASSIGNMENT 2:7
Make a copy of the federal court structure diagram found in this chapter and add any explanatory notes you feel will be useful to you in the future. Include in your diagram the

names of U.S. district courts that sit in your state and the U.S. court of appeals that covers the circuit in which your state is situated.

Make a similar explanatory diagram for the court system of your state. Research the material to be placed in the diagram, including any jurisdictional amounts, by looking under "courts," "judiciary," and "jurisdiction" in the index of your state statutes or constitution, usually located in the law library. Some states have an administrative office of the courts at the capitol, which may provide preprinted state court diagrams.

Place both diagrams in the court section of your litigation system folder. (See appendix.)

ASSIGNMENT 2:8

Consult the state's legal directory in the library to obtain all court addresses, names of clerks of court, important telephone numbers, and so on. Research state statutes for the subject matter jurisdictions of your state's highest, intermediate, and trial courts. Place this data on separate sheets in the court structure portion of your system folder.

Venue

Venue, literally "neighborhood," is the concept that determines where a case should be heard. Generally it means the defendant's neighborhood and/or the neighborhood where the incident occurred giving rise to the legal claim in the lawsuit. In most states this means the county where the defendant resides and the county where the incident happened. Some states have passed statutes or rules of procedure that define what court has venue generally and in specific kinds of situations such as in probate or property matters. Learn the venue requirements for your state.

The venue requirements for the United States District Court, 28 U.S.C. § 1391, states:

(a) A civil action wherein jurisdiction is founded only on diversity of citizenship may, except as otherwise provided by law, be brought only in (1) a judicial district where any defendant resides, if all defendants reside in the same State, (2) a judicial district in which a substantial part of the events or omissions giving rise to the claim occurred, or a substantial part of property that is the subject of the action is situated, or (3) a judicial district in which the defendants are subject to personal jurisdiction at the time the action is commenced.

(b) A civil action wherein jurisdiction is not founded solely on diversity of citizenship may, except as otherwise provided by law, be brought only if (1) a judicial district where any defendant resides, if all defendants reside in the same State, (2) a judicial district in which a substantial part of the events or omissions giving rise to the claim occurred, or a substantial part of property that is the subject of the action is situated, or (3) a judicial district in which any defendant may be found, if there is no district in which the action may otherwise be brought.

(c) For purposes of venue under this chapter, a defendant that is a corporation shall be deemed to reside in any judicial district in which it is subject to personal jurisdiction at the time the action is commenced. In a State which has more than one judicial district and in which a defendant that is a corporation is subject to personal jurisdiction at the time an action is commenced, such corporation shall be deemed to reside in any district in that state within which its contacts would be sufficient to subject it to personal jurisdiction if that district were a separate State, and, if there is no such district, the corporation shall be deemed to reside in the district within which it has the most significant contacts.

(d) An alien may be sued in any district.

(e) A civil action in which a defendant is an officer or employee of the United States or any agency thereof acting in his official capacity or under color of legal authority, or an agency of the United States, or the United States, may, except as otherwise provided by law, be brought in any judicial district in which (1) a defendant in the action resides, (2) a substantial part of the events or omissions giving rise to the claim occurred, or a substantial part of property that is involved in the action is situated, or (3) the plaintiff resides if no real property is involved in the action. Additional persons may be joined as parties to any such action in accordance with the Federal Rules of Civil Procedure and with such other venue requirements as would be applicable if the United States or one of its officers, employees, or agencies were not a party.

The summons and complaint in such an action shall be served as provided by the Federal Rules of Civil Procedure except that the delivery of the summons and complaint to the officer or agency as required by the rules may be made by certified mail beyond the territorial limits of the district in which the action is brought.

(f) A civil action against a foreign state as defined in section 1603(a) of this title may be brought—

(1) in any judicial district in which a substantial part of the events or omissions giving rise to the claim occurred, or a substantial part of property that is the subject of the action is situated;

(2) in any judicial district in which the vessel or cargo of a foreign state is situated, if the claim is asserted under section 1605(b) of this title;

(3) in any judicial district in which the agency or instrumentality is licensed to do business or is doing business, if the action is brought against an agency or instrumentality of a foreign state as defined in section 1603(b) of this title; or

(4) in the United States District Court for the District of Columbia if the action is brought against a foreign state or political subdivision thereof.

Venue is distinct from jurisdiction. It does not address which court has personal or subject matter jurisdiction. Rather, it addresses a location that should be fair to the parties and is likely to be close to witnesses, evidence, or the property in question. It might help to think that subject matter jurisdiction presents the question of *what court* handles this kind of case. Personal jurisdiction asks *whom* can this court enforce a judgment against, and venue asks *where*, in relationship to the parties, the event, or the property, can this case be heard. If venue is improper, the court can dismiss the case or transfer it to a court that has venue [28 U.S.C. § 1406(a)]. Normal venue considerations are frequently altered in special circumstances by either state or federal law. In interpleader cases, for example, federal venue rests in any judicial district where one or more of the claimants to the contested property reside (28 U.S.C. § 1397). In probate matters, state court venue is usually where the estate is located. Objection to venue, if not made early in the suit, will be waived, unlike objections to subject matter or personal jurisdiction.

Choosing a Court: The Relationship between Jurisdiction and Venue

Here is a review of the factors that must be taken into consideration in deciding what court can hear a matter. First, the court must have subject matter jurisdiction. Most state courts, unless they are specialized courts, are courts of general jurisdiction and can hear most matters. The federal courts have limited jurisdiction and can hear only those matters defined by law for them to hear.

Once it is determined which courts have subject matter jurisdiction, it must be determined which courts have venue. Keep in mind that in most states, venue rests with the court in the county where the defendant resides and in the county where the incident occurred giving rise to the lawsuit. Some state statutes define the venue for specific matters. Federal venue is defined by statute and, in cases where jurisdiction is based solely on diversity, venue exists in any federal district:

1. where any defendant resides when all defendants reside in the same state; or
2. where a substantial part of the claim (events or omissions) arose, or the property in dispute is located; or
3. where personal jurisdiction exists over all of the defendants [28 U.S.C. § 1391 (a)(1–3)].

Venue exists in federal question and other cases in any federal district:

1. where any defendant resides when all defendants reside in the same state; or
2. where a substantial part of the claim (events or omissions) arose, or the property in dispute is located; or
3. where any defendants may be found, if no other district has venue [28 U.S.C. § 1391 (b)(1–3)].

Also remember that for venue purposes, corporations, insurance companies, aliens, foreign states, and actions in which a defendant is the United States or one of its officials or agencies are treated specially and the specific statute should be consulted.

Of the courts that have both subject matter jurisdiction and venue, it remains to be determined which, if any, of these courts have personal jurisdiction (or in the case of property like real estate, which has in rem jurisdiction over the property). To gain personal jurisdiction over the defendant, the defendant must be served with a summons and complaint. The summons is generally valid only in the geographical area over which the court has authority. Generally, therefore, federal district courts can serve a summons on persons only in the district in which the court sits. State courts can get personal jurisdiction only over persons within the boundaries of the state in which that court sits. State statutes called long-arm statutes can extend personal jurisdiction beyond a state's borders to persons living in other states if those persons have had or do have sufficient contact with the state seeking personal jurisdiction. For example, if Florida has passed a long-arm law to reach across state boundaries, a motorist from New York driving in Florida generally is deemed to be subject to the personal jurisdiction of the Florida courts for wrongful acts (negligence) while operating a motor vehicle in Florida. This is true even if the motorist has returned to New York. In diversity cases, the law of the state in which the federal court sits determines the reach of the federal court. In addition, specific federal statutes may give the federal district courts personal jurisdiction beyond each court's district boundaries. Long-arm statutes will be discussed further in chapter 6.

Corporations are subject to personal jurisdiction in any state where the law invokes personal jurisdiction if the cause of action arises out of the corporation's "doing business," "transacting business," or registration to do business in that state. Usually, if a corporation regularly does business in a state, it is subject to personal jurisdiction in the state. If the corporation is subject to personal jurisdiction in a state, it is also deemed subject to personal jurisdiction of the U.S. district court in that state.

Now, how good are you at applying these general rules to determine in which courts an action can be filed? Assume that X, a California resident, wants to sue Y, a resident of western New York, for $60,000 in damages stemming from an automobile accident in northern California. Which courts have subject matter jurisdiction? At least the state trial courts of California and New York have the original and general jurisdiction to hear the case. The federal district courts in the Northern District of California and the Western District of New York have the needed limited subject matter jurisdictions, that is, diversity jurisdiction involving more than $50,000.

Which courts have venue? One California state trial court has venue—the trial court located in the county where the accident occurred. A New York trial court has venue in the county where defendant Y resides. Federal venue rests in the Northern District of California because this is a diversity of citizenship case and in such cases venue is located where a substantial part of the events or omissions arose. Federal venue also rests in the Western District of New York because in diversity cases, venue exists where any defendant resides when all defendants reside in the same state.

Assuming there is no long-arm statute, which courts can get personal jurisdiction? Courts, normally, can get personal jurisdiction only in the state or federal district in which they sit. Therefore, only the New York state trial court and the federal district court for the Western District of New York have the defendant residing in their geographical boundaries. Therefore, X must bring suit in either the New York state court or the federal court for the Western District of New York. A chart showing which courts can hear the case of *X v. Y* looks like this:

	Subject Matter Jurisdiction	Venue	Personal Jurisdiction
California State Court	Yes	Yes	No
California Federal Court	Yes (diversity)	Yes	No
New York State Court	Yes	Yes	Yes
New York Federal Court	Yes	Yes	Yes

With this information, the attorney would have to consider the judges in each court, possible bias in state court, convenience to witnesses and evidence, and all other factors that would work either in X's favor or to X's disadvantage in deciding which of the two courts would be best.

If, in the prior action, Z is also a defendant and lives in Utah, where could X sue? Add the following to the previous breakdown:

	Subject Matter Jurisdiction	Venue	Personal Jurisdiction
Utah State Court	Yes	Yes (for Z only)	Yes (for Z only)
Utah Federal Court	Yes	Yes (for Z only)	Yes (for Z only)
N.Y. Federal Court	Yes	Yes (for Y only)	Yes (for Y only)

Utah cannot qualify for joint federal venue because all of the defendants do not reside in Utah, no personal jurisdiction exists over all the defendants, and the substantial events or omissions did not occur there. This is also true for the federal court in New York. Therefore, no federal court will work for suing both defendants simultaneously or individually, so X must sue Y and Z separately in their respective state or federal courts. Note that in federal actions with one defendant, all the defendants reside in one state. Therefore, venue exists in the district of the defendant's residence.

X could sue Y and Z in California state or federal court only if California had a long-arm guest motorist statute giving California courts personal jurisdiction over out-of-state residents involved in automobile accidents in California.

If the original X and Y example involved a federal question, such as a violation of a constitutional right, the federal venues would be the same as in the preceding diversity example. State venue would exist in the county in which the action arose and where defendant resides (the proper county in New York.) But again, without a long-arm statute, only the district court in New York and the state court in New York have personal jurisdiction.

This time, you try to determine where A and B can sue under the following circumstances. A resides in Wyoming and B resides in Colorado. They wish to sue C, a corporation, for a contract violated in Colorado in the amount of $100,000. C is incorporated in Delaware and has its principal place of business in Colorado. Take a minute to work this out. Hey! Do not read further until you have tested your understanding. Give it a try.

If you sued in Delaware and Colorado state courts, you are correct. Here is why. Each state in question has subject matter jurisdiction. Diversity jurisdiction for a federal court action does not exist—diversity must be complete, and B is from Colorado and so is defendant C (principal place of business). Without diversity jurisdiction, the federal courts are out of the picture. Since state venue normally exists in the county of the defendant's residence as well as the county where the action arose, venue exists in Delaware and Colorado. The only state courts with personal jurisdiction are those where the defendant resides—in this case Delaware and Colorado, if Colorado state law holds that the principal place of business is sufficient for personal jurisdiction to exist. The action, therefore, can be heard in state courts in Colorado or Delaware.

But what if C's principal place of business is Chicago, Illinois, instead of Colorado? Then we have plaintiffs from Wyoming (A) and Colorado (B) and a defendant (C) from Delaware (state of corporation) and Illinois (principal place of business). Because of general jurisdiction, each of the named states has subject matter jurisdiction. Federal diversity jurisdiction exists in each of the district courts—the districts of Colorado, Wyoming, Northern Illinois, and Delaware. State venue exists in Delaware and Illinois (residence of defendant) and in Colorado (where case arose). Federal venue, under 28 U.S.C. § 1391(c), for a *defendant* corporation lies in any district in any state where under that state's law the corporation does enough business that the state has personal jurisdiction over the corporation. Personal jurisdiction can be obtained at least in Delaware and in Illinois and, if there is enough business, in Colorado and Wyoming. Federal venue, therefore, would exist in these states and double in Colorado because that is where the cause arose. A chart of the possibilities appears as follows:

	Subject Matter Jurisdiction	Venue	Personal Jurisdiction
Colorado State Court	Yes	Yes	? (depends on contacts)
Wyoming State Court	Yes	No	? (depends on contacts)
Delaware State Court	Yes	Yes	Yes
Illinois State Court	Yes	Yes	Yes
Colorado Federal Court	Yes	Yes	?(depends on contacts)
Wyoming Federal Court	Yes	?	? (depends on contacts)
Delaware Federal Court	Yes	Yes	Yes
Illinois Federal Court	Yes	Yes	Yes

Plaintiffs would definitely have four courts to choose from and possibly as many as eight because of the defendant corporation venue rule and the expanded personal jurisdiction through corporate contacts in the state.

ASSIGNMENT 2:9

Determine in which courts subject matter jurisdiction, personal jurisdiction, and venue exist in the following problems. The answers are in your teacher's instruction manual.

1. A, a resident of Florida, sues B, a resident of Washington, who is also the secretary of the interior, in a First Amendment freedom of speech issue arising in southeast Georgia.
2. M, a resident of Wisconsin, and O, a resident of Minnesota, sue Corporations X and Y for industrial injuries amounting to $40,000 for each plaintiff resulting from an accident that occurred in Illinois. X is incorporated in Delaware and Ohio, and Y is incorporated in North Carolina with its principal place of business in Ohio.
3. J and K reside in Oregon and sue R, who resides in Kentucky, and S, who resides in Washington, for a tort (libel) amounting to injuries exceeding $70,000 each, which occurred in Washington.
4. What happens in problem 3 if S is a Canadian citizen living in Louisiana?
5. E sues Great Britain for damages exceeding $500,000 for the illegal impounding of E's commercial plane.

Transfer of Cases

Under 28 U.S.C. § 1404 and similar state laws, courts have the discretion to transfer a case to a more convenient court if the current court is inconvenient, even though the plaintiff may have met all the jurisdiction and venue requirements. This is a legal concept known as *forum non conveniens*. If a defendant demonstrates that the current forum is truly inconvenient (unfair, too costly, too far from evidence, and so on) and that another court exists with all the requisite jurisdiction and venues, then the court may transfer the case to the better forum.

Figure 2:9   Case Roadmap

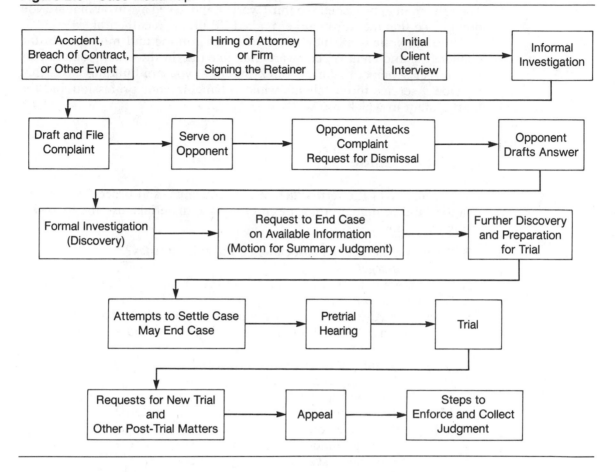

A Case Roadmap

Figure 2:9 sets out the various steps in handling a case from start to finish. Although you will be learning the process in more detail later, this case roadmap will help you to know where you are headed when working on a case. You should photocopy this diagram and place it in your system folder.

Concluding Comments

The *Paralegal Handbook* has introduced you to the law firm, its structure, the kinds of cases it handles, the role of the paralegal, office procedures, ethical considerations, and the methods to be employed in your training. In addition, the handbook has emphasized techniques for thriving in the law office, your professional development, and a review of courts and jurisdictions. These are fundamentals essential to a good beginning and to your career.

There is the story of a man who encountered three workers. Stepping up to the first worker, the man asked, "What are you doing?" The first worker replied, "Making a buck." Going on to the second worker, he repeated the question, "What are you doing?" The second worker said, "Laying bricks." Then the man approached the third worker and asked again, "What are you doing?" To this the third worker replied, "Building a cathedral."[15]

Although your work may range from the routine and mundane to the challenging and creative, be aware that, like the third worker, you are part of a larger scheme of things. Brick by brick, you are building cases that provide a service to our clients while enhancing your profession and the legal system in which you work.

Study Guide

As a summary of the terms, definitions, concepts, and procedures in this chapter, and to prepare for an exam on these materials, use the following study questions:

1. What is a partner, an associate, and a staff attorney?
2. Define *paralegal*.
3. What is your "chain of command" in this firm?
4. Define *litigation*.
5. What is the difference between a personal injury case based on negligence and a products liability case? An antitrust and a civil rights case?
6. Why is a paralegal valuable to a law firm?
7. Describe the steps in the timekeeping procedure.
8. Describe the steps in the deadline control procedure.
9. Why are timekeeping and deadline control important?
10. Which law office errors most often lead to malpractice claims?
11. What are the techniques for thriving in the law office?
12. What is a litigation system and why is it beneficial?
13. What is the sequence of a litigation case from start to finish?
14. Define *professional ethics* in the context of the practice of law.
15. Why are professional ethics so important to a law firm?
16. What are the things a paralegal may not do?
17. What are the seven criteria that assure a paralegal's actions will not be or cause a breach of ethics?
18. How does a paralegal preserve client confidences?
19. What is a conflict of interest?
20. What is the significance to paralegals of the expression "Chinese wall"?
21. What are the characteristics of the common components of court systems in the United States?
22. What is jurisdiction? Define the various kinds of jurisdiction: geographical, personal, general, and so on.
23. What are the names and jurisdictions of the various levels of courts in both the federal and your state system?
24. What federal circuit is your state in?
25. What three things must a court have in order to hear a case and bind a party to the court's decision? Be able to apply these concepts to determine what court or courts can hear a lawsuit depending on domiciles of the parties and other factors.

26. Be able to explain why and give examples of when a court might have personal jurisdiction but still not be able to hear a case.
27. Why are professional integrity and honesty so important?
28. What is meant by the term *professional loyalty* as applied to your fellow workers? The client? The practice of law?
29. What is personal professional development? Why is it important?

Endnotes

1. STERNGARD, HORDLINGER & FELIX-RETZKE, A PRACTICAL GUIDE TO PREVENTING LEGAL MALPRACTICE (1983). Report results of Virginia Bar Study (1963–73); Southern Conferences of Bar Presidents' Study (1974–77); and the more recent National Legal Malpractice Data Center Study, 8–12.
2. Id., 17–19.
3. Judd, *Beyond the Bar: Legal Assistants and the Unauthorized Practice of Law*, 3 LEGAL ASSISTANTS UPDATE 12 (1983).
4. See Schairer, *Paralegals and the Imputed Firm Disqualification Rule*, JOURNAL OF PARALEGAL EDUCATION AND PRACTICE 1–22 (Oct. 1990).
5. Pub. L. No. 100–352, 102 Stat. 662 (1988).
6. *Owen Equipment & Erection Co. v. Kroger*, 437 U.S. 365, 373 (1978).
7. *National Mutual Insurance Co. v. Tidewater Transfer Co.*, 337 U.S. 583 (1949).
8. See CHEMERINSKY, FEDERAL JURISDICTION 250 (1989) and WRIGHT, MILLER & COOPER, FEDERAL PRACTICE AND PROCEDURE § 13B, at 530–33 (1984).
9. CHEMERINSKY, *supra*, at 250.
10. Id.
11. Id., 251.
12. Id., 252–53.
13. *Saint Paul Mercury Indemnity Co. v. Red Cab Co.*, 303 U.S. 283, 288 (1983).
14. Id., 256–58.
15. JEANS, TRIAL ADVOCACY 48 (1975).

3

The Initial Interview

- Introduction
- The Interview Plan
- The Interview
- Summarizing the Interview
- Keeping the Client Informed

Note: If students have not yet had a course on torts and contracts, an expanded discussion of torts and contracts and the pertinent principles of law is included in appendices B and C.

■ Introduction

Today you have the opportunity to begin working on a case. (Please reread Case I.) Mr. White has met with Ann Forrester, who will be coming to the office for her initial interview for a personal injury negligence case. It is your job to prepare and conduct the interview with Ms. Forrester.

The client interview is a significant step. First, it sets the tone for the entire relationship between the prospective client and the law firm. The client should leave feeling comfortable with the relationship and confident that matters will be handled competently. Second, it sets the tone for the critical relationship between the client and the paralegal that may last months or even years. Third, it is the important beginning of investigation, a fact-gathering process requiring other interviews and techniques that will be discussed in the chapters to follow. The initial client interview and subsequent interviews determine the basis of the lawsuit (or its defense), the firm's acceptance of the case, and the fee.

ASSIGNMENT 3:1
List the task and the purpose(s) of the task at the beginning of the interview section in your system folder.

The Interview Plan

You will need to set up an interview plan in order to derive maximum benefit from the time spent with the client. Use the following Interview Plan Checklist in developing your interview plan.

Interview Plan Checklist

Step 1   Review all available information on the case.
Step 2   Locate or develop an appropriate interview form.
Step 3   Select a location for the interview.
Step 4   Schedule the interview (tentatively); check with attorney.
Step 5   Determine what information the client should bring.
Step 6   Set up the appointment with the client.
Step 7   Anticipate and arrange for any special needs.
Step 8   Review all pertinent ethical and tactical considerations.
Step 9   Review recommended interview techniques.
Step 10   Prepare orientation and instruction materials for client.
Step 11   Prepare any forms for the client's signature.
Step 12   Prepare the interview site.

ASSIGNMENT 3:2
Place a copy of the "Interview Plan Checklist" in your system folder. Label twelve sheets of paper with the twelve steps in the plan (one step per page), and place them in order after the checklist. Any additional information or documents can be added behind the appropriate step sheet.

The Interview Plan in Detail

Step 1

Review all available information on the case. Check the file for news clippings, and note any other readily available information. Any background you can gain about the incident will direct you in researching additional information.

ASSIGNMENT 3:3
The case file for Ann Forrester consists of the information in Case I of chapter 1. Reread that case before proceeding.

Step 2

Locate or develop an appropriate interview form. An interviewer needs to identify what information is needed from the client and what questions will best elicit that information. A form questionnaire can save preparation time and serve as a guide for the interviewer. Such forms can usually be found in the firm's form files, or in trial practice manuals readily available at the firm or local library. Our firm has an interview form for personal injury– automobile negligence cases. These forms are contained in figures 3:1(a)and (b).[1]

Figure 3:1(a)   Checklist Form: Client Background Information

Please type or print neatly. If more space is needed, please use back or extra sheets

1. Why did you choose this office? _____

2. Have you hired any other attorney on this matter? _____

3. _____ 4. _____
                    Name   Soc. Sec. No.

5. _____
                        Address, Including County   Zip Code   Years at

List Prior Addresses and Approximate Dates on Back

6. _____ 7. _____ 8. _____ 9. _____ 10. _____
     Home Phone   Work Phone   Date of Birth   Age   Sex

11. _____ 12. _____ 13. _____
       Maiden Name   Other Names Used   Nationality, Race, Religion

14. _____
                    If minor, guardian's name, address, if different from 3. above

15. S __ M __ D __ W __ Other __ 16. _____ 17. _____
         Marital Status   Spouse's Name   Date of Birth

18. _____ 19. _____ 20. _____
         Address if Different from 3. above   Home Phone   Work Phone

21. _____ 22. _____
             Spouse's Place of Employment   Spouse's Job Title

23. _____   _____   _____

    _____   _____   _____

    _____   _____   _____

         Children's Names   Ages   Addresses

24. _____ 25. If other marriages, list date, spouse, and children on back.
         Date of Marriage/Divorce

26. _____
                    If divorced, status of maintenance or child support

27. _____
             Other Close Relative   (Name, Address, Phone)

28. Current _____   _____   _____   _____   _____

    _____   _____   _____   _____   _____

    _____   _____   _____   _____   _____

         Employer   Address   Job Title/Salary   Phone   Dates

List Others on Back

29. _____
             If self-employed, nature of business, address, phone, partners, salary or approximate income

30. Education: highest grade or degree completed _____

_____

_____

School   Dates   Degree   Area of Study

31. Gross income _____ **32.** Attach tax returns from last three years.
33. Property: List all real estate owned/if held solely, jointly, etc./value, mortgage, etc.

_____

34. If requested, attach list of personal property (bank accounts, stocks and bonds, autos, furniture, etc.).
35. If you have been involved in any prior litigation, please give details, type of action, plaintiff-defendant, attorney, court, year, result.

_____

_____

_____

Figure 3:1(b) Checklist Form: Automobile Accident

PARTIES—GENERAL INFORMATION

( ) Plaintiff _____ Age ____ Sex ____ Phone _____

( ) Address _____ City _____ County _____ State _____ Z.Code _____

( ) Bus. Address _____ City _____ County _____ State _____ Phone _____

( ) Ins. Carrier _____ Address _____ Phone _____

    Amt. Ins. Liab. _____ P.D. _____ Med. _____ Collision _____

    Uninsured Motorist _____ Any Coverage Deductible? Which? _____

( ) Defendant 1. _____ Age _____ Sex _____ Phone _____

( ) Address _____ City _____ County _____ State _____ Phone _____

( ) Bus. Address _____ City _____ County _____ State _____ Phone _____

( ) Ins. Carrier _____ Address _____ Phone _____

    Amt. Ins. Liab. _____ P.D. _____ Med. _____ Collision _____

    Uninsured Motorist _____ Any Coverage Deductible? Which? _____

( ) Co-Defendants 2. _____ Age _____ Sex _____ Phone _____

              3. _____ _____ _____ _____

( ) Address 2. _____ City _____ County _____ State _____ Z.Code _____

              3. _____ _____ _____ _____ _____

( ) Bus. Address 2. _____ City _____ County _____ State _____ Phone _____

              3. _____ _____ _____ _____ _____

( ) Ins. Carrier 2. _____ Address _____ Phone _____

3. _____   _____   _____

Amt. Ins. Liab. 2. _____ P.D. _____ Med. _____ Collision _____

3. _____   _____   _____   _____

Uninsured Motorist 2. _____ Any Coverage Deductible? Which? _____

3. _____   _____

2. _____

3. _____

FACTS OF ACCIDENT

( ) Date of Accident _____ Time _____ Material Facts _____

_____

_____

_____

_____

Res Gestae Statements _____

_____

( ) Type of Case (Check Applicable Subject Matter)

( ) Animals ( ) Assault & Battery ( ) Drainage & Pollution ( ) Employer, Employee & Independent Contractor ( ) False Imprisonment ( ) Fraud & Deceit ( ) Invitees & Licensees ( ) Malicious Arrest or Prosecution ( ) Malpractice ( ) Municipal ( ) Products Liability ( ) Real Estate ( ) Slander or Libel ( ) Transportation—Airplane, Automobile or Train ( ) Trespass ( ) Wrongful Death ( ) Workers' Compensation ( ) Other _____

_____

( ) Diagram Accident Scene if Physical Facts Important

_____

_____

( ) Indicate & Note on Diagram. Answer Yes or No Where Applicable

( ) Width of Streets or Roads Measured _____

( ) Number of Lanes _____ Any Peculiar Curves or Hills _____

( ) Yellow Lines _____ Stop Signs or Traffic Devices _____

( ) Skid Marks _____ Position of Vehicles After Accident _____

( ) Type of Road Surface. Asphalt or Concrete _____

( ) Dry or Wet _____ Weather—Fog, Rain, Drizzle, Sleet, or Snow _____

_____

( ) Visibility—Good or Bad _____ Day, Night, Dusk, or Dawn _____

_____

( ) Clear or Cloudy _____ Other _____

( ) Ascertain if Pictures Were Taken of Accident Scene _____

( ) When _____ By Whom _____

( ) Address _____ Phone _____

( ) If Not, Take Pictures of Accident Scene immediately

( ) Place Pictures Obtained or Taken in Evidence File

( ) Miscellaneous Comments _____

_____

( ) Automobile information

    ( ) Plaintiff Vehicle

        ( ) Year _____ Make _____ Model _____ Color _____

        ( ) Cylinders _____ Horsepower _____ Weight _____ Manuf. I.D. _____

        ( ) Tag No. _____ Power or Regular Steering _____ Brakes _____

        ( ) Defects of Vehicle—Brakes _____ Lights _____ Motor _____

            Steering _____ Tires _____ Other _____

            Comments as to Condition _____

        ( ) Location of Vehicle—Garage _____

            Address _____ Phone _____

            Were Pictures Taken of Automobile _____

            When _____ By Whom _____

            Address _____ Phone _____

        ( ) If Not, Take Pictures at Garage & Place in Evidence File

            Taken By _____ When _____ Address _____

        ( ) Note Alleged Speed Prior to Collision _____

        ( ) Indicate Impact Points on Vehicle Diagram & Note Interior Damage

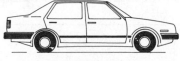

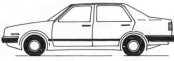

Right Side
Length ____ ft.   Front
                       Width ____ ft.   Rear   Left Side

( ) Owner of Plaintiff Vehicle _____ Age _____ Sex _____

( ) Address _____ City _____ State _____ Phone _____

( ) Business Address _____ City _____ State _____ Phone _____

( ) Ins. Carrier _____ Address _____ Phone _____

Amt. Ins.—Liab. _____ P.D. _____

Med. _____ Collision _____

Uninsured Motorist _____ Any Coverage Deductible? Which? _____

_____

( ) Driver Plaintiff Vehicle _____

( ) Relationship to Owner _____

Driving With Permission _____

( ) Destination & Purpose _____

( ) Impediments of Driver—Intoxication _____ Glasses _____

Hearing _____ Other Physical Defects _____

Passengers   Seat Location in Vehicle

_____

_____

( ) Defendant Vehicle

( ) Year _____ Make _____ Model _____ Color _____

( ) Cylinders _____ Horsepower _____ Weight _____ Manuf. I.D. _____

( ) Tag No. _____ Power or Regular Steering _____ Brakes _____

( ) Defects of Vehicle—Brakes _____ Lights _____ Motor _____

Steering _____ Tires _____ Other _____

Comments as to Condition _____

( ) Location of Vehicle—Garage _____

Address _____ Phone _____

Were Pictures Taken of Automobile _____

When _____ By Whom _____

Address _____ Phone _____

( ) If Not, Take Pictures at Garage & Place in Evidence File

Taken By _____ When _____ Address _____

( ) Note Alleged Speed Prior to Collision _____

( ) Indicate Impact Points on Vehicle Diagram & Note Interior Damage

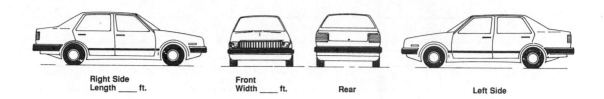

Right Side
Length _____ ft.   **Front**
                          Width _____ ft.   **Rear**   **Left Side**

( ) Owner of Defendant Vehicle _____ Age _____ Sex _____

( ) Address _____ City _____ State _____ Phone _____

( ) Business Address _____ City _____ State _____ Phone _____

( ) Ins. Carrier _____ Address _____ Phone _____

   Amt. Ins.—Liab. _____ P.D. _____

   Med. _____ Collision _____

   Uninsured Motorist _____ Any Coverage Deductible? Which? _____

   _____

( ) Driver Defendant Vehicle _____

( ) Relationship to Owner _____

   Driving With Permission _____

( ) Destination & Purpose _____

( ) Impediments of Driver—Intoxication _____ Glasses _____

   Hearing _____ Other Physical Defects _____

   Passengers   Seat Location in Vehicle

   _____

   _____

   _____

( ) Traffic Violations by Plaintiff & Defendant

   Charges Against   Court   Hearing Date   Result

   _____

   _____

( ) Get Copy Traffic Court Testimony if Recorded & Place in Evidence File

( ) Witnesses to Accident including Parties

Witnesses	Address	County	State	Age	Phone

( ) Statement Record—Use Checklist in Taking Statements

Last Name Witness	Taken by Plaintiff	Given to Defendant	When?	Written, Recorded, Or Oral	Copy Retained
Plaintiff					
Defendant					

( ) Place All Statements in Evidence File

( ) Impeachment of Parties & Witnesses (Note Unfavorable Military Record)

Name	Crime Conviction	Date	Good or Bad Character

( ) Parties' Prior Accidents

Plaintiff _____

_____

Defendant _____

_____

MEDICAL

( ) Plaintiff—Summary of Injuries <u>(Indicate Degree of Disability) (Restriction of Activities in Work,</u>
<u>Sports, etc.)</u>

_____

_____

( ) Note Injuries on Diagram   ( ) <u>Indicate Plaintiff's Area of Pain</u>

( ) Symptoms   ( ) Trunk

    ( ) Headaches   ( ) Shoulders
    ( ) Dizziness   ( ) Spine
    ( ) Nausea   ( ) Thoracic
    ( ) Nervousness   ( ) Scapula
    ( ) Insomnia   ( ) Lumbar
    ( ) Appetite   ( ) Sacrum
                ( ) Coccyx
( ) Head   ( ) Pelvis
                ( ) Hips
    ( ) Brain
    ( ) Forehead   ( ) Legs (Rt. or Left)
    ( ) Ears
    ( ) Eyes   ( ) Thighs
    ( ) Nose   ( ) Upper
    ( ) Mouth   ( ) Lower
    ( ) Teeth   ( ) Knees
                ( ) Ankles
( ) Neck   ( ) Feet
                ( ) Toes
    ( ) Muscles
    ( ) Spine   ( ) Indicate Radiations of Pain
    ( ) Throat
                ( ) <u>Note Cuts, Bruises, Burns,</u>
( ) Chest   <u>Bumps, Sutures. Fractures,</u>
                Missing Teeth, Swelling,
    ( ) Heart   Contusions, Points of
    ( ) Lungs   Bleeding, Unconsciousness, etc.
    ( ) Ribs

( ) Abdomen

( ) Internal Injuries

    ( ) _____
       _____

( ) Arms (Rt. or Left)

    ( ) Upper
    ( ) Forearm
    ( ) Elbows
    ( ) Wrist
    ( ) Hands
    ( ) Fingers

PLAINTIFF MEDICAL & PAIN AREAS

( ) Same Information for Defendant's Injuries (If Any)

( ) Ambulance, Hospital & Doctor Service, Findings & Treatment

    ( ) Ambulance Service—By Whom? _____ Other _____

    Any First Aid Administered? If So, What? _____

    Note Time Ambulance Arrived at Accident Scene _____

    ( ) Hospitals   Address   Phone   Period of Treatment   Surgery

    1. _____

    Treatment _____

    _____ X-Rays Taken? When? _____

    2. _____

    Treatment _____

    _____ X-Rays Taken? When? _____

    3. _____

    Treatment _____

    _____ X-Rays Taken? When? _____

    ( ) Doctors   Address   Phone   Period of Treatment   Surgery

    1. _____

    Diagnosis, Treatment & Prognosis _____

    _____ X-Rays Taken? When? _____

    2. _____

    Diagnosis, Treatment & Prognosis _____

    _____ X-Rays Taken? When? _____

    3. _____

    Diagnosis, Treatment & Prognosis _____

    _____ X-Rays Taken? When? _____

    4. _____

    Diagnosis, Treatment & Prognosis _____

    _____ X-Rays Taken? When? _____

    ( ) Summary Comments as to Percentage of Disability & Patient Prognosis

    _____

    _____

PRIOR MEDICAL TREATMENT—PLAINTIFF & DEFENDANT

(   ) Plaintiff—Prior Medical Treatment

Doctors & Hospitals	Address	Phone	Period of Treatment
1.			
2.			
3.			

Treatment _____

_____

(   ) Note Relationship of Prior to Present Injuries _____

_____

_____

(   ) Prior Claims of Any Nature? When? Where? _____

_____

_____

(   ) Defendant—Prior Medical Treatment

Doctors & Hospitals	Address	Phone	Period of Treatment
1.			
2.			
3.			

Treatment _____

_____

(   ) Note Relationship of Prior to Present Injuries _____

_____

_____

(   ) Prior Claims of Any Nature? When? Where? _____

_____

_____

(   ) Summary Degree of Prior Disability

    (   ) Plaintiff _____

    (   ) Defendant _____

DAMAGES—PLAINTIFF

( ) Plaintiff Employment Subsequent & Prior to Accident

Subsequent to	Dates	Position	Annual Earnings	Per Diem

Prior to (Last 2 Yrs.)	Dates	Position	Annual Earnings	Per Diem

( ) Education & Job Training—( ) Elementary   ( ) High School   ( ) College   ( ) Graduate

( ) Other _____

_____

( ) Family Situation

Spouse & Children	Relationship	Age

( ) Computation of General Damages—Note Age of Injured Party _____

( ) Pain & Suffering (Past, Present & Future) Estimate of Party—Value Assessed Per

Day $_____ × _____ Days $_____ × Life Expectancy _____ $_____

( ) Diminution Capacity to Labor as Element of Pain & Suffering

(Past, Present & Future) Estimate of Party-Value Assessed Per Day $_____

× _____

( ) Days $_____ × Life Expectancy _____ $_____

Loss of Consortium—Estimate of Party—Value Assessed Per Day $ _____

× _____ Days $_____ × Life Expectancy _____ $_____

( ) Computation of Special Damages (Date Accident _____)

( ) Loss of Earnings

( ) Past & Present to Date of Trial—Days in Hospital _____)

( ) Past & Present Continued—(At Home _____ Returned To Work—Date _____)

( ) Total Days _____ × Per Diem Wages $_____ $_____

( ) Annual Average Earnings $_____ (Capacity Reduced _____%

Disability $_____) × _____ Use Annuity Table _____%

Column to Reduce to Present Cash Value) or × _____ Life Expectancy

(for Gross When Reduction Not Required) $_____

( ) Hospitals, Nurses, Doctors, Drugs (Supports & Braces) & Ambulance Expenses

Hospitals	Period	Amount	
_____		$_____	
_____			
_____			
_____			
		$_____	$_____

Nurses	Period	Amount	
_____		$_____	
_____			
		$_____	$_____

Doctors	Period	Amount	
_____		$_____	
_____			
_____			
_____			
_____			
		$_____	$_____

Pharmacy	Period	Amount	
_____		$_____	
_____			
		$_____	$_____

Ambulance	Period	Amount	
_____		$_____	
		$_____	$_____

( ) Funeral Expenses—Mortician's Name & Address _____

_____ $_____

( ) Property Damage

    ( ) Automobile—Fair Market Value Before $_____ $_____

       Less Fair Market Value After Accident $_____

       Diminution in Value $_____ $_____

    ( ) Reasonable Hire _____ Days × Rental Value $_____ $_____

Use the interview form as an aid; do not rely on it entirely. Each case is unique, and there will be times when you will need to add or delete questions.

Some cases will require you or the attorney (or both of you) to develop a special interview form or set of questions to cover in the interview. Until you become more experienced, this should be done in close consultation with the attorney working on the case. In order to develop your own questionnaire, you will need to review the file. If necessary, ask the attorney to identify the cause of action: negligence, breach of contract, sexual harassment, or other.

Research the cause of action and identify the elements that need to be proven to establish a case or its defense. Jury instruction books and legal encyclopedias will provide a quick overview of the key elements for a particular cause of action and its defenses.

A BRIEF LOOK AT THE SUBSTANTIVE LAW OF NEGLIGENCE

Law is divided into two major areas: substantive law and procedural law. Substantive law defines the duties owed by one person to another. Procedural law defines the steps that must be followed in a lawsuit. The substantive law of negligence states that all individuals have a duty to conduct themselves in their activities so as not to create an unreasonable risk of harm to others. The elements that must be proven to show that negligence exists include the following:

1. *Duty:* the existence of a **duty** of due care owed by one person to another. For example, in Case I, Mr. Hart had a duty to drive the van without creating an unreasonable risk of harm to any other drivers or pedestrians, such as Ms. Forrester.
2. *A breach of that duty:* failure to conform to the required standard of care. The required standard of care is that which is reasonable under the circumstances. What is reasonable is a matter of experience and common sense. For example, if Mr. Hart were speeding, especially on icy roads, and/or was not paying close attention to the road, his conduct would fall short of what is reasonable under the circumstances to protect others.
3. *The cause of the injury:* that the conduct in question was the natural and **proximate** (probable) **cause** of the resulting harm. Some states define it as a substantial cause of the injury. If Ms. Forrester could have crossed the road safely had it not been for

Mr. Hart's excessive speed, then Mr. Hart's speed would be the natural and proximate cause of Ms. Forrester's injuries.

4. *Injury in fact:* an actual injury or loss must have resulted from the incident. If Ms. Forrester, for example, suffers a broken hip as a result of the negligent act, then that is sufficient to provide this fourth element of negligence. It is also important that the injury be a foreseeable consequence of the negligence and not some quirk.

The defenses to negligence include the following:

1. *Contributory negligence.* Although most states have abolished contributory negligence as a defense, its use should be understood. If the action of the plaintiff, the person suing for injuries, was a contributing factor in the accident, the plaintiff cannot recover her losses from the defendant, the person being sued. For example, if a jury found that plaintiff Ms. Forrester had contributed to her own injuries by failing to look both ways before crossing the highway, she would be barred from any recovery, even if defendant Mr. Hart was found to be primarily responsible for the accident. The harshness of this rule explains why it has been abolished in many states. Assume that contributory negligence is not the law in Columbia unless your instructor indicates otherwise.

2. *Last clear chance* is a doctrine that permits parties to recover damages who normally could not because of their contributory negligence. In that sense, it is a defense to the defense of contributory negligence. It applies when the plaintiff, through her own negligence, is placed in the defendant's path so that the defendant has the last clear chance to avoid an accident. If the defendant does not react as a reasonable person should (is negligent), causing injury to the plaintiff, the plaintiff may recover regardless of her initial contributing negligence. For example, assume that Ms. Forrester carelessly ran across the ice on the road, slipped, and fell, leaving her directly in the path of Mr. Hart's van. Also assume that Mr. Hart had a last clear chance to avoid the accident. If he was inattentive and did not avoid the accident, Ms. Forrester could still recover damages in spite of her own negligence.

3. *Comparative negligence* is the law in the majority of states and in Columbia (unless your instructor indicates otherwise). The doctrine of comparative negligence permits a plaintiff who is contributorily negligent to recover, but the award is reduced proportionately by the percentage of the plaintiff's negligence. For example, if Ms. Forrester stepped onto the highway without looking, then slipped as she tried to retreat, a jury might find her 30 percent negligent. If Mr. Hart was driving too fast to stop, a jury might find him 70 percent negligent. If Ms. Forrester's damages came to $100,000, the award would be reduced by 30 percent to $70,000. In some states, Ms. Forrester would be barred from any recovery if her comparative negligence was found to exceed 50 percent.

4. *Assumption of risk* states that plaintiffs may not recover for damages if they knowingly place themselves in danger. For example, if Ms. Forrester had decided to stay in the middle of the road and thumb her nose at any oncoming vehicle, she would be assuming the risk of injury, and Mr. Hart would have a defense to Ms. Forrester's action for negligence.

After identifying the elements of the action, draft questions that elicit information that will help prove or disprove the elements or defenses. Forming questions to elicit information is a matter of applying common-sense to the elements that must be proven. For example, to determine if the defendant has created an unreasonable risk of harm to the plaintiff under the circumstances, the interviewer would need to find out what the circumstances were. The question should be asked, "What are all the possible circumstances that might have a bearing on the accident?" Each factor that comes to mind should be listed.

Circumstances possibly affecting an accident:

Time (such as rush hour, dusk, night)
Weather (such as cold, rainy, foggy)
Lighting (such as bright, dim, dark)
Road conditions (such as slippery, dry, oily, rough)
Road structure (such as lanes, narrow shoulders, curve, straight, level)
Location of parties (including specific measurements in feet, inches)
Dress of parties (as pertinent to cause of accident)
Condition of parties (such as intoxicated, drugged, tired)
Disabilities of parties (such as poor eyesight, poor mobility, poor hearing)
Obstructions (such as limitations on view of parties, bushes, trees, terrain, sun glare)
Traffic (such as heavy, light)
Caution signs (including all traffic signals, barricades, posted signs, etc.)
Relevant ordinances (such as speed limit, school zone, crosswalk)
Helplessness of parties (facts indicating parties inability to avoid or extract themselves from the peril)

The next question is, "Is there any evidence that an unreasonable risk of harm was created [carelessness]?"

Evidence of creating an unreasonable risk of harm:

Speed of vehicle(s)
    Plaintiff's opinion
    Underlying basis for opinion (observability)
    Skid marks—length and location
    Time intervals and distances to estimate speed
    Police report information
Attentiveness of defendant
    Plaintiff's view of defendant
    Witness's view of defendant
    Direction driver was looking
    Distractions at point in road

Time interval between when driver should have observed plaintiff and
first attempt to brake or take evasive action

Distance between point where driver should have first seen plaintiff
and start of skid marks

Lack of skid marks

Sounding of horn

Obstructions under the control of defendant

Broken windshield

Frost, condensation, ice on windshield

Stickers

Car ornaments

Unsafe vehicle

Immediate loss of control (brakes, steering, bald tires)

Lack of skid marks (brakes)

High engine roar (stuck accelerator)

Dipped down on one side (springs, shock absorbers, overload)

Creating questions or areas for inquiry is a brainstorming process that
raises a variety of possibilities. This process should be repeated for each of
the elements as well as the defenses. Complete your interview form with the
following information:

■ Add the standard general information questions (name, address,
phone) found on most interview forms to complete the new interview
form.

■ Have the attorney review the draft interview form and make suggestions for other questions.

■ Amend the form where appropriate.

Once you understand this method of creating an interview form, you
should be able to create a form or expand an existing one in any area of law.

ASSIGNMENT 3:6
Adapting the methods you have learned to a variety of circumstances is an important
process. The ability to adapt is invaluable to the law office and should give you
confidence. Test your understanding of the methodology described in this section by
creating an interview form for a breach of implied warranty or other type of case. If
needed, see the appendix on contracts to review the elements for an implied warranty
case. If each student or group of students is to prepare interview forms for different types
of lawsuits, it would be good to exchange copies of these forms to expand the interview
section of your system folder.

Step 3

Select a location for the interview. Most interviews will take place in the
convenience of the office. This gives the interviewer control over outside
interruptions and assures privacy, which is a paramount consideration. A
disabled or ill client, however, may require a personal visit. Sometimes it is
advantageous to conduct all or part of an interview at the scene of the
accident or where a view of some evidence would be particularly helpful.
Before conducting an outside interview, however, approval should be
sought from the supervising attorney. When the client is contacted to
schedule the appointment, it should be determined if the site you have
chosen is convenient.

Step 4

Schedule the interview to provide for some flexibility in its length. This allows a more relaxed atmosphere for the client, and provides the opportunity for the interviewer to take more time should circumstances warrant it. The time of the interview should be coordinated with the supervising attorney to allow the attorney to meet with the client prior to the interview. This meeting helps establish the attorney-client relationship and may be used to answer the client's questions about the firm's fees. Occasionally, this meeting with the attorney is not possible and the paralegal will be directed to proceed accordingly.

Step 5

Determine what information the client should bring. Before calling the client, review the interview form and make a list of those items the client should bring to the interview. Typically, in a personal injury case, the client should bring all medical bills and dates of treatment; accident reports; pertinent names, addresses, and phone numbers; a diagram of the accident; and any other relevant documents.

In contract cases, the client should bring key dates surrounding the contract; the time, place, and nature of negotiations preceding the contract; the names, addresses, and phone numbers of people present during the negotiation or during discussion if it was an oral contract (lawyers, all parties, accountants, and so on); points of disagreement and how they were resolved; all drafts of the contract and the contract as signed by the parties; all papers, correspondence, memoranda, and so on, relating to the contract; anything indicating an attempt to modify the contract; and any documentation relating to actual damages or attempts to minimize damages.

ASSIGNMENT 3:7

Review the interview forms in figures 3:1(a) and 3:1(b) and compile a list of the names, addresses, phone numbers, medical records, insurance information, and so on, that you would like Ms. Forrester to bring to the interview. Make a copy of the list and place it in the system folder. This list will be useful when you call or write the client and will serve as a checklist for future cases.

Step 6

Set up the appointment with the client. Telephone the client to set the time for the interview. The following conversation is an example.

Paralegal: Ms. Forrester, this is Terry Salyer. I am a paralegal with the firm of White, Wilson, and McDuff. Mr. White asked me to arrange an appointment for you to come to our office and discuss your case. Would Wednesday afternoon, June twenty-ninth, at 2:30 be convenient?

Client: Yes, it would.

Paralegal: We will be sending you a letter to remind you. There are some things we would like you to collect and bring with you at that time, and I will list those in the letter. Do you know where our office is located?

Client: Yes.

Paralegal: There is parking behind the building. See you at 2:30 on the twenty-ninth. I look forward to our meeting. Good-bye.

You may also choose to use the phone conversation to assess whether the client has any special disabilities or needs that could affect the interview, such as language or other barriers.

Following the phone conversation, you should fill out a deadline control slip noting any tasks, such as preparation of a letter confirming the appointment or preparation of any documents to be signed by the client at the interview. The date should be noted on your calendar, Mr. White's calendar, and that of the legal secretary who will greet Ms. Forrester. Then draft or dictate a letter confirming the appointment. You may choose to draft your own letter or copy a similar letter from another file. Have your supervising attorney review the letter and send it. An example of such a letter is shown in figure 3:2. This letter can be easily adapted for a contract dispute or other type of case.

Figure 3:2 Confirmation of Appointment Letter

WHITE, WILSON & McDUFF

ATTORNEYS AT LAW
FEDERAL PLAZA BUILDING, SUITE 700
THIRD AND MARKET STREETS
LEGALVILLE, COLUMBIA 00000
(111) 555-0000

June 24, 19____

Ms. Ann Forrester
1533 Capitol Drive
Legalville, Columbia 00000   Your Case File No. PI 3750

This is to remind you of your appointment on Wednesday, June 29, at 2:30 p.m. at our office. The purpose of the appointment will be to discuss in detail the accident you were involved in on February 26 of this year. The appointment is for an hour, or more if necessary.

Please bring the items checked in the following list, if they are available:

(X) Social security number
(X) Insurance carrier, policy limits, address, and phone number
(X) Name(s) of the other party or parties and any information you have about them, including insurance carrier
(X) Photos of accident, injuries, or other damage
(X) Photos of accident scene

(X) Diagram of accident and location
(X) News clippings regarding accident
(X) Names, ages, birth dates of spouse and dependents
(X) Description of vehicle(s) in accident, license number, owner, damage
(X) Medical bills, treating physicians, medical insurance, medical history
(X) Occupation and salary information, time lost
(X) Accident or injuries subsequent to this incident
(X) Any correspondence regarding accident
(X) Names, addresses, and phone numbers of other witnesses
(X) Be prepared to describe accident
( ) Other_____

We appreciate your gathering as much of the information as you can. I look forward to meeting you. In the meantime, I can be reached at 555-0000.

Terry Salyer

Litigation Paralegal

ASSIGNMENT 3:8
Make the letter in figure 3:2 into a form letter for your system folder. Retype the letter, leaving blank those areas of the letter that will contain the variable information (names, addresses, date, and so on) for each new client. Once your form is set up, it can be placed in your system folder and in the memory of a word processor or automatic typewriter, requiring the entry of only the variable information for each repeated use. Throughout this training period, follow this form-making procedure for letters and other documents that will be used repeatedly from one case to the next.
   Note: Keep track of your time by filling out the time log.

Step 7

Anticipate and arrange for any special needs. These might include arranging for an interpreter, having a diagram board ready, preparing for unique ethnic or occupational jargon, or reviewing special medical terminology. If a child is to be interviewed, a few toys might be helpful. Some evidence suggests that young children talk more freely in a play setting and describe what happened to them more easily when using a doll or other props for demonstration purposes.

Step 8

Review pertinent ethical and tactical considerations. The paralegal handbook has already set out for you some of the significant ethical considerations that you must keep in mind while interviewing any client. It might be useful to review those prior to each interview until you have such considerations firmly in mind.

The interview is a time when clients want to ask you questions: What does my case look like? Will I be liable? What is your fee? Don't you think I ought to sue? Anticipate such questions and prepare a response. Use the opportunity to make clear your status as a paralegal. Your response to the previous questions could be the following:

> I am sorry, but I am not permitted to answer that question because it calls for legal advice. Paralegals are not permitted to give legal advice, but Mr. White will be glad to respond to that question. I will pass your questions on to him.

Avoid tape-recording or having the client sign a written statement, unless otherwise directed by your supervising attorney. The opponent may be able to acquire the client's recorded statement under some state rules of civil procedure and would try to use that statement against the client. You may take notes of the interview and record your impressions of the facts and the client's demeanor and truthfulness. Such records are normally protected under the attorney-client privilege.

ASSIGNMENT 3:9
List the pertinent ethical considerations for interviewing a client. Place them in your system folder.

Step 9

Review recommended interview techniques. The following techniques have proven to be useful.

Interview techniques

1. Have the client meet with the attorney first. This will give the attorney the opportunity to explain the role of the paralegal and what that means to the client in reduced cost. The attorney can then introduce the paralegal. This sequence should help develop client confidence in the firm's professionalism and in the paralegal.
2. Make the client comfortable. Offer refreshments and break the ice with light, pleasant conversation.
3. Be friendly and respectful. Address the client as Mr., Mrs., Ms., or Dr., as appropriate.
4. Create a private environment free of interruptions. Have your calls held. If necessary, place an Interview in Progress sign on the office door.[2]
5. Explain the purpose of the interview and let clients know you need their help.
6. Inform the client that you, the attorney, and any employees of the law office are required to protect the information provided by the client and that such information is held in the strictest confidence. Explain that honesty is essential and that it can be disastrous to hold back any information, no matter how personal or embarrassing it might be. On the other hand, explain that it is human to forget, and it is not unusual that something forgotten now can be recalled later. Discuss, also, that it is normal for people to want to fill in gaps in their memory; that they need to be careful about presenting information they do not remember clearly.

7. Express confidence about what you are doing. Thorough preparation and planning will help you be more confident. It is equally important to avoid trying to impress the interviewee with all of your legal knowledge and vocabulary.

8. Avoid being condescending. Try to put yourself in the client's position and think how you would like to be addressed.

9. Take accurate, detailed, and legible notes.

10. Be a good listener. Silences during the interview process are inevitable and can be productive periods of thought and recall.[3] Avoid the temptation to end the silence quickly. Be patient, supportive, and accepting. Encourage the expression of feelings, and avoid making value judgments.[4]

11. Be mindful of the client's body language or idiosyncratic mannerisms, but only in the sense of how a jury might react. Do not fall into the trap of drawing conclusions about truthfulness or personality traits from body language. This can lead to gross misjudgments, despite popular literature to the contrary.

12. Let clients tell their stories. It is important to them. Come back later to pick up significant details.

13. Use open narrative questions such as "What happened? What happened next?" This allows clients to proceed at their own pace and encourages a freer flow of information, which is more conducive to fact gathering.

14. Avoid questions that suggest an answer. For example, "Ms. Forrester, you did look both ways before you stepped onto the highway, didn't you?" This is a **leading question** and encourages clients to respond as they perceive you want them to respond, and not necessarily with the truth. This type of question restricts the flow of information.

15. Avoid "why" questions, which are often viewed by the interviewee as a sign of disapproval.[5] A less confrontational approach might be "Try to help me understand this" or "Would you please elaborate on your reasons for doing that?"

16. Probe the accuracy of judgments, such as to speed, distance, color, time, or size. Determine, if possible, the basis of the judgment or test its accuracy through example or comparison to some similar item or distance.

17. Be mentally prepared to deal with very sensitive or personal matters in a forthright yet empathetic manner. Avoid skirting the issue and the use of euphemisms. Such shyness or hesitancy on the part of the interviewer can encourage dishonesty.[6]

18. Deal tactfully but directly with suspected dishonesty. Do not be afraid to indicate that a response doesn't seem to stand up or to follow from the other evidence.

19. Restate the client's information when necessary to make sure you understand: "Now let me see if I have this right. You said you stepped out . . .?"

20. Be very thorough in asking about the accident or other alleged wrong and any damages. The more details you can obtain, the better.

Interviewing is an art and, like most art, requires practice and experience. Techniques that work well for some people do not work well for others. Experiment and develop your own style.

ASSIGNMENT 3:10

Prepare a list of these interview techniques for step 9 in this section of the system folder. If you choose to study interview techniques in more detail, research the topics Interviewing, Interrogation, and Listening in the library and add to your list of techniques.

Step 10

Prepare orientation and instruction materials for the client. Clients will normally have a variety of questions concerning the litigation process as well as what will be expected of them. Some firms have developed a videotape that the client views either before or after the initial interview. This firm has a pamphlet that is designed to provide guidance and information to the client. Whether through the pamphlet or otherwise, make sure the client leaves with information on the following matters.[7]

Information to be given to the client at the initial interview

1. The attorney is your legal advocate whose function is to assume responsibility for your case and represent you to the best of the attorney's ability.
2. The paralegal assists your attorney in handling your case, providing you with a more thorough preparation at a lower cost.
3. You will need to provide your attorney with all the information that you can gather and recall about the incident, your injuries and losses, and any statements you have made to others.
4. It may be necessary to provide your attorney with very personal information. Expect that the information you give will be held in the strictest of confidence consistent with the highest standards of professional loyalty.
5. Refrain from making any statements to others about the incident or about your injuries or losses. Such statements may be used against you in court and could weaken your case.
6. Refrain from signing any documents releasing others from liablity or accepting payments for injuries. Do not file an accident report without first checking with your attorney.
7. Begin a daily medical journal in which you will record the condition of your injuries and medical treatment. Daily references to pain, suffering, sleeplessness, limitations on normal activity, changes in condition, and trips to the hospital or physician should be noted. Keep a record of your expenses: mileage, prescriptions, drugs, crutches, wheelchair, private nurse, and so on.
8. Record all employment losses: days missed; lost pay and benefits; and missed raises, promotions, merit pay, and bonuses. Also note the date of your return to work and any subsequent effects your injuries have on your ability to do your job.
9. Make a record of all damages to property and estimates for repair. Do not discard, give away, or sell such property without consulting your attorney.
10. List your expenses in hiring others to perform domestic work and maintenance or child care needed as a result of your injuries.
11. Apprise your attorney or paralegal of your medical, property, and disability insurance coverage in order that steps may be taken to inform the companies of the incident and claims made. You do not

want to waive your right to a claim; such claims may provide necessary cash for living expenses. Money paid by your insurance company will be reimbursed to the insurance company if it is awarded to
you in the lawsuit for the same damages previously paid for by the
insurance.

12. You should be aware that most cases are settled before trial; your
case may be settled through negotiation prior to trial.

13. The filing of a case is important because it keeps the case moving,
provides access to the opponent's information, and encourages a
more timely resolution of the matter. Once a case is filed, it may
take from one year to several years before it comes to trial. No
settlement will be agreed upon without your full knowledge and
acceptance.

14. Keep the paralegal informed of any new information that arises or
that you recall. Inform us of any change in address, extended vacation plans and so on. Refrain from asking others questions about
your case. This frequently leads to confusion and incorrect information. If you have questions about your case, please ask us. We will be
glad to help.

15. Prior to trial you will be called to the office to review information
and to prepare for trial. You may be asked to provide sworn testimony about the incident at a deposition. This is required by law.
You will be given time to prepare for this deposition. You may
also be asked to undergo an examination by a physician chosen by
the opponent in order to verify your injuries. This is permitted
by law.

16. Your case may not end following a decision by the court. Frequently
appeals are filed before a case is final. This can take a long time.

ASSIGNMENT 3:11
Place the "Information to be Given to the Client at the Initial Interview" checklist in step
10 of the interview section. As you gain experience, you will probably add to the list.

Step 11

Prepare any forms for the client's signature. The interview is a good time to
have the client sign several documents. The attorney and the client should
have discussed the fee arrangement. If so, the interview is a good time to
have that signed (executed). There are two typical fee agreements. The
first is for representation based on an hourly rate. The second is for
representation based on a percentage of the award won by the plaintiff,
allowing for no fee if the plaintiff does not win. This is called a **contingent
fee.**

Many client-attorney fee disputes arise because the nature of the fee was
not made clear to the client from the beginning and because the fee
arrangement was not put in writing. Be prepared to explain the fee contract
and have the client sign the written fee agreement. In some firms only the
attorney will take this responsibility, but even then, the paralegal may be
responsible for drafting the fee agreement (see figures 3:3 and 3:4).[8] Court
rules dictate the nature and limits of contingent fee agreements in some
states.

Figure 3:3 Fee Agreement

LEGAL REPRESENTATION AGREEMENT

I hereby employ the firm of _____, with the

understanding that attorney _____ will represent me and provide

legal services for me in: _____

_____

_____

and I authorize the firm to commence an action in this matter as may be advisable in the judgment of the firm, subject to my approval. I also understand that the law firm may assign other or additional attorneys to represent me, with my approval, as may be required from time to time.

Attorneys' fees and expenses

I agree that the following method is to be used for determining the proper amount of legal fees:

1. FEES:

The attorney's fees for services performed under this agreement shall be based upon a rate of $____ per hour. Hourly billing will be to the tenth (1/10th) of an hour. (If more than one attorney, or paralegal, at differing rates, then so specify.)[a]

2. RETAINER: (Choose one):

A. In order to secure the time and services of the attorney for this matter, I agree to make an initial, nonrefundable payment in the amount of $____ toward my attorney's fees and expenses. I understand this is the minimum fee I will be charged for services and expenses.

B. In order to secure the time and services of the attorney for this matter, I agree to make an initial payment in the amount of $____ toward my attorney's fees and expenses. This retainer fee shall be a credit against hourly attorney's fees and costs advancements. It will be refunded to the extent it has not been utilized for this purpose.

3. COSTS:

A. I authorize my attorney to retain any individual and entities to perform services necessary for investigation or completion of legal services. I agree to pay the fees or charges of every person or entity hired by the attorney to perform necessary services.

B. I acknowledge that my attorney may incur various expenses in providing services to me. I agree to reimburse the attorney for all out-of-pocket expenses paid. If I am billed directly for these expenses, I agree to make prompt direct payments to the originators of the bills. Such expenses may include, but are not limited to, service and filing fees, courier or messenger services, recording and certifying documents, depositions, transcripts, investigations, witnesses' fees, long distance telephone calls, copying materials, overtime clerical assistance, travel expenses, postage, notarial attestations and computer research.

Billing

I agree to the following schedule of billing:

1. Fees, charges and expenses will be billed on at least a monthly basis as they accrue.

2. The retainer shall be paid in full upon the execution of this agreement. The retainer shall be a credit against monthly bills.[b]

3. I agree to make payments promptly. I understand that failure to make payments is sufficient reason for the attorney to withdraw from representing me in this matter, whether or not litigation has been commenced. I will be notified in writing prior to any withdrawal. I agree that a letter to my last known address is sufficient notice.

Consultations

I understand that personal and telephone consultations with my attorney shall be part of my representation and I will be billed by the attorney for the time spent on such consultation.

Discharge of attorney

I may, if unsatisfied with the services for any reason, discharge the attorney at any time; however, it is understood that the attorney will be paid or arrangements will be made for the payment of all fees and costs.

Representation

It is expressly agreed and understood by me that no promises, assurances or guarantees as to the outcome of this matter have been made by the attorney. Payment is not contingent upon the outcome of this matter.

I have read this fee agreement, and have had opportunity to discuss it with my attorney or any other attorney. I understand, agree and accept all of the terms within this agreement.

Dated this _____ day of _____ 19 _____

Attorney _____ Client _____

---

[a]Note that any additional reservation of right to increase the fee in the future for increased hourly rates must be specifically stated.
[b]Modify paragraph if retainer is nonrefundable. Any other agreement on applying or retaining the retainer should be specifically drafted.

Figure 3:4   Contingent Fee Agreement

GENERAL CONTINGENT FEE AGREEMENT

1. I, _____, having been injured on _____,

hereby agree to retain _____, of the law firm of _____

_____ as my attorney to make claims or bring suit against anyone necessary.

2. My attorney is to receive ____% of the gross settlement or judgment for legal services. This percentage will increase to ____% of the gross settlement or judgment in the event of an appeal of the final judgment to the court of appeals or supreme court. My attorney is hereby given a continuing lien in my claim and the proceeds thereof for the amount of the contingent fee, pursuant to Wis. Stats. section 757.36.

3. I UNDERSTAND THAT I COULD RETAIN THE ATTORNEY TO REPRESENT ME IN THIS ACTION AND COMPENSATE HIM/HER ON AN HOURLY BASIS, BUT I EXPRESSLY DECLINE TO DO SO, SUBJECT TO PARA. 8.

4. I also have been informed that I am responsible to pay for costs and disbursements including, but not limited to:

_____

_____

My attorney may, but is not obligated to, advance these and other costs he or she believes are reasonable and necessary for preparing and presenting any claim. Any costs advanced by the attorney for which he or she was not reimbursed shall be paid to the attorney from the gross recovery after calculation of attorneys' fees. In the event there is no attorney's fee, I agree to reimburse the attorney for costs within 30 days of receiving a written statement therefore.

5. I understand that if no recovery is obtained for me, no attorneys' fees shall be due; however, I will remain responsible for costs and disbursements. I also understand that settlement shall not be made without my approval or the approval of my guardian.

6. I understand that by signing this agreement, I am promising not to release the names of any experts and/or consultants hired in regard to my case. I further understand that the names of any experts and/or consultants hired in regard to my case are the property of the attorney and law firm and are not my property. I expressly agree that my attorney may promise experts/consultants that their names and/or reports will not be revealed to anyone, including me.

7. I understand that my attorneys may withdraw if they believe my case lacks merit or is not fiscally responsible to pursue.

8. I understand that in the event that, contrary to the advice of my attorneys, I instruct my attorneys to discontinue the matter, the matter shall be discontinued and I shall pay the law firm a reasonable hourly rate, plus expenses, for the time they have expended on my behalf.

9. I have read and my attorney has explained the above eight points of this agreement and I understand the same.

Dated: _____ Client _____

Witness: _____

(Law Firm) _____

Attorney _____

Signed documents are of considerable assistance to the paralegal in subsequent investigative work. Among these forms are authorizations signed by the client permitting those holding confidential information, such as doctors, to release that information to the lawyer. Figure 3:5 is a standardized release form designed to cover a variety of needed information. It can be used when one is not yet sure of the entire range of things that will need to be requested.

In the following chapters, more specialized authorization forms are presented and discussed. These may be preferable for a particular situation than a form that attempts to meet all needs.

ASSIGNMENT 3:12
Place copies of the fee and release forms in your system folder.

Step 12

Prepare the interview site. On the day scheduled for the interview, prepare the interview site. In this case, it will be your office. You will need to make sure the office is neat and that your desk is clear of all other files. A clean, neat office and desk suggest to clients that you have everything under control. In addition, the clients will realize that you have set aside this time especially for them. We all like to feel important, and clients are no exception. If your office and your manner convey to clients that they are important, your interview will be that much more productive.

Make sure the office is equipped with everything you and the client will need. You should have paper for taking notes and drawing diagrams, extra pens or sharpened pencils, and ice water, coffee, and tea. Be sure to have your own diagram present if you intend to work from that, and any photographs or other items you will be using or referring to. All the forms that you drafted should be at hand for the client's signature.

Figure 3:5   Standardized Release Form

WHITE, WILSON & McDUFF

ATTORNEYS AT LAW
FEDERAL PLAZA BUILDING, SUITE 700
THIRD AND MARKET STREETS
LEGALVILLE, COLUMBIA 00000
(111) 555-0000

Address

Date

RE: (Name of client, date of birth, Social Security number)

This form authorizes _____ to release to my attorney, White, Wilson & McDuff, or their designated representative, all of the following information about me as indicated (X), and to discuss it, send it, make it available for inspection, or photocopy it as they may request.

( ) All medical and hospital records, including medical history, tests, test results, diagnoses, treatment, x-ray reports, current medical status, prognosis, bills, and any other information designated in the attached letter relevant to treatment on _____ 19 ___ to _____ 19 ___.

( ) Employment records: description of position, length of employment, pay, benefits, absences, performance, accumulated sick leave, etc.

( ) Academic and school records: attendance dates; evaluations; grade performance; psychological, aptitude, and achievement tests; class ranking; teachers, etc.

( ) Military records

( ) All state and federal tax returns for the years _____

( ) Other: _____

_____   _____
Client   Date

_____
Address

You might also want to give some thought to the arrangement of the office and what you feel will be most comfortable for the client: facing each other across a desk; sitting side by side at a table for paperwork; or in a more conversational arrangement of chairs.

In addition, you will want to remind the secretary to hold your calls and to help head off other interruptions.

As a part of your preparation, be sure you know the procedure to follow in the event of an emergency. It does happen, though rarely, that the interviewee will faint, have a heart attack or seizure, or otherwise create a medical emergency. The office should have a regular procedure that you should know so that you can react quickly and confidently to such a situation.[9] If there is anyone in the office or the building that has special training in giving emergency aid, you should be aware of it.

You have now gone through a fairly thorough preparation process for the interview. The interview, whether it is your first or one hundred and first, will go more smoothly and the client will have more confidence in you because of it. With this kind of preparation, little can go wrong.

ASSIGNMENT 3:13
Develop your own checklist of the items you will need at the interview site. Such a checklist will be a quick reference for preparing your office or a conference room for the interview. Include the necessary forms and directions. Place this material in the system folder.

■ The Interview

You are now prepared to conduct the initial interview with Ms. Forrester. The following are some examples of how you might conduct the interview. Assume that Ms. Forrester has already met with Mr. White and that he brings the client to your office. (Ms. Forrester is in a wheelchair.)

The Introduction

Mr. White:	Ms. Forrester, I would like you to meet Terry Salyer, who is the paralegal that will be assisting me with your case. Terry, this is Ms. Ann Forrester, who, as you know, suffered injuries in a car-pedestrian accident this past year and is seeking our firm's assistance.
Paralegal:	How do you do, Ms. Forrester. We have spoken on the phone, and I have looked forward to meeting you.
Mr. White:	I'll leave you with Terry, who will be asking you some important questions. We will meet again later. It was good to see you.

Another frequent scenario for an introduction occurs when the secretary or receptionist informs you that your appointment has arrived. Clear your desk and go out to meet the client, letting her know that you are eager to meet and work with her.

Interviewing is more than just asking questions. What techniques can you use to elicit your client's story?

Paralegal: Please come into my office. I would be happy to fix you a cup of coffee or tea. We also have some soft drinks. Would you care for anything?

Ms. Forrester: Not now, thank you, maybe later.

Close the office door, return to your chair, and speak briefly about the weather, ask about her family, or about how she is doing with the wheelchair. Proceed to explain your role as a paralegal and the purpose of the interview. Ask for the information that Ms. Forrester was requested to bring.

Paralegal: Thank you for taking the time to gather this material. It will be very helpful. I have some questions I need to cover with you. You can start by telling me your full name.

Ms. Forrester: Ann Brooke Forrester.

Paralegal: Your home address is 1533 Capitol Drive, Legalville, Columbia, Zip 00000?

Ms. Forrester: Yes.

You can now proceed to work through the questions on the form that you have prepared, listening carefully, recording all pertinent information, and drawing from the information brought in by the client as needed.

Assume that Ms. Forrester goes on to describe the accident summarized as follows. It was a partly sunny, windy, cold morning. There was ice on the road in front of the Forrester house. Ms. Forrester crossed the highway to mail a letter. The point of crossing sits in a depression in the road with knolls rising to the east and west, obscuring some vision. A van came over the east knoll, slid and hit Ms. Forrester, who was seriously injured.

Questions on Circumstances of the Accident

Now you need to focus on specific details. The following questions demonstrate the necessary detail that must be inquired into to see if there is evidence to establish the elements of proof of breach of duty. (*P* stands for paralegal and *F* stands for Ms. Forrester.)

P: Ms. Forrester, you mentioned in your description of the accident that the road was icy. I'd like to go back to that. Did you personally observe that the road was icy?

F: Yes, when I walked across the road.

P: Was it icy enough for you to alter your normal walk?

F: Yes, I kind of shuffled over the icy patches.

P: The ice did not cover the entire road?

F: That's right.

P: Was the ice thick?

F: No, just a thin layer, like heavy frost. Some had already begun to melt in the sun and other areas were completely dry.

P: Did you notice the condition of the road on the downslope from where the van approached?

F: Not really. It was in the early morning shadows, however, and what ice was there probably did not melt.

P: On what do you base that opinion?

F: Several days before the accident we had similar weather. That slope remained icier because of the shadows.

P: Is there anyone besides yourself and the defendant who might have observed the ice on the road?

F: Yes.

P: Their names and addresses, please.

The questioning must be very detailed. Listen carefully and take advantage of the opportunity to get witnesses' names on this particular point. It is a good idea when receiving such names to use a local phone directory immediately to confirm the spelling of the names as well as addresses and phone numbers.

P: Ms. Forrester, I would like to go back to what you said about the van seeming to keep coming at you. Did the defendant see you first, or did you see the defendant first?

F: I am not sure; however, when I looked up, the van was already coming down the slope, so the defendant should have seen me first.

P: When you first saw the van, was there any indication that the driver was taking evasive action?

F: No, in fact, the van just kept coming for what must have been at least four seconds, it felt that long. Before it hit me I heard a skidding sound and the van began to fishtail.

P: Describe what you mean by "fishtail."

F: The rear of the van began to move sideways—back and forth.

It is important that you call attention to words that might not be clear (in this case, *fishtail*) and ask for further explanation. It is also a good idea to clarify the meaning of all words you do not understand or that may be misused by the client.

The Issue of Contributory or Comparative Negligence

P: Earlier, you mentioned wearing a warm winter coat with a high, furry collar. Was the collar high enough to go over your ears?

F: Yes, it was.

P: Do you always wear it that way?

F: No, but I did on this day. The wind was cold, and I pulled my collar up and tucked my head into it.

P: Did you tuck your head into it far enough that your vision was obscured?

F: It was not obscured looking forward, but, yes, it was, I guess, on the sides.

P: By "sides" do you mean your peripheral vision?

F: Yes.

P: Help me on this. You said "I guess," referring to the coat's obstruction of your vision. Was your side vision obscured?

F: Yes, it was.

P: Would you have seen the van sooner had you not pulled the coat up around your head?

F: I don't know. It's possible. I did look to the left and then the right before stepping onto the road.

P: What were you looking at once you stepped onto the road?

F: The road immediately in front of me. I did not want to slip on the ice.

Note several things. First, a high collar might be a hearing obstruction. Second, the client said she tucked her head into the collar, raising the possibility of a sight obstruction. And third, responses such as "I guess" are insufficient. Tactfully press the client for a more precise response.

The Extent of Injury and Sensitive Inquiry

The following questions come after a fairly extensive description by the client of severe injuries to the left hip, pelvic region, lower back, and left leg.

The client has stated that she is nearly paralyzed on her left side from the waist down. At this point in the interview, the client begins to weep. The paralegal gets up from behind the desk and comes over to the client, placing a gentle hand on the client's shoulder.

P: Ms. Forrester, I know these must be very difficult times for you. Let's take a short break. How about a glass of water or maybe some soda?

(Ms. Forrester nods. Leave the room to give the client a few moments of privacy and time to regain her composure. Bring her a glass of water.)

P: May I get you anything else?

F: No, but thank you. I feel better now.

P: I realize it must be difficult to talk about your injuries. The more you can help me with information, however, the better job we can do for you.

F: I understand. Let's go on.

P: Ms. Forrester, have you had any problems as a result of the injuries regarding normal bodily functions?

F: Yes, I have some difficulty controlling my bladder.

P: I need to make sure I understand this correctly. You urinate regardless of any effort to control the urination process on your part?

F: That is correct.

P: Now, it is important for me to determine how this inconvenience and anxiety affect you.

Go on to explore the details, including any sense of humiliation, frustration, or degradation. Do not let the sensitivity of the issue stop the detailed inquiry. In most cases, sensitive issues must be dealt with forthrightly, using straightforward vocabulary. Avoid euphemisms.

One thing to be observed in reading through these interview segments is the need to ad lib questions. Such questions will follow naturally as long as you listen carefully and keep in mind the elements of the action as well as the defenses.

ASSIGNMENT 3:14
Conduct an interview of Mr. Ameche (Case II). Do this in class in a role-playing setting unless told to do otherwise by your instructor. Divide the interview into various segments (introduction, personal information, events leading up to accident, the accident, injuries, and so on). Different students should take the responsibility of interviewee and interviewer for each segment. The class should critique each segment of the interview according to the following criteria:

1. Friendly and effective introduction
2. Clarity of questions
3. Application of specific interview techniques
4. Willingness to probe
5. Attitude toward client
6. Effective conclusion of interview
7. Overall preparation

Concluding the Interview

In concluding the interview, give the client a list of all the information that remains for the client to gather. Also remind the client to notify you of any new information regarding the accident, witnesses, injuries, and so on. Provide the client with the client information brochure. It might be helpful to give the client her own file folder in which to keep records and documents over the course of the lawsuit. Attach your business card to the folder. Then explain the documents that need to be executed and have them signed. After one last reminder to the client not to make any statements about the case and not to discuss the case with others, the interview can be concluded. Some interviewers choose at this time to turn off the billing clock and visit informally with the client to show their interest in the client. This is an effective technique, especially if used sincerely. Tell clients that you will keep them informed periodically on the progress of their case.

Confirming the Statute of Limitations

Once you have found out the date of the occurrence and the nature of the action, it is important to check the **statute of limitations.** This may have been done already, but if not, it should be done now. The statute of limitations is the date by which an action must be filed. If it is not filed by the required time, the defendant has a defense to the action, and the case will be dismissed. Rarely is there an excuse of sufficient degree for a judge to permit an action to be filed after the required date. Therefore, the paralegal must unfailingly check to see what the statute of limitations is for the particular type of action involved. The time periods vary depending on the type of action and the state. Usually someone in the office will have previously made a quick reference list of the common time limits. If not, statute books will list the time limits under the topic Statute of Limitations or by the type of case: negligence, contract, products liability, and so on.

The time period involved in the statute of limitations is a specified time such as one year or two years. When claims are based on federal laws with unspecified statutes of limitations, federal courts must look to parallel limits in the law of the state in which they are located. Title 28 U.S.C. § 1658 sets a uniform four-year limit in all such actions based on federal laws enacted after December 30, 1990. Normally the statute of limitations starts with the date of the injury, accident, breach of contract, and so on. In such circumstances, the lawsuit must be filed before one year elapses if it is a one-year statute of limitations or before two years elapses if it is a two-year statute, and so forth. If the injury is of a nature that its precise origin is not apparent or the symptoms of the injury are not likely to manifest themselves for some time after the event that caused them (for example, in black lung cases in coal mining or in cancer cases caused by long-term exposure to radiation), then the statute begins to run at the time the symptoms were first noticeable or at a time a reasonable person should have noticed the symptoms or problem. A fifteen-year coal miner might not show symptoms of black lung until ten years after leaving the mines. That miner can still sue, even though the injuries actually occurred many years earlier. The action must be started before the statute runs; it does not have to be concluded in that time. The statute of limitations is so significant that it should be conspicuously noted on the front of the case file and placed in the deadline calendaring system.

ASSIGNMENT 3:15
Locate the common statutes of limitations through the index to the state's statutes. Compile a list of the statute numbers and time limits for cases involving personal injury, property damage, wrongful death, contracts (oral and written), and any others requested by your instructor. Place the list into the system folder.

■ Summarizing the Interview

After the interview, the paralegal should have the interview notes typed. From the notes and the interview form, a summary of the interview should then be prepared. A summary sheet appears in figure 3:6; the completed version is in figure 3:7. One copy of the summary should go into the file and another copy should be given to the supervising attorney.

ASSIGNMENT 3:16
Enter into a computer the notes from your interview with Mr. Ameche. Using a duplicate of these notes, delete extraneous material and organize the remaining important information into a summary according to the format in figure 3:6.

Figure 3:6   Summary Sheet: Initial Interview of Client

File no.   Date opened: Interviewer:
Client: (M) Spouse: (C) Children, ages: (P) Phone:
Party opponent(s):

Date of incident:

Type of action: Statue of limitations:

Summary of facts of action:

Noteworthy facts related to elements of action:

Noteworthy facts related to possible defenses:

Witnesses:

Summary of injury and treatment to date:

Total medical bills to date:

Summary of business or wage loss:

Total business or wage loss to date:

Evaluation of client as witness:

Other comments:

Things to do:

Figure 3:7   Summary Sheet: Initial Interview of Client (Completed)

File no. PI 3750   **Date opened:** 6/23/ ___   **Interviewer:** T.S. 6/29/ ___
Client: (P) Ann Forrester   (M) William Forrester   (C) Michael, 8   (P) 555-1111
                                                              Sara, 4
Party opponent(s):   (D) Richard Hart (Ohio resident)
                                Mercury Parcel Service (Ohio resident, Hart's employer)
Date of incident: 2/26/ ___
Type of action: P.I. negligence, auto-pedestrian
Statute of limitations: 2/26/ ___
Summary of facts of action:
   P walked across Highway 328 three miles west of Legalville, Columbia, to mail letter. Coming back
was stuck by van owned by Mercury Parcel Service. Crossing point was in depression in road obscuring
long-range vision of both pedestrian and driver. Road had patchy ice. D was driving at about 40 mph in
35-mph zone. P was struck on left side and thrown to side of road. Van went off road and struck tree.
Noteworthy facts related to elements of action:
   Breach of duty: P states D going too fast for icy conditions, slid on ice. Also P states D delayed evasive
action and may have been inattentive. P says her husband felt D looked quite tired. According to P's
husband, van windshield partially fogged over.
Noteworthy facts related to possible defenses:
   Comparative negligence: P was in hurry to mail letter to leave for work, had head tucked into coat
and vision to side obscured. Thinks she looked to left, not sure; did look to right. Didn't see van until it
was headed down slope toward her. Didn't hear van coming.
Witnesses:
   Ms. Freda Schnabel saw accident from crest of opposite hill while driving her car toward accident.
Her address is 1625 Capitol Dr.
   P's husband, William Forrester, also saw some of accident.
   Officer Jeremy Burton was first police officer on scene.
Summary of injury and treatment to date:
   Several fractures of left hip, pelvis, and left leg. Partial paralysis on left side from waist down. Loss of
bladder control. Considerable pain in injured area. Permanent disability likely, currently confined to
wheelchair. Emergency treatment: 2/26/ ___ Good Samaritan Hospital, 4600 Church St., Legalville,
Columbia.
Treating physician(s): Albert Meyer, M.D.; orthopedic surgeon
                                   Medical Arts Building, 4650 Church St.
Consultant: Robert S. Ward, M.D., urology
Total medical bills to date: $22,000
Summary of business or wage loss:
   Full-time teacher, Legalville Board of Education, $24,000 annually.
   Unable to work since accident. Note: Wage loss could be substantial if injury permanent.
Total business or wage loss to date: $12,000
Evaluation of client as witness: Client is pleasant, intelligent, and should be good witness.
Other comments: Client wanted to know if she should file a lawsuit. I explained she needed to discuss
this with Mr. White, who would be meeting with her.
Things to do: Gather medical records, interview witnesses, locate van.

■ Keeping the Client Informed

A significant improvement that paralegals have brought to the law office is
increased communication with clients. Lack of communication from the
law office is a frequent complaint of clients. Therefore, the paralegal should
assume the primary responsibility of keeping the client well informed.

Schedule a report letter to be sent to the client at least once a month. Try to respond to all the client's inquiries as soon as possible and acknowledge receipt of any information sent to you by the client. This personal attention assures clients that they are not merely a case file number.

Study Guide

1. For what reasons is the initial interview with the client important?
2. Why is planning an interview important?
3. What are the twelve steps in the interview plan? Explain how each step is accomplished.
4. Explain how to develop an interview form.
5. Identify and define the four legal elements that must be proved by the plaintiff in a negligence case.
6. What is the difference between contributory negligence and comparative negligence? Which of these two doctrines is the rule of law in your state?
7. What is the doctrine of last clear chance? What is the assumption of risk? Give examples of each.
8. How does one develop pertinent questions for an interview?
9. Create ten questions probing the existence and nature of injuries suffered in an occurrence.
10. What are some of the considerations in selecting a location for the interview?
11. Why is scheduling a flexible time for the interview important?
12. What types of things should the client bring to the interview?
13. What is the simple process for developing a form letter?
14. Identify the special needs one should anticipate in planning an interview.
15. What special ethical and tactical concerns must a paralegal be aware of when interviewing a client?
16. Restate as many of the interview techniques as you can.
17. In the "Information to be Given to the Client" checklist, which suggestions, if not followed, may adversely affect the client's case?
18. Be able to prepare a variety of releases and a fee agreement.
19. List those things to be considered in preparing the interview site.
20. Be able to prepare and conduct an entire interview.
21. What is a statute of limitations? When should it be checked? When does a statute of limitations begin tolling in various circumstances?
22. How should you summarize or evaluate an interview?
23. How can the paralegal play a key role in keeping the client informed of the status of the client's case?

Endnotes

1. ELLIOTT & ELLIOTT, A TORT RESUME FOR USE IN PROSECUTION AND DEFENSE OF ALL DAMAGE CLAIMS 1ff., with permission of Agnes M. Elliott.
2. THE NATIONAL ASSOCIATION OF LEGAL ASSISTANTS, MANUAL FOR LEGAL ASSISTANTS 255 (1979) [hereinafter cited as NALA MANUAL].

3. SHAFFER, LEGAL INTERVIEWING AND COUNSELING 117 (1976) (quoting suggestions by Annette Gerret).
4. Id., 117–18.
5. Id., 80 (quoting Alfred C. Kinsey).
6. Id., 124 (quoting Alfred Benjamin).
7. Suggested in part by JEANS, TRIAL ADVOCACY 62–72 (1975).
8. Katzman, *Using Written Fee Agreements*, WISCONSIN LAWYER (Dec. 1990), reprinted with permission of the Wisconsin Bar Association.
9. NALA MANUAL, 269.

4

Evidence and Investigation

■ Introduction
■ The Relationship of Evidence Law to Investigation
■ Planning the Investigation
■ Ethical and Related Considerations
■ Gathering the Evidence
■ Preserving Evidence
■ Reviewing the Informal Investigation

■ Introduction

Mr. White has given you your next assignment. He wants you to do the investigation of the *Forrester* case and the *Ameche* case.

Investigation is the formal and informal process of gathering information to determine what the facts are in a case. Formal investigation, involving exchanges of information between opposing attorneys as governed by court rules and sanctions, is called *discovery*. This is the focus of chapter 8. Chapter 4, however, focuses on informal investigation. Fact gathering in informal investigation is achieved by interviewing the client (chapter 3); interviewing witnesses; and reviewing documents, records, physical evidence, and test results. The purposes of the investigation are listed next.

1. To identify and locate the factual evidence that may be used by both sides to support or defeat each element of a cause of action
2. To locate persons and property
3. To establish expert opinion evidence
4. To develop evidence to discredit (impeach) a witness or opponent
5. To determine if there is sufficient factual evidence to support or defend the cause of action at trial or to form the basis for a settlement
6. To find additional evidence if necessary
7. To preserve evidence for trial
8. To organize the evidence for trial

Investigation requires the search of all the evidence, pro and con, and is so important a process that cases are won or lost on the degree of diligence devoted to investigation.

ASSIGNMENT 4:1
List the purposes of investigation at the beginning of the investigation section of your system folder.

▉ The Relationship of Evidence Law to Investigation

Introduction

The purpose of investigation is to accumulate evidence for trial. That evidence must be evaluated to determine if it is admissible—whether it can be used in a court of law. Although investigative decisions should be made in close consultation with the supervising attorney, the more the paralegal knows about the rules of evidence, the more assistance the paralegal can provide. An efficient investigator uses a fundamental knowledge of the rules of evidence to evaluate the usefulness and admissibility of the evidence as it is gathered. Knowledge of the rules also guides the investigator to the most valuable evidence, thus saving time and money. Job satisfaction is enhanced if the paralegal understands the underlying reasons for investigative tasks.

Evidence in General

Evidence is a distinct body of law that defines and regulates what information may be presented at trial. It is the information that the trier (jury or judge) uses to decide whether the plaintiff has proved the case. The rules of evidence help to ensure the fairest possible trial through the efficient presentation of reliable and understandable evidence. Truth and justice are the rules' ultimate goal. Rules of evidence exist for the federal court system as well as for the system of each state. The rules for the federal system are the Federal Rules of Evidence, cited as FED.R.EVID. Some state systems have adopted the Federal Rules, and the rules of most other states have much in common with the Federal Rules. This section will focus on the Federal Rules of Evidence.

Evidence is categorized as direct or circumstantial. **Direct evidence** is that which is directly observable and proves the truth asserted. In Case I, for example, if the neighbor saw the van hit Ms. Forrester, a statement to that effect in court by the neighbor would be direct evidence that the van did hit Ms. Forrester. On the other hand, if the neighbor saw a damaged van and Ms. Forrester lying near it, a statement to the effect by the neighbor would be circumstantial evidence that the van hit Ms. Forrester. **Circumstantial evidence** is evidence that merely suggests the existence of some other occurrence or thing. Both types of evidence may be valuable to a case.

Admissible Evidence

Admissible evidence is evidence that may be presented in court prescribed by the rules of evidence. To be admissible, evidence must be relevant. **Relevance** has two components: the evidence must be **material**—of consequence to the determination of the action—and it must tend to prove or refute a fact of consequence (FED.R.EVID. 401). Being of consequence to the determination of the action (materiality) means that it bears a meaningful relationship to the determination of the issues at hand. For example, if the issue is whether Mr. Hart was careless when operating his van, would the color of his hair be of consequence to the determination of the issue? No. Would Mr. Hart's testimony that he was driving at thirty miles per hour be of consequence to the action? Yes. Speed in conjunction with the circumstances can be an indication of carelessness or carefulness; therefore, the testimony is material.

To be relevant, however, evidence must also tend to prove or refute a fact of consequence. If the fact of consequence is that Mr. Hart was traveling at thirty miles per hour, would his testimony that he was driving about thirty miles per hour tend to prove or refute this fact? Yes, it helps prove he was going thirty miles per hour (a fact of consequence). Therefore, the testimony meets both tests and is relevant and generally admissible.

Limits to Relevancy

Even relevant evidence is not always admissible. The evidence is inadmissible if the **probative value of evidence**—its strength to prove what it purports to prove—is outweighed by other factors deemed harmful to the trial process. These factors are identified in Rule 403 of the Federal Rules of Evidence and similar provisions in state rules of evidence. The rule states:

> Although relevant, evidence may be excluded if its probative value is substantially outweighed by the danger of unfair prejudice, confusion of the issues, or misleading the jury, or by considerations of undue delay, waste of time, or needless presentation of cumulative evidence [FED.R.EVID. 403].

The danger of unfair prejudice means that relevant evidence can be excluded if it is very likely to cause a jury to decide an issue because it evokes undue sympathy, contempt, horror, or strong emotion. If a judge, for example, believed that a photograph showing Ms. Forrester's little girl crying over her injured mother would so evoke the jurors' sympathy that it would distract them from the actual injury portrayed in the photograph, the judge could exclude the photograph despite its relevance. The key is whether the danger of unfair prejudice substantially outweighs the probative value of the evidence.

If the evidence is very likely to create confusion—that is, create unnecessary side issues or simply be too complex for most jurors—it may be excluded under this rule. Or if the evidence is too misleading and likely to cause jurors to place more weight on the evidence than fairness dictates, it may be excluded. For example, a jury may put too much credence on the results of a lie detector test or an unscaled model of the scene of an accident.

The remaining concerns under Rule 403 are directed at saving time and money in the trial. Thus, if the probative value of evidence is substantially outweighed by its consumption of court time, it can be excluded. Similarly, if it wastes time or is merely a repetitious accumulation of evidence already adequately presented, the court may exclude it. Another consideration here is if repeated or extended presentations on a certain point would cause jurors to unduly emphasize its importance, such evidence may be limited or excluded if its probative value is substantially outweighed by its detrimental effect.

Evidence of a person's character or a particular trait offered as proof that a person's conduct conformed to that trait on a particular occasion is inadmissible (FED.R.EVID. 404). One major exception to this rule occurs when character, or a trait of character, is an element of a claim. To illustrate, truth would be a defense to an action for making false and damaging statements about another. Hence, evidence of truthfulness and specific instances of such conduct would be admissible [FED.R.EVID. 405(b)]. When evidence of character is admissible, a witness may testify to the reputation of the person or render an opinion on the person's character [FED.R.EVID. 405(a)]. In these situations, inquiry into specific instances of relevant conduct is permissible on cross-examination of the witness. Any permissible testimony on reputation or opinions on a person's character focuses on reputation in the subject's neighborhood (residence) or among associates.

Evidence of habit or routine to prove that conduct on a specific occasion conformed to the habit or routine is generally admissible (FED.R.EVID. 406). **Habit** is the semiautomatic, repeated response to a specific situation. Brushing one's teeth each morning or automatically fastening the seat belt every time one rides in a car are examples of habit. **Routine** (custom) is the equivalent of habit for organizations. Products may be routinely inspected for defects, accounts routinely inspected for improper expenditures, and prospective employee references routinely checked. It is the nearly invariable regularity of habit and routine that makes them valid as evidence. Acts similar to the act in question, however, are not generally admissible as evidence because they may be remote in time to the occurrence in question or may lack the reliability of the invariable frequency of actions that is characterized as habit or routine.

Evidence of offers to compromise on payment of medical expenses is inadmissible, as well as evidence of insurance coverage and subsequent repairs to correct a defect that caused damages.

Privileged Communications

Privileged communications are also a limitation on relevancy. Privilege makes inadmissible certain communications of a confidential nature because of their social utility: husband-wife, physician-patient, attorney-client, social worker–client, priest-penitent. The law of the local jurisdiction must be consulted for unique rules on privileged communications.

Evidence Admissible from a Party

The relevant admission of an opposing party (party-opponent) is admissible. It may be oral, written, or nonverbal conduct. The admission is generally damaging to the party making the admission and, at the very least, suggests a belief or position inconsistent with the one the admitting party is taking at trial. This damaging nature, however, is not a requirement for admission. Therefore, the often-used designation of "admission against interest" is a misnomer under the federal rule and similar state rules.[1] According to Federal Rule of Evidence 801(d), such an admission is admissible under the following rules:

1. If it is the party-opponent's own statement either in an individual or a representative capacity (if the latter, the statement must be relevant to the context of the representation; both types of admissions can include relevant pleas of guilty);
2. If the opponent has in words or conduct manifested an adoption or belief in the truth of the statement or manifested such belief by remaining silent when normally a denial would be expected;

3. If the statement is by a person authorized by the party-opponent to make such a statement (a party's books and records may be entered under this rule);[2]
4. If the statement is made by a party-opponent's agent or servant concerning a matter in the scope of his or her agency or employment;
5. If the statement is made by a co-conspirator in the course of the conspiracy.

Common law and some state evidence provisions make admissible against the party-opponent any statements made by one jointly interested in privity (sharing a common right in property or contract) with the party-opponent. Any such provision has been omitted in the Federal Rules and many state rules because of the lack of probative value.[3]

Rules Regarding the Testimony of a Witness

Requirement of Firsthand Knowledge

The testimony of witnesses must be based on firsthand knowledge. In other words, the witnesses must have seen, heard, smelled, touched, or otherwise directly observed the subject of their testimony (FED.R.EVID. 602).

Opinion

Federal courts and those of many states allow laypersons to give opinions. One such type of opinion is based on perceived facts leading to opinions on speed, weight, height, distance, and so on. A second type of opinion is that of a skilled lay observer. This opinion is based on repeated observations permitting identification of a specific signature or voice, or an assessment of the sanity of a person the observer knows.

Expert Opinion

Highly specialized, educated experts are permitted to give their opinions on matters at issue that relate to their field (FED.R.EVID. 702). Doctors, for example, are permitted to give their opinion regarding an injury, the cause of an injury, and the prognosis (outlook). Typically, engineers and scientists are among those experts permitted to give opinions.

Evidence of Character and Conduct of a Witness

It is important for a paralegal to remember that the jury's perception of a witness's truthfulness (credibility) may make the difference between winning and losing a case. Therefore, any evidence that bears on the truthfulness of a witness should be noted.

Under the Federal Rules of Evidence, it is permissible for others to enter an opinion on a witness's truthfulness or reputation for truthfulness. Specific acts of conduct that bear on a witness's truthfulness may be inquired into by the attorneys but cannot be proven by independent evidence. Criminal convictions less than ten years old are also significant if the possible punishment was for more than one year in prison and/or the crime reflected dishonesty or untruthfulness. Religious beliefs are not admissible to show credibility. Rules 607 to 610 of the Federal Rules of Evidence apply to evidence of a witness's character and conduct.

Prior Statements of a Witness

A paralegal should take note of any statements of a witness on matters likely to be important at trial that may be used to challenge or support a witness's truthfulness. For example, if a witness testifies that Mr. Hart's van was going forty-five miles per hour at the time of the accident, and the same witness told a police officer that the van was going about twenty-five miles per hour, the prior inconsistent statement could be very damaging to the witness's credibility.

Capacity to Observe, Record, Recollect, or Narrate

Any witness may be examined for the ability to observe, record, recollect, or narrate in order to demonstrate any weaknesses. Extrinsic evidence— evidence other than the testimony of the witness in question—may be used to prove such weaknesses. Mental capacity, intelligence, distractions, distance from the event observed, lighting conditions, influence of drugs or alcohol, and a multitude of other matters that affect reliability may be inquired into or proved by other evidence.

Hearsay

Hearsay is evidence that relies on the firsthand observation of another person rather than the person testifying. For example, Ms. Schnabel, the neighbor, might testify that Mr. Forrester told her that Mr. Hart's van was going forty-five miles per hour. Since that statement is based on Mr. Forrester's observation and not on the firsthand observation of Ms. Schnabel, it is hearsay as to the speed of the van. Hearsay is considered unreliable and is generally inadmissible. The paralegal, therefore, must not rely on hearsay but should seek out the original firsthand source for needed evidence.

There are, however, some important exceptions to the hearsay rule. These are found in the Federal Rules of Evidence, beginning with Rule 801(d), and in similar state rules.

Prior statements of a witness   A statement previously made by a witness is admissible at trial if the witness is subject to cross-examination and any of the following elements are present:

1. The statement is inconsistent with the witness's trial testimony and given under oath.
2. The prior statement is consistent with the witness's testimony and is offered to meet an attack on the declarant's honesty or motives.
3. The statement was one identifying a person after seeing the person.

Admission by party opponent   A previous statement made by a party may be admitted against that person by the opponent. See the preceding section, "Evidence Admissible from a Party."

Present sense impression   A statement made during or immediately after an event is observed or a condition is described is admissible. (Example: Mr. Johnson said, "That car is gong too fast to make that curve!")

Excited utterance An excited utterance is admissible. (Example: "My husband said, 'Look out! That car is coming into our lane!'")

Then-existing mental, emotional, or physical conditions This exception is designed to admit some evidence other than conduct to reveal a person's state of mind regarding intent, plan, motive, emotion, and pain. (Example: "Ms. Forrester said, 'My hip hurts so much I can barely stand it.'" Example: "Mr. Hart said, 'I'll get those brakes fixed next month.'") Statements that are present sense impressions, excited utterances, or about then-existing mental, emotional, or physical conditions are called **res gestae statements.**

Statement made to receive a medical diagnosis (Example: "Ms. Forrester said to me [doctor], 'My left hip is very painful.'") Such a statement is admissible.

Recorded recollection A statement recorded when a witness's memory was fresh is admissible when the witness cannot recall the contents of the statement.

Records Records kept in the regular course of business, such as motel registration or time cards, are admissible.

Statement of reputation When it concerns family history, boundaries, or a person's character, such a statement is admissible.

Court judgment A conviction of fraud, for example, would be admissible if offered to prove any fact essential to the case.

Unavailability of witness Some hearsay evidence is admissible only if the declarant is unavailable to testify (Fed.R.Evid. 804). Unavailability means the witness is dead, is unavailable through reasonable efforts, refuses to testify or is protected from testifying, or can't remember.

Former testimony: If a witness is unavailable at trial, the witness's former testimony is admissible as long as it was subject to cross-examination at the time by one having a similar interest to the opponent's.

Statements under belief of impending death (dying declarations): A statement made by a person who believed his or her death was imminent is admissible when offered to show the person's belief regarding the cause or circumstances of death. Under common law the person must have died; in the Federal Rules the person must be unavailable.

Statements against interest: The law has assumed that a person would not make a statement against his or her financial, business, or legal interest unless it were true. Therefore, when a witness is unavailable, that witness's previous statement against his or her interest is admissible.

Rules Regarding Physical Evidence and Authentication

Physical evidence is evidence that one can see, hear, touch, or otherwise perceive firsthand: the scene of an accident, a contract or other written instrument, an x-ray, the viewed injuries or scars of the plaintiff, or a photograph. Because such evidence is perceived firsthand by the trier of fact and not through the description of a witness, it can be very persuasive. Physical evidence needs to be authenticated in order to be admissible. In other words, it must be shown to be what it purports to be. Therefore, the paralegal must also determine what is necessary to have that evidence authenticated. Rule 901(b) of the Federal Rules of Evidence suggests several ways that evidence can be authenticated:

1. Testimony of a witness who has knowledge that a matter is what it is claimed to be. (Example: "I made the entries in the log describing which deliveries Mr. Hart was to make the day of the accident, and that is the log.")
2. Testimony of a nonexpert on someone's handwriting. (Example: "I have seen Mr. Hart's signature many times, and that is his signature.") This method can apply to voice identification as well.
3. Testimony of an expert witness based on adequate comparison. (Example: "I have examined exhibit A and several samples of handwriting known to be Mr. Brown's; it is my opinion that exhibit A is Mr. Brown's handwriting.")
4. Testimony about distinctive characteristics. (Example: "My wife's coat was all hand sewn, and the aunt who made it sewed her initials, B.J., into the lining. Yes, that is my wife's coat.")
5. Testimony about a telephone conversation determining whether the other person was the person in question. (Example: "I called Richard Hart at the extension number listed for him at the Mercury Parcel Service, and he answered and said, 'This is Richard Hart.' ")

If an item of evidence is not unique, such as an automobile tire, it can be shown to be the tire in question by establishing a **chain of custody.** A chain of custody is a chronological history of the storage or use (or both) of an item since the event in question. Testimony demonstrating a complete chain should remove any reasonable doubts as to the authenticity of the item.

Scientific evidence resulting from blood, breathalyzer, and other scientific analyses requires testimony that the theory underlying the test is valid and the equipment used is reliable.

Some evidence is self-authenticating, requiring only a government seal, official attestation, or the signature of an official in charge of such documents. Federal and state documents and public records come under this category. Official publications, such as books and pamphlets, are self-authenticating, as are newspapers and periodicals, trade inscriptions, notarized documents, commercial paper, or any other signature or document declared so by act of Congress.

The context of writings, recordings (including mechanical recordings), and photographs (including x-rays, motion pictures, and videotapes) also require authentication. These things fall under the **best evidence** rule (FED.R.EVID. 1002). By this rule, only the original document or item is admissible. This is to prevent admission of altered or fraudulent copies. Therefore, an investigator must strive to secure the original item. In some circumstances, however, copies may be substituted. This is so when the authenticity of the original is not in question, when use of a duplicate will not be unfair to the other party, or when the original is lost or destroyed (unless in bad faith by the proponent). Writings, recordings, or photographs too voluminous for practical court use may be summarized.

Other Evidentiary Concepts

Judicial Notice

Judicial notice permits a judge to admit certain evidence without authentication. Such evidence can be judicially noticed if it is a fact not subject to reasonable dispute and meets one of two criteria: (1) the fact must be commonly known in the territorial jurisdiction of the court, or (2) the fact is readily verifiable through undisputed sources (FED.R.EVID. 201). By eliminating the need for authentication, judicial notice saves time and expense. A court might take judicial notice of acts and records of the court, geographic and historical facts, matters of public record, or the viability of the underlying basis for a scientific test, such as for the presence of alcohol in the blood.

Stipulations

A **stipulation** is an agreement between the parties that permits evidence to be admitted as true without authentication. Stipulations are formally received by most courts because they save time and often reduce the need for witnesses. For example, in a contract dispute, the parties might stipulate that the signatures are authentic or that the contract is the original, eliminating the need of proof of these facts.

Burden of Proof

Even in the earliest stages of investigation, it is important for the paralegal to understand which party has the **burden of proof** and on which points. Having that information, the paralegal will be of more assistance in ferreting out evidence useful to the client's case.

The plaintiff is the accuser and the one seeking a remedy. Therefore, the law places the burden on the plaintiff to plead and prove the allegations set out in the complaint. Only when the plaintiff has satisfied the minimum burden does it become necessary for the defendant to rebut the plaintiff's evidence with evidence of his or her own. The defendant, however, bears the burden of proving affirmative defenses such as self-defense, payment of the alleged debt, or assumption of risk. If a party is in a position to have the only knowledge of a fact, that party bears the burden on the fact.

In civil cases, the person who bears the burden of proof must meet that burden by a **preponderance of the evidence.** "Evidence preponderates when it is more convincing to the trier than the opposing evidence," and the burden is met by "proof which leads the jury to find that the existence of the contested fact is more probable than its nonexistence."[4]

In some types of civil cases (citizenship, fraud, mutual mistake, and content of lost deeds), the standard is proof by clear and convincing evidence. **Clear and convincing evidence** is a higher standard of proof than "preponderance of evidence" and requires that the matter be shown to be very probable. Criminal cases require the highest burden of proof: proof beyond a reasonable doubt. **Proof beyond a reasonable doubt** is proof that is so strong it excludes any other reasonable hypothesis or explanation— almost a certainty.

Presumption

An evidentiary **presumption** is a mechanism that presumes a certain fact to be true when certain other preliminary evidence is established. Thus, if it is proved that Ann Forrester mailed a letter to Richard Hart, and the letter was never returned to Ann Forrester as unclaimed, a presumption takes over that says Richard Hart received the letter. By presuming the existence of an unestablished fact, that Hart received the letter, a presumption helps one side establish facts that otherwise might be difficult, time-consuming, or awkward to prove. Unless Hart comes forth with evidence to rebut the presumption, such as, "I never received the letter," the jury will be instructed that the delivery has been established.

Sources for Evidentiary Research

Keep in mind that rules of evidence are more complex than can be covered here, and occasions arise in the law office when you will need more information on a particular rule of evidence. When you do, there are several sources to consider: *Wigmore on Evidence*, the hornbook *McCormick on Evidence*, and the legal encyclopedias. The Nutshell books published by West, Rothstein's *Evidence*, and Graham's *Federal Rules of Evidence* are good for quick reference. The Federal Rules of Evidence with drafter's comments and the evidentiary statutes and rules of each state should not be overlooked. Imwinkelreid's book, *Evidentiary Foundations*, can be useful as a quick guide to what evidence is necessary to establish proper foundation. An evidentiary foundation is that testimony necessary to establish that a person was in a position to have observed or have knowledge of the facts to which he or she will be testifying. It establishes firsthand knowledge.

ASSIGNMENT 4:2
The following is a list of possible evidence in Case I. Based on your understanding of the necessary elements in a negligence case from chapter 3, the information in this chapter, and the rules of evidence for both the federal (F) and your state courts (S), indicate whether the listed items of evidence are admissible (A) or inadmissible (I). State any applicable reason and rule number.

Evidence	Fed.	State	Reason	Rule(s)
Witness: "Mr. Hart is a good baseball player."	(I)	(I)	irrelevant	401(F)(S)
1. Witness: "Mr. Hart smelled of beer."	( )	( )		
2. Bloody video of Ms. Forrester's hip repair	( )	( )		
3. Witness: "Mr. Hart is a cautious person."	( )	( )		
4. Routine practice of Mercury to check all brakes of vehicles	( )	( )		
5. Forresters' offer to Mercury to settle for $50,000	( )	( )		
6. Hart told wife he was too tired to be driving	( )	( )		
7. Forrester's letter to friend stating she didn't look for traffic	( )	( )		
8. Friend's opinion that signature on letter is Forrester's	( )	( )		
9. Doctor's testimony that van caused Forrester's injuries	( )	( )		

10. Independent evidence that van caused Forrester's injuries   ( )   ( )
11. Testimony from Hart's minister that Hart is honest   ( )   ( )
12. Independent evidence that doctor previously said falling   ( )   ( )
    on the ice was cause of injury
13. Witness: "Mr. Forrester said, 'Hart was going fast.' "   ( )   ( )
14. Witness at scene: "That van driver didn't even try to stop."   ( )   ( )
15. Nearby service station attendant: "Hart said before accident,   ( )   ( )
    'I'm going to scrape off that windshield.' "
16. Mercury vehicle service log   ( )   ( )
17. Relevant former testimony of unavailable witness   ( )   ( )
18. Duplicate photograph of left front fender of van where   ( )   ( )
    authenticity of original in question
19. Witness identification of bald tires from Hart's van with   ( )   ( )
    proper chain of custody

ASSIGNMENT 4:3

Locate a copy of the Federal Rules of Evidence. Note how a photocopy of the table of contents for these rules can serve as a quick reference guide to evidence. You may choose to photocopy the table of contents to the rules of evidence and write the state equivalent next to each rule. Record whether evidence is admissible (A) or inadmissible (I). Place the reference guide in the investigation section of your system folder.

■ Planning the Investigation

With some of these evidentiary concepts and principles in mind, you can begin the investigation. There are three stages in the investigation procedure: planning the investigation, gathering the evidence, and preserving the evidence.

Thorough planning is extremely important to a good and efficient investigation. Some cases can be characterized as bottomless pits that can sap the energy and time of the paralegal and the financial resources of the client. Proper planning allows for a thorough yet sensible approach that works to the benefit of paralegal and client alike.

A sound approach to planning an investigation should include the following steps:

1. Review the file and other available information.
2. Identify the essential elements of proof as defined by the appropriate substantive law.
3. Identify what facts will be needed to prove each of these elements.
4. Determine what sources, including witnesses, may provide those facts.
5. Record the investigation plan.
6. Consult with the attorney in selecting the most appropriate sources and methods of investigation to be followed.

Review the File and Other Available Information

Review the file to familiarize yourself with the client, the facts, the cause of action, and the leads to evidence and witnesses.

ASSIGNMENT 4:4

Review the factual descriptions of Case I and the summary of Ms. Forrester's interview.

Identify the Essential Elements of Proof

The realization that evidence is gathered to prove or disprove the specific elements of a cause of action is essential for effective investigation. Such knowledge permits the paralegal to immediately narrow and focus the investigation. Chapter 3 explained the process of identifying the key elements of a cause of action through research, particularly research in a good jury instruction book. To review, the elements that our client, Ms. Forrester, must prove are:

1. Duty of care (as dictated by conditions)
2. Breach of duty (carelessness)
3. Injury
4. Causal relationships between breach and injury
5. Damages

In addition, Ms. Forrester must disprove comparative negligence.

Identify What Facts Will Be Needed

Drawing from practical experience and common sense, list facts that need to be gathered to prove the elements in the case. Typical facts for several key elements are listed in the following table.

Breach of Duty	Injuries	Comparative Negligence
Carelessness	Fractures	Attentiveness
Road conditions	Pain	Obstructions to sight and sound (coat)
Mechanical defects	Disabilities	Haste (carelessness)
Speed of van	Insomnia	
Driver's condition		

Determine What Sources, Including Witnesses, May Provide Facts

Identifying possible sources for information and evidence is a process of applying the information already gathered in the file, as well as a knowledge of investigative sources of information and common sense. Some typical sources of information and evidence are included in table 4:1.

Table 4:1   Checklist of Evidentiary Sources

FOR NEGLIGENCE CASES

Source	Likely Information
Client	Occurrence, other witnesses, damages, etc.
Witnesses	Occurrence, other witnesses, injuries, etc.
Scene of accident	Obstructions, distances, special circumstances
Police reports	Details of accident, witnesses, officer at scene, photos, sobriety tests
Department of Motor Vehicles	Accident reports, driving records
News accounts (newspapers, microfilm, videotapes)	Details, witnesses, reporters

FOR NEGLIGENCE CASES (continued)

Source	Likely Information
Reporters (notes)	Details, photos, witnesses
Emergency personnel (ambulance crew, paramedic, tow truck operator)	Details, injuries
Fire marshal (reports)	Causes of fire, witnesses
Transcripts of related trials or hearings (criminal, traffic)	Statements of witnesses and parties, admission
U.S. Weather Bureau	Official weather reports
Licensing and inspection authorities	Code and licensing violations
Police agencies (local police, FBI)	Criminal records for impeachment
Public or university library (reference section)	General reference information
	Directories for scholarly and professional associations
	Experts in pertinent field, consultants
	Business information
	Corporate information
	Federal and state agencies
	Census reports

Federal Agencies[a]

Source	Likely Information
Federal Aviation Administration (FAA) (202) 426-4000	Airline accidents, safety standards
Department of Transportation (202) 426-4043	Vehicle safety standards
National Oceanic and Atmospheric Administration (310) 655-4000	Certified weather reports
National Climatic Center, Asheville, NC	Certified weather information by state
Department of Agriculture (202) 655-4000	Aerial photos, plants, wildlife
Department of Interior (Geologic Survey)	Maps
Internal Revenue Service (202) 566-4021	Former tax rates and schedules
Census Bureau (202) 372-2000	Demographic statistics
Occupational Safety and Health Administration (OSHA) (202) 523-8165	Job safety standards
Government Agencies, Greenwood Press (1983)	Federal agencies and services

State Agencies[b]

Source	Likely Information
Department of Transportation	Traffic flow, highways, bridges, signals, signs
Department of Labor and Industry	Industrial safety rules and regulations, statistics
Department of Geology	Geological surveys
Office of Secretary of State (corporations)	Corporate addresses, officers
Department of Insurance	Auto liability coverage, insurance company requirements
Department of Business and Professions	Licensing requirements of trades and businesses
Bureau of Vital Statistics	Certified records of birth, death, divorce, etc.
Department of Revenue	Personal property licenses, taxes, ownership, transactions
Wright and Allen, *The National Directory of State Agencies*, Information Resource Press (1983)	Directory of state agencies

County and Local Agencies[c]

Source	Likely Information
Tax Assessor's Office	Ownership, location, taxes, and assessed value of property
Voter Registration	Voter's address, age, sex, race, and voting precinct

Table 4:1   Checklist of Evidentiary Sources (continued)

FOR NEGLIGENCE CASES (continued)

Source	Likely Information
District, County, or City Attorney's Office	Criminal records, location of person
Coroner's Office	Cause of death and related hearings, records
Chamber of Commerce	Local businesses, services, literature
Department of Public Works and Traffic	Street blueprints, timing of traffic lights, expert witnesses, statistics
Universities and colleges	Experts in a variety of fields

FOR PERSONAL INJURY CASES

Source	Likely Information
Hospital	Emergency case, names of nurses, doctors, technicians, x-rays, medication, related medical records, pain and suffering, bills
Physicians	Consulting physicians, treatment history, diagnosis, prognosis, disabilities, pain and suffering, bills
Physical therapists	Disabilities, necessary treatment, likelihood of success
Ambulance attendants	Witnesses
Close relatives, friends, and neighbors	Effects of the injury, disabilities
Medical literature	Injuries, medication, side effects, prognosis
Department of Vocational Rehabilitation	Expert witnesses, statistics on job rehabilitation and earning potential
Injured party's employer	Performance records, wages, firings, promotion potential

FOR PRODUCTS LIABILITY CASES

Source	Likely Information
Consumer Product Safety Commission Washington, D.C. (202) 634-7700	Product safety standards
Advertisements	Claims about safety and use of product
Department of Commerce, Patents, and Trademarks (703) 577-3158	Claims of safety of product
Headquarters of various manufacturing associations	Recommended manufacturing and safety standards, expert witnesses
American National Standards Institute	Product standards
Toy safety associations	Information on unsafe products

FOR CONTRACT CASES

Source	Likely Information
Trade and industrial associations	Pertinent contract vernacular, performance standards

FOR CONTRACT CASES (continued)

Source	Likely Information
Better Business Bureau and other regulatory agencies	Evidence of fraud or patterns of improper business conduct
Department of Labor (202) 737-8165	Employment standards, wages or salary loss, statistics
Federal Trade Commission, Bureau of Consumer Protection (202) 523-3625	Credit discrimination practices, fraud
Department of Commerce, Small Business Administration	Small business losses, statistics
Public records	State and federal contracts, deeds, liens, taxes
Appraiser	Property evaluations
Scene	Evidence of breach of warranty, damages

[a]Bruno, Paralegal's Litigation Handbook, 107–10 (1980).
[b]Id., 110.
[c]Id., 111–13.

Data Bases: A Wealth of Information

Because law firms have become increasingly computerized, volumes of information are quickly accessible. Some of the more common data bases that can be accessed by computer include the following.[5]

Legal: **LEXIS** and **WESTLAW** provide full-text information on case decisions, statutes, and administrative regulations and may be used to access other data bases. **LEGAL RESOURCE INDEX** provides indexing of law jounals and law newspapers (1980 to present). **LABORLAW** provides decision summaries on labor relations, fair employment, wage and hours, and occupational safety and health (1930 to present). **TRADEMARKSCAN** provides records on currently active trademark applicants and negotiations (1984 to present).

News: **NEXIS** provides full-text coverage of national and international newspapers, magazines, and wire services. **VU/TEXT** provides full-text coverage of local newspapers. **NATIONAL NEWSPAPER INDEX** provides indexing of the *Christian Science Monitor,* the *New York Times,* and the *Wall Street Journal* (1979 to present). **NEWSEARCH** provides textual coverage of prominent newspapers for the current month and day.

Legislative: **PUBLIC AFFAIRS INFORMATION** contains all bills and enactments for the current session in every state. **CONGRESSIONAL RECORD ABSTRACTS** provides abstracts of the *Congressional Record,* **CONGRESSIONAL INFORMATION SERVICE** provides abstracts of all Congressional, Office of Technology Assessment, and Congressional Budget Office publications.

Business: **DUN & BRADSTREET'S MILLION DOLLAR DIRECTORY** contains business information such as corporate credit and financial profiles on U.S. companies worth $500,000 or more. **DUN'S MARKET IDENTIFIERS** provides information on U.S. business establishments that have ten or more employees. **PTS, F & S INDEXES,** and **PTS PROMPT** provide information on products, mergers, forecasts, and so on, on domestic and international companies. **DISCLOSURE II** contains extracts of SEC reports filed by publicly owned corporations.

Securities: **DOW JONES SPECTRUM PROFILES** offers extracts of SEC reports on institutional holdings, investment company holdings, beneficial ownership, tender offers, and insider trading. **SECURITIES DATA CORP** contains information on offerings of stocks and bonds.

Medicine: **PHARMACEUTICAL NEWS INDEX** offers current news on drugs, cosmetics, medical devices, and related health fields. **CHEMICAL EXPOSURE** provides information on chemicals found in the human body and food chain (1974 to present). **MEDLINE** indexes and abstracts articles from the major medical journals of the world (1966 to present).

Miscellaneous: **AMERICAN STATISTICS INDEX** offers a thorough index of statistical publications from U.S. governmental agencies: population and economic censuses, CPI reports, unemployment and vital statistics. **ENVIRON LINE** offers abstracts of publications on the world environment.

Some data bases like **DIALOG,** owned by Lockhead, contain hundreds of information services, including many of those just mentioned.

Methods for Gathering Information or Evidence

Once the potential sources of information have been identified, it is necessary to choose the method most suitable to obtain that information.

- The telephone. Pinpointing the best source of information, especially if it involves leaving the office, interviewing people, going through files, and so on, can be a costly and time-consuming process. A preliminary assessment of these sources by telephone can reduce the amount of time and money spent. For example, if there were several witnesses to a particular occurrence, it might be wise to call each of them for a preliminary interview to determine whether an in-person visit is warranted.
- Mailed requests. Some information is obtainable through a relatively inexpensive request by correspondence. Medical, school, employment, and agency records can frequently be obtained in this manner if the request includes the proper authorization to release the information. Examples of particular requests by correspondence will be covered later in this chapter.
- The modem. A modem is an electronic device that permits an office computer to link up through a telephone connection with a designated computer network anywhere in the country. It is through the modem that the data bases previously mentioned are accessed. Although there is a fee for on-line data base searches, the cost can be relatively inexpensive compared with more cumbersome and traditional methods of gathering information. Any office having a personal computer, a modem, and the necessary software can access a data base. Should you find yourself without access to the office modem, some public and university libraries will conduct on-line searches for a fee. The average search takes about ten to twenty minutes, and costs are reasonable.
- Personal interview. In most circumstances involving key witnesses, there is no substitute for a personal interview. Personal interviews take time, careful planning, and skill. Because of costs, it may not be feasi-

blc to interview less important witnesses in person. The phone can be a big help in this case. It is better, however, to err on the side of too much interviewing than too little. Interviews produce good evidence as well as the opportunity to assess the ability of the witness to testify.

- Professional research and search services. There are times when it pays to hire professional search services. These companies provide a highly experienced and well-trained staff who can open the door when you cannot, or who have access to documents all over the country to which you do not. Although these services are often expensive, they should be employed when the information sought is critical or needs to be gathered quickly (or both). A variety of professional search services are available: **PARASEC** (916-441-1001) provides document retrieval from anywhere in the country, including county services. It will also conduct searches of records and statements filed with secretaries of state. The **DOCUMENT BANK** (202-833-9220) offers same-day service on federal documents. **Corporation Service Company** (800-441-9975) offers a wide array of corporate information search services. **INFOSEARCH** (800-833-9848) provides Uniform Commercial Code and Corporate Information searches.
- Legal research. An important part of any investigation involves going to the law library or general library to locate pertinent statutes, rules, and regulations; news articles; scholarly articles on particular points of law, investigation, and use of evidence; medical information; commercial information; sources for expert witnesses; and other sources.
- Visit the scene of the incident. In many cases, not just personal injury cases, a specific location may offer significant evidence. A visit to the location (office, scene of accident, factory) is essential.
- Photos. Photography or videotaping (or both) not only preserves evidence but also may be the only way to effectively gather and demonstrate evidence. If the photo is critical, a professional photographer may be employed.
- Scientific tests. Re-creations, chemical analysis, and other forms of testing may be the only way to support the theory of the plaintiff or defense. The employment of state and private laboratories is normally essential in such circumstances.
- Expert. Related to testing, the use of scientists, professors, engineers, mechanics, medical personnel, and other experts in the relevant field is increasingly essential to win cases. Sometimes victory hinges on which side has the best expert. See *Locating Scientific and Technical Experts*, 2 AM. JUR. *Trials* 302–56; *Locating Medical Experts*, 2 AM JUR. *Trials* 112–33; and THE LAWYER'S DESK REFERENCE.

ASSIGNMENT 4:5
Using the sources of information and methods mentioned earlier, make lists of investigative sources that may prove beneficial. Title the list "Investigative Sources" and list the agencies, contact persons, addresses, and phone numbers of offices you are likely to use on a regular basis. Do this for federal as well as your state and local agencies. Do some work in the reference library to determine what data bases and professional research services are available in your area. These lists should be placed in the investigation section of your system folder. As you gain experience, you will want to add new sources and contact persons to the list. Creating and maintaining such lists in one ready location should save you considerable time in the long run.

Record the Investigation Plan

Keeping in mind evidentiary considerations, the elements of the cause of action or its defenses, the potential sources of information, and the methods and costs of gathering that evidence, write out the detailed investigation plan as demonstrated in Table 4:2.

Consult with the Supervising Attorney

Take the completed investigation plan to the attorney. A brief discussion should be held to determine the most feasible approach regarding sources, methods, and available time and money. You will be better able to assist in making decisions about sources and methods as you gain experience. The investigation plan should be amended as indicated by the attorney. At this time it should be made clear who is responsible for carrying out each step of the investigation, especially if the attorney regularly assumes some of this responsibility.

ASSIGNMENT 4:6
Following the steps and examples of planning an investigation as presented in this chapter, create an investigation plan for Case II. Develop the elements and facts to be proved, the sources, and the methods to be used in a format similar to that in table 4:2. Place an example of an investigation plan into your system folder.

Ethical and Related Considerations

Investigation brings the paralegal into more contact with the public than at any other stage of litigation. The manner in which the paralegal approaches and conducts these contacts will reflect upon the reputation of the paralegal, the firm, and the paralegal profession. If the contacts are thoughtful and ethical, the process will benefit the firm and help establish a responsive network of individuals who will be willing to help in future cases. Conversely, if the contacts are tactless and unethical, the consequences will be uncooperative witnesses, unsatisfactory information, a loss of confidence in the paralegal and the firm, and possible disciplinary action. Therefore, when investigating a case, keep in mind the following ethical considerations.

Be thorough in preparing and investigating a case, an important aspect of "competency" required in Rule 1.1 of the Model Rules of Professional Conduct. Similarly, be diligent and prompt to avoid the loss of important evidence (Rule 1.3). Exercise independent judgment so as not to become unduly influenced by the client or the client's directives to engage in unlawful or even unethical conduct. Know the limits to the scope of representation (Rule 1.2). Good investigation is essential for you to keep your client informed and able to make knowledgeable decisions (Rule 1.4). Seek all the evidence, both pro and con, and report your findings so the attorney can adequately advise the client—even if this includes information the client does not want to hear (Rule 2.1).

While investigating and researching, be aware of the attorney's as well as your own obligation to be candid with the court. Inform the attorney of any

Table 4:2 Investigative Plan

Possible to Prove or Acquire	Possible Source of Information	Method	Cost
Defendant	Dun's Market Identifiers	Modem (on-line data search)	
Mercury Express—financial status, service agent, home office, etc.	Corporation Service Co.	Professional search service	

Breach of Duty

Possible to Prove or Acquire	Possible Source of Information	Method	Cost
Weather conditions	Certified copy of weather conditions from National Climatic Center	Mail	
Mechanical defect	Inspection of vehicle	Hire mechanic	
	Police report	Mail	
	Vehicle maintenance records	Mail request	
	Mechanic who services vehicle	Phone/interview (deposition)	
Condition of driver	Police report	Mail	
	Police officer	Phone/personal interview	
	Copy of breathalyzer report	Mail	
		Clerk of court file	
	Ms. Schnabel (witness)	Personal interview	
Conditions at scene	Scene of accident	Visit scene (photograph)	

Plaintiff's injuries

Possible to Prove or Acquire	Possible Source of Information	Method	Cost
Immediate injuries, broken bones, etc.	Doctors' reports	Mail	
	Emergency room records	Mail	
	Hospital records	Mail	
	X-rays	Mail	
	Doctors' testimony	Interview, letter, reports evaluated	
Immediate and long-term disabilities	Doctors' reports (follow-up visits)	Mail	
	Doctors' testimony	Interview (after reports evaluated)	
	Ms. Forrester	Initial interview	
	Mr. Forrester	Interview	
	Nurse	Phone (followed by interview)	
	Friends	Phone (followed by interview)	
Pain	Ms. Forrester's testimony (pain log)	Initial and follow-up interviews	
	Mr. Forrester	Interview	
	Nurse	Phone (follow-up interview)	
	Hospital and doctors' reports	Mail	
	Doctors' testimony	Interview	
	Ambulance assistants	Phone	
	Ms. Schnabel (witness)	Interview	

Comparative Negligence

Possible to Prove or Acquire	Possible Source of Information	Method	Cost
Attentiveness of plaintiff (haste of plaintiff)	Police report	Mail	
	Insurance and Mercury accident reports	Mail (discovery)	
	Ms. Forrester	Interview	
	Mr. Forrester	Interview	
	Ms. Schnabel	Interview	
	Mr. Hart	Deposition	
Obstruction of sight and sound by coat worn by plaintiff	Coat itself	Obtain from Ms. Forrester	
	Possible re-creation tests with coat at scene	(Suggestions from supervising attorney)	
	University consultant	Phone	

Note: This table is for illustrative purposes. It is not complete as to possible facts to prove, sources, or methods.

relevant evidence that is false or appears false; record all legal authority so the attorney can inform the court of clear opposing authority if the other side fails to present it; avoid inflating the importance of any evidence that might make the attorney appear to be presenting false statements to the court; correct false evidence presented to the court by informing the attorney; and in cases where there is only one side (ex parte), see to it that the attorney can present all material facts, both pro and con, to the court [Rule 3.3(a) and (d)].

Fairness to the opposition is also essential. Avoid any act that obstructs others' access to evidence or unlawfully alters, destroys, or conceals evidence [Rule 3.4(a)(b)]. It is also unethical to instruct a third person to refrain from speaking to or from giving information to the opposition unless the person is an employee or agent of the client [Rule 3.4(f)]. Paralegals can be involved in cases that attract public attention; in such circumstances and as a general rule, make no comments to the press. Attorneys may, but under strict guidelines (Rule 3.6). False statements to others on important facts are violations of the code [Rule 4.1(a)]. In some circumstances, there is a duty to speak up to prevent a client from committing fraud or a crime [Rule 4.4(b)]. If you are aware that your client is planning a fraudulent contract or agreement, the supervising attorney should be informed so remedial measures can be taken.

When speaking with others, always identify yourself as a paralegal from your firm or office so there can be no misunderstanding of your title or purpose. If the need arises to speak with a person who is represented by an attorney, speak with that person only with the permission of or through that person's attorney (Rule 4.2). If the person is not represented by an attorney, avoid implying your neutrality and correct any misunderstanding about whom you represent (Rule 4.3). Remember that you may not violate the rights of others (stealing a key document or harassing a potential witness, for example) or do anything for the purpose of embarrassment, delay, or to burden another (Rule 4.4). Keep in mind that to breach any of these ethical standards could subject your supervising attorney to disciplinary action, since the attorney is responsible for the ethical conformance of each employee (Rule 5.3).

Attorney's Work Product

Another matter of which a paralegal must be aware is the law regarding an attorney's work product. Under Rule 26 of the Federal Rules of Civil Procedure and the rules of most states, a party may obtain from another party information that is relevant to the subject matter involved in the action. This information includes the existence, description, nature, custody, condition and location of any books, documents, or other tangible things, and the identity and whereabouts of persons having knowledge of disclosable matter. This exchange of information is called **discovery.**

Excepted from discovery under Rule 26(b)(3) are the mental impressions, conclusions, opinions, or legal theories of the attorney or the attorney's agent. This exception is called the **attorney's work product.** As a tactical measure, each party will try to protect as much material as possible from discovery while trying to discover as much as they can from the opponent. The primary concern is to recognize that the work product exception exists to prevent divulging information that should not or need not be disclosed.

Revealing Information to a Witness

It is possible for a witness or other source of information to turn the tables on the investigator by finding out more from the investigator than the investigator does from the source. Some investigators, especially novices, seem to feel that if they generously answer the questions of the other person, the other person will in turn generously answer their questions. This approach is unproductive and can lead to the revealing of confidential or undiscoverable information. Avoid this situation by stating that you are bound to preserve confidentiality and may not discuss what you know about the case. The majority of witnesses will accept this explanation with no effect on their willingness to participate.

To summarize this section, a paralegal must always be careful to avoid violating ethical standards, exposing the attorney's work product to discovery, and revealing confidences. Paralegals must also take care not to conduct themselves in a manner that will negatively reflect on the law firm and result in the drying up of useful contacts and sources of information.

ASSIGNMENT 4:7
Citing the relevant Model Rules of Professional Conduct, what should you do under the following circumstances?

1. You need to see one last critical witness who you are fairly sure will not speak with you if you tell the witness you are representing Ann Forrester. You arrive at the witness's apartment and she answers the door. What should you do?
2. You are investigating a low profit case where your elderly client is trying to hang onto the only house and property she has ever had. Yet to interview the key witness in the case will cost more than the case will bring to the firm. What should you do?
3. Your firm is representing a federal judge in a civil suit. You have come to admire this judge and know that the firm believes he is a very valuable client. One night you are working with the judge on his case. There is a letter in the file that the judge received from a third party. The judge asks you to change one word in the letter because he knows that is what the party said he meant in the first place. The judge has offered you a terrific federal job at the close of this case. What would you do?
4. As you are preparing a legal memo on a case for your supervising attorney, your fellow paralegal tells you not to deal with or cite two of the strongest cases against you because that is likely to help the other side—especially if they failed to find these cases. What should you do?

ASSIGNMENT 4:8
Read those Model Rules of Professional Conduct located in appendix E that cover the ethical questions raised in this chapter. Also read Rule 26 of the Federal Rules of Civil Procedure and the state equivalent. Draft a sheet titled "Ethical Applications to Investigation," and write out a one- or two-word topic head for each applicable rule and cite it. Then place them in your system folder.

Gathering the Evidence

Introduction

When you have in mind an investigation plan as well as an awareness of ethical, evidentiary, and other considerations, it is time to actually gather the information. The three significant investigative procedures that will be emphasized in this section include: gathering reports, records, and other documents; investigating the scene of the accident; and taking the statements of witnesses.

Gathering Reports, Records, and Other Documents

The investigation plan indicates that evidence needs to be gathered regarding the injuries of the plaintiff, including pain and suffering. A complete plan would also call for evidence of doctor and hospital bills. The task at hand is to gather that information. The most common method of verifying the plaintiff's injuries and bills is to request the medical records and doctors' reports describing the treatment rendered. Such records not only will help prove the plaintiff's case but also will provide a well-documented record that will be useful in settling the case.

Records regarding the treatment of the plaintiff in Case I, Ms. Forrester, can be obtained by writing the medical records librarian of the hospital, in this case the Good Samaritan Hospital in Legalville, Columbia. As long as such requests are accompanied by the authorization to release medical information executed by Ms. Forrester at the time of her initial interview, there should be no difficulty in obtaining the desired information. The medical authorization must be current (signed within sixty days of the request for information in some areas). If the authorization is not current, it will have to be reexecuted. If the patient about whom information is requested is dead, the authorization must be signed by the executor or administrator of the patient's estate. The defendant's paralegal, having no such authorization, can get these records only by court order or subpoena. In these cases the statutes on medical records should be consulted. The hospital will charge a per-page fee for the reports. In many jurisdictions, the medical records librarian is not required to send the records unless the fee is paid in advance. Most record requests are phrased as "any and all records" pertaining to the treatment for an injury occurring on a specific date; but it is preferable to mention specifically emergency room reports, outpatient reports, and the face sheet of the patient's chart (which contains good background information plus a physician diagnosis in some cases), since these records will not necessarily be automatically included in the response. The records that might be available to the requesting paralegal are as follows:

- Physician's discharge summary
- Emergency room and outpatient reports
- Patient's chart
- History and physical information
- Reports from operating room
- Pathology reports
- X-ray reports (summary plus film impression)
- Lab reports (summary)
- Progress notes by physician or interns
- Doctors' orders to nurses regarding medication and other care
- Consulting physicians' reports
- Nurses' notes

The following records are not usually requested; however, they can prove useful in specific situations or in malpractice cases. Because these records technically belong to the hospital, a subpoena may be needed to obtain them.

- Incident reports (if previous records reflect a fall or other accident)
- Statistical reports (by physician, disease, type of patient, etc.)
- Departmental records (radiology, physical therapy, etc.)
- Committee minutes and reports (problems and solutions)
- Peer review (licensing and accreditation reports)

Prior to making a request for records, contact the records librarian to find out the fee and any particular rules or procedures that should be followed. Draft a letter to the medical records librarian of the hospital, giving the full name, address, date of birth, and Social Security number of the person whose records are requested, and stating the inclusive dates of treatment and specific records requested. The authorization for release of medical records should be attached. Special authorization procedures and forms for release of information on treatment for drug or alcohol abuse may be required. It is a good idea to call the hospital records librarian to determine proper form and procedure. An example of a form letter adapted to Ms. Forrester's case is included in figure 4:1. An example of an Authorization to Release Medical Information form is shown in figure 4:2.

ASSIGNMENT 4:9
Copy the list of available medical records, the standardized record request letter shown in figure 4:1, and the Authorization to Release Medical Information form shown in figure 4:2. Place these in your system folder.

Another source of valuable medical information will be a narrative medical report prepared by the treating physician or physicians. A request for such a narrative is a simple matter, but not without pitfalls. Doctors charge $500 or more for such summaries, which frequently contain unneeded information. The better practice is to obtain the hospital records first, review them, and then request from the physician the specific information needed.[6] Since the paralegal and the firm are likely to be working periodically with the physician and nurse or assistant, it is a good idea to develop a pleasant relationship with them. Noting the name of the physician's nurse for your file, for example, will expedite future contacts. Such connections can be helpful when gathering information.

When requesting information from a doctor, many paralegals use a standardized letter. Unfortunately, such a letter is likely to lead to a rather general or incomplete response. A letter to the doctor needs to be as specific as possible and based on detailed information gathered from the medical records and the complaints identified by the client. It is a good idea to confirm with the client each matter complained of to the doctor so the report will be complete. An example of such a letter appears in figure 4:3. Occasionally a doctor needs a follow-up letter such as in figure 4:4.

Figure 4:1   Request for Medical Records

WHITE, WILSON & McDUFF

ATTORNEYS AT LAW
FEDERAL PLAZA BUILDING, SUITE 700
THIRD AND MARKET STREETS
LEGALVILLE, COLUMBIA 00000
(111)555-0000

Ms. Betty Noble
Medical Records Librarian
Good Samaritan Hospital
4600 Church Street
Legalville, Columbia 00000

Re: Medical Records of Ms. Ann Forrester

> 1533 Capitol Dr., Legalville, Columbia 00000
> Soc. Sec. No. 123-45-6789
> Birthdate: 4/23/—
> Dates of Care: 2/26/—
>   to discharge 3/29/—

Dear Ms. Noble:

The firm of White, Wilson, and McDuff has been retained to represent the above-named individual.

Enclosed is a current Authorization to Release Medical Information executed by our client.

Would you please send copies of the following records to me:

(X) Discharge summary
(X) ER and outpatient reports
(X) Patient's chart
(X) History and physical
(X) Operative and pathology reports
(X) X-ray reports
(X) Lab reports
(X) Progress noted by physicians and nurses
(X) Doctors' orders
(X) Consultation reports
(X) Nurses' notes

( ) Alcohol and drug treatment notes

( ) Others _____

On receipt of the records, our firm will promptly submit payment for any preparation fee.

Thank you for your assistance.

Sincerely,

Terry Salyer
Paralegal

Enclosure: Authorization to Release Medical Information

Figure 4:2 Authorization to Release Medical Information

Patient's Name _____

Social Security No. _____ Date of Birth _____ Age _____

Address _____ Phone _____

   By my signature below, I authorize and request _[name and address of hospital or other institution]_

to provide __[name of law firm and representative]___with access to all my medical records and copies thereof as may be requested pertaining to my stay and treatment from _____ to _____ (if no limitation is preferred, so state) including any treatment for alcohol and drug abuse.

   I request that this authorization remain valid until further notice from me. [Some states have a ninety-day limit.]

Signature _____ Date _____

_____ Date _____

Signature of Parent, Guardian, or Authorized Representative

Relationship _____

ASSIGNMENT 4:10

Assume that you have received the hospital reports for the treatment of Mr. Ameche in Case II, and these reports confirm the injuries described by him in his initial interview (chapter 3 instructor's manual). Draft a letter to Mr. Ameche's physician requesting a medical report. Use the letter in figure 4:3 as a guide. Remember, however, to keep the letter specific to Mr. Ameche's injuries. Place both your letter and copies of letters 4:3 and 4:4 into your system folder.

If the plaintiff has died, another report of value is the autopsy report. This report represents the findings of the medical examiner or coroner on the

Figure 4:3   Request for Physician's Narrative Medical Summary

---

WHITE, WILSON & McDUFF
ATTORNEYS AT LAW
FEDERAL PLAZA BUILDING, SUITE 700
THIRD AND MARKET STREETS
LEGALVILLE, COLUMBIA 00000
(111)555-0000

Albert Meyer, M.D.
Medical Arts Building
4650 Church St.
Legalville, Columbia 00000

Re: Ms. Ann Forrester, Soc. Sec. No. 123-45-6789

Dear Dr. Meyer:

Ms. Forrester has retained this office to represent her regarding injuries sustained from being struck by a van on February 26, 19___. Ms. Forrester suffered multiple fractures of the pelvis and left leg, and also had spinal and internal injuries. As a result of these injuries, Ms. Forrester is currently bound to a wheelchair and may not be able to return to work for some time.

To assist Ms. Forrester, we would appreciate it if you would send us a report on the following:

1. Your diagnosis of Ms. Forrester's mental, emotional, and physical injuries
2. Your opinion as to the cause of Ms. Forrester's injuries
3. A description of the treatment given Ms. Forrester
4. Likely degree of pain and discomfort related to such injuries
5. Mental, physical, and emotional limitations as they relate to employment, recreational activities, and enjoyment of life
6. Future treatment needed
7. Prognosis
8. Likelihood of Ms. Forrester being able to return to work. If so, when?

In addition, please send an itemized bill for all your services related to these injuries. The necessary authorization is enclosed. Upon receipt of your report, this office will promptly pay any preparation fee.

Please keep us informed regarding Ms. Forrester's future visits to your office and any change in condition or prognosis.

Thank you for your cooperation.

Terry Salyer
Paralegal

Enclosed: Authorization to Release Medical Information

cc: Ms. Ann Forrester

cause of death and the medical evidence to support the conclusion. Such reports may be obtained through the office of the coroner or medical examiner.

Another area of importance to Ms. Forrester's case is her loss in gross wages as a result of the accident. Such losses are recoverable and can make up an important part of a damage claim. That is why Ms. Forrester was asked to execute the authorization for release of employment information at the initial interview. Send a copy of the authorization along with a request letter to the personnel office where Ms. Forrester is employed. Remember that a person may have more than one employer or source of income. The letter should request a brief history of annual earnings; current salary or hourly wage; days of work missed since the accident; and overtime and bonuses missed. Request information on disability insurance to assist the client in meeting expenses.

If the client is self-employed, an average weekly gross income would have to be determined from the client's records or from the client's accountant. Keep in mind the following formula: average gross weekly income, less normal costs not incurred because of injury (such as the purchase or sale of goods, phone bills, and mileage), equals weekly amount claimed.[7]

In serious injuries, or in the case of death, loss of future earnings is also an important component of damages. Inquiry should be made about labor contracts that dictate pay into the next several years; possible loss or reduction in fringe benefits; and any schedule of eligibility for promotion, bonuses, overtime, stock options, and profit sharing; or other special considerations. In addition, it is wise to seek the assistance of a qualified vocational expert or economist (or both) to form a sound claim for future loss of earnings or to challenge such a claim. One source of assistance is the American Board of Vocational Experts.

Other records or documents may be obtained on behalf of the client as long as the proper authorizations have been signed. Information from the federal as well as some state governments may be obtained through forms and procedures described in the particular Freedom of Information Act.

Check documents immediately. Regardless of what information is requested, you will need to ensure that the information received is correct and clear. Requests for corrections or explanations should be made

Figure 4:4   Request for Medical Update

WHITE, WILSON & McDUFF

ATTORNEYS AT LAW
FEDERAL PLAZA BUILDING, SUITE 700
THIRD AND MARKET STREETS
LEGALVILLE, COLUMBIA 00000
(111)555-0000

Albert Meyer, M.D.
Medical Arts Building
4650 Church St.
Legalville, Columbia 00000

Re: Ms. Ann Forrester, Soc. Sec. No. 123-45-6789

Dear Dr. Meyer:

Your report of September 9, 19___ on Ms. Forrester was very helpful. Six months have passed since that report, and we need an update. Please provide us with detailed information on the following:

[List those points where specific elaboration is needed beyond the first request. Add a catchall question asking for information on any new or otherwise significant developments.]

Please include copies of itemized bills for your services to Ms. Forrester since September 9.

Thank you again for your assistance.

Terry Salyer
Paralegal

cc: Ms. Ann Forrester

immediately where errors exist or information is not clear. It is also important to have a guide to reading medical records, a medical dictionary, or some guide to the vernacular of the particular subject area. Do not assume that these words are correctly used or that someone else in the office, particularly the attorney, will be able to decipher the language. See chapter 9 on interpreting medical records and medical terminology.

Investigating the Scene of the Accident

Viewing the scene of the accident or source of the claim at the time of the injury or as soon thereafter as possible is essential to sound investigation. Secondhand reports and photos are certainly useful, but they do not substitute for a personal visit to the scene.

The time at the scene can be more efficiently spent with some advance planning. A quick review of the information in the file, including the summary of the client's interview, and the elements of proof critical to the case will help focus attention on the most important facts. It will also help to anticipate the need of any special investigative tools.

There are some typical tools necessary for investigating the scene. A quad-ruled tracing paper pad and clipboard are useful for diagramming the scene of the accident. (See figures 4:8–4:10 for tips on diagramming an accident.) Tape measures of varying length, plus a walk-along, wheeled measuring device for longer distances, are essential. A reliable 35-mm camera with flash is necessary, and a color video camera, if available, would certainly be helpful. Other useful tools that conjure up visions of Sherlock Holmes include a flashlight, magnifying glass, compass (to ensure accurate directions), tape recorder, stopwatch, protractor (for measuring angles), labeling tags, and various sizes of plastic bags (for storing evidence). Occasionally a specific type of case may require some other useful instruments.

A checklist form of things to note and record at the scene appears in figure 4:5.

Figure 4:5 Accident Scene Checklist

---

1. Nature of area: urban, rural, intersection, highway, school zone, other _____

2. Weather (if at scene soon enough to observe) _____

3. Other conditions: visibility _____

        road surface _____

        lanes _____

        curves _____

        grade _____

        speed limit _____

        other _____

4. Witness   Position to view accident   View, obstructions

_____   _____   _____

_____   _____   _____

_____   _____   _____

5. Possible distractions that might cause inattention _____

6. Measurements of critical distances[a]

skid marks _____

road width _____

distance vehicle traveled after impact _____

distance from witness position to scene _____

other _____

7. Traffic control

signs _____

lane markings _____

other _____

8. Sun or other lighting conditions at time of day accident occurred

from plaintiff's position _____

from defendant's position _____

from witness's position _____

other _____

9. Temporary conditions

construction _____

parked vehicles _____

other _____

10. Flow of traffic, same time of day, same day of week _____

11. All possible causes of accident _____

_____

12. Evidence of damage

vehicles _____

signs _____

trees _____

buildings _____

other _____

13. Photograph and videotape important items noted above from different angles to show relevant conditions or defects such as a pothole in the street, uneven sidewalk, slippery spots, etc.

14. Carefully note pertinent directions (N, NE, E, SE, S, SW, W, NW) _____ _____

_____

15. Locations of other possible witnesses regularly at the scene

homes _____

businesses _____

joggers _____

dog walkers _____

farm workers _____

maintenance or public works people _____

other _____

16. Other physical evidence relevant to case _____

17. Special needs

expert to view scene _____

professional photographer to capture lighting, angles (good source: International Council of Evidence Photographers) _____

aerial photograph _____

other _____

18. Carefully preserve evidence.

_____

ªA handy formula for converting speed to distance (and vice versa) is mph × 1.5 = ft per sec.

ASSIGNMENT 4:11
Subsequent to any class discussion in which other items may arise to add to the checklist in figure 4:5, draft your own accident scene checklist and place it in the system folder.

ASSIGNMENT 4:12
Investigate an actual accident scene. Use whatever tools and measuring devices you have at your disposal and follow the accident scene checklist from figure 4:5.

Acquiring the Statements of Witnesses

Locating the Witnesses

Locating witnesses as soon as possible is important to investigation. Memories fade quickly, making it difficult for witnesses to recall important details. Witnesses also tend to develop an attachment to the side that contacts them first, creating an impediment for the opposing investigator. Being first to the witness gives you an advantage. The following list contains ideas for locating witnesses:

■ Ask the client, other known witnesses, the reporting police officer, emergency personnel, and so on.
■ Review photographs for bystanders, license numbers, and other leads.

- Locate news reporters, camera operators, and free-lance photographers.
- Visit the scene at the same time of day and week to locate persons who might routinely frequent the area (joggers, walkers, delivery personnel, school crossing guards).
- Canvass the immediate area for local residents and businesses, or farm workers in rural areas.
- Place an ad in the local newspaper with a photo of the accident, asking witnesses or people with information to call.

If only a photo of the person is available:

- Canvass the area asking people who are likely to know many people, such as local politicians and officials, police, bankers, or school officials.
- Place an ad with the photo requesting information.

If only a name is available:[8]

- Use the telephone book, voter registration lists, or the city directory.
- Consult postal officials (you may need to use post office Freedom of Information form 1478 for forwarding address).
- Call contacts at utility companies and public service offices.
- Check with local credit bureaus (you may find restrictions or conditions).
- Check with the motor vehicle and licensing bureau.

If only the name and occupation are available:[9]

- Contact the personnel office of a likely employer (possible restrictions).
- Speak with co-workers.
- Seek information from the licensing agency if it is a regulated profession.
- Contact unions or trade associations.

If only the avocation or school is known:

- Contact sports leagues or hobby societies.
- Consult alumni groups.

If a witness is particularly critical and hard to locate, the office may have no choice but to hire a private investigation firm to locate the person.[10]

Locating Expert Witnesses

There are times when a case may involve the highly complex and technical principles of medicine, mechanics, engineering, electronics, or other fields. In such cases it may be necessary to locate an expert witness, not only to interpret information but also to translate it to a jury and to give an opinion relevant to the issues. The supervising attorney or the senior member of the firm will make the decision to hire an expert. The decision is an important one because hiring an expert can be expensive.

Nevertheless, it may fall to the paralegal to locate an expert. Some ways to locate an expert are as follows:

- Check office files for previously compiled lists of experts.

- Locate pertinent articles in professional journals or books on the topic and contact the authors (frequently considered experts in the field).
- Ask other firms who have had similar cases to recommend an expert they have used.
- Contact professional societies.
- Contact the applicable department or research facility at a college or university.
- Contact pertinent government agencies (local, state, and national) that often employ experts in a particular field.
- Check national legal newspapers, bar association, and paralegal publications for advertisements by experts. Request references and names of former clients.
- Review expert lists in *The Lawyer's Desk Reference,* a resource book for lawyers.

ASSIGNMENT 4:13
Create a Suggestions for Locating Witnesses and Experts list and place it in your system folder.

Planning the Interview

Once the potential witness is located, it may be best to call the witness to see what information can be obtained. This step should be bypassed if the witness is evasive or seems likely to be so. If a personal visit is necessary to have the witness sign a written statement, the interview should be planned. The planning process and the techniques are essentially the same as those for planning and conducting an interview with the client (see chapter 3).

Determining the purpose of the interview is absolutely necessary. Some witnesses are interviewed to provide a broad look at events—the witness to

Technology, communication skills, common sense: how can you best use your resources to conduct a good investigation?

the accident, for example. Other witnesses, such as the mechanic who checked the brakes on Mr. Hart's truck, will be interviewed to explore entirely different information, possibly with a very narrow focus. Each witness is therefore sought out for a purpose, and that purpose should be clearly in mind, dictating the extent and nature of preparation.

As an initial step in planning the interview, locate or develop any helpful forms and checklists. The law firm often has copies of such forms. These forms are designed to make sure the interviewer covers the essentials. Figure 4:6 is the Witness Information Cover Sheet to be filled out at the interview and used later for quick reference.

Figure 4:6 Witness Information Cover Sheet

1. _____ Date   2. _____ Interviewer   3. _____ Place

4. _____ Client   5. _____ File No.   6. _____ Type of Case

Photo

7. _____ Full Name of Witness   8. For Def. _____ Pltf. _____

9. Summary of Statement _____

_____

_____

10. Availability _____

BACKGROUND

11. _____ Address, City, County, State, Zip Code   (_____) Years at   12. _____ Alias/Maiden Name

13. _____ Home Phone   Work Phone   14. Citizen (_____) Yes (_____) No   15. _____ Nationality/Race

16. _____ Date of Birth   17. _____ Age   18. _____ Sex   19. _____ If Minor, Guardian's Name

20. _____ Close Relative or Friend (Not Immediate Family)   21. _____ Address/Phone

22. S__ M__ D__ W__ Other _____   23. _____ Spouse's Full Name

24. _____ Spouse's Address If Other than 11.   25. _____ Spouse's Place of Employment   26. _____ Phone

27. _____ Spouse's Job Title   28. Children's Names, Ages, Addresses (other than 11.)

a. _____ ( ) _____

b. _____ ( ) _____

c. _____ ( ) _____

29. List other marriages on back.

EMPLOYMENT

30. _____
                      Witness's Employer   Address   Job Title

31. _____ 32. _____ 33. _____
              Supervisor   Phone   Date Started Employment

34. Other Jobs: Employer/Address/Phone/Supervisor/Dates/Job Title

   a. _____

   b. _____

   c. _____

35. Education: School/Address/Degree or Diploma/Date

   a. H.S. _____

   b. Voc. _____

   c. Coll. _____

   d. Grad. _____

   e. Other _____

36. Experience as Witness (_____) (_____) _____ _____ _____
                                      Yes   No   Date   Location   Type of Case

37. Ever been convicted of fraud, theft, or other dishonesty? Give details.

_____

_____

_____

Figure 4:7, Checklist for Witness Interview, should be easily adaptable to any personal injury case. It can be used as a guide for asking questions and, more important, as a check to see that all significant items have been covered in the interview. This list should be checked prior to drafting the written statement.

Figure 4:7 Checklist for Witness Interview

☐ 1. Complete Witness Information Cover Sheet.
☐ 2. Identify taker of statement, time, date, place.
☐ 3. Witness's activity just prior to accident:
      ☐ location ☐ time ☐ date
      ☐ witness's activity ☐ view of scene ☐ distance from scene
      ☐ obstruction ☐ location of plaintiff and defendant
      ☐ activity of plaintiff ☐ activity of defendant ☐ others present
      ☐ names ☐ their location ☐ activities
      ☐ other possible witnesses ☐ others in vehicle
      ☐ key issue questions
☐ 4. Setting at time of accident:
      ☐ time ☐ weather ☐ lighting conditions ☐ road conditions
      ☐ wind ☐ unforeseen obstructions (repair work, children, animals, fallen trees or rocks, etc.) ☐ dangerous conditions

☐ traffic flow ☐ speed limits ☐ traffic signs
☐ school zone ☐ intersection ☐ type of road ☐ hills
☐ curves ☐ shoulders ☐ any unusual or particularly notable activity of parties or others (recklessness, inattentiveness, evidence of influence of alcohol or drugs, etc.)
☐ speed of vehicles ☐ distance between plaintiff and defendant
☐ vehicle window obstructions ☐ other conditions of importance
☐ when witness's attention first drawn to plaintiff and defendant
☐ other key issue questions

☐ 5. The accident:
☐ time ☐ general description of sequence
☐ attempt to evade (sound horn, brake, head for shoulder, etc.)
☐ skidding ☐ sounds of contact
☐ detailed description of what happened to plaintiff and defendant (thrown from car, hit windshield, fell, etc.)
☐ detailed description of what happened to vehicles
☐ exact point of contact ☐ exact position of parties at time of contact ☐ position of other people ☐ opinion as to cause of accident
☐ diagram ☐ other key issue questions

☐ 6. Setting after accident:
☐ witness's description of scene (diagram)
☐ position of plaintiff and defendant ☐ position of vehicles
☐ injuries and damage (persons and property)
☐ description of sequence of events after accident
☐ time of arrival and activity of all emergency personnel
☐ care rendered at scene to injured ☐ other persons and witnesses present after accident, including reporters, photographers, investigators ☐ cleanup activities (name of tow truck)
☐ who, if anyone, made or recorded statements ☐ conversations overheard (parties, witnesses, emergency personnel, etc.)
☐ opinion as to truthfulness and character of parties and witnesses
☐ witness's record of character and honesty ☐ any conversation with any of the parties since accident about accident or injuries
☐ other key issue questions

☐ 7. Record statement and have witness read, sign, and date it.
☐ 8. Check to see if witness made statements about the accident to anyone else. If so, to whom and what kind (oral, written, recorded)?
☐ 9. Assess witness's abilities
☐ voice ☐ sincerity ☐ power of observation ☐ confidence
☐ appearance ☐ appreciation of importance of truthfulness
☐ recognition of evidence, persons, photos, etc. ☐ objectivity
☐ truthfulness ☐ vulnerability to impeachment
☐ willingness to testify ☐ availability for trial

In addition to using this general questionnaire, the paralegal needs to take the planning stage further by developing questions that focus on the key issues of the case as they relate to elements and defenses in negligence. For example, in Ms. Forrester's case, some initial questions must be probed in detail with one key witness, Ms. Schnabel. Some of these questions for each of the key elements are as follows:

Element. Duty (defined by conditions at the time).

Issue. Was ice a factor in determining degree of caution required?

Questions. Was ice on the road the morning of the accident? How much of the road near the scene and at the scene of the accident was covered by ice? Where was the ice? Had you experienced any difficulty on the ice yourself? Did your tires slip? Did you have control problems?

Element. Breach of duty.

Issue. Was Mr. Hart driving too fast under the icy conditions?

Questions. How fast were you driving? How fast do you normally drive at that point? How fast was Mr. Hart driving? From your observations, how did the ice affect or enter into the accident? In your opinion, was Mr. Hart driving too fast for the icy conditions? Explain the basis for your answer.

Element. Breach was proximate cause of injury.

Issue. Was Mr. Hart's speed under the icy conditions the cause of Ms. Forrester's injuries?

Questions. In your opinion, what was the primary cause of the accident? Explain. Do you feel there were any other contributing causes? If so, what were they? Explain. Which cause was most significant? Explain.

This question-planning process should be followed for any issues that might prove pivotal in the success of the case. Other key factors in the *Forrester* case include speed related to obstructions caused by the hills, inattentiveness of pedestrians, position of pedestrians, reaction times of the drivers, evidence of mechanical defects, and so on. Questions need to be planned to gather information on the key points of contention for each of the elements. This requires thorough preparation. Such preparation will help clarify the objectives of the particular interview and will make the interview much more valuable to the outcome of the case.

ASSIGNMENT 4:14
Place these items in your system folder: Checklist for Witness Interview, Witness Information Cover Sheet, and a brief description of how to create interview questions.

Another part of the planning process is deciding where the interview should take place. Occasionally a witness will agree to come to your office, but more than likely the interview will take place in the home, at the witness's place of employment, in a restaurant, in a car, or at the scene of the accident. Whenever possible the location should offer as much freedom from outside interruption and influence as possible. Witnesses should not be interviewed together.

As in the initial interview, special problems or needs should be anticipated. Will you need a translator? Will you need a special setting for an interview with a child? Should you arrange for someone else to be present if the witness is likely to be hostile or accuse you of unethical behavior? Will the witness expect to be paid? (Expert witnesses expect to be paid.) Check the office for the local practice and appropriate fee. Be sure that the fee is approved before incurring the expense.

Conducting the Witness Interview

Because the personality and attitude of each witness can be quite different, there is probably no standard method of approaching a particular witness. You will have to draw upon experience, intuition, and common sense as the situation dictates. There are, however, some pointers worth remembering. Courtesy should be of the first order. Calling ahead to arrange the interview is an important consideration. In some circumstances, such as in the case of a hostile witness, when it may be better not to call, you should choose a time likely to be convenient to the witness. Make it clear to the witness who you are, your status, which party you represent, and your purpose. If the witness is a friend of your client, or simply neutral, introducing some information about your client that will evoke sympathy may encourage the witness to help you. Keep in mind, however, the ethical responsibility not to be misleading or deliberately dishonest.

If witnesses are unwilling or hesitant to grant the interview, emphasize that you need their help and that it could be instrumental in bringing this matter to a quick, just, and less costly resolution. Cooperation now might reduce the time they would have to spend in the future. Also, delaying the interview may cause memory to fade, and valuable evidence will be lost. If this doesn't work, tell the witness that your firm can subpoena them to testify under oath, and it would be easier and more convenient to go ahead now than to do so under the subpoena. If this strategy fails, there is probably little choice but to withdraw and consider having them formally deposed, as discussed in chapter 8.

The Witness Information Cover Sheet (see figure 4:6) should be completed at the outset and clipped to the witness's statement. When organizing items for settlement or trial, you may refer to the cover sheet for a quick review of the witness and what he or she had to say.

The investigator's approach to the interview will depend on the witness. Some will want to tell you the entire story, while others will need regular questioning to focus their thoughts and to keep them on relevant information. Take notes, but listen carefully; do not be so concerned about your next question that you do not listen carefully to the answer to your last one. When you are not clear on a point, restate what the witness has said and ask if you have understood correctly. Be ready to employ the variety of interview techniques designed for the initial interview in chapter 3. Do not try to compose a statement for the witness until you are sure that you know the information well.

The following are sections of an interview with Ms. Forrester's neighbor, Ms. Schnabel. The purpose of this example is to illustrate several things: an approach to setting up an interview, a sequence to follow, a way to elicit detailed facts instead of beliefs, and a method to implement aspects of the interview plan (most particularly the key issue questions).

Illustrative Interview: Case 1

Setting up the interview   Setting: The doorstep of witness's home (*I* stands for interviewer; *W* stands for witness).

I: Good afternoon, Ms. Schnabel. I'm Terry Salyer, a paralegal with the law firm of White, Wilson, and McDuff. I'm the one who spoke with you on the phone earlier this week. I appreciate your willingness to talk with us. As you know, we are trying to help Ms. Forrester recover compensation for the terrible injuries inflicted on her in an accident last February.

W: Well, I have been thinking about this, and my husband feels that I shouldn't get involved. We are terribly busy and I just don't have the time to be going to court. I'm really not sure how helpful I can be anyway. I'd like to help Ms. Forrester, but I think I'd better stay out of it.

I: I can understand your concern, Ms. Schnabel, but one of the things we hope to accomplish in interviewing you is to get a better picture of what happened. It is likely that what you tell me could actually shorten this case, possibly make your testimony at a trial unnecessary, and allow for an early and just settlement of this matter. Frankly, it may be better for everyone involved in this incident, especially Ann Forrester, for you to tell us what you observed now, than to wait until months down the road when you might have to testify in court and you have forgotten much of what happened. I ask you to put yourself in Ms. Forrester's place—if you were her, not only would you want the help, but you would need it. I'll make every effort to be as brief as my job will permit. May I come in?

W: Well, I guess so. My husband won't like it, but I'll do what I can.

I: Thank you. You have a lovely home.

W: Thank you. Please sit down.

I: I'll be asking you several questions about what you observed at the accident and then ask you to reconfirm what you said in a written statement. I have several background questions to ask you. [Follow the Checklist for Witness Interview, or use the checklist to make sure you have covered everything at the conclusion of the interview.]

Questions regarding witness's activity prior to accident

I: Ms. Schnabel, do you remember the date on which the accident involving Ms. Forrester occurred?

W: Yes, it was February 26, 19__, the day after my husband's birthday.

I: What were you doing that morning immediately prior to the accident?

W: I was driving my grandchildren to school.

I: What way did you go that morning?

W: I turned onto Highway 328 and headed toward town.

I: What direction would that be?

W: East.

I: What was the weather like that morning?

W: It was a cold, windy morning. I recall that the road was slippery. [It might be best to finish questions about the weather, and then go on to questions about it being slippery.]

Questions regarding the conditions at the time of the accident

I: Could you describe in more detail what you mean by "slippery"?

W: Yes, there were patches of ice on the road. I remember that my wheels spun when I turned onto the highway. I noticed several more slippery spots, so I drove quite slowly.

I: How far did you drive before you came to where you observed the accident?

W: Oh, about a quarter of a mile.

I: Were there other slippery spots on that quarter mile of road?

W: Yes, there were several.

I: What percentage of the road was slippery?

W: Oh, I'd say about 20 percent.

I: Was there ice on both sides of the road?

W: Yes.

Questions regarding the accident

I: Ms. Schnabel, would you please draw me a diagram of the accident location?

W: Yes.

I: Using the diagram, describe the sequence of events of the accident itself.

W: Ann Forrester was walking on the road toward her house. The van was coming down the hill in her direction. Suddenly, the back of the van began to swerve from side to side. Ms. Forrester tried to get out of the way but the van kept sliding into the middle of the road and hit her. Ms. Forrester was thrown to the side of the road.

Using follow-up questions to gain greater factual detail

I: How close was the van to Ms. Forrester when it started to skid and turn?

W: Pretty close.

I: Please state the distance in feet.

W: About thirty-five to forty feet.

I: What would you estimate to be the distance between your front window and your mailbox? [This gives an indication of the witness's judgment of distance. The actual distance can be measured later.]

W: Around sixty to seventy feet.

I: Was there any observable attempt by the driver of the van to warn Ms. Forrester or to avoid the accident?

W: Not that I recall.

I: Not even a sounding of the horn?

W: No.

I: Not any braking?

W: Well, yes. It sounded like the wheels locked on the van. There was some sliding and some skidding.

I: Describe those sounds, please.

Probing further for details

I: Could you see the driver of the van just before the accident?

W: Not really.

I: Were the windows of the van fogged over?

W: I really didn't notice.

I: How fast was the van going when you first saw it?

W: He seemed to be going pretty fast.

I: How fast was that?

W: Oh, I'd say about forty to forty-five miles per hour.

I: Help me understand how you arrived at that estimate.

W: Well, thirty years of driving for one thing, but also because the van came over the hill so quickly and seemed to cover the ground between it and Ann so fast, even after the driver tried to brake the van.

I: What was the distance between the van when you first saw it crest the hill and Ms. Forrester?

W: I'd say about one hundred feet—maybe a little more.

I: Did you see if Ms. Forrester looked before she stepped onto the road?

W: No, she was already on the road when I came over the hill.

I: Where was Ms. Forrester's attention directed when you first saw her?

W: I can't be certain, but she seemed to be looking at the road.

I: Please describe that in more detail.

W: She was looking down and straight ahead.

I: Was her head tucked into her coat collar?

W: I kind of recall her collar being up around her neck and ears—but I'm really not sure.

(Note the absence of expressions such as "poor Ms. Forrester" or "poor Ann," which might suggest a strong bias held by Ms. Schnabel, thus weakening the possible effectiveness of her testimony at trial.)

The remaining part of the interview concerns the witness's impression of the situation immediately after the accident. Here, a good investigator would concentrate on the witness's observation of injuries to either party, especially on any overt indications of pain and suffering endured by Ms. Forrester. Prior to writing the statement, review the checklist to make sure all areas of the planned inquiry have been covered.

I: Ms. Schnabel, is there anything else you would like to add? [This avoids accusations of restricting what the witness was allowed to say.]

W: Not that I can think of.

I: Ms. Schnabel, I will take what you have told me and draft a written statement for you to review and sign. This will take me a few minutes, so if you have something to do in the meantime, please go ahead and I will let you know when we are ready to resume.

ASSIGNMENT 4:15
Drawing from the information in this section on conducting an interview, draft a Checklist of Considerations for Conducting a Witness Interview and place it in your system folder.

Drafting the Statement

The statement of a witness is taken for several reasons, as we have seen in other contexts. It tells the attorney what facts can be corroborated or refuted, which determines what the issues in the case will be and how good the evidence will be on those issues. In other words, it helps reveal whether the client's case is a strong one or a weak one. More directly, the statement serves as a record of the witness's recollection of the facts, which can be used months and even years later to refresh the memory of the witness. It can also be used in cross-examination to impeach the testimony of a witness who later contradicts the earlier statement. Statements of opposing parties can also serve as admissions that can be used against them in court. In addition, if a statement is sufficiently convincing and corroborates key facts, it may help bring about an early settlement of the case.

There are several different ways to record a statement. One method is to have witnesses write their own statements and sign them. This process is inexpensive, but few witnesses are willing to do this, and if they are, the information often lacks factual detail. Another method is to have a court reporter (stenographer) accompany the paralegal and record the statement. This approach may be particularly helpful when interviewing an adverse party or witnesses partial to the opposition. It is not, however, recommended for witnesses favorable or partial to the client because any initial inaccuracies or misjudgments of the witness will be recorded prior to any corrections, making the witness appear uncertain.[11] This method is also more expensive. Another method is to bring a neutral third party to hear the interview and sign the statement as a verification witness, or to record in a memorandum what the witness said, especially if the witness refuses to sign a statement. The advantage to these last two methods is that they provide a neutral third party to refute any statements by the witnesses that they did not read the statements; that the words in the statements are not their words; or that improprieties occurred. Without the neutral third party, the paralegal might have to testify to refute such an allegation. Unfortunately, the paralegal has a specific interest in the case and would probably not be viewed by the jury as a neutral witness.

The most common method involves interviewing the witness and drafting a statement for the witness to read and sign. In addition to these methods, statements may be taken by audio or video recorder or recorded over the telephone. Tape recordings or phone recordings should be conducted only with the full knowledge and permission of the witness and should be done so as to guarantee that the recordings are not subsequently tampered with or altered.

Tips for Taking and Drafting an Effective Statement

1. Visit the scene of the accident first to gain insights that will aid in taking a statement.
2. Note facts as opposed to beliefs ("twenty feet" as opposed to "too close").
3. Avoid references to automobile insurance; they can make the statement inadmissible.[12]
4. Take statements from likely witnesses who say they didn't see anything; a change in their stories will subject them to impeachment.
5. Note, but do not include in the statement, the names of other witnesses. (The jury may wonder why some of these people are not called later at trial.)[13]
6. Do not pay a witness for a statement without the attorney's approval. Fees for a statement are viewed skeptically by jurors, but reimbursement for expenses actually incurred by a witness, such as travel or missed work, is typical.[14]
7. Do not probe further when you receive a favorable answer to a question, especially if the interview is witnessed by a court reporter or other third party. Further inquiry often reveals weaknesses or qualifications, which may impede a favorable settlement. (There are two schools of thought here. One says if you get what you need for settlement, stop. If you need more information later for trial, go back. The other school says get all the information you can at this point—even if it hurts. Ask your supervising attorney for guidance on this one.)
8. Do not give the witness a copy of the statement unless told to do so by the attorney. (It can fall into opponent's hands.)[15]
9. Use diagrams to aid the witness's explanations.
10. Avoid a witness's tendency to use qualifiers such as "I think," "maybe," and "could have," which weaken a favorable statement.[16]
11. Draft the statement in the best light for the client without being misleading or inaccurate, or substituting interviewer's vocabulary and grammar for that of the witness.

ASSIGNMENT 4:16
After any class discussion, which might add other tips to the previous list, draft your own list of tips for taking and drafting an effective statement and place it in your system folder.

The statement should be drafted in the following sequence:[17]

1. Begin with a background paragraph to identify the witness, address, date, time, marital status, occupation, and so on. If you use a form such as the Witness Information Cover Sheet, more detailed background is not necessary in the statement.
2. A second section should state the date of the accident, the setting prior to the accident, the witness's purpose in being there, and so on.
3. A third section should describe the sequence of events as observed by the witness (the accident or other occurrence).

4. A fourth section describes what happened following the accident.
5. Conclude with a brief statement to be signed: "I, _____, have read the above statement comprising _____ pages, and it is true to the best of my knowledge. I have initialed each page and sign this in the presence of _____ this _____ day of _____, 19__."

If the witness is partial to the client and really wants to help, the statement could be drafted at the office and returned for signature at some later time. Otherwise it is best to complete the process at the interview.

ILLUSTRATIVE STATEMENT

I am Freda C. Schnabel and I reside at Box 20, Route 328, Legalville, Columbia. I was born on May 16, 19__, and am fifty-eight years of age. I am married, have three grown children, and am a housewife. I worked as a department store clerk for eight years.

On February 26, 19__, about 7:35 A.M., I was driving my grandchildren to school. We went east on Highway 328. It was a cold, windy day and there were patches of ice along the road. About 20 percent of the highway was covered with ice. Because of the ice, I was driving twenty-five to thirty miles per hour. As we got to Forresters' house, I saw Ms. Forrester crossing the road at a low spot in the highway. We were at a rise in the highway about 250 feet west of the spot where Ms. Forrester was crossing. There is another rise in the highway a little more than 100 feet east from the same low spot. Until the car reaches the top of either rise, the driver cannot see the bottom of the low spot. There are other hills and low spots and some tricky curves on Highway 328 east of the point where the accident took place.

I started to slow down for Ms. Forrester. A white van on the down-slope east of Ms. Forrester came on down the hill a ways. I'd estimate its speed to be about forty to forty-five miles per hour. It started to swerve from side to side. Ms. Forrester hesitated, not knowing which way to go. She then headed for my lane, which was the south side of the road. I heard a few squeals of tires as the van veered toward the middle of the road. I heard a thud and saw Ms. Forrester thrown to the side of the road where she landed like a sack of potatoes—very still and limp. The van kept veering left, crossed over my lane and hit a tree.

I pulled my car over to the side of the road near the van. The driver got out of the van. He was limping and had a cut on his forehead. Ms. Forrester was lying face up. She kept screaming, "God help me, it hurts, oh, God, I'm dying, please help me." I told Mr. Forrester to call an ambulance and that I'd stay with his wife. Soon my grandchildren got some blankets to cover Ms. Forrester. She was bleeding at her left side and leg. I remember her left foot pointing inward at an odd angle. The ambulance eventually arrived and took Ms. Forrester and her husband. I offered to stay with the children.

I did get a chance to see the driver of the van a little later at the scene. He appeared tired—his face was pale; he had a five o'clock shadow; his voice was hoarse; and I noticed his clothes were wrinkled.

I, _____, have read the above statement comprising _____ pages and it is true to the best of my knowledge. I have initialed each page and sign this in the presence of Terry Salyer, this 3d of September, 19___.

The witness should then read the statement. Corrections should be made where needed, and the witness should indicate approval of the correction by initialing the correction. If a major change is required, or one that suggests uncertainty where you do not want uncertainty, the statement may need to be redrafted. This is where a portable word processor and printer could be useful. The witness should initial each page to verify that he or she has read each page, and then sign at the end of the statement. A third party might also sign to indicate that this is the witness's statement and was read and signed in the third party's presence.

ASSIGNMENT 4:17
Following the directions of your instructor and the procedure set out in this chapter and chapter 3 on interviewing, conduct an interview with Robert Warren, a witness to the incident in Case II. After the interview, prepare a witness's statement according to the recommended procedures and tips covered in this chapter.

Concluding the Witness Interview

You might ask to take a photograph of the witness, which can be helpful in assessing the witness's impact on the jury and in recognizing the witness at a later time. Thank the witness for the assistance and leave a business card. Remind the witness to call you if he or she will be moving or will be gone for any extended period of time, or if additional information is recalled.

After the interview, review your interview notes and check the witness's statement for inaccuracies, typos, and leads that should be followed immediately. Make note of the leads and enter them on your deadline calendar. Unpursued leads can be damaging to the case and embarrassing to the paralegal and the firm, especially when settlement negotiations or trial is imminent and it is realized that the lead should have been followed up months ago.

After reviewing your notes and the witness's statement, summarize the essence of the witness's statement in the appropriate place on the "Witness Information Cover Sheet." Place the completed sheet and statement in the client's folder.

■ Preserving Evidence

Learning to preserve evidence is essential for a good paralegal. Techniques for preserving evidence are examined in the following material excerpted from the *NALA Manual for Legal Assistants*.[18]

Identification

Identifying potential "evidence" is perhaps the most difficult aspect of the investigator's duty. An investigator at an accident scene works under certain time constraints before the cleanup activity begins and, of course, there is always a substantial amount of confusion regarding the circumstances of the event as well as the number and variety of people interested in the matter. Police, fire department, and public safety personnel all have responsibilities in any accident involving major property damage or injury to life.

The first step most investigators follow at an accident scene is to preserve that scene as best they can through immediate photography and/or sketches. This frequently requires a quick orientation sketch on which a diagram of the camera angles and distances is plotted [see figure 4:8]. One technique for creating good proportionate sketches is to carry a quad-ruled tracing paper pad. After making a basic sketch with the major geographic features (whether of an intersection or a room), it is torn off the pad and slipped beneath the next sheet. Retrace the major

Figure 4:8   Photograph Index Sketch

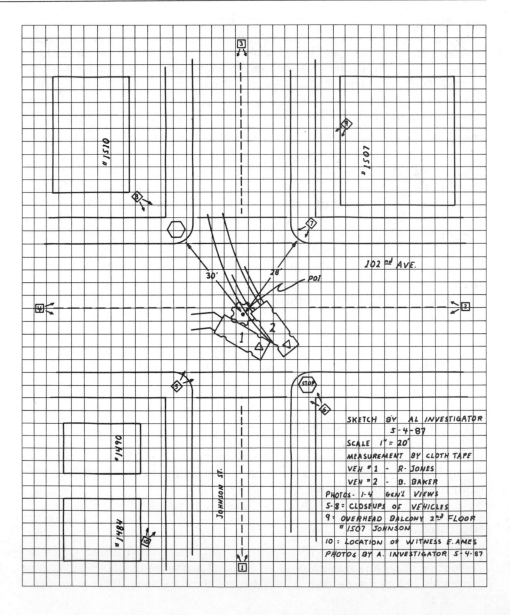

features and add the specific data desired for that sketch. One sketch may be the photo reference sketch; another might be the positions of the vehicles (if it is a traffic collision); and, thirdly, a highly helpful technique is marking a clear basic sketch with the data supplied by each percipient witness. That data might include the location of the witness, the first point at which the witness saw each vehicle, the locations of other vehicles or witnesses. These "witness sketches" can be amplified by trees, shrubs, buildings, parked vehicles, and supplemented by the investigator placing himself at the "witness" location to determine whether the story of the witness is physically possible. A composite sketch can be used to locate each witness graphically [see figure 4:9].

The diagram may be used to record such things as skid marks, significant buildings, vegetation, safety control devices, and the relationships of the objects

Figure 4:9   Witness Location Sketch

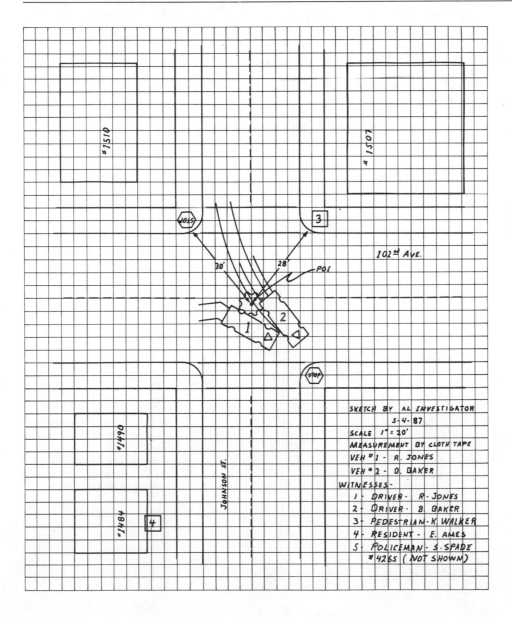

involved in the incident. At an explosion scene, for instance, where a gas heater is considered to be the origin of the explosive material, a photograph including both the thermostat and heater in one picture is desirable, if possible. If not, a sketch must be used to carefully reconstruct that relationship, keying the multiple photographs together with the sketch.

At accident scenes involving automobiles, the road ways, traffic control devices, visual obstructions (trees, fences, bridges, parked cars, etc.), skid marks, point of impact and positions at rest of the involved vehicles is essential. While photographs can do this to a certain extent, detailed sketches are also necessary. In extremely important cases, these details should be surveyed by a qualified surveyor to ensure the accuracy and later admissibility of the sketch at trial [see figure 4:10].

Figure 4:10   Basic Scene Sketch

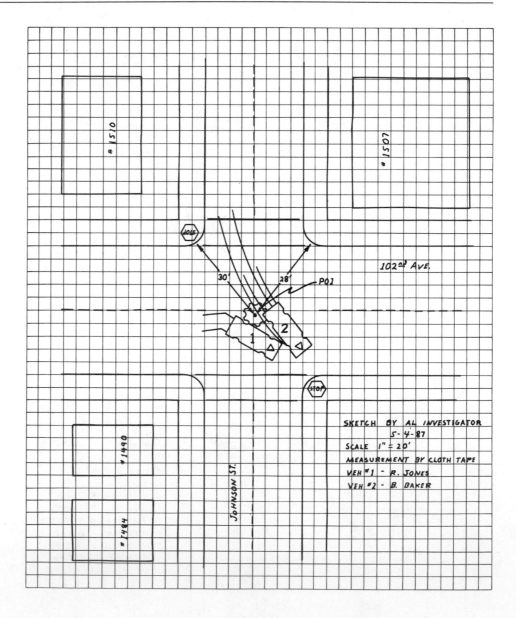

Physical Evidence

Every time an object is identified as potential evidence the investigator faces the problems of "How do I acquire it?" "How do I preserve it?" "How do I identify it for future reference and retrieval for introduction at trial?" "How do I create the foundation for the admissibility of this particular item?" In many cases, the investigator does not have legal title to the evidence he wishes to take into custody. Frequently, the ownership of the item is in question and the propriety of taking custody is one which calls the investigator's judgment to the test. In most cases of doubt, take custody of the documents, objects, or things, and leave a receipt indicating the name, identity, and the means by which people can contact the investigator if they wish to exert their ownership rights in the matter. Often police, fire, or safety investigators will be on the scene, and notification can be left with them if they allow the investigator to take possession of the item.

Control and Retrieval

Possession of the item of evidence carries the responsibility of control and for future identification of the object as being *that very item.* The investigator imposes upon the object some minor, but unique, marking to allow absolute and unequivocal identification of that particular object as being the one taken into custody on the date and at the time involved. The investigator thus must create a document which details the manner of taking custody and of marking this item for future reference as well as establishing the first step in the "chain of evidence" which will terminate with the introduction of the item at trial. Many investigators carry little copper wire and lead seals with a sealing tool. It allows the copper wire to be passed around the object, then through the seal. Special sealing tools (pliers) squeeze the seal tightly around the wire and can impress designs, a logo, or numbers on the soft lead. For larger objects, nylon cable-ties can be obtained in a range of sizes. Some objects are too large or unsuitable for such seals, and a unique marking can be engraved on the object; initials and the date are best. Small objects can be placed inside plastic bags or envelopes and sealed with tape on which the date and initials can be written. Any system may be used, so long as it provides a means of distinguishing that one object from all others similar to it and to provide a credible basis for testifying that the object is the very one collected as evidence on a given date.

From the time that object is identified as potential evidence, the custody of that particular item must be substantiated by a document trail showing every transfer of custody from the point of the incident or event to the trial, whenever it occurs. That chain is based on the proper procedure of the investigator or legal assistant in creating the first step in proper, ethical, and careful manner, and detailed recording of each subsequent transfer.

Caveat. "Documents" pose a special identification and storage problem for the investigator. They are most valuable to the attorney in their "unaltered" state. Yet the investigator usually must attach them to a report, describe them, provide a foundation for their use, and refer to them as "attached". When the document is a letter, written memorandum, pamphlet, etc., many investigators mark the document "EXHIBIT _____" or "ATTACHMENT _____" and staple it to the report. Convenient? Yes! But very poor technique, since the attorney now has an *altered* document and the convenient title "EXHIBIT _____" or "ATTACHMENT _____" must be explained in the future.

A better technique is to place the document in a transparent envelope (or even an opaque paper one) and apply the "EXHIBIT _____" or "ATTACHMENT

_____" label to the envelope together with a thorough description of the document (date, document type, author, addressee, topic or title, number of pages, and any attachments), as well as a short statement of the source of the document, the custodian, and the relevance of the document to the case. Alternatively a "face sheet" can carry this information. A photocopy of the document can be used as a "work copy" during preparation of the case.

Occasionally the investigator will find a document to be used in an interview or any situation where underlining, marginal annotation, or writing on the document might occur. This cannot be allowed to happen to the *original* document (whether the true original, a duplicate true copy, or a photo copy). *Evidence* must be preserved in the *discovered state.* If a copy is needed, it is photocopied and that new copy *must be marked as a copy,* preferably with a marginal label "Copy of a document in the file _____ vs. _____". This avoids the problem of "creating" yet another piece of *evidence* which would confuse the future admissibility of the "original" document at the trial.

Other forms of "documents", such as movie films, tape recordings, even photographs are not quite so susceptible to contamination as paper "documents"; however, safeguards should be considered for any item which may become "evidence" at trial.

Storage

Obviously, once the document or object is in custody, it cannot simply be placed on a file cabinet in an uncontrolled environment where anyone can obtain access to it, remove it, alter it, or damage it. Therefore, the investigator or the attorney must provide a safe and controlled environment within which the object is stored. Each event between the time of taking custody and its introduction to trial where people wish to examine the object should be recorded in detail to include the date and time, the person authorizing the particular examination or movement, the person benefiting from such activity or movement, the duration, and the return of the object to the place of storage. Anyone taking possession of the object must sign it out with a statement that it will be safeguarded and returned or preserved in the exact same condition. Polaroid photos may be appropriate for memorializing the transfer. A suitable form for controlling "evidence" is shown in figure 4:11.

Testing and Examination

Often evidence connected with an event over which litigation is to transpire must be tested, examined, or disassembled to validate its concept as "evidence". Sometimes the examination, disassembly, or test will damage or destroy the object. If this situation arises, the attorney will ensure that the adversary and all other parties to the action have an opportunity to have representatives present. The investigator generally is charged with taking custody of the item, removing it to the place of examination, and documenting the steps of the examination. The purpose of the examination and the anticipated method should be planned and the scenario described and noticed in timely fashion to all parties of the action to allow them or their "expert" to participate or observe the necessary examination. The whole process may be recorded through the use of still photographs, movies, or, more recently, videotape. The investigator records the presence of all witnesses, including their full identification and their association with their respective parties in the matter. All experts should be fully identified as to name, address, specialty, and

Figure 4:11 Evidence Log

EVIDENCE LOG			
CASE:		EVENT:	
EVIDENCE:			
HOW ACQUIRED:		DATE:	
		BY:	
IDENTIFYING MARKS:			
		BY _____ DATE _____	
STORAGE LOCATION:			
CUSTODIAN	DATE	RELEASED TO	DATE/PURPOSE

employer. Remember, any examination, testing, or disassembly of the item which destroys or changes the physical characteristics of the item, and if not accomplished with the knowledge, consent, and participation of all of the parties may prevent the use of any developed information at trial.

Demonstrative Evidence

Demonstrative evidence in the form of sketches, drawings, or surveys, created as a means of preserving transitory physical evidence into retrievable form, will require a certain amount of documentation for use at future times. The presence of a "scale" and the date and the name of the person who rendered the drawing is essential. Obviously, the means and method of making the measurement represented in the drawing will be subject to question and must be supported by the proper foundation. The date of the examination and measurements are essential, particularly if they are different from the date of the event in question. It is helpful to support these drawings with photographs of the same area.

In the event that the demonstrative evidence is to be a model, a replica, a reconstruction, or an exact duplicate of the object involved in the case, the same foundation will be necessary to establish the dates, times, scale, methods of calculation, sizes, and measurements. It probably still will be subject to questioning on the accuracy of the representation. Many of these demonstrative evidence procedures are very expensive and obviously should be discussed with and authorized by the attorney before initiating steps for their generation.

Sketches and Drawings

Certain injury litigation cases and regulatory agency actions can benefit from the use of renderings by artists. Medical illustrators are particularly talented in clarifying what otherwise might be very difficult explanations of X-rays (even if produced as positives) by converting them into easily understood colored drawings at relatively little cost. Illustrators can show a proposed development or project in simplified (even idealized) form to assist the presentation for permits, zoning, etc.

Photography

Photography is both a blessing and a curse in litigation. It is a truism that almost any photograph related to an event is potentially admissible at trial. The opposite side of the coin is that almost any photograph may be subject to argument over its admissibility. The judgment of the person taking the photograph and his expertise are always subject to question. The average investigator or legal assistant who chooses to take his own photographs rather than to employ professional photographers must be prepared to defend the representations in his photographs. For this reason, many investigators have resorted to "snap shots" taken with simple nonadjustable cameras or "Polaroid" varieties of photographic equipment. If the investigator is an expert, then he understands that the use of an adjustable lens camera which allows him to shoot wide angle, normal angle, and telephoto views of the same scene, also changes perspective as those changes in focal length are used. In order to ensure that he can, at a later time, defend the photographic representation, he should employ some form of photo log.

Every photograph taken should have recorded the focal length, "f" stop, film speed, film type, filters, and whether or not artificial lighting equipment was used. If possible, each photograph should be related to a sketch indicating the location of the camera and the direction it was pointed to get the view in the photograph [see figure 4:12].

Use of filters is arguable at best and difficult to explain to a jury. At worst, the photograph will be excluded. If filters are used, an unfiltered shot of the same view should be made. A great deal of judgment must be exercised by the investigator or legal assistant in deciding whether or not to shoot photographs.

Obviously, if the client is a plaintiff and the accident investigation involves an automobile collision with injury, photographs of the amount of blood spilled in the vehicles may be a desirable quality to memorialize by photography. If the client is a defendant, "gory" photographs can be no help at all. It is not enough to take them and destroy them because then the photographs must be explained and the destruction must also be explained. The skilled legal assistant considers the

Figure 4:12 Recorder Log Slip

Case Number and/or Name		Recorded By:
Day, Hr. & Date	Tape No.	Reel Size:
Recorder No. & Type:		Tape Speed 7½ 3¾ 1⅞ 15/16 S
Typing Requested:	By:	Reason:
Typed By:	Trans. No.	Date Typed:

Counter Rdg		Description of Recording
Side 1	Side 2	
		Date of Accident RECORDER LOG SLIP FIELD OPERATION

Case Number and/or Name *Jones vs. Baker* *Eldorado Sup Ct No 1273*		Recorded By: *A.B. Allen*
Day, Hr. *Monday, 10:30 A.M.* & Date *Sept 6, 1992*	Tape No. *74-ABA-52*	Reel Size: *Cassette*
Recorder No. & Type: *Sony Ex-9*		Tape Speed 7½ 3¾ 1⅞ ~~15/16~~ S
Typing Requested: *Feb. 6, 1993*	By: *G. Lawyer*	Reason: *comply w/ discovery*
Typed By:	Trans. No.	Date Typed:

Counter Rdg		Description of Recording
Side 1	Side 2	
00-246		*Statement - E. Ames (Eye witness) 1484 Johnson St,* *Pleasantville, CA*
246-256		*Blank*
256-300		*description of scene from physical examination*
		Date of Accident RECORDER LOG SLIP *5-4-92* FIELD OPERATION

evidentiary value of each photograph he intends to take—both its benefits and its detriments—and then decides whether the benefits outweigh the detriments.

Counsel for plaintiffs often find photographs of bodily injuries very early in the incident are shockingly persuasive to the jury to demonstrate the obvious pain and suffering caused by the injury. It is important to consider the type of camera used and the type of film that was used in making these photographs. For instance, a black and white photograph of a person showing massive bruises of an extremely dark nature may be the result of the use of black and white film specially sensitive to the color red and generating a higher contrast than otherwise may be present. Similarly, color photographic film can be obtained with a definite tendency to show red very strongly, blue very strongly, or green very strongly, depending on the representation desired by the person taking the photograph.

The use of lighting will often have an effect on the imagery presented by the photograph. Daylight provides one form of reflected light accepted by the camera while incandescent light tends to throw a warmer red-toned color on the same object. Fluorescent lighting tends to provide more yellow-green and, of course, the flash bulbs, depending on their size and nature affect the color quality of the image produced. Infra-red film provides even more dramatic effects. Infra-red can be highly informational in some cases involving vegetation growth, decline and death or in heat gain and loss disputes.

When the investigation begins some time after the incident giving rise to the case there are a wide variety of sources of photographs which always should be explored. The police often take photographs, as do the fire departments and, of course, newspapers, wire services, and free-lance photographers. The more important, dramatic, and long term incident produces a veritable flood of photographs to which the legal assistant can gain access. Occasionally a neighborhood canvass can locate snapshots of the immediate area.

It is always possible, and often desirable, to employ a professional photographer to take selected photographs for specific purposes. They are relatively expensive but professionals can usually qualify their photos for introduction as evidence. Be specific in the request.for the number, sizes, black and white or color, and views desired. Every photograph should have a purpose beneficial to the case or the understanding of the jury.

Do not ignore the possibilities of overhead views which can be obtained through aerial photos by a wide variety of sources. The U.S. Coast and Geologic Survey has a tremendous collection of aerial photos in different scales, both recent and historical. The U.S. Department of Agriculture, too, uses aerials in its studies. Forestry departments, state and federal highway projects or departments, city and county public works and planning departments turn more and more to aerial photographs for planning, zoning, and traffic study work. Many have aerial photographs of diverse locations. Any area subject to land management or reclamation probably has been photo-mapped by the U.S. Department of the Interior. These governmental sources generally provide fine, full-frame prints at nominal cost, but with a built-in bureaucratic time delay problem. Using private aerial photograph sources often permit enlargements of all of a negative or only a portion, at the lawyer's election. The cost is a little greater for the custom work but is well worth the price.

Individually, photographs from an upper story window or rooftop can be helpful. Or, a photograph from a chartered airplane may be desirable. It is difficult for these photographs to be used "to scale" however, and that is one of the major benefits of professional aerial photographs—the exact determination of scale. [Distinguish between photos that will be used for trial and those simply to provide perspective and insight in planning the case. The latter require less care and backs can be written on. These might be photos of a witness, a piece of physical evidence, or a piece of land.]

Preserving Recorded Statements

The preservation of the recorded statement is a special problem since it is a form of "evidence". A special storage facility for such recordings should be maintained, together with a numbering system, a log, a cross reference to the case file, and a suspense device to dispose of the recording following resolution of the case. An easy system combines the last two digits of the year, the initials of the investigator, and the number of the tape (an increasing sequential series) to be affixed to the tape.

ASSIGNMENT 4:18
Draft a detailed checklist for preserving evidence and file it in your system folder.

◼ Reviewing the Informal Investigation

Investigation may continue in its various stages, including continuing to follow leads and gathering documents, right up until trial. After this initial stage of informal investigation, however, the attorney will want a report on how you have progressed. Providing a simple summary of what you have found on each of the elements will accomplish this task. Often the attorney will simply review the file containing the client interview, medical and other records, a description and diagrams of the scene, photos, statements of the witnesses, and any other gathered information. From the review of this information, the attorney can determine whether a complaint should be filed to start the action.

◼ Summary

Because there is a lot of material covered in this chapter, the key for you is to separate out the material that is clearly reference material. Know it is there and note that you can find it in the future as needed. Focus on those concepts and terms that are significant and will be helpful when you are not next to a legal dictionary or not in a law library—when you are talking with a client or out in the field gathering evidence, for example. The study questions at the end of this chapter will help identify most, but not all, of this material.

   The purposes of investigation can be summed up as the need to provide your client with the knowledge to make informed decisions and to provide your attorney with the best available evidence to assess and hopefully win the case. Investigation of any type is not likely to be effective, however, without a good grasp of the rules of evidence, what is admissible and what is not, as set out in both the state and federal rules. Generally, evidence must be relevant, which means it must be material and tend to provide or refute a fact of consequence. But even relevant evidence may not be admissible because of its prejudicial or detrimental value. Unreliable evidence such as hearsay is excluded except when its source or nature suggests reliability.

Understanding the rules of evidence helps you develop a plan for investigation, from understanding the elements of the law that must be proved or refuted to developing a list of likely sources for obtaining information. Learning your ethical responsibilities is extremely important in giving you a mooring in safe harbor at troubling moments. In investigation, a paralegal needs to be thorough, prompt, objective, and honest; must avoid falsehoods, misrepresentations, and the revealing of attorney-client privileged information; and must remain independent in professional responsibility. To do otherwise can jeopardize the case and the attorney's and paralegal's reputations.

Gathering the evidence requires a knowledge of where to look, the most efficient methods and technologies, and the relationship between the economics of the case and the cost of the investigation. Interviewing witnesses is a critical part of this process and requires diligence, planning, and tact. Drafting a good statement that is an accurate reflection of the witness's point of view is an art that improves with practice.

Finding all the evidence in the world is of little value if you do not know how to preserve it. This can be done by diagramming, photographing, storing, testing, and properly inventorying all evidence. Evaluate the evidence and report to the attorney on what has been gathered so decisions about filing or defending a lawsuit can be made.

Study Guide

1. What are the purposes of investigation?
2. Why does an investigator need to understand the relationship between investigation and evidence law?
3. Define *evidence law*.
4. What is the difference between direct and circumstantial evidence?
5. What requirements must be met for evidence to be admissible?
6. What is relevant evidence?
7. When will relevant evidence not be admissible?
8. What are the rules of evidence (for federal and for your state) governing the following areas?

Character	Hearsay
Habit or routine	Physical evidence
Privilege	Authentications
Requirement of witness to testify	Best evidence
Admission of party opponent	Judicial notice
Lay opinions	Reputation for truthfulness
Expert opinion	

9. Define *preponderance of evidence* and *clear and convincing evidence*.
10. Define *presumption of evidence*.
11. What are some typical sources for the rules of evidence?
12. Why is it necessary to plan an investigation thoroughly?
13. What are the six stages in planning an investigation?

14. Review, but do not attempt to memorize, the checklist for evidentiary sources.
15. Define *data base;* explain how one is used and how it is useful, and review the list of data bases.
16. What are the major methods of investigation, and what should be considered in selecting a particular method?
17. What information should go into a written investigation plan?
18. Discuss the major ethical and related concerns (including attorney's work product) that are particularly applicable to investigation.
19. How should a paralegal gather medical and employment information about the client? What recommendations should be followed?
20. Why is it essential to immediately check documents that have been returned pursuant to the paralegal's request?
21. What procedures should be followed in investigating the scene of an accident?
22. List some good techniques for finding a witness and for finding an expert witness.
23. Why is it important to interview a witness as soon as possible after the accident?
24. What needs to be done to plan a witness interview?
25. Why are the elements of a cause of action important to planning an interview?
26. How does an interviewer gain the cooperation of a witness?
27. Describe useful techniques in interviewing a witness. (Review the appropriate section of chapter 3.)
28. What are the purposes of taking a statement?
29. How does a paralegal draft a good statement?
30. Why should a paralegal review a statement immediately after it has been taken?
31. Describe the purpose for preserving evidence and some good techniques for preserving evidence.

Endnotes

1. Graham, Federal Rules of Evidence in a Nutshell 251 (1981).
2. Id., 256.
3. Id., 253.
4. McCormick, McCormick on Evidence (3d ed. 1984).
5. Johnson, *Modems and International Data Bases Equal Worldwide Resources,* 58 Wisconsin Bar Bulletin 64 (1985); and Chung, *Online Databases,* 2 Legal Assistant Today 23 (1984).
6. Memo from C. Wilson to J. McCord (March 23, 1986).
7. Weinstein, Introduction to Civil Litigation 59 (2d ed. 1986).
8. Suggested in part by National Association of Legal Assistants, Manual for Legal Assistants 296–99 (1979) [hereinafter cited as NALA Manual].
9. NALA Manual, 299.
10. Id.
11. Morrill, Trial Diplomacy 175 (2d ed. 1972) [hereinafter cited as Morrill].
12. Lay, *A Trial Lawyer Speaks to the Investigator,* 2 Practical Lawyer 68–81 (1956) (quoted in Statsky, Torts: Personal Injury Litigation 151 [1982]).

13. Bruno, Paralegal's Litigation Handbook 122 (1980) [hereinafter cited as Bruno].
14. Morrill, 172.
15. Bruno, 123.
16. Morrill, 174.
17. Id.
18. Reprinted by permission of NALA Manual for Legal Assistants 310–23. Copyright 1979 by West Publishing Company. All rights reserved.

5

Drafting the Complaint

- ■ Introduction
- ■ The Complaint in Detail
- ■ Exhibits and Appendices
- ■ System Checklist for Drafting a Complaint
- ■ Sample Complaints
- ■ Injunctions

■ Introduction

The Task: Draft a Complaint

Now that you have gathered some significant evidence through informal investigation, your next task assignment from Mr. White is to draft complaints for the *Forrester* and *Ameche* cases. It will be Mr. White's duty to review and sign the complaints.

Before you draft the complaint for this case, you will learn the purpose for the complaint, the structure and components of both state and federal complaints of various kinds, how to ensure the complaint states a cause of action, and how to properly include exhibits and appendices. Further, you will practice drafting complaints according to a checklist, learn about pleading for an injunction (another form of action), and continue to expand your litigation system.

Learning to draft effective complaints and similar pleadings is an art; like other arts it takes time and, above all, practice. This art is an important one. If done well, the complaint is succinct, adequate, and permits the action to proceed. If done poorly, the complaint will lead to costly delay, negative impressions of the advocate's ability, and worst of all, dismissal and possible loss of the client's cause of action. Like other skills addressed in this text, learn this one well and your value to firm and client increases significantly.

Definition and Purpose

The Fifth and Fourteenth amendments of the Constitution of the United States guarantee that a person shall not be deprived of "life, liberty, or property" without **due process of law.** Most civil lawsuits attempt to

139

deprive the defendant of money or other property. Therefore, the procedure used in deciding whether that person will be deprived of that property must meet the requirement of due process. In other words, the procedure must be fair. One way to ensure fairness is to require that all parties be informed of the basis of the lawsuit. This is initially accomplished through formal documents called pleadings that must be filed in court.

Pleadings are formal documents that state and clarify the issues in a case by setting out the claims and defenses of the parties. There are a variety of state and federal pleadings that are allowed by the respective rules of each state and the federal rules. Some pleadings are claim pleadings; they state a claim against the other party. These pleadings include the complaint, counterclaim, cross-claim, and third-party complaint. Other pleadings are defense pleadings that respond to the claim and may state defenses. These include the answer, reply to counterclaim, answer to cross-claim, and a third-party answer. Most of these pleadings are discussed in subsequent chapters.

One of the pleadings, and the focus of this chapter, is the **complaint.** The purpose of the complaint is to (1) introduce the cause of action, (2) invoke the court's jurisdiction, and (3) present the facts, thus (4) informing the defendant about who is suing him or her, for what reason, and for how much money or other award. This gives the defendant time to respond to the allegations and to prepare adequately for trial. Thus, the complaint helps ensure fairness and compliance with procedural due process.

An Example

In preparing to draft a complaint, it is useful to obtain a copy of a previously filed complaint. One can be obtained from another case file, the firm's form file, or from form books in the law library. Most state rules of civil procedure and the Federal Rules of Civil Procedure provide examples of complaints. A sample complaint appears in figure 5:1.

Figure 5:1   Sample Complaint (State)

STATE OF COLUMBIA	CAPITOL COUNTY	CIRCUIT COURT

caption

MARY E. JOHNSON, Plaintiff

v.   Civil Action, File No. <u>00000</u>

ARTHUR HENDRICKS, Defendant

COMPLAINT FOR NEGLIGENCE

The Plaintiff states that:

body

1. The court has jurisdiction in this matter under Section 403A, Title 23 of the Columbia Revised Statutes.

2. Plaintiff is a paralegal and resides at 433 South Senate Avenue, Legalville, in Capitol County, Columbia.

3. Defendant is a baker and lives at 500 Maple Street, Legalville, in Capitol County, Columbia.

4. Defendant owns and operates the Deli Bakery at 508 Maple Street, Legalville, in Capitol County, Columbia.

5. On August 23, 19—, at said bakery, Defendant sold Plaintiff a chocolate eclair, which was negligently prepared so as to contain pieces of glass.

6. Plaintiff ate said pastry, causing the following damage:

      a. Great pain and suffering

      b. Internal injuries

      c. Medical and hospital bills

      d. Loss of income

prayer for relief   WHEREFORE, Plaintiff demands judgment in the amount of seven thousand dollars ($7,000), together with the costs and disbursements of this action.

_____

Plaintiff's Attorney
407 E. Second Avenue
Legalville, Columbia

State of Columbia
County of Capitol

verification   Mary Johnson, on oath deposes and states that she has read the foregoing complaint, and that the matters stated therein are true to the best of her knowledge, information, and belief.

_____

Mary Johnson
Subscribed and sworn to before
me this 12th day of October, 19__.

_____

Notary Public

My commission expires: _____

■ The Complaint in Detail

Caption

The caption of the complaint is the heading that identifies the location of the action, the court, the docket or file number, and the title of the action. The title includes the parties and sometimes the nature of the action (e.g., complaint for negligence). The attorney will inform you of the appropriate court and parties.

The following shows you how the caption would look in the *Forrester* case in both state and federal courts.

EXAMPLE OF CAPTION: STATE COURT

STATE OF COLUMBIA   CAPITOL COUNTY   CIRCUIT COURT

ANN FORRESTER, Plaintiff
      v.   Civil Action, File No. <u>1000</u>
RICHARD HART and
MERCURY PARCEL SERVICE, INC., Defendants

COMPLAINT FOR NEGLIGENCE

EXAMPLE OF CAPTION: FEDERAL COURT

UNITED STATES DISTRICT COURT FOR THE EASTERN DISTRICT
OF COLUMBIA Civil Action, File Number <u>1001</u>

ANN FORRESTER,
              Plaintiff
    v.
                         COMPLAINT
RICHART HART and
MERCURY PARCEL SERVICE, INC.,
              Defendants

Rule 10 of the Federal Rules of Civil Procedure designates what must be included in a pleading filed in federal court. Form 1 and subsequent forms in the Federal Rules appendix of forms give recommended examples. Likewise, parallel state rules and forms should be consulted.

ASSIGNMENT 5:1
Research the rules of civil procedure for your state for the recommended caption form. If the rules of your state do not have sample forms, go to a book on forms for civil action in your state. Place a copy of the state caption form with copies of the prior captions at the beginning of the complaint section of your system folder. Also list the applicable rules and forms.

The Parties

The caption requires designation of the parties to the lawsuit. In order for parties to sue or be sued, they must meet certain minimal requirements. First, they must be a **real party in interest** [Rule 17(a)]. A real party in interest refers to both the injured person and the person who allegedly caused the injury. The real party in interest cannot be a friend or cousin or some other stand-in; it must be a person directly involved. Substantive law of each state defines when a party has a cause of action, such as for negligence, and when a party is liable for a wrong committed against another. In the *Forrester* case, Ann Forrester is the injured party, and thus, a real party in interest. Richard Hart is the alleged wrongdoer from whom compensation is sought, and thus, a real party in interest.

In addition, a party must have the **capacity** to sue or be sued [Rule 17(b)]. Persons have such capacity unless they are under the age of majority (eighteen in most states), are incompetent, insane, or dead. The law of each state determines whether a person has the capacity to sue. Capacity in the federal courts is determined by the law of the state in which the person resides (domicile). In those cases where persons do not have legal capacity, they may sue or be sued through a legal representative, or have a **guardian ad litem** (a representative just for the action) appointed by the court [Rule 17(c)]. When a party dies or becomes incompetent during a lawsuit, another party may be substituted as long as it is done within ninety days of notice of the death to the court (Rule 25).

Corporations are considered "persons" under the law, and therefore have the capacity to sue and be sued. Consequently, because Mercury Parcel Service corporately owns the van that caused Ann Forrester's injuries and is also the employer of Richard Hart, it is a real party in interest and a co-defendant.

There is no limit to the number of parties to a lawsuit. Rule 20(a) of the Federal Rules of Civil Procedure and the rules of most states permit the **joinder of parties.**

> All persons may join in one action as plaintiffs if they assert any right to relief jointly, severally, or in the alternative in respect of or arising out of the same transaction, occurrence, or series of transactions or occurrences and if any question of law or fact common to all of these persons will arise in the action. All persons (and any vessel, cargo or other property subject to admiralty process in rem) may be joined in one action as defendants if there is asserted against them jointly, severally, or in the alternative, any right to relief in respect of or arising out of the same transaction, occurrence or series of transactions or occurrences and if any question of law or fact common to all defendants will arise in the action. A plaintiff or defendant need not be interested in obtaining or defending against all the relief demanded. Judgment may be given for one or more of the plaintiffs according to their respective rights to relief, and against one or more defendant according to their respective liabilities.

For example, the spouse of an injured party may be joined as a plaintiff for the loss of love, affection, and service of the injured party; or the estates of several victims of an airline crash may be combined as plaintiffs in an action against the airline. Also, Mr. Hart and the company he works for may be joined as defendants in the suit by Ms. Forrester.

Rule 22, the **interpleader** rule, permits a plaintiff to join as defendants those parties who have claims against the plaintiff when the plaintiff is exposed to multiple liability. For example, if defendant A has a counterclaim to plaintiff's property as does B, the plaintiff may interplead B as a defendant and let the court decide who gets the property. If done in separate suits, the plaintiff could be found liable to both parties.

Class actions are permitted under Rule 23. For such actions, one or more members of a class may sue or be sued as representative of the entire class if the following elements are present:

1. The members of the class are too numerous for joinder.
2. There are common questions of law and fact.

3. The claims of the representative are typical of those of the class.
4. The representative will protect the interests of the class.
5. Separate actions would be likely to bring inconsistent results.
6. Separate actions might hinder or preclude the action of the other members of the class.
7. The adverse party has acted or failed to act in a manner applicable to the entire class.
8. A class action is the superior action under the circumstances.

See the forms of various types of complaints at the end of this chapter for an example of a complaint for a class action suit.

In this same vein, Rule 24 permits a party to intervene in an action either as a plaintiff or as a defendant when specifically permitted by U.S. law; when the action may impede or impair the intervenor's interest which is otherwise unrepresented by the existing parties; or when the applicant's claim or defense raises the same question of law or fact as the existing claim. Intervention is accomplished by a *motion to intervene* [Rule 24(C)].

The policy behind these joinder rules is that it is much better to resolve all related claims with all needed or likely parties in one action than to have a whole series of costly and time-consuming actions. A 1990 law, 28 U.S.C. § 1367, reinforces the authority of federal courts to join cases or parties for which there is no federal jurisdiction independent of the original federal case. When considering adding such claims or parties, consult this statute and the pertinent Federal Rules of Civil Procedure.

Here are examples of caption formats for a variety of circumstances and parties. Add them to your system folder.

PARTY CAPTION FOR SUIT BY CHILD

BARRY SMITH
a minor by his parents and guardians,
SAMUEL and EDNA SMITH,
                              Plaintiff

v.

JOHNSON MOTORS, INC.,
                              Defendant

PARTY CAPTION FOR SUIT BY DECEASED PERSON

HAROLD WEBER,
Executor of the estate of
[(or) Personal Representative for the Estate of]
MARY WEBER,
                              Plaintiffs

v.

FRANCIS LONG,
                              Defendant

PARTY CAPTION FOR SUIT BY MULTIPLE PARTIES

SAMUEL HARRIS
            and
IRENE BOND,
                    Plaintiffs
            v.
EDWARD SUMMER
            and
SPIKES, INC.,
            and
JOHNSON   MANUFACTURING
COMPANY, INC.,
                    Defendants

PARTY CAPTION FOR SUBSEQUENT PLEADING IN PRECEDING CASE

SAMUEL HARRIS, et al.,
                    Plaintiffs
            v.
EDWARD SUMMER, et al.,
                    Defendants

"Et al." is an abbreviation for the Latin *et alii,* meaning "and others." Rule 10(a) of the Federal Rules of Civil Procedure and parallel state rules require that all parties to an action be listed in the caption. Pleadings that come after the complaint, however, may state the name of the first party on each side followed by the "et al." abbreviation. This can save paper and time in actions involving numerous parties.

Jurisdictional Allegations

As we have seen in chapter 2, jurisdiction is the authority of a court to decide a case and enforce its decisions. Subject matter jurisdiction is the court's authority to hear certain types (subjects) of cases. An allegation of jurisdiction must be included in complaints filed in federal courts because those are courts of limited subject matter jurisdiction. A plaintiff must demonstrate to a federal court through the jurisdictional allegation that the court has the subject matter jurisdiction to hear the case.

Although the trial courts of most states are courts of general jurisdiction, it is best to allege jurisdiction unless you are absolutely positive that your state rules do not require such an allegation. More than likely, you will need the names and domicile of the parties, the cause of action and its location, a reference to any controlling jurisdictional state statute, and any jurisdictional amount. These are stated in the first paragraphs of the complaint.

Since paralegals are often responsible for drafting complaints, they must know the jurisdictional requirements for the pertinent court and take care that the amount or other jurisdictional requirements are properly alleged. The determination of whether the client's case meets the jurisdictional requirement, and what court the case should be filed in, will be left to the attorney. Nevertheless, it is important to know the jurisdictional fundamentals needed for drafting jurisdictional allegations and for understanding the attorney's choices. A review of these fundamentals as discussed in chapter 2 may be useful at this time.

Typical formats for allegations of subject matter jurisdiction for a complaint to be filed in federal district court follow.

JURISDICTIONAL ALLEGATION OF DIVERSITY

Sample 1

1. Jurisdiction of this court is based on diversity of citizenship and the amount in controversy exceeds the sum of $50,000, exclusive of interest and costs.

Sample 2

1. Plaintiff is a [citizen of the State of Columbia] [corporation incorporated under the laws of the State of Columbia having its principal place of business in the state of Columbia] and defendant is a corporation incorporated under the laws of the State of Ohio having its principal place of business in [Ohio] [a state other than the State of Columbia]. The matter in controversy exceeds, exclusive of interest and costs, the sum of $50,000.00

Sample 2 is based on Form 2(a) in the appendix of forms of the Federal Rules of Civil Procedure. Note that diversity for a corporation is based on two locations: the state of incorporation and the state where the corporation has its principal place of business. These should be two separate states. If either of those locations is the same in which the opposing party is located, diversity does not exist.

JURISDICTIONAL ALLEGATION FOR FEDERAL QUESTION CASES

1. The action arises under [the Constitution of the United States, Article _____, Section _____]; [the _____ Amendment to the Constitution of the United States, Section _____]; [the Act of _____, _____ Stat. _____; U.S.C., Title _____, § _____]; [the Treaty of the United States (here describe the treaty)].

The preceding example is based on Form 2(b) in the appendix of forms of the Federal Rules of Civil Procedure. Jurisdictional amount is no longer alleged in federal question cases.

JURISDICTIONAL ALLEGATION FOR CASES ARISING UNDER FEDERAL STATUTE

Sample 1

1. The action arises under the Act of _____, Stat. _____, U.S.C., Title _____, § _____.

Sample 2

1. The action arises under the National Environmental Policy Act of 1969, § 102; _____ Stat. 852; 42 U.S.C. § 4332 (1970).

Samples 1 and 2 are based on Form 2(c) in the appendix of forms. In those states where jurisdictional allegations are required, the following formats may be appropriate.

JURISDICTIONAL ALLEGATION WHERE CASES ARISE UNDER STATE STATUTE AND WHERE JURISDICTIONAL AMOUNT IS NECESSARY

1. The jurisdiction of this court arises under Section 335, Title 17, of the State Code of Columbia. The amount in controversy exceeds $2,500, exclusive of interest and costs.

Note: In the prior example, it was necessary to allege the $2,500 in order to get into the state circuit court, in this case the highest-level trial court in the state.

Identification of the Parties

The complaint should state the domicile of the plaintiff and the defendant. Jurisdictions and form books vary on whether "domicile" requires you to include the complete address of the parties or simply the city, county, and state. The following examples include addresses.

---

2. Plaintiff resides at 301 South Short Street, in the City of Legalville in the County of Capitol in the State of Columbia.
3. Defendant resides at 5130 West North Avenue, in the City of Lancaster in the County of Capitol in the State of Columbia.

In some jurisdictions it is necessary to have the names and addresses of the parties stated in the complaint to demonstrate that the court has proper venue. This is true if venue is to be based on the convenience of the parties. If venue is to be based on the location of the incident precipitating the lawsuit, then that location (state, city, and county) must be made clear in the body of the complaint. In the federal system, proper venue does not have to be alleged in the complaint; it is considered a matter for the defendant to raise.[1] Venue may be waived by the defendant; jurisdiction may not be.

The Body of the Complaint (the Cause of Action)

The body is the heart of the complaint. It states the *claim upon which relief may be granted,* often called the **cause of action.** The writing of this section of the complaint is critical to the initial success of the plaintiff's lawsuit, for if it is not done correctly, either the action will be dismissed or the complaint will have to be amended.

What Must Be Alleged?

The specific answer to what must be alleged lies in the law of each jurisdiction. It would be comforting to all of us if drafting an adequate body of a complaint were an exact science. Unfortunately, it often depends on the history of pleadings in a particular jurisdiction, that is, the case law on adequate pleading and the rules of civil procedure for the pertinent court. Therefore, regardless of the specific points to be covered here, it is absolutely essential that you become familiar with what is acceptable in the court in which the action will be filed. This can be done by reviewing copies of successful pleadings previously filed in that court, but preferably by researching the applicable rules of procedure and the case law applicable to that particular court. Regardless of the differences among jurisdictions, there are some factors that are applicable to most complaints.

Think of the claim as a syllogism.[2] A syllogism is a logical formula for an argument based on three parts: a major premise, a minor premise, and a

Where can you find local standards for pleadings?

conclusion. The claim or cause of action is essentially a syllogism. The major premise is the rule of law. It is stated like this: if A, B, and C exist, then the plaintiff is entitled to relief X. The minor premise consists of the facts to support the rule of law: that A, B, and C exist. Then the conclusion is: since A, B, and C exist, the plaintiff is entitled to X. Let us look at this from the perspective of a negligence case.

The rule of law or major premise in a negligence case would develop this way: if (A) there is a duty to the plaintiff, (B) a breach of that duty occurred, (C) injury or damage to the plaintiff resulted, and (D) the breach of duty was the substantial cause of injury, the plaintiff is entitled to compensation for the resulting damages.

In order to have in mind the major premise underlying a successful complaint, *you must know the applicable rule of law for the claim and each element of that rule of law* (duty, breach, injury, etc.). Chapter 3 discussed how you can research the elements of the rule of law in jury instruction books, legal encyclopedias, and the particular statute involved.

The minor premise in the syllogism is A, B, and C exist. In terms of a negligence action, it is stated: (A) the defendant was operating a motor vehicle on the highway and had a duty to drive safely; (B) the defendant drove negligently by speeding, failing to keep proper lookout, and failing to keep his vehicle under control; (C) the plaintiff suffered several broken bones, internal injuries, and considerable pain; and (D) the plaintiff's injuries were substantially caused by the defendant's breach of duty (allowing his vehicle to strike her). In brief, these are the facts that support the allegation that A, B, C, and D exist. In other words, *you must state facts to satisfy each element of the rule of law.* These facts must be alleged in the body of the complaint, for if the alleged facts can be proven to exist through evidence presented by the plaintiff at trial, then the minor premise is established, bringing the syllogism to its conclusion (the designated relief to the plaintiff). Should the drafter carelessly omit facts needed to support one of the required elements of the rule of law, the syllogism is incomplete, and the complaint is defective and subject to dismissal.

Keep in mind that the major premise—the rule of law and each of its elements—is not stated in the body of the complaint. Its function is to determine what facts must be alleged in the complaint and what remedy is available. The complaint drafted with an understanding of these logical and necessary relationships will be a superior complaint.

Guidelines and Techniques for Drafting the Body of the Complaint

In addition to thinking through the legal syllogism, there are several other guidelines and techniques that you should have in mind before drafting the body of the complaint.

■ Be clear and concise. Get to the point quickly, state it simply, and eliminate all unnecessary words and phrases. Avoid archaic, redundant, and obscure legalese. Do not get caught in the trap of perpetuating the obscure language found on many legal forms and documents. Judges, juries, and others will read the complaint or hear it being read. If it is unnecessarily wordy or obscure, it will waste time and be a source of irritation for those persons you want on your client's side.
■ Which of the following would you rather read?

Complaint. Example 1

Comes now the above named plaintiff, by his attorney, Albert Grey, for his complaint, respectfully shows to the court and alleges as follows:

At all times hereinafter mentioned, Plaintiff was and still is a resident of Legalville, Columbia, residing at 201 Short Street.

Complaint. Example 2

Plaintiff resides and has resided in the City of Legalville in the County of Capitol in the State of Columbia.

Several good books on plain English and effective legal writing are: Wydick's *Plain English for Lawyers* (1979), Good's *Mightier Than the Sword* (1984), Mellinkoff's *The Language of the Law* (1963), Goldfarb and Raymond's *Clear Understandings* (1983), and Hurd's *Writing for Lawyers* (1984).

- Use brief, numbered paragraphs. Short paragraphs are best for the sake of clarity, and the numbers provide easy reference. Avoid complex, run-on paragraphs by limiting each paragraph to a single idea.
- Be an advocate when drafting. Strive for language that is assertive, persuasive, evokes sympathy for the client, and conveys a confident attitude toward the claim. "The Plaintiff was hit by the van" is colorless and evokes little emotion. "The Plaintiff was struck down by the van" would be a more assertive statement. On the other hand, do not overdo it. You do not want to sound phony or theatrical.
- Avoid impertinent, scandalous, or immaterial language. A complaint is not to be used for harassment or any other improper purpose (Rule 11). If language is improper, it subjects the complaint to attack and the inappropriate language will be stricken [Rule 12(f)]. Furthermore, the use of such language makes suspect the motive of the plaintiff and the judgment of the law firm.
- Organize the paragraphs of the complaint so that they flow logically. A complaint should tell an interesting, chronological story. One paragraph should lead into the next. This not only makes the complaint read more smoothly but also enhances clarity and effectiveness.
- Reveal no more of the facts than necessary. Your client gains no advantage by having the complaint reveal too much. To do so may simply show weaknesses or contradictions in the case, or even suggest defenses to the opposition.
- Do not state evidence or conclusions. It is not the purpose of the complaint to prove the case. Allegations such as "The Defendant had 300 feet in which to avoid the accident, according to skid marks, but did not apply his brake until only 100 feet were left" do not belong. A conclusion such as "Defendant breached his duty of care" is excluded because it serves no useful function other than possibly to prejudice a jury. Some conclusions such as "Defendant negligently operated the vehicle" have been accepted as useful to a general understanding of the specific cause of action. Regardless, including evidence or conclusions will make the body of the complaint intolerably long-winded as well as subject to attack. Stick to alleging the facts.
- Be truthful. Keep in mind at all times when drafting pleadings that the supervising lawyer is under a serious ethical responsibility of truthfulness and can be severely disciplined for pleadings that reflect a disre-

gard for the truth. Model Rule 3.3(a)(1) of the American Bar Association's Model Rules of Professional Conduct, which has been adopted by most states, requires truthfulness in pleadings.

■ When the truth of the matter is uncertain but there is some basis for a statement, make the statement on the basis of information and belief. For example: "On information and belief, Defendant Hart was an employee of the Mercury Parcel Service at the time of the accident."

■ Do not anticipate defenses. When the facts of a case may raise defensive issues, such as contributory negligence, payment of the debt, or self-defense, the complaint should not include any direct attempt to address those concerns. An allegation that "Plaintiff did not fail to keep a lookout prior to crossing the street" or "Plaintiff was exercising due care for her safety at all times prior to the accident" are subjects to be raised by the defendant and not the plaintiff.

■ When there is uncertainty or alternative parties or causes, that uncertainty is permissible in the complaint. Suppose a piece of rodent was found in some corn served to a customer at a restaurant. The culprit could be the packager of the corn or the server of the corn. An acceptable allegation in the complaint would be: "Defendant City Cafe or Defendant Green Grower Canning Company negligently or willfully allowed animal remains to be mixed with corn served to the Plaintiff at said cafe, causing Plaintiff to become violently ill."

■ Do not state the law. It is not the function of the complaint to serve as a vehicle to argue the law or to cite cases in support of the client's case. The law, however, should appear in the complaint in the following instances: if the action is brought pursuant to the specific provisions of a particular statute, administrative rule, or ordinance; and if the action is brought in one state and the plaintiff is relying on the law of another state.

■ It is better to state the various types of damages incurred by the plaintiff in one concise paragraph as opposed to several wordy paragraphs when permitted by the rules of the particular jurisdiction.

> As a consequence of Defendant's negligence and the aforesaid resulting injuries, the Plaintiff has incurred, and will incur, substantial monetary losses for hospital and medical care, loss of income and benefits, and property damage.

The law in some jurisdictions, however, requires that each type of damage be stated separately and in detail, including the specific part of the body that was injured. The rules on damages do differ and need to be consulted. One must be careful as well to allege damages in an amount sufficient to meet any jurisdictional amount.

■ State separate claims or theories for claims in separate counts: Count One for negligence, Count Two for breach of warranty, and Count Three for battery. Each count will have its own separate body of allegations, damages, and demand for judgment. Information alleged in the introductory paragraphs or that would be repeated from Count One, may be incorporated in the other counts. For example:

COUNT THREE

> Plaintiff hereby incorporates by reference the allegations contained in paragraphs 1 through 7 of Count One.

Fact (Code) Pleading

Columbia, as is true of a number of other states, requires **fact pleading.** The body of the complaint must state the ultimate facts (the minor premise) in support of each element of the rule of law or claim (the major premise). In other words, there must be sufficient detail alleged to tell the defendant the basis of the complaint. The difficulty in this type of complaint is knowing what is enough without unnecessarily revealing too much. The answer to this dilemma lies in the experience, rules, cases, and statutes of the particular jurisdiction in which the claim will be filed. An example of an adequately alleged claim for Columbia follows. The labels on the left side of the page indicate the elements and other requirements of the complaint that are met by that particular paragraph.

SAMPLE BODY OF A NEGLIGENCE COMPLAINT FOR A FACT PLEADING STATE

date/time
duty/conditions

venue

connection
to other
defendants

4. On February 26, 19—, at approximately 7:30 A.M., Defendant Hart was operating a motor vehicle on a hilly and partially icy section of Highway 328 about three miles west of the City of Legalville, County of Capitol, in the State of Columbia. Defendant Hart was driving a vehicle owned by Defendant Mercury Parcel Service for whom Hart is an employee and for whom he was working at all times in the course and scope of his employment.

breach of
duty

alternative
theories

5. Defendant Hart operated his vehicle in a negligent manner and without regard for Plaintiff by:
   (a) operating the vehicle at an excessive rate of speed under the circumstances;
   (b) failing to exercise a proper lookout and attentiveness;
   (c) failing to exercise adequate control of said vehicle; and
   (d) otherwise failing to exercise due and adequate care under the circumstances.

substantial
cause of
injury

6. As a direct consequence of Defendants' negligence, Plaintiff was struck down and seriously injured by Defendants' vehicle as she was walking south across Highway 328.

injuries

7. As a result of said negligence, Plaintiff suffered fractures of the left leg and hip; damage to the lower spine; torn muscles, tendons, tissue, and nerves; insomnia; inability to walk; confinement to a wheelchair; intense depression; and other maladies; all of which, now and in the future, will cause her intense pain, great suffering, and considerable inconvenience.

damages

8. As a consequence of Defendants' negligence and the aforesaid injuries, the Plaintiff has incurred and will incur the loss of considerable sums of money for hospital and medical care, loss of income and benefits, property damage, and domestic expenses.

[Compare to the traditional allegation of damages in paragraphs 8–10.]

ALTERNATIVE

medical expenses (damages)	**8.** As a further consequence of the injuries, Plaintiff has been and will continue to be obligated to pay large sums of money for medical and hospital bills.
other damages	**9.** As a result of these injuries, Plaintiff has and will continue to be unable to fulfill her daily duties and will be unable to do so for an indefinite time, to her loss.
other damages— loss of income	**10.** As a further consequence of Defendants' negligence, Plaintiff has been unable to pursue her regular or any other employment and will be unable to do so for an indefinite period of time causing her considerable loss of income and benefits.

Notice Pleading

The Federal Rules of Civil Procedure, which have been adopted by many state jurisdictions, require a briefer form of pleading called **notice pleading.** One purpose of notice pleading is to eliminate some of the uncertainty and resulting litigation concerning what factual allegations are sufficient. Notice pleading simply informs the defendant of the claim and the general basis for the claim (notice). Rule 8(a) of the Federal Rules of Civil Procedure states that the body of the complaint must contain "a short and plain statement of the claim showing that the pleader is entitled to relief." Rule 8(c)(1) states: "Each averment of a pleading shall be simple, concise, and direct. No technical forms of pleadings or motions are required." More specialized rules of pleading are found in Rules 8, 9, and 10. Form 9 in the Federal Rules sets out the necessary allegations. The following is based on Form 9.

SAMPLE BODY OF NEGLIGENCE COMPLAINT FOR FEDERAL OR OTHER NOTICE PLEADING JURISDICTION

2. On Feburary 26, 19__, on Highway 328 in Capitol County, Columbia, Defendant negligently drove a motor vehicle striking down Plaintiff who was then crossing said highway.

3. As a result, Plaintiff fractured her left leg and hip bones and was otherwise seriously injured. She has been prevented from transacting her business, and has suffered and will continue to suffer great physical and emotional pain. In addition, she has incurred and will continue to incur expenses for medical attention and hospitalization in the sum of $750,000.

Note: Despite the brevity of the body of the complaint, there are effective allegations on each essential element of the syllogism.

Remedies and the Prayer for Relief (Demand for Judgment)

The complaint should contain a prayer for relief (demand for judgment), which is commonly referred to as the "wherefore" clause. This clause demands that judgment be entered for the plaintiff and that relief be granted accordingly.

Some of the typical remedies that the plaintiff may demand are damages, recovery of property, injunctions, and specific performance.

1. Damages are sums of money awarded to compensate the plaintiff for a variety of injuries and losses. **General damages** are those damages that are a natural and direct result of the defendant's wrong and the resulting injury, for example: pain and suffering or emotional trauma. General damages do not have to be pleaded in the complaint in order to prove them at trial.

   Special damages are damages that are incurred but do not necessarily follow from the defendant's wrong. For example, pain is the natural and direct consequence of being struck (general damage), but one does not necessarily incur hospital bills for being struck, so the hospital bill would be a special damage. It is the result of the injury but not necessarily the natural result. Other special damages could be doctors' fees, loss of income, loss of profits in a contract situation, and property damage. Special damages must be specifically alleged in most jurisdictions, including the federal courts.

   Exemplary damages or *punitive damages* are damages awarded to the plaintiff when the defendant's conduct is particularly aggravated, malicious, or reckless. Such damages are designed to punish the wrongdoer and to deter similar conduct. The award is in addition to all other damages.

2. Recovery of property is a remedy available to a plaintiff when property has been wrongfully taken, transferred, sold, or otherwise kept from its rightful owner. In such cases, the property may be seized (attached) by the court and returned to the rightful owner. The eviction of a tenant is an example of a recovery of property remedy.

3. Injunctions are remedies designed to prevent future harm and, in some cases, correct past harm. There are **prohibitory injunctions** that order the defendant to refrain from a specific course of conduct and **mandatory injunctions** that require the defendant to continue or take some course of conduct. For example, an ornate fence divides the property of two new residents of a subdivision. Neighbor A wants the fence torn down, claiming it to be his fence. Neighbor B loves the fence and wants it to remain. Owner B can get an injunction against A ordering A not to tear the fence down until it can be determined who owns it.

4. Specific performance is a remedy unique to contract law. Instead of granting damages when a breach of contract occurs, the court can require the offending party to live up to the specific terms of the contract. If one party agrees to sell an original painting and then reneges,

damages are of little value to the party who wanted the painting. In this case, the court may require the seller to surrender the painting called for by the contract.

Rule 8(a) of the Federal Rules of Civil Procedure requires a demand (wherefore) clause. Should a complaint contain more than one claim or count, each count needs to have a separate "wherefore" clause. The plaintiff is not bound by the relief requested if it is inappropriate or inaccurate as revealed later in trial. The court, however, may not grant the plaintiff more than that requested in the complaint if the defendant defaults (fails to oppose the action) according to Rule 54(c). A sample of a typical prayer for relief follows.

SAMPLE PRAYER FOR RELIEF (DEMAND)

WHEREFORE plaintiff demands judgment against defendant in the sum of seven hundred and fifty thousand dollars ($750,000), together with the costs and disbursements of this action.

A Brief Guide to Causes of Action and Remedies

Knowing what elements to allege and what remedies to claim is essential to drafting complaints. Here is a brief guide to the common causes of action and their respective remedies.[3]

Breach of Contract

In any type of contract action, the existence of the contract and the type of contract must be proven. The law recognizes three types of contracts:

1. Oral contracts

In the complaint, the plaintiff must allege the terms of the contract including the consideration for the contract.

2. Written contracts

The plaintiff must allege the terms of the contract or attach a copy of the contract to the complaint as an exhibit.

3. Implied contracts

An implied contract may exist when, despite no formal agreement, the actions of the parties cause the court to find that a contract exists. For example, a person operating a restaurant may be found by the court to have an implied contract to provide the public with healthy, wholesome food. If the patrons in the establishment are suddenly struck with hepatitis, a suit for breach of this implied contract may result.

In a suit of breach of implied contract, the following facts must be alleged in the complaint:

—The performance by the plaintiff of the contract terms or the excuse for his non-performance;

—The facts which caused the defendant to fail to fulfill his part of the contract; and

—The damages suffered by the plaintiff as the result of the defendant's non-performance.

Remedies available

■ General damages

Compensation for the injuries suffered by the plaintiff directly stemming from the defendant's breach.

■ Special damages

Compensation for the "out-of-pocket" expenses suffered by the plaintiff due to the breach, such as loss of earnings, medical expenses, and injury to property.

■ Attorney's fees

Attorney's fees are available in any contractual action if called for under the terms of the contract.

■ Costs of suit

Costs of suit are available in any action at the discretion of the court.

■ Liquidated damages

Some contracts include in their terms a "liquidated damages" provision, spelling out specific sums payable by a party upon breach of the contract. These provisions may have an effect on the damages awarded to the plaintiff.

■ Exemplary damages

Recently, some state courts have recognized and approved the award of exemplary or punitive damages in a breach of contract case, if the breach is found by the court to have been "willful or malicious." Exemplary damages are awarded by the court to punish the defendant because of the particularly reprehensible nature of his actions.

■ Pre-judgment interest

Some contracts have provisions for the payment of interest by the defendant on any sums which are to be found due and owing to the plaintiff.

Anticipatory Breach of Contract

If one party to a contract unilaterally repudiates the contract before the time of performance, the injured party may either:

■ Wait until the time for performance of the contract, and bring suit for breach of contract; or
■ Bring immediate suit for anticipatory breach of contract.

The defendant's repudiation of the contract may take one of two forms: 1) Expressed; when defendant's repudiation is clear, positive, and unequivocal; or 2) Implied; when the actions of the defendant make performance of the contract impossible.

An example of this cause of action would be a farmer who contracts with a laborer to plow his field on a given date. Prior to the date of the plowing, the laborer communicates to the farmer that he will not plow the field (expressed anticipatory breach), or the farmer learns that the laborer will be out-of-town on the date set for the plowing (implied anticipatory breach). In either of the above instances, the farmer will have a cause of action for anticipatory breach of contract.

In bringing suit for anticipatory breach of contract, all the following elements must be pled:

■ Existence of a contract;
■ The actions of the defendants which caused the anticipatory breach;
■ That these actions happened before the time of performance of the contract;
■ That the plaintiff has performed his duties under the contract; and
■ That plaintiff has been injured by the actions of the defendant.

Remedies available

The following remedies are available in an action for anticipatory breach of contract:

■ Compensatory damages

The measure of the compensatory damages is the amount that will fully compensate the plaintiff for the damages caused by the breach, or that will result from the breach in the ordinary course of events.

■ Future damages

The plaintiff is entitled to any damages that he may foresee as the result of the breach, but only at their present value.

■ Limitation on damages

The damages awarded for anticipatory relief are limited to "reasonable damages." No punitive or exemplary damages may be awarded, nor can the plaintiff receive a greater amount than he would if the contract had been performed.

Specific Performance

The remedy for a cause of action for specific performance is a court order that the contract in question be performed exactly as it was written and negotiated. This remedy is not available for the following types of contracts:

■ Personal service contracts;
■ Contracts to employ another;
■ Contracts for acts which the party charged with performing the act has no legal power to do at the time of the contract. An example of this bar would be a contract to sell a piece of property before the selling party had in fact purchased it; and
■ Agreements to obtain the consent of a third party.

The elements making up the specific performance cause of action are:

■ Existence of the contract;

As well as containing the elements listed in [Breach of Contract], the complaint must also state that performance of the contract was possible for both parties.

■ That the plaintiff has performed his duties under the contract;
■ That the defendant has failed to perform his duties under the contract; and
■ That the plaintiff has an inadequate remedy at law. This means that an award of money will not compensate the plaintiff for the damages he has suffered. It is this element that separates a cause of action for specific performance from a cause of action for breach of contract.

Remedies available

The following remedies are available in an action for specific performance:

■ In general

—An order for performance of the contract;
—An adjustment for the losses suffered by the parties because of the delay in performance;

■ In actions involving real property:

—Rents and profits which would have accrued to the plaintiff had he obtained the property under the contract;
—The buyer of real property may be awarded interest on any money deposited in escrow;
—The seller of real property may be awarded interest on any money he would have received had the property been bought; and
—The seller may recover the upkeep expenses of the property, such as taxes and insurance costs.

■ Injunctive relief

Injunctive relief is an order by the court that an action be done or to prevent someone from performing a specified action.

Contractual Reformation

Contractual reformation is a request to the court to change the terms of a contract because of an error made by the parties. The elements to prove this cause of action are:

■ Existence of the contract;
■ The mistake which arose between the parties; and
■ The grounds for the reformation which include:

—Mutual mistake of fact; or
—Fraud, which occurs when one party falsely represents that modifications will be made to the written agreement conforming with the original agreement between the parties.

Remedies available

The sole remedy for a cause of action for contractual reformation is correction of the error made in the contract.

Rescission

This action calls upon the court to cancel a contract on any of the following grounds:

■ the agreement was made under a mistake of fact or law;
■ that the party requesting the rescission was mentally incompetent;
■ that there was a material breach of the contract;
■ that all parties to the contract agreed to the rescission;
■ that the agreement was induced by fraud, duress, menace or undue influence; or
■ that the contract was unlawful or against the public interest.

The elements which must be pled in the complaint are:

- existence of a contract;
- the grounds for the rescission as listed above; and
- that the plaintiff suffered a material injury.

Remedies available

The following remedies are available in an action for rescission:

- Implied damages

    This remedy includes the repayment of any contractual consideration provided by the plaintiff and all incidental damages that may have been suffered as the result of the contract.

- Attorney's fees

    In a rescission action, the court may award attorney's fees, even if not called for in the contract.

- Exemplary damages

    These may be awarded if it is found that the defendant fraudulently induced plaintiff to enter into the contract.

Quantum Meruit

This cause of action arises when the defendant fails to pay for goods or services supplied by the plaintiff at the request of the defendant. The elements necessary to plead this cause of action are:

- The defendant requested plaintiff's performance;
- The plaintiff performed the services requested:
- The services rendered by the plaintiff had a fair and reasonable value; and
- The defendant(s) failed to pay for the goods or services rendered.

Remedies available

The following remedies are available in an action for quantum meruit:

- Damages equal to the value of the goods and services rendered:
- Special damages, which include the costs incurred by plaintiff in attempting to enforce the contract;
- Attorney's fees;
- Costs of suit; and
- Liquidated damages, if called for in the contract.

Negligent Torts Causes of Action

The types of torts in this classification include the following:

- personal injury
- wrongful death
- attorney malpractice
- medical malpractice
- infliction of emotional trauma; and
- wrongful termination.

In any negligent tort, the following elements must be pled:

■ The existence of a duty owed by the defendant to the plaintiff

There is no hard and fast rule for determining the existence of a duty. The general rule is the question: how would a "reasonable" person have acted in the role of the defendant? If this reasonable person would have performed differently than the defendant and would have taken steps to prevent or lessen the injury suffered by the plaintiff, then a duty exists for the defendant to act in the same manner.

■ Breach of the duty
■ Plaintiff suffered an injury caused by defendant's breach of duty.

Remedies Available in a Negligent Tort Action

In any negligent tort action, the plaintiff may recover the following:

■ Compensatory damages

The plaintiff may recover damages for the detriment he suffered as a result of the defendant's negligent conduct.

■ Lost earnings

Plaintiff may recover any wages he has lost because of the defendant's negligent conduct. The amount of lost earnings to be awarded to the plaintiff is based upon the plaintiff's possible future earnings, not past income.

■ Lost profits

This remedy is available when it can be proven that the plaintiff had a reasonable expectation of earning profits based upon his prior earnings.

■ Injury to personal property

The plaintiff can be awarded damages based upon the damage and the loss of use of personal property.

■ Personal injuries

The plaintiff can recover damages to compensate him for the injuries incurred because of defendant's negligent actions and any injuries the plaintiff can reasonably expect to incur in the future.

■ Pain and suffering

Plaintiff can recover for past pain and suffering, and if his injury is permanent, for the pain and suffering expected to occur in the future.

■ Emotional distress

Recoverable by the plaintiff in most states only if he has suffered a physical injury.

■ Loss of consortium

Recoverable by spouse of the plaintiff for loss of the love and affection of a spouse.

■ Exemplary damages

Exemplary or punitive damages are available where it can be shown that the defendant acted with malice or criminal indifference.

Relief Available in a Wrongful Death Action

The damages available in wrongful death actions differ from those available in other negligent torts as follows:

■ General damages

In most states, the monetary damages awarded in a wrongful death action are based upon a formula which takes into account the future monetary contributions and the value of any personal service, training, or advice that may have been given by the decedent to his heirs.

■ Spousal damages

A surviving spouse may recover for the loss of the decedent's love and affection and the value of future earnings.

■ Parental damages

The parents of a deceased child may recover for loss of the child's comfort and society. The parent's future costs for the child's support and education may be discounted in the award.

■ Emotional and mental distress

Damages for these factors are available when death is not instantaneous.

■ Exemplary damages

The laws of most states disallow the awarding of exemplary damages in a wrongful death action.

■ Funeral expenses

The decedent's survivors are entitled to the reasonable cost of all funeral expenses.

■ Damages otherwise available to the decedent

The administrator of the decedent's estate is permitted to maintain any action on behalf of the decedent that would have accrued had the decedent survived, such as an action for damage to personal property. Such actions are usually joined in the wrongful death complaint.

Other Torts

Aside from the negligence torts, there is also a class of tort which relates to the conduct of business and business relationships.

Unfair Competition

To bring an action for unfair competition, the following facts must be pled in the complaint:

■ The plaintiff must be engaged in a business affected by the interference of the defendant;
■ The defendant must have engaged in improper conduct, an unlawful, unfair, or fraudulent business practice or have been engaged in unfair, untrue, or misleading advertising; and
■ Defendant's conduct must have resulted in injury to the plaintiff.

Remedies available

The following remedies are available in unfair competition actions:

■ Injunctive relief

Injunctive relief is available to the plaintiff where the court finds that general damages will not fully compensate the plaintiff.

■ Restoration of property

The court may order the defendant to provide an accounting of the monies or property earned by the defendant from the unfair competition and that any such monies be paid to the plaintiff.

■ Exemplary damages

These damages are awarded if the court finds the defendant's actions to have been malicious.

Inducing Breach of Contract

To bring an action for inducing breach of contract, the following conditions must be pled:

■ The existence of valid contract between the plaintiff and a third party;
■ Knowledge of the existence of the third party contract by defendant;
■ Defendant's intention to cause the breach of the third-party contract;
■ Breach of the contract by the third party;
■ That the defendant was the cause of the breach of contract; and
■ Injury to the plaintiff resulted.

Remedies available

The following remedies are available in an action for inducement of breach of contract:

■ Injunctive relief
■ General damages;
■ Special damages, including any damage to plaintiff's good will; and
■ Exemplary damages on the showing of maliciousness by the defendant.

Tortious Interference with Prospective Economic Advantage

To bring an action for tortious interference with prospective economic advantage the following facts must be pled in the complaint:

■ Existence of relationship between the plaintiff and a third party

This relationship must contain the possibility of an economic or monetary benefit accruing to the plaintiff.

■ Knowledge of this relationship by the defendant

This includes relationships of which the defendant has direct knowledge and those that the defendant *should have reasonably known to have existed.* For example, if there are only two manufacturers of a certain type of widget, the defendant can reasonably be expected to know that any third party using these widgets obtained them from one of the two sources.

- The defendant's intent to interfere with the economic relationship;
- Disruption of the relationship; and
- Injury to the plaintiff caused by the disruption.

Remedies available

The following remedies are available in an action for tortious interference with prospective economic advantage;

- Injunctive relief;
- General damages;
- Special damages, including any damage to plaintiff's good will (good will is defined as the manner in which a business is perceived by the public); and
- Exemplary damages on the showing of maliciousness by the defendant.

Misappropriation of Trade Secrets

To bring an action for misappropriation of trade secrets, the following facts must be pled in the complaint:

- Existence of a trade secret

An exact definition of a trade secret is not possible. However, it must be a scientific or technical process which gives the possessor a unique advantage over a competitor. It has also been held that certain elements of the retail trade, such as customer lists, constitute trade secrets.

- Defendant must owe a duty not to disclose the information;
- Disclosure of the secret by the defendant;
- Damage suffered by the plaintiff by the disclosure.

Remedies available

- Injunctive relief;
- Compensatory damages including the loss of value to plaintiff's business suffered because of defendant's disclosure; and
- An accounting of all profits earned by the defendants because of the misappropriation.

Separate Counts

Rule 18 of the Federal Rules of Civil Procedure states that "[a] party asserting a claim to relief . . . may join . . . as many claims . . . as he has against an opposing party." Rule 8(e)(2) also permits claims to be set out in separate statements or counts.

It is not uncommon for a single occurrence to result in several claims for relief. In the rodent-in-the-corn example mentioned earlier, the victim had at least two claims against each of the defendants. One claim was for willful or negligent conduct stated in the alternative. The other was for a breach of warranty that the food was edible and safe. The negligence claim could be alleged as Count One and the breach of warranty claim as Count Two. It is also possible, as in our contract case (Case IV, in which the doll clothing company was unable to fulfill its obligation to the dollmaker), that instead of one contract there could be several contracts, each with a specific delivery date: May 15, July 15, September 15, and October 15. Each of these contracts could be joined in one complaint and alleged in four individual counts. Another possibility exists in the *Forrester* case. If Ann's husband had been joined as one of the parties, the complaint could also allege that William Forrester has suffered and will continue to suffer the loss of consortium (marital affection) of his wife due to the negligence of the defendant. The form of the second count is demonstrated next.

SAMPLE SEPARATE COUNT

COUNT TWO

1. Plaintiffs hereby incorporate by reference paragraphs 1 through 6 of Count One.
2. Because of Defendants' negligence, Plaintiff William Forrester has suffered loss of the consortium of his wife, Ann Forrester, in the amount of twenty thousand dollars ($20,000).

WHEREFORE, Plaintiff William Forrester demands judgment against Defendant in the sum of twenty thousand dollars ($20,000) and costs and for such other relief as this court may deem just and proper.

Note: Each separate count should have a separate "wherefore" clause.

Demand for Jury Trial

Rule 38(b) of the Federal Rules indicates that a demand for a jury may be placed in the complaint. This is advisable in both federal and state courts. Verify with the attorney the desirability of making a demand for a jury trial before including it in the complaint. The demand can be made later (ten days after service of the last pleading), but by putting the demand in the complaint, a strategic and embarrassing oversight can be avoided. The demand should be in a conspicuous place, such as in the lower right corner of the caption or at the end of the "wherefore" clause above the attorney's signature, as shown in the next sample.

SAMPLE SUBSCRIPTION AND DEMAND FOR JURY TRIAL

Plaintiff demands trial by jury.
October, 19___

Arthur White
White, Wilson & McDuff
Attorneys at Law
Federal Plaza Building
Suite 700
Third and Market Streets
Legalville, Columbia 00000
(111) 555-0000

Subscription

The complaint must be signed by the attorney for the plaintiff. In federal pleadings (Rule 16), the address of the signer should be included. Some jurisdictions require the phone number. The signature certifies that the attorney has read the pleading; that it is well grounded in fact based on knowledge, information, and belief; that it is warranted by existing law or a good-faith argument to change the law; and that it is not brought to harass or cause delay, or for any other improper purpose.

Verification

The certification method used in the federal system and many states makes verification unnecessary in those jurisdictions. Where verification is required, it consists of a brief affidavit sworn to by the party stating that the party has read the pleading and it is true except for statements made on information and belief. The purpose of the verification is to deter the filing of false claims by imposing the threat of criminal prosecution for false swearing.

The filing of a pleading, especially a complaint, is a serious matter that can have a serious impact on the lives of others. When the pleading is sworn to and signed by the client, special care should be given to see that the client reads it carefully; is given the opportunity to ask questions; is asked to raise the right hand and repeat the oath; and is asked to sign the pleading. Above all, if you act as notary, you must witness the client's signature to affirm that the oath was sworn and signed in your presence.

SAMPLE PLEADING VERIFICATION

State of Columbia
County of Capitol

Ann Forrester, being first duly sworn on oath according to law, deposes and says that she has read the foregoing complaint and that the matters stated therein are true to the best of her knowledge, information, and belief.

_____
Ann Forrester

Subscribed and sworn to before me this 1st day of October, 19___

_____
Notary Public

My commission expires January 1, 19 ___.

■ Exhibits and Appendices

There are times when it is helpful to attach exhibits or an appendix to the complaint. It is required in some jurisdictions, most commonly in contract cases where the contract or a copy of the contract is included. Exhibits will normally include contracts, promissory notes, bills of lading, correspondence, and other documents at issue. An appendix will often be used to further explain technical language used in the documents. Exhibits and appendices can be helpful to the parties, but especially to the judge and jury.

Exhibits or appendices are attached following the verification or certification, and essentially become a part of the complaint. The drafter includes references to the attachments in the body of the complaint, as shown in the following example.

> 6. That the Defendant prepared a contract that was entered into with the Plaintiff on June 15, 19___, a copy of which is attached and marked "Exhibit A," and incorporated into this complaint.

The exhibits and appendix could appear as follows (first page after verification or certification):

Agreement between Plaintiff and Defendant.

EXHIBIT A

[here insert language of contract]

APPENDIX A

[here insert explanatory note or term defined]

"Extra Ordinary Whole Life 13" refers to a special insurance policy that . . . ."

When all aspects of the complaint are ready, they should be placed in their proper order and bound together. The paralegal sees to it that copies are prepared by the legal secretary.

■ System Checklist for Drafting a Complaint

If the complaint is to be filed in state court, consult state rules for differences from the federal rules.

Preparation

☐ Review the file for the names and addresses of the parties, the type of claim, and so on.
☐ Ask in what court the action should be filed.
☐ Research the existence of venue, subject matter jurisdiction, and personal jurisdiction if requested.
☐ Research the necessary elements for each cause of action to be alleged.
☐ Formulate those elements into a legal syllogism to form the body of each count of the complaint. (If A, B, and C exist, then plaintiff is entitled to X.)
☐ Identify the facts needed to support each element of the syllogism.
☐ Identify the appropriate remedies.
☐ Consult with the supervising attorney to confirm all of the above.
☐ Make corrections as the attorney indicates, and do further research or investigation as needed.

☐ Check your system folder for appropriate samples of both federal and state complaints or sections thereof.

☐ Obtain one good copy of a recent complaint for the type of claim or claims to be alleged and for the specific court in which the action is to be filed.

☐ Check court rules for size of paper, backing sheets, color, and any other requirements.

Drafting

☐ Draft the caption.
    ☐ Indicate the court (branch if several branches) and its location.
    ☐ Indicate the parties, the joinder thereof; check spelling and the addresses if included; capacity, real party in interest, and so on. Federal Rule 17(a)(b)(c), 19(1), 20(1); State rule _____; system folder page _____.
    ☐ Indicate the docket or court file number of the action if available, or leave an appropriate space.
    ☐ Indicate the type of complaint (negligence, breach of contract, etc.).
    ☐ Include the references to federal and state rules and forms on drafting. Federal Rule 10(a), Form 1; State Rule _____, Form ; system folder page _____.
    ☐ Include a demand for jury trial if so instructed.

☐ Draft simple, concise, and direct statements. Avoid repetition.

☐ Use double spacing; quoted matter should be single spaced.

☐ Draft the jurisdictional allegation, if required, including any monetary amount. Federal Rule 8(a)(1), Form 2; State Rule _____; system folder page _____.

☐ Make sure all allegations regarding venue, if required, are included (not necessary in the federal system): location of incident and addresses of parties. State Rule _____; system folder page _____.

☐ Draft the body of the complaint.
    ☐ Include facts to support each element of the claim.
    ☐ Use brief, numbered paragraphs limited to one idea. Federal Rule 10(b); State Rule _____; system folder page _____.
    ☐ Add just enough detail to meet the minimum requirement for fact pleading or for notice pleading, depending on applicable rules. Federal Rule 8(a)(2), 8(e)(1), Forms 3-17; State Rule _____; system folder page _____.
    ☐ Do not state evidence or conclusions.
    ☐ Avoid impertinent, scandalous, or immaterial language. Federal Rule 11, 12(f); State Rule _____.
    ☐ Be truthful; make sure there are provable facts to support a good-faith allegation. Model Rule 3.3(a)(1).
    ☐ State those allegations that are uncertain but have some basis on information and belief.
    ☐ Do not anticipate defenses.
    ☐ Plead hypothetically, in the alternative, and state uncertainty when necessary. Federal Rule 8(e)(2); State Rule _____; system folder page _____.

- [ ] Do not plead the law, except (1) when the action is under a specific statute or administrative rule, or (2) when the action is in one state but relies on the law of another state.
- [ ] List various damages in one paragraph, unless local rules or practice dictates otherwise.
- [ ] Check to see that all separate claims are alleged and all separate counts included. Federal Rule 8(e)(2), 18; State Rule _____; system folder page _____.
- [ ] Check to see that paragraphs flow logically and tell an interesting and easy-to-read story.
- [ ] Choose assertive, persuasive words to evoke sympathy and convey confidence.
- [ ] Check that all incorporations by reference (including exhibits and appendices) have been accurately stated where needed.
- [ ] Draft in special matters as they arise.
  - [ ] Aver the capacity of the parties unless not required by local rules. It is not required in the federal system [Rule 9(a)].
  - [ ] Aver the circumstances supporting the allegation of fraud or mistake with particularity [Rule 9(b)].
  - [ ] Aver malice, intent, knowledge, or other condition of the mind generally [Rule 9(b)].
  - [ ] Aver the performance of all conditions precedent generally [Rule 9(c)]; aver the denial of performance with particularity.
  - [ ] Aver that an official document was issued or act done in compliance with the law [Rule 9(d)].
  - [ ] Aver a judgment or decision of domestic or foreign court, administrative tribunal, or of a board of officers without alleging facts showing jurisdiction to render it.
  - [ ] Aver time and place [Rule 9(f)].
  - [ ] Aver specifically any special damages [Rule 9(g)].
- [ ] Draft the prayer for relief (demand for judgment).
  - [ ] State relief in the alternative when necessary. Federal Rule 8(a)(3); State Rule _____; system folder page _____.
    - [ ] damages   [ ] recovery of property
    - [ ] injuries   [ ] specific performance   [ ] other
- [ ] Draft the subscription and see to it that the attorney's address and phone number are included. Federal Rule 11; State Rule _____; system folder page _____.
- [ ] Draft verification if required (not required in federal pleadings). Federal Rule 11; State Rule _____; system folder page _____.
- [ ] Have the client swear to the truthfulness of the complaint and sign it in your presence if you are a notary.
- [ ] Attach exhibits and appendices.
- [ ] See that the complaint is typed with sufficient copies.

ASSIGNMENT 5:2

Following class discussion on drafting complaints, especially regarding state court rules, copy the System Checklist for Drafting a Complaint, complete the state and system folder reference blanks in the checklist, and place in your system folder.

■ Sample Complaints

Drawing from the checklist and information in the chapter, a fact-pleading complaint in the *Forrester* case appears as follows.

COMPLAINT FOR ANN FORRESTER CASE

STATE OF COLUMBIA   CAPITOL COUNTY   CIRCUIT COURT

ANN FORRESTER and
WILLIAM FORRESTER,
        Plaintiffs
        v.   Civil Action, File No. <u>1000</u>
RICHARD HART and
MERCURY PARCEL SERVICE, INC.,
        Defendants   Plaintiff Demands Trial by Jury.

COMPLAINT FOR NEGLIGENCE

The Plaintiffs make the following allegations:

1. The jurisdiction of this court is based on the amount in controversy in this action which is more than $2,500.
2. Plaintiff Ann Forrester is a teacher and homemaker and resides at 1533 Capitol Drive, Legalville, in Capitol County, Columbia.
3. Plaintiff William Forrester is the husband of Ann Forrester and resides with her.
4. Defendant Richart Hart is a driver employed by Defendant Mercury Parcel Service, Inc., and resides at 1223 Penny Lane, Cincinnati, Ohio.
5. Defendant Mercury Parcel Service, Inc., is incorporated in the state of Delaware with its principal place of business located at 603 Stoker St., Cincinnati, Ohio.
6. On February 26, 19___, at approximately 7:30 A.M., Plaintiff Ann Forrester was walking across a hilly and partially icy section of Highway 328 in the City of Legalville, County of Capitol, in the State of Columbia.
7. At that time, Defendant Hart was driving a van on behalf of his employer and the owner of the van, Defendant Mercury Parcel Service, Inc.
8. Defendant Hart operated the van negligently by:
   (a) driving the vehicle at an excessive rate of speed under the circumstances;
   (b) failing to exercise a proper lookout;
   (c) failing to exercise adequate control of said vehicle; and
   (d) otherwise failing to exercise due and adequate care under the circumstances.
9. As a direct consequence of the Defendants' negligence, the Plaintiff was struck down by the Defendants' van and seriously injured.

10. Because of said negligence, the Plaintiff suffered fractures of the left leg and hip; damage to the lower spine; torn muscles, tendons, tissue, and nerves; insomnia; paralysis that confines her to a wheelchair; depression; and other maladies, causing her intense pain and great suffering and considerable inconvenience which will continue in the future.

11. As a consequence of the Defendants' negligence and the aforesaid injuries, the Plaintiff has incurred and will incur substantial monetary losses for hospital and medical care, loss of income and benefits, domestic services, and property damages to her coat and clothing.

WHEREFORE the Plaintiff demands judgment in the amount of seven hundred and fifty thousand dollars ($750,000), together with the costs and disbursements of this action and for such other relief as this court may deem just and proper.

COUNT TWO

12. The Plaintiffs hereby allege and incorporate by reference paragraphs 1 through 9 of Count One.

13. Because of the Defendants' negligence, Plaintiff William Forrester has suffered the loss of consortium with his wife, Ann Forrester, in the amount of twenty thousand dollars ($20,000).

WHEREFORE, Plaintiff William Forrester demands judgment against the Defendants in the sum of twenty thousand dollars ($20,000) and costs and for such other relief as this court may deem just and proper.

Arthur White
White, Wilson & McDuff
Attorneys at Law
Federal Plaza Building
Suite 700
Third and Market Streets
Legalville, Columbia 00000
(111) 555-0000

STATE OF COLUMBIA }
County of Capitol _____ } ss.

Ann Forrester and William Forrester, being duly sworn on oath according to law, depose and state that they have read the foregoing complaint and that the matters stated therein are true to the best of their knowledge, information, and belief.

Ann Forrester

William Forrester

Subscribed and sworn to before me this 1st day of October, 19___.

_____
Notary Public

My commission expires January 1, 19___.
[attach exhibits if any]

_____

ASSIGNMENT 5:3

Using the checklist and examples in this chapter, draft a complaint for Ann Forrester to be filed in the United States District Court for the Eastern District of Columbia alleging diversity jurisdiction. Place copies of the federal (notice) complaint and the previous state (fact) complaint into your system folder.

ASSIGNMENT 5:4

Draft both a fact and a notice complaint for the _Ameche_ case (Case II in chapter 1) using the facts you found through investigation in chapter 4.

Examples of complaint forms for other types of actions follow. Keep in mind that these are forms for your guidance and that any particular case may require important amendments.

CONTRACT

Elements of a claim for breach of contract include the following:

A. A promise by Defendant, e.g., to pay money or do something by a certain date
B. Consideration for promise, e.g., $25,000
C. Performance of condition by Plaintiff, e.g., payment of $25,000
D. Defendant's breach, i.e., failure to perform promise by a certain date
E. Plaintiff's injury, e.g., loss of $25,000 plus additional cost to enforce performance of promise.

The syllogism would be: If A, B, C, D, and E exist, then the plaintiff is entitled to damages. Facts should be alleged in the body of the complaint to show A through E exist.

FORM FOR COMPLAINT IN CONTRACT

[include caption]   Jury Trial Is Demanded
The Plaintiff makes the following allegations:

1. That the court has jurisdiction over this matter because the Plaintiff is a resident of the State of Columbia, and the Defendant is a resident of the State of Ohio, and the amount in controversy exceeds sixty thousand dollars ($60,000), exclusive of interest and costs.
2. That on [date], a written contract was entered into by the Plaintiff and the Defendant in which the Defendant agreed to _____. [state promise].

3. That the agreed upon consideration for said promise was payment to the Defendant of _____.
4. That a copy of said contract is attached to this complaint as "Exhibit A" and incorporated herein by reference.
5. That the Plaintiff _____ [state the Plaintiff's performance of condition, e.g., rendered payment] and all other conditions precedent have occurred or have been performed by the Plaintiff.
6. That the Defendant failed to _____ [restate promise] even though the Plaintiff made a demand on the Defendant to do so.
7. That as a consequence of the Defendant's breach of contract, the Plaintiff has _____ [state the injury or injuries, e.g., purchased at a higher price, lost profit, interest, lost other contracts].

WHEREFORE, the Plaintiff demands judgment against the Defendant for the sum of _____ dollars with interest at the rate of _____ per annum from the date of the Defendant's breach, together with the Plaintiff's costs and disbursements.

_____
Attorney for Plaintiff
[Address]
[Phone]

FORM: COMPLAINT ON A PROMISSORY NOTE

1. Allegation of jurisdiction
2. The Defendant, on or about June 1, 1935, executed and delivered to the Plaintiff a promissory note [in the following words and figures: *(here set out the note verbatim)*]; [a copy of which is hereto annexed as Exhibit A]; [whereby the Defendant promised to pay the Plaintiff on order on June 1, 1936, the sum of _____ dollars with interest thereon at the rate of six percent per annum].
3. Defendant owes the Plaintiff the amount of said note and interest.

WHEREFORE the Plaintiff demands judgment against the Defendant for the sum of _____ dollars, interest, and costs.

Signed:_____
Attorney for Plaintiff
Address:_____
[Phone]

Source: FED.R.CIV.P. Form 3

FORM: COMPLAINT FOR ANTITRUST ACTION[4]

[Title of Court and Cause]

The plaintiff, _____, a corporation, (hereinafter referred to as "B_____"), by _____ & _____, its attorneys, complains of the defendant, _____, a corporation (hereinafter referred to as "G_____") as follows:

1. [*Allegations of jurisdiction based on federal statute and diversity of citizenship.*]

2. Defendant G_____, a _____ corporation, has its principal place of business at _____, and is a manufacturer and seller of watch bands and other merchandise to the wholesale jewelry trade in the State of _____ and in various other states in the United States of America, and is and has been at all times referred to herein engaged in interstate commerce between various states and including such commerce between the States of _____ and _____. By reason thereof, the defendant G_____ is subject to and bound by the provisions of the Sherman Antitrust Act, being Sections 1 through 33, inclusive, Title 15, United States Code Annotated.

3. The plaintiff, B_____, a _____ corporation, has its principal place of business in _____, and is engaged in the wholesale jewelry trade in the State of _____ and in various other States of the United States of America.

4. Prior to _____, 19__, the plaintiff B_____, had been appointed and had acted as a wholesale distributor of G_____'s products to the retail jewelry trade in the State of _____ and in various other States of the United States of America.

5. At all times while plaintiff had been so appointed and engaged as a wholesale distributor for defendant G_____, plaintiff followed and adhered to G_____'s announced policy of selling G_____ products to retailers at G_____'s factory suggested list prices.

6. On _____, 19__, G_____, through its Vice President in Charge of Marketing, and its Chicago representative, advised plaintiff B _____ that the philosophy of G_____ is that all watch bands sold by a G_____ distributor, whether manufactured by G_____ or by its competitors, must be sold by the G_____ distributor at the factory suggested selling prices, and that to continue to be a G_____ distributor, B_____ would have to price other factory lines, that is, watch bands manufactured by G_____'s competitors and sold by B_____, at factory suggested selling prices, and not at prices otherwise determined by B_____.

7. B_____ refused so to do, and G_____'s Vice President in Charge of Marketing thereupon, then and there, and on the same day, and at the same conference, on, to-wit, _____, 19__, summarily advised B_____ that B_____'s distributorship of G_____'s products was terminated and G_____ would no longer sell B_____ any G_____ merchandise because of B_____'s refusal to comply with G_____'s policy regarding the price at which B_____ sold watch bands manufactured and sold by G_____'s competitors.

8. That the defendant, G_____ thereby attempted to engage in a wrongful and unlawful combination and conspiracy,

a. To prevent and restrict the sale and distribution of G_____'s products, by reason of its refusal, for the unlawful reason stated by G_____ as aforesaid, to sell its products to B_____;

b. To prevent and restrict the sale and distribution of products manufactured and sold by G_____'s competitors;

c. To, and did, discriminate against a wholesale distributor, to-wit, B_____, who would not combine and conspire with G_____ to price competitors' lines as directed and dictated by G_____;

d. To force and compel B_____ to enter into a contract or agreement providing for the establishment and maintenance between wholesalers of minimum resale prices on products competitive to the G_____ line; and

e. To force and compel B_____ to enter into a contract or agreement providing for the establishment and maintenance of minimum resale prices between persons, firms, or corporations in competition with each other; and that such acts have unreasonably restrained, do unreasonably restrain, and will continue unreasonably to restrain trade and commerce in violation of the anti-trust laws of the United States of America above cited.

9. That by reason of G_____'s wrongful and unlawful termination of B_____'s distributorship of G_____ products and its refusal to thereafter sell such products to B_____ for the reason forbidden by the antitrust laws, as aforesaid, and in restraint of trade and commerce, as aforesaid, the plaintiff, B_____, has been injured in its business and property to an amount in excess of _____ (_____), and hereby demands of the defendant G_____ threefold the damages by it sustained, and the costs of this action, including a reasonable attorney's fee to be fixed and determined by this Court.

_____
Plaintiff

By _____
President

FORM: COMPLAINT FOR CLASS ACTION[5]

Class Action Allegations—Action for Damages
[FED. R. CIV. P 23(a), (b)]

2. Plaintiffs bring this action on behalf of themselves and, under Federal Civil Procedure Rule 23(a) and (b)(3), on behalf of all other Lake _____ lakeshore landowners and lakeshore lessees similarly situated and located in the Towns of _____ and _____, County of ____, State of _____; the said lakeshore landowners and lakeshore lessees in the Towns of _____ and _____ number approximately two hundred (200), and it is therefore impracticable to bring them all before Court.

3. There are questions of law and fact common to the entire class of lakeshore landowners and lakeshore lessees similarly situated and located in the Towns of _____ and _____; the claims of the Plaintiffs herein are typical of the claims of the said class; and the Plaintiffs will fairly and adequately protect the interest of and represent said class; the common questions of law and fact predominate over any questions affecting only individual members, and a class action is superior to other available methods for the fair and efficient adjudication of this controversy.

    4. The Plaintiffs, _____ and _____, are the owners of certain lands and premises having lake frontage on the easterly edge of Lake _____ in the Town of _____, _____, namely, all and the same lands and premises conveyed to the Plaintiffs _____ by Warranty Deed of _____, dated _____, 19__, and recorded in _____, said lands including over _____ feet of lakeshore frontage.

    5. The Plaintiffs, _____ and _____, are the owners of certain lands and premises having lake frontage on the easterly edge of Lake in the Town of _____, _____, being all and the same lands and premises conveyed to the Plaintiffs _____ by Deed of _____, dated _____, 19__, and recorded in _____, said lands and premises including over _____ feet of lakeshore frontage.

ASSIGNMENT 5:5

Add the previous form complaints to your system folder. Be sure to check the pleading rules of your own state. Gather examples of local complaints by researching the firm's files and recent editions of legal forms and pleading books, or by going to the pertinent clerk of court and reviewing pleadings in recent case files. Try to locate a full range of examples of complaints that include pleading in the alternative, pleading in the hypothetical, joined parties, and joined claims and counts.

■ Injunctions

At times the attorney will instruct the paralegal to draft a request for an injunction or temporary restraining order to accompany the complaint. This is necessary in some circumstances to prevent further deterioration in the subject of the lawsuit, or some other violation of a party's rights. For example, when the defendant is sued over a boundary dispute, a preliminary injunction may be in order to prevent the defendant from cutting down trees on the disputed property until the suit is resolved.

    Rule 65 sets out the difference between a preliminary injunction and a temporary restraining order. The important thing to remember, however, is that these documents are filed to require the other party either to do or refrain from doing some act. Without such action, it is possible the plaintiff will suffer irreparable harm.

    The injunction or temporary restraining order should be filed with the complaint along with a proposed order prohibiting or demanding the action in question. The request is often supported by a memorandum of law, covered in detail in chapter 7. A surety bond must also be filed with the court.

    Figures 5:2[6] and 5:3[7] are examples of forms for injunction and the temporary restraining orders.

ASSIGNMENT 5:6

Copy the injunction forms for your system folder and note that they are filed with the complaint and require a surety bond.

Figure 5:2   Motion for Preliminary Injunction—General Form

[Fed. R. Civ. P. 65(a)]

[*Title of Court and Cause*]

Plaintiffs, _____ and _____, move the Court for a preliminary injunction in the above entitled cause enjoining the defendants, and _____ and _____, their agents, servants, employees, and attorneys, [and those persons in active concert or participation with them] from _____

The grounds in support of this motion are as follows:
1. _____
2. _____

Unless restrained _____ and _____ will immediately [*state action defendants will take unless restrained*].

Immediate and irreparable injury, loss, and damage will result to the plaintiffs by reason of the threatened action of the defendants, as more particularly appears in the verified complaint filed herein and the attached affidavit of _____. The plaintiffs have no adequate remedy at law.

If this preliminary injunction be granted, the injury, if any, to defendants herein, if final judgment be in their favor, will be inconsiderable and will be adequately indemnified by bond.

[Add if appropriate: Plaintiffs further move the Court that the trial of this action on the merits be advanced and consolidated with the hearing of this motion for preliminary injunction. The grounds in support of consolidation are as follows: *Add matter similar to matter in second paragraph of form in § 5272*].

_____,

Attorneys for Plaintiffs.

Address: _____

Figure 5:3   Motion for Temporary Restraining Order

[Fed. R. Civ. P. 65(b)]

[*Title of Court and Cause*]

Plaintiff moves this court to grant [(1) forthwith and without notice to defendant or his attorney] a temporary restraining order restraining and enjoining the defendant [his agents, servants, employees, and attorneys, and those persons in active concert and participation with him] from [*describe actions sought to be enjoined by motion*] pending a hearing and disposition of plaintiff's motion for a preliminary injunction filed herein on _____, 19__, [and scheduled by the court for a hearing on _____, 19__] on the ground that immediate and irreparable loss, damage, and injury will result to plaintiff [(2) before defendant or his attorney can be heard in opposition] and before [notice can be served and] a hearing can be had on plaintiff's motion for a preliminary injunction, if defendants are permitted to [*describe actions sought to be enjoined*], as more fully appears from plaintiff's verified complaint herein and the attached affidavits of _____ [(3) and the attached certificate of applicant's attorney certifying the efforts which have been made to give defendant [and his attorney] notice, and the reasons notice of this motion should not be required].

[*Date*]

_____,

Attorney for Plaintiff.

Address: _____

Summary

Drafting good pleadings is an important art that increases your value to the law firm. The first pleading to be drafted in litigation is the complaint. It introduces the cause of action, invokes the court's jurisdiction, presents the facts of the case, and provides due process notice to the defendant. A complaint consists of three main parts: the caption, the body, and the prayer for relief. What must be stated in these sections is established by court rules, the nature of the action, remedies available, and techniques of drafting. A checklist for drafting complaints and sample forms are provided in the chapter as guides to be adapted for state or federal court. The assignments in the chapter emphasize your need to practice applying the techniques and procedures outlined in the chapter.

In addition, you have learned about the pleadings needed to file for an injunction. An injunction may be sought as a lone action or as a remedy in conjunction with another action. Its purpose is to request a court to prohibit the action of another or to command that the other party take some action. Injunctions are an important tool in our legal system to prevent damage before it occurs. Sample motions for an injunction have been provided for your use. Familiarity with and practice at each of the tasks presented in this chapter will increase your ability and confidence as a paralegal.

Study Guide

1. What is procedural due process of law?
2. What is the relationship between due process and a complaint?
3. Describe the various sections of a complaint, their contents, and the functions of each section.
4. What are the minimum requirements in order for a person to be eligible to sue or be sued? What happens when a person has grounds for a lawsuit but does not have the legal capacity to sue?
5. What is the federal and your state rule on joinder of parties in a lawsuit?
6. Why is jurisdiction important to the drafter of a complaint?
7. What role do jurisdictional amounts play in both federal and state courts?
8. Be able to draft an adequate jurisdictional allegation.
9. Why is venue important to the drafter of a complaint? When venue must be alleged, what specifically needs to be included?
10. What should a paralegal do to be sure that a claim is properly alleged in a particular jurisdiction?
11. What is a syllogism? A major and minor premise? How can it be useful to the drafter of a complaint?
12. For an adequate allegation of a claim, what must a paralegal know about the legal basis of such a claim?
13. Review the guidelines and techniques for drafting the body of the complaint.
14. What ethical consideration must a paralegal keep in mind when drafting a complaint? Cite the disciplinary rule.
15. What is the difference between fact pleading and notice pleading?

16. What federal rules set out guidelines for pleading?
17. How can a paralegal determine the extent of facts to allege in a fact-pleading jurisdiction?
18. What is the difference, if any, between a prayer for relief, a demand for judgment, and the "wherefore" clause?
19. What are damages?
20. What is the difference between general and special damages? Which must be alleged with particularity (applicable rule)?
21. Describe and define the other common forms of relief: recovery of property, injunction, and specific performance.
22. What does it mean to have multiple counts in a complaint? Should there be a "wherefore" clause in each count?
23. What is the proper method of incorporating paragraphs of one count into another?
24. What must a paralegal keep in mind regarding a demand for a jury trial? What federal rule applies?
25. What does an attorney certify in signing a complaint where verification is not required?
26. What is the proper procedure for notarizing a verification?
27. What is the purpose of an appendix to a complaint? What is the proper way to reference either an exhibit or an appendix?
28. Review the system checklist for drafting a complaint.
29. Be prepared to draft both a fact and a notice complaint.

Endnotes

1. MOORE, TAGGART & WICKER, MOORE'S FEDERAL PRACTICE § 0.140 (1–4) (2d ed. 1959).
2. The following discussion on the syllogism is drawn in part from KARLEN, PROCEDURE BEFORE TRIAL IN A NUTSHELL 45–48 (1972).
3. From *Litigation Paralegal* by Philip J. Signey. Copyright 1991 by James Publishing, Inc.; reprinted with permission of the publisher.
4. WEST'S FEDERAL FORMS § 1585, v. 2A, with permission of West Publishing Company.
5. Id., § 3065, v. 3, with permission of West Publishing Company.
6. Id., § 5271, v. 4, with permission of West Publishing Company.
7. Id., § 5297, v. 4, with permission of West Publishing Company.

6

Filing the Lawsuit, Service of Process, and Obtaining a Default Judgment

- Introduction
- Preparing Documents for Filing an Action and for Service of Process
- Filing the Lawsuit
- Service of Process
- Filing and Service of Pleadings and Papers Subsequent to the Complaint
- Obtaining a Default Judgment

▊ Introduction

The Tasks: Filing the Lawsuit, Serving the Summons, Obtaining a Default Judgment

Mr. White has met with Ms. Forrester and reviewed her case. She has decided to go forward with her lawsuit. You have been assigned the following tasks:

1. Prepare the necessary documents to file the action.
2. Deliver the documents to the court clerk for filing.
3. Serve each defendant with the summons and complaint.
4. If the defendant does not respond, prepare the necessary documents to obtain a default judgment.

Purpose of the Tasks

Filing the lawsuit is the first formal step in the litigation process. It establishes the date when the case officially begins, and all deadlines in the case ultimately stem from that date. If the claim has not been filed prior to the running of the statute of limitations, the opposition has a defense to the action and the case will be dismissed. The filing of the action informs the court of the suit and makes the claim a matter of public record.

Service of process (delivery of a copy of the summons and complaint) officially notifies the defendant of the lawsuit and the defendant's need to

179

respond (answer). Service also gives the court personal jurisdiction over the defendant, which is necessary for the court to impose a binding judgment on the defendant. Discussion of the default judgment is reserved for later in this chapter.

ASSIGNMENT 6:1
Write a brief outline of the tasks as previously listed. Place it in your system folder.

■ Preparing Documents for Filing an Action and for Service of Process

Determine What Documents Are Needed

There are several ways to determine what is needed to file an action. One method is to ask another paralegal, a legal secretary, or an attorney in your law firm. A better method, until you are familiar with the requirements, is to visit the clerk of court in which the action will be filed. The clerk will explain to you what is needed and will probably give you copies of some of the forms you will need. Do not be afraid of appearing uninformed. The clerks are there to help you and want you to have a good start.

This visit will acquaint you with the clerk's personnel, who will be of considerable help to you in the years to come. If you treat these individuals with courtesy and respect, remembering that they are also under pressure and time constraints, your relationship with the clerk's office should develop on a pleasant and productive basis.

Take the time to study filing and service requirements for both the federal and state courts. Frequently, these courts have their own local rules in addition to the standard rules that dictate what documents must be prepared and filed.

Confirm with the attorney the method of service of process to be used. This method has an impact on what documents are necessary. For example, the documents that must be delivered to the clerk of court for service by mail of an instate individual are different from those needed when service is made to the secretary of state to serve a foreign corporation. When it is determined what documents are needed, make a prefiling checklist as shown in figure 6:1.

Figure 6:1 A Prefiling Checklist

FOR FEDERAL COURT SERVICE BY MAIL (MOST COMMON)

Need
1. Original complaint, checked for accuracy and attorney's signature
2. Copy of original complaint to be returned to the client's file after being stamped by clerk
3. A copy of original complaint for each defendant to be served
4. Original summons with all necessary information, accurately spelled, and so on
5. Copy of original summons for each defendant
6. A Civil Cover Sheet (Form 18-A), completed and signed by the attorney
7. A Stipulation to have case tried by magistrate (only if requested by attorney)
8. Check for $120 filing fee

SERVICE THROUGH SECRETARY OF STATE OR OTHER STATE OFFICIAL FOR FOREIGN CORPORATION

Need

1. Varies according to state statute in which federal district court is located
2. Original complaint
3. One copy of original complaint for client's file to be stamped by clerk
4. Two copies of original complaint to be attested as true copies of the complaint by the clerk
5. One other copy of original complaint if state statute requires plaintiff to also mail a copy to defendant
6. Completed original summons, checked for accuracy
7. Two copies of original summons for clerk to mail
8. Civil Cover Sheet
9. Stipulation
10. Plain envelope for clerk to mail documents, plus postage
11. The green receipt from the post office for certified mail if required
12. Fee, as set by state statute, for each defendant to be served
13. Check for $120 filing fee

FOR STATE COURT, GENERALLY (VERIFY IN YOUR STATE FOR PARTICULARS)

Need

1. Original complaint, checked for accuracy and client verification or attorney's signature depending on jurisdictional requirements
2. One copy of complaint for client's file and one or two copies for each defendant, depending on local sheriff's requirements
3. Original summons checked for accuracy, plus one or two copies for each defendant based on sheriff's requirements
4. Praecipe [request] for Summons if required
5. Request for Service of Process if required
6. Civil Cover Sheet if required
7. Checks for filing fee plus service of process fee

ASSIGNMENT 6:2

If possible, visit the clerk of court's office for both the federal and state court in your area. Do this as an entire class at a prearranged time out of courtesy to the clerk's office. Make a list of the documents required to have a civil action properly filed and served on the defendant. Request copies of the necessary documents.

Amend the Prefiling Checklist (figure 6:1), especially the state court section, as the rules indicate and place the checklist in your system folder.

As you gain experience, you will prepare documents for other types of service that will be explored later in this chapter. As you become familiar with the prefiling needs of each type of service of process, make a prefiling checklist for that particular type of service and add it to your folder. This is a good time to see that your system folder contains the names, addresses, and phone numbers for the clerks of the courts in which you are likely to be working.

Gather and Prepare the Documents Necessary for Filing and Service

Once the required documents are identified, draft the necessary information into the forms, or, in some cases, draft the entire document. The document is then typed by the legal secretary. Gather or prepare the following forms.

The Complaint

The complaint has been prepared, but this is a good time to check its accuracy and to see that it has been signed by the attorney or verified by the client as required by the jurisdiction. The secretary should then be directed to prepare the necessary copies. Blue backings may be required by the state; they are not required in federal court.

The Summons

Rule 4(b) states the requirements for a valid summons in federal court. All states have similar requirements. The summons should identify the court and the parties, be directed to the defendant, and give the name and address of the plaintiff's attorney and the time within which to appear and defend. Failure to do so will result in judgment being entered for the plaintiff in the amount demanded. Most clerks of court have preprinted copies of the summons. All that remains is for you to see that it is properly and accurately filled out. Obtain a copy of the summons for a state court action or for any other local court in your jurisdiction. Figure 6:2 is a federal summons completed for the Ann Forrester case. Remember that the necessary copies of the summons need to be prepared for each defendant.

Civil Cover Sheet

A Civil Cover Sheet should be prepared for each civil case filed in federal district court. Some states require the completion of a similar form. Figure 6:3 is a completed version of the federal Civil Cover Sheet (Form 18-A). Always make sure that this cover sheet is signed by the attorney.

Notice and Acknowledgment of Receipt of Summons and Complaint

In the federal system, the most common method of service of process is by mail. When service is made by mail, Federal Rule 4(c)(2)(C)(ii) requires that the plaintiff send two copies of the Notice and Acknowledgment of Receipt of Summons and Complaint to each defendant. These forms are available at the district court clerk's office. The necessary information should be added. The clerk will provide the civil case number at the time the complaint is filed. The attorney should sign the notice. Figure 6:4 shows the form for the Acknowledgment.

Request for Service of Process

Because the mail has become the primary mode of service in the federal system, it is unlikely that you will need to prepare a federal form requesting service of process by the United States marshal. However, when the marshal does serve process, Form USM-285, Process Receipt and Return, must be completed by the law firm and filed with the action. An example of this form is shown in figure 6:5.

This form is available through the marshal's office. The fee for the marshal's service is minimal, but must be included when filing the Process Receipt and Return.

Many state courts also require the filing of a request for service of process. Filed with the clerk of the state court, this request is then given to

Figure 6:2   Summons in a Civil Action (Completed Form)

AO 440 (Rev. 5/85)   Summons in a Civil Action

United States District Court

DISTRICT OF

ANN FORRESTER and
WILLIAM FORRESTER, Plaintiffs

V.

RICHARD HART and
MERCURY PARCEL, INC., Defendants

SUMMONS IN A CIVIL ACTION

CASE NUMBER:

TO: (Name and Address of Defendant)

Richard Hart
1223 Penny Lane
Cincinnati, OH

YOU ARE HEREBY SUMMONED and required to file with the Clerk of this Court and serve upon

PLAINTIFF'S ATTORNEY (name and address)

Arthur White
White, Wilson & McDuff
Attorneys at Law
Federal Plaza Building, Suite 700
Third and Market Streets
Legalville, Columbia 00000

an answer to the complaint which is herewith served upon you, within _____20_____ days after service of this summons upon you, exclusive of the day of service. If you fail to do so, judgment by default will be taken against you for the relief demanded in the complaint.

J. D. Walterson
_____
CLERK

10/2/--
_____
DATE

_____
BY DEPUTY CLERK

Figure 6:2   (Continued)

AO 440 (Rev. 5/85)   Summons in a Civil Action

<table>
<tr><td colspan="2" align="center">**RETURN OF SERVICE**</td></tr>
<tr><td>Service of the Summons and Complaint was made by me[1]</td><td>DATE</td></tr>
<tr><td>NAME OF SERVER</td><td>TITLE</td></tr>
</table>

Check one box below to indicate appropriate method of service

☐ Served personally upon the defendant. Place where served : _____
_____

☐ Left copies thereof at the defendant's dwelling house or usual place of abode with a person of suitable age and discretion then residing therein.
Name of person with whom the summons and complaint were left: _____

☐ Returned unexecuted: _____
_____
_____

☐ Other (specify): _____
_____
_____

STATEMENT OF SERVICE FEES

TRAVEL	SERVICES	TOTAL

DECLARATION OF SERVER

I declare under penalty of perjury under the laws of the United States of America that the foregoing information contained in the Return of Service and Statement of Service Fees is true and correct.

Executed on _____   _____
              Date   *Signature of Server*

_____
Address of Server

1) As to who may serve a summons see Rule 4 of the Federal Rules of Civil Procedure.

Figure 6:3 Civil Cover Sheet (Completed Form)

JS 44
(Rev. 07/86)

CIVIL COVER SHEET

The JS-44 civil cover sheet and the information contained herein neither replace nor supplement the filing and service of pleadings or other papers as required by law, except as provided by local rules of court. This form, approved by the Judicial Conference of the United States in September 1974, is required for the use of the Clerk of Court for the purpose of initiating the civil docket sheet. (SEE INSTRUCTIONS ON THE REVERSE OF THE FORM.)

I (a) PLAINTIFFS

Ann Forrester and
William Forrester

DEFENDANTS

Richard Hart and
Mercury Parcel Service, Inc.

(b) COUNTY OF RESIDENCE OF FIRST LISTED PLAINTIFF __Capitol__
(EXCEPT IN U.S. PLAINTIFF CASES)

COUNTY OF RESIDENCE OF FIRST LISTED DEFENDANT __Hamilton__
(IN U.S. PLAINTIFF CASES ONLY)
NOTE: IN LAND CONDEMNATION CASES, USE THE LOCATION OF THE TRACT OF LAND INVOLVED

(c) ATTORNEYS (FIRM NAME, ADDRESS, AND TELEPHONE NUMBER)
Arthur White
White, Wilson & McDuff
Federal Plaza Building, Suite 700
Third and Market Streets
Legalville, Columbia 00000

ATTORNEYS (IF KNOWN)
Harold Ott
Ott, Ott, and Knudsen
444 Front Street
Cincinnati, OH

II. BASIS OF JURISDICTION (PLACE AN × IN ONE BOX ONLY)

☐ 1 U.S. Government Plaintiff

☐ 2 U.S. Government Defendant

☐ 3 Federal Question
(U.S. Government Not a Party)

☒ 4 Diversity
(Indicate Citizenship of Parties in Item III)

III. CITIZENSHIP OF PRINCIPAL PARTIES (PLACE AN × IN ONE BOX FOR PLAINTIFF AND ONE BOX FOR DEFENDANT)
(For Diversity Cases Only)

	PTF	DEF		PTF	DEF
Citizen of This State	☒ 1	☐ 1	Incorporated or Principal Place of Business in This State	☐ 4	☐ 4
Citizen of Another State	☐ 2	☒ 2	Incorporated and Principal Place of Business in Another State	☐ 5	☐ 5
Citizen or Subject of a Foreign Country	☐ 3	☐ 3	Foreign Nation	☐ 6	☐ 6

IV. CAUSE OF ACTION (CITE THE U.S. CIVIL STATUTE UNDER WHICH YOU ARE FILING AND WRITE A BRIEF STATEMENT OF CAUSE.
DO NOT CITE JURISDICTIONAL STATUTES UNLESS DIVERSITY)

28 USC 1332, 1441 Action for damage to pedestrian due to negligent operation of motor vehicle.

V. NATURE OF SUIT (PLACE AN × IN ONE BOX ONLY)

CONTRACT	TORTS		FORFEITURE/PENALTY	BANKRUPTCY	OTHER STATUTES
☐ 110 Insurance	**PERSONAL INJURY**	**PERSONAL INJURY**	☐ 610 Agriculture	☐ 422 Appeal 28 USC 158	☐ 400 State Reapportionment
☐ 120 Marine	☐ 310 Airplane	☐ 362 Personal Injury— Med Malpractice	☐ 620 Food & Drug	☐ 423 Withdrawal 28 USC 157	☐ 410 Antitrust
☐ 130 Miller Act	☐ 315 Airplane Product Liability	☐ 365 Personal Injury— Product Liability	☐ 630 Liquor Laws		☐ 430 Banks and Banking
☐ 140 Negotiable Instrument	☐ 320 Assault, Libel & Slander	☐ 368 Asbestos Personal Injury Product Liability	☐ 640 R.R. & Truck	**PROPERTY RIGHTS**	☐ 450 Commerce/ICC Rates/etc.
☐ 150 Recovery of Overpayment & Enforcement of Judgment	☐ 330 Federal Employers' Liability		☐ 650 Airline Regs	☐ 820 Copyrights	☐ 460 Deportation
☐ 151 Medicare Act	☐ 340 Marine	**PERSONAL PROPERTY**	☐ 660 Occupational Safety/Health	☐ 830 Patent	☐ 470 Racketeer Influenced and Corrupt Organizations
☐ 152 Recovery of Defaulted Student Loans (Excl. Veterans)	☐ 345 Marine Product Liability	☐ 370 Other Fraud	☐ 690 Other	☐ 840 Trademark	☐ 810 Selective Service
☐ 153 Recovery of Overpayment of Veteran's Benefits	☒ 350 Motor Vehicle	☐ 371 Truth in Lending	**LABOR**	**SOCIAL SECURITY**	☐ 850 Securities/Commodities/ Exchange
☐ 160 Stockholders' Suits	☐ 355 Motor Vehicle Product Liability	☐ 380 Other Personal Property Damage	☐ 710 Fair Labor Standards Act	☐ 861 HIA (1395ff)	☐ 875 Customer Challenge 12 USC 3410
☐ 190 Other Contract	☐ 360 Other Personal Injury	☐ 385 Property Damage Product Liability	☐ 720 Labor/Mgmt. Relations	☐ 862 Black Lung (923)	☐ 891 Agricultural Acts
☐ 195 Contract Product Liability			☐ 730 Labor/Mgmt. Reporting & Disclosure Act	☐ 863 DIWC (405(g)) ☐ 863 DIWW (405(g))	☐ 892 Economic Stabilization Act
REAL PROPERTY	**CIVIL RIGHTS**	**PRISONER PETITIONS**		☐ 864 SSID Title XVI	☐ 893 Environmental Matters
☐ 210 Land Condemnation	☐ 441 Voting	☐ 510 Motions to Vacate Sentence	☐ 740 Railway Labor Act	☐ 865 RSI (405(g))	☐ 894 Energy Allocation Act
☐ 220 Foreclosure	☐ 442 Employment	☐ 530 Habeas Corpus	☐ 790 Other Labor Litigation	**FEDERAL TAX SUITS**	☐ 895 Freedom of Information Act
☐ 230 Rent Lease & Ejectment	☐ 443 Housing/ Accommodations	☐ 540 Mandamus & Other	☐ 791 Empl. Ret. Inc. Security Act	☐ 870 Taxes (U.S. Plaintiff or Defendant)	☐ 900 Appeal of Fee Determination Under Equal Access to Justice
☐ 240 Torts to Land	☐ 444 Welfare	☐ 550 Civil Rights		☐ 871 IRS—Third Party 26 USC 7609	☐ 950 Constitutionality of State Statutes
☐ 245 Tort Product Liability	☐ 440 Other Civil Rights				☐ 890 Other Statutory Actions
☐ 290 All Other Real Property					

VI. ORIGIN (PLACE AN × IN ONE BOX ONLY)

☒ 1 Original Proceeding

☐ 2 Removed from State Court

☐ 3 Remanded from Appellate Court

☐ 4 Reinstated or Reopened

☐ 5 Transferred from another district (specify)

☐ 6 Multidistrict Litigation

☐ 7 Appeal to District Judge from Magistrate Judgment

VII. REQUESTED IN COMPLAINT: CHECK IF THIS IS A **CLASS ACTION** ☐ UNDER F.R.C.P. 23

DEMAND $ 750,000 Check YES only if demanded in complaint:
JURY DEMAND: ☒ YES ☐ NO

VIII. RELATED CASE(S) IF ANY (See instructions):

JUDGE _____ DOCKET NUMBER _____

DATE
10/21/--

SIGNATURE OF ATTORNEY OF RECORD
Arthur White

UNITED STATES DISTRICT COURT

Figure 6:4   Notice and Acknowledgment of Receipt of Summons and Complaint

EDKY Form 18-A

United States District Court

EASTERN DISTRICT OF KENTUCKY

Civil No.

Plaintiff

v.

Defendant

NOTICE AND ACKNOWLEDGMENT OF RECEIPT OF SUMMONS AND COMPLAINT

NOTICE

TO:

The enclosed summons and complaint are served pursuant to Rule 4(c)(2)(c)(ii) of the Federal Rules of Civil Procedure.

You must complete the acknowledgment part of this form and return one copy of the completed form to the sender within 20 days.

You must sign and date the acknowledgment. If you are served on behalf of a corporation, unincorporated association (including a partnership), or other entity, you must indicate under your signature your relationship to that entity. If you are served on behalf of another person and you are authorized to receive process, you must indicate under your signature your authority.

If you do not complete and return the form to the sender within 20 days, you (or the party on whose behalf you are being served) may be required to pay any expenses incurred in serving a summons and complaint in any other manner permitted by law.

If you do complete and return this form you (or the party on whose behalf you are being served) must answer the complaint within the time specified in the summons. If you fail to do so, judgment by default will be taken against you for the relief demanded in the complaint.

I declare, under penalty of perjury, that this Notice and Acknowledgment of Receipt of Summons and Complaint was mailed on _____.

(date)

_____

Signature

ACKNOWLEDGMENT OF RECEIPT OF SUMMONS AND COMPLAINT

I declare, under penalty of perjury, that I received a copy of the summons and complaint, in the above-captioned matter at _____

(insert address where received)

on the _____ day of_____, 19_____.

_____   _____

Signature   Date of Signature

_____

Relationship to Entity/Authority to Receive Service of Process

Figure 6:5   Process Receipt and Return

U.S. Department of Justice
United States Marshals Service

PROCESS RECEIPT AND RETURN
See Instructions for "Service of Process by the U.S. Marshal"
on the reverse of this form.

PLAINTIFF	COURT CASE NUMBER
DEFENDANT	TYPE OF PROCESS

SERVE
➤
AT

NAME OF INDIVIDUAL, COMPANY, CORPORATION, ETC., TO SERVE OR DESCRIPTION OF PROPERTY TO SEIZE OR CONDEMN

ADDRESS *(Street or RFD, Apartment No., City, State and ZIP Code)*

SEND NOTICE OF SERVICE COPY TO REQUESTER AT NAME AND ADDRESS BELOW:

Number of process to be served with this Form - 285	
Number of parties to be served in this case	
Check for service on U.S.A.	

SPECIAL INSTRUCTIONS OR OTHER INFORMATION THAT WILL ASSIST IN EXPEDITING SERVICE *(Include Business and Alternate Addresses, All Telephone Numbers, and Estimated Times Available For Service):*
Fold   Fold

Signature of Attorney or other Originator requesting service on behalf of:	☐ PLAINTIFF ☐ DEFENDANT	TELEPHONE NUMBER	DATE

SPACE BELOW FOR USE OF U.S. MARSHAL ONLY — DO NOT WRITE BELOW THIS LINE

I acknowledge receipt for the total number of process indicated. *(Sign only first USM 285 if more than one USM 285 is submitted)*	Total Process	District of Origin No.	District to Serve No.	Signature of Authorized USMS Deputy or Clerk	Date

I hereby certify and return that I ☐ have personally served, ☐ have legal evidence of service, ☐ have executed as shown in "Remarks", the process described on the individual, company, corporation, etc., at the address shown above or on the individual, company, corporation, etc., shown at the address inserted below.

☐ I hereby certify and return that I am unable to locate the individual, company, corporation, etc., named above *(See remarks below)*

Name and title of individual served *(if not shown above)*	☐ A person of suitable age and discretion then residing in the defendant's usual place of abode.
Address *(complete only if different than shown above)*	Date of Service Time am pm
	Signature of U.S. Marshal or Deputy

Service Fee	Total Mileage Charges *(including endeavors)*	Forwarding Fee	Total Charges	Advance Deposits	Amount owed to U.S. Marshal or	Amount of Refund

REMARKS:

the local sheriff or constable with the summons and complaint. Determine if there is a request for service required in your state and place a copy of the request form in your system folder.

Motion for Special Appointment to Serve Process

In some circumstances your attorney may feel that service should be made by a person specially appointed by the court [Rule 4(c)(2)(B)(iii)]. If so, such a motion should also be prepared. Figure 6:6 is an example of the motion.[1]

Affidavit of Return of Service of Summons and Complaint

When service is performed by a specially appointed process server, an affidavit of return of service must be completed pursuant to Rule 4(g). There are times when your state court may also require such an affidavit. An affidavit appropriate for federal court is shown in figure 6:7.[2]

Figure 6:6 Motion for Special Appointment to Serve Process

THE UNITED STATES DISTRICT COURT FOR
THE CENTRAL DISTRICT OF COLUMBIA

Civil Action, File No. _____

_____,
                     Plaintiff

    v.   Motion for Special Appointment
                                      to Serve Process
_____,
                     Defendant

Pursuant to Rule 4(c), Federal Rules of Civil Procedure, _____ moves this Court to specifically appoint _____ to serve the _____ on _____ in this action. Said person to be appointed is not less than eighteen years of age and is not a party to this action. Said appointment will bring a savings in costs to the United States Marshal.

_____
Attorney

Order

IT IS ORDERED this _____ day of _____, 19___, that _____ be appointed to serve the _____ on _____ in this action.

Proof of such service shall be made by affidavit in accordance with Rule 4(g), Federal Rules of Civil Procedure.

By the Court

_____
United States District Court Judge

Figure 6:7 Return of Service of Summons and Complaint

UNITED STATES DISTRICT COURT FOR
THE CENTRAL DISTRICT OF COLUMBIA CIVIL ACTION,

File No. _____

_____,
                    Plaintiff

   v.

_____,
                    Defendant

Return of Service of
Summons and Complaint

I certify that I personally served the summons and complaint in the above captioned matter at _____ on the _____ day of _____, 19___, on the following person, corporation, agency, etc:
  time

Name:

Address where served:

Under penalty of perjury, I declare that the foregoing is true and correct.

_____

Signature of process server

_____

Name (typed or printed)

_____

Date

Stipulation for Trial by Magistrate Judge

This document is drafted only on the specific direction of the attorney. Its purpose is to inform the court that the parties agree to have the matter tried by a federal magistrate judge rather than the district court judge. If so directed, this document should be prepared and presented to the clerk at the same time the complaint is filed. It will then have to be signed by the defendant and returned to the clerk of court. Figure 6:8 is an example of such a stipulation.

Obtain the Check for the Filing Fees

After the documents are prepared and checked for accuracy and necessary signatures, a check for the filing fee should be obtained. Each firm will have its own procedure in this regard. If the procedure is not in the office procedures manual, ask an experienced secretary or the office manager. If the action is to be filed in state court, include any necessary service of process fee. This is paid to the clerk in some states and directly to the sheriff in others. If the summons is to be served in a jurisdiction beyond that of the local sheriff, the sheriff in the foreign jurisdiction is generally paid directly and in advance for serving the documents.

Figure 6:8   Stipulation for Trial by Magistrate Judge

UNITED STATES DISTRICT COURT
EASTERN DISTRICT OF KENTUCKY

Civil Action No. _____

_____	Plaintiff
v.	
_____	Defendant

STIPULATION

Pursuant to the provisions of the Federal Magistrate Act, the undersigned counsel for (Plaintiff or Defendant) hereby consents and/or stipulates that a Magistrate Judge may conduct any or all proceedings in the trial and enter a judgment in the case, 28 U.S.C. 636(c)(1) and (2).

A copy of this stipulation has this _____ day of _____, 19__, been mailed to counsel for all parties.

Signed _____

Attorney for _____

ASSIGNMENT 6:3

Obtain a fee schedule for the federal, state, and local courts. Include any fees for service of process and the person to whom such service fees should be paid. Contact the appropriate clerk of court for this information. The fee schedule will include the fees for the filing of subsequent pleadings and motions. Place the fee schedule(s) in your system folder with a reminder to update the information periodically.

ASSIGNMENT 6:4

Prepare the necessary documents for filing Case II, the *Ameche* case, for both federal and your state court. Use the sample forms set out in this chapter and the completed forms as a guide. Assume there is diversity of jurisdiction. Check for accuracy. Place copies of the federal and your state summons, the Civil Cover Sheet, the Notice and Acknowledgment of Receipt of Summons and Complaint, federal and state forms for requesting service of process, the motion for special appointment to serve process, the affidavit of return of service, and the stipulation for trial by magistrate in your system folder.

■ Filing the Lawsuit

It frequently becomes the responsibility of the paralegal to file the action. Although filing the summons, complaint, and subsequent papers is occasionally done in a rush, it is a simple procedure. The prepared documents are taken to the clerk of the court in which the action is to be filed. Personal delivery of the papers to the clerk is the most common method of filing, but mailing the summons, complaint, and other necessary documents to the clerk is permitted. Fax machines (electronic mail) are beginning to change the way pleadings and other documents may be filed. Some clerk's offices are now permitting filing by electronic mail, even after regular business

What does service of process accomplish?

hours. This not only gives parties more time to file but also avoids the frantic eleventh-hour trip to the courthouse frequently experienced by paralegals.

The clerk stamps the date on the original complaint and, in the federal system, immediately assigns the action a civil case number and possibly a judge. The action commences in federal court upon the delivery of the complaint to the clerk (Rule 3). In state courts, the action officially commences when a complaint and summons are served upon the defendant.

The court clerk then issues a summons with the court seal and the clerk's signature. As time permits, the clerk may assist by checking to see if the summons is properly done. The cover sheet, if required, is also checked. The clerk in federal court then asks what method of service will be used. This is done to see that all needed documents are presented. A summons for each defendant is then either returned to be served on the defendant (federal court) or delivered to the sheriff for service (state court).

For all practical purposes, the procedure is the same in all federal district courts. The procedure in state courts is similar but varies to some degree by state.

■ Service of Process

Once the action is filed, it is essential to serve the summons and complaint on the defendant in order for the court to gain personal jurisdiction over the defendant. In state court this is usually necessary to begin the action. The court's judgment is not binding against the defendant unless personal jurisdiction has been obtained by service of process. Consequently, it is an extremely important step.

Most Common Methods of Service

Mail

The most common method of service of process in the federal courts and most state courts is by mail [Rule 4(c)(2)(C)(ii)] This is accomplished in the following manner (variation may occur in any state):

1. Present documents to court clerk.
2. Clerk issues summons and copies [Rule 4(a)].
3. Mail copy of summons and complaint with two copies of the Notice and Acknowledgment and a return self-stamped envelope to the defendant [Rule 4(c)(2)(C)(ii)].
4. Send first-class mail or certified mail; mark green certified mail card for Restricted Delivery Only. (This means that only the person intended to receive service may receive it.)
5. Defendant acknowledges receipt and returns it.
6. Fill out Return of Service on original summons and file it along with signed Acknowledgment with clerk.

Personal Service

If the defendant fails to return the Acknowledgment within twenty days after the date of mailing (for which the person may incur costs unless there is a good reason), personal delivery must be tried, which can also be used as an alternative to mailing.

Who Can Serve?

1. Any person not a party and at least eighteen years old [Rule 4(2)(A)] (this can include the use of process serving companies who charge a fee for the delivery),
2. The local sheriff or constable, or
3. The U.S. marshal or other court-approved person *only:*
   a. If the plaintiff is a seaman (Title 28 U.S.C. § 1916) or is a person proceeding *in forma pauperis* (without funds)(Title 28 U.S.C. § 1915),
   b. If the plaintiff is the United States or an officer or agency of the United States, or
   c. If pursuant to a special court order [Rule 4(c)(2)(B)].

When service is complete, the process server fills out the Return of Service and files it with the clerk of court.

How to Serve

1. Personally hand a copy of summons and complaint to defendant or authorized, registered, or statutory agent [Rule 4(d)(1)].
2. If the defendant is not available, leave a copy of summons and complaint at the individual's residence with a person of suitable *age* (fourteen in many jurisdictions) and *discretion* residing there [Rule 4(d)(1)]. Leaving the complaint with another person is not permitted in some states.

3. Serve the documents during reasonable hours including Sundays and holidays and during the night shift if that is when the defendant works.

Service in Special Circumstances, to Infant or Incompetent Person

Using mail or personal delivery:

1. Serve the legal guardian or appointed representative, or
2. As otherwise prescribed by state law [Rule 4(d)(2)].

Corporation or Other Business (in State or Registered with State)

1. Serve the officer, managing or general agent, or other person authorized by appointment or law to receive service [Rule 4(d)(3)].
2. Serve the agent authorized by statute to receive service and also mail a copy to the defendant [Rule 4(d)(3)]. The secretary of state in many states is the statutorily designated official.

United States, Officer, or Agent

1. Serve the U.S. attorney for the district in which the action is brought or an assistant U.S. attorney or clerical employee designated by the U.S. attorney in writing filed with the clerk of the court, *and*
2. Send a copy of the summons and complaint by registered or certified mail to the attorney general of the United States in Washington, D.C., *and*
3. In any action against an officer or agency of the United States or in any action attacking the validity of an order of an officer or agency of the United States not made a party, also serve such officer or agency by registered or certified mail, *and*
4. If the U.S. agency is a corporation, by service as designated for corporations above. The enabling statutes of most agencies indicate the service requirements [Rule 4(d)(4-5)].

State, Municipal Corporation, or Other Governmental Entity Subject to Suit

1. Serve its chief executive officer, or
2. Serve as prescribed by state law.

Party Outside the State

1. *State action:* Serve according to state long-arm statute (to be discussed). Typical procedure includes:

   ■ The original and two copies of the complaint are filed with the clerk of court.
   ■ The clerk issues the summons and mails two copies of the summons and complaint by certified mail to the secretary of state or other designated officer.
   ■ The secretary of state's office sends a copy of the summons and complaint to the nonresident defendant by certified mail, Return Receipt Requested.

- On return of the receipt, the secretary of state's office certifies to the clerk of court that service has been made.
- If the secretary of state's office cannot gain service, the state statute normally sets out alternatives for service.

2. *Federal action:* Serve according to statute of the state in which the federal district court sits [Rule 4(e)], or according to the federal statute authorizing the cause of action [Rule 4(f)].
3. *Federal action:* If a nonresident is added to the suit as third-party defendant or as a necessary party to counterclaim or cross-claim and lives within 100 miles of the federal district court in which the action is filed [Rule 4(f)], serve according to the federal rules outlined earlier for service on individuals, corporations, the United States, and so on. [Rule 4(d)(1-6)].

Party in Foreign Country

1. Serve pursuant to pertinent state or federal statute and according to the laws of the foreign country, or
2. As directed by the foreign authority in response to a letter rogatory, or
3. In person or in the case of a corporation to an officer or general agent, or
4. By mail dispatched by the clerk of court and requiring a signed receipt, or
5. As directed by order of the court [Rule 4(i)].

Party in In Rem Cases (Discussed Below)

Serve person holding the property in the appropriate manner described earlier.

Party in Quasi In Rem Cases (Discussed Below)

Serve defendant by mail to last known address or, if address is not available, by constructive service (publication).

Note that these procedures are based on the federal rules. The rules of each state should be checked for similarities, differences, and reliance of the federal rules on the rules of the state in which the federal court is located.

Long Arm Statutes

At one time it was very difficult, if not impossible, to serve defendants who resided beyond the borders of a particular state or who had passed briefly through the state and had caused injury. This injustice has been corrected in some states with the passage of **long-arm statutes.** The key to these statutes is whether the defendant has sufficient minimum contacts with the state to justify personal jurisdiction. Under such statutes, courts have been able to gain jurisdiction over nonresident motorists and operators of planes and vessels; persons who commit torts in the state; property owners; foreign corporations and manufacturers; and persons who contract to sell goods or services in the state. Courts have upheld the validity of these statutes on the logic that the cause of action should be remedied where the harm occurred.

This is true as long as the minimum contacts are present and the nonresident is treated fairly (given due process).

ASSIGNMENT 6:5
Memo to: Terry Salyer, Paralegal
From: Isadora Pearlman
Subject: Research
Completion Date: Three days from today

Issue: What are the necessary minimum contacts required by our state statute to gain jurisdiction over a foreign corporation? Over a nonresident tort feasor?

Task: Prepare a short memorandum on the state and constitutional law on this subject.

Guidelines: Check the annotated state statutes under "long-arm statutes," "foreign corporations," and "nonresident tort feasors" for case law. Also try the state digest under similar key phrases. Since the state's long-arm statute affects both our federal and state court, decisions in both jurisdictions are helpful. See the section on researching and drafting a memorandum of law in chapter 7.

The long-arm statute identifies which public official in the state must be served. For example, it is typical for out-of-state corporations doing business in the state to be served through the state's secretary of state; insurance companies through the commissioner of insurance; and out-of-state motorists through the commissioner of highways.

Prior to filing an action using the long-arm statute, read the state's long-arm statute to determine what official should be served and with what documents. A typical procedure for gaining service of process under a long-arm statute is described earlier under "Party Outside the State."

The federal courts follow the long-arm procedure of the state in which the federal district court is located [Rule 4(c)]. A few federal long-arm provisions provide for nationwide personal jurisdiction. This is true of some antitrust and securities laws as well as interpleader actions, which resolve a special type of property dispute. It pays to consult the specific statute under which a federal claim is brought to see if such extended jurisdiction exists. In addition, Rule 4(f) gives a federal district court jurisdiction over parties later added to an action who reside within 100 miles of the district court regardless of state boundaries.

Service may also be made on a defendant in a foreign country. In such circumstances, consult the state's statute on the subject, the rules of the specific federal district court, and Federal Rules 4(e) and (i). The last volume of *The Martindale Hubbell Law Directory* contains information on foreign service as established by treaty.

Service in In Rem and Quasi In Rem Cases

An **in rem action** is an action involving the attachment of property to resolve claims to the property. Since the jurisdiction is over the property, service is gained by delivery of the summons and complaint to the person holding the property.

A **quasi in rem** action is one in which the court uses the property of a defendant over whom it does not have personal jurisdiction to pay a judgment against the defendant entered in an action unrelated to the property. One might characterize quasi in rem statutes as "short-arm" statutes. Service of process in such cases is made by mail to the last known address of the defendant.

When such an address is unavailable, many jurisdictions authorize **constructive service.** This involves publication of the summons in a newspaper of general circulation in the area where the property is located. The newspaper will generally provide an affidavit of publication and the attorney will file an affidavit of compliance plus copies of the publication. Some publication statutes deem personal service of the defendant in another state to be adequate publication.

ASSIGNMENT 6:6
Look up "service of process by publication" in your state statutes. Find out when publication is required or permitted, what time limits must be observed, and what procedure must be followed. Make a short checklist of these and add them to your system folder.

Service of process for a state court is somewhat different from federal court. Therefore, it is important to check with the clerk of the state court in which the action is to be filed to be confident of the proper procedure. Generally, the sheriff (or constable) delivers the summons and complaint for state court actions.

Time for Service

The summons and complaint must be served on the defendant within 120 days of the filing of the complaint [Rule 4(j)]. Unless good cause is shown for failing to comply with this time limit, the action may be dismissed without prejudice. This rule does not apply to service on persons in a foreign country. For similar time limits in your state, check state rules.

ASSIGNMENT 6:7
Using the methods of service list as a guide, draft a state service of process checklist for your system folder. Look up any needed information in your state's rules of civil procedure or state statutes to complete your checklist.

Immunity from Service of Process

In some instances, a person may not be legally served with a summons and complaint because of immunity from service of process. Commonly, defendants and witnesses attending a trial, or traveling to or from the trial, are immune from service. So too are defendants brought into a state by force or served in some fraudulent manner.

Locating the "Invisible" Defendant

In most instances, you will be asked to locate the defendant as early in the case as possible to determine how and where service can be made. Even if the sheriff will be serving the papers, he or she will need directions. Therefore, it is helpful to know ways to locate people who are difficult to find. Chapter 4 set out several methods to locate hard-to-find witnesses; many of those methods are applicable to locating hard-to-find defendants. Here are some of the better techniques for locating the "invisible" defendant.

Checklist for Locating Defendants

1. If you are trying to locate a corporation, call the secretary of state's corporate division for your state or for the state in which the corporation is likely to be incorporated or have its principal place of business. Many of the techniques used to locate individuals are applicable to corporations and other business organizations.
2. Check telephone and city or county directories.
3. Send an envelope addressed to the last known address of the defendant with the words "Forwarding Address Requested" written in the lower left-hand corner of the envelope. The envelope should have the firm's return address on it and the necessary return postage enclosed.[3] The post office may require the submission of Form 1478 for a forwarding address under the Freedom of Information Act.
4. Send a plain envelope addressed to the defendant by registered mail marked "Return Receipt Requested" and check the box on the green card entitled "Show to whom, date, and address of delivery." The mail carrier will request the defendant to sign the card. Out of courtesy, a brief note requesting payment of plaintiff's charges could be included.[4]
5. Telegraph the defendant through Western Union's Report, Delivery, and Address service.[5]
6. Contact the defendant's former landlord or neighbors to obtain a new address, the name of the moving company, or the names of relatives or friends who might know the new address or provide additional information. Sources providing such information include: churches, schools, or colleges attended; former employers, present employer, co-workers; professional or trade associations; health insurance carriers; sports clubs, civic clubs, country clubs, vets' organizations; and banking institutions.
7. Check voter registration lists, tax rolls, land transfer records (for names of persons involved in recent property transfers who might know the defendant's whereabouts, such as a buyer, a real estate agent, or a bank employee), civil and criminal court records, and vital statistics records.
8. Check with utility, telephone, cable television, newspaper, and other community-based companies for the address.
9. Check with credit and banking institutions. One way to locate the institutions used by the defendant is to ask a former employer to review old paychecks for the name of the bank where the checks were cashed. Review the bank's checking account records for business, service, and organizations paid by the defendant.[6]
10. Contact the pertinent state's auto registration and driver's licensing division.
11. Check with local tax accounting firms.
12. Place an ad in the newspaper with a reward for information that leads to the location of the defendant.
13. Hire a private investigator.

A word of caution is in order here. Prior to contacting employers, neighbors, relatives, and so on, review the consumer protection and collection laws for your jurisdiction, including the Federal Collections Act. Note especially the section on what constitutes harassment or otherwise illegal collection practices.[7] If you do not, you may find yourself in violation of the law and subject to serious penalty.

ASSIGNMENT 6:8
After class discussion on locating difficult-to-find defendants, add additional techniques to the Checklist for Locating Defendants. Place the checklist in your system folder.

Keep Good Records of Service

Keep good records of the filing, service, and receipt of service of all the outgoing and incoming pleadings, notices, subpoenas, and motions in the entire case. Certified mail, Return Receipt Requested provides green receipts for the necessary documentation. If an item is delivered by hand, a receipt that lists the delivered item, the date it was delivered, and the signature of the person acknowledging receipt should be used. These receipts should be attached to a file copy of the pertinent document. If you are acknowledging service on behalf of your firm (check to see when, if ever, your attorney wants you to do this), keep one copy of the acknowledgment or signed receipt in the client's file with the pertinent document.

■ Filing and Service of Pleadings and Papers Subsequent to the Complaint

Once the lawsuit is started, there will be pleadings, motions, notices, orders, and other documents that must be served on the adverse party. Rule 5 of the Federal Rules of Civil Procedure sets out the procedure to follow to serve documents subsequent to the complaint. The original and supporting documents are filed with the clerk of court "either before service or within a reasonable time thereafter" [Rule 5(d)]. One copy of the documents should be served on each of the parties.

When it becomes clear that a party is represented by an attorney, service should be on the attorney [Rule 5(b)]. Service is achieved by mailing a copy of the document to the attorney's last known address; if no address is available, then by delivering it to the clerk of court. Service is also achieved by handing it to the attorney, leaving it at the attorney's office with a clerk or other person in charge, leaving it in a conspicuous place, or leaving it at the attorney's usual place of abode with a person of suitable age and discretion. The court, on its own motion, may alter the requirement that service be made on every party when there is an unusually large number of defendants [Rule 5(c)].

ASSIGNMENT 6:9
Draft a brief Checklist for Filing and Service of Documents Subsequent to the Complaint—Federal and a similar one for your state. Note the applicable rules for future reference. Place the checklists in your system folder.

■ Obtaining a Default Judgment

Mr. White says the defendants in the Ann Forrester case are in default. He wants you to prepare the necessary documents to obtain a **default**

judgment. This will involve the drafting and proper service of several forms.

The Federal Rules of Civil Procedure and those of many states require the defendant to respond in twenty days after being served with the summons and complaint. If the defendant does not file an answer to the complaint or a motion attacking the complaint or otherwise respond in the prescribed twenty days, the defendant is in default and judgment may be entered against the defendant without a trial. In other words, the plaintiff wins the action. The purpose of the task, therefore, is to have a default judgment entered against the defendant for the amount of the claim.

ASSIGNMENT 6:10
Enter the task and its purpose in your system folder.

The Procedure and Necessary Forms

Default judgments help clear the court docket of cases that would otherwise languish for lack of a desire to defend or for some other reason. Their purpose is not to give the plaintiff an advantage, and for that reason they incorporate some safeguards for the defendant. These include satisfactory proof of service of the summons and complaint and the opportunity to have the default set aside if there is adequate justification.

Most states and the federal courts require a two-step process. The first step is the filing of a request to the clerk of court for entry of default [Rule 55(a)]. The request for entry of default normally requires an affidavit stating that the defendant has failed to respond to the summons or otherwise has failed to appear in the action within the required time period. This step is significant because the entry of default generally prevents the defendant from doing anything further to contest his or her liability. Therefore, it is advantageous to prepare the necessary request so it can be filed as soon as the twenty days or other applicable time period has elapsed. See figure 6:9 for examples of these forms.[8]

Step two requires the filing of a request for entry of a default judgment. Note that there is a distinct difference between the entry of default, which simply establishes the point in time of the default, and the judgment, which is a determination that the plaintiff has won the action and is entitled to a specific amount of money or other remedy. Step two is the request for this judgment.

In some jurisdictions this is done simultaneously with the filing of the request for entry of default. In other jurisdictions the filing of the request for entry of default has been eliminated. Some jurisdictions have a statutory waiting period before the judgment can be requested, and in others a default judgment may be lost if it is not pursued within a statutory period of time. Consult the specific rules of the court in which you have filed the action to determine the exact procedure and time limits. It is best to file for the judgment at the first possible opportunity.

Once the default is entered, the federal rules provide for two approaches to obtain the default judgment. If the suit is for a sum certain, meaning not readily challengeable nor subject to reasonable dispute, the request for judgment is submitted to the clerk with an accompanying affidavit attesting to the amount. Judgment is then entered by the clerk. Figure 6:10 is an

Figure 6:9   Request for Entry of Default

(Caption omitted)

REQUEST TO CLERK FOR ENTRY OF DEFAULT

The Plaintiff requests the clerk for the _____*[name of court]*_____ to enter the Defendant's default in the above entitled action. The Defendant has failed to appear or otherwise answer the complaint, and is therefore in default as set out in the accompanying affidavit.

_____

Attorney for Plaintiff
(Address)
(Phone number)

**AFFIDAVIT OF DEFAULT IN SUPPORT OF REQUEST FOR
ENTRY OF DEFAULT**

State of _____
                            } ss.
County of _____

_____, being duly sworn, deposes and says;

1.   That s/he is Plaintiff's attorney and has personal knowledge of the facts set forth in this affidavit.

2.   That the Plaintiff, on the _____ day of _____, 19__, filed his complaint against the Defendants.

3.   That the Defendants were served with a copy of the summons and the Plaintiff's complaint, on the _____ day of _____, 19__.

4.   That more than 20 days have elapsed since the Defendants were served with the summons and complaint.

5.   That the Defendants have failed to answer or otherwise defend as to the Plaintiff's complaint, or serve a copy of any answer or other defense which it might have had, upon _____ and _____, attorneys of record for the said Plaintiff.

6.   That this affidavit is executed in accordance with Rule No. 55(a) of the Federal Rules of Civil Procedure, for the purpose of enabling the Plaintiff to obtain an entry of default against the Defendants.

[Jurat]

_____

Attorney for Plaintiff

example of a request for default judgment by the clerk with an accompanying affidavit.

Most jurisdictions also require submission of an affidavit of nonmilitary service, as shown in figure 6:11.[9] Also draft a judgment for signature unless told not to do so. See an example in figure 6:12.

If the claim is not for a sum certain, the request for default judgment is submitted to the court for determination [Rule 55(b)(2)]. Similar documents are required. The court may require a hearing in which evidence is required to prove the amount of the damages. When the defendant enters a special appearance to be heard on the damage issue, or when the defendant is a minor or incompetent, notice of the application for judgment must be served on the defendant at least three days prior to the hearing on the application. The form appears in figure 6:13.[10]

Figure 6:10 Request for Entry of Default Judgment by Clerk

(Caption omitted)

REQUEST FOR ENTRY OF DEFAULT JUDGMENT BY CLERK WITH SUPPORTING AFFIDAVIT

The Plaintiff in the above entitled action requests the clerk of __*[name of court]*__ to enter judgment by default against the Defendant __*[name of defendant]*__ in the amount of __*[state sum]*__ , plus interest at the rate of __*[state rate]*__ , and costs.

_____
Attorney for Plaintiff
(Address)
(Phone number)

AFFIDAVIT

State of _____ ⎫
                        ⎬ ss.
County of _____ ⎭

__*[name of attorney]*__ , being duly sworn, deposes and states:

1. That s/he is the attorney for Plaintiff in the above entitled action.
2. That Defendant's default in this action was entered on __*[date default entered]*__ .
3. That the amount due Plaintiff from Defendant is a sum certain in the amount of __*[state amount]*__ .
4. That the Defendant is not an infant, incompetent person, or in military service.
5. That the amount indicated is justly owed Plaintiff no part of which has been paid.

_____
Attorney for Plaintiff

[Jurat]
(A brief statement of amount due may be included.)

When the documents are completed, signed, and notarized, they should be filed with the clerk of court, and any required notice served on the defendant. If the court holds a hearing on the application, additional preparation on behalf of the attorney may be required.

Once the default judgment is entered, enforcement of the judgment is obtained in the same manner as for any other judgment (see chapter 12). The plaintiff is limited to the amount of damages requested in the complaint and may not increase the amount.

Default and Multiple Defendants

Exercise special caution when seeking a default judgment when only one defendant is in default. Some jurisdictions permit only one judgment in an action, which might preclude proceeding against the other defendants. This is avoided in some jurisdictions by placing language in the judgment that states this judgment will be "joint and several" with any judgments granted against the remaining defendants. Seek the advice of your supervising attorney after checking the pertinent rules and cases.

Figure 6:11 Affidavit of Nonmilitary Service of Defendant

[FED. R. CIV. P. Rule 55(b)]

[*Title of Court and Cause*]

State of _____
County of _____

   I, _____ being first duly sworn, on oath state:
   1. My age is *legal* years.
   2. I reside at No. _____, _____ Street in the City of _____, State of _____.
   3. My occupation is attorney at law.
   4. I am the duly authorized agent for the plaintiff in the above entitled and numbered cause and as such have full knowledge of the facts relating thereto.
   5. With reference to the matter in issue in the above cause, I have conversed with the defendant _____ over the telephone; that at the said time said defendant _____ was at his place of business in the City of _____, and I have had representatives of this office call on him for the purpose of inducing him to comply with the demand set forth in the complaint filed herein; that from all of said facts, this affiant says that the said defendant _____ is engaged in the business of _____ in the City of _____, and is not in the military service of the United States.

_____

   Subscribed and sworn to before me this _____ day of _____, 19___.

Notary Public

_____

Figure 6:12 Judgment of Default

[*Title of Court and Cause*]

JUDGMENT

   Defendant _____ having failed to answer plaintiff's complaint or otherwise appear in this action and having his/her default entered, and on plaintiff's application and affidavit that defendant owes plaintiff the sum of _____ ($_____),
   It is ORDERED and ADJUDGED
   that plaintiff _____ recover from defendant _____ the sum of _____ ($_____), with _____ percent interest from (date) _____ and costs of the action.

Clerk of Court

Dated _____

Checklist for Default Judgment

Stage One

☐ Check calendar (deadline control system) for upcoming expiration of deadline to answer or otherwise defend case.
☐ Review case file and date and proof of service.

Figure 6:13 Notice of Motion for Default Judgment by Court to Defendant Who Has Appeared in Action

---

[FED. R. CIV. P. Rule 55(b)]

[*Title of Court and Cause*]

Take notice, that the plaintiff will move this court, at _____ Building in the city of _____, on the _____ day of _____, 19___, at _____ o'clock in the _____ noon, or as soon thereafter as counsel may be heard, for a default judgment for the relief demanded in the complaint.
  [*Date*]

_____,
Plaintiff's Attorney
Address: _____

[*Address to defendant's attorney.*]

☐ If defendant defaults, take action to file request and affidavit with clerk as soon after default (twenty-first day in most jurisdictions) as possible.
☐ Draft entry of default and affidavit.
☐ Attach copies of proof of service of summons and complaint.
☐ Have the documents signed and notarized.
☐ File with clerk and obtain clerk's entry of default.

Stage Two

☐ As soon after entry of default as local rules and statutes permit, take action to request judgment of default. (Note: If there are multiple defendants and not all are in default, consult with attorney.)
  ☐ If the award is for a sum certain, draft a request for entry of default judgment by the clerk [Rule 55(b)(1) and your state rule].
  ☐ If the award requested is not for a sum certain, draft a request for entry of default judgment by the court [Rule 55(b)(2) and your state rule].
☐ Include the attorney's affidavit, the affidavit regarding military service, breakdown of debt, affidavit of costs, proof of service if required, and the judgment.
☐ Have appropriate documents signed and notarized.
☐ Deliver to clerk of court.
☐ Obtain date for hearing if needed.
☐ If hearing is required, draft notice of hearing on application and have it signed and served on defendant at least three days prior to hearing [Rule 55(b)(2)].
☐ Notify all nondefaulting defendants of application for judgment or as directed by attorney.

ASSIGNMENT 6:11
Copy the previous checklist and place it in the system folder. Research the rules and forms for your state applicable to obtaining a default judgment, and add a state checklist for default judgment. Make a copy of each of the forms required for a default judgment for both federal and your state and place them in the system folder.

ASSIGNMENT 6:12
Assume for purposes of this assignment that Mr. Hart is an incompetent person; that he is the only defendant in the Ann Forrester Case; that Mr. Hart's guardian has been served with a summons and complaint; and that s/he did not respond within the required twenty days. Draft the necessary state documents to obtain a default judgment in the case. Use your checklist.

Setting Aside a Default Judgment

Despite any excellent forms you may have drafted to obtain a default judgment, the defendant may be able to have a default judgment set aside [Rule 55(c)]. If so, the defendant can attack the complaint or file an answer as if the twenty-day period had not expired. The court will set aside the default judgment for *good cause*. Those things constituting good cause are enumerated in Rule 60(b):

> (1) mistake, inadvertence, surprise or excusable neglect; (2) newly discovered evidence which by due diligence could not have been discovered in time to move for a new trial under Rule 59(b); (3) fraud . . . , misrepresentation, or other misconduct of adverse party; (4) the judgment is void; (5) the judgment has been satisfied, released, or discharged or a prior judgment upon which it is based has been reversed or otherwise vacated, or it is no longer equitable that the judgment should have prospective application; or (6) any other reason justifying relief from the operation of the judgment.

In more concrete terms, good cause might exist if a person has been incapacitated due to illness or injury, and is unable to attend to business; or if the attorney is ill or unavailable.

The motion must be made in reasonable time (up to one year from the date of judgment) for items 60(b)(1), (2), and (3). The form for a motion to set aside a default judgment appears in figure 6:14. We will discuss motion practice in more detail in the next chapter.

ASSIGNMENT 6:13
Copy the motion to set aside default judgment and the notice of motion and place them in your system folder.

ASSIGNMENT 6:14
Assume that you work for the firm that is representing Richard Hart and that for purposes of this problem, Mr. Hart is elderly and not well educated. He comes to your firm six months after a default judgment has been entered against him. Your attorney assigns you the task of determining if limited capacity brought on by aging and lack of education is sufficient good cause to have a default judgment set aside. Research the issue and prepare a brief outline on what facts are sufficient good cause to set aside a default judgment.

ASSIGNMENT 6:15 (SPECIAL EMPHASIS)
Two rules in this chapter give specific time limits that must be met. They are Rule 55(b)(2), which requires that notice of a hearing on an application for default judgment be served on the defendant or representative at least three days prior to the hearing, and Rule 60(b), which requires a motion to set aside a default judgment to be filed within one year from the date of the judgment in specified circumstances. Keeping track of time requirements and calendaring them is extremely important. Your system folder should have a guide to both federal and state time limits. See the Pleadings, Motions, and Time Limits table in chapter 7. Verify both state and federal deadlines for default judgments and all other deadlines as they arise.

Figure 6:14 Motion to Set Aside Default Judgment

THE UNITED STATES DISTRICT COURT FOR

THE _____ DISTRICT OF _____

Civil Action, File No. _____

_____,

Plaintiff

v.

_____,

Defendant

MOTION TO SET ASIDE

DEFAULT JUDGMENT

(NOTICE OF MOTION)

The Defendant moves the Court for an order to set aside the default judgment entered in the above action on _____, 19__, on the grounds that _____

_____

_____

_____

Attorney for Defendant
(Address)
(Phone number)

Notice of Motion
To: _____
Attorney for Plaintiff

Please take notice that the undersigned will bring the above motion on for hearing before this Court at Room _____, United States Courthouse, _____, on the _____ day of _____, 19__, at _____ o'clock in the _____ of that day, or as soon thereafter as counsel can be heard.

_____

Attorney for Defendant
(Address)

Summary

Chapter 6 has focused on the specific tasks that you must perform to commence a lawsuit officially, serve the opponent properly, and get a judgment should the defendant default. The purpose of filing the lawsuit is to notify the court and the defendant of the action and to establish its official beginning date.

You must determine what documents are needed to file the action, always including the summons and complaint, and see that they are prepared, signed, and copied. The original documents are then delivered to the clerk of the appropriate court, who stamps the complaint and assigns it a case number. A summons is issued.

Subsequently, the plaintiff must acquire personal jurisdiction over the defendant through service of the summons and a copy of the complaint. This can be accomplished by mail or personal service; the exact process is determined by whether the defendant is a person, a corporation, an out-of-state citizen, or a foreign citizen, and according to the federal or state rules of procedure. Citizens and corporations of other states may be served if there is an applicable long-arm statute and there are adequate minimal contacts to make the application of the statute constitutional. Constructive service requiring publication may be available to plaintiff—especially in in rem actions.

If the defendant is properly served and fails to answer the complaint or otherwise appear in the action, the plaintiff may seek a default judgment. Such a judgment ends the case and may award the plaintiff the sum or damages sought plus costs. No trial is held. You must consult local rules of court and local form books to determine default procedure. Normally the default should be officially entered as soon after its occurrence as possible, with the request for judgment following as soon as the law permits. If there is good cause for the defendant's default, the judgment may be set aside.

Study Guide

1. What purposes are achieved by filing the action and service of process?
2. What event marks the commencement of a lawsuit in the federal court system? What usually commences the action in most state systems?
3. What is the best method of determining which documents and how many are needed to properly file a civil lawsuit?
4. Review the Prefiling Checklist for both the federal system and your amended version of the state checklist. From memory, be able to state what documents are needed and to whom they will go.
5. Be able to prepare each of the documents needed for filing an action and for service of process in both the federal and state court systems.
6. Although the complaint has been drafted, what should be checked on the complaint before filing?
7. Who should sign the Civil Cover Sheet?
8. What must be filed with the clerk to authorize a paralegal to deliver service of process in the federal system? In your state system?
9. What is the filing fee to file a civil action in federal court? In your state court?
10. What does it mean for the clerk of court to issue a summons?
11. What is the clerk of federal court likely to ask the paralegal at the time of filing?
12. The court cannot gain personal jurisdiction over the defendant until what happens?
13. What is the practical goal of service of process?
14. Be prepared to explain who is to be served process when the defendant is one of the following:
   a. An individual: Federal? State?
   b. An infant or incompetent: Federal? State?
   c. A domestic or foreign corporation: Federal? State?
   d. The United States
   e. An officer or agency of the United States
   f. A state or a municipal corporation or other governmental organization thereof subject to suit
   g. A party outside the state or in a foreign country

15. What are long-arm statutes? What injustice do they attempt to remedy? What is meant by "minimum contacts"?
16. What classes of persons and businesses will the long-arm statute reach in your state?
17. What is (are) the method(s) of service required to comply with the long-arm statutes in your state?
18. What federal statutes permit nationwide service of process?
19. Who is served process in an in rem action?
20. Describe each step required in the federal system for service of process by mail. What items are needed?
21. How is service of process generally achieved in your state court system? What items are needed?
22. What are the alternative methods to service by mail in the federal system?
23. Who is immune from service of process and when?
24. What are ten techniques or sources for locating hard-to-find defendants?
25. How does a paralegal keep good records of service?
26. What is a default judgment?
27. What is the benefit to the plaintiff of a default judgment?
28. What are the applicable rules and procedures for obtaining a default judgment?
29. Be able to draft the necessary forms to obtain a default judgment for both state and federal court.
30. How and why may a default judgment be set aside?

Endnotes

1. Adapted from exhibit 4:18, WEINSTEIN, INTRODUCTION TO CIVIL LITIGATION 94 (2d ed. 1986) with permission of West Publishing Company.
2. Id., 95, with permission of West Publishing Company.
3. Memo from J. Burton to J. McCord (March 27, 1986).
4. BRUNO, PARALEGAL'S LITIGATION HANDBOOK 180 (1980).
5. Id.
6. Id., 182.
7. Id., 179.
8. Affidavit adapted from WEST'S FEDERAL FORMS, § 4663, v. 4, with permission of West Publishing Company.
9. Id., § 4672, with permission of West Publishing Company.
10. Id., §4670, with permission of West Publishing Company.

7

Defending and Testing the Lawsuit: Motions, Answers, and Other Responsive Pleadings

■ Introduction

When the complaint is received, the defendant may do one or more of the following: do nothing and default, attack the complaint through appropriate motions, file a petition to have the case removed from state court to federal court, and file an answer. The opponent may respond, amend, oppose, or reply as necessary.

Beyond this stage of the pleadings, both sides may test the lawsuit with hope of ending it through a motion for judgment on the pleadings and a motion for summary judgment. We will look at motion practice first through the defendant's motion to dismiss and other motions attacking the complaint.

■ Motions in General

A **motion** is a request to the court for an order granting relief favorable to the moving party. An **order** is a directive from a judge requiring some act or restraint from some act in a lawsuit—for example, an order to dismiss the case. Motions may be made before, during, and after trial. It is frequently the task of the paralegal to draft motions and supporting documents and to research the law in support of the motion.

Purpose

Motions have several purposes: to obtain judicial relief such as dismissal of the action, exclusion of evidence, new trial, and so on; to narrow the issues for trial; and to establish a record for appeal. The first of these purposes needs no explanation. The second, to narrow the issues for trial, reflects that motions are used for a variety of matters, some central to the cause of action that may eliminate the lawsuit altogether, and some of lesser impact to clarify and refine the lawsuit. The third purpose, to establish a record for appeal, indicates that motions raise questions of law that affect the outcome of the case and must be decided by the judge. The judge's decision on these questions is often appealed. The motion establishes the fact that an issue was raised in a proper and timely manner, thereby preserving the right to have the issue heard on appeal.

Requirements and Components of the Motion

Federal Rule 7(b) and parallel state rules set out the basic requirements for a motion: it must be made in writing, unless it is made at trial or hearing; its grounds must be stated with particularity, setting forth the order sought; it should have the same caption as the complaint with the exception that et al. (meaning "and others") may be used after the name of the first plaintiff or defendant rather than a list of all the other parties; and addresses need not to be included. Rules 7(b) (3) and 11 require that all motions be certified by the attorney's signature and include the attorney's address.

In addition to the motion, a notice of motion must be prepared. The purpose of the notice is to inform the opponent that a motion has been filed and will be heard by the court at a specified time and place. Due process requires that the adverse party be given notice and a fair chance to prepare for the hearing and to refute the motion. The Federal Rules permit the motion and notice of motion to be combined in one document called the notice of motion [Rule 7(b)].

Motions are frequently accompanied by an affidavit or a **memorandum of law.** Both provide the judge with information for a ruling on the motion. An affidavit sets forth additional facts not in the complaint. A memorandum of law presents the legal authority (statutes and case decisions) that the submitting party hopes will persuade the judge to decide the motion in the party's favor.

Procedure: Filing, Service, and Time Limits

When the documents are prepared and signed, the motion must be filed and served on the opponent's attorney consistent with the procedure set out in Rule 5 and as discussed in chapter 6.

A motion must be served not less than five days before the scheduled hearing on the motion [Rule 6(d)]. State requirements may vary. Affidavits may be served no later than one day before a hearing on the motion [Rule 6(d)]. The adverse party may file a responsive affidavit or memorandum.

ASSIGNMENT 7:1
Locate in your state rules the requirements, procedures, and time limits that apply to motions. Write a checklist for drafting, filing, and serving motions for both state and federal court, and place it in your system folder. Verify the time limits pertaining to motions in the Pleadings, Motions, and Time Limits table at the end of this chapter. Add state deadlines.

Motion to Dismiss

The Task

Mr. McDuff has just received the complaint in a case similar to Ms. Forrester's. In the new case, however, our firm represents the defendant, Allen Howard. Mr. McDuff would like you to look over the complaint to see if it can be attacked. After your review, Mr. McDuff will go over the complaint. If there are weaknesses in the complaint, your task will be to draft a motion to dismiss the opponent's complaint.

Purpose

The purpose of a motion to dismiss is to have the court dismiss the complaint. Reasons for this motion include lack of jurisdiction, improper venue, defective service, and so on, to be discussed later. Filing the motion to dismiss or related objections to the complaint is also a common tactic to gain time to prepare the required answer to the complaint, because the twenty-day limit to answer is suspended until the motion is decided. This tactic is not ethically defensible when the basis for the motion is without substance (frivolous) and is submitted solely for delay.

If the complaint is dismissed, the plaintiff will probably respond by amending the complaint. Occasionally, however, the plaintiff is unable to correct the defect, and the case ends, much to the delight of the defendant. The savings in cost, time, and anxiety can be substantial. In other words, if the opponent can be kept out of court, our client cannot lose the lawsuit.

A motion to dismiss the complaint says that the complaint does not state a claim for which relief can be granted. In some states the demurrer is used for the same purpose.

Determining What to Attack

What weaknesses should you look for? If you will recall our discussion on drafting complaints (chapter 5), the key to a successful complaint is a logical syllogism based on a rule of law, such as, if A, B, and C exist, then the plaintiff is entitled to remedy X. This rule is the major premise. The minor premise is stated in the complaint: A + B + C do in fact exist, therefore plaintiff should receive remedy X. This opens two avenues for attack. The first is to determine whether a required element of the minor premise is missing in the complaint. If so, the minor premise is incomplete and the complaint fails to state a claim. The second avenue of attack is to look beyond the complaint to the major premise. The complaint may be based on an inaccurate or misconceived reading of the law. If so, there can be no claim. The court occasionally does, however, decide to accept a new rule of law.

Let us look at the body of the negligence complaint filed against Mr. Howard.

4. On September 2, 19___, Defendant was operating a motor vehicle on South Maple Drive.
5. Defendant operated said vehicle in a negligent manner by failing to maintain a lookout and by failing to keep his automobile under control.
6. Plaintiff suffered great pain, broken ribs, and head injuries.
7. As a result of said injuries, plaintiff has incurred and will continue to incur doctor and hospital bills and loss of income and benefits.

Assume that you have researched the rule of law for a cause of action for negligence and find it to be: if A (duty) + B (breach) + C (injury) + D (breach is substantial cause of injury) exist, plaintiff is entitled to damages. Now apply the law to the complaint at hand to see if facts have been alleged to support each of the required elements of negligence. Paragraph four indicates that the defendant was operating a motor vehicle, which requires a duty of care toward others; therefore, a proper allegation of duty is present. Paragraph five alleges facts to show a breach of that duty. Paragraphs six and seven state facts in support of an injury to the plaintiff. So far, so good. But what is missing? The plaintiff has failed to allege facts to demonstrate D, that the defendant's breach of duty was a substantial cause of the plaintiff's injury. Because an entire element of the law is unalleged and unsupported, the complaint does not state a claim and is subject to a motion to dismiss. It is true that the omission may be easily corrected. On the other hand, there may not be a substantial connection between the defendant's negligence and the plaintiff's injuries, or the plaintiff may not have sufficient facts to demonstrate the connection. If the latter is true, the motion to dismiss will end the case against your client.

The body of the negligence complaint against Mr. Howard might read:

4. On September 2, 19___, Defendant was operating a motor vehicle on South Maple Drive.
5. Defendant operated said vehicle in a negligent manner by failing to maintain a lookout and by failing to keep his automobile under control.
6. Plaintiff no longer feels safe operating a vehicle on South Maple Drive.

Here the complaint alleges that A + B + E (plaintiff's fear) exist, therefore the plaintiff is entitled to X damages. Research shows the underlying rule of law to be that $A + B + C + D$, not E, invoke the right to a remedy. The complaint does not match the law. Because it is based on an erroneous reading of the law, the major premise implied in the complaint does not hold up, and no cause of action is stated.

In the previous examples, the complaint is missing the proper allegations to state a claim on which relief can be granted. A third avenue of attack arises when the complaint alleges too much, revealing a defense to the action. Consider this premise: if $A + B$ exist, and if W does not exist, then the plaintiff is entitled to relief. The existence of an element W, such as self-defense, would be a defense to the action. If in the factual allegation of the complaint, the plaintiff states that he was struck while lunging at the defendant, it might be sufficiently clear that W (self-defense) does exist. The motion to dismiss for failure to state a claim would be granted. Although oversimplified for purposes of illustration, these examples can be useful as a basic pattern in applying a syllogism to attack a complaint.

Prior to drafting the motion to dismiss the complaint, inform the supervising attorney of any apparent weaknesses in the opponent's complaint. This gives the attorney a chance to review the complaint, identify other weaknesses that need to be pursued, and assign any legal research needed to develop a basis for the motion founded in legal authority.

ASSIGNMENT 7:2

You are directed to look over another complaint for negligence. The body of the complaint reads as follows:

5. On March 22, 19___, Defendant owned and operated the Bay View Motel.
6. On that date Plaintiff was descending a stairway at the motel and, as a result of Defendant's conduct, tripped and fell down the stairway.
7. As a result of Defendant's conduct, Plaintiff suffered a broken wrist, a brain concussion, and numerous bruises over much of his body.
8. Because of the above injuries, Plaintiff had extensive medical bills and lost six weeks of work, to the sum of $25,000.

Using the method suggested in this section, determine if the body of this complaint is defective, and if so, why. Explain how the syllogism method of finding defects applies to this case. Be prepared to defend your conclusion.

The Memorandum of Law

Mr. McDuff agrees that the opponent's complaint is inadequate and assigns you the tasks of researching the legal basis for the motion to dismiss; writing a rough draft memorandum in support of the motion to dismiss; and drafting the motion to dismiss the complaint. You are also aware that the motion must be filed and served within the twenty days permitted by the rules.

You might start by asking Mr. McDuff if he recalls any recent cases where a similar motion was raised. The forms and authority used in such a case could cut your research and drafting time substantially. Another source of help is the firm's form file or memorandum of law file. A recent edition of a state civil practice manual may provide examples and some authority for your memo. Researching the question, however, provides the latest authorities and gives you more confidence.

Legal authority may provide the leverage to win a lawsuit. What authority can you find to attack your opponent's pleadings and motions?

Begin by going to the law library and finding the state or federal digest, as appropriate. Look up key words that focus on the issue at hand, such as "negligence," with subcategories of "complaint for," and further subcategories of "sufficiency" or "insufficiency," then turn to that section of the digest and pocket part to find cases like the one you are working on. Cases stating the general requirements of an adequate complaint are also persuasive. Cases that are relevant to the case at hand are *on point*. Read opinions in the state or federal reporter to be sure they apply, then Shepardize them: check the case citations in the appropriate state or federal *Shepard's Citations* to confirm that the cases are still good precedent and have not been overruled by more recent cases.

Drafting the Documents

When research is complete, draft the motion to dismiss the complaint. Figure 7:1 is an example of such a motion. Draft the notice of motion using the format demonstrated in figure 6:13. If a state uses the demurrer, it appears as in figure 7:2.

In some states a demurrer must contain the supporting authority for the demurrer, often eliminating the need for a memorandum of law.

The remaining task is the writing of the rough draft memorandum of law in support of the motion. Although the memorandum should be drafted with the highest standards, it is useful to consider it a rough draft to emphasize to both yourself and the attorney that the memorandum needs to be reviewed and probably revised by the attorney before filing at the courthouse. Figure 7:3 is a brief example of how a rough draft memorandum might look in Mr. Howard's case.

Figure 7:1   Motion to Dismiss Complaint

STATE OF COLUMBIA   CIRCUIT COURT   CAPITOL COUNTY

MARY ANN JAMES,
                        Plaintiff
            v.   Civil Action, File No. <u>22222</u>
ALLEN HOWARD,
                        Defendant

MOTION TO DISMISS COMPLAINT

Defendant moves the court pursuant to Rule 12(b)(6) of the Columbia Rules of Civil Procedure to dismiss the action because the complaint fails to state a claim against the Defendant upon which relief can be granted.

James McDuff
Attorney for Defendant
(Address)

Figure 7:2   General Demurrer

STATE OF COLUMBIA   CIRCUIT COURT   CAPITOL COUNTY

MARY ANN JAMES,
                        Plaintiff
            v.   Civil Action, File No. <u>22222</u>
ALLEN HOWARD
                        Defendant

DEMURRER

Defendant demurs to Plaintiff's complaint, specifying:
I
That said complaint does not state facts sufficient to constitute a cause of action against Defendant.
    WHEREFORE, Defendant prays that Plaintiff be awarded nothing by reason of his complaint and that he be dismissed with his costs of suit paid by Plaintiff.

James McDuff
Attorney for Defendant
(Address)

In some jurisdictions the court requires that the motion be accompanied by a draft of the order for the judge to sign. It is a good idea to do this whether it is required or not. Figure 7:4 is an example of such an order.
    Each of these documents should be proofed for accuracy, reviewed by the attorney, typed, and then signed by the attorney. Before filing the

Figure 7:3 Memorandum of Law in Support of Defendant's Motion to Dismiss Complaint

STATE OF COLUMBIA	CIRCUIT COURT	CAPITOL COUNTY

MARY ANN JAMES,
     Plaintiff

   v.   Civil Action, File No. <u>22222</u>

ALLEN HOWARD,

     Defendant

MEMORANDUM OF LAW
IN SUPPORT OF DEFENDANT'S MOTION TO DISMISS COMPLAINT

Defendant argues to the court that the Plaintiff's complaint should be dismissed on the grounds that it does not state a claim against the Defendant on which relief can be granted. In support of said motion, Defendant states the following.

That Plaintiff's complaint does not allege facts in support of a critical element of a claim for negligence. A long-standing precedent in the state of Columbia is the case of *Winthrup v. Walters*, 200 Col. 392, 105 W.W. 63 (1934).* That case established the rule of law that a civil complaint must allege and state facts in support of each element of the cause of action, and that failure to do so made the complaint defective and upheld the lower court's dismissal of the complaint for its failure to state a cause of action.

In the recent case of *Arnold v. Taggie*, 592 Col. 365, 354 S.W.2d 615 (1992)* where the plaintiff failed to allege that the defendant's negligent operation of a van was the cause of plaintiff's injuries, the court held the dismissal of the complaint for failure to state a cause of action was proper.

Plaintiff's complaint in this action does not allege that the Defendant's conduct caused her injuries, nor does it allege any facts to support such a conclusion.

Therefore, Plaintiff's complaint is defective and should be dismissed.

Date _____

              _____

              James McDuff
              Attorney for Defendant
              (Address)
              (Phone number)

*Citations in this memorandum are fictitious.

documents with the clerk, a hearing date for the motion should be acquired from the clerk to be placed on the notice of motion. One copy of each document should be kept in the file; the original should be delivered to the clerk's office; and one copy of the motion, memorandum of law, and notice of motion should be served on the plaintiff's attorney as previously indicated and set out now in your system folder.

Remember that in the Federal Rules and those of most states, the defendant must respond within twenty days of receipt of the complaint, and any motion must be served not later than five days before the time specified for the hearing on the motion, unless the rules or order of the court indicate otherwise. Local rules should always be checked. The opposing party may file a responsive memorandum of law.

Occasionally, one side or the other in a lawsuit may need an extension of time for some good reason. The paralegal may have the responsibility of drafting a stipulation between the parties for an extension of time. Since the court is likely to grant such a request, the parties generally cooperate and eliminate the need for court intervention. An example of such a stipulation appears in figure 7:5.

Figure 7:4 Order Granting Motion to Dismiss Complaint

STATE OF COLUMBIA   CIRCUIT COURT   CAPITOL COUNTY

MARY ANN JAMES,
                              Plaintiff
                      v.   Civil Action, File No. <u>22222</u>
ALLEN HOWARD,
                              Defendant

ORDER

On ____[date]____ Defendant motioned this Court for an order dismissing Plaintiff's complaint for failure to state a cause of action. The Court considered the motion, memoranda of law, and oral arguments heard by this Court on ____[date]____ .

For **GOOD CAUSE SHOWN**, this Court finds that facts in support of several elements of the cause of action are insufficiently alleged failing to state a cause of action and that Defendant's motion to dismiss should be granted. SO ORDERED.

Date _____

_____
Signature of Judge

Figure 7:5 Stipulation for Extension of Time

STATE OF COLUMBIA   CIRCUIT COURT   CAPITOL COUNTY

MARY ANN JAMES,
                              Plaintiff
                      v.   Civil Action, File No. <u>22222</u>
ALLEN HOWARD,
                              Defendant

STIPULATION FOR EXTENSION OF TIME

It is stipulated among counsel for Plaintiff and Defendant in the above action that Plaintiff shall have an extension of time to October 1, 19__, to respond to Defendant's memorandum of law in support of the motion to dismiss the complaint in this action.

Date _____

_____
Attorney for Plaintiff
(Address)
(Phone number)

_____
James McDuff
Attorney for Defendant
(Address)
(Phone number)

ASSIGNMENT 7:3
Copy each of the documents necessary to file a motion to dismiss the complaint and place them in your system folder.

ASSIGNMENT 7:4
To enhance your research and motion practice skills, follow the research steps outlined in the section of this chapter entitled "The Memorandum of Law." Locate a case from your state or federal jurisdiction that upheld the dismissal of a complaint for failure to state a claim. Make a copy of the complaint in the case and then draft the necessary motion and memorandum of law, plus all supporting documents. Citations in the court opinion and the case itself give authority for your memorandum. Gear your caption to the jurisdiction of the researched case. Make a copy of the case to hand in to your instructor with the completed assignment.

Other Motions to Dismiss

The most common motions to dismiss are contained in Rule 12(b) of the Federal Rules of Civil Procedure:

1. Lack of jurisdiction over the subject matter
2. Lack of jurisdiction over the person
3. Improper venue
4. Insufficiency of process
5. Insufficiency of service of process
6. Failure to state a claim upon which relief can be granted (previously discussed in this chapter)

Although it is beyond the scope of this book to discuss separate examples of each of these, the motion procedure previously discussed in this chapter applies to these motions as well as other motions presented in this text. Referral to a form manual, such as West's *Federal Legal Forms* or *American Jurisprudence Pleadings and Practice Forms* (rev. ed.), should provide you with any examples of the forms that you might need. The digests should provide leads to the case precedents needed to draft a memorandum in support of any of these 12(b) motions.

Form 19 of the Federal Rules gives an example of a motion to dismiss for failure to state a claim, for lack of service of process, for improper venue, and for lack of jurisdiction under Rule 12(b). Form 19 is duplicated in figure 7:6.

The Federal Rules and the rules of those states adopting the Federal Rules permit Rule 12(b) motions to be filed as part of the answer or other appropriate pleadings, or they may be filed separately as illustrated in this chapter.

Other Motions Attacking the Complaint

The Motion to Strike

There are two other motions commonly used to attack the complaint: a motion to strike and a motion to make more definite and certain. Rule 12(f) states, "Upon motion . . . the court may order stricken from any pleading any insufficient defense or any redundant, immaterial, impertinent, or

Figure 7:6   Form 19. Motion to Dismiss, Presenting Defenses of Failure to State a Claim, of Lack of Service of Process, of Improper Venue, and of Lack of Jurisdiction Under Rule 12(b)

The defendant moves the court as follows:

1. To dismiss the action because the complaint fails to state a claim against defendant upon which relief can be granted.

2. To dismiss the action or in lieu thereof to quash the return of service of summons on the grounds (a) that the defendant is a corporation organized under the laws of Delaware and was not and is not subject to service of process within the Southern District of New York, and (b) that the defendant has not been properly served with process in this action, all of which more clearly appears in the affidavits of M.N. and X.Y. hereto annexed as Exhibit A and Exhibit B respectively.

3. To dismiss the action on the ground that it is in the wrong district because (a) the jurisdiction of this court is invoked solely on the ground that the action arises under the Constitution and laws of the United States and (b) the defendant is a corporation incorporated under the laws of the State of Delaware and is not licensed to do or doing business in the Southern District of New York, all of which more clearly appears in the affidavits of K.L. and V.W. hereto annexed as Exhibit C and D respectively.

4. To dismiss the action on the ground that the court lacks jurisdiction because the amount actually in controversy is less than fifty thousand dollars exclusive of interest and costs.

Signed: _____
Attorney for Defendant

Address: _____

Notice of Motion

To: _____
   Attorney for Plaintiff

_____

Please take notice that the undersigned will bring the above motion on for hearing before this Court at Room _____, United States Court House, Foley Square, City of New York, on the _____ day of _____, 19__, at 10 o'clock in the forenoon of that day or as soon thereafter as counsel can be heard.

Signed:_____
Attorney for Defendant

Address: _____

scandalous matter." Hence, the purpose of the motion to strike is to keep pleadings lean, to the point, and free of spurious and prejudicial language. The motion to strike can be an effective mechanism to keep pleadings sensible and fair.

The Motion to Make More Definite and Certain

Rule 12(e) of the Federal Rules authorizes a motion when the complaint or other pleading is so vague or so devoid of facts that it is difficult to determine if a claim for relief or a defense to a claim has been stated. This motion is similar in function to a *special demurrer,* which is still used in some states to attack the complaint for insufficiency of facts. A request for a **bill of particulars,** which asks the opponent for more details, is used in some states. The purpose of the motion to make more definite and certain, the special demurrer, and the bill of particulars, however, is essentially the same: to provide the opponent with sufficient facts to determine the claim or defense, and the opportunity to respond.

You can assist the supervising attorney by reviewing outgoing or incoming pleadings for such defects, calling them to the attention of the attorney, and drafting the necessary motions and supporting documents. Rule 12(e) requires that the motion to make more definite and certain specify the defects complained of and the details desired.

Review the following excerpts from a complaint filed in federal district court. Do grounds exist for either a motion to strike or a motion to make more definite and certain?

COUNT ONE

1. . . .
2. Defendant negligently drove a vehicle against Plaintiff who was crossing the highway.
3. As a result, Plaintiff was injured to the sum of twenty thousand dollars.
   WHEREFORE . . .

COUNT TWO

4. . . .
5. Defendant negligently caused injury to Plaintiff.
6. As a result, Plaintiff has suffered serious emotional trauma to the sum of thirty thousand dollars.
   WHEREFORE . . .

This example demonstrates how problems may arise when a complaint is poorly drafted or without substance. Counts I and II of this complaint could be subject to a motion to make more definite and certain for several reasons: there is no date specified in the complaint, no location is given, and no facts are presented to support the claim that the defendant was driving negligently. The defendant can only guess at the accusation. Without more detail, it may be impossible to determine if there is a defense. For example, the defendant may have been in South America at the time of the alleged accident. The motion to make more definite and certain eliminates guesswork for the defendant regarding the basis for the claim. It is not to be used to provide details to the defendant such as weather conditions, names of witnesses, and other facts that can be found out in discovery. The motion to make more definite and certain appears in figure 7:7.

A motion to strike will not be allowed unless there is a very clear reason to do so. In the preceding example it appears as if Count Two may be a restatement of Count I, but alleging a different injury, emotional trauma. The statement of two counts could make the jury think the defendant had committed two wrongs instead of one. Assuming that the motion to make more definite and certain revealed that Count II simply repeated Count I, a motion to strike under Rule 12(f) for redundant material is in order. Emotional trauma would then be included in the damages clause to Count I. Figure 7:8 is how such a motion appears.

Figure 7:7   Motion to Make More Definite and Certain

(Caption omitted)

MOTION TO MAKE MORE DEFINITE AND CERTAIN

Defendant, pursuant to Rule 12(e) of the Federal Rules of Civil Procedure, moves this court for an order requiring Plaintiff to provide a more definite statement of the claim against the Defendant.

As grounds, Defendant states the Plaintiff's complaint is so vague and ambiguous that Defendant cannot reasonably frame a response thereto.

The complaint is defective for the reasons stated below:

1. In both Counts One and Two Plaintiff does not state on what date the alleged incident occurred.
2. Nor does Plaintiff indicate the location of said occurrence, and
3. Insufficient facts are alleged in support of the claim of negligence or any other cause of action.

Defendant requests Plaintiff provide the following:

1. The date of the alleged incident.
2. The specific location of the incident, and
3. Facts describing how the Defendant was negligent.

(Attorney's signature and address)
(Notice of motion omitted)

Figure 7:8   Motion to Strike Redundant, Immaterial, Impertinent, or Scandalous Matter from Pleading

(Caption omitted)

MOTION TO STRIKE

Defendant, pursuant to Rule 12(f) of the Federal Rules of Civil Procedure moves the court for an order striking Count Two of the Plaintiff's complaint on the grounds that it is redundant, repeating the same cause of action as Count One, causing confusion and prejudicing Defendant at trial.

(Attorney's signature and address)
(Notice of motion omitted)

Apply what you learn in reviewing pleadings for weaknesses to improve the drafting of your own complaints and other pleadings.

ASSIGNMENT 7:5
Make copies of the Motion to Strike and the Motion to Make More Definite and Certain, and place them in your system folder.

Ethics Reminder

Remember that the attorney's signature on a pleading, including a motion, certifies: that the attorney has read the document, that it is well grounded in fact, that it is warranted by law or a good-faith argument to alter the law, and that it is not offered for any improper purpose (Rule 11). Keep this in mind while drafting and reviewing pleadings.

Response to Motions

When the plaintiff receives the defendant's motion, check to see if it was filed within the time limit provided (in the case of a complaint, within the twenty days), that it contains the requisite information (in writing, particular grounds, relief sought, and any necessary affidavit [Rule 7(b)]), and that it contains the necessary signatures under Rule 11 or similar state rule.

To respond, you may need to research the matter (and brief it if the court has required it) and draft any opposing affidavit. After consulting with the attorney and obtaining needed signatures, serve the response to the motion not later than one day before the hearing on the motion [Rule 6(d)] unless an enlargement of time is granted [Rule 6(b)]. Any legal authority or supporting evidence that you have gathered becomes the basis for a possible oral argument before the judge. If the motion to dismiss is denied, the defendant must proceed to file an answer; if successful, either the case will be dismissed with the possibility of a new start if the defect can be corrected, or the court may permit the plaintiff an opportunity to amend the complaint without dismissal.

■ Removal of State Action to Federal Court

The Task

Mr. McDuff wants you to draft the necessary documents and follow the necessary procedure to have Allan Howard's case removed from the state court to the federal district court. This task can be important to the defendant's case, but the task itself is relatively simple.

Purpose

The objective of removal is to have the case transferred from the jurisdiction of the state court to that of the federal court. The defendant is given this privilege under 28 U.S.C. § 1441 et seq. It affords the defendant the same opportunity that the plaintiff has to choose either the state or federal court when their respective jurisdictions are concurrent. A case may not be removed unless the federal district court has original jurisdiction over the subject matter of the lawsuit. An attorney may choose federal court for a variety of strategic reasons:

1. A different judge, considering that federal judges have more control over the case and may comment on the evidence;
2. A more competent jury (it is generally harder for business people and others to get excused from federal jury duty);
3. A twelve-person jury requiring a unanimous verdict in contrast to many state juries that are six in number, often requiring a 5/6 or 3/4 verdict in civil cases;
4. A chance to have the case removed to an even more convenient federal court through the liberal transfer and venue rules within the federal system; and
5. A more complete discovery of evidence under the federal discovery rules than some state rules.

Although some of these considerations can be quite complex, the end result can be an increased likelihood of winning the case.

Cases That May Be Removed and When

The United States Code Title 28 § 1441(a) states that

> any civil action brought in a state court of which the district courts of the United States have original jurisdiction, may be removed by the defendant or the defendants, to the district court of the United States for the district and division embracing the place where such action is pending.

Therefore, if federal original subject matter jurisdiction exists, as it does in diversity of citizenship and federal question cases, then the case may be removed. Only defendants have the right of removal, and all defendants must agree to the removal. Removal is a statutory and not a constitutional right, so any close questions about the appropriateness of removal are to be decided against removal. Any officer of the United States or any officer of a United States agency may have a case against the officer removed to federal court [28 U.S.C. § 1442(a)]. Civil rights cases where a person is denied the opportunity to have a federal right honored because of some unique aspects of state law can be removed to federal court (28 U.S.C. § 1443). Cases that may not be removed include workers' compensation cases, specified actions against railroads, and some actions against interstate (common) carriers [28 U.S.C. § 1445(a–c)]. The state court no longer must have jurisdiction for the federal court to hear the case [28 U.S.C. § 1441(e)].

The right to remove a case must exist when the action is commenced and at the time of the petition for removal. The right to remove related cases along with the federal jurisdiction case was limited significantly by the Judicial Improvement Act of 1990. Formerly, actions subject to state jurisdiction could be removed to federal court only if they were related to any federal jurisdiction action and the removal allowed the federal court to adjudicate all claims at one time. Congress now permits this joinder of actions only in federal question cases—no longer can state cases be removed along with diversity of citizenship cases [28 U.S.C. § 1441(c)].

Procedure

The procedure for removing a case to federal court is governed by 28 U.S.C. § 1446. This statute was recently amended requiring the following procedure:

1. File a "notice of removal" in the federal district court encompassing the area where the state action is pending. The notice must be signed in compliance with Rule 11 of the Federal Rules of Civil Procedure [28 U.S.C. § 1446(a)].
2. The notice should contain a "short plain statement of the grounds for removal, together with a copy of all process, pleadings, and orders served upon . . . defendants" [§ 1446(a)]. The notice should include:
   a. The statute conferring federal jurisdiction;
   b. Facts in support of federal jurisdiction;

    c. The date of receipt of the initial pleadings in the state action;
    d. The applicable removal statute [28 U.S.C. § 1446(b)]; and
    e. That all defendants have joined in the removal action.
3. The notice of removal must be served on all parties and filed within thirty days after commencement of the state action or, if the original action is not removable but becomes removable, thirty days after amendment or service of papers from which it can be determined that the action has become removable.
4. The requirement of filing a bond has been abolished, even though some overlooked language about the bond remains in the statute [§ 1446(d)].
5. A copy of the notice must be "promptly" filed with the state court; the state court must proceed no further.

The plaintiff can challenge the removal through a motion to remand because of defects in the removal process. This motion must be filed within thirty days after the filing of the notice of removal (28 U.S.C. § 1447). The district court's subject matter jurisdiction can be challenged any time up to the entry of judgment. If after removal the plaintiff joins additional defendants whose joinder defeats subject matter jurisdiction, the district court may deny joinder, or it may permit joinder and remand the case to state court [28 U.S.C. § 1447(c)]. Figure 7:9[1] is a suggested format for the notice of removal.

Figure 7:9 Notice of Removal

[28 U.S.C.A. §§ 1441, 1446]

[*Title of Federal Court and Cause as in State Court*]

To: The United States District Court for the _____ District of _____, _____ Division; and to: _____ Counsel for Plaintiff(s) from: _____, Counsel for Defendants.
    1. Pursuant to 28 U.S.C. §§ 1441 and 1446(b) take notice that the above entitled action is removed to the above mentioned United States District Court.
    2. The above entitled action was commenced in the _____ Court of _____ county, State of _____ and is now pending in that court. Process was served on the petitioner on the _____ day of _____, 19__. A copy of the plaintiff's _____ (complaint, declaration or other initial pleading) setting forth the claim for relief upon which the action is based was first received by the petitioner on the _____ day of _____, 19__.
    3. The action is a civil action for _____ [*state briefly nature of case*] and the United States District Court for the District of _____ has jurisdiction by reason of the diversity of citizenship of the parties.
    4. Plaintiff is a citizen of the State of _____ and defendant is a citizen of the State of _____. The matter in controversy exceeds, exclusive of costs and disbursements, the sum [*or value*] of $50,000. No change of citizenship of parties has occurred since the commencement of the action.
    5. All defendants have joined in this removal action (if applicable).
    6. Copies of all process, pleadings and orders served upon petitioners are filed herewith.

Dated _____, 19__.

                                        _____
                                        Attorney for Petitioner

                                        Address: _____

ASSIGNMENT 7:6
Copy the form for removing an action to federal court in figure 7:9 and place it in your system folder. You may also choose to develop your own brief checklist for the required procedural stages and place that in your system folder.

ASSIGNMENT 7:7
Draft the Notice of Removal to have the case against Allen Howard removed to federal court, as Mr. McDuff requested.

■ Computation of Time

In this chapter we have discussed a variety of procedures and responses that require one side or the other in the lawsuit to meet a deadline imposed by the rules "within twenty days," "not less than five days before the hearing," or some other limit. You must be able to compute these time periods accurately, either to comply with the deadlines or to know when the adverse party is not in compliance. Federal Rule 6(a) states what days should be included or excluded in calculating the time period. The day the pleading is served or mailed, and the day the hearing is held, for example, are not counted. The last day of any time period may not fall on a Saturday, Sunday, or a legal holiday. When it does, the next regular business day is considered the final day of the period. When the period of time is less than eleven days, Saturdays, Sundays, and legal holidays shall not be counted. The legal holidays include New Year's Day, Martin Luther King, Jr.'s Birthday, Presidents' Day, Memorial Day, Independence Day, Labor Day, Columbus Day, Veterans' Day, Thanksgiving Day, Christmas Day, and any other days so designated by the president or Congress, or by the state in which the district court is held. When working in state court, the state's rules on time should be consulted.

Confusion arises when the rule or order states the time as "two months" rather than "sixty days" or "to" July 1 rather than "until" July 1. In these instances it is best to consult local rules. If they are unclear, consult the judge or a knowledgeable clerk. Generally speaking, however, "two months" means the specific number of calendar days in each of the next two months (twenty-eight, thirty, or thirty-one days). Two months from a specific date is that same numerical date—say the fourth—two months later (two months from June 4 = August 4). Sixty days is simply sixty calendar days starting with the first day after service or other required act. "To" a certain day usually means "up to" and does not include the designated day. "Until" normally means until the close of business on the specified day. An enlargement of time that has been granted by the court begins at the time the original time limit expires (i.e., if the answer was originally due on October 1, a thirty-day extension would run through October 31). It bears no relationship to the date on which the court grants the motion to extend the time.

Here is a formula for computing the due date: date of service + the number of days in the prescribed time period — the number of days in the month if the days in the time limit exceed the number of days left in the month = due date. To calculate the due date for an answer to a complaint served on September 20, the formula would work as follows:[2]

Date of Service: September   20
Prescribed time limit   20
Total   40
Less days in September   30
Due Date   10th of October (unless Saturday,
                                     Sunday, or holiday, then add
                                     days to next business day)

Remember that when service is by mail, three days shall be added to any prescribed period [Rule 6(e)]. Failure to calculate time accurately can result in some serious consequences including default, loss of a claim or defense, payment of penalties or costs, and possible malpractice claims against the law firm.

ASSIGNMENT 7:8
Add the rules for calculating time for both the federal and your state jurisdiction [see Rule 6(a)] to your system folder. Include the formula and the previous example on how to calculate the due date.

◼ Drafting the Answer, Counterclaim, and Cross-Claim

For the purposes of this section, assume that you are a paralegal in the firm of Ott, Ott, and Knudsen, which is representing Mercury Parcel Service. You receive the following interoffice memo:

Memo to: Chris Sorenson
From: Lynn Ott
Subject: Forrester v. Hart and Mercury Parcel

Date: October 1, 19__
    We have twenty days to file an answer to the complaint against our client, Mercury Parcel. Please draft the answer including a counterclaim against Ms. Forrester for her negligence which resulted in injury to Mr. Hart, our need to replace him temporarily, and damage to our van. Please ask me if you need any assistance.

The purpose of the answer is to give the defendant a chance to respond to the complaint and identify the issues to be contested. It contains a statement of what the defendant admits and denies, and what defenses to the claim, if any, will be presented.

General Requirements

Time

Rule 12(a) of the Federal Rules and parallel state rules require the answer to be served on the plaintiff within twenty days after receipt of the summons and complaint. The time limit varies from state to state. The United States is given sixty days to file an answer. Consult the rules for your state to be sure of the time limit. The summons may state the time limit. On receipt of the summons and complaint, note the due date in the deadline control system.

ASSIGNMENT 7:9
Verify the required time limit for filing an answer and the applicable federal and state rules in the Pleadings, Motions, and Time Limits table.

Style and Content of the Answer

The answer should be drafted similarly to the complaint:

- Be clear and concise [Rules 8(b) and (e)(1)].
- Use numbered paragraphs addressing point by point the elements of the complaint, each paragraph being a statement of a single set of facts [Rule 10(b)].
- Avoid impertinent, scandalous, or immaterial language [Rule 12(f)].
- Follow the complaint logically.
- Reveal no more facts than necessary.
- Avoid evidence and conclusions, and
- Be truthful [Rule 11 and Disciplinary Rule 7–10(a)].
- State that the defendant lacks knowledge or information sufficient to form a belief as to the truth of the matter alleged, when that is the case [Rule 8(b)].
- State separate defenses in separate paragraphs.

The difference between notice pleading and code pleading applies to answers as it does to complaints. An answer drafted for a code pleading jurisdiction requires more detail than an answer for a notice pleading jurisdiction. Check local procedure and forms for guidance.

ASSIGNMENT 7:10
Draft a list of the previous style and content suggestions and place it in your system folder.

Structure of the Answer

The answer may have several components: legal defenses, admissions, denials, affirmative defenses, counterclaims, and cross-claims. After reviewing the complaint, the defendant's attorney indicates to the paralegal what needs to be done. The attorney may scribble directions on a copy of the complaint. For complex complaints, use a color-coded system: yellow highlight for facts admitted; blue for facts denied; and pink for allegations lacking knowledge to form a belief. The paralegal for the plaintiff would find this a useful method for keeping track of what has been admitted or denied by the defendant.[3]

Defenses

Defenses using the Rule 12(b) motion to dismiss for failure to state a claim, for lack of jurisdiction, for insufficient process, and others are commonly filed as separate motions. They may also be a part of the answer [Rule 12(b)(1) and (2)], where they are set out following the caption. If these defenses have not been filed separately, the attorney should be consulted to see if they are to be added to the answer. This is important because a defense of lack of personal jurisdiction, improper venue, insufficiency of process, or insufficiency of service of process is waived unless raised in the first responsive pleading [Rule 12(h)(1)] or unless the court permits an amendment under Rule 15(a).

Denials

Rule 8(d) requires a party in a responsive pleading to deny the allegations of the other party or they will be deemed admitted. The answer, therefore, should contain a section where the opponent's allegations are denied, when the facts justify the denial. General denials, however, are discouraged by the rules of most jurisdictions. A general denial is a brief statement that denies all allegations and claims of the plaintiff. Because it fails to narrow the contested issues and encourages a sweeping, thoughtless response, it is not favored by the courts. Instead, Rule 8(b) requires the denials to be written in short, plain terms with a separate admission or denial for each of the plaintiff's allegations. The denial should make clear what language in what paragraph of the complaint is being denied.

Plaintiff's allegation:

4. Defendant's vehicle was traveling in excess of the speed limit at the time of the accident.

Defendant's corresponding answer would use the same paragraph number as the complaint and state a short, plain denial:

4. Defendant denies the allegation of paragraph 4 of the complaint.

Or if the defendant agreed with the allegation, the response would be:

4. Defendant admits the allegation of paragraph 4 of the complaint.

It may be necessary to split a response and admit some and deny some of the allegation [Rule 8(b)].

Plaintiff's allegation:

5. Defendant is the owner of said van which struck Plaintiff.

Defendant's response:

5. Admitted in part and denied in part. It is admitted that Defendant owns said van. It is denied that said van struck the Plaintiff.

If the defendant has insufficient knowledge or information to form a belief as to the truth of the matter, then the response should so state [Rule 8(b)]. However, this type of denial should be made in good faith and not simply to avoid an admission, reveal a denial, or cover up an unwillingness to investigate the fact. The penalty assessed in such circumstances is a finding that the allegation is admitted.[4] A response based on lack of knowledge follows.

Plaintiff's allegation:

6. As a result of Defendant's negligence plaintiff has suffered loss of employment.

Defendant's response:

6. Defendant lacks knowledge sufficient to form a belief as to the truth of the allegation in paragraph 6 of Plaintiff's complaint, and therefore denies same.

Denials should not be ambiguous. For example, if the plaintiff alleges that the defendant is the owner of the car that struck the plaintiff at the corner of Jefferson and Wells streets, and the defendant simply states "denied," it is impossible to know what is being denied—ownership of the car, location of the accident, or the fact that the car struck the plaintiff. The denial should be more specific. Denials that state facts suggesting a defense, but in fact are not really defenses, are called **argumentative denials.** For example, if the plaintiff alleges an accident occurred in Gary, Indiana, on the evening of March third and the defendant replies, "Defendant was in Chicago on March 3," there is an implication that the defendant was elsewhere. However, that is not necessarily the case, since the person could travel to both places on the same day. This type of answer is only confusing and should be avoided.[5]

Here are some other suggestions for drafting successful denials.[6] If the defendant faces making a multitude of denials covering words as well as phrases, it might be easier to state the defendant's own version of the facts, using the following format:

As to paragraph _____ of the complaint, [Defendant] alleges that [own version of facts]. Except as so alleged, Defendant denies the remaining allegations of paragraph _____.

When the term of a contract or other document is characterized in the pleading, it is best to deny the opponent's characterization and state that the documents speak for themselves.

When a co-defendant faces allegations or counts addressed to the other defendant, the language of Rule 8(b) does not excuse the defendant from denying claims asserted against a co-defendant. The following response is suggested:

As to paragraph _____ of the complaint, [Defendant] denies having sufficient knowledge to form a belief.

Paragraphs _____ to _____ [of Plaintiff's complaint] do not apply to this Defendant, but insofar as they do refer to, may refer to, or may apply to this Defendant, each allegation is denied.

If lack of capacity is alleged or performance of a condition precedent is denied, such must be done specifically and with particularity as required by Rule 9 on pleading special matters.

Table 7:1 summarizes the denials available and their purposes.

ASSIGNMENT 7:11
Drawing from the entire subsection on denials, make a list of suggestions for drafting successful denials and add it to the system folder. Add table 7:1, Forms of Denial in Pleadings, to your system folder.

Affirmative Defenses

An affirmative defense says, "There are facts present which defeat the plaintiff's claim." These facts are not denials; they are "new matters" and

Table 7:1 Forms of Denial in Pleadings

TYPE	FORM [each answer after "reasonable inquiry" must be accurate and submitted in good faith (Rule 11)]	EFFECT
Deny	Defendant denies the allegations of paragraph _____ of the complaint, or Denied (depending on jurisdiction).	Denies each allegation of that paragraph; any allegation not denied is admitted [Rule 8(d)].
Without knowledge	Defendant is without knowledge or information sufficient to form a belief as to the allegation that (state specific allegation) of paragraph _____ of the complaint.	Works as denial but provides flexibility as more information comes to light. Defendant has burden to make "reasonable inquiry."
Admit in part	As to paragraph _____, defendant admits to operating the van on (date) but denies the balance of the allegations in the paragraph.	Makes the admission specific, but denial of remainder of paragraph avoids having to list and possibly omitting a response to some of the items.
Leave to proof	As to paragraph _____, defendant neither admits; or denies but leaves plaintiff to his/her proof.	Works as denial by requiring plaintiff to prove facts at trial.
Own allegation	Defendant denies the allegation in paragraph _____ and alleges that (own version of facts).	Gives defendant the opportunity to be free from certain implications of plaintiff's language and to state more accurately what happened.
No answer/ conclusion of law	The allegation in paragraph _____ of the complaint improperly states a conclusion of law.	Protects defendant but points out that pleadings are not to allege conclusions of law, just facts in support of the conclusions.
Denial on information and belief	Defendant, on information and belief, denies the allegation in paragraph _____ of the complaint.	Generally used by corporations to deny based on the best information they have at the time from their employees. Permits change if necessary.
Note applicable to defendant	Paragraphs _____ to _____ of the complaint do not apply to this defendant, but insofar as they do refer to, may refer to, or may apply to this defendant, each allegation is denied.	Provides notice that defendant feels the allegation does not apply to this defendant but protects defendant in case it is intended to apply.

say, "Even if all of the plaintiff's allegations are true, the defendant has a defense to the claim and should prevail."

Affirmative defenses are defined by substantive law. Each action or claim established by substantive law has one or more defenses that will defeat the claim. A civil action for battery can be defeated by proving self-defense; slander by proving the statement is true; negligence by proving contributory negligence (where it still exists as a defense) or assumption of risk; and so on.

It is the responsibility of the defendant's attorney to determine if the substantive law provides a defense to the claim, and whether there are sufficient facts to support a good allegation of that defense. As it is true that each element of a claim must be supported by facts in the complaint, so it is that each element of an affirmative defense must be supported by facts in the answer.

The attorney may tell you what defenses, if any, are to be drafted into the answer. Nevertheless, you need to know how to determine what defenses are available to the claim and what facts must be alleged to support the elements of the defense. The procedure for locating defenses is similar to the procedure for locating the elements of a claim as described in chapter 5:

Identify the descriptive word for the claim (negligence, contract, anti-trust, etc.).

In the index to the appropriate jury instruction book, look up the descriptive word for the claim and search for the subcategory on defenses or a separate section in the index on affirmative defenses. Turn to the designated instruction, which should define the affirmative defense and set out the elements that must be proven.

Go to a legal encyclopedia and look up the descriptive word for the claim and the subcategory under that topic on defenses. Here the defenses are defined and the elements set out.

If the claim is defined by statute, consult the index of the annotated statutes to find the pertinent statute and defenses.

Review the applicable digest of cases under the topic of the affirmative defense. These cases may shed light on what elements must be alleged and typical fact situations that invoke the defense.

Compare this information with the facts known about the case at hand, determining what defenses are applicable and what facts, if any, support an allegation of the defense.

ASSIGNMENT 7:12
Draft a list of the steps in locating affirmative defenses and add the list to the system folder.

ASSIGNMENT 7:13
Review the basic facts set out in chapter 1 for Case IV, *Briar Patch Dolls, Inc. v. Teeny Tiny Manufacturing Co.*, a contract case. Using the method described in this section, make an initial determination of what affirmative defenses under the topic "discharge" might be available to the defendants. Make a list of these defenses and suggest some facts that might be necessary to support the defense. Because there are numerous defenses in contract law, confine yourself in this assignment to those defenses within the concept of "discharge."

Federal Rule 8(c) sets out the defenses that must be alleged affirmatively:

Accord and satisfaction	Discharge in bankruptcy
Arbitration and award	Duress
Assumption of risk	Estoppel
Contributory negligence	Failure of consideration

Fraud	Res judicata
Illegality	Statute of frauds
Injury by fellow servant	Statute of limitations
Laches	Waiver
License	Any other avoidance or affirma-
Payment	tive defense
Release	

For the definition of these terms, see appendices B and C on torts and contracts and a legal dictionary.

Federal Rule 8(e)(2) indicates that affirmative defenses may be pleaded in the alternative, hypothetically, and even inconsistently. Therefore, in a negligence case a defendant might admit to the negligence but allege the running of the statute of limitations, or might allege that the plaintiff is comparatively negligent as well as having assumed the risk.

Affirmative defenses are placed immediately after the denials in the answer and appear as follows.

FIRST AFFIRMATIVE DEFENSE
Plaintiff did not file this action before the one-year statute of limitations elapsed.

SECOND AFFIRMATIVE DEFENSE
Plaintiff signed a release on November 8, 19__, relieving Defendant of all liability in this matter.

In some states the affirmative defenses fall in a section on the answer titled "New Matter." The length and detail of the affirmative defense depend on the practice in a particular jurisdiction. In a notice pleading jurisdiction, the defenses may be stated quite briefly. In a code or "fact" pleading state, more detail may be required.

Under modern rules of pleading, the plaintiff is not required to plead responsively to the defenses. They are assumed to be controverted. The plaintiff, however, may choose to attack the defenses in the same manner as the defendant attacks the complaint: through a motion to strike or to dismiss, or through a demurrer in some jurisdictions.

Wherefore Clause

The answer includes a "wherefore" clause:

> WHEREFORE, Defendant demands a jury trial, requests that Plaintiff's complaint be dismissed, and that judgment be entered for the Defendant for his/her costs and disbursements.

A single "wherefore" clause is all that is necessary in most jurisdictions regardless of the inclusion of affirmative defenses or the number of affirmative defenses. Some attorneys prefer and some local practices require one "wherefore" clause after the denials and another after the affirmative defenses. Verify the local practice. The demand for a jury trial should be included in the answer; some drafters prefer to place it in the caption, while others place it in the "wherefore" clause. In some states a demand for a jury trial must be made in a separate document called a *notice of issue.*

Counterclaims

The counterclaim is a claim asserted by the defendant against the plaintiff. It may arise out of the same circumstances as the plaintiff's claim or from unrelated circumstances. It is a suit within a suit. For example, a bishop used tennis courts at the United States Naval Academy on a regular basis for a number of years. He was never charged for his use of the courts. When the bishop injured his leg playing tennis, he sued the Naval Academy for negligence. The Naval Academy in turn counterclaimed against the bishop for all the accumulated fees owed the academy for use of the court.[7]

Rule 13 of the Federal Rules of Civil Procedure permits two basic types of counterclaims: compulsory and permissive.

Compulsory counterclaims are those that arise out of the original circumstances leading to the plaintiff's action against the defendant. For example, if Mercury Parcel thought Ann Forrester was responsible for the auto-pedestrian accident, it could counterclaim against Ms. Forrester for the loss of business and damage to their van. Since this claim arose out of the same transaction as Ms. Forrester's claim, Federal Rule 13(a) requires it to be brought in the answer. If not asserted, the claim could not be raised against the plaintiff in a separate lawsuit. The purpose of this rule is to have all claims related to a single occurrence resolved at one time. In some states where the Federal Rules have not been adopted, there are no compulsory counterclaims.

Counterclaims may also be brought against the plaintiff for claims unrelated to the original action [Rule 13(b)]. Assume that Ann Forrester had owed money for services provided to her by Mercury Parcel. Mercury Parcel could assert a *permissive counterclaim* against Ms. Forrester for the debt. The purpose of this rule is to use the one suit to resolve all outstanding matters between the parties rather than doing so through separate lawsuits. The defendant, however, may choose to assert the claim in a separate lawsuit and is not barred from doing so. If the claim is asserted in the answer, an independent source of jurisdiction for the unrelated action must be asserted. A court will not permit the original action to be left in limbo for failure of the court to get jurisdiction over the counterclaim.

Counterclaims are added to the answer following the "wherefore" clause after the affirmative defenses. Appropriate portions of the complaint may be incorporated by reference. The claim must be drafted according to the same rules as the body of the complaint and assert facts necessary to support the elements of the claim.

The defendant may add other parties besides the plaintiff [Rule 13(h)], and the amount of the claim may exceed that of the original action [Rule 13(c)]. Should a counterclaim against the plaintiff arise after the answer has been filed, or if the defendant realizes that a counterclaim has been inadvertently missed, Rules 13(e) and (f), respectively, permit the subsequent filing of those claims by leave of the court. There is a filing fee for the counterclaim.

The counterclaim is subject to the same attack and motions as the complaint, and the plaintiff is required to reply to the counterclaim with denials and defenses in the same fashion that the defendant answers the complaint. The plaintiff's response to the counterclaim is called a reply and must be served on the defendant within twenty days after service of the answer and counterclaim [Rule 12(a)].

Cross-Claims

When two or more persons are sued in an action, it is not unusual for one party to believe the other party should bear the liability. For example, if a builder of an office building is sued over defects in the building, the builder may believe that any damages owed the plaintiff were caused by and should be the responsibility of his co-defendant, the architect who designed the building. In such circumstances, the builder may file a cross-claim against the architect. Rule 13(g) permits a cross-claim to be filed against a co-party only if the cross-claim arises out of the original action or a counterclaim or relates to any property that is the subject matter of the original action. Cross-claims, therefore, do not require an independent source of jurisdiction. A party may choose to cross-claim or sue independently.

A cross-claim must meet all the pleading requirements of any other claim. It is placed in the answer after the counterclaim or may be placed in a separate document. A cross-claim does not require a summons for service.

Should the original action be dismissed or otherwise disposed of, the court will still try a remaining cross-claim or counterclaim. If a cross-claim or counter-claim is made a part of the answer, the title of the document should be changed from "Answer" to "Answer, Counterclaim, and Cross-Claim."

If either a counterclaim or cross-claim or both are drafted into the answer, an additional "wherefore" clause is required in the answer, demanding judgment to be entered for the person bringing the claims for the sum requested, plus costs and interest. A party receiving a cross-claim has twenty days to answer.

Certification and Verification

All that is required to certify the answer under the federal rules of pleading is the signature and address of the defendant's attorney. If the state rules require verification, the defendant must read the pleading, sign it, and have it notarized. As you may recall, a verification is the defendant's sworn statement that the defendant has read the pleading and that all the facts alleged are true or otherwise stated on information and belief. For this reason, it may be best not to plead inconsistent facts where verification is required.[8] Local practice should be determined.

Sample Answer, Counterclaim, and Cross-Claim

The general requirements and components of an answer have been reviewed. The task assigned is to draft an answer for Mr. Hart to the complaint filed against him by Ms. Forrester and her husband. The Forresters' complaints (both notice and code-pleading examples) appear in figures 7:10 and 7:12. Following each complaint is the corresponding answer (see figures 7:11 and 7:13). Note the difference between the two answers in the factual detail required.

Figure 7:10   Forrester Complaint: Notice Pleading

UNITED STATES DISTRICT COURT FOR
THE EASTERN DISTRICT OF COLUMBIA

Civil Action, File No. _____

ANN FORRESTER 　　　　and WILLIAM FORRESTER, 　　　　　　Plaintiffs 　　　　v. RICHARD HART 　　　　and MERCURY PARCEL SERVICE, INC., 　　　　　　Defendants	COMPLAINT FOR NEGLIGENCE Jury Trial Demanded

COUNT I

1. Plaintiffs are citizens of the State of Columbia and Defendant Hart is a citizen of the State of Ohio; Defendant Mercury Parcel Service, Inc., is a corporation incorporated under the laws of the State of Delaware, having its principal place of business in the State of Ohio. The matter in controversy exceeds, exclusive of interest and costs, the sum of $50,000.
2. On February 26, 19___, on Highway 328 in Capitol County, Columbia, Defendant Hart, an employee of Defendant Mercury Parcel, Inc., negligently drove a motor vehicle striking down Plaintiff who was crossing said highway.
3. As a result, Plaintiff fractured her left leg and hip bones and was otherwise seriously injured; has been prevented from transacting her business; has suffered and continues to suffer, great pain of body and mind; has incurred, and will continue to incur, expenses for medical attention and hospitalization, all to the sum of $750,000.

WHEREFORE Plaintiff demands judgment against Defendant in the sum of $750,000.

COUNT II

4. Plaintiff William Forrester hereby alleges and incorporates by reference paragraphs 1 through 3 of Count One.
5. Because of Defendant's negligence, Plaintiff has suffered loss of the consortium of his wife, Ann Forrester, in the amount of $20,000.

WHEREFORE, Plaintiff demands judgment against the Defendant in the sum of $20,000.

Arthur White
Attorney for Plaintiffs
(Address)
(Phone number)

Figure 7:11 Answer and Counterclaim to Forrester Complaint: Notice Pleading

UNITED STATES DISTRICT COURT FOR
THE EASTERN DISTRICT OF COLUMBIA

Civil Action, File No. _____

ANN FORRESTER
and
WILLIAM FORRESTER,
        Plaintiffs
v.
RICHARD HART
and
MERCURY PARCEL SERVICE, INC.,
        Defendants
	DEFENDANTS' ANSWER
	AND COUNTERCLAIM

COUNT I

1. Admitted.
2. Denied that Defendant negligently drove vehicle.
3. Defendant lacks knowledge sufficient to form a belief regarding the truth of the allegation in paragraph 3 of Plaintiff's complaint, and therefore denies same.

FIRST AFFIRMATIVE DEFENSE

Plaintiff was more than 50 percent negligent in causing the accident, and is therefore barred from recovery.

COUNT II

4. No answer required.
5. Denied.

COUNTERCLAIM

On February 26, 19__, on Highway 328 in Capitol County, Columbia, Plaintiff Ann Forrester negligently tried to cross the road in front of Defendant's vehicle, causing injury to Defendant Hart.

As a result of Plaintiff's negligence, Defendant Hart suffered lacerations and contusions and lost days of work all to the sum of $2,200.

SECOND COUNTERCLAIM

Defendant Mercury Parcel incorporates by reference the facts as alleged in the first counterclaim and alleges the Plaintiff's negligence caused damage to the defendant's vehicle and required the hiring of an extra employee for one week all to the sum of $4,250.

WHEREFORE, Defendants request that Plaintiffs' action be dismissed and demand judgment against the Plaintiffs for $2,200 for Defendant Hart and $4,250 for Defendant Mercury Parcel Service, Inc., plus interest and costs.

_____
Attorney for Defendants
(Address)
(Phone number)

Figure 7:12 Fact Complaint for Forrester Case

STATE OF COLUMBIA   CAPITOL COUNTY   CIRCUIT COURT

ANN FORRESTER
          and
WILLIAM FORRESTER,
                    Plaintiffs
                    v.   Civil Action, File No. ____
RICHARD HART
          and
MERCURY PARCEL SERVICE, INC.,
                    Defendants   Plaintiff Demands Trial by Jury

COMPLAINT FOR NEGLIGENCE

Plaintiffs allege the following facts:

1. The jurisdiction of this court is based on the amount in controversy in this action which is more than $2,500.
2. Plaintiff Ann Forrester is a teacher and homemaker and resides at 1533 Capitol Drive, Legalville, in Capitol County, Columbia.
3. Plaintiff William Forrester is the husband of Ann Forrester and resides with her.
4. Defendant Richard Hart is a driver employed by Defendant Mercury Parcel Service, Inc., and resides at 1223 Penny Lane, Cincinnati, Ohio.
5. Defendant Mercury Parcel Service, Inc., is incorporated in the State of Delaware with its principal place of business located at 603 Stoker St., Cincinnati, Ohio.
6. On February 26, 19___, at approximately 7:30 A.M., Plaintiff Ann Forrester was walking across a hilly and partially icy section of Highway 328 in the City of Legalville, County of Capitol, in the State of Columbia.
7. At that time, Defendant Hart was driving a van on behalf of his employer and the owner of the van, Defendant Mercury Parcel Service, Inc.
8. Defendant Hart operated the van negligently by:
   a. driving the vehicle at an excessive rate of speed under the circumstances;
   b. failing to exercise a proper lookout;
   c. failing to exercise adequate control of said vehicle; and
   d. otherwise failing to exercise due and adequate care under the circumstances.
9. As a direct consequence of Defendant's negligence, Plaintiff was struck down by Defendant's van and seriously injured.
10. Because of said negligence, Plaintiff suffered fractures of the left leg and hip; damage to the lower spine; torn muscles, tendons, tissue and nerves; insomnia; paralysis that confines her to a wheelchair; depression; and other maladies, all of which cause her intense pain, great suffering, and considerable inconvenience, and will continue to do so in the future.
11. As a consequence of Defendant's negligence and the aforesaid injuries, the Plaintiff has incurred, and will incur, considerable expense for hospital and medical care, loss of income and benefits, domestic services, and property damages to her coat and clothing.

     WHEREFORE, Plaintiff demands judgment in the amount of seven hundred and fifty thousand dollars ($750,000), together with the costs and disbursements of this action and for such other relief as this court may deem just and proper.

COUNT II

12. Plaintiffs hereby allege and incorporate by reference paragraphs 1 through 9 of Count I.
13. Because of Defendant's negligence, Plaintiff William Forrester has suffered loss of the consortium of his wife, Ann Forrester, in the amount of twenty thousand dollars ($20,000).

WHEREFORE, Plaintiff William Forrester demands judgment against Defendants in the sum of twenty thousand dollars ($20,000) and costs and for such other relief as this court may deem just and proper.

(verification)

_____

Arthur White
White, Wilson & McDuff
Attorneys at Law
Federal Plaza Building
Suite 700
Third and Market Streets
Legalville, Columbia 00000
(111) 555-0000

Assume for illustrative purposes that Richard Hart and Mercury Parcel Service are each represented by different attorneys and that Richard Hart has decided to cross-claim against Mercury Parcel. The cross-claim is placed in Hart's answer after the counterclaims, and the drafted language appears as follows:

CROSS-CLAIM

22. Defendant incorporates by reference paragraphs 1-21 of his answer.
23. Sometime during the week of February 20, Defendant Mercury Parcel Service negligently failed to check and maintain the van driven by Defendant Hart on February 26 as required by (state any applicable statutes or regulations).
24. Because of Defendant Mercury Parcel's negligence, the brakes on said vehicle were not functional, causing the wheels to lock and the vehicle to go out of control. The malfunctioning caused said vehicle to strike Plaintiff Ann Forrester, go off the highway, and strike a tree.
25. As a consequence of Defendant Mercury Parcel's negligence, Plaintiff and Defendant have both suffered the injuries and loss of income set out in the complaint and answer.

WHEREFORE, Defendant Hart demands judgment be entered against Defendant Mercury Parcel for him for $2,200 and for any liability Defendant Hart is required to pay Plaintiffs as a consequence of this lawsuit.

ASSIGNMENT 7:14

Figure 7:14 is a copy of the code (fact) complaint in Case II, the _Maple Meadows Campground_ case. Assume that your firm is defending the owner of the campground. Review the complaint and draft an Answer and Counterclaim for a code-pleading state. Then draft one for a notice-pleading jurisdiction. Make a copy of each of the answers and place them in your system folder. Place a copy of the sample cross-claim illustrated in your system folder.

Figure 7:13   Answer and Counterclaim to Forrester Complaint: Code (Fact) Pleading

STATE OF COLUMBIA   CAPITOL COUNTY   CIRCUIT COURT

ANN FORRESTER
                and
WILLIAM FORRESTER,
                            Plaintiffs
                    v.   Civil Action, File No. _____
RICHARD HART
                and
MERCURY PARCEL SERVICE, INC.,
                            Defendants   Jury Trial Demanded

DEFENDANTS' ANSWER, NEW MATTER, AND COUNTERCLAIM

1. Admitted.
2. Admitted.
3. Admitted.
4. Admitted.
5. Admitted.
6. Admitted.
7. Admitted.
8. Denied. Defendant specifically denies negligence in the following areas:
   a. Driving the vehicle at an excessive rate of speed under the circumstances.
   b. Failure to exercise a proper lookout.
   c. Failure to exercise adequate control of vehicle.
   d. Failure to exercise due and adequate care under the circumstances.
9. Admitted in part, denied in part. Defendant admits the Plaintiff was struck by Defendant's van and denies the balance of the allegations in the paragraph.
10. Denied. Defendant, after reasonable investigation, lacks sufficient knowledge to form a belief regarding the truth of Plaintiff's allegation of injuries, and therefore denies same.
11. Denied. Defendant, after reasonable investigation, lacks sufficient knowledge to form a belief as to the truth of Plaintiff's allegation of loss of money, and therefore denies same.

WHEREFORE, Defendants request the Plaintiffs' complaint be dismissed and that judgment be entered for Defendants for their costs and disbursements.

NEW MATTER

12. Defendants incorporate by reference paragraphs 1 through 11 of their answer.
13. Defendant alleges that Plaintiff is more than 50 percent responsible for the accident and resulting injuries and therefore barred from recovery due to the following:
    a. Failing to stop, look, and listen for oncoming traffic prior to stepping onto the highway.
    b. Failing to maintain a lookout for oncoming vehicles while crossing said highway.
    c. Not taking care for her safety and the safety of others in light of the ice on the highway.

WHEREFORE, Defendants request that Plaintiff's complaint be dismissed and that judgment be entered for Defendants for their costs and disbursements.

ANSWER TO COUNT II

14. No response to Plaintiffs' paragraph 12 is required.
15. Denied. Defendants specifically deny being negligent or responsible for Plaintiff's alleged injuries. Defendant, after reasonable investigation, lacks sufficient knowledge to form a belief regarding the truth of Plaintiff's allegation of loss of consortium of his wife and the amount of the loss.

WHEREFORE, Defendants request that Plaintiffs' complaint be dismissed and that judgment be entered for Defendants for their costs and disbursements.

NEW MATTER COUNT II

16. Defendants incorporate by reference paragraphs 12 and 13 of their answer alleging the Plaintiff is more than 50 percent responsible for the accident and is barred from recovery.

WHEREFORE, Defendants request that Plaintiffs' complaint be dismissed and that judgment be entered for Defendants for their costs and disbursements.

DEFENDANTS' COUNTERCLAIM

17. Defendants incorporate by reference paragraphs 1 through 16 of their answer.
18. On February 26, 19___, Plaintiff Ann Forrester negligently walked onto Highway 328 in Capitol County, Columbia by failing to take the following precautions:
   a. Stop, listen, and look for oncoming traffic
   b. Maintain a lookout while crossing said highway.
   c. Exercise due care for her own safety and that of others in light of the ice on the highway.
19. As a result of Plaintiff's negligence, Defendant Hart had to take emergency evasive action, unsuccessfully avoiding Plaintiff, and causing his vehicle to leave the road and strike a tree.
20. Because of Plaintiff's negligence, Defendant Hart suffered lacerations to his head and legs, bruises to various parts of his body and head, intense emotional anxiety, insomnia, and substantial pain and suffering.
21. As a further consequence of Plaintiff's negligence and the aforesaid injuries, Defendant Hart has incurred the expense of hospital and medical care, and a loss of income totaling two thousand two hundred dollars ($2,200).

COUNT II

22. Defendants incorporate by reference paragraphs 1 through 21 of their answer.
23. Because of Plaintiff Ann Forrester's negligence, Defendant Mercury Parcel Service suffered damage to their delivery van and expenses necessitated by a replacement employee for Mr. Hart for one week, totaling four thousand two hundred and fifty dollars ($4,250).

WHEREFORE, Defendants demand judgment against Plaintiff Ann Forrester for Defendant Hart in the amount of $2,200, and for Defendant Mercury Parcel Service in the amount of $4,250, plus their costs and disbursements.

_____
Attorney for Defendants
(Address)
(Phone number)

State of Columbia   ⎤
                     ⎬ ss.
Capitol _____   ⎦

Richard Hart, being duly sworn on oath according to law, deposes and states that he has read the foregoing Answer and Counterclaim, and that the matters stated therein are true to the best of his knowledge, information, and belief.

_____
Richard Hart

Subscribed and sworn to before me this _____ day of _____, 19__.

_____

Notary Public

My commission expires January 1, 19__.

State of Columbia ⎫
⎬ ss.
County of Capitol_____ ⎭

  Sandra Franz, being duly sworn on oath according to law deposes and states that she is the president and duly authorized representative of Mercury Parcel Service, Inc., and has read the foregoing Answer and Counterclaim, and that the matters stated therein are true to the best of her knowledge, information, and belief.

_____

Sandra Franz

Subscribed and sworn to before me this _____ day of _____, 19__.

My commission expires January 1, 19__.

_____

Notary Public

Figure 7:14   Fact Complaint Case II

STATE OF COLUMBIA   CAPITOL COUNTY   CIRCUIT COURT

CARL AMECHE
            and
ZOE AMECHE,
                        Plaintiffs

            v.   Civil Action, File No. ____
MARGIE CONGDEN
            and
LEROY CONGDEN,

                        Defendants   Plaintiffs Demand Trial by Jury

COMPLAINT FOR NEGLIGENCE

Plaintiffs allege that:

1. The jurisdiction of this court is based on the amount in controversy in this action which is more than $2,500.
2. Plaintiff Carl Ameche is an accountant and resides at 222 2nd Street, Thorp, Ohio.
3. Plaintiff Zoe Ameche is the wife of Carl Ameche and resides with him.
4. Defendants Margie and Leroy Congden are the owners of the Maple Meadows Campground and reside at the campground which is located at Star Route 2, Highway 66, in the city limits of Legalville, Capitol County, Columbia.
5. On August 21, 19__, Plaintiffs rented campsite 36 in the Maple Meadows Campground.
6. Defendants had negligently placed a worn extension cord running to campsite 36.

7. As a direct consequence of the Defendants' negligence, a fire was started that encircled the Plaintiffs' son, Zachary, requiring Carl Ameche to place himself in peril in order to rescue his son.
8. Because of said negligence, Carl Ameche suffered severe burns to his face, hands, and legs that have caused him intense pain, suffering, physical disability, considerable inconvenience, and permanent scarring.
9. As a consequence of the Defendants' negligence and the aforesaid injuries, Carl Ameche has incurred and will incur considerable expense for hospital and medical care, loss of income and benefits, and property damage to his clothing and camper.

WHEREFORE, Plaintiff demands judgment in the amount of three hundred and fifty thousand dollars ($350,000), together with the costs and disbursements of this action, and for such relief as this court may deem just and proper.

COUNT II

10. Plaintiffs hereby allege and incorporate by reference paragraphs 1 through 8 of Count I.
11. Because of the Defendants' negligence, Plaintiff Zoe Ameche has suffered loss of the consortium of her husband, Carl Ameche, in the amount of fifteen thousand dollars ($15,000).

WHEREFORE, Plaintiff Zoe Ameche demands judgment against Defendants in the sum of fifteen thousand dollars ($15,000), together with costs, and for such relief as this court may deem just and proper.

> Arthur White
> White, Wilson & McDuff
> Attorneys at Law
> Federal Plaza Building
> Suite 700
> Third and Market Streets
> Legalville, Columbia 00000

(verification)

Third-Party Practice

Prepare the summons and a third-party complaint; file the third-party action with the clerk of court; have it served on the third-party defendant.

Purpose

The purpose of third-party practice is similar to that of the cross-complaint: to litigate all the claims that arise from a single set of circumstances. Third-party practice is governed by Rule 14 of the Federal Rules of Civil Procedure and parallel state rules. Rule 14 gives the person who is defending against a claim the right to bring in a third party. A third-party complaint essentially says, "If I am going to be held liable in this action, then so are you because you are at fault." For example, Ms. Forrester is suing Mercury Parcel for the injuries suffered in the pedestrian accident. Mercury Parcel may choose, in turn, to sue the van dealer or manufacturer for defects that contributed to or caused the accident. One of the advantages of such a suit is that one jury or one judge may hear all sides, rendering a more uniform decision. A third-party action may be based on *indemnification*, a theory that says if B is found liable, C owes B for the amount of the judgment. Or it may be based on *joint liability*, meaning B and C share the liability. Title 28 U.S.C. should be consulted to see what parties and claims may be heard by the federal court when the parties or claims do not have an independent source of federal jurisdiction.

Procedure

The original defendant drafts a third-party complaint, files it with the clerk of court, and then serves a summons and a copy of the complaint on the new party. The original defendant is called the third-party plaintiff, and the new party is called the third-party defendant.

Rule 14 gives the third-party plaintiff the right to implead another party without leave of court if the third-party complaint is filed within ten days after the answer. If it is filed after the ten days, a motion to implead must be filed to obtain the court's permission.

The third-party complainant must get personal jurisdiction over the other party, following the same procedure for service of process of the complaint outlined in chapter 6 and Rule 4(f). A small filing fee is required. Independent subject matter jurisdiction is not required.

The third-party defendant may respond to the third-party complaint like any other defendant, including Rule 12 motions, counter- and cross-claims, and even a third-party action. Any claim against the original plaintiff may be asserted. The original plaintiff may implead as the respondent to any counterclaim [Rule 14(b)].

Follow these steps in preparing and filing a third-party action:

1. Obtain all necessary information on the third-party defendant.
2. Draft a motion for a third-party complaint unless the action is filed within ten days of the answer [Rule 14(a)].
3. Draft a summons and third-party complaint.
4. File with the clerk of court using the summons and complaint as exhibit A.
5. On notice that the motion is approved serve the summons and a copy of the third-party complaint in the same manner that the original complaint is served [Rule 4(f)].
6. Note the calendar for the due date for the third party's answer.

Figures 7:15, 7:16, and 7:17 are examples of the third-party summons, complaint, and motion. They are based on forms 22A and 22B in the appendix to the Federal Rules of Civil Procedure.

ASSIGNMENT 7:15
From the steps for preparing and filing a third-party complaint, create a checklist for third-party practice and place it in your system folder. See Federal Forms 22A and 22B.

ASSIGNMENT 7:16
Make copies of the third-party summons, complaint, and motion and place in your system folder.

Figure 7:15 Summons Against Third-Party Defendant

[FED. R. CIV. P Rule 14]

UNITED STATES DISTRICT COURT FOR
THE SOUTHERN DISTRICT OF ————
Civil Action, File Number ————

A.B., Plaintiff

v.

C.D., Defendant and Third-Party Plaintiff } Summons

v.

E.F., Third-Party Defendant

To the above-named Third-Party Defendant:

You are hereby summoned and required to serve upon ————, plaintiff's attorney whose address is ———— and upon ————, who is attorney for C.D., defendant and third-party plaintiff, and whose address is ————, an answer to the third-party complaint which is herewith served upon you within 20 days after the service of this summons upon you exclusive of the day of service. If you fail to do so, judgment by default will be taken against you for the relief demanded in the third-party complaint. There is also served upon you herewith a copy of the complaint of the plaintiff which you may but are not required to answer.

———————————————
Clerk of Court

[Seal of District Court]

Dated: ————

Figure 7:16 Third-Party Complaint

[FED. R. CIV. P. Rule 14]

[*Title of Court and Cause*]

1. Plaintiff A.B. has filed against defendant C.D. a complaint, a copy of which is hereto attached as "Exhibit A."

2. (*Here state the grounds upon which C.D. is entitled to recover from E.F., all or part of what A.B. may recover from C.D. The statement should be framed as in an original complaint.*)

WHEREFORE C.D. demands judgment against third-party defendant E.F. for all sums that may be adjusted against defendant C.D. in favor of plaintiff A.B.

Signed: ———————————
Attorney for C.D.,
Third-Party Plaintiff

Address: ———————————

Figure 7:17   Motion to Bring in Third-Party Defendant

[FED. R. CIV. P. Rule 14]

[*Title of Court and Cause*]

Defendant moves for leave, as third-party plaintiff, to cause to be served upon E.F. a summons and third-party complaint, copies of which are hereto attached as Exhibit X.

_____

Attorney for Defendant,

C_____ D_____

Address: _____

Amending and Supplementing the Pleadings

Purpose

The parties to the lawsuit are permitted by the Federal Rules and the rules of adopting states to amend and supplement their pleadings freely. Amendments are generally used to repair defective pleadings that may have omitted necessary elements of a cause of action, improperly or inadequately alleged subject matter jurisdiction, or used language that is too general or states evidence. An amendment might even be used to change a defense or other legal theory. The amendment, however, cannot state a whole new claim unrelated to the first.

A supplemental pleading allows a party to add facts that have occurred since the original pleadings were filed. For example, Ms. Forrester may want to supplement her pleadings if her injuries resulted in blindness or a stroke after the original pleading was filed; or a farmer who is suing a contractor for failure to complete a barn by winter may lose some cattle as a consequence after the complaint is filed. Federal Rule 15(d) authorizes supplemental pleadings.

Rule 15 of the Federal Rules of Civil Procedure states that permission to amend pleadings should be given freely. The purpose of the rule is to make it easy for parties to correct procedural oversights and bad drafting so the issues and evidence are accurately reflected in the pleadings. If amendments and supplements were not freely permitted, the parties would be hamstrung in their efforts to present the best possible case on clearly defined issues, and cases would be dismissed for procedural errors rather than tried on the real substance or merit.

Procedure

A party is permitted to amend a pleading anytime before the responsive pleading is served. If no responsive pleading is required, and if the action is not on the trial calendar, the pleading may be amended within twenty days after the pleading is served. Otherwise pleadings may be amended only with leave of the court or with written consent of the opponent. [Rule 15(a)].

It is necessary to respond to an amended pleading either within the remaining period to respond to the original pleading or within ten days of service of the amended pleading, whichever period is longer, unless otherwise ordered by the court [Rule 15(a)].

When leave of court is required to amend a pleading, the request is made by motion. Because of the policy to freely allow amendments to conform to the evidence, such motions can be brought any time, even after judgment [Rule 15(b)]. An amended pleading dates from the filing of the original pleading as long as the claim or defense asserted in the amended pleading arose out of the conduct, transaction, or occurrence set forth in the original pleading. This avoids the statute of limitations problems, especially for a party that filed the original pleading just before the deadline. If a party, however, tries to amend the pleading with an entirely new claim based on a different fact situation, this is a new pleading and will not date from the original.

The amended pleading should combine the amended language plus what remains of the original pleading. Pleading one complete, amended document is easier for the court and the parties than referring to both the original document and the amended one.[9] The amended pleading should be captioned "Amended" or "Supplemented" for clarity.

Amended and supplemental pleadings are served on the adverse party's attorney by mailing or delivering a copy of the pleading to the attorney or as otherwise directed in Rule 5. The amended pleading should be filed with the clerk of court. Most state jurisdictions freely permit the filing of amended pleadings; local rules, however, should be consulted.

Figure 7:18 is an example of an amended pleading,[10] and Figure 7:19 shows the format for a notice of motion and motion to amend the complaint.[11]

ASSIGNMENT 7:17
Make a copy of the amended complaint and the motion to amend and place in your system folder.

ASSIGNMENT 7:18
Verify in the Pleadings, Motions, and Time Limits table the deadlines for amended pleadings set out in this section and in Rule 15. In addition, draft a checklist of procedures and time limits regarding amended pleadings and add it to the system folder.

Figure 7:18 Amended Complaint

[FED. R. CIV. P. Rule 15(a),]

[*Title of Court and Cause*]

The plaintiff in accordance with Rule 15(a), Federal Rules of Civil Procedure, amends the complaint in this action as follows:

[*State amended pleadings.*]

Attorney for Plaintiff

Address: _____

Figure 7:19 Notice of Motion and Motion for Leave to Amend Complaint

[FED. R. CIV. P. Rule 15(a)]

[*Title of Court and Cause*]

To the Above Defendant and Its Attorneys, Messrs. _____:

    You and each of you will please take notice that the plaintiff in the above-entitled case upon the

affidavit of C_____ D_____ hereto annexed as Exhibit A, will at Room _____, United States

Courts and Post Office Building, City of _____ on the [*date*], at the hour of _____ o'clock ___.M., or as soon thereafter as the court will hear counsel, move for an order permitting the plaintiff to file her proposed amendment to her complaint, a copy of which is hereto annexed as Exhibit B and herewith served upon you.

    Dated: [*date*].

_____

Attorneys for Plaintiff

Address: _____

▪ Motion for Judgment on the Pleadings

You may be asked to draft a motion for judgment on the pleadings when all the required pleadings have been filed and the supervising attorney believes the opponent's claim or defense is by law inadequate. The pleadings are normally closed after the filing of the complaint, answer, and reply to the counterclaim. Once the pleadings are closed, Rule 12(c) and parallel state rules permit the filing of the motion for judgment on the pleadings.

Purpose

The purpose of the motion is to end the litigation. In effect the motion says, "Even if what the opponent says is true, no claim is stated on which relief can be granted," or conversely, "No adequate defense is stated, and therefore I should win." For example, even if Ms. Forrester's allegations in her complaint are considered to be true, if Richard Hart and Mercury Parcel could show that the statute of limitations had run prior to the action being filed, the defendants' motion would be granted.

    On the other hand, if Richard Hart and Mercury Parcel's only defense is not recognized in the state, then the court is within its authority to grant the motion for the plaintiff. Their motion is to be considered without the assistance of the affidavits and matter outside the pleadings. If outside matter is presented with the court's permission, Rule 12(c) requires the motion to be considered a motion for summary judgment (to be taken up in the next section). A motion on the pleadings often results in an amendment to the pleadings rather than dismissal.

    The motion is drafted, filed, and served in the same manner as other motions discussed in this chapter.

ASSIGNMENT 7:19
Be sure to note the time requirements for a motion for judgment on the pleadings in the Pleadings, Motions, and Time Limits table.

◼ Motion for Summary Judgment

Draft a motion for summary judgment and the necessary supporting documents.

Purpose

A successful motion for summary judgment wins the case without the necessity of a trial. The motion does more, however, than a motion to dismiss or a motion for judgment on the pleadings because it asks the court to look behind the pleadings at additional evidence. This evidence can be affidavits, statements made under oath by parties and witnesses (called depositions and interrogatories), admissions of facts, and stipulations of facts. Only admissible evidence is considered. A motion for summary judgment and the supporting evidence must allege two things: that there is no genuine issue of material fact (no crucial questions of fact that must be answered by a jury at trial) and that, according to the law, the movant is entitled to judgment [Rule 56(c)]. If the opponent's evidence can show that there is a genuine issue of fact, the motion is denied.

A summary judgment might be granted in the following situation. Ann Forrester files a complaint for negligence against Hart and Mercury Parcel. The defendants' answer admits all the allegations, but as a defense, states that Forrester signed a release freeing the defendants from all liability. Since defenses are deemed controverted, there appears to be a factual issue: was a release signed? If, after filing a motion for summary judgment, the defendant can prove that the release exists, or present affidavits of witnesses who read the release and saw it signed, the court can grant summary judgment. There is no longer an issue of fact because the evidence proves the release was signed. As a matter of law, the release bars recovery. If the plaintiff could prove facts to the contrary, or show that the release was only a partial release, then the motion would be denied, or at best granted in part. Whether or not the party opposing a motion for summary judgment must rebut the movant's evidence varies in state practice. If a party cannot rebut the motion because the evidence needed is not yet available, the court may not grant the motion and has the option of granting a reasonable continuance until the evidence is available [Rule 56(f)].

Procedure

Rule 56(a) states that any party seeking to recover on a claim, counterclaim, or cross-claim may, after twenty days following commencement of the action, move for summary judgment or do so after service of a motion for summary judgment by the adverse party. Any party defending against a claim, counterclaim, or cross-claim may move for a summary judgment any time. Either party may move for a summary judgment against the other. This is called a *cross-motion*.

The motion must be served at least ten days (more than the five days normally required in motion practice) before the hearing on the motion, and the opponent must file responding affidavits at least one day prior to the hearing [Rule 56(c)].

The documents required to file the motion are typical of those required for most motions: the motion itself, the notice of motion, attached affidavits plus exhibits, a memorandum of law in support of the motion, and an order for the court to sign. The motion is filed and a copy served on the opponent. Proof of service is filed with the clerk of court. Following are examples of the motion (Figure 7:20),[12] notice of motion (Figure 7:21)[13] and an affidavit in support of the motion for summary judgment (Figure 7:22).[14]

Figure 7:20   Motion for Summary Judgment by Plaintiff

[FED. R. CIV. P. Rule 56(a)]

[*Title of Court and Cause*]

Plaintiff by his attorneys and, pursuant to Rule 56 of the Federal Rules of Civil Procedure, moves the Court to enter summary judgment for the plaintiff on the ground that there is no genuine issue as to any material fact, and the plaintiff is entitled to judgment as a matter of law.

In support of this motion, plaintiff refers to the record herein including the amended complaint, the answer thereto, the defendants' amendment to the answer, plaintiff's annexed affidavit sworn to the _____ day of _____, 19__, and _____.

_____,

Attorney for Plaintiff

Address: _____

Figure 7:21   Notice of Motion for Summary Judgment

[FED. R. CIV. P. Rule 56(a)]

[*Title of Court and Cause*]

Sir:

Please Take Notice, that upon the complaint herein, the affidavits of _____, sworn to _____, 19__, and the affidavit of _____, sworn to _____, 19__, and [the annexed statement in accordance with Rule 9(g) of the General Rules of this Court], the undersigned will move this Court at a motion part thereof, to be held at Room _____, United States District Courthouse, _____, _____, on the _____ day of _____, 19__, for an order granting plaintiff summary judgment pursuant to Rule 56 of the Federal Rules of Civil Procedure, on the ground that there is no genuine issue as to any material fact, and that plaintiff is entitled to judgment as a matter of law.

Dated: _____, _____, _____, 19__.

_____

Attorney for Plaintiff

Address: _____

To: _____, [Address]

Figure 7:22 Affidavit in Support of Motion for Summary Judgment—General Form

[FED. R. CIV. P. Rule 56(e)]

State of _____

                                    ss

County of _____

_____, being first duly sworn, deposes and says:

I am _____, and have personal knowledge of the facts herein set forth.

This affidavit is submitted in support of the plaintiff's [*or* defendant's] motion for summary judgment herein, for the purpose of showing that there is in this action no genuine issue as to any material fact, and that the plaintiff [*or* defendant] is entitled to judgment as a matter of law.

[*State all the evidentiary facts within affiant's personal knowledge in support of motion.*]

_____

[*Jurat*]

ASSIGNMENT 7:20

Place copies of the motion, notice of motion, and affidavit in support of motion for summary judgment in your system folder.

ASSIGNMENT 7:21

Verify the time limits set out in Rule 56 in the Pleadings, Motions, and Time Limits table. Enter state equivalents.

■ Keeping a Pleading Record

Pleadings require good record keeping. It can be beneficial if a quick glance in the file tells the reader exactly what pleadings have been filed, served, and replied to, and the applicable dates. A pleadings log in each file can provide this information. Figure 7:23 is an example of a pleadings log that can be regularly updated as each pleading is exchanged.[15]

ASSIGNMENT 7:22

Make a copy of the File Pleading Log and place it in your system folder.

■ Pleadings, Motions, and Time Limits

Table 7:2 displays the most common pleadings in approximate chronological order, their purpose, any applicable time limit, and the pertinent federal rule.

ASSIGNMENT 7:23

Fill in the state rule and deadline section of the Pleadings, Motions, and Time Limits Table (table 7:2) and add the table to your system folder.

Figure 7:23   File Pleading Log

Title of Case _____   Client   _____

_____   File No. _____

Our Pleading	Date Filed	Date Served	Opponent Acknowl. of Service	Opponent Response Due	Opponent Pleading	Date of Service	Our Response Due
Summons and complaint Reply to counterclaim					Answer and counterclaim		

Table 7:2   Pleadings, Motions, and Time Limits

Pleading/Act	Purpose If Not Clear	Due	Federal Rule	State Rule/Due
PLEADINGS/PARTIES				
Complaint				
Service of summons and complaint	For personal jurisdiction	120 days after filing complaint	4,4(j), 5	
Request for Entry of Default and Judgment of Default	To prevent defendant's response after time limit for answer, to get judgment concluding case and awarding remedy	Entry best sought on first day after expiration of time limit for answer. Judgment sought as soon after as possible. Notice of hearing on application for default—three days prior to hearing when required.	55, 54(c)	
Motion to set Aside Default Judgment		In reasonable time and not more than one year after judgment	55(c), 60(b)	

Table 7:2 Continued

Pleading/Act	Purpose If Not Clear	Due	Federal Rule	State Rule/Due
Motions Attacking Complaint or Action (in general)	To dismiss action for lack of subject matter jurisdiction, personal jurisdiction, improper venue, insufficiency of service, failure to state a claim, and failure to join a party, or to make complaint more definite or to strike language, or for *forum non conveniens*	Twenty days, generally; motion to dismiss for lack of subject matter jurisdiction can be made any time, including on appeal	12(b), (e), (f), 28 U.S.C. § 1406(a), 28 U.S.C. § 1404	
Notice of Motion plus affidavit		Served at least five days before hearing	6(d)	
Responsive Motion plus affidavit		Served one day before hearing on motion, generally	6(d)	
Amendment to Pleadings (generally)	To correct errors, vagueness, or other inadequacies	Prior to service of a responsive pleading *or* within twenty days after service. If in response to order to make more definite, ten days after notice of order.	15(a), 12(e)	
Answer	To admit, deny, or state defenses to plaintiff's allegation; may include counterclaim and motions attacking complaint	Twenty days after service of complaint (U.S. has sixty days) or in ten days after decision on motion attacking complaint	12(a)	
Answer in Response to amended complaint		In remaining time to respond to original or within 10 days, whichever is greater	15(a)	
Counterclaim	To state a claim defendant has against plaintiff, usually arising out of same transaction alleged by plaintiff	At same time answer is served or as permitted by court	13	

Table 7:2 Continued

Pleading/Act	Purpose If Not Clear	Due	Federal Rule	State Rule/Due
Cross-Claim	To state a claim against a party on the same side of the action and may allege that the party is the one fully or partially liable for claim alleged in complaint or counterclaim	With answer, reply to counterclaim, or other appropriate pleading	12(g)	
Reply to Counterclaim or Cross-Claim	To admit, deny, or state defenses to allegations in counterclaim or cross-claim. May include motions attacking these pleadings.	Twenty days after service of answer or twenty days after service of notice of order to reply to counterclaim or as otherwise directed (U.S. has sixty days)	12(a)	
Third-Party Complaint	To bring in third party who may be liable to one of the original parties for the claim or counterclaim brought against the original party	Ten days after service of original answer (counterclaim) or by leave of court	14(a)	
Third-Party Answer	To attack, or to admit, deny, or state defenses to the third-party complaint (may include counter and cross-claims)	Twenty days	14(a), 12(a)	
Motion to Dismiss: Not Real Party in Interest	To attack jurisdiction of court and to avoid harassment of defendant by parties having no right to claim	Twenty days/in time permitted for regular response to complaint	17(a)	
Motion to Join a Party	To add either plaintiffs or defendants for the purpose of adjudicating all claims of all parties arising from same or series of transactions	In reasonable time after action begins	19, 20	

Table 7:2 Continued

Pleading/Act	Purpose If Not Clear	Due	Federal Rule	State Rule/Due
Motion to Add Interpleader	To add a party to resolve all possible claims against a third party	In reasonable time after action begins	22	
Motions Regarding Class Actions	To certify a group of plaintiffs as a class or to dismiss or compromise	As soon as practicable after start of action	23(c)(1)	
Motion to Intervene	To permit party to enter lawsuit so can protect interest or where statute permits intervention	In reasonable time after start of action	24, 5	
Motion for Substitution of a Party	To permit continuation of action by substituting a party in the case of death, incompetency, transfer of interest, or resignation of office	Ninety days after death, etc., made part of record	25	
Motion for Enlargement of Time	To gain extension from original date pleading is due	In time within which pleading is originally due or after if due to excusable neglect	6(b)	
Motion for Judgment on the Pleadings	To get final judgment in case based solely on the pleadings	After pleadings closed but not so late as to delay trial	12(c)	
Motion of Application for Seizure of Property (Writ of Attachment)	To secure property so that if suit is successful, judgment can be paid. Also final remedy to collect judgment.	After filing of lawsuit (generally) or after judgment	64 (incorporating state law)	
Motion or Application for Injunctions Including Temporary Restraining Order, Preliminary Injunction, and Permanent Injunctions	To prevent irreparable damage to persons or property involved in the original action, to require another party to do some act or to refrain from some act	After filing of lawsuit (temporary restraining order good for up to ten days unless extended by court for good cause); after ten days must secure preliminary injunction	65	

Table 7:2   Continued

Pleading/Act	Purpose If Not Clear	Due	Federal Rule	State Rule/Due
Motion for Summary Judgment	Seeks final judgment based on pleadings and supporting affidavits (may come after discovery). Alleges no genuine issue in case.	Plaintiff: twenty days after filing complaint or after being served with such motions by adverse party. Defendant: Any time after action filed. Notice: Served ten days prior to hearing on motion.	56	
DISCOVERY				
Petition for Deposition Before Action or Pending Appeal	To preserve testimony or other evidence before action or appeal started	Notice to each party due twenty days before hearing on petition	27(a)1-2)	
Motion for Discovery Conference	To have court conference to plan and set out discovery	After start of action	26(f)	
Objections or Additions to Matters Set Forth in Motion for Discovery Conference		Ten days after service of motion	26(f)(5)	
Notice to Take Deposition (notice to all other parties)	To gather evidence from the oral or written statements of others	After start of action and for defendant after thirty days after service of summons and complaint on defendant or by leave of court (generally)	30(a), 30(b)(1)	
Motion to Enlarge or Shorten Time for Taking Deposition			30(b)(3)	
Notice to Take Deposition on Written Questions	Requested when oral deposition impractical	After start of action cross questions within thirty days of service of original questions; redirect and recross questions within ten days of service of follow-up questions	31(a)	

Table 7:2 Continued

Pleading/Act	Purpose If Not Clear	Due	Federal Rule	State Rule/Due
Objections to Form of Written Deposition Questions		In time permitted for response as stated above and in five days after service of the last question	32(d)(3)(c)	
Interrogatories	To discover evidence through written questions to any party	To plaintiff after start of action, to defendant with or after service of summons and complaint	33(a)	
Answers or Objections to Interrogatories		Thirty days after service of questions, or if defendant in forty-five days after service of summons and complaint on defendant	33(a)	
Request for Production of Documents and Things and Entry to Land	To inspect documents (writings, photos, data collections, etc.) and land to gather evidence	Served on plaintiff after start of action or any other party after service of summons and complaint on that party	34(a)(b)	
Response to Request for Production, Etc.		Thirty days after service of request. If defendant, in forty-five days after service of summons and complaint on defendant.	34(b)	
Motion for order to Submit to Physical or Mental Exam	To require a party to submit to exam when condition in question (injury, emotional illness, other) relates to cause of action or damages	After start of action	35(a)	
Request for Admission(s)	To get opponent to admit to certain facts so they do not have to be proven at trial by separate evidence	After start of action for plaintiff, otherwise after service of summons and complaint	36(a)	

Table 7:2   Continued

Pleading/Act	Purpose If Not Clear	Due	Federal Rule	State Rule/Due
Answer or Objection to Request for Admission		Thirty days after service of request. If defendant, forty-five days after service of summons and complaint on defendant.	36(a)	
Duty to Supplement Discovery Responses	To keep discovery current	Seasonable	26(e)(1)	
Motion to Compel Discovery	To get court to order party to provide discovery	On reasonable notice to all parties	37(a)(d)	
Motion for Protective Order	To get order permitting party not to respond to certain aspects of discovery or to prevent abuse of discovery by opponent	In reasonable period of time	26(c)	
Motion to Enforce Subpoena	To require person to appear and/or produce documents for examination	After notice of request for deposition or for production of documents	45	
Motion to Modify or Quash Subpoena Duces Tecum	To change or stop the enforcement of subpoena	Promptly and before time for compliance with subpoena	45(b)	
PRETRIAL				
Demand for Jury Trial		To all parties any time after action starts but no later than ten days after the last pleading directed to such issue	38(b)	
Motion for Involuntary Dismissal	To dismiss action for failure of plaintiff to prosecute	At point lack of prosecution becomes obvious or, if at nonjury trial, after close of plaintiff's evidence	4(b)	

Table 7:2 Continued

Pleading/Act	Purpose If Not Clear	Due	Federal Rule	State Rule/Due
Consolidation of Actions or Separation for Trial	To combine actions for the sake of judicial economy or to provide separate trials where combined trial would cause prejudice or inconvenience	In reasonable time before trial	42(a)(b)	
Motion for Voluntary Dismissal	So plaintiff or parties can agree to action dismissal	By notice of dismissal at any time before service by adverse party of an answer or motion for summary judgment, whichever occurs first, or by filing stipulation signed by all parties appearing in action	41(a)(1)	
Motion to Use Deposition at Trial	To use deposition as testimony at trial	Reasonable time before trial	32(a)(3)	
Motion in Limine	For protective order against prejudicial questions or statements by adverse party	Reasonable time before trial or reasonable time after selection of jury		
Motion to Exclude Evidence	To exclude evidence for a variety of reasons	Reasonable time before trial or as matter arises at trial		
TRIAL				
Motion for Directed Verdict	To have court enter verdict for moving party for failure to prove prima facie case	At close of evidence presented by opposing party	50(a)	
Motion for Judgment Notwithstanding Verdict	To have court enter judgment contrary to that returned by jury on basis jury verdict goes against weight of evidence (may be joined with motion for new trial)	Ten days after jury discharged or judgment if party previously moved for directed verdict	50(b)	

Table 7:2 Continued

Pleading/Act	Purpose If Not Clear	Due	Federal Rule	State Rule/Due
POST-TRIAL				
Motion for new Trial or to Alter or Amend Judgment	To have judgment set aside and new trial ordered because of error or other injustice at first trial	Ten days after entry of judgment	59, 52(b)	
Response to Motion for new Trial/Affidavits	To oppose motion for new trial	Ten days after service of motion or twenty more days with leave of court	59(c)	
Motion to Correct Clerical Errors in Judgment		Any time	60(a)	
Motion for Stay of Execution of Judgment Pending Post-Trial Motions		Ten days after entry of judgment or with motion for post-trial relief	62(b)	
APPEAL				
Notice of Appeal	To notify all parties of appeal	Thirty days after judgment or order; sixty days if U.S. or officer or agency	Rule 4(a) of Appellate Procedure	
Stay on Appeal	To prevent execution of judgment until appeal decided	At filing notice of appeal or soon after	62(d)	

Summary

Chapter 6 emphasized the role of formulating and filing a case, the offense; chapter 7 emphasizes the defense, how to attack the weaknesses in the complaint or action, how to remove a case to federal court, and how to respond in the form of an answer to the complaint.

The defendant, in most jurisdictions, has twenty days to respond to the complaint. The first likely response includes a host of motions to have the complaint dismissed or modified. These motions are your first introduction to what today has become an extensive motion practice. Motions drafted by the parties to the action request the court for some relief concerning the proceedings. That relief is a court order directing the other side to comply, backed up with contempt of court or other sanctions for failure to do so. Because they can result in specific court action against one or more of the parties, motions are critical to sound representation.

The first motions to be filed in a case seek orders dismissing or modifying the complaint [Rule 12(b)]. These motions can attack jurisdiction, service, or venue; or they may attack a complaint for stating an incomplete, inaccurate, or misconceived premise. Your tasks are to review the complaint and spot its weaknesses, and to research and draft the motion and supporting documents, including memoranda of understanding and affidavits. If the motion is successful, the complaint may be dismissed or simply amended. If the latter, then the defendant must file the answer.

If the case is filed in state court but could be heard in federal court, the defendant may choose to have the case removed to federal court. This is accomplished through the drafting and filing of a Notice of Removal.

The defendant must answer the complaint regardless of removal. The answer is the formal pleading that states the defendant's specific admission, denial, or other responses to each of the plaintiff's assertions in the complaint. What determines the needed detail in the response is whether the jurisdiction is a notice pleading or a code (fact) pleading jurisdiction.

The answer must include affirmative defenses, such as the expiration of the statute of limitations if the defense plans to assert these defenses at trial. In addition, counterclaims that the defendant has against the plaintiff should be asserted with the answer. Cross-claims against co-parties can be included in the answer after the counterclaim or may be filed as separate documents. To litigate all the claims arising from a single set of circumstances, the parties may bring in nonparties as third-party defendants. These are persons who may be liable to the defendant for part or all of the plaintiff's claim, or may be liable to the plaintiff for part or all of the defendant's counterclaim.

The filing of each of the pleadings and motions mentioned in this chapter follows strict time deadlines that, if not met, may result in default, the loss of the right to assert or claim a defense, or the loss of the case. One of your important roles is knowing each of the time limits and then seeing to it that they are met. It also involves noting when the other parties fail to meet their deadlines.

Pleadings may be liberally amended or supplemented under Rule 15 as long as the time limits for doing so are followed. When the pleadings are closed after the filing of the complaint, answer, and reply to counterclaim, either party may file a motion for judgment on the pleadings. A judgment on the pleadings essentially asserts that even if what the adversary says is true, there is no claim or there is no defense. A motion for summary judgment is similar, but goes further by asking the court to look behind the pleadings to consider additional evidence. Because of the importance of each of these pleadings and motions and their respective time deadlines as set out in state and federal rules, it is helpful for you to keep an accurate and timely pleading record.

Study Guide

1. What is a motion? State the purposes of motions in general.
2. What does it mean to preserve an issue for appeal?
3. What are the requirements for a motion under federal and your state rules? Identify the particular rules that apply.

4. What is a notice of motion and what purpose does it serve? Do the Federal Rules permit it to be combined with the motion?

5. What is the purpose of a supporting affidavit in motion practice? A supporting memorandum of law? What is the difference between the two?

6. Describe the detailed procedure for filing and serving motions. What federal and state rules apply?

7. What time deadlines must be heeded in motion practice? State the applicable rules.

8. Have you developed a checklist for drafting and filing motions?

9. What is a motion to dismiss? What purpose does it serve?

10. What is a demurrer? What purpose does it serve?

11. What method should you use to determine the weaknesses in a complaint subject to a motion to dismiss the complaint? Explain how the method works.

12. What procedure should be followed in researching the legal basis for a memorandum of law in support of a motion to dismiss the complaint?

13. Be able to draft the necessary documents to obtain an order dismissing the complaint.

14. Explain the procedure, applicable rules, and time deadlines for filing and serving a motion to dismiss in both federal and your state courts.

15. What are the other Rule 12(b)motions? Must they be made separately?

16. What are the other motions attacking the complaint? State their purposes.

17. Be able to draft (a) a motion to strike and (b) a motion to make more definite and certain. What are the applicable rules?

18. If your state makes use of the special demurrer or the bill of particulars, be able to draft either.

19. When may an action be removed to federal district court?

20. What is the correct procedure and what form is needed to remove an action to federal court?

21. What is the formula for calculating time limit due dates?

22. What is the purpose of the answer? When must it be filed? What rule is applicable?

23. Be able to list style and content considerations for drafting an answer, including those that apply to denials.

24. What are the components of an answer? Be able to define each of them.

25. What is the procedure for locating the possible defenses to a claim?

26. Be able to draft an answer, including all the possible components.

27. What is the purpose of the following: third-party practice, amending and supplementing the pleadings, a motion for judgment on the pleadings, and a motion for summary judgment?

28. Be able to draft the documents needed for third-party practice, amending and supplementing the pleadings, a motion for judgment on the pleadings, and a motion for summary judgment.

29. What time deadlines apply to the variety of pleadings covered in this chapter?

Endnotes

1. Adapted from WEST'S FEDERAL FORMS, § 1101, v. 2, with permission of West Publishing Company.
2. Adapted from BRUNO, PARALEGAL'S LITIGATION HANDBOOK 186 (1980) [hereinafter cited as BRUNO].
3. Memo from J. BURTON to J. McCord (March 27, 1986).
4. KARLEN, PROCEDURE BEFORE TRIAL IN A NUTSHELL 134 (1972) [citing Nieman v. Long, 31 F.Supp. (E.D.Pa.1934)].
5. Id., 136–37.
6. VETTER, SUCCESSFUL CIVIL LITIGATION: HOW TO WIN YOUR CASE BEFORE YOU ENTER THE COURTROOM 43–47 (1977) [as cited in BRUNO, 188–90].
7. NATIONAL LAW JOURNAL (June 1985), last page.
8. BRUNO, 191.
9. WEINSTEIN, INTRODUCTION TO CIVIL LITIGATION 122 (2d ed. 1986).
10. Adapted from WEST'S FEDERAL FORMS, § 2717, v. 3, with permission of West Publishing Company.
11. Id., § 2701, with permission of West Publishing Company.
12. Id., § 4723, v. 4, with permission of West Publishing Company.
13. Id., § 4722, with permission of West Publishing Company.
14. Id., § 4726, with permission of West Publishing Company.
15. Suggested by J. WARM in a memo to J. McCord (March 24, 1986).

8

Discovery

- Overview of Discovery
- Compelling Discovery and Sanctions
- Interrogatories
- Depositions
- Production of Documents and Things and Entry Upon Land for Inspection and Other Purposes
- Request for Physical and Mental Examination
- Request for Admission (Rule 36)
- The Freedom of Information Act

◼ Overview of Discovery

Discovery is the process in a lawsuit during which the parties request and exchange information, exhibits, and documents according to specific rules of procedure. That information helps form the basis for both sides of the lawsuit. The exchange involves the following procedures or devices listed in Federal Rule 26:

1. Interrogatories: written questions submitted to a party
2. Deposition: sworn oral testimony of a witness or litigant taken prior to trial
3. Production of documents, tangible items, or entry to property for inspection
4. Expert's report and opinion: the name, subject matter, and substance of the report of scientists and other experts to be used at trial
5. Medical examinations: requirement upon motion that a party submit to a physical or mental examination by a doctor chosen by the opposing party
6. Request for admission: asking the opponent to admit certain facts in writing, which then do not have to be proven at trial

Employ these devices more or less in proportion to the complexity of the case and the amount in dispute. Small cases use discovery sparingly, large cases extensively. This chapter emphasizes the full use of discovery. Read the discovery section of table 7:2 in chapter 7 for a helpful overview of the discovery devices, rules, and time limits that pertain to each.

The Purpose of Discovery

Justice is better served when a case is tried on its merits (the evidence) rather than on some tactic of surprise or deception. "Trial by ambush" is no longer accepted. The rules of discovery attempt to achieve this result by making it possible for both sides in a lawsuit to be informed about the evidence and witnesses that will be presented by the opponent. More information should result in better preparation by both sides, which in turn provides the trier of fact with better information for ascertaining the truth.

More practical purposes exist as well. Discovery helps reveal whether there is in fact a basis for the lawsuit or a basis for its defense. If there is no basis, discovery may lead to summary judgment or voluntary dismissal, ending the lawsuit, and saving the time, expense, and anguish of a trial. The early access to information provided by discovery is more likely to lead to an early settlement based on a more accurate assessment of the case. Discovery also serves to identify factual areas where there are no disputes, leaving for trial only those issues clearly in conflict. Fewer issues may result in a shorter, less expensive trial.

Another purpose of discovery is to gather information from the opponent that can strengthen one's own case or allow one to be better prepared to refute the accuracy of the evidence presented by the other side. For example, if a witness says one thing at a deposition and another at trial, the earlier statements can be used to weaken the inconsistent trial testimony. Discovery also helps preserve evidence. If a witness gives testimony at a deposition and is later unavailable for trial, the court might permit the prior testimony to be entered at trial.

The Scope and Limits of Discovery

Federal Rule 26(b) and similar rules in most states permit the parties to discover a wide range of information as long as it is not privileged, is relevant to the pending action, and appears that it is or will lead to admissible evidence. Under this liberal approach to discovery, one party may be required to reveal the names of persons known to have knowledge of relevant information, pertinent documents and business records, insurance agreements, other physical evidence, scientific and medical reports, and a variety of other items. Rule 26(b)(3) authorizes a party and nonparty to obtain any statement they have made relevant to the lawsuit. This is permitted to avoid the inordinate emphasis often placed on inconsistencies between what a witness recalls saying and what was actually said. Even the name of an expert witness and the substance of the expert's likely testimony is discoverable.

You must know the limits to discovery in order to draft requests for discovery, recognize when the opponent's request exceeds the scope of discoverable matter, and prevent the unnecessary revelation of evidence protected by privilege or the attorney work product rule.

The liberal approach to discovery has resulted in some abuses. Lawyers have waited until the other side has gathered all the information before asking for it, cutting their time and expense for investigation. Requests for volumes of documents requiring lengthy and expensive production has been used to cause delay. Some well-financed parties have used such tactics to force unfair settlements on their less well-financed opponents. Now the rules give the court the power on motion (or its own initiative) to limit discovery if the following conditions are present:

The discovery sought is unreasonably burdensome, cumulative, or duplicative, or is obtainable from a more convenient and less expensive source.

The party seeking discovery has had ample opportunity to obtain the information sought; or

The discovery is unduly burdensome or expensive, taking into account the needs of the case, the amount in controversy, limitations of the parties' resources, and the importance of the issues at stake in the litigation [Rule 26(b)(1)].

Discovery should not reach privileged information. Communication between attorney-client, priest-penitent, and the like are not discoverable (see chapter 4).

The other major limitation on the scope of discovery is the attorney's work product exception. It bears repeating that documents and tangible things prepared in anticipation of litigation or trial may be discovered *only* if the party wanting discovery can prove obtaining the information any other way would cause undue hardship. This rule protects the work of the attorney as well as that of those who work for the attorney (agents) [Rule 26(b)(3)]. This rule especially protects from disclosure the mental impressions, conclusions, opinions, and legal theories of the attorney. Although Rule 26 leaves the federal judge some discretion, this protection is absolute in some states. It takes time and considerable experience for a paralegal to learn the delicate boundaries of what is protected and what is not. This chapter presents some specific applications.

Rule 26(b)(4) also places limits on the discoverability of the facts known and opinions held by experts in preparing for trial. Through interrogatories, a party can request the identity of each expert witness to be called at trial, the subject matter of the expert's testimony, the substance of the facts and opinions to be expressed, and a summary of the grounds for each opinion [Rule 26(b)(4)(A)(i)]. An example of how to provide information on an expert in response to interrogatories or a demand for exchange of expert witness information follows.[1]

Ursala Workharder

15) Ms. Workharder has agreed to testify at trial.

16) Ms. Workharder is a Certified Public Accountant.

17) Ms. Workharder will testify on the damages allegedly suffered by Plaintiff as a result of Defendant's actions.

18) In forming her expert opinion, Ms. Workharder relied upon her examination of Plaintiff's financial records.

19) Ms. Workharder is sufficiently familiar with the pending action to submit to a meaningful oral deposition concerning the testimony described above, including his [sic] expert opinion and the basis thereof.

20) Ms. Workharder's fee for providing deposition testimony is $250.00 per hour.

The facts known or opinions held by an expert or a consultant who has been retained by a party but who will not testify at trial are discoverable *only* on a showing by the other party of exceptional circumstances that make it impracticable to obtain like information elsewhere, or as permitted under Rule 35(b) governing medical examinations. The court has the authority to require the discovering party to pay the expert witness for the time spent responding to the discovery request, or to share the entire expense for the expert with the other party [Rule 26(b)(4)(c)].

ASSIGNMENT 8:1
Drawing from the prior discussion on the scope and limitation of discovery plus the pertinent rules of evidence discussed in chapter 4, indicate whether the following would be discoverable in the Ann Forrester case. If an item would be discoverable only on a showing of undue hardship, indicate that as well. The first item is completed for you as an example. D = discoverable, ND = not discoverable, R = reason not discoverable, E = exceptional circumstances.

Item	D	ND	R	E
1. Photo of accident scene taken by plaintiff's attorney		x	work product	substantial need/ undue hardship
2. Defendant Hart's driving schedule for day of accident and previous week				
3. Mercury Parcel's maintenance schedules on van				
4. Hart's statement to his attorney				
5. Forrester's medical bills				
6. Identification and opinion of plaintiff's trial expert on auto defects				
7. Statement Hart made to Mr. Forrester in plaintiff's possession				
8. Defense attorney's diagram of accident				
9. Forrester's alleged confession to her priest that she felt responsible for accident				
10. Plaintiff's request for a second copy of Hart's driving schedule				
11. Statement of Forrester tape recorded by her attorney's paralegal				
12. Letters between attorneys for defendants discussing strategy				

■ Compelling Discovery and Sanctions

Chronologically, the effort to compel discovery comes after preparation of discovery requests. It is covered here, however, because it is important for you to realize before drafting discovery documents, reviewing discovery responses, and responding to requests, that discovery can be compelled by the court and that failure to cooperate in the discovery process can result in costly sanctions including the costs incurred by a party who is forced to ask the court to intercede on a request to compel discovery. Before accepting or providing a half-hearted response to a request for discovery, consider the costs and sanctions that may be in the balance. Caution and close work with the attorney are in order. In some recent cases judges have imposed stiff sanctions.

The federal discovery rules and those in most states are designed to encourage cooperation in the mutual discovery process with a minimum of court involvement. This eases the burden on both the litigants and the court by reducing the need for court orders, hearings, and conferences.

Despite the emphasis on cooperation, there are times when the court must become involved. When one of the parties refuses to respond or cooperate in a request for discovery, the requesting party can invoke the power of the court to compel that party to produce the information or give valid reasons for not doing so.

A party may seek the aid of the court when the other party does not answer questions in interrogatories or a deposition, when a corporation or other entity fails to designate the person who will provide the required interrogatory or deposition answers, when a party does not permit the inspection of documents, or when a party provides an evasive or incomplete answer [Rule 37(a)(2) and (3)].

Motion, Order, and Sanctions

When a party has failed to cooperate, the adverse party may file a motion requesting an order to compel discovery. The court may then order the uncooperative party to pay the costs and attorney fees incurred by the other side in bringing the motion, unless the failure was substantially justified. Conversely, if a motion to compel is filed, denied, and found to be without substantial justification, the filing party may be ordered to pay costs [Rule 37(a)(4)].

If the motion is filed, and the court orders compliance but the party does not comply, the court may impose a number of severe sanctions. The court in the district where the deposition is taken may fine the uncooperative party for contempt of court if the person has refused an order to answer a deposition question [Rule 37(b)(1)]. If a party or the designated person for an entity fails to obey an order to permit discovery, the court may impose certain sanctions:

a. Order that the matter or evidence sought be considered proved for the benefit of the party requesting the order;
b. Order the uncooperative party not to oppose certain claims or defenses or not to introduce designated matter into evidence;
c. Order the pleadings or parts thereof be stricken;
d. Stay (stop) further proceedings until the order is obeyed;
e. Dismiss the action, or any part thereof;
f. Render a default judgment against the disobedient party;
g. Find the party in contempt of court;
h. Order sanctions a, b, and c, when there is a refusal to submit to a medical exam unless the person can show s/he cannot produce the person to be examined [Rule 37(b)(2)(A-E)].

In lieu of or in addition to these sanctions, the court may impose the payment of costs, including attorney's fees, unless such failure to respond is substantially justified [Rule 37(b)(2)]. Local rules may provide different sanctions and should be consulted.

If a party receives a request for admission and fails to admit the genuineness of any document or the truth of any matter as requested under Rule 36, and the other party proves the genuineness or truth of the matter, the court on motion may order the refusing party to pay the other party's expenses in proving the matter [Rule 37(c)]. The court will not order payment of costs if the request for admission was objectionable, pertained to something insubstantial, provided reasonable grounds to believe the request would be unsuccessful, or if payment would otherwise not be appropriate.

If a party or an officer, director, or managing agent of a party or a designate for a corporation or other entity fails to appear at the deposition after receiving proper notice, or fails to serve answers or objections to interrogatories after proper service, or to serve a written response to a properly served request for inspection, the court may on motion impose the sanctions previously mentioned including payment of costs, except contempt of court.

If pursuant to Rule 26(f) a party requests a discovery conference to set up a discovery plan and the other party fails to participate in good faith in the framing of a discovery plan, the court may impose the payment of costs incurred by the other party, including attorney fees, due to the failure to cooperate.

Procedure for Compelling Discovery

When the opponent has not responded to the request for discovery within the usual thirty days required by the rules, the supervising attorney should be informed. If the decision is made to compel discovery and seek sanctions, you should draft the necessary documents to file the motion to compel discovery. The documents include the motion, the notice of motion, usually a memorandum of law, the desired order, and the certificate of service. Before you draft the motion, however, the attorney must decide what court should receive the motion. A motion for an order to compel a party may be filled in the court where the action is pending, or on matters relating to a deposition, the court in the district where the deposition is being taken. If the deponent is not a party, the motion should be made in the court in the district where the deposition is being taken [Rule 37(a)(1)]. The caption should be drafted accordingly. An adaptable form for a motion to compel appears in figure 8:1,[2] the affidavit in support of the motion is figure 8:2,[3] and a proposed order to compel in figure 8:3.[4]

A copy of the motion and supporting documents should be reviewed by the attorney and served on the attorney for the adverse party. All documents plus proof of service should be filed with the appropriate clerk of court. These procedures and the need for a supporting memorandum of law may vary in state practice.

ASSIGNMENT 8:2
Use an outline format to define and list the purposes of discovery. Also list the key federal and state rules on discovery stating the scope, limits, means to compel, and sanctions related to it. Place these in your system folder.

Figure 8:1   Motion to Compel Production, Inspection, and Copying of Documents in Case of Objection or Failure to Respond—General Form

[FED. R. CIV. P. Rules 34(b), 37(a)]

[*Title of Court and Cause*]

Defendant, _____, moves the court for an order requiring plaintiff, _____, to produce and to permit defendant to inspect and to copy or photograph each of the following documents [*here list the documents and describe each of them*]. This motion is made on the ground that the defendant served a written request upon the plaintiff for production, inspection, and copying or photographing the above-mentioned documents, a copy of which is attached hereto as Exhibit A, and that the plaintiff objected to said production by a response, a copy of which is attached hereto as Exhibit B [*or and that plaintiff has failed and refused to respond to defendant's request as required by Rule 34, Federal Rules of Civil Procedure*]. The documents requested by defendant contain relevant and material evidence in the above-entitled action and their production is necessary for defendant to prepare for trial, as indicated in Exhibit C hereto attached.

Attorney for Defendant

Address: _____

Figure 8:2   Affidavit in Support of Motion to Compel

[FED. R. CIV. P. Rules 34, 37(a)]

[*Title of Court and Cause*]

[*Venue*]

_____, being first duly sworn, on his oath states:

That he is one of the attorneys for the above named defendant and he makes this affidavit in support of the Motion for Production of Documents and Things for Inspection, Copying and Photographing which is attached hereto; that the production of the documents, papers, statements and things requested is made in good faith; that he has been informed and therefore believes that the matters and things so sought in said motion are competent as evidence in said cause and are especially competent by reason of the fact that, _____; that the facts sought to be elicited are facts necessary to be shown and produced in said cause in the furtherance of justice and in securing all the facts competent upon the issues to be tried.

The motion herein made is made in good faith and the affiant as one of counsel for defendant desires to inspect said documents solely for the purpose of establishing facts to be used as evidence in the above-entitled cause and affiant does not intend to use said information for any other purpose or to convey the same to any other party or persons.

Dated this _____ day of _____, 19__.

[*Jurat*]

_____

ASSIGNMENT 8:3

Based on the information in this section of the chapter, draft a brief checklist on the procedure to follow to compel discovery; photocopy the motion to compel and the order compelling discovery, and place these in the system folder.

Figure 8:3 Order That Interrogatories Concerning Personal Jurisdiction Are Answered and That Personal Jurisdiction Is Established

[FED. R. CIV. P. Rule 37(b)(2)]

[*Title of Court and Cause*]

Ready for decision is the plaintiffs' motion to impose sanctions for failure to comply with order of the court, filing _____.

On _____, 19__, an order was entered, filing _____, requiring the defendants to file answers to designated written interrogatories on or before _____, 19__. No such filing has been made to the present day, and no motion has been made for an enlargement of time in which to comply with the order.

Sanctions under Rule 37(b) of the Federal Rules of Civil Procedure are therefore appropriate.

It appears to the court that the unresolved issues to which the interrogatories went are those designated in Exhibit C of the order on pretrial conference, filing _____, as:

"1. Personal jurisdiction on The _____ Company, a _____ corporation.

(a) Was The _____ Company, a _____ corporation doing business in _____?

(b) Was the involvement of The _____ Company substantial enough to give this court jurisdiction over this defendant?"

Those questions will now stand as answered in the affirmative, and personal jurisdiction waived by that defendant.

It may be that the interrogatories are relevant to other issues described in the order on pretrial conference. If so, the plaintiffs may make a showing brief or otherwise pointing out what other issues, and consideration will be given to imposition of further sanctions.

IT IS THEREFORE ORDERED.

1. That the motion to impose sanctions for failure to comply with order of the court, filing is granted to the extent that it hereby is determined: That the defendant The _____ Company, a _____ corporation, was doing business in _____ and its involvement was substantial enough to give this court jurisdiction over that defendant; that personal jurisdiction over the defendant The _____ Company, a _____ corporation, is deemed admitted and established and the issue of personal jurisdiction over the defendant is waived by that defendant;

2. That the defendant The _____ Company shall pay within fifteen days of the date of this order to the plaintiffs' counsel the amount of $_____ as the expense of obtaining this order; and

3. That because The _____ Company, a _____ corporation, is now known as _____ Corp., wherever in this order there is reference to _____ Company, a _____ corporation, it is applicable to _____ Corp.

[*Date*]

_____
United States District Judge

Objecting to Discovery: Protective Orders

A discovery request may go too far. It may request privileged information or attorney work product, be unduly expensive, or be excessive in some other way. When this happens, it is necessary to object to the specific question or request. If the requesting party persists with a motion to compel discovery, the resisting party may by motion request a protective order from the court. The court has the duty to protect a party or person from annoyance, embarrassment, oppression, or undue burden or expense. It is empowered to provide these remedies set out in Rule 26(c):

1. Deny the requested discovery;
2. Grant discovery on specific terms and conditions, including time and place;

3. Grant discovery if another method (such as interrogatories) is used;
4. Grant discovery provided certain items are not inquired into, or if the scope of the inquiry is limited;
5. Grant discovery but only in the presence of certain individuals named by the court;
6. Grant discovery provided the deposition is sealed and opened only by court order;
7. Deny discovery of trade or commercial secrets, or grant discovery in a limited way;
8. Grant discovery only if parties simultaneously file specified information or documents in sealed envelopes to be opened as directed by the court.

The court has the power to deny the motion and order the resisting party to permit the discovery. If the motion is denied and justice requires, the court may order the resisting party to pay the costs and attorney fees incurred by the party seeking discovery [Rules 26(c) and 37(a)(4)].

Updating Discovery

It is no secret that many civil cases can drag on for years. Information supplied in discovery can become dated and inaccurate, defeating the purpose of discovery to avoid surprise at trial. Rule 26(e) partially prevents that by requiring periodic updating of certain discovery information. Under this rule, parties have an obligation to update their list of witnesses and expert witnesses. It is necessary to amend a prior response to a discovery request if the responding party realizes that the response is no longer accurate. Failure to amend will constitute a knowing concealment. The duty to update responses may be imposed and expanded by the court or by agreement between the parties. A party may also request a supplementation of prior responses. There is no other duty to update responses under Rule 26(e).

Because paralegals work so closely with discovery information, they are frequently the ones in the law firm who know when responses need updating. A good paralegal notices outdated or inaccurate information and calendars in regular reminders to seek supplementation of discovery from the opponent and to reciprocate.

Ethical Considerations

Discovery offers a significant improvement over the traditional form of trial by surprise and concealment. Preserving the benefits of discovery, however, demands vigilance, honesty, and cooperation. The paralegal and attorney who fail to adhere to the relevant ethical standards do a disservice not only to their profession, but also to the fairness that is the goal of discovery.

There are numerous ethical provisions that directly or indirectly apply to discovery. Several are worth noting. The ABA's Model Rules of Professional Conduct has a rule that addresses fairness to the opposing party and counsel. Rule 3:4 reads in part:

A lawyer shall not:

(a) unlawfully obstruct another party's access to evidence or unlawfully alter, destroy or conceal a document or other material having potential evidentiary value. A lawyer shall not counsel or assist another person to do any such act;

(b) falsify evidence, counsel or assist a witness to testify falsely or offer an inducement to a witness that is prohibited by law;

(c) knowingly disobey an obligation under the rules of a tribunal except for an open refusal based on an assertion that no obligation exists;

(d) in pretrial procedure, make a frivolous discovery request or fail to make reasonably diligent effort to comply with a legally proper discovery request by an opposing party; . . .

(f) request a person other than a client to refrain from voluntarily giving relevant information to another party [emphasis added].

This rule reflects many of the standards in the older Code of Professional Responsibility that remains in effect in some states. Unlike the Code, however, the new Rules reflect the contemporary importance of discovery by addressing it specifically . Some of the relevant provisions of the older Code state that a lawyer "shall not suppress any evidence that he [she] or his [her] client has a legal obligation to reveal" [DR7-109(A)]; "shall not [i]ntentionally or habitually violate any established rule of procedure or of evidence" [DR7-106(C)(7)]; "shall not participate in the creation or preservation of evidence when he [she] knows it is obvious that the evidence is false" [DR7-102(A)(6)]; "shall not disregard . . . a standing rule of a tribunal . . ." [DR7-106(A)]; and shall not ask a question "intended to degrade a witness or other person" [DR7-106(C)(2)].[5]

The essence of these rules rests in the attorney's obligation to cooperate in discovery and avoid any concealment of discoverable evidence. That obligation is shared by the paralegal along with the obligation to resist any attempt to have the paralegal destroy or manufacture evidence.

Another area of ethical concern previously addressed is the attorney work product and attorney-client privilege. These have been addressed principally in light of the concern for revealing more information to the opponent than is necessary. There is, however, the more serious matter of inadvertently revealing the confidences of a client during the discovery process. Careless review and screening of materials by a paralegal or an attorney may result in the improper revelation of a client's confidences or secrets in direct violation of the code of ethics. The old Code states this in DR4-101 "Preservation of Confidences and Secrets of a Client":

(A) "Confidence" refers to information protected by the attorney-client privilege . . . , and "secret" refers to other information gained in the professional relationship that the client has requested to be held inviolate or the disclosure of which would be embarrassing or would be likely to be detrimental to the client.

(B) Except when permitted under DR4-101(C) a lawyer shall not knowingly:

(1) Reveal a confidence or secret of his client.

And

(C) A lawyer may reveal:

(1) Confidences or secrets with the consent of the client . . . , but only after a full disclosure to them.

The Model Rules of Professional Conduct replaces the language of DR4-101 with New Model Rule 1.6:

> (a) A lawyer shall not reveal information relating to representation of a client unless the client consents after consultation, **except for disclosures that are impliedly authorized in order to carry out the representation** [emphasis added].

The new rule covers information gained before and after the representation and does not require the client to indicate what is to be held secret; nor does it ask the lawyer to speculate what is embarrassing or detrimental.[6] The new rule does permit a lawyer to make disclosures when there is implied authorization. The example given in the commentary to Rule 1.6 applies directly to the discovery process and states that a lawyer may, for example, disclose information by admitting facts that cannot properly be denied.[7]

Regardless of whether the attorney's conduct is governed by the older Model Code or the new Model Rules, you must strive to identify any confidential information or secret that has been given to the attorney by the client and consult with the attorney prior to disclosing that information to anyone outside the firm. This guideline for paralegal conduct is extremely critical and cannot be overemphasized.

ASSIGNMENT 8:4
In your system folder add a list of the pertinent ethical sections from both the new Model Rules and the older code (if applicable in your state) and restate the essence of those rules in your own words in outline form.

▌ Interrogatories

Mr. White wants you to draft a set of **interrogatories** in the next three days to be answered by a yet-unidentified officer at Mercury Parcel Service, Inc.

Purpose of Interrogatories

Interrogatories are written questions submitted to another party and answered by that party in writing and under oath. They are authorized in Federal Rule 33 and parallel state rules. Their primary purpose is to provide a relatively inexpensive way to gather initial information from the opposing party. Useful information on the parties, witnesses, documents and records, evidence, and leads thereto can be obtained through questions like the following:

- State the name and address of each person who has knowledge concerning . . .
- Identify and give the location of each document or record in your possession regarding . . .

The answers to the questions can aid in drafting other interrogatories or in preparing for depositions, and can provide the supporting information for summary judgment.

Interrogatories have some outstanding advantages. They are relatively inexpensive and the answering party cannot say "I do not know" or "I have forgotten." The rules impose a duty on the answering party to seek out the answer if the information is in the possession or control of that party. Interrogatories are especially helpful in "piercing the corporate veil" to gain information about internal structure, policies, and records of a corporation or agency.

Procedure

Interrogatories must be carefully planned and drafted. They may be served by any party on any other party as early as the service of the summons and complaint. Each question of the interrogatory must be answered separately and completely, or objections noted in lieu of the answer. The answers to the interrogatories must be returned within thirty days of service of the interrogatories or within forty-five days if served with the summons and complaint [Rule 30(a)]. The court can grant an extension or reduction in the time required for response.

Interrogatories must be answered by the party, or by a designated official or agent in the case of a corporation or other entity. The answers are actually drafted by the attorney and the paralegal.

In some cases it is not fair to place the time-consuming and difficult burden solely on the responding party to search through documents and locate the exact information. Rule 33(c) is designed to reduce that burden by permitting the responding party to identify the specific documents and records where the information is likely to be found and giving the requesting party the opportunity to review the documents and locate the specifically requested information.

If a party objects to a question or refuses to answer, the requesting party can seek the assistance and sanctions provided by Rule 37(e). The scope of the interrogatories is the same as that for any discovery device as set out in Rule 26(b) and the Rules of Evidence. Interrogatory practice is generally the same in most jurisdictions. There are some local differences, however, so you should become familiar with the local practice.

ASSIGNMENT 8:5
Review and verify the deadlines for interrogatory practice by checking the Pleadings, Motions, and Time Limits Table in chapter 7 or in your system folder. Draft an outline to include the definition, purpose, scope, and procedure for interrogatories. Place the outline in your system folder.

Planning the Interrogatories

Interrogatories can be extremely useful as a discovery tool if they are planned carefully. If they are not planned carefully, the opponent may pose valid objections that preclude or delay discovery or produce information that is so general that it is useless.

Interrogatories are generally used to obtain the following information:[8]

1. Identities of persons who provided statements
2. Identities of persons interviewed
3. Facts elicited from a person interviewed who is now unavailable
4. Identity of documents, witness statements, and physical evidence, including the nature, condition, location, and custody

5. Information on all correspondence written by, read by, or mentioning a specific party, witness, or other person involved in the case
6. Summary explanations of technical matter, data, and documents
7. Transactions relating to the parties prior or subsequent to the events of the case
8. Similar incidents related to the case involving the parties or others
9. Information on the business or corporation including its organization, principal place of business, and other relevant data
10. Information on the finances, related records, and status of the business or party
11. Licenses relevant to party's business or conduct
12. Identities of experts who will testify at trial and their opinions and bases for each opinion
13. Insurance coverage
14. Data on time, speed, distance, and other relevant measurements, tests, or estimates
15. Information on property and other assets for purposes of pre- or postjudgment collections
16. Jurisdictional facts
17. Protected work product where sufficient cause exists

Interrogatories may be done in several sets. One set, for example, may be submitted early in the litigation to obtain leads for further investigation and discovery, and another set submitted later to obtain detailed information on a particular subject. In planning interrogatories, the drafter must be aware of any limitations on the number of questions that may be submitted. In some jurisdictions courts limit the number of questions to as few as fifteen. Determine if there are any such limitations and plan accordingly. If the limit seems unworkable due to the complexity of the case, the supervising attorney may choose to move the court to expand the limit.

Determine the Objectives of the Interrogatories

A significant step in the planning of interrogatories is determining what information suitable for interrogatories is needed from the opponent. Ultimately the attorney will decide this, but you will often have the task of initiating the work. How is this done?

1. Keep the task clearly in mind, noting any special directions. In this case the task is to draft interrogatories to be submitted to Mercury Parcel Service.
2. Review the case file including the pleadings and any other documents exchanged, as well as information obtained through informal investigation. Note areas that need clarification or more information. Review the complaint, answer, and counterclaim found in chapters 5 and 7. Also review the information obtained in the informal investigation stages found in chapter 4.
3. Review or determine the elements of the cause of action according to the method outlined in chapter 4. This includes knowing the elements of any alleged defense and counterclaim.
4. Determine the broad goals to be accomplished against the defendant at trial. In this case, the goal is to show that Mercury Parcel is Rich-

ard Hart's superior and therefore liable for the negligent actions of Mr. Hart, its agent. Interrogatories would be needed to establish agency and to establish the following facts:

That Mercury is a business
That Hart was in the employ of Mercury on the date of the accident
That Mercury owned the vehicle driven by Hart
That Hart was working within the scope of his employment
That Mercury had insurance to cover Hart and the vehicle

A further goal is to establish that Mercury was liable as a matter of its own fault. By applying imagination, one might produce the following possibilities for Mercury's negligence:

That the van was defective
That regular maintenance was ignored
That complaints of defects were ignored
That a pattern of poor maintenance procedures existed
That maintenance reports were falsified to cover up poor or hurried maintenance procedures
That drivers were asked to work unusually long shifts
That Hart was asked to work an unusually long shift
That hiring procedures disregarded or did not adequately screen for poor driving records

5. Determine what information is needed to reveal evidence or lead to evidence that supports such theories. The specific elements of the cause of action should be used as focal points for ideas on what information, witnesses, records, procedures, and so on might reveal evidence supportive of the proferred theories. Under each element, the following may prove helpful.

Duty of Care

- Laws or regulations imposing standards of care, such as a mandatory program for maintenance and vehicle and driver safety
- Records that must be kept to prove compliance with legal requirements
- The names of those responsible for recording and storing these records
- The existence of a company policy on maintenance or a regular maintenance program and records verifying such
- The existence of drivers' schedules, in-out reports, mileage, and so on
- The existence, quality, and use of a safety program and safety library

Breach of Duty

Specifically on the van operated by Hart on the day of the accident:

- Maintenance records since the vehicle was purchased
- Source of purchase (new or used vehicle), name and address of previous owner(s)
- Records containing drivers' complaints or notes on performance
- Names and addresses of mechanics or others who worked on the vehicle

- Records relating to the history of maintenance and repair
- Maintenance and repair records for all vehicles covering the eighteen months prior to accident
- Names and addresses of all persons responsible for implementing and supervising vehicle maintenance and repair
- Names and addresses of all drivers who operated the van
- Record of Richard Hart's driving schedule one month prior to the accident
- Dispatch logs for one month prior to the accident through the date of the accident
- Records of road hours put in by all drivers eighteen months prior to accident
- Names and addresses of all drivers employed within the last eighteen months prior to accident

Breach Was Substantial Cause of Injury

- Possible expert witness to testify at trial denying that any defect caused or contributed to the accident
- Possible expert witness to testify at trial that no defect existed at the time of the accident.

The previous lists are by no means exhaustive, but illustrate the type of brainstorming process helpful in developing goal-related questions.

6. It usually proves helpful to consult form or "canned" interrogatories. Although determining your own specific objectives will lead to better-focused and more useful interrogatories, the form interrogatories can act as a reminder of goals or specific objectives that you may have missed. Form interrogatories are often available in the firm's form files or in the case folder of a similar case. The advantage to the latter is that the answers to the questions are available and can tell the drafter if the questions were too easily avoided or otherwise unproductive. Form interrogatories may also be found in the law library, in books written specifically on interrogatories and arranged by topic, or in various litigation practice manuals and form books. Remember, however, that form interrogatories are good sources for ideas but bad sources for the final product. It is the rare form interrogatory that will meet the drafter's specific needs.

7. Once you have set out the goals and specific related objectives, organize them by topics. One approach is to use the elements of the action and defenses as topics. Another is to follow the paragraphs in the pleading. No one method is best. Each law firm or each case may require a different approach. The following list contains frequently used topics in particular types of actions.

Contract

1. Identification of parties, addresses, background
2. Events leading up to breach of contract
3. Details of the breach
4. Events following the breach
5. Communications between parties
6. Documents relating to breach, location, other evidence

7. Defenses raised
8. Damages
9. Basis for calculation of damages

10. Witnesses/statements
11. Elements, information, documents, and so on related to counterclaim

Personal Injury Case

1. Identification of parties, addresses, background
2. Jurisdictional matters (for example, to determine if there really is diversity of citizenship)
3. Duty of care
4. Breach of duty
5. Damages/basis for calculation

6. Breach is substantial cause of damages
7. Defenses
8. Documents and related information
9. Witnesses/statements
10. Elements, information, documents, and so on related to counterclaim

Products Liability

1. Parties, addresses, place of business, and so on
2. Product's purchase and use
3. Advertising, warranties, representations, operator's manual, posted cautions, and so on
4. Events leading to injury
5. History of product/similar incidents and claims
6. Product testing and related re-

ports
7. Details of injuries or damages (emotional, mental, and physical)
8. Basis for calculations of damages
9. Witnesses/statements
10. Documents
11. Defenses

Based on these three types of cases, one might construct a list of common categories:

1. Parties, addresses, background, and so on
2. Events leading up to injury or incident
3. Injury
4. Damages
5. Basis for damages

6. Witnesses/statements
7. Related documents
8. Defenses
9. Elements, information, documents, and so on related to counterclaim

Regardless of the topics suggested here, usually other topics or subtopics are unique to the case and require special attention.

8. Interrogatories may be a valuable discovery device, but they are not without pitfalls. Interrogatories should not be used to cover an area exhaustively; their primary function is to get background information, determine the existence and location of evidence, and to elicit leads to other evidence. Determining the detailed content of the evidence is best left to other discovery devices such as depositions and document production. Using interrogatories exhaustively will likely elicit valid objections for length, scope, and harassment, and achieve unsatisfactory results. The practice will also engage the parties in a costly and inefficient paper war.

Extensive interrogatories may encourage an otherwise busy and unconcerned opponent to study the case thoroughly, giving the opponent insight and awareness that could impede settlement and enhance the opponent's preparedness for trial.

Large numbers of interrogatories are likely to lead to evasiveness, incompleteness, and laziness on the part of the opponent, making it necessary to demand more information or to seek assistance of the court.

Therefore, interrogatories are best used prudently, with very clear objectives in mind, with an awareness of the specific benefits of the other discovery devices, but also with the understanding that they are invaluable for their limited purposes in almost every case.

Drafting the Interrogatories

Although most jurisdictions have similar rules on the style and format for interrogatories, consult the local rules and acquire examples of interrogatories used in that particular jurisdiction. They will serve as important guides to drafting.

Introductory Paragraphs

After the case caption, an introductory paragraph should be drafted. These come in a variety of formats, but generally state to whom the interrogatories are directed, that an answer is required within a specified period of time, and the appropriate state or federal rule. For example:

Plaintiff hereby requests defendants to answer under oath, pursuant to Rule 33 of the Federal Rules of Civil Procedure, the following interrogatories within __* days of the date service is made upon you. *[Under Rule 33(a) the defendant may have up to forty-five days if the interrogatories are served with the summons and complaint; otherwise it is thirty days.]

The introductory paragraph addressed to a corporation or other company might appear as follows:[9]

[Caption]

To _____ Company, Defendant:
The plaintiff requests that the following interrogatories be answered under oath by any of your officers competent to testify in your behalf who know the facts about which inquiry is made, and that the answers be served on plaintiff within _____ days from the time these interrogatories are served on you.

Definitions and Abbreviations

The interrogatories should be preceded by a section on definitions and abbreviations. This provides clarity and makes it unnecessary to define terms repeatedly throughout the questions. An example of such a section follows.[10]

I. DEFINITIONS

A. As used herein, the words "document" or "documents" include any written, printed, typed or graphic matter of any kind or nature however produced or reproduced, now in the possession, custody, or control of a defendant, or in the possession, custody or control of the present or former officers, agents, representatives, employees of a defendant or any and all persons acting in its or his/her behalf, including documents at any time in the possession, custody or control of such individuals or entities, or known by the defendants to exist.

B. As used herein, the words "identify," "identity," or "identification" when used in reference to a natural person mean to state his or her full name and present or last known address, and his or her present or last known position and business affiliation; when used in reference to a document mean to state its date, its author, the type of document (e.g., letter, memorandum, telegram, chart, photograph, sound reproduction, etc.) or, if the above information is not available, some other means of identifying it, and its present location and the name of each of its present custodians. If any such document was but is no longer in your possession or subject to your control, or in existence, state whether it is (a) missing or lost, (b) has been destroyed, (c) has been transferred voluntarily or involuntarily to others, or (d) otherwise disposed of, and in each instance, explain the circumstance surrounding and authorization for such disposition thereof and state the date or approximate date thereof.

C. The words "you" or "your" mean the defendants, their present or former members, officers, agents, employees, and all other persons acting or purporting to act on their behalf, including all present or former members, officers, agents, employees, and all other persons exercising or purporting to exercise discretion, making policy, and making decisions.

(Include any abbreviations or acronyms [ABA for example] if appropriate.)

Instructions

It has become increasingly common to include a section of instructions. This provides the opposition with some guidance and allows the questioner to shape the form of the answers. An example follows.[11]

II. INSTRUCTIONS

1. To the extent that information sought by any Interrogatory can be furnished by reference to the Answer furnished to another Interrogatory, appropriate reference will be acceptable to the plaintiff. However, a separate answer should be accorded to each Interrogatory, and Interrogatories should not be joined together and accorded a common answer.

2. Each Answer should be preceded by identification and verbatim quote of the Interrogatory to which the Answer regards.

3. Separate interrogatories have been prepared for each defendant. Each Interrogatory should be answered separately by each defendant. If an Interrogatory Answer provided by one defendant contains information responsive to an Interrogatory directed to another defendant, that defendant may incorporate such Answer by reference.

4. If any Interrogatory is objected to by you as inquiring into privileged matter, set forth fully in the objection the facts which form the basis for your objection.

5. If any document, report, study, memorandum, or other written material is withheld or not identified under claim of privilege, furnish a list identifying each such document for which the privilege is claimed, together with the following information: date, author, sender, recipient, persons to whom copies were furnished, together with their job titles, subject matter of the document, the basis on which the asserted privilege is claimed, and the paragraph or paragraphs of these Interrogatories to which the document responds.

Another typical instruction reads: Divulge in your Answer all pertinent information in your possession, or in possession of the corporation, or your attorney's agents, investigators, employees, or other representatives.

Questions for the Body of the Interrogatories

General background interrogatories Following the introductory paragraphs is frequently one or more questions on the general background of the person or corporation being questioned. For example:

Please state your:	Please state:
Full name	The full name of the corporation
Age	The date and place of incorporation
Current address	tion
Marital status	The corporation's principal place
Employment address	of business
Employment position	Type of corporation
Education	

Interrogatories that cover the pleadings Good interrogatories elicit information based on the most recent pleading of the opponent. Since the pleading states factual allegations to show that the elements of the cause of action exist or are denied or state a defense, the opponent has the right to discover the underlying basis of the alleged facts: the who, what, when, where, why, and how (the five W's and an H) of the factual allegations. Therefore, the pleading in question should be reviewed carefully and interrogatories should be drafted to acquire information on each allegation. For example, assume the complaint alleges the following in paragraph 3:

> Defendant operated vehicle in a negligent manner by failing to keep a proper lookout and by operating said vehicle at an excessive rate of speed.

The defendant should draw upon the five W's and an H to formulate questions to elicit information that is clear and complete. For example:

> Regarding paragraph 3 of Plaintiff's Complaint, describe and explain all the specific facts on which you rely to support your contention that the defendant failed to keep a proper lookout.

> Regarding paragraph 3 of Plaintiff's Complaint, describe and explain all the specific facts on which you rely to support your contention that the defendant "operated vehicle at an excessive rate of speed."

On the other hand, the plaintiff should draft questions to elicit information that forms the basis for the defendant's answer. For example, assume defendant's answer to paragraph 3 was "Denied," an appropriate interrogatory would be:

> Regarding paragraph 3 of Defendant's Answer, describe and explain all the specific facts on which you rely to support your denial of the allegation that defendant failed to keep a proper lookout.

In another paragraph of the complaint, assume that the following allegation is made:

> As a consequence of Defendant's negligence, Plaintiff has incurred numerous expenses for doctor bills, hospital bills, nursing care, and medications to the sum of $17,000.

In a section on damages in the interrogatories, the defendant might request the following information:

> In regard to paragraph 8 of Plaintiff's Complaint, identify each doctor, hospital, source of nursing care, and medication and all records related thereto to support the allegation that Plaintiff incurred expenses "to the sum of $17,000."

Interrogatories that cover the basic areas of the case   The next section of the interrogatories goes beyond the pleadings and focuses on areas not yet addressed by the questions on the pleadings. This is the area where the ideas generated in the brainstorming process are molded into questions. Recall the ideas and areas for inquiry implicating Mercury Parcel in the negligence apart from the negligence of Mr. Hart. The ideas generated in the planning stage might take the following form in the drafting stage. Some of the ideas generated under duty of care were: laws or regulations imposing standards of care such as a mandatory program for maintenance and vehicle and driver safety, records that must be kept to prove compliance with legal requirements, the names of those responsible for recording and storing these records, and the existence of a company policy on maintenance or a regular maintenance program/records indicating such.

Interrogatories based on these points should then be drafted:

1. Identify any state or federal laws, rules, or regulations that require your compliance regarding:
   a. Regular maintenance of your delivery vehicles
   b. Repair of your delivery vehicles
   c. Driver safety (including training, required breaks, limits to operating hours, vehicle safety checks, precautions on ice, speed, etc.)
   d. The maintaining of records on a.–c.

2. Identify all types of records kept by your company on a.–c. in interrogatory no. 1.

3. Identify all records and communications (both oral and written) on a.–c. in interrogatory no. 1 specifically pertaining to Mr. Hart and the van operated by Mr. Hart that was involved in the accident of February 26, 19___.

Because "identify" has previously been defined, it is not necessary to repeat all the requests associated with the term "identify." Following this method, you should be able to continue drafting pertinent questions to cover all the necessary points for each element of the cause of action.

It is also appropriate to ask questions about insurance coverage (company, coverage, limits), the existence of physical things (evidence), persons with knowledge of the facts, witnesses and exhibits to be relied on or "may" be relied on, and the identity of persons who helped prepare the interrogatories or acted as consultants.

Interrogatories on opinions and legal and factual contentions   Rule 33(b) and parallel state rules permit questions calling for "an opinion or contention that relates to fact or the application of law to fact." The information gained in the answer to such a question reveals the opponent's position on a key point of possible contention and calls for the opponent to reveal the facts and other evidence relied on to support the contention. If it is revealed that the matter is not contended, or the opponent is without evidence to support the contention, the area could be a productive one for the party seeking the answer. An example of such a question appears as follows:

Do you contend that Defendant Hart was not operating the van at an excessive rate of speed at the time of the accident? If so:
On what do you base your contention?
What is the identity of every person who has knowledge of these facts?
Have any of these people, to your knowledge, made statements to you or others regarding these facts?
What is the identity of any documents, physical things, or other evidence that you believe supports your contention?

This type of question is often reserved until the end of the discovery period to gain maximum information and avoid responses like "not sure yet," or "investigation still continuing," or "not available at this time." This type of question can be more effective than a request for admission because it calls for the basis of the contention.[12]

General concluding or summary interrogatories   Some general interrogatories should be drafted to cover any oversights and prevent the opponent from later using evidence at trial that should have been elicited in the interrogatories. Here are some examples:[13]

Do you have any additional information relevant to the subject of this lawsuit not previously set out in your answers above?
Have you listed and contacted all individuals that you know have, or might have, information pertaining to this lawsuit?
Please identify and state the capacities of all persons who helped you obtain answers to these interrogatories, specifying the answer with which they assisted.

Concluding Material

Notice to supplement answers The opponent should be advised of the continuing obligation to supplement the answers to the interrogatories. This can be done in the instructions or as a concluding reminder at the end of the interrogatories. Here is an example:

> Take notice that you have a continuing obligation to supplement your answers to these interrogatories as information is acquired by you, your agents, attorneys, or representatives.

Signature and certificate of service The interrogatories should end with a signature line for the attorney and the address of the firm or office. A certificate of service should be included. For example:

CERTIFICATE OF SERVICE

A copy of PLAINTIFF'S CONTINUING INTERROGATORIES SET ONE was served on Defendant Mercury Parcel Service, Incorporated's attorney, Lynn Ott, located at 518 So. Maple Street, Cincinnati, Ohio, by U.S. Mail this 21st day of November, 19___.

> Arthur White
> Attorney for Plaintiff
> (address)

Specific Drafting Techniques

These are some specific pointers for drafting well-written interrogatories.

Test the appropriateness of the question by asking if the information requested will lead to evidence that is admissible. There is no restriction that the information requested be admissible.

Draft the question as concisely and precisely as possible. Keep it simple and easy to understand. If you do, the answer will be more to the point.

Avoid an excessive number of questions.

Number the questions sequentially with extra sets starting where the last set left off.

Use the following techniques when the number of interrogatories is severely limited.[14] Avoid numbering or lettering sublistings. Do not make your subtopics conspicious; avoid "and," "or," "the," semicolons, and colons. For example, do not write "Please state the names, addresses, and phone numbers of the defendant's employers for each job held by the defendant during 1980, 1981, 1982, 1983, 1984, and to the present." Write "Please identify all the defendant's employers beginning with 1980." Reduce lengthy phrases to a single word or class. For example, instead of asking the defendant to "list all repairs to the wheels, brakes, engine, exterior, hood, etc.," ask the defendant to "list all repairs to the car." Ask singular questions that require multiple answers rather than the other way around. For example, instead of saying, "State the name of the corporate president, vice president, and associate vice president," say, "Identify each corporate officer by name and office held." Use multiple choice questions if appropriate, unless you do not want to suggest the answer: "State whether the bonds in question are Series E bonds, Series F bonds, or Series Y bonds."

Draft interrogatories in the correct tense. Interrogatories should be stated in the proper verb tense. "Who had custody of the documents?" is a different question and may elicit quite a different answer than "Who has custody of the documents?" The careful drafter must be sure the correct question is being asked. If it is not, lost time and a permanently lost answer may be the consequence.

Phrase questions to determine if an answer is based on firsthand knowledge and if impediments to accuracy exist. It is important for evidentiary reasons to determine whether an answer is based on firsthand knowledge or secondhand knowledge, the latter being less reliable and likely to be excluded as hearsay. Therefore, the questions should be phrased to determine whether knowledge is first or secondhand.[15] "Did you personally observe ice on the road?"

Questions should also be devised to determine the ability of the party to observe the facts.[16] "Was there anything obstructing or limiting your view of the pedestrian? If so, explain the nature of the obstruction or limiting factor, and how it affected your view of the pedestrian. Are you required to wear glasses with corrective lenses when you drive? Were you wearing your glasses at the time of the accident?"

Keep in mind, however, that the deposition may be a better time to ask some of these questions because the answers will be more spontaneous. If answered in the interrogatories, the answer will be carefully planned and probably more self-serving than a deposition answer. The most appropriate discovery device for each type of question needs to be weighed carefully.

Avoid questions that allow a yes or no answer unless you include a follow-up.[17] Questions that permit the answering party to respond yes or no rarely provide much useful information. Normally such a question should be followed by others that require more detail or an explanation of the answer.

Evaluate and proofread the questions. The purpose of an interrogatory is to force the opponent to relinquish information that you need.[18] It should be drafted to restrict the answering party's ability to provide an uninformative though truthful answer. Evaluate each question drafted to see if it is sufficiently restricted by trying to see how the question could be evaded. If it can be, it requires redrafting or more specific questions. It is essential to go through this evaluation process prior to giving the interrogatories to the attorney for review.

Further, the interrogatories should be proofread carefully to eliminate typos, misspellings, grammatical mistakes, and so on. Such mistakes, if left uncorrected, not only will create a negative impression of your abilities but also will frequently result in confusion, unresponsive answers, and the time-consuming and embarrassing process of asking the opponent to stipulate to a correction.

ASSIGNMENT 8:6
Make a copy of the checklist in figure 8:4. Add any explanatory details from the text material that you choose to, then place this checklist in your system folder.

Figure 8:5 contains sample interrogatories for an auto accident case.[19]

Figure 8:4   Checklist for Planning and Drafting Interrogatories

I. Planning the Interrogatories
  A. Have the attorney's directions for the task firmly in mind.
  B. Review the file, especially the pleadings, and all related information discovered to date.
  C. Review the elements of the claim, defense, counterclaim, and so on.
  D. Determine the goals to be accomplished.
    1. Review the pleadings for areas needing more detail or explanation.
    2. Brainstorm on each element of the claim, defense, counterclaim, and so on, to develop useful theories of liability and areas of inquiry.
    3. Determine what must be discovered (witnesses, documents, physical evidence, etc.) and the likely leads to it.
  E. Acquire and read form interrogatories for suggested areas of inquiry, format, and questions.
  F. Organize areas of inquiry by logical topics.
  G. Avoid pitfalls.
    1. Do not try to cover entire areas exhaustively if other methods of discovery are available and better lend themselves to the specific objective.
    2. Keep brief to avoid setting off a paper war.
    3. Avoid forcing the other side to prepare their case.

II. Drafting the Interrogatories
  A. Acquire the civil practice rules for interrogatories and locate samples of interrogatories in the jurisdiction for the particular case.
  B. Draft an introductory paragraph stating to whom the interrogatories are directed, applicable rules, and time required for a reply.
  C. Provide a definition and abbreviation section.
  D. Provide an instruction section so the answer and any objections will be placed in a format most useful to the questioner.
  E. Draft questions that focus on finding out more about the basis for the allegations in the opponent's pleadings.
  F. Draft questions that cover the theories of liability and defenses thereto as they relate to the elements of the offense.
  G. Draft questions calling for opinion and legal and factual contentions [Rule 33(b)].
  H. Draft concluding or summary interrogatories.
  I. Include notice of continuing obligation to update answers.
  J. Provide for attorney's signature and certificate of service.

III. Specific Drafting Techniques
  A. Ask whether the question elicits information that is likely to lead to admissible evidence.
  B. Keep questions concise, precise, and easy to understand.
  C. Avoid excessive questions.
  D. Number questions and sets of questions sequentially.
  E. If the number of interrogatories is limited:
    1. Do not number or letter subdivisions.
    2. Avoid making subtopics conspicuous: avoid "and," "or," "the," semicolons, and colons.
    3. Reduce lists to single word or class.
    4. Ask singular questions that require multiple answers.
    5. Use multiple-choice questions where appropriate.
  F. Use correct verb tense.
  G. Phrase questions to determine if answers are based on firsthand knowledge and if impediments to accuracy exist.
  H. Avoid questions that permit yes or no answers unless more detail is requested.
  I. Phrase questions to restrict evasiveness in the answer.
  J. Proofread carefully prior to submitting to attorney for review.

IV. Final Preparation and Service of Interrogatories

Figure 8:5   Sample Interrogatories

State of _____ ⎫
Count of _____ ⎬
Civil Court Branch   ⎭

Dennis Diamond
346 Redgrove Street
City of _____, State   Plaintiff,
of _____ 45890
                              v.   } CIVIL ACTION NO. ____
Janet McDonald
781 4th Street
City of _____, State   Defendant,
of _____ 45966

INTERROGATORIES TO _____

Pursuant to section _____, _____ hereby submits the following interrogatories to _____. These interrogatories are to be answered by _____ under oath and served on the attorney for _____ within _____ days.

INSTRUCTIONS FOR USE

A. All information is to be divulged which is in the possession of the individual or corporate party, his attorneys, investigators, agents, employees or other representatives of the named party and his attorney.
B. A "medical practitioner" as used in these interrogatories is meant to include any medical doctor, osteopathic physician, podiatrist, doctor of chiropractic, naturopathic physician, or other person who performs any form of healing art.
C. Where an individual interrogatory calls for an answer which involves more than one part, each part of the answer should be clearly set out so that it is understandable.
D. Where the terms "you," "plaintiff," or "defendant" are used, they are meant to include every individual party and separate answers should be given for each person named as a party, if requested.
E. Where the terms "accident" or "the accident" are used, they are meant to mean the incident which is the basis of this lawsuit, unless otherwise specified.

NAME

1. State your full name, age and place of birth.
2. Have you ever been known by any other name and, if so, give the other name or names and state where and when you used such names.
3. Has your name ever been legally changed and, if so, state when, where and through what procedure.

RESIDENCE

4. State your present residence address and the period during which you have resided at said address.
5. List all other addresses at which you have resided during the past ten years and the dates of the use of each.

MARRIAGE

6. Are you married at the present time and, if so,
   a. Give your spouse's full name.
   b. If a female, her maiden name.
   c. His or her address for the five years before your marriage.

d. The date and place of your marriage.

e. State whether or not your spouse is now living with you.

f. If not, when the separation occurred, and

g. Your spouse's present address.

7. If you were previously married, state for each previous spouse:

    a. The name and present residence address of each spouse.

    b. The dates of commencement and termination of each marriage.

    c. The place where you were married to each spouse.

    d. For each marriage, please state the manner in which it was terminated.

    e. If any marriage was terminated by divorce, state for each such divorce the county and state or place where the action was filed and the grounds alleged in said action and whether filed by you.

PAST EMPLOYMENT

8. For the ten years immediately preceding the date of the incident referred to in the complaint, state

    a. The names and addresses of each of your employers.

    b. The dates of commencement and termination of each such source of employment.

    c. Detailed description of the services or work performed for each source of employment.

    d. Your average weekly wages or earnings from each place of employment.

    e. For each employer, whether a physical examination was required, and if so, state the date, place and person giving the physical examination.

    f. For each employer, whether or not you made any representations in writing or answered in writing any questions concerning your physical condition.

    g. The name of your immediate boss, foreman or other superior to whom you were responsible at each of the places of employment listed above.

PRESENT EMPLOYMENT

9. What was your business or occupation at the time of the incident referred to in the complaint and are you still engaged in such business or occupation and if not state

    a. When you ceased working in such business or occupation.

    b. Your present business or occupation, the date you entered it and your present income from such business.

    c. Any other business or occupations prior to your present one and after the date set out in answer to paragraph (a) above.

10. Have you lost any time from your business or occupation since the incident referred to in the complaint and if so, state

    a. The cause of such loss of time.

    b. The number of days lost and the dates.

    c. The amount of any wages or income lost.

11. If employed at the time of the incident referred to in the complaint, state

    a. The name and address of the employer.

    b. The position held and the nature of the work performed.

    c. Average weekly wages for the preceding year.

12. If employed since the incident referred to in the complaint, state

    a. Name and address of present employer.

    b. Position held and nature of work being performed.

    c. Hours worked per week.

    d. Present weekly wages, earnings, income or profit.

    e. Name of your immediate boss, foreman or other superior to whom you are responsible.

    f. Whether a physical examination was required and if so, state the date, place and person giving the examination.

    g. For each employer, whether or not you made any representations in writing or answered in writing any questions concerning your physical condition.

SOCIAL SECURITY AND WORKERS' COMPENSATION

13. What is your social security number?

14. Have you ever drawn social security benefits for disability and if so, state
  a. Your residence at the time.
  b. The social security office through which you filed your claim.
  c. The nature and extent of the disability.
  d. The length of time of such disability and the beginning date.

15. Are you now receiving or have you ever received any disability pension, income or insurance or any workers' compensation from any agency, company, person, corporation, state or government and if so, state
  a. The nature of any such payment.
  b. Dates you received such income.
  c. For what injuries or disability did you receive it and how such injury occurred or disability arose.
  d. By whom paid.
  e. Whether or not you now have any present disability as a result of such injuries or disability.
  f. If so, the nature and extent of such disability.
  g. Whether or not you have any disability at the time of the incident referred to in the complaint.
  h. If so, the nature and extent of such disability.

INCOME AND TAX RETURNS

16. With respect to each of the past five years, state
  a. Your yearly gross income.
  b. Your yearly net income.
  c. The name and address of the person, firm, or corporation having custody of any papers pertaining to your income.

17. Did you file income tax returns with the Director of Internal Revenue for any of the past five years or with any state tax authority or department? If so, state
  a. The office of the Director of Internal Revenue with which each return was filed.
  b. The amount reported in each return as earned income.
  c. The years for which filed as to Director of Internal Revenue.
  d. The state tax authority or authorities with whom such returns were filed.
  e. The years for which filed with such state tax authority or authorities.
  f. The amount of tax shown to be due on each return.

EDUCATION

18. State the name and address of each school, college, or educational institution you have attended, listing the dates of attendance and the courses of study.

ARMED FORCES

19. Have you ever served in the Armed Forces or performed services for any branch of any governmental agency? If so, state
  a. The name of each such organization and the particular branch for whom you performed services.
  b. The dates and places of such services.
  c. Your serial or identification number.
  d. A detailed description of the services performed.
  e. Whether or not a physical exam was required, and if so, the dates and places of such exams.
  f. The date of termination of such services.
  g. A detailed description of the reason why the services were discontinued.

20. Have you ever been rejected for military or government service for physical reasons? If so, state
  a. The date thereof.
  b. The condition for which rejected.
  c. The agency so rejecting you.

21. Have you ever received a discharge from military or government service for physical reasons? If so, state
    a. The date thereof.
    b. The condition for which discharged.
    c. The agency so discharging you.

HOBBIES AND RECREATION

22. List all hobbies and forms of recreation in which you have participated in the last ten years.
23. State all social clubs, lodges, or associations of any nature in which you have participated or of which you were a member in the last ten years.

OTHER CLAIMS

24. Have you made claim for any benefits under any medical pay coverage or policy of insurance relating to injuries arising out of said incident? If so, state
    a. The name of the insurance company or organization to whom said claim was made.
    b. The date of the claim or application.
    c. The claim number and policy number.
25. Have you ever made claim for any benefits under any insurance policy, or against any person, firm or corporation for personal injuries or physical condition which you have not heretofore listed in your answers to these interrogatories? If so, state
    a. The injury or condition for which such claim was made.
    b. The name and address of the person, firm or corporation to whom or against whom it was made.
    c. The date it was made.
    d. The nature and amount of any payment received therefor.

PRIOR OR SUBSEQUENT INJURIES AND DISEASES

26. Have you ever suffered any injuries in any accident either prior or subsequent to the incident referred to in the complaint? If so, state
    a. The date and place of such injury.
    b. A detailed description of all the injuries you received.
    c. The names and addresses of any hospitals rendering treatment.
    d. The names and addresses of all medical practitioners rendering treatment.
    e. The nature and extent of recovery, and, if any permanent disability was suffered, the nature and extent of the permanent disability.
    f. If you were compensated in any manner for any such injury, state the names and addresses of each and every person or organization paying such compensation and the amount thereof.
27. Have you ever had any serious illness, sickness, disease, or surgical operations, either prior or subsequent to the incident referred to in the complaint? If so, state
    a. The date and place.
    b. A detailed description of your symptoms.
    c. The names and addresses of any hospitals rendering treatment.
    d. The names and addresses of all medical practitioners rendering treatment.
    e. The approximate date of your recovery.
    f. If you did not recover fully, give the date your condition became stationary and a description of your condition at that time.

LIFE INSURANCE

28. Have you ever been turned down or rated by any such company for accident, health, or life insurance? If so, state
    a. The name and address of such company or companies.
    b. The date thereof.
    c. The reason therefor.

WEIGHT

29. Please give your average weight for the two years preceding the injuries complained of, your weight at the time of such injuries, and your weight at this time.

CRIMES OR IMPRISONMENT

30. Have you ever pleaded guilty to or been convicted of any crime other than traffic violations and if so, please state
   a. The nature of the offense.
   b. The date.
   c. The county and state in which you were tried.
   d. The sentence given you.
31. Have you ever entered or been committed to any institution, either public or private, for the treatment or observation of mental conditions, alcoholism, narcotic addiction, or disorders of any kind and if so, state
   a. The name and address of such institution.
   b. The length of your stay and the dates thereof.
   c. The purpose or reason for your entry into such institution.
   d. The name and address of the doctor who treated you for such condition.

TRAFFIC VIOLATIONS

32. Please list all violations of the motor vehicle or traffic laws or ordinances to which you have pleaded guilty or nolo contendere and to which you have been found guilty, the date of such offense, the court in which the case was heard and the nature of the violation charged.

DRIVER'S LICENSE

33. At the time of the incident referred to in the complaint did you have a valid license to operate a motor vehicle and if so, state
   a. The state issuing it.
   b. The expiration date.
   c. The number of such license.
   d. Whether there were any restrictions on said license and if so, the nature of the restrictions.
34. Have you ever had a license to operate a motor vehicle suspended or revoked, and if so, state
   a. When and where it was suspended or revoked.
   b. The period of such suspension or revocation.
   c. The reasons for such suspension or revocation.
   d. Was such suspension or revocation lifted?

PURPOSE OF TRIP

35. Please state the point of origin and the point of destination of the particular travel in which you were engaged on the date and time of the occurrence, and please state the following:
   a. the date and time on which you left your point of origin;
   b. the names and addresses of all passengers who may have been with you between the point of origin and the point of accident;
   c. the date and time and specific location of each place that you may have stopped between the point of origin and the point of accident;
   d. the number of miles between the point of origin and the point of accident;
   e. the estimated time you were expecting to arrive at your intended point of destination;
   f. the purpose of your travel.

FACTS OF ACCIDENT

36. State in detail the manner in which you assert that the incident referred to in the complaint occurred, specifying the speed, position, direction, and location of each vehicle involved during its approach to, at the time of and immediately after the collision.

PRECEDING 48 HOURS

37. Did you consume any alcoholic beverage of any type, or any sedative, tranquilizer or other drug, medicine or pill during the 48 hours immediately preceding the incident referred to in the complaint? If so, state

    a. The nature, amount and type of item consumed.

    b. The amount of time over which consumed.

    c. The names and addresses of any and all persons who have any knowledge as to the consumption of these items.

REPAIRS TO VEHICLE

38. State whether or not the vehicle in which you were riding was repaired. If so, state

    a. The date thereof.

    b. The name and address of the person or corporation making such repairs.

    c. The nature of such repairs.

    d. The cost of such repairs.

    e. If written records or memoranda were made of such repairs, state where, when and the names and addresses of the people making such records or memoranda, the present whereabouts of the memoranda, and the name and address of the person in possession or custody of such records or memoranda.

39. If the vehicle was not repaired, state whether or not an estimate of the necessary repairs was made. If so, state

    a. The name and address of the person making such estimate.

    b. If it was written, the name and address of any person having custody of a copy thereof.

STATEMENTS BY PLAINTIFF

40. State whether you have made any statement or statements in any form to any person regarding any of the events or happenings referred to in your complaint, and if so, state

    a. The name and addresses of the person or persons to whom such statements were made.

    b. The date such statements were made.

    c. The form of the statement, whether written, oral, by recording device or to a stenographer.

    d. Whether such statements, if written, were signed.

    e. The names and addresses of the persons presently having custody of such statements.

WITNESSES

41. State the full name and last known address, giving the street, street number, city and state of every witness known to you or to your attorneys who has any knowledge regarding the facts and circumstances surrounding the happening of the incident referred to in the complaint or your alleged injuries including, but not being limited to, eyewitnesses to such event, as well as medical witnesses and other persons having any knowledge thereof.

42. If any of the witnesses listed above or whom you propose to use at the trial are related to you or to each other, please state the nature of such relationship.

DEFENDANT'S STATEMENT

43. State the full name and last known address, giving the street, street number, city and state, of every witness known to you or to your attorneys who claims to have seen or heard the defendant make any statement or statements pertaining to any of the events or happenings alleged in your complaint.

44. Supply the following information with respect to each individual whose name you have given in the answer to the preceding interrogatory:

    a. The location or locations where the defendant made any such statement or statements.

    b. The name and address of the person or persons in whose presence the defendant made any such statement or statements.

    c. The time and date upon which the defendant made any such statement or statements.

    d. The full name and address of any other person who was present at the time and place the defendant made such statement or statements.

e. Whether you or anyone acting on your behalf obtained statements in any form from any persons who claim to be able to testify to the statement or statements made by the defendant.

45. If the answer to paragraph (e) above is in the affirmative, then state
    a. The names and addresses of the persons from whom any such statements were taken.
    b. The date upon which said statements were taken.
    c. The names and addresses of the employers of the persons who took such statements.
    d. The names and addresses of the persons having custody of such statements.
    e. Whether such statements were written, oral, recording device or by court reporter or stenographer.

WRITTEN STATEMENTS OF WITNESSES

46. State whether you, your attorney, your insurance carrier or anyone acting on your or their behalf obtained statements in any form from any persons regarding any of the events or happenings that occurred at the scene of the incident referred to in the complaint immediately before, at the time of, or immediately after said incident, and if so, state
    a. The name and address of the person from whom any such statements were taken.
    b. The dates on which such statements were taken.
    c. The names and addresses of the persons and employers of such persons who took such statements.
    d. The names and addresses of the persons having custody of such statements.
    e. Whether such statements were written, by recording device, by court reporter or stenographer.

EXPERT AND MEDICAL EVIDENCE

47. State the names and addresses of any and all proposed expert witnesses, and the technical field in which you claim they are an expert.
48. Do you intend to rely upon any medical text in your cross-examination of this defendant's medical experts? If so, state
    a. The exact title of each medical text upon which you intend to rely.
    b. The name and address of the publisher of each such medical text.
    c. The date upon which each such medical text was published.
    d. The name of the author of each such medical text.

DIAGRAMS AND PHOTOS, SURVEYS, MAPS

49. Do you, your attorney, your insurance carrier or anyone acting on your or their behalf, have or know of any photographs, motion pictures, maps, drawings, diagrams, measurements, surveys or other descriptions concerning the events and happenings alleged in the complaint, the scene of the accident, or the areas or persons of vehicles involved made either before, after or at the time of the events in question, including any photographs made of the plaintiff at any time since the incident referred to in the complaint and if so, as to each such item, state
    a. Its nature.
    b. Its specific subject matter.
    c. The date it was made or taken.
    d. The name and last known address of the person making or taking it.
    e. What each such item purports to show or illustrate or represent.
    f. The name and address of the person having custody of such item.

INJURIES

50. Please state in detail the nature of the injury or injuries you allege that you suffered as a result of the incident referred to in the complaint.
51. With respect to the injuries allegedly suffered, state
    a. The extent and nature of any disability.
    b. Describe in detail the location of any pain suffered and the duration and intensity of such pain.
    c. Whether or not you suffered any restraint of your normal activities due to the injuries allegedly suffered, and describe in detail the nature of such restraint and the dates you suffered the pain.

52. If you receive any treatment with respect to the injuries allegedly suffered, state
  a. The name and address of each hospital at which you were treated or admitted.
  b. The dates on which said treatment was rendered, including the dates of entry and discharge into and from said hospital or hospitals.
  c. Itemize the charges rendered by each of the hospitals listed above.
  d. State the name and address of each medical practitioner of any type whatsoever who has examined or treated you or conferred with you with respect to the injuries alleged.
  e. Itemize the cost and expenses of such examinations or treatments by the medical practitioners listed above.
53. State the treatment, or procedures or operations that have been performed in connection with the alleged injuries at any hospital and give the name of the hospital and the name of the medical practitioners giving the treatment or performing the procedures and the dates upon which they were given or performed.
54. Since the date of the incident referred to in your complaint, have you been treated by or examined by or conferred with or consulted with any other medical practitioner of any type whatsoever whose name you have not heretofore supplied, and if so, state
  a. The name and address of each medical practitioner of any type whatsoever who has examined, treated, conferred, or consulted with you and the dates of the same.
  b. The condition for which said care or treatment or attention was rendered.
55. If you have incurred any medical bills in connection with the alleged injuries not heretofore listed, please state
  a. The total amount of each such bill.
  b. The person to whom such amount was paid.
  c. The service or thing for which the bill was rendered.
56. If you are still receiving medical services or treatment of any nature whatsoever, state
  a. The name or names of the person or persons attending you.
  b. The approximate frequency of said treatment or service.
  c. The date you last received said treatment or service.
57. State the dates during which you were confined following your discharge from the hospital.
  a. To your bed.
  b. To your home.

BRACES OR APPLIANCES

58. Have you worn any type of orthopedic appliance and if so, state
  a. The name of the medical practitioner who fitted or prescribed said appliance.
  b. Describe the appliance and state its cost.
  c. When did you start wearing said appliance.
  d. When did you stop wearing said appliance.
  e. Was said appliance worn constantly or intermittently during the foregoing period, and if both state the period in which it was worn constantly.
59. At the time of the incident referred to in the complaint, did you have any condition for which you wore eye glasses or for which eye glasses had been prescribed for you and if so, state
  a. A brief description of the condition.
  b. Were you wearing glasses at the time in question?
  c. The name and address of the person who prescribed eye glasses for you.

MEDICINE

60. Please list all medicine purchased or used by you in connection with the treatment of the injuries complained of, the cost thereof, and the store from which purchased.

CHARGE OR TRIAL CONCERNING INCIDENT COMPLAINED OF

61. Were you charged with any violation of law arising out of the incident referred to in your complaint, and if so, state
  a. The plea entered by you to such charge.
  b. The court in which the charge was heard.

c. The nature of the charge.

d. Whether or not the testimony at any trial on said charge was taken down or recorded in any manner whatsoever.

62. If such testimony was taken down or recorded, state by whom it was recorded and whether a transcript has been made of such recording.

    a. If a transcript has been made state who has possession of the transcript at this time.

    b. If there was a hearing or trial on any such charge, please state

        1. The date of the hearing or trial.

        2. The names and addresses of person or persons who were subpoenaed or who appeared as witnesses.

OTHER ACTIONS

63. Have you ever been involved in any other legal action, either as a defendant or as a plaintiff? If so, state

    a. The date and place each such action was filed, giving the name of the court, the name of the other party or parties involved, the number of such actions and the names of the attorneys representing each party.

    b. A description of the nature of each such action.

    c. The result of each such action, whether or not there was an appeal and the result of the appeal and whether or not such case was reported and the name, volume number and page citation of such report.

LOSSES NOT OTHERWISE COVERED

64. Have you sustained any additional financial losses as a result of the incident complained of, other than those covered by preceding interrogatories? If so, state

    a. The nature and amount of such losses.

    b. The date thereof.

    c. The names and addresses of any persons to whom any money so claimed as an additional loss was paid.

WITNESSES AND EXHIBITS

65. List the names, addresses, official titles (if any), and other identification of all witnesses, including expert witnesses, who, it is contemplated, will be called upon to testify in support of your claim in this action, indicating the nature and substance of the testimony which is expected will be given by each such witness, and stating the relationship, if any, to the plaintiff(s).

66. List specifically and in detail each and every exhibit you propose to utilize upon the trial in this matter. This Interrogatory is directed both to exhibits you intend to use upon the trial and exhibits you may use.

67. With reference to the exhibits listed in the previous Interrogatory, please state the source of the exhibit, the nature of the exhibit, (i.e., whether said exhibit is documentary, a picture, or other), who prepared each exhibit, and the date on which same was prepared.

CONTINUING INTERROGATORIES

68. These interrogatories shall be deemed continuing so as to require supplemental answers if you or your attorneys obtain further information between the time answers are served and time of trial.

Procedure for the Final Preparation and Service of Interrogatories

After the attorney has received the interrogatories, all corrections should be made and submitted to the secretary or word processing center for typing. Make sure that copies are prepared for each defendant, the court, and the client's file. Prior to service, the attorney's signature should be obtained. Service is made pursuant to Rule 5 of the Federal Rules and parallel state rules that permit service by mail or in person to the opponent's attorney. The original is filed with the court. The certificate of service should be executed, and some acknowledgment of service requested from the other attorney. In some circumstances the court may not require the filing of interrogatories [Rule 5 (d)].

ASSIGNMENT 8:7
After verifying the correct procedure for your state, draft a concluding section of the Checklist for Planning and Drafting Interrogatories (figure 8:4) on the procedure for the final preparation and service of interrogatories (see section IV of the checklist) for both state and federal practice. Add this to the checklist previously inserted in your system folder.

ASSIGNMENT 8:8
Drawing from the material in this chapter on planning and drafting interrogatories (including the checklist in figure 8:4), and using the form interrogatories as a guide, draft a set of carefully planned interrogatories on behalf of Ms. Forrester to Mercury Parcel Service. For the purposes of this assignment, confine your drafting to the following:

1. Caption and instructions
2. Questions on:
   a. Background information, employment, and agency of Hart
   b. Inadequate maintenance of van and possible defects
   c. Time standards for operation of vehicles by drivers, and Hart and Mercury Parcel's compliance prior to accident
3. Concluding questions and directions
4. Signature and certificate of service

ASSIGNMENT 8:9
To gain additional practice and confidence, reverse the situation and draft a set of interrogatories from Mercury Parcel to Ms. Forrester. Confine your drafting to:

1. Caption and instructions
2. Questions on:
   a. Her background information (current employment information only)
   b. Her statements to others about the accident
   c. Her own possible negligence
3. Concluding questions and directions
4. Signature and certificate of service

Procedure for Answering Interrogatories

Review Task, Note Deadline

Typically, the attorney will come to you saying, "Here are the interrogatories in the Forrester case. Please begin preparing answers to these questions. We have thirty days to respond. Let me know if you need any help." First fill out a deadline slip to ensure the deadline will be met. Failure to answer on time waives any objections to the questions, except questions that are grossly improper or call for privileged information or an expert's opinion.[20]

Review Case File in Detail

Become thoroughly familiar with the facts and all the evidence and sources of evidence that might be called on in answering the interrogatories. This will make answering easier and give you confidence that there are facts and evidence to support the answers.

Review Possible Objections

Before reading the interrogatories, have firmly in mind what kinds of objections can be raised to any particular question. Then read through the interrogatories and note questions believed to be objectionable. These common types of objections are based on the definition of what is discoverable found in Rule 26(b)(1):

Irrelevant   A question is objectionable if its ultimate aim is to elicit evidence information that is not relevant to the issues in the case.

Privileged   A question that calls for information protected by the attorney-client, husband-wife, and like privileges is objectionable.

Work product   If a question calls for the mental impressions, conclusions, legal theories, and like matters related to the attorney's preparation for trial, it need not be answered. Objectionable questions typically ask for the names of witnesses that will be called at trial and for the names and opinions of experts who are hired as consultants and not as trial witnesses. The work product objection, however, is often invoked too broadly and abused.

Vague, ambiguous, and unintelligible   Occasionally a question is so unspecific or worded so unclearly that it requires the answering party to guess at the meaning of the question. Such a question is objectionable.

Too Broad   A question can be so inclusive that its limits are excessive. For example, a question calling for the names of all the documents gathered over the last twenty years pertaining to the incident in question is so sweeping in its coverage that it is overly burdensome, while also calling for irrelevant material. Questions requesting information covering an unduly lengthy time span are objectionable. The scope of the question must be reasonable.

Unduly burdensome   Paragraph (c) of Rule 26 allows a party to seek a protective order from unduly burdensome or expensive discovery requests. It is a valid objection to a particular interrogatory or an entire set of interrogatories. If a question or set of questions requires a response that is excessively detailed, costly, time-consuming, or embarrassing relative to the opponent's need for the requested information, then the question or set of questions is objectionable.

Questions can also be too numerous, call for previously disclosed information, be premature, call for purely legal conclusions, or for information that is just as easily obtainable by the other side. The last is especially true if the information is not in the answering party's custody or is in the public domain.[21] Requesting the attachment of documents or other evidence is objectionable if a request for production of documents and things [Rule 34] has not been submitted; therefore, interrogatories are often submitted with a Rule 34 production request.

Some common objections that are not valid are: that the information is already known by the opponent; the question calls for inadmissible evidence (it may); seeks an admission (it may); better obtained at deposition (so what!); seeks factual opinions, conclusions, and legal contentions (it may); and "it's no business of the questioning party."[22]

There are some strategic concerns to have in mind. Although the decision to object is the realm of the attorney, keep in mind that it is sometimes better to answer an objectionable question than to have to request the court for a protective order. This is especially true if the information to be revealed does not hurt the answering party or might improve their case in the eyes of the opponent.[23]

ASSIGNMENT 8:10
In your system folder include a list of the objections discussed here.

Read Questions Thoroughly and Note Observations

Photocopy the interrogatories so that notes can be written on the copy. Then read each question thoroughly, noting any observations in the margin. These observations might include questions, ideas on where to gather information, possible objections, or a note that an objectionable question might be answered without harm to the case.

Review Questions and Observations with Attorney

Before attempting to answer the questions, confer with the attorney to discuss the questions and your notes. As each question is approached, note on the photocopied set of interrogatories any comments, suggestions, or possible sources of information from the attorney.

Gather and Record Information for the Answers

The client and the client's agents, representatives, investigators, and attorney will provide most of the information needed to answer the interrogatories. It is well-accepted practice for the attorney to take this information and, with your help, mold it into the answers for the client. The client should become involved as early as possible in the interrogatory process. To do this, copy each question on a separate sheet of paper and send the questions to the client with a cover letter and instructions. Some firms will ask the client to answer the questions and return them to the firm, as requested in the letter in figure 8:6. Other offices prefer to have the client come in to go over each question and possible answer. This process takes more time but may be best in the long run. Check with your supervising attorney to see which procedure is preferred.

ASSIGNMENT 8:11
Create a form letter to the client from the letter in figure 8:6 and place it into your folder. You may choose to use the copying and editing features of a computer to do this assignment.

Prepare a working copy of each question and its comments on a separate page. Organize the pages in a three-ring binder or other expandable system so that all information gathered can be kept in order with the appropriate question. This prevents loss and simplifies the task of drafting answers to the questions.[24]

The primary source of information must be the party requested to answer the interrogatories. In the case of a corporation or agency, it must be those officers or employees, either individually or collectively, who have the

Figure 8:6   Letter to Client on Answering Interrogatories

WHITE, WILSON & McDUFF

ATTORNEYS AT LAW
FEDERAL PLAZA BUILDING, SUITE 700
THIRD AND MARKET STREETS
LEGALVILLE, COLUMBIA 00000
(111) 555-0000

November 1, 19___

Ms. Ann Forrester
1533 Capitol Drive
Legalville, Columbia 00000

Dear Ms. Forrester:

I have enclosed a set of questions called "interrogatories" submitted by the attorney for Mercury Parcel Service. The rules of the court require your full cooperation in answering each of the questions. We are permitted to assist you.

Each of the attached questions is on a separate sheet of paper so that you can answer them fully. Add extra sheets if you need them.

We must have your answers no later than November 15. Failure to return the answers when they are due may be harmful to your case. On receipt of your answers, we will review them, possibly amend some, and return the answers for your review and signature. Should it be necessary to have you come to the office to discuss your answers, we will inform you.

Please begin gathering all the documents and other information needed to answer the questions. When writing answers to the questions, keep the following in mind:

1. Answer all questions completely but concisely.
2. Always be truthful.
3. Do not try to withhold information or be evasive. For example, if asked about witnesses (and you know of three), name all three; or, if you are asked about prior injuries, lawsuits, or criminal convictions, state them with identifying dates, times, location, etc. Any evasiveness is a serious matter and can definitely affect the outcome of the case.
4. Look up all dates, amounts, times, and other information requested.
5. You are not required to make an unreasonable search or incur unreasonable expense. If you do not have access to the information, you are not required to provide it. State any reasons for not answering a question.

After answering the questions, return them in the enclosed envelope.

Thank you for your assistance. If you have questions, please let me know.

Sincerely,

Terry Salyer
Paralegal
White, Wilson & McDuff

knowledge to answer the questions. In the case of multiple parties with duplicate sets of interrogatories, answering may be a joint effort or the work of the party having the requested information.[25]

If you have become familiar with the case, it should not be difficult to determine where the information will come from. Some of the techniques discussed in chapter 4 on investigation might be drawn on to answer interrogatories properly.

When gathering information, keep in mind that the answer should be based on reasonable investigation; it does not require the searching of every possible nook and cranny; and the questions require a reasonable interpretation, not an irrational or hypertechnical one.[26]

Review the Techniques for Answering Interrogatories

- Precede each answer with a restatement of the applicable question. This is called *engrossing* the question.
- Write the answer clearly and concisely. Avoid confusing answers that lead the opponent to the answers of several previous questions or to answers in other documents (depositions) incorporated by reference.
- Write out objections by stating with particularity the nature of the objection and its basis. This may be done in the interrogatory or separately. Here is an example of how an objection would appear in the answer to an interrogatory:

   Defendant objects to this interrogatory because it requests information that is irrelevant and cannot reasonably lead to evidence that is admissible on any issue in this action.

- Answer ethically with accurate and complete information; do not be evasive or deceptive. If an interrogatory asks for the name and location of a person, it would not be adequate to state only his first name and "I do not remember where he lives."
- Disclose as little harmful information as possible, but not by deliberate concealment or unreasonable interpretation of the question.
- Place the client in the best possible light without distorting or misrepresenting the facts.
- Use the alternative option to produce business records found in Rule 33(c), which places the burden on the opposing party to search or audit your client's records. In such cases one need only identify the documents available. This should not be done, however, if other information sensitive or harmful to the client will be revealed.

■ Use the following techniques for answers you are unable to complete or are unsure of:[27]

Indicate supplements will follow.
State on information or belief or based on secondhand information
State according to person Y or records in office X
Indicate do not know answer but received information that _____.

■ Inform the attorney when an extension of time is needed to answer a question fully. The extension may be obtained informally through the opponent or, if need be, through a motion to the court.

Draft the Interrogatories and Have Them Reviewed, Signed, and Served

The interrogatories should be drafted, incorporating the information gathered on the pertinent pages of the loose-leaf notebook. The attorney should then review the answers. Once prepared in final form, the person answering the interrogatories (usually the client, or in the case of a corporation, a representative of the corporation) must sign the document (Rule 33). Any necessary exhibits should be attached. A certificate of service should be prepared and service made according to Rule 5, or as dictated by state rules.

Continue to Update Answers

In many jurisdictions there is a continuing obligation to respond to questions as the answering party becomes aware of additional information or discovers inaccuracies in the answers previously submitted. A good way to do this is to simply replace the out-of-date page of the former answer with a revised one. The new page should restate the question accompanied by the complete new answer.

ASSIGNMENT 8:12
Drawing from the material covered in this section of the chapter, and any information added in class, draft a Checklist for Answering Interrogatories and place it in your system folder. The checklist should cover the basic steps and techniques for preparing, drafting, serving, and updating interrogatories.

Analyzing the Answer and Compelling a Response

When the opponent's answers to interrogatories are received, promptly read each answer, carefully noting the opponent's objections and any deficits in completeness, responsiveness, or clarity. Inform the attorney of each objection and defect. If the attorney believes some clarification or other action is needed, the following options are available:

1. The attorney will handle the matter at this point.
2. You will contact the opponent's attorney or paralegal and request more information, possibly offering an extension of time. This should be followed by a confirming letter identifying the incomplete answer, acknowledging the extension of time granted, and stating that the time for a Motion to Compel Further Answers will be assumed tolled until the opponent files a corrected response or does not make a correction within the allotted time.[28]
3. You will draft a motion to compel with an accompanying affidavit and have it filed and served.

ASSIGNMENT 8:13
Exchange the interrogatories you drafted in assignments 8:8 and 8:9 with a classmate, then draft answers to the classmate's interrogatories using the checklist you developed. For practice, object to at least one question and explain the basis of the objection. Also assume you do not trust the accuracy of the information you have for the answer to one other question. You may have to create some information to adequately answer the questions.

In the alternative, assume that you are the paralegal whose firm is representing Carl Ameche in Case II, the campground fire case. Draft answers to the sample set of interrogatories (figure 8:5). Also practice objections and how to respond when unsure of your information in your answers.

▇ Depositions

A **deposition** is a significant discovery device permitting a party's attorney to question a witness (including parties) before trial. The witness, called a **deponent,** is under oath and must respond orally to the questions.

Purpose

Depositions are the most commonly used discovery device and have a multiplicity of purposes. Depositions are used to discover information or leads to information based on the deponent's testimony and any accompanying physical evidence. They are used to find out more information about the opponent's case, to evaluate their witness and the opposing attorney. Because the answers offered at the deposition may be used later in court, depositions have purposes related to their potential use at trial. Rule 32 and parallel state rules allow depositions to be used to impeach the trial testimony of the deponent. If the deponent testifies at trial that the van was going twenty-five miles per hour, but said at the deposition that it was going fifty-five miles per hour, the earlier answer may be used to throw doubt on the reliability of the trial testimony. Likewise, if a party takes the stand at trial, the party's answers at the deposition may be used as an admission of key facts or for impeachment of the party [Rule 32(a)(2)]. Further, if a witness is unavailable for trial (dead or out of the country, for example) that witness's deposition may be offered into evidence at the trial as if the witness were present [Rule 32(a)(3)].

Scope of the Deposition

One real advantage of the deposition over interrogatories is that persons besides the parties may be deposed: bystanders, experts, document custodians, character witnesses, and the like. Rule 30(c) requires that the deposition, examination and cross-examination be conducted in accordance with the Federal Rules of Evidence. In all other respects the scope is the same as that for other discovery devices [Rule 26(b)].

Types of Depositions

There are three types of depositions set out in the federal and parallel state statutes. They are: depositions on oral exam, depositions on written questions, and depositions before the action is filed. The most commonly used of the three is the deposition on oral examination (Rule 30), and for that reason will constitute the primary basis for discussion in the following section. Depositions on oral examination simulate a trial-like, sworn, question-and-answer session absent a jury and a judge.

Depositions on written questions are an under used device where direct questions from one party and cross questions from the opposing party are read to the deponent who orally answers the questions in the presence of a person authorized to administer oaths. This procedure is governed by Rule 31 and is used primarily to gain information on noncontroversial matters or on documents from a person other than a party.

The third type of device is the taking of a deposition before the action and is governed by Rule 27. The purpose of this device is to preserve testimony that may be unavailable later. This might arise when a witness or party is very ill and may not be available to testify at the trial, or when a witness will be out of the country for a long time. In circumstances like these, a person may, with court permission, take the deposition of a person before an action is filed. Rather strict requirements set out in Rule 27 must be met before the court will grant permission. When you are asked to assist the attorney on depositions of written questions or depositions before trial, it is important to check Rules 31 and 27 and parallel local rules for any limitations or special procedures that must be followed.

Description of Procedure

The party conducting the deposition must set a time and place and arrange for a person authorized to administer oaths and able to record the testimony. Notice of the deposition is then sent to each party. The witness is subpoenaed by the court and must be present at the designated time and place. The other parties may also attend and ask questions. At the deposition the officer swears in the witness, and the attorney requesting the deposition asks the witness questions. The opponent may cross-examine. All questions and answers are recorded by the officer, a court reporter, or other recording device. The record is reviewed by the witness and certified as accurate.

ASSIGNMENT 8:14
Write a brief outline on the definition, purpose, scope, applicable rules, and the procedure of depositions to place in your system folder.

Preliminary Tasks

Determine Whom to Depose

The decision concerning who should be deposed must rest with the attorney. A well-informed paralegal, however, can be helpful in indicating potential witnesses and facts that might provide guidance to the attorney in identifying people to be deposed. Before such planning is done, thoroughly review the facts of the case, the key elements, the pleadings, information gained through investigation, and especially the opponent's answer to any interrogatories. The process should lead to a list of persons whose testimony could provide important information. Such a list will help the attorney in this selection.

Your understanding that the basis for deciding whom to depose is both practical and tactical is also helpful to the attorney, who must decide if the expected information is worth the expense of the deposition. Little benefit is derived from deposing friendly witnesses or opposition witnesses who are very old or ill, or those who have previously provided a favorable statement.[29]

Conduct a Preliminary Interview

The list of persons to be deposed is narrowed by conducting preliminary interviews. Paralegals are frequently assigned this task. The purpose of the interview is to determine if the person possesses information worth an expensive deposition. It might also reveal that the person is gravely ill or will soon be leaving the country, thus enhancing the decision on whether to depose. Before conducting such an interview, obtain from the attorney a clear idea of what is needed from that particular witness. Then proceed in the manner described in chapter 4 on investigation. Occasionally a brief phone call may be all that is necessary to make the determination.

Coordinate the Deposition

Arrange for Site and Necessary Components

Time Before setting up the time for the deposition, check the date the action commenced. Rule 30(a) states that a deposition may not be taken within thirty days of service of the summons and complaint without leave of the court. Therefore, unless otherwise directed by the attorney, the deposition should be scheduled after the thirty days. Then check with the attorney, the client (if attending), the parties, and possibly the person to be deposed. Taking the time to coordinate the date may be time-consuming, but it will save rescheduling and paperwork in the future. Be sure to have the deposition calendared into the deadline system.

ASSIGNMENT 8:15
Enter in the deposition and time deadline portions of your system folder that depositions may not be taken within thirty days of service of the summons and complaint without leave of the court [Rule 30(a)].

Site In most instances, the site for the deposition is a standard one often used by the firm: a conference room at the office, or if a more formal atmosphere is sought, a room at the courthouse. Occasionally a deposition must be taken in another jurisdiction. In such circumstances, a law firm in that area might permit use of a room, or a clerk of court in the foreign jurisdiction may be able to arrange for a room. When an overnight stay is required, a conference room at a hotel may be convenient. In determining the location for the deposition, remember that the plaintiff can be required to attend a deposition in the jurisdiction where the action was brought. For other persons it is the jurisdiction where they live and work. Occasionally the deposition of a doctor is taken in the doctor's office. Regardless of the location, a suitable room should be reserved well in advance. Suitability may depend on atmosphere, adequate space, power outlets, and convenience to refreshments, meals, and rest rooms.

Method of recording   There are several options in determining the method of recording the deposition. The most common is the use of a certified court reporter, who is also authorized to administer oaths, to stenographically record the deposition. Another option of increasing popularity is to record the deposition by videotape. Permission to do so is required, however, and that may be obtained either by stipulation between the parties or by motion and court order. Rule 30(b)(4) requires that the stipulation or order "designate the person before whom the deposition shall be taken, the manner of recording, preserving and filing the deposition, and may include other provisions to assure that the recorded testimony will be accurate and trustworthy."

Videotaping a deposition provides the jury with the nearest thing to a real picture of a since-deceased individual, of a laboratory demonstration conducted by an expert witness, or testimony describing a thing or location inaccessible or inconvenient to the jury. Some disadvantages accompany the use of video, such as improper camera angles, bad or misleading lighting, and poor sound quality. Consequently, in arranging a video deposition or reviewing a stipulation for video recording, make sure that the camera is inobtrusive, the operator is well trained, the lighting and setting are fair, the audio is of high quality, and that the camera angles are fair but sufficiently varied for interest. The camera operator should not totally exclude the examiner from view. Two cameras permit a split-screen image of the witness as the dominant view and the examiner as the smaller view.

Rule 30(b)(7) permits a deposition to be taken by phone if the parties so stipulate or the court so orders. This could result in considerable cost savings if it avoids travel and lodging expenses.. It would be difficult, however, to evaluate such a deponent as a potential witness unless the deponent were simultaneously videotaped. Telephone depositions are not very common. If the deposition is on written questions, it is still necessary to reserve a site and to have the answers recorded.

Oath officer   Regardless of the type of deposition or the method used to record the deposition, a person is needed to administer the oath and, when necessary, to certify the deposition. Occasionally the person operating the recording equipment has the required authorization. If not, the court can appoint the operator to administer the oath [Rule 28(a)]. The clerk of court and the law firm are likely to have lists of court reporters and video operators available for recording depositions and administering oaths.

Prepare and Serve Notice of the Deposition

After the arrangements are made, you must serve notice of the deposition on the deponent and each of the other parties. This is required by Rule 30(b)(1). If a party, or a person designated to represent a party, is to be deposed, service of the notice of deposition is all that is needed, and failure to attend is subject to sanctions under Rule 37(d). A nonparty deponent must be subpoenaed, as discussed later.

The notice must state the time and place, the name of the attorney conducting the examination, and the name and address of each person to be deposed. If the name of the person is not known, Rule 30(b)(1) permits a general description sufficient to identify the person or his or her class or group. If the deponent is a business, association, or agency, the notice should describe in some detail the matters that the examination will cover. If documents, books, papers, or tangible things are requested to be brought to the deposition, they should be designated in the notice to take deposition. An example of a Notice of Taking Deposition appears in figure 8:7.[30]

The notice should be drafted and served on the deponent, all parties, and the court reporter. A certificate of service should be executed. If the deposition is rescheduled or other changes occur, draft a letter notifying the deponent, all parties, and the court reporter. If a party does not want a deposition taken, the party must petition the court and have good grounds for the request.

Subpoena the Deponent

Obtain the subpoena A **subpoena** is a document issued by the clerk of court commanding a person to be present and, if indicated, bring physical items to a specified place at a designated time. Failure to comply with the subpoena may result in contempt of court and appropriate penalties. Subpoenas are the documents used to require attendance of witnesses at depositions and at trial. Rule 45 of the Federal Rules and parallel state rules set out the requirements for a subpoena and its service. There are two types of subpoenas; the most common is a subpoena for a person to give testimony. The second type is a **subpoena duces tecum,** which requires a person to appear and produce books, papers, documents, or tangible things [Rule 45(b)]. Because parties to an action do not have to be subpoenaed, it is appropriate to serve a Rule 34 request for production of documents with the notice of the deposition. This serves the same function as the subpoena duces tecum for nonparties.

To obtain a subpoena for a deponent, provide the appropriate clerk of court with a copy of the notice to take deposition and proof of service on the parties. In the federal system the subpoena must be issued by the clerk in the district where the deposition is to be taken. In some states it is issued

Figure 8:7 Notice of Taking Deposition of a Witness Including Reference to Materials Designated in Attached Subpoena

[*Fed. R. Civ. P. Rule 30(b)(1)*]

[*Title of Court and Cause*]

TO: [*Attorney for Plaintiff*]
    [*Law firm*]
    [*Address*]

PLEASE TAKE NOTICE that pursuant to Rule 30 of the Federal Rules of Civil Procedure, Plaintiff will take the oral deposition of L _____ before a notary public on _____, _____, 19___, at ___ p.m. and thereafter from day to day until completed, at the offices of [*law firm name and address*]. Defendant requests that deponent bring to said deposition all documents described in the attached ADDENDUM to Civil Subpoena.

_____

Attorney for Defendant

Address: _____

where the action is pending. Consult local rules. The clerk will sign the subpoena *in blank* in most jurisdictions. This means that you will need to fill in the necessary information.

Following the dictates of Rule 45, be sure that the following information is on the subpoena: the name of the court; the title of the action; the name of the paralegal's attorney; the witness's name and address with directions for the witness to attend and give testimony; and the date, time, and place for the deposition. If the production of documents is commanded, the clerk will issue a subpoena for that purpose. Add the details just mentioned and designate the documents or physical evidence to be produced, inspected, and copied. It is good practice to include the attorney's declaration that the items requested are necessary to the deposition, relevant to the case, and either constitute potential evidence or will lead to its discovery.[31] If the items are numerous or require a lengthy description, a rider may need to be attached to the subpoena. An example of a combined subpoena and subpoena duces tecum appear in figure 8:8.[32]

Attach fees   Before serving the subpoena, determine if it is necessary to attach witness and mileage fees. The Federal Rules require that such fees be tendered at the time of service of the subpoena to have a valid subpoena (28 U.S.C. § 1821). Determine the distance to be traveled by the deponent and calculate the round trip mileage. A call to the federal clerk of court will give you the most recent witness fee and the mileage allowance. Prepare a check and attach it to the subpoena for service. The procedure is the same for most states. Some states require a witness fee only for witnesses from outside the county where the deposition is to be taken. Generally speaking, deponents may not be required to go beyond the county in which they reside or work or transact personal business, or forty miles from the place of service of the subpoena [Rule 45(d)(2)].

Serve the subpoena   The subpoena and attached fee must be personally served on the deponent. Because a subpoena can be unnerving to its recipient, it may be a good idea, if your attorney approves, to warn the witness and explain why the subpoena is necessary. This might keep a witness in your camp. In the federal system a subpoena may be served by a marshal, a deputy, or a person not less than eighteen years of age. Service in the states is performed by a sheriff, special bailiff, or any person of legal age (check local rules). Paralegals are frequently asked to serve subpoenas. Professional servers are available in some areas. When delivering the subpoena or directing someone else to do so, make sure the server fully understands the correct way to serve a subpoena. Consult local rules, but in most instances, the subpoena must be personally handed to the deponent and the deponent told what the subpoena is, where the deponent is to go, and what is expected of the deponent. The server must then acknowledge service in writing on a copy of the subpoena or execute an affidavit of service.

When service is to be on an out-of-town deponent, it is best to call the local clerk of court for the correct procedures and, if necessary, call each day to ensure issuance of the subpoena and service on the witness.[33] If a person objects to the commands of the subpoena, objections must be served on the deposing attorney within ten days of service of the subpoena, or on or before the deposition if it is scheduled in less than ten days from service.

Figure 8:8 Subpoena for Taking Oral Testimony and Production of Documents (Duces Tecum)

[Fed. R. Civ. P. Rule 45(a)]

[*Title of Court and Cause*]

To: _____

_____

_____

_____

Greeting:

We command you, that all business and excuses being laid aside, you and each of you attend before an officer authorized by law to take deposition at the offices of _____ & _____, Room _____, [*complete address*] [at *city*], in the District aforesaid, on the _____day of _____, 19__, at _____ A.M., to testify and give evidence on behalf of the defendant in a case pending and undetermined in the Northern District of _____ wherein _____ is plaintiff and _____ is one of the Defendants, No. _____. And this you shall in nowise omit, under the penalty of the law in that case made and provided, and that you also diligently and carefully search for and bring with you and produce at the time and place aforesaid the documents described in the attached schedule "A."

To the Marshall of the Northern District of _____ to execute and return in due form of law.

_____

Clerk of the United States
District Court for the _____
District of _____

By: _____
Deputy Clerk

Dated _____, 19__.

Schedule "A" to Subpoena

The period of time covered by each of the following categories of documentary materials shall be _____, 19__ to date unless otherwise specifically indicated.

The word "records" shall be construed to refer to and include every document, report, summary, bulletin, manual, purchase order, purchase contract, release, map, policy statement, notation, worksheet, memorandum, letter or other written record reflecting the indicated information.

[*List of records*]

The attorney serving the subpoena must then seek a court order to have the subpoena complied with [Rule 45(d)(1)].

ASSIGNMENT 8:16
Draft a checklist on serving subpoenas and place it and documents shown in this section as forms in your system folder. Note the time limits for objection to a subpoena in this section and in your time deadline section.

Prepare for Deposition

Draft Questions or an Examination Outline

Although the attorney will determine what questions will be asked the deponent, you can provide considerable assistance by drafting a proposed set of questions or a detailed outline for the examination indicating each point to be addressed. The outline may be better because it is less time-consuming, often more complete, and easily amended, and provides flexibility during the examination. Adequate preparation is important.

Carefully review all file information, paying particular attention to those things the witness is likely to be able to prove and to provide information and leads on. This includes any documents or physical items that can or need to be introduced through this witness. Pay special attention to answers to interrogatories or admissions from this case or other cases made by the witness. If the witness is a party, these items just mentioned will permit you to eliminate some areas of questioning, especially if the other party has already admitted certain facts. Make notes.

Meet with the attorney, review the notes, and determine as specifically as possible what the attorney wants from this witness. For example, the attorney for Ms. Forrester may wish to examine Mr. Hart to determine his version of the facts, lock him into that version, and establish any breaches in company policy or defects in the vehicle that may have contributed to the accident. The attorney may want to depose the head of Mercury Parcel's maintenance shop to produce his records of repairs on the van, explain the shop procedures and policies to see if they were followed in this case, or reveal any problems or defects in the van. Or the attorney for Mercury Parcel might want to depose Ms. Forrester to lock her into her story, assess how high the jury sympathy factor will be, probe her attitude on any negligence on her part, or to hear her description of her injuries and pain. Or Mercury's attorney may want to depose Ms. Forrester's surgeon and other doctors to get detailed assessment of injuries, possible causes, treatment, and prognosis. Since the witness has been previously identified, you will find that it is easier than you might think to determine what the witness needs to be asked and what can be eliminated. The discussion with the attorney ought to make clear the objectives and areas of examination.

Look at similar witness examinations from other office files or form depositions. Several publishing companies have published detailed outlines to cover a variety of type of witnesses. Simply go to the law library and find what is available. An example of such a predrafted deposition outline appears in figure 8:9.[34]

The outline in figure 8:9 can be adapted to a particular witness and set of facts. If there is no sample available, check the objectives carefully and brainstorm topics and subtopics that must be covered. In most circumstances, it is necessary to get detailed information on the witness's background (including possible areas for future impeachment), and then on the details of the event, documents, or other matters relevant to the case. Remember that in a deposition the attorneys have more latitude in the types of questions the may ask than they have at trial. The scope is confined to what is relevant to the case, is admissible evidence, or might reasonably lead to admissible evidence. Therefore, hearsay may be legitimate, as is the identification of other possible witnesses, documents, and physical evidence. In deposition preparation it is probably better to err on the side of going too far rather than being too cautious.

One of the best techniques for generating questions for an outline is to sit down with your notes, form depositions, and a tape recorder and dictate every question you can possibly think of to elicit the desired information.

Figure 8:9 Deposition Checklist Plaintiff—Automobile

PRELIMINARY INFORMATION

Title of Case _____

_____

Court Number _____

Deponent's Name _____

Place of Deposition _____

Date _____ Time _____

Lawyer(s) for Plaintiff(s): _____

_____

_____

_____

_____

Lawyer(s) for Defendant(s): _____

_____

_____

_____

_____

Lawyers in Attendance

_____ for _____

_____ for _____

_____ for _____

_____ for _____

_____ for _____

Type of deposition: Evidence or Discovery _____

Is signature waived? _____

Is witness sworn? _____

Is a statement made for the record (e.g., the type of deposition or the rules by which it is being conducted)?

_____

Make the following statement:

"If I ask any question that you do not understand, please tell me and I will re-phrase it. Do you understand?"

IDENTIFICATION OF DEPONENT

Name _____

Address _____

City & State _____

Bus. Phone _____ Home Phone _____

Names and addresses of people who will always know of deponent's whereabouts:

_____

_____

Has deponent ever used an alias? _____

If yes, explain: _____

Has deponent ever been convicted of a crime?

_____

If yes, explain: _____

_____

Has deponent been a party or witness in a lawsuit?

_____

If yes, explain: _____

_____

_____

Social Security Number _____

Driver's License Number _____

Selective Service Number _____

Height _____ Weight _____ Sex _____

Color of eyes _____ Color of hair _____

Race _____ Citizenship _____

Date of birth _____ Place of birth _____

Mother's maiden name _____

Further Details: _____

_____

_____

Names and Addresses of Parents, Brothers and Sisters

Name _____ Relationship _____

Address _____

City & State _____

Name _____ Relationship _____

Address _____

City & State _____

Name _____ Relationship _____

Address _____

City & State _____

Name _____ Relationship _____

Address _____

City & State _____

Others: _____

_____

_____

_____

_____

_____

_____

_____

_____

Children

Name _____ Birth date _____

Name _____ Birth date _____

Name _____ Birth date _____

Name _____ Birth date _____

Name _____ Birth date _____

Others: _____

_____

_____

_____

_____

Who supports the children? _____

Educational background of deponent: _____

_____

_____

Other special training: _____

_____

_____

Residence Addresses for the Past Ten years

Address _____ Dates _____

City & State _____

Address _____ Dates _____

City & State _____

Address _____ Dates _____

City & State _____

Address _____ Dates _____

City & State _____

Address _____ Dates _____

City & State _____

Marital Status _____

Spouse's full name _____

Maiden Name _____

Any other marriages? _____

If yes, explain: _____

_____

_____

_____

Military Service Experience: _____

_____

Injuries in service: _____

_____

Prior traffic convictions: _____

_____

_____

Has driver's license ever been revoked? _____

If yes, explain: _____

_____

Does deponent have restrictions on driver's license?

_____

If yes, explain: _____

_____

Does the deponent carry liability insurance? ____

Name of company _____

Policy number _____

Liab. limits _____ Med. limits _____

Effective period _____

Did the deponent settle with any other person

involved in this occurrence? _____

If yes, explain: _____

_____

_____

Was any reimbursement received for medical expenses, loss of income, property damage, or

Workmen's Compensation, or other? _____

If yes, explain: _____

_____

Were any oral or written statements given? ____

If yes, explain: _____

Were income tax returns filed in the past 5 years?

_____

Where? _____ Jointly? _____

Does the deponent have copies? _____

Is deponent acquainted with or related to any

party in this suit? _____

If yes, exlain: _____

_____

_____

_____

EMPLOYMENT BACKGROUND

Name of employer _____

_____

Address _____

City & State _____

Job description: _____

_____ Rate of pay _____

Immediate Supervisor _____

_____

Employment for the Past Ten Years

Employer _____ Dates _____

Address _____

City & State _____

Job description: _____

Employer _____ Dates _____

Address _____

City & State _____

Job description: _____

Employer _____ Dates _____

Address _____

City & State _____

Job description: _____

If not employed for the past 10 years, was

deponent ever employed? _____

Explain: _____

_____

Further Details: _____

_____

_____

_____

_____

_____

_____

DETAILS OF DEPONENT'S VEHICLE

Make _____ Model _____

Year _____ Color _____ No. of doors _____

Unusual accessories on car: _____

_____

Owner's name _____

Address _____

City & State _____

Approximate mileage on a car at time of accident

_____

When did car last have repairs? _____

Where were repairs performed? _____

_____

Nature of last repairs before accident: _____

_____

Approximate mileage on tires at time of accident

_____

Condition of:

    Tail lights _____   Tires _____

    Headlights _____   Horn _____

    Turn signals _____   Steering _____

    Windshield _____   Wipers _____

                        Brakes _____

When was the last safety check before the accident? _____

_____

Was the auto ever in a previous accident? _____

If yes, explain: _____

_____

What portion of the vehicle was damaged as a result of the above previous accident? _____

_____

Was the car repaired after the previous accident?

_____

If so, where and what was the cost of repair: ___

_____

In how many previous accidents had this automobile been involved? _____

Details: _____

_____

_____

_____

_____

_____

OCCUPANTS IN DEPONENT'S CAR

L.F. (1)

Name _____ Age _____

Address _____

City & State _____

Bus. Phone _____ Home Phone _____

M.F. (2)

Name _____ Age _____

Address _____

City & State _____

Bus. Phone _____ Home Phone _____

R.F. (3)

Name _____ Age _____

Address _____

City & State _____

Bus. Phone _____ Home Phone _____

L.R. (4)

Name _____ Age _____

Address _____

City & State _____

Bus. Phone _____ Home Phone _____

M.R. (5)

Name _____ Age _____

Address _____

City & State _____

Bus. Phone _____ Home Phone _____

R.R. (6)

Name _____ Age _____

Address _____

City & State _____

Bus. Phone _____ Home Phone _____

Others

_____

_____

Did driver ask passengers to wear seat belts? ___

_____

Which passengers were wearing seat belts? ____

_____

Did passengers have a clear view of the accident?

Explain: _____

_____

What were passengers doing before impact (e.g., sleeping, talking, drinking, touching controls, yelling, etc.)? _____

_____

_____

Did any passengers warn the driver of impending

danger? _____

Explain: _____

_____

Did any passengers complain of the driving? ___

Explain: _____

_____

Was anyone giving directions to the driver? ___

Explain: _____

_____

Were any occupants injured? _____

If yes, what did deponent notice about injuries to

other occupants? _____

_____

DESCRIPTION OF ACCIDENT SCENE

Diagram

```
            |  N  |
 _____|     |_____
 W                           E
 _____      _____
            |     |
            |  S  |
```

Other Diagram—Draw Below

==

Location of accident: _____

_____

Number of driving lanes for each road: _____

Number of parking lanes for each road: _____

Direction of each road: _____

_____

_____

Describe each road (e.g., level, hilly, divided, etc.)

_____

_____

Type of surface (e.g., dirt, gravel, asphalt, brick,

concrete, blacktop, etc.) _____

_____

Condition of roads (e.g., holes, icy, dry, wet, etc.)

_____

Were lanes marked?

Explain: _____

_____

_____

Type of area (e.g., residential, business, rural, etc.)

_____

Describe structures located at or near scene (e.g., building at each corner).

_____

_____

_____

_____

Was there anything obstructing the driver's view

(e.g., buildings, smoke, signs, dust, etc.)? _____

Explain: _____

_____

_____

Describe the traffic controls and location of each (e.g., stop signs, caution signs, arrows, etc.).

_____

_____

_____

_____

What was the speed limit? _____

Where was the speed limit sign? _____

_____

Were traffic signals functioning? _____

Were there artificial lights at the scene? _____

State the approximate width of each street: _____

_____

_____

Is the deponent familiar with the accident scene?

_____

Explain: _____

_____

_____

_____

_____

DETAILS SHORTLY BEFORE OCCURRENCE

Where was deponent going at time of accident?

_____

_____

Where was the deponent coming from? _____

_____

_____

What route was taken? _____

_____

_____

At what time was the deponent to arrive at his destination?

_____

Was the deponent early or late? _____

Explain: _____

_____

What was the last stop made before the accident, other than for traffic?

_____

_____

_____

Was the deponent talking to anyone in the car?

_____

If so, state to whom and the nature of the conversation.

_____

_____

Was the deponent:

Smoking? _____ Drinking? _____

Did he have both hands on the wheel? _____

When is the last time before the accident that the deponent had anything of an alcoholic nature to

drink? Explain: _____

_____

_____

_____

State the names and addresses of all persons present with the deponent at all times during the five hours preceding the occurrence.

_____

_____

_____

Was the deponent under medication at the time

of the occurrence? _____

Explain: _____

_____

_____

When was the last time prior to the accident that the deponent slept and how much sleep did he have?

_____

_____

Was the deponent:

Sleepy? _____ Emotionally upset? _____

Ill? _____ Other? _____

If yes, explain: _____

_____

_____

_____

During the 24-hour period before the accident, did the deponent consume—

A tranquilizer? _____   A narcotic? _____

A prescription? _____   Aspirins? _____

If yes, explain: _____

_____

Did any passengers pay for the ride or share expenses?

Explain: _____

_____

Was the driver acting as agent for anyone? _____

List details (business trip, etc.). _____

_____

_____

Did driver have the owner's permission to drive car? Details (e.g., express or implied consent):

_____

_____

_____

_____

_____

DETAILS OF OCCURRENCE

In what direction and on which street was the deponent traveling?

_____

_____

What was the direction and street for the other car(s)?

_____

_____

_____

Other traffic present: _____

_____

_____

When the deponent first became aware of the other vehicle, how many feet was he from the point of impact? _____

How many seconds from point of impact? _____

What was his speed at this time? _____

In which lane of traffic was he? _____

Did he change lanes within one block of the point of impact? _____

Explain: _____

_____

Did the deponent perform any maneuver to avoid the impact? _____

Explain: _____

_____

Did the deponent try to signal or warn the other party of danger? _____

Did he:

   sound the horn? _____

   use flashing lights? _____

   other? _____

What was the deponent doing when he first became aware of danger (e.g., talking, looking the opposite way, etc.)?

_____

When the deponent first saw the other car, where was it (lane, direction of travel, distance from point of impact, etc.)? _____

_____

_____

What was the other car's speed? _____

Did the other car warn the deponent by:

   sounding the horn? _____

   flashing lights? _____

   other: _____

_____

How many feet from the intersection was the deponent when he could first see the other car?

_____

Did the deponent look for the other car at the first possible point he could see it? _____

Explain: _____

_____

Did the other driver do anything to indicate he saw the deponent? _____

Explain: _____

_____

Did the deponent take evasive action at the point when he first observed the other car? _____

Explain how many seconds elapsed between the time he saw the car and the time he reacted. __

How many feet did he travel? _____

Did the deponent apply his brakes? _____

How far (feet) from the point of impact? _____

What was the speed of the deponent:

   one block from the point of impact? _____

   ½ block from the point of impact?   _____

   100 feet from the point of impact?   _____

   50 feet from the point of impact?   _____

   at the point of impact?   _____

What was the speed of the other vehicle:

   one block from the point of impact? _____

   ½ block from the point of impact?   _____

   100 feet from the point of impact?   _____

   50 feet from the point of impact?   _____

   at the point of impact?   _____

Did deponent use:

   hand brake? _____ shift gears? _____

Did the brakes decrease the speed? _____

Describe the point of contact on the deponent's auto:

_____

_____

_____

_____

Describe all remaining contact points: _____

_____

_____

Describe all damage to deponent's auto: _____

_____

_____

In relation to the intersection, describe the exact point of impact (use intersecting point of lanes in which cars are):

_____

_____

Where did the deponent's vehicle come to rest in relation to the point of impact?

_____

_____

Describe the point of contact concerning the other auto(s):

_____

_____

_____

Describe remaining contact points: _____

_____

Was there debris to mark point of impact? _____

Explain (e.g., broken glass, vehicle parts, dirt or mud, water or radiator fluid, gas, oil, or grease, etc.): _____

_____

_____

_____

In which direction was each car facing at the final resting point? _____

_____

Was there anything about either automobile which may have caused or contributed to the accident? _____

Explain: _____

_____

Was there anything about the road or its surface that may have caused or contributed to the accident? _____

Explain: _____

_____

Describe the location of each party to this suit after the cars came to their final resting places:

_____

_____

Was anyone removed by ambulance? _____

Who? _____

_____

Was first aid rendered at the scene? _____

To whom? _____

_____

By whom? _____

_____

Nature of treatment: _____

_____

_____

Was there any evidence of drinking at the scene?

_____

Explain: _____

_____

Did any person at the scene appear:

   to be intoxicated? _____

   to have been drinking? _____

Who? _____

_____

_____

Did the deponent talk to anyone at the scene? __

If yes, to whom and what was said: _____

_____

_____

_____

What conversation(s) did the deponent overhear at the scene? Between whom was the conversation and what was said? _____

_____

_____

_____

_____

_____

POLICE INVESTIGATION

Did police respond? _____

What police department? _____

_____

How many police cars? _____

How many policemen? _____

Was a traffic citation issued? _____

To whom? _____

_____

What was (were) the charge(s)? _____

_____

Court date: _____

What was the disposition of the traffic hearing (e.g., plea of guilty, found guilty or not guilty)?

_____

Were the proceedings in traffic court recorded (e.g., court reporter, tape recorder)?

Details: _____

_____

_____

Were photographs taken? _____

Details: _____

_____

Did the police take measurements? _____

How (e.g., tape measure, walking, etc.)? _____

_____

Further Details: _____

_____

_____

_____

_____

_____

_____

_____

_____

_____

WITNESSES

Were there any occurrence witnesses? _____

If Yes, List

Name _____

Address _____

City & State _____

Bus. Phone _____ Home Phone _____

Name _____

Address _____

City & State _____

Bus. Phone _____ Home Phone _____

Name _____

Address _____

City & State _____

Bus. Phone _____ Home Phone _____

Name _____

Address _____

City & State _____

Bus. Phone _____ Home Phone _____

Others: _____

_____

_____

_____

Describe where witnesses were: _____

_____

_____

_____

_____

_____

_____

Describe deponent's conversation with witnesses:

_____

_____

_____

_____

_____

_____

Did any witnesses arrive later? _____

Explain (e.g., passing motorist, friends, etc.): ___

_____

_____

_____

_____

Were any people in the immediate area? _____

Explain (e.g., gas station attendant, mailman, people waiting for a bus, etc.):

_____

_____

_____

_____

Did any articles appear in the newspapers? ___

Explain: _____

_____

_____

_____

_____

Further Details: _____

_____

_____

_____

_____

_____

_____

INJURIES AND MEDICAL INFORMATION

Description of injuries: _____

_____

_____

_____

Name of treating Dr.: _____

Address _____

City & State _____

Phone No. _____

Names and Addresses of Specialists

Name _____ Specialty _____

Address _____

City & State _____

Phone No. _____

Name _____ Specialty _____

Address _____

City & State _____

Phone No. _____

Name _____ Specialty _____

Address _____

City & State _____

Phone No. _____

Name of Hospital _____

Address _____

City & State _____

Phone No. _____

Describe medical treatment received together with dates, and identify doctors giving treatment.

_____

_____

_____

_____

_____

_____

PRIOR MEDICAL HISTORY

Prior Injuries

Date _____ Where? _____

Details: _____

_____

_____

Date _____ Where? _____

Details: _____

_____

_____

Prior Hospitalization

Date _____ Where? _____

Details: _____

_____

_____

Date _____ Where? _____

Details: _____

_____

_____

Date _____ Where? _____

Details: _____

_____

_____

Does deponent have any physical or mental illnesses or is he being treated for any condition?

_____

Explain: _____

_____

_____

_____

Any prior claims or lawsuits? _____

Explain: _____

_____

_____

_____

DAMAGES TO DATE

Hospital _____ $ _____

Ambulance Service _____ $ _____

Private Nurses _____ $ _____

Dr. _____ $ _____

Dr. _____ $ _____

Dr. _____ $ _____

Dr. _____ $ _____

Drugs & Prescriptions _____ $ _____

X-rays _____ $ _____

Loss of Income _____ $ _____

Property Damage _____ $ _____

_____ $ _____

_____ $ _____

_____ $ _____

_____ $ _____

             Total To Date $ _____

Further Details: _____

_____

_____

_____

_____

_____

_____

_____

_____

_____

_____

_____

_____

_____

_____

ATTORNEY'S APPRAISAL OF DEPONENT

Physical description, general appearance and characteristics, handicaps, or impairments—hearing, eyesight, speech, etc.

_____

_____

Does the deponent describe the accident in a clear, rational and understandable manner? If not, why not?

_____

_____

Does the deponent show any marked tendency to engage in conjecture and speculation?

_____

_____

Can the deponent be easily confused, swayed, or led?

_____

_____

Do deponent's normal activities and past experiences qualify with respect to estimating speeds, distances, etc.? State the qualifications, if any.

_____

_____

General attitude—favorable, unfavorable, or passive?

_____

_____

General Impression: From your observations of the deponent, state whether the deponent's appearance, personality, and demeanor shall normally invite belief or disbelief in his version of the accident or occurrence, as the deponent tells it.

_____

_____

_____

_____

_____

_____

Submitted by: _____
　　　　　　　　　　Name of Attorney

You will be surprised once you get rolling how many useful questions you can generate. Trying to write the questions in longhand or on a word processor takes too long and is not as productive as the tape recorder. Have a working document typed that you can edit and add to as needed.

As you are going through materials and generating questions, be sure to write down each document that needs to be gathered for your attorney for use or to be introduced at the deposition. A possible format for the outline appears in figure 8:10.[35]

The advantage of such an outline form is that it lists the questions or topics on one side and permits comments, notations, documents that need to be introduced, or evaluation of the answer on the other side. This will help the attorney at the deposition. It also permits highlighting of questions that the attorney may choose to use out of chronological sequence to elicit a more spontaneous and less planned answer from the deponent.

Figure 8:10   Deposition Outline

CASE: Smith vs Jones   DEPO DATE: 6 Jan 1988

DEPONENT: Albert Smith - Plaintiff   LOCATION: 1421 - 6th Avenue
                                                  Sacramento

ATTYS: E. Gibson for Jones
       N. Mason for Smith

Items to cover	Known facts ?
ID: Albert Smith	√
Age	43
Res	2130 "I" St., Sacramento
SSN	238 - 45 - 9726
Educ.	Wilson HS Sacramento
Employ:	State of Cal. Dept of Highway 51 - 79

Once the outline is in good draft form, it should be reviewed by the attorney. Amendments should be added, and a final outline typed by the legal secretary. Extra copies should be made for the form file if there are no other good examples.

Gather and Prepare Documents and Exhibits

Each of the documents or photographs the attorney plans to introduce for authentication or needs for reference should be gathered and placed in separate, clearly labeled manila folders. Sufficient copies of each document should also be in the folder, allowing the attorney to mark up one copy as needed or to give copies to the other attorneys at the deposition. Other physical items requiring introduction should be gathered.

Some exhibits may need to be located, purchased, or prepared. Preparation of exhibits will be discussed later in the chapter on preparing for trial. Most attorneys agree that witnesses have an easier time and are more accurate if they refer to a diagram or some other visual exhibit. These should also be organized in the order they will be needed by the attorney.

ASSIGNMENT 8:17
Draft a checklist that includes coordinating the deposition and planning and preparing an outline for taking a deposition based on the steps and recommendations made here, and place it in your system folder.

Set Up Witness Files

Important to conducting a good deposition is a good witness file. You can begin to organize a witness file as it becomes clear that a particular witness will play a role at deposition and probably later at trial. The file should be organized prior to the scheduled deposition of the witness and should contain the following:

A witness information sheet (see chapter 4)
The deposition outline or questions
Documents by or concerning the witness arranged chronologically or as
    needed at the deposition
An extra set of documents that you or the attorney may mark on during
    the deposition
Discovery information gained through interrogatories, admissions, or
    other requests
Allegations in the pleadings
Notice of deposition, subpoenas, and certificate of service

The witness file should be arranged according to the specifications of the supervising attorney. A small three-ring binder with all pertinent documents placed loosely at the back in separate, clearly labeled folders seems to aid organization and quick access. A separate witness file should be maintained for each witness to be deposed or later examined at trial.

ASSIGNMENT 8:18
Copy the Checklist for Preparing Witness Files and place it in your system folder.

Assist in the Preparation of the Client or Witness for Testimony

Preparing clients or witnesses for deposition testimony is extremely important, because what they say, how effective they appear, and how

Preparing the client for deposition: a team effort.

certain they are of the facts may well determine whether the case is settled in the client's favor or heads for a full-blown expensive trial. Further, if the case does go to trial and the witnesses' answers are not well thought out, there is considerable likelihood that the opponent will use the deposition to show inconsistencies and inaccuracies that will harm the witnesses' credibility in the eyes of the jury.

You can play an important role in seeing to it that the witnesses do the best job they can. In many law offices the paralegal's role is primarily one of communication, keeping the witness informed on what to expect and when to expect it. This involves timely correspondence, phone calls, and coordinating meetings with the attorney. In some offices the paralegal is used even more effectively by working directly with the witness. In this case the client or witness comes to the office, where the paralegal assists the attorney by addressing the witness's anxiety, counseling on testifying techniques, and answering questions. Frequently the firm takes the witness through a mock examination. The paralegal can help by having questions ready that are likely to be asked by the opponent.

The experienced paralegal occasionally participates in questioning the witness during the mock examination.

You may have the responsibility of informing the client or witness what to expect and how to handle the deposition. The law office frequently does this by a letter or brochure on testifying. One often-used brochure is titled "About Your Deposition" and is published by the Lawyers and Judges Publishing Company in Tucson, Arizona. Many law firms, however, have developed their own list of suggestions; you should check with the office.

There are numerous ways you can assist at a preparation conference: making suggestions to the witness, observing the witness in mock examination and noting weak or ineffective areas, doing the questioning while the attorney notes problems, and other possibilities. You may need to be assertive at this stage in suggesting ways to render assistance.

Figure 8:11 is a sample letter that serves two purposes; first, it shows the form of a letter that many paralegals are called on to draft and send to clients, and second, it covers the most significant tips that should be passed on to a client, whether by letter or in a conference at the office. Some attorneys are uncomfortable with sending out detailed instruction letters to clients. Such letters may be used against the client or attorney, so they prefer to handle such things in an office visit. Check with your supervising attorney. The proposed letter can always be used as a checklist on what to tell the client at such an appointment.

A letter such as in figure 8:11 should be followed by an appointment with the attorney, and possibly including yourself. At that time any additional directions can be conveyed. If given responsibility for guiding the witness, keep in mind some matters of concern:

1. It is unethical for an attorney or attorney's agent to tell a client what to say to answer questions, either at deposition or at trial. To do so greatly influences the witness, and may unintentionally lead to perjury or cause the witness to believe that you or the attorney condones such dishonesty. Even if you or the attorney knows a particular answer is true, specific answers should not be suggested. Any breach of this ethical standard is extremely serious and the slightest implication of impro-

priety can be damaging to the case and the reputation of the attorney.

2. In going over questions that might be asked the witness, watch for questions that call for privileged information or the attorney's work product. Such matters should be called to the attention of the attorney so the client can be instructed accordingly and any necessary protective orders can be sought.

3. When working with a witness as opposed to a client, many of the same suggestions apply. One additional suggestion is to stress to the witness the importance of impartiality. If the witness appears too sympathetic to the client or too eager to help, it may cause the jury to question the reliability of the witness and possibly discount the testimony.

4. It is not a good idea to have witnesses, including clients, review documents and recorded statements prior to depositions or trial. The other side is entitled to a copy of a document that a witness has reviewed to refresh his or her memory of the events. Such a document can be damaging and especially useful to the opposition for impeaching the friendly witness. The best approach is to try to get the client to recall facts by asking questions and discussing information rather than having the client read the document.

5. A set of form deposition questions can be used to simulate the deposition. An attempt to anticipate unusual questions that will likely be asked by the opponent is usually well worth the effort.

Figure 8:11 Letter to Client Regarding Deposition

WHITE, WILSON & McDUFF

ATTORNEYS AT LAW
FEDERAL PLAZA BUILDING, SUITE 700
THIRD AND MARKET STREETS
LEGALVILLE, COLUMBIA 00000
(111) 555-0000

Ms. Ann Forrester
1533 Capitol Drive
Legalville, Columbia 00000

November 1, 19___

Dear Ms. Forrester:

As we previously discussed, the time has come when you will need to testify about the accident and your injuries at a deposition. We will work with you to prepare for the deposition. Mr. White will be with you and is confident you will do just fine.

The deposition is scheduled for Wednesday, December 2, 19___, at 10:00 a.m. in room 202 in the Federal District Court Building at Third and Race Streets. Parking is available at the Municipal Parking facility behind the courthouse. Please be there by 9:30 a.m.

A deposition is an examination of a witness under oath by the opposition and in the presence of a court reporter. The examination is to determine the witness's version of the facts, the evidence in support of those facts, and the location of the evidence and names and addresses of persons having information about the evidence. It is an important stage in the lawsuit because the other side will be evaluating you as a witness, including your appearance, ability to recall facts, and truthfulness, etc. Depositions produce evidence that might lead to a settlement of the case. They may also be used at trial to test the consistency and credibility of a witness. Therefore, good preparation on your part is important. It will give you confidence.

In preparing for the deposition, please keep the following in mind.

1. Depositions are occasionally postponed, and if so, you will be informed.
2. Chronologically review the facts of the case up through your current medical status; anticipate questions on dates, times, directions, distances, speeds, weather, clothes, events, injuries, medical treatments, expenses, witnesses, statements, etc. If you do not know distances and the like for sure, reasonable approximations are acceptable. A return to the scene of the accident to check distances, obstructions, and other details before your deposition might be helpful.
3. Be sure you have informed your attorney of all matters about the incident and those that reflect on your own honesty and credibility. Do not allow your attorney to be surprised to your detriment.
4. Expect the opponent's attorney to do most or all of the questioning. Your attorney will object when it is necessary.
5. Dress neatly, be pleasant, and speak up.
6. Listen to each question carefully. If you do not understand the question, *do not guess at its meaning,* simply state you do not understand.
7. Think about your answer; do not blurt out answers. Be cautious of a series of questions in quick succession that intend to lead you to the answer your opponent desires. Answer thoughtfully at your own pace.
8. Above all, tell the truth. You will be under oath and should avoid giving in to the temptation to fill in gaps of information. Do not guess. Should you want to correct an earlier answer, simply indicate your desire to do so. The attorney will assist you.
9. If you are asked, "Did you speak with your attorney about testifying today?" answer "yes." There is nothing wrong with speaking with your attorney about testifying. If the question is, "Did your attorney tell you what to say?" the correct answer is, "He told me to tell the truth." Other than that, your attorney will not tell you what to say.
10. While testifying, it is preferable that you not seek guidance from your attorney. You must answer the question as best you can. If your attorney feels a question is improper, an objection will be stated. An objection is a signal to you to stop answering.

11. A common technique of adverse attorneys is to remain silent after your answer. This is frequently done in the hope that you will feel compelled to add more information. It can be damaging information. Therefore, resist the temptation to add information and to fill silences.

12. Avoid discussing your case and any aspect of your testimony with anyone other than your attorney. Casual conversation about your case can be damaging.

13. You may be asked at the deposition to sketch a diagram of the accident scene. If you try some practice sketches, you should not have any difficulty with this.

14. During the deposition you may be given documents, diagrams, photographs, or other items to identify. Be sure to examine such items carefully to see that they accurately reflect what they intend to reflect before you agree to their accuracy.

15. Be prepared to describe your injuries and medical treatment in detail. Do not exaggerate or understate.

16. Be prepared to discuss any injuries you suffered or claims you made before this accident.

17. Bring any documents that you have been requested to bring.

18. Be prepared to discuss changes such as loss of pay, property damage, and other out-of-pocket expenses.

19. It is not necessary to memorize possible answers and is probably better if you do not.

In summary, you will do the best job at your deposition if you are well prepared, thoughtful, deliberate, and truthful. I will be contacting you very soon to set up a time when you and Mr. White can meet to discuss the deposition. Meanwhile if you have any questions or concerns, please feel free to contact me or Mr. White.

Very truly yours,

Terry Salyer
Paralegal

ASSIGNMENT 8:19
Draft a copy of the letter in figure 8:11 and place it in your system folder. Draft and add a separate list on preparing witnesses for testifying, including the preceding five items and any items mentioned in class by your instructor.

Attend and Review the Deposition

You will often be asked to attend the deposition with the supervising attorney. Ideally, you should have the opportunity to attend one or more depositions prior to doing any deposition work. That experience provides a better understanding of the entire process and leads to a better job of assisting the attorney and the witness in all steps of deposition practice.

At the deposition your most important role is to listen carefully. If your attorney is doing the questioning, follow along on the outline of questions.

The paralegals for both sides should take notes on significant information, objections, and observations about the effectiveness of the witness and opposing counsel. Listening and observing carefully are important factors because the supervising attorney will occasionally be too distracted to be a good listener. You should be able to make suggestions, catch topics or questions that have been missed, and detect evasiveness or lies. You can also make sure information and documents are quickly retrieved when needed, that the law is researched on a point that arises in the deposition, or that an important phone call is made.

Immediately following the deposition, compare notes with the attorney and draft a summary of the deposition based on those notes and other impressions. This summary allows discovery to progress and avoids having to write for the typed transcript before other discovery decisions are made.

Following the deposition, the court reporter will prepare the transcript. Rule 30(e) of the Federal Rules and parallel state rules require that the transcript of the deposition be made available to the deponent to review for accuracy and to sign. The deponent's signature may be waived, but sound practice advises against it. A signed deposition is stronger evidence when used at trial for impeachment or other reasons. If the deponent finds an error or wants to correct testimony, that is permitted under Rule 30(e). The court reporter must enter the changes on the deposition with a statement of the reasons given by the witness for making them.

Check to see that the witness signs the transcript. If the witness refuses to sign it, the court reporter should sign it and state the reason why the witness would not sign. Verify that the court reporter has certified that the witness was duly sworn by the officer and that the deposition is a true record of the testimony given by the witness [Rule 30(f)]. The deposition is then filed with the court. Again, verifying that the requirements have been met assures the deposition's effective use at trial if needed.

On receipt of the deposition transcript, you may be asked to review it. Any questions omitted by the attorney should be noted so they can be asked through interrogatories or at trial. Inconsistencies in a witness's testimony should also be noted. For example, in one part of the transcript the witness might say the van was traveling at thirty-five to forty miles per hour and twenty pages later say it seemed like less than thirty. Such inconsistency can be used to impeach the witness. The review may also reveal inaccuracies or omissions in the reporting. Digesting depositions will be covered in the next chapter.

ASSIGNMENT 8:20
Prepare a Checklist for Attending and Reviewing the Deposition and place it in your system folder.

ASSIGNMENT 8:21
Assume you represent Mr. Hart. Prepare a deposition outline for your attorney to use in examining Ms. Forrester. Try using a tape recorder if one is available to dictate questions or topics. Use the sample outline and sample checklist from the chapter (figures 8:9 and 8:10) as guides for your work. Then shift roles and prepare an outline for Ms. Forrester's attorney to examine Mr. Hart.

█ Production of Documents and Things and Entry Upon Land for Inspection and Other Purposes

Introduction

A discovery device that has grown in significance is the Rule 34 production of documents and things. This is a request made of one party by the other to physically produce and make available for the requesting party's inspection documents, physical evidence, and land and buildings. Its purpose is to make evidence available to both sides to assess its value and to prevent surprise at trial. More specifically, the requesting party uses the device not only to discover what evidence the other side has, but also to locate evidence damaging to the other side that supports any theories propounded by the requesting party. The request for production and inspection is particularly valuable in business cases and for accessing any tests or information used to form the basis for the testimony of the adversary's expert witnesses. Information discovered in this manner can be valuable in preparing for depositions, settlement proposals, or trial.

Scope

Rule 34(a) defines the scope of the request and includes the following evidence:

> Writing, drawings, graphs, charts, photographs, phone records, and other data compilations from which information can be obtained, translated, if necessary, by the respondent through detection devices into reasonably usable form, or to inspect and copy, test, or sample any tangible things which constitute or contain matter within the scope of Rule 26(b) and which are in the possession, custody or control of the party upon whom the request is served; or (2) to permit entry upon designated land or other property in the possession or control of the party upon whom the request is served for the purpose of inspection and measuring, surveying, photographing, testing, or sampling the property or any designated object or operation thereon, within the scope of Rule 26(b).

The scope of the rule has expanded to cover new technology, including computer data banks and usable printouts. The request, however, cannot be unreasonably burdensome, oppressive, or unduly disruptive, such as when going to observe the internal workings of a business or manufacturing plant. Businesses are not expected to disclose commercially valuable trade secrets like the twelve (or is it eleven?) secret herbs and spices that go into the batter for Colonel Sanders' chicken. Of course, privileged and work product information that is irrelevant or cannot reasonably be expected to lead to relevant evidence is beyond the reach of the rule.

Procedure

The request for production and inspection can be made with the service of the summons and complaint, or at any time after the action starts. It can be made to any other party. Third persons can be asked to produce documents only through the subpoena duces tecum [Rule 45(b)].

The request may be served directly on the other party without leave of the court and must state the items to be inspected either by individual item or by category with reasonable particularity. It shall also specify a reasonable time, place, and manner for conducting the inspection [Rule 34(b)].

The responding party must file a reply within thirty days of receipt of the request or within forty-five days if the request was served with the summons. The court may, on request, require a shorter time for the response. The reply should indicate compliance and any objections, specifying the particular part or section of the request objected to (Rule 34). The requesting party may move for a court order under Rule 37(a) if it is felt that the refusal or objection is improper. Most states have either parallel or similar procedures, but it is always wise to check. If the request involves some expense, such as for photocopying documents or developing negatives of photos, the requesting party must pay for the expense of production.

Preparing for Production and Inspection

Decide what to request, keeping in mind the facts of the case and the legal theories gained through a review of the file. Give particular attention to the answers to interrogatories or deposition questions that identify pertinent documents. It might be useful to determine the types of documents or things often used in a particular industry or business.[36] Clients may help here, or persons in similar businesses and trade and professional associations. The attorney should be consulted to mutually arrive at a list of specific items or categories of items that should be requested.

Establish a time and place for the production and inspection by agreement with the other party's attorney. Frequently the examination occurs in a room in the office of the attorney whose client has possession of the documents. In some cases it involves arranging to go to a particular building to inspect machinery, or observe a production process or a test. If so, a time and manner of inspection should be agreed on that is reasonable and not disruptive. This may require setting a time outside normal business hours; otherwise, most requests are timed for normal business hours.

Drafting the Request for Production and Inspection

A good sample of a request, preferably in a similar case, should be obtained for reference. Office copies or the standard form books should be consulted. Figure 8:12 is a general form for a Request for Production.[37]

It is helpful to remember the following things.

1. The items or categories must be described with sufficient specificity so that a person of average intelligence has enough information to know what must be produced. The standard is flexible and is determined by how much the requesting party can reasonably be expected to know and whether the respondent has sufficient knowledge to determine what is requested.[38] Phrases such as "financial records" or "all correspondence between" have been found to be inadequate descriptions.[39] More specificity in name, topic, and time is required.

Figure 8:12 Request for Production, Inspection, and Copying of Documents, and Inspection and Photographing of Things and Real Property—General Form

[Fed. R. Civ. P. Rule 34]

[*Title of Court and Cause*]

Plaintiff A_____ B_____ requests defendant C_____ D_____ to respond within _____ days to the following requests:

(1) That defendant produce and permit plaintiff to inspect and to copy each of the following documents:

[*Here list the documents either individually or by category and describe each of them.*]

[*Here state the time, place, and manner of making the inspection and performance of any related acts.*]

(2) That defendant produce and permit plaintiff to inspect and to copy, test, or sample each of the following objects:

[*Here list the objects either individually or by category and describe each of them.*]

[*Here state the time, place, and manner of making the inspection and performance of any related acts.*]

(3) That defendant permit plaintiff to enter [*here describe property to be entered*] and to inspect and to photograph, test, or sample [*here describe the portion of the real property and the objects to be inspected*].

[*Here state the time, place, and manner of making the inspection and performance of any related acts.*]

_____

Attorney for Plaintiff

Address: _____

2. The request should be organized by the type of evidence requested (see figure 8:12) and, if possible, include a paragraph on the continuing obligation of the respondent to produce pertinent documents that come into the respondent's possession after the original production date.[40]

Assume that Mercury Parcel has indicated in its answer to Ms. Forrester's interrogatories that the following items do exist: rules and regulations of the Interstate Commerce Commission on the required maintenance of vehicles used in interstate commerce, copies of Form ICC-2010 needed to report compliance with those rules on a quarterly basis, Form ICC-2010A used to record regular maintenance information on a specified vehicle, and Form ICC-2015 for recording specific complaints and resulting repairs to a specific vehicle. Also assume that the answer revealed that the van was vehicle number 23 and that photographs had been taken of the van and the accident scene. Although more records might be available, this should be sufficient for purposes of illustration. Assume Mr. White has asked you to draft that request. After reviewing the file and forms and consulting with the attorney, you might draft a form that looks like the one on the next page.

Service of the Request for Production

The request should then be signed by the attorney, and you should serve the request by mail and execute the appropriate certificate of mailing. A copy

UNITED STATES DISTRICT COURT
FOR THE EASTERN DISTRICT OF COLUMBIA

ANN FORRESTER,
                            Plaintiff
            v.   } Civil Case, File No. _____
MERCURY PARCEL SERVICE, INC.,
                            Defendant

PLAINTIFF'S REQUEST FOR PRODUCTION AND INSPECTION OF DOCUMENTS, THINGS, AND REAL PROPERTY

According to Rule 34 of the Federal Rules of Civil Procedure, Plaintiff requests Defendant Mercury Parcel Service to respond within thirty days to the following requests:

1. That Defendant produce and permit Plaintiff to inspect and to copy each of the following documents:
   a. The specific rules and regulations of the Interstate Commerce Commission requiring regular safety checks, maintenance, and repair of vehicles used in interstate commerce.
   b. Defendant's file copies of all Form 2010's submitted to the ICC between Feb. 19__ and Jan. 19__.
   c. All Form ICC-2010A's recording the regular maintenance and safety checks on van number 23 over the two-year period preceding the accident on February 26, 19__.
   d. All Form ICC-2010A's for all other Defendant's delivery vehicles over the two years preceding the accident.
   e. All Form ICC-2015's recording complaints and needed repairs and subsequent repairs made to van number 23 for the two years preceding the accident.
   f. All Form ICC-2015's on all other vehicles for the two years preceding the accident.
   g. All photographs or negatives thereof that Defendant had taken of the accident scene and the damage to the van. Plaintiff will inspect and copy these items at the office of Plaintiff's attorney on November 1, 19__ at 9:00 A.M., or at any other reasonable time and place convenient to counsel in this action.

                            _____
                            Arthur White
                            Attorney for Plaintiff
                            (address)

should be kept for the file. It is good practice to file a copy of the request and certificate of service with the court as well. The response date should be noted on your calendar and in the deadline calendar so that the failure of the other party to respond will not go unnoticed. The attorney should be informed if no reply is forthcoming so remedial measures can be taken. Figure 8:13 is an example of the length of records that might be requested in a business case.[41]

Figure 8:13 Request for Production of Documents—Business Records

[Fed. R. Civ. P. Rule 34]

[*Title of Court and Cause*]

To: _____
　　Attorney for Plaintiff

　　Address: _____

　　Plaintiff, _____ requests defendant, _____, to respond within 30 days to the following requests pursuant to Rule 34, Federal Rules of Civil Procedure:

　　Plaintiff requests that defendant _____ produce, give access, and make available to the plaintiff, or his duly appointed attorneys-at-law, accountants, or agents, at _____ Street and/or _____ Avenue, _____, and permit the said plaintiff or his duly appointed attorneys, accountants or agents to inspect and/or copy all of the books, accounts, papers, records and other documents of the defendant, M_____ Company, a co-partnership, which said books, accounts, papers, records or other documents relate or pertain to transactions and affairs of said partnership, and on which any of the affairs of said partnership are recorded; or any other books, accounts, papers, records or other documents in the possession of defendants, or either of them, which pertain to any transactions or engagements which they or either of them have made or entered into for or on behalf of or ir the name of said partnership from the date of its inception on _____, 19___, to the date of this order; which said books, accounts, papers, records and other said documents shall include, but not by way of limitation, the following:

　　All books of general ledger, general journal, purchase journal, sales journal, cash receipts journal, cash disbursements journal, accounts receivable ledger, accounts payable ledger, canceled checks, bank statements, duplicate deposit slips, check register, purchase orders, shop orders, packing slips, invoices to customers, customers' orders, invoices from credits, payroll records, Social Security and unemployment compensation records, daily record of machine production, record of daily shipments, all vouchers in support of disbursements, all inventory records, machine rental contracts, record of all machine rentals, all audit reports, all working papers of accountants, bookkeepers, or other persons employed by defendants or either of them relating to the said partnership transactions, records of fixed assets, depreciation schedules, all correspondence and other miscellaneous papers concerning or relating to said partnership business, all documents relating to the purchase, use and disposition of materials, all deeds, assignments or other documents evidencing the assignment of fixed assets of the partnership, all income or other federal or state tax returns prepared or filed for or on behalf of said partnership, records of quantity, type and size of material required for the production of any item produced by the said partnership, together with all shop time cards, slips and other summaries of original entry, all daily progress records of customers' orders concerning the shipment of parts for customers, all letters, forms or other records pertaining to renegotiation or termination of war contracts, all records pertaining to all insurance policies, and any and all other records, papers, documents or other legible evidence relating or pertaining to transactions and engagements of the said partnership business.

　　It is further requested that plaintiff and/or his attorneys-at-law, accountants or agents be permitted the right of access to or to inspect or make copies of said books, records, and other papers only during the regular business hours of week-day prior to _____ 19___, and only in the presence of an employee or agent, or employees or agents, of defendants, or either of them. It is further requested that defendants, and each of them, at all such business hours of all week-days have in said premises an employee or agent, in whose presence such inspection or copying can be done by plaintiff, or his attorneys-at-law, accountants or agents herein authorized.

Dated: _____, 19___

Attorney for Plaintiff

Address: _____

Responding to a Request for Production and Inspection

If asked to respond to a request for production and inspection, you must identify and screen documents and things. A discussion of the procedure for gathering and organizing documents is reserved for chapter 9. In consultation with the attorney, determine what documents and things are to be produced, and draft a response to the request. Figure 8:14 provides a suggested format for that task.[42]

Should a party fail to reply or object without sufficient grounds, you may be asked to draft a motion to compel production. Figure 8:15 is an example of such a motion,[43] and figure 8:16 is the affidavit.[44]

Assisting at Production

In reviewing the opponent's documents, it is a good idea to be sure that there is a photocopying machine available and a phone to reach the attorney in case any questions arise. Determine what method will be used to identify

---

Figure 8:14 Response to Request for Production—General Form

[FED. R. CIV. P. Rule 34]

[*Title of Court and Cause*]

_____

Attorney for Plaintiff

Address: _____

In response to plaintiff's request to produce and for inspection in the above-entitled action, served upon plaintiff _____, 19___, the inspection and related activities requested will be permitted at [if a different place than requested] with respect to each item and category as requested [add with the exception of Items as follows, _____, to which inspection defendant objects, respectfully on the following grounds: list each request objected to, the objection and reasons _____] [or, the inspection and related activities requested are objected to on the ground that _____].

Yours, etc.

_____

Attorney for Defendant

Address: _____

the documents. One method is to take a mechanical numbering device and sequentially number each document selected by the attorney. It is also a good idea to take along a dictaphone and dictate a description of the significant documents. That may be necessary if the other side refuses to

Figure 8:15 Motion to Compel Production, Inspection, and Copying of Documents in Case of Objection or Failure to Respond—General Form

[FED. R. CIV. P. Rules 34(b), 37(a)]

[*Title of Court and Cause*]

Defendant, _____, moves the court for an order requiring plaintiff, _____, to produce and to permit defendant to inspect and to copy or photograph each of the following documents [*here list the documents and describe each of them*]. This motion is made on the ground that the defendant served a written request upon the plaintiff for production, inspection, and copying or photographing the above-mentioned documents, a copy of which is attached hereto as Exhibit A, and that the plaintiff objected to said production by a response, a copy of which is attached hereto as Exhibit B [*or and the plaintiff has failed and refused to respond to defendant's request as required by Rule 23, Federal Rules of Civil Procedure*]. The documents requested by defendant contain relevant and material evidence in the above-entitled action and their production is necessary for defendant to prepare for trial, as indicated in Exhibit C hereto attached.

_____
Attorney for Defendant
Address: _____

Figure 8:16 Affidavit in Support of Motion to Compel Production

[FED. R. CIV. P. Rules 34, 37(a)]

[*Title of Court and Cause*]

[*Venue*]

_____, being first duly sworn, on his oath states:

That he is one of the attorneys for the above named defendant and he makes this affidavit in support of the Motion for Production of Documents and Things for Inspection, Copying and Photographing which is attached hereto; that the production of the documents, papers, statements and things requested is made in good faith; that he has been informed and therefore believes that the matters and things so sought in said motion are competent as evidence in said cause and are especially competent by reason of the fact that, _____; that the facts sought to be elicited are facts necessary to be shown and produced in said cause in the furtherance of justice and in securing all the facts competent upon the issues to be tried.

The motion herein made is made in good faith and the affiant as one of counsel for defendant desires to inspect said documents solely for the purpose of establishing facts to be used as evidence in the above-entitled cause and affiant does not intend to use said information for any other purpose or to convey the same to any other party or persons.

Dated this _____ day of _____, 19___.

[*Jurat*]

allow the documents to be stamped. All extraneous writing on the document should be noted, in addition to the type of document, date, author, addressee, number of pages, and attachments. Such scribbles often provide valuable insights, or even evidence, against the opponent. it is important to see if all documents requested are produced, and whether the opponent has a list of each document not produced under the claim of privilege.

If, on the other hand, you are "sitting" the client's documents at the production, see that the documents are kept in order and that no documents leave the room. Occasionally documents disappear or are lost. Request that a phone be made available in the production room so that you do not have to leave the documents unattended to call the attorney with a question.[45]

ASSIGNMENT 8:22
Write an Outline on the Definition, Purpose, Scope, and Procedure for Requests for Production and a Checklist for Preparing a Request for Production of Documents and Things, and place them with copies of the pertinent forms and examples in your system folder.

ASSIGNMENT 8:23
Draft a response to Ms. Forrester's request for production of documents and things. Also make a brief checklist of pointers for assisting at a production of documents, and place the response and checklist in your system folder.

■ Request For Physical and Mental Examination

Purpose and Scope

Rule 35 and parallel state rules permit an adverse party, with good cause, to have the other party submit to a medical examination. The exam is requested to confirm the opponent's allegations of mental or physical injury and to prevent fraudulent claims. The exam may be to confirm a child's blood type in a paternity action, the permanency of a physical injury in an automobile accident, or the mental capabilities and awareness of a person who may be the victim of undue influence in a will challenge.

The request may reach parties and persons who are in the custody or legal control of a party. For example, a mother suing for paternity may need to bring the child for a blood test, or a guardian ad litem may be requested to produce an incompetent person to have injuries examined that the guardian alleges disabled that person in an automobile accident. Co-parties may also be reached under the rule.

According to Rule 35(a) an examination may be ordered if two tests are met: that the alleged condition is in controversy (i.e., the nature and extent of the condition is at issue), and second, that good cause exists to have the examination. In this context, good cause means that there must be a legitimate need to confirm the injury or to discover information that is likely to have a direct bearing on the case. Because of the potential for abuse, and the obvious and sometimes painful intrusion into the privacy of the person subject to examination, the courts tend to interpret "good cause" rather strictly and deny motions for medical examinations if the information can be acquired through less intrusive means. Medical examinations are most routinely ordered in personal injury cases.

Procedure

Attorneys for the parties are usually quite cooperative regarding such exams. Often a phone call and a confirming letter are all that is needed to secure the examination. However, a request to a party to undergo an exam does not require the party to undergo the exam. If an informal overture is rejected or ignored, a motion for a court order is required. A refusal to submit to the exam in violation of a court order may result in dismissal of the case [Rule 37(b)]. The party subject to the exam may object or seek a protective order.

Once the exam is completed, a physician's report is prepared for the party requesting the exam, who then is responsible to forward a copy of it to the examined party.

Set Up the Exam

You may be asked to perform several tasks in conjunction with the Rule 35 examination. Contacting the other party's attorney to see if there are any objections to the exam and proceeding informally will be the initial task. Consult with the supervising attorney to see if a confirming letter or a more formal stipulation is appropriate, or if a motion is required.

Contact the physician to discuss the purpose of the exam and the method of payment. Schedule an appointment and convey this information to the party to be examined.

Draft the Documents

Draft the necessary documents. An example of a motion for compulsory physical examination appears in figure 8:17.[46]

The motion requires a notice of motion, an accompanying affidavit, and a proposed order for the judge. See chapter 7 on motion practice. The notice and motion should be reviewed by the attorney, signed, and served on the other party. After the exam, obtain a report from the doctor and consult with the supervising attorney. When the report is approved, send a copy to the opposing party. Pay the doctor and record the expense so it can be added to the client's bill.

ASSIGNMENT 8:25
Write an Outline on the Definition, Purpose, Scope, and Procedure for a Request for Physical and Mental Examination and make a copy of the Motion for Compulsory Physical Examination. Place both in your system folder.

Inform the Client

If it is your party subject to the exam, tell the client as soon as it is determined that the exam should be taken. Although the client may have been forewarned of a possible exam, the reality of it calls for further explanation, support, and instruction. This may be done by letter as in the figure 8:18 example.

The client might also be instructed, as indicated in the previous letter, at the office. In some circumstances you may be asked to accompany the client to the exam. In a Colorado case, a judge ruled that a paralegal could

Figure 8:17 Motion for Compulsory Physical Examination

[FED. R. CIV. P. Rule 35(a)]

[*Title of Court and Cause*]

Defendant, _____, moves the court for an order requiring the plaintiff, _____, to submit to a physical examination [to be made by _____ describe examiner or examiners, or by a competent _____ describe type of examiner or examiners designated by the court, at _____ or as the court shall order,] for the purpose of determining the exact nature and extent of his [or, her] injuries, if any, and the disabilities, if any, resulting there from [or for an order requiring the plaintiff _____, the Guardian of _____ to produce _____, for whose injuries the above entitled action is brought, to submit, etc, or include appropriate designations of the party and person under his legal custody and control].

The ground of this motion is that there is a controversy between the plaintiff and defendant as to the physical injuries, if any, sustained by the plaintiff [or _____], and the disability, if any, resulting therefrom, and that the physical examination of the plaintiff [or _____] is necessary in order that the defendant, _____, may be in a position to defend as to the claimed injuries of the plaintiff [or _____], as is more fully shown in the affidavit of _____ hereunto annexed as Exhibit A [designate record and any other supporting documents].

[Date]

_____

Attorney for Defendant

Address: _____

Figure 8:18 Notice to Client of Physical Examination

WHITE, WILSON & McDUFF

ATTORNEYS AT LAW
FEDERAL PLAZA BUILDING, SUITE 700
THIRD AND MARKET STREETS
LEGALVILLE, COLUMBIA 00000
(111) 555-0000

Ms. Ann Forrester   December 15, 19___
1533 Capitol Drive
Legalville, Columbia 00000

Dear Ms. Forrester:

You may recall I mentioned in our initial interview the possibility that the other side in this case may request an examination by a doctor of their choosing to confirm the existence and extent of your injuries. Lynn Ott has contacted me to request such an exam.

The exam is scheduled for January 23, 19___, at 1:30 in the afternoon. The examining physician is Dr. Melissa Ward, whose office is at 1644 Fountain Drive near exit 103 off I-275 in Legalville. Please make arrangements to be at Dr. Ward's office at the appointed time.

The exam will consist of a routine examination of your injuries, brief strength and movement tests, and a discussion with the doctor about your injuries and disabilities. The exam should last about an hour.

Before going to the examination, you may choose to make a list of your injuries, treatments, pain, disabilities, and current status. A review of your injury diary should help you.

You should cooperate fully in the exam and be sure neither to overstate or understate the progress of your condition.

Mr. White believes the exam will be beneficial to your case. If you have any concerns, please let me know.

Very truly yours,

Terry Salyer
Paralegal

---

attend the Rule 35 physical exam of the paralegal's client. The court ruled that the exam was more adversarial than medical, giving rise to the need of the paralegal to protect the client from overreaching and unfair questioning.[47]

Request the Report

Following the exam, check with the supervising attorney on whether to request a copy of the report. Once the report is requested by the examined party, Rule 35(b)(2) says all privilege regarding other examinations had by that party pertaining to the condition in question is waived. Normally this would not be a problem, but in some unusual cases it may be. You may be asked to review and summarize the report noting any significant findings or comments for the attorney.

ASSIGNMENT 8:25
Make a copy of the Notice to Client of Physical Examination (fig. 8:18) and place it in your system folder.

■ Request for Admission (Rule 36)

A request for admission is a document that sets out questions on specific facts, opinions, or the application of law to facts for the other party to admit or deny. Once admitted, the matter cannot be controverted. The purpose of admissions is to clarify what matters are no longer in dispute and, thus, unnecessary to prove at trial. This device is authorized by Rule 36 of the Federal Rules and parallel state rules. By narrowing the issues and related areas of proof, admissions can reduce the amount of time devoted to investigation and discovery, as well as the number of witnesses needed for trial. The need for the trial itself can be eliminated by clarifying the desirability of a settlement or possibility of a summary judgment. In short, it aims to achieve efficiency and frugality. The request for admission generally follows other discovery devices. It is not a request for information like a deposition or an interrogatory, but a confirmation of the truthfulness and accuracy of the previously discovered information.

The scope of the request is defined by Rule 26(b) and for all practical purposes is the same as that for the other discovery devices. The request may be directed to any other party in the lawsuit and its use is limited solely to the particular lawsuit. In addition to facts, opinions, and application of law to facts, the request may seek admission on the genuineness of documents, photographs, exhibits, and physical evidence (things).

Procedure

The steps in requesting admission include the following:

1. The request for admission must be served with attached documents on the responding party with copies to other parties.
2. The request may be served with the summons and complaint (served early to clear up obvious admissions and later to narrow the proof needed at trial).
3. The response must be made within thirty days (forty-five if request served with summons and complaint) or matters are deemed admitted unless extension of time is requested and granted.
4. The party responding may choose to seek a Rule 26(c) protective order on any particular matter. If so, other parties must be notified, the motion argued, and order entered.
5. The party responding may withdraw an answer and amend it with leave of the court. A timely withdrawal is granted if the original response is inaccurate and has not prejudiced the other party's case. If a party relied on the truthfulness of a response, and as a result did not pursue an expert opinion or evidence at that time available but now lost, the withdrawal can be denied.
6. The party requesting admission may accept the opponent's replies and objections or seek an order compelling either an answer or an expanded answer through an order on the sufficiency of the response [Rule 37(a)].
7. Motions for court-imposed sanctions may be made if a denial is ruled improper or the challenge to an objection improper. The court may then require the other party to pay for costs of having to bring or ar-

gue a motion or for having to prove the matter at trial when it should have been admitted (Rules 36 and 37).

Preparing the Request for Admission

Your role in working with requests for admissions can range from simply keeping track of what has been admitted and what has not, to a more intensive involvement, including the drafting of questions and answers for such requests. The following is a list of suggested steps in assisting the attorney with requests for admissions.

1. Review the pleadings, interrogatories, depositions, statements, and other relevant information if it is not fresh in your mind.
2. Prepare a list of admissions you need from the opponent. In the *Forrester* case it would be helpful if Mercury Parcel admitted that Mr. Hart was their employee and on duty at the time of the accident, or that Mr. Hart had exceeded the recommended number of shift hours just prior to the accident, if discovery had so revealed. Depending on the nature of the case, the list could become quite lengthy.
3. Seek suggestions and comments on the list from the attorney.
4. Draft a set of requests, keeping the following suggestions and techniques in mind.

   Check to see if court rules impose any limits on the number of admissions that may be requested. The Federal Rules have no such limitations.

   Locate a form for requests for admissions to learn format, types of questions, style, detail, and other matters that will help in visualizing the task.

   Set forth each point in a separate request or clearly delineated subsection. Combining points can be confusing and may lead to evasive or misleading answers.

   Write brief and concise questions that elicit yes or no or otherwise brief answers. Eliminate unnecessary qualifiers from the questions.

   Avoid use of incorporations by reference unless it is the only alternative.

   Number questions sequentially and from the end of one set of requests to the beginning of another.

   Research any request formats that raise questions of appropriateness.

   Request admissions that relate to facts, statements or opinions of fact, or of the application of law to fact. Include admissions regarding the genuineness of documents or other physical evidence including diagrams and exhibits [Rule 36(a)].

An example of request for admission of a fact:

   Please admit:
   That Mr. Hart was driving said vehicle on the date of said accident.

An example of a request eliciting an admission of an opinion:

> Please admit:
> That Defendant Hart was tired at the time of the accident.

An example of a request relating the application of law to fact:

> Please admit:
> That Defendant Hart was acting in the scope of his agency to Defendant Mercury Parcel at the time of the accident.

Agency and its scope are defined by law; therefore this question requires the application of legal principles on agency to the specific facts of the case.

An example of a request related to a document:

> Please admit:
> That exhibit 5, a form MSA dated June 12, 19___, signed by Mr. Hart:
> **a.** is an accurate copy of the original document,
> **b.** is kept in the ordinary course of Mercury Parcel Service's business,
> **c.** is a document used for drivers to report complaints about Mercury Parcel's vehicles.

This example demonstrates how a document should be identified and how a question on one item can be broken down to elicit admissions on each important subpoint. These points, if admitted, not only establish the copy of the document as a true copy, but also seek an admission that will lay the necessary foundation for the document to be admitted into evidence at trial. If admitted, these points will eliminate the need of a special witness to lay the foundation.

Usually a copy of the document is also included as an exhibit for review by the opponent; however, attaching the document is not necessary if the other party has the original document or a copy acquired through discovery. The description of the document must be sufficiently detailed to enable the other party to determine what document is addressed.

5. Have the request for admission reviewed, signed, and served on all parties.

Figure 8:19 is the form for a request for admissions based on Official Form 25 of the Federal Rules of Civil Procedure.

Figure 8:19   Federal Form 25. Request for Admission Under Rule 36

[Caption]

Plaintiff A.B. requests Defendant C.D. within _____ days after service of his request to make the following admissions for the purpose of this action only and subject to all pertinent objections to admissibility which may be interposed at the trial:

1. That each of the following documents, exhibited with this request, is genuine. (Here list and describe each document.)

2. That each of the following statements is true. (Here list the statements.)

Signed: _____
Attorney for Plaintiff

Address: _____

ASSIGNMENT 8:27
Create a Checklist for Drafting Requests for Admissions and place it and the form in figure 8:19 in your system folder.

ASSIGNMENT 8:28
Using the checklist you created, the form in figure 8:19, and examples of the types and forms of questions to ask, draft a set of requests for admissions from Ms. Forrester to Mercury Parcel that covers:

■ Caption
■ Introductory material, if any
■ Admissions on employment and agency of Hart
■ Admissions on speed and exhaustion
■ Admissions on forms that reflect irregular maintenance—as well as inaction on complaint about wheels locking when braking

Assume that you have previously discovered certain facts needed to justify the requests.

Responding to a Request for Admission

1. Fill out a deadline control slip entering the necessary response date figured on the basis of thirty or forty-five days.
2. Review the request thoroughly and the particular case file as needed.
3. Consult with the supervising attorney on how to respond to each request.
4. Draft the response keeping the following in mind:
   Answer each question unless told to do otherwise. Failure to answer means the item is admitted.
   Engross questions and then add the corresponding response for purposes of convenience and clarity.
   Answer with one of the following choices: admit, deny, qualify, object, move for extension of time, or move for a protective order.
   You must admit if you believe the matter is at least substantially true; however, if you have a reasonable doubt, such as when the **veracity** (truthfulness) of a witness is doubted, a denial is permissible.[48] Misspellings and other minor inaccuracies are not sufficient grounds for denial unless they go directly to the substance of the dispute.
   If an item is denied, you must state "denied," not "refuse to admit" or "not accurate."[49]
   You may admit in part and deny in part, but be clear.
   You may qualify a response and say, "Cannot admit or deny," as long as you give adequate reasons such as, "After reasonable inquiry, there is insufficient information to admit or deny" [Rule 37(c)].[50]
   If an objection is made, the reason must be stated.
   You may object if a specific question does not fall within the usual scope of discovery. The most common objections are irrelevancy and privilege. Other acceptable objections may include: vagueness, trade secrets, compound question, and others.[51] Typical invalid objections include: request presents issue for trial, disputable matter, factual opinion, mixed question of law and fact, other party already knows the answer, and requesting party has burden of proof.[52]
5. Have the draft reviewed, typed, signed, and served on all parties.

Figure 8:20 is the form for the Response to Defendant's Requests for Admissions.[53]

ASSIGNMENT 8:29
Create a Checklist on Responding to Requests for Admissions and place it in your system folder.

ASSIGNMENT 8:30
Photocopy the form for a Response to Defendant's Requests for Admissions and place it in your system folder.

ASSIGNMENT 8:31
Exchange the requests for admissions you drafted in assignment 8:28 with a classmate. Draft a response to their request. Assume the facts are such that you can admit, deny, admit in part and deny in part, object, and state you cannot admit or deny with reasons at least once each in the response.

Review of and Reply to Response

1. List all admissions, denials, objections, or improper responses.
2. Consult with the supervising attorney concerning the response and the list you made on it.
3. Draft motions to test the appropriateness of answers or objections as instructed.
4. Keep a record of all costs related to proving points denied by the other party for recovery if denial is shown to be improper.

Figure 8:20   Response to Defendant's Requests for Admissions

(Caption omitted)

The Plaintiff, _____, in answer to the Defendant's request for admissions served on the _____ day of _____, 19___, in the above stated matter, says:

1. Denied. However, Plaintiff admits that, apart from the fact that the premiums were waived by the terms of the policies on account of Plaintiff's then existing total and permanent disability, premiums would have become due as set out in that statement.

2. Admitted.

3. Admitted in part and denied in part. Plaintiff admits that the check referred to in Statement No. 2, when deposited by the Defendant, was not honored by the bank. Plaintiff denies that the check was not paid thereafter.

4. Plaintiff objects to Request No. 4, which request is as follows: _____. The objection is: _____. (State as ground for objection that the requested admission is privileged, irrelevant or otherwise improper.)

5. Plaintiff can neither admit nor deny Request No. 5, which request is as follows: _____. This is because Defendant refused to permit Plaintiff to review the document in question pursuant to a proper request for production, and without said production, Plaintiff does not have the knowledge to admit or deny the request.

Attorney for _____
(address)

Amending Responses

If a response is discovered to be untrue because of inaccuracies or change in facts, you may be requested to draft a motion for a court order to withdraw the answer and to submit an amended response [Rule 36(b)]. The paralegal on the other side may have to draft a response to the motion demonstrating that the client would be prejudiced by the withdrawal. A party may be prejudiced, for example, if he or she had stopped discovery on an issue or failed to seek witnesses because of reliance on the admission.

■ The Freedom of Information Act

Definition and Purpose

In 1976, the Freedom of Information Act, 5 U.S.C. § 552 (FOIA) was passed to provide the general public access to the records of many government agencies. The public policy underlying the law is that a more informed public will enhance the accountability and performance of government agencies and officials. Such openness is deemed desirable and consistent with our democratic form of government. Several states have passed similar laws.

Unlike the other devices mentioned in this chapter, the FOIA was not created as a discovery device for purposes of litigation. Its intent is to benefit the public as a whole and not specific litigants or private interests. All the same, it can be an important tool in the discovery or investigative process. A wealth of information can be obtained that might be helpful in a suit against a particular government agency or in a suit against a private party. Both U.S. and state agencies store a wide range of information that would otherwise be unavailable. The Consumer Products Safety Commission, for example, might be able to provide information on the safety record of the make of van involved in Ms. Forrester's accident, on the type of extension cord used by the campground in Case II, or on the three-wheeled all-terrain vehicle that led to the death of Sean Coleman in Case III.

Use of the FOIA offers some advantages over most other discovery devices:

1. It is not necessary to file an action or order to gain access to the information. In the examples just given, a request for information about faulty products could be submitted well before the filing of the action, and could be useful in determining whether the manufacturer of the product in question should be joined as one of the defendants in the case.
2. Because the law is not oriented toward litigation, the Rule 26(b) prerequisite of relevancy does not apply. Consequently, one can go on "fishing expeditions" regardless of relevancy in the hope of turning up something useful.
3. Access is available to anyone with a bona fide request.
4. The request is not restricted to information from a party as is true of most discovery devices; therefore, the range of information that can be obtained is greater.[54]

Procedure and Limits

The requesting party invokes the FOIA by submitting a request to the pertinent agency through that agency's designated information officer. The request must demonstrate that the information requested is in the records of an agency covered by the act. Specific exemptions to the disclosure requirement are listed in section 552(b) of the act:

- Properly classified national defense or foreign policy documents
- Internal personnel rules and practices
- Material specifically exempted from disclosure by statute
- Trade secrets and commercial or financial information obtained from a person which are of a privileged or confidential nature
- Inter- and intra-agency communication (letters and memos) otherwise not available through discovery in actions against an agency
- Personnel, medical, and similar files of a private nature
- Law enforcement records and information if disclosure would impede investigation, violate personal privacy, or permit circumvention of the law
- Reports related to the regulation or supervision of financial institutions
- Geological and geophysical information on oil and natural gas wells

Once the request is submitted, the agency must indicate within ten days whether it will comply or deny the request [§ 552(a)(6)(A)(i)]. That decision may be appealed, and if so, a determination must be made within twenty days [§ 552(a)(6)(A)(ii)]. If the agency upholds the decision to withhold the information, the administrative remedies are exhausted and relief must be sought in federal district court.

A reasonable fee for producing the information will be charged. The agency may waive the fee, however, if release of the information is likely to contribute significantly to public understanding of the operation or activities of government and is not primarily in the commercial interest of the requester [5 U.S.C. § 552(a)(4)(A)(iii)].

The Role of the Paralegal

Your task as paralegal regarding a request for information under the FOIA will be to draft the request. Figure 8:21 is a form that can be used as a guide when drafting the document.[55]

You may also be called on to research the likely availability of particular information and whether it is accessible under the act. Knowing the act exists and that the procedure is relatively simple should help you recognize opportunities to utilize this unique means of discovery and investigation. An excellent resource on making FOIA requests is a Bureau of National Af-fairs pamphlet entitled "The Freedom of Information Act: Business Uses."

ASSIGNMENT 8:32
Draft a Procedural Checklist for Making a Request Pursuant to the Freedom of Information Act and place it in your system folder with the sample request.

Figure 8:21   Freedom of Information Act (FOIA) Sample Request Letter

Agency Head or FOIA Officer
Title
Name of Agency
Address of Agency
City, State, zip

Re: Freedom of Information Act
Request.

Dear _____:

   Under the provisions of the Freedom of Information Act, 5 U.S.C. 552, I am requesting access to [*identify the records as clearly and specifically as possible*].

   If there are any fees for searching for, or copying, the records I have requested, please inform me before you fill the request. [*Or:* * * * please supply the records without informing me if the fees do not exceed $_____]

[*Optional*]

I am requesting this information [*state the reason for your request if you think it will assist you in obtaining the information.*]

[*Optional*]

As you know, the act permits you to reduce or waive fees when the release of the information is considered as "primarily benefiting the public". I believe that this request fits that category and I therefore ask that you waive any fees.

   If all or any part of this request is denied, please cite the specific exemption(s) which you think justifies your refusal to release the information, and inform me of the appeal procedures available to me under the law.

   I would appreciate your handling this request as quickly as possible, and I look forward to hearing from you within 10 days, as the law stipulates.

Sincerely, _____

_____
[*Signature*]
[*Name*]
[*Address*]
[*City, State, zip*]

■ Summary

Your work often focuses on the stage of litigation called discovery. This is the formal process of investigation that invokes the cooperation of all parties in producing and exchanging information so that facts can be determined, evidence revealed, and issues narrowed before the matter goes to trial.

   The scope of discovery is broadly defined in Rule 26(b) of the Federal Rules and corresponding state rules. Exchange is allowed as long as what is being sought is evidence pertinent to the action or material believed to lead to such evidence. Only requests that are unreasonable, unnecessary, or seek privileged information or information that is the attorney's work product may be excluded [Rule 26(b)(3)]. In such cases protective orders may be sought under Rule 26(c) and corresponding state rules. If a party refuses to respond to a discovery request, the party may be compelled to do so by the court under Rule 37. Sanctions for refusing to comply vary, but can include not being able to use the evidence wrongfully protected and having to pay costs to the other party for trouble and expense due to the refusal. Refusal to cooperate may also create some serious ethical breaches under most state codes of professional conduct.

The tools employed for discovery vary depending on the magnitude of the case and the financial strength of the client. The available tools include interrogatories; depositions; requests to produce and inspect documents, land, and other things; requests for physical and mental examination; request for admission; and use of the Freedom of Information Act.

You must be adept at employing and responding to each of these tools to gain the maximum benefit for your client within the scope, limits, and ethical standards applied to discovery. Discovery is an area quite suitable for the talents of the paralegal. When exercised knowledgeably, these discovery talents are extremely valuable to the law firm, the client, and you.

Study Guide

1. Define the term *discovery* and describe its purposes in the context of litigation practice.
2. List and define the six discovery devices set out in the Federal Rules of Civil Procedure.
3. What is the scope of discovery as defined by Federal Rule 26(b) and parallel state rules?
4. Has your state adopted the Federal Rules of discovery? If so, cite the statute or rule numbers.
5. What are the specific limits on discovery?
6. Under what circumstances are the facts known and opinions held by experts discoverable?
7. Under Rule 37, when can a party seek the aid of the court to compel discovery?
8. What sanctions can be imposed on a party by the court for failure to cooperate and adequately comply with a discovery request, or for failure to comply with a court order compelling discovery?
9. What is the procedure for compelling discovery and the role of the paralegal?
10. What does the obligation to update discovery consist of? Can you play a key role here? Explain.
11. What are the important ethical rules that apply to discovery? What is their significance?
12. What are interrogatories, their purpose and advantages? What federal and state rules govern interrogatories?
13. What are the basic procedures that must be followed when utilizing interrogatories?
14. What are the specific steps in planning a set of interrogatories?
15. What kinds of information lend themselves to exploration through interrogatories?

16. What are the typical divisions of and types of questions that make up a set of interrogatories? Explain their usefulness.
17. Be able to draft a set of interrogatories or any specific portion thereof.
18. What are the basic reasons discovery requests are objectionable under Rule 26(b)(1)? Explain each objection.
19. What are the steps to be followed in preparing answers to interrogatories?
20. What should you do on receipt of the opponent's answers to a set of interrogatories?
21. What is a deposition? What is the purpose of a deposition?
22. Is there anything unique about the scope of depositions?
23. How many kinds of depositions are there, and what are their unique functions?
24. What is the procedure for setting up and conducting a deposition?
25. What is your role in the deposition process?
26. How do you obtain a subpoena for a deponent? What is the appropriate clerk? What should be included on the subpoena?
27. When are witness and mileage fees required under Rule 45?
28. What should you do to plan and draft an outline for taking a deposition?
29. What should be included in a witness file for the attorney?
30. Why is it important to prepare friendly witnesses or clients for deposition testimony?
31. What are some of the most significant things a witness can be told in preparing for the deposition?
32. What are significant ethical and other considerations that you need to be aware of in working with witnesses?
33. What is your most important role at the deposition? Why?
34. Why should the deponent's signature on the certified copy of the deposition not be waived in most instances?
35. What should you check for on receipt of the record of the deposition from the court reporter?
36. What do you look for when reviewing a deposition?
37. Be able to draft an outline for the attorney for conducting a deposition.
38. What is the definition, purpose, and scope of the request for production of documents and things?
39. What are the procedural steps and time requirements involved in the production of documents?
40. How do you determine what documents and things should be requested for a production of documents and things?
41. Know the requirements and techniques for drafting a Request for Production, Inspection, and Copying of Documents and its response.
42. What is the purpose of a Rule 35 mental or physical exam? What nonparties may be reached through this rule, and what showing is needed for such a request to be granted?
43. What are the procedures and tasks you perform in working with requests for compulsory medical examination?
44. What is the definition, purpose, and scope of Rule 36 requests for admissions?

45. What are the steps in the procedure for requesting admissions and responding to them?
46. Describe in detail your role regarding requests for admissions.
47. Be able to draft a request for admissions and its response.
48. What is the Freedom of Information Act? Why is it potentially useful to you as a litigation paralegal?
49. What materials are excepted from the FOIA?
50. What must be demonstrated to be granted a FOIA request, and what procedure must be followed to have such a request approved?

Endnotes

1. SIGNEY, LITIGATION PARALEGAL 5-82–83, § 593(1989).
2. WEST'S FEDERAL FORMS §§ 3559, v. 3A, with permission of West Publishing Company.
3. Id., § 3560, with permission of West Publishing Company.
4. Id., §3721.5, with permission of West Publishing Company.
5. MODEL RULES OF PROFESSIONAL CONDUCT Rule 3.4 (Model Code Comparisons 1983).
6. Id., Rule 1.6.
7. Id., Comments to Rule 1.6.
8. HAYDOCK & HERR, DISCOVERY: THEORY, PRACTICE, AND PROCEDURES 187–89 (1983) [hereinafter cited as HAYDOCK].
9. Adapted from WEST'S FEDERAL FORMS, § 3512, v. 3A, with permission of West Publishing Company.
10. Id., adapted from § 3513.10, with permission of West Publishing Company.
11. Id., with permission of West Publishing Company.
12. THE NATIONAL ASSOCIATION OF LEGAL ASSISTANTS, MANUAL FOR LEGAL ASSISTANTS 383–85 (1979) [hereinafter cited as NALA MANUAL].
13. BRUNO, PARALEGAL'S LITIGATION HANDBOOK 212 (1980) [hereinafter cited as BRUNO].
14. HAYDOCK, 205–7.
15. STATSKY, TORTS: PERSONAL INJURY LITIGATION 218 (1982).
16. Id.
17. Id.
18. INSTITUTE FOR PARALEGAL TRAINING, INTRODUCTION TO CIVIL LITGATION 229 (1977) [hereinafter cited as INSTITUTE].
19. Adapted from Smith, *Form Interrogatories in Personal Injury Actions*, 32 INSURANCE COUNSEL JOURNAL 453, 458ff. (July 1965). Reprinted from Insurance Counsel Journal (now Defense Counsel Journal). Copyright 1965, International Association of Insurance Counsel, now International Association of Defense Counsel.
20. HAYDOCK, 208 [citing Renshaw v. Ravert, 82 F.R.D. 361, 362 (E.D.Pa.1979); Williams v. Krieger, 61 F.R.D. 142, 145 (S.D.N.Y.1973); and Bohlie v. Brass Rail, Inc., 20 F.R.D. 224 (S.D.N.Y.1957)].
21. Id., 210.
22. Id., 210–11.
23. Id., 212.
24. NALA MANUAL, 377.
25. HAYDOCK, 213.
26. Id.
27. Adapted from HAYDOCK, 217–18.
28. NALA MANUAL, 387.
29. MORRILL, TRIAL DIPLOMACY 181 (2d ed. 1972).

30. West's Federal Forms § 334.5, v. 3A, with permission of West Publishing Company.
31. NALA Manual, 393.
32. West's Federal Forms § 4011.5, v. 3A, with permission of West Publishing Company.
33. Memo from J. Schuller to J. McCord (March, 1986).
34. Selected from Morrill, Trial Diplomacy, Selected Text 200–11 (2d ed. 1972) ("Deposition Checklist Plaintiff—Automobile"), with permission of the author, Alan E. Morrill.
35. NALA Manual, 391, with permission of West Publishing Company.
36. Institute, 237.
37. West's Federal Forms, § 3551, v. 3A, with permission of West Publishing Company.
38. Underwood, A Guide to Federal Discovery Rules 222 (2d ed. 1985) [hereinafter cited as Underwood].
39. Id.
40. Bruno, 219.
41. West's Federal Forms, § 3552, v. 3A, with permission of West Publishing Company.
42. Id., § 3557, with permission of West Publishing Company.
43. Id., § 3559, with permission of West Publishing Company.
44. Id., § 3560, with permission of West Publishing Company.
45. Several suggestions in the last two paragraphs are from a memo from J. Burton to J. McCord (March 27, 1986) and from the NALA Manual, 416.
46. West's Federal Forms, § 3601, v. 3A, with permission of West Publishing Company.
47. *Boulder Colorado Judge Rules to Allow Paralegals to Attend R. 35 Examinations*, NFPA Alert (July 1989).
48. Haydock, 277.
49. Id.
50. Id., 279.
51. Id., 281.
52. Id., 282.
53. Adapted from Forms § 3632 and §3635, West's Federal Forms, v. 3A, with permission of West Publishing Company.
54. Underwood, 315–23.
55. West's Legal Forms, § 20.2, v. 27 (1986), with permission of West Publishing Company.

9

Discovery Analysis and Document Control

■ Introduction
■ Producing Documents
■ Reviewing and Interpreting Documents: Medical Records
■ Digesting Depositions and Other Documents
■ Organizing Files

■ Introduction

Paralegal skills related to discovery go beyond knowing the various discovery devices and the techniques related to effective drafting. You must also know how to prepare documents for production; read complex, technical material such as medical and financial reports; digest and summarize large amounts of information; and organize materials so specific information can be retrieved quickly. Such skills are essential for proper management of litigation and can provide invaluable assistance to the attorney. Learn them well, since these are the skills that you will be using much of your time as a paralegal.

■ Producing Documents

Mr. White has asked that you oversee the production of a sizable number of documents pursuant to a request for production submitted by the adverse party in one of our cases. The following section will suggest to you a variety of techniques and steps to follow in performing this task.

The number of documents to be screened and produced in compliance with a request for production may range from a few in a simple personal injury case to hundreds of thousands in a complex antitrust or other commercial case. The purpose of production is to provide the opponent an opportunity to review documents pertinent to the case to determine if and how the documents support the facts to be alleged at trial. From the point of view of the person producing the documents, the more practical objectives are to locate and produce documents thoroughly, accurately, and efficiently. In order to do this effectively, the documents must be well organized and easy to retrieve. The entire process should interfere as little as possible with the daily business needs of the client or the client's employees.

Procedure for Producing Documents

Whether the task involves relatively few or volumes of documents, thorough preparation is necessary.[1] To do otherwise invites delays, errors, inefficiency, and wasted hours of retracking and paper shuffling. Failure to plan can result in embarrassing losses of valuable documents, discovery sanctions, or the loss of the client's case for want of one piece of paper at a crucial moment at trial.

The first step is to review the case and carefully read the opponent's production request. As you read the request, note the items requested, possible objections, privileged information, likely location of the items, and, if possible, the number of documents involved.

Estimate what materials are needed for production: file labels, Post-it notes, expandable files, storage boxes, three-ring binders, prepunched photocopying paper. Also estimate needed personnel, equipment, and space. Note whether any special expertise may be needed to review highly technical or arcane documents, and whether potential resources or assistance such as personnel and storage space can be provided by the client. Consider what method for locating, controlling, and retrieving the documents best suits the circumstances. This method is already established in most offices. If so, other personnel and former files can be consulted for assistance in planning and estimating. For the paralegal who is the first on the block to confront such an assignment, suggestions from paralegals in other offices and from books on law office management and document control can be helpful.

Discuss these matters with the attorney who should provide detailed guidance on the issues in the case and what to watch for regarding privilege, work product, and other sensitive material. Decisions on how to allocate resources, the specific control method to use, whether the documents should be numbered, and so on, are made by the attorney. A decision may need to be made on whether the production process will be computerized or strictly manual. The more voluminous the project, the greater the need for a computer to provide assistance in locating documents. The plan should also set out the critical classification and topics into which the documents will be sorted with a uniform system of codes or abbreviations for designating those classifications.

Locate Documents

The difficulty in locating documents varies with the particular case. Locating the medical records on Ms. Forrester's injuries and treatment and her employment records is relatively easy. Locating all the records pertaining to the manufacture, maintenance, and operation of the van driven by Mr. Hart could be more difficult. Much more difficult is locating all pertinent documents generated by a large multinational corporation with numerous subsidiaries and branch offices.

The location of most documents and their likely custodian is usually apparent. When it is not, use your imagination to generate possible sources and alternatives. Frequently, the client is the most helpful. Company division heads should know where most documents are stored, and if not, should be able to provide leads to someone who will know. In some cases it is important to become aware of the "chain of command" to locate sources for documents. Prepare a list of probable sources that contains the name of the custodian, the department or office, and the subject matter and types of documents needed. If nothing is found at a source, indicate such on the form.

Notify office supervisors of the reason for the search and the subject matter and types of documents needed. If practical, arrange a meeting with the supervisor or an appointed liaison to create an atmosphere of cooperation. Be sensitive to the need for keeping disruption of the office routine to a minimum. In some instances, the office personnel can do a preliminary search, but the utilization of trained paralegals working closely with the custodian of the documents is most effective.[2]

Pull Files and Documents

In coordination with each custodian or liaison, and carefully following the guidelines set up by the attorney, pull the files or individual documents likely to contain the responsive information. As each relevant file is pulled, you must do the following:

- Pull the file and fill out a file checkout card or leave a temporary replacement sheet or file cover indicating by whom the file has been pulled, for what case, its next location (office or room number), and the date. When in doubt whether to pull a file, the best practice is to pull it.
- Check with the custodian to see if the file is so critical to daily operations of the office that an immediate copy of the file or of certain documents needs to be made for the convenience of the office. If so, have the document or file photocopied. Tape a legend reading: "Copy: original in case file _____ vs. _____" to the photocopy machine so it will appear on each copy. This provides notice that the new file is a copy and indicates where the original can be located.[3]
- Label each file or document as it is pulled to indicate its place in the case file. For example, the first file pulled for the *Forrester* case could be labeled F-1 indicating that it is now in the first file folder of the *Forrester* case.
- Prepare a log of each file pulled. The log should contain at a minimum the source of the file, a description of the file (exact title is best), the new working file number (F-1, F-2) assigned to it, and the custodian. The log might also contain other information as indicated in figure 9:1, which shows an original source log.
- The original source log provides immediate information on the source of the document or file and is invaluable when the files or documents are returned.
- If any files cannot be found, this should be noted on the log, and a memo so indicating should be addressed to the case file and attached to the log. This protects you from accusations of sloppy work and the firm from possible sanctions from the court for failure to comply with a discovery order.

Figure 9:1 Document Production Original Source Log

New File No.	Description	Source
F-1	maint. form 20's 19—	Merc. Parcel Rm 108 drawer 31 Ralph Johnson
F-2	maint. form 20's 19—	Merc. Parcel Rm 108 Dr. 31 R. Johnson
F-3	Driver Hour Logs 19—	Merc. Parcel Rm 108 Dr. 81 Betty Robinson

- Log books, journals, or other unique items should be specially noted to indicate their unique nature for easier identification in the future.
- Remove the pulled files and documents to a separate office or screening room with limited access. This ensures control over the documents and should greatly enhance the efficiency of additional screening. If there are a large number of documents, the files should be placed into file boxes and labeled—for example, Box 1 files F-1 to F-50, Box 2 files F-51 to F-100, and so forth.
- As a courtesy, inform the custodian what documents have been removed.

Screen Pulled Files and Documents

This next stage lies at the very heart of good document control and production. It involves the detailed and sometimes laborious job of reviewing each piece of paper for its relevancy to the request and for any privileged or sensitive material. The objectives and guidelines for this step of the document production process should be specific.

The objectives of this step normally include the following:

- To identify documents that are responsive to each particular request for production
- To number those documents, if so directed, for easy identification and retrieval
- To identify documents that are privileged or sensitive to avoid disclosure of that information
- To classify documents for rapid identification, retrieval, and return
- To prepare documents for copying
- To have documents readied for review by the attorney

The tasks in this procedure involve the following. Aim to pass through all documents once and to record all necessary information at that time. If several people are reviewing, logs should be maintained by each person to show who has reviewed what.

Place the files and documents on their sides in boxes. As each relevant document is identified, the document should not be removed from the file but placed in an upright position so it protrudes from the file.[4] See figure 9:2.

Figure 9:2   Place Documents in an Upright Position

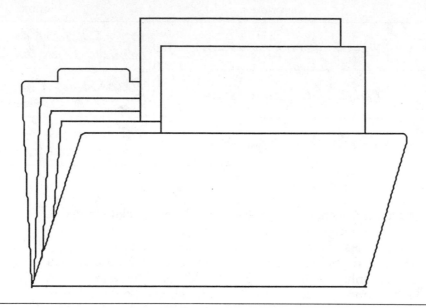

Do the following as each document is turned up. Number each document page in sequential order as the pages are turned up. Since these are the original documents and need to be preserved in their original state, a decision must be made by the attorney if numbering and other notations should be penciled on the document or a Post-it label used on which to record the necessary information. If the Post-it labels are the type that reliably stay on and can be removed without damaging the original document, this is probably the best method. Some firms number the documents directly; others do not. Numbering at this stage, however, can save much time later.

Indicate the number on each document, the set and paragraph of the production request to which it is responsive, the numbered source file in which it belongs (F-1, F-2), how many copies of the document are needed, and what cross files the copies of the document should go to. The files normally kept include three files of original documents: one as numbered, one of privileged and other undiscoverable documents, and one of unresponsive documents. Copies of all the files and documents are made to be returned to the original custodian. Additional copies of the numbered documents go into cross files: chronological files and files sorted by production request set and paragraph. Some firms also want copies of the documents sorted into files by issue and by person. Systems may become even more detailed than this.

Indicate whether the document is privileged or contains work product or other sensitive material. In such cases a colored cover sheet should be placed in front of the document so it can be readily identified and pulled when necessary.

Index the documents. The number of indices maintained will depend on what the supervising attorney has requested. A master index should record the number of the document, subject matter on the document, and its nature (memo, letter, tax return, phone log, etc.), the new file number, the date of the document, the author of the document, the recipient of the document, whether the document is privileged or otherwise undiscoverable, the set and item of the production request that it responds to, and eventually whether the document was produced to the adversary. If other files, such as personality files, are requested, information such as names of persons mentioned or receiving carbon copies of the document might be included. This master index or collection of file cards can then be used to create other indices.

A Standardized Numbering System

A standardized or uniform numbering system will prove most efficient and can be adapted to most cases in the office. Many attorneys set up a numbering system as it occurs to them in a particular case, resulting in confusion for others not privy to its logic. Further, such haphazard systems often prove inadequate as the case expands, or result in telltale gaps in the numbering system as privileged or attorney work product documents are removed. The method used by many law firms is the decimal system. The numbers become a shorthand description of the document, and the system can be used for all appropriate cases. Here is how the system works.[5]

First, an estimate of the number of documents involved must be made. The number of documents equals the degree of digits needed for numbering. Ninety-nine (99) or fewer documents is a second-degree case, 100–999 documents equals a third-degree case, 100,000 documents equals a sixth-degree case, and so forth. The number of digits needed for numbering is based on the formula: degree + 3 = digits needed. Therefore, a third-degree case is simply calculated: degree = 3 + 3 = 6 digits. A sixth-degree case calculates: 6 + 3 = 9 digits (xxx,xxx,xxx).

The first digit refers to the first assigned category or grouping. In many firms this first grouping is the *role* the document will play in the proof process according to the elements of the case and related factors. A sample group one in a negligence case might appear as follows:

Group I, Role in Case

1. Jurisdiction (to establish or challenge)
2. Parties (to identify)
3. Existence of duty
4. Breach
5. Causal connection to damage/injury
6. Damages
7. Defenses
8. Others

If the first document to be numbered for production (or the first to be received in response to a request for production) pertains to the existence of a duty, the very first digit will be numbered 3xx,xxx,xxx. In other words, anyone familiar with the categories will know at a glance the expected role the document will play in the case. The other digits, as you will see, provide similar information at a glance. This information will be based on categories carefully planned by the attorney. The categories will generally be the same for all negligence cases or all products liability cases. The attorney-paralegal team, however, can alter these categories as the unique nature of a case dictates.

A document might play several roles. In that case, number it for its major role, but also number a reference insert page according to the secondary role, which refers the searcher back to the original numbered document. When the documents are sorted by categories, this will prevent a document with dual purposes from being overlooked and may make an extra copy of a lengthy document unnecessary.

The second digit may be designated to show the *source* of the document. Group two, therefore, might appear as follows:

Group II, Source of Document

1. Ms. Forrester
2. Dr. Harris
3. Mr. Hart
4. Mercury Parcel Service
5. Others

If the first document came from Ms. Forrester, the numbered document would appear as 31x,xxx,xxx. Other groupings for remaining digits could include the *type* of document (correspondence, memo, others), *production mode* (how produced—with pleadings, pursuant to a request for production, subpoena duces tecum, etc.), *potential for evidentiary exclusion* (admissible, privilege, hearsay, etc.), and any other grouping predetermined by the attorney.

The order in which the document was pulled or received can be indicated by using the right-hand digits in the number. If your first document is numbered by all its categories and appears at 318,720,001, it would be recorded on the general index as the first document. The next document (whatever its categories would indicate) would end in xxx,xxx,xx2 and would be the second document entered into the general index. If there are numerous groupings, digits may have to be added to accommodate the sequential numbering. If the document is multipaged, pages are indicated simply by inserting a decimal and the page number. The ninth page of your first document would be numbered 318,720,001.9. This uniform decimal system is compatible with computer use.

Have the Attorney Review the Documents

The documents should be reviewed by the attorney to verify that the documents are responsive to the production requests, that all privileged and other undiscoverable documents have been identified, that the documents have been kept in original format (stapled, bound, paper-clipped), and that the necessary copies will be prepared.

Extract Privileged Documents

Each of the privileged or sensitive documents should be pulled from the original file and placed in a separate folder. The colored privileged document sheet should be pulled with it. This folder should be placed in a locked facility. A sheet of paper with the document's number on it should be substituted in the original file.

Have Documents Copied

The person so assigned makes copies following your indication of how many copies of each document are needed. Usually four or five are necessary: one to replace the originals in the files of origin, one to duplicate the original file, one for a chronological file, one for each item of the response request, and any other need such as a personality or issue file. The copier substitutes a sheet in the original file indicating what documents are being copied and by whom. The copies should contain a legend indicating that they are a copy of the original and where the original can be found, as described previously. The copies should be in the same format, paper-clipped, stapled, and so on, as the original. Unless it is impractical, an entire document should be copied even if only one page of the document is responsive. All oversized, reduced, and otherwise nonreproducible or altered documents should be noted. Any bad copies should be destroyed. The copies should then be sorted into expandable file folders or boxes as initially indicated on the original. The originals should be placed in an original document file in numerical order as they were identified. A copy of the originals should be reinserted in the files of origin, and they may be returned to their custodians and refiled. A letter of return to the custodian should be drafted and the copy placed in the case file. The custodian should be directed to keep the files in their original state. It is wise to request a receipt. The process described thus far is most pertinent to large cases. Some of these techniques may work for smaller cases as well. If a case is small, it may be adequate just to set up a three-ring binder and place the copied documents into the needed categories or according to the sets of the discovery requests with a simple table of contents at the front.

Prepare Documents for Examination

A copy of the documents should be arranged and noted according to the set and item of the request they pertain to. Some firms prefer to renumber the documents at this time. (This is not necessary with the decimal numbering system.) Others wait for the examination and number only those documents selected by the opponent. Either way, an index showing the original number of the document, the item to which it responds, that it was produced, and if it was selected by the adversary should be kept. Be sure to keep a copy of all documents produced to the opponent.

Retrieve the Documents

During the case it may become necessary to retrieve a particular document or several documents. This could be necessary to prepare for a deposition, to find documents for an expert to review, to prepare for the examination of a witness, or to make a critical rebuttal point at trial. Using the indices that have been prepared, you can retrieve the pertinent documents efficiently with one or more of the following: the date of the document, the name of the author or recipient, the number of the document, the issue that it pertains to, and so on. A checkout system for all documents should be carefully maintained.

Return the Documents and Retain Indices

At the close of the case, usually after all appeals have been exhausted, the original documents may be returned to their original locations. The return of each document or identifiable group of documents should be logged and receipted.[6] Any of the client's original documents filed with the court or in the possession of the other parties should be retrieved and returned. All copies should then be shredded or burned.[7] All the indices, return letters, and receipts should be kept in the case file.

If your task is to review the documents sent by the opponent in response to a request for production submitted by your firm, a similar system of selecting and organizing can be used.

ASSIGNMENT 9:1
Draft a thorough Checklist for Document Production and place it in your system folder.

Document Production and Computers

Document control in discovery cases can become costly and cumbersome, and retrieval of those documents may be painfully slow in especially complex and voluminous cases. The method many offices have chosen to resolve this problem is **automated litigation support**—the application of the computer to litigation tasks. A few years ago it was reserved for only the most complex and costly cases. Today, however, the relatively inexpensive computer and corresponding document-control software make its application to a variety of cases both practical and efficient. Computers are most helpful in cases involving hundreds of thousands of documents, but cases with 1,000 or even fewer documents may also lend themselves to automated litigation support.

You need to find one document among thousands. What methods can you use?

Litigation paralegals are increasingly assigned to assist in computerized document-control cases, and they need to have a basic understanding of the task. Application of the computer does not relieve the paralegal of the tasks of finding, analyzing, and classifying documents. In fact, computerizing documents adds work at that stage of the process. Work savings for the paralegal is at the retrieval stage, when a single or an entire group of documents can be retrieved instantly.

Necessary Knowledge and Skill

The key to the rapid retrieval provided by automation is the use of a classification system that relies on a uniform set of words that logically describe the classes of documents and the data most important to the case. Once the documents are analyzed, classified, and entered into the computer according to that uniform word system, a variety of document sortings and retrievals can be achieved by using carefully constructed searches (queries) based on logical use of the uniform word system.

You do not need to know the technical components of the computer, how it works, or how to program, but need the ability to think logically and categorically. Logical use of language to identify classifications and to formulate effective retrieval queries determines success in automated document control.

Typing skills are valuable for working the computer keyboard in the entry and retrieval of data.

Initial Decision

Many law firms already have a computerized system in place by the time the new paralegal arrives on the scene. Usually, the system has been purchased to handle a variety of functions such as docket control, billing, form and brief storage, storage of client files, and other areas beyond discovery document control. Even if the office is computerized, every new case requires document-control evaluation. The supervising attorney must determine the nature of the case and the need for automated litigation support.

The use of a computerized system depends on many factors: how technical and complex the case will be, how many parties are involved, how many documents are likely to be reviewed and produced, whether the system is capable of handling the load, whether it would be more cost effective to use the client's system or hire a private vendor, what personnel would be needed, and whether the case could be handled just as well manually. Observing the evaluation process will help you develop the knowledge to assist in future decisions. If automated litigation support is being considered for the first time in this office, advice of vendors or a consultant could help you start off on a realistic basis. Some state bar associations offer consulting services in law office management and automated litigation support.

Things to Look For in System and Software

Most document production cases can be handled with a 20-megabyte memory; a 40-megabyte system is a little more expensive but offers storage for numerous cases. A *bit* is one letter or character, a *byte* is 8 bits, a *kilobyte* is 1,000 bytes, and a *megabyte* is 1,000 kilobytes or, if my math is correct, 8 million characters. The speed with which a system works is called a *baud*. The higher the baud, the faster information is transmitted from the memory disk to the screen.

A hard drive is convenient and provides rapid retrieval, but can crash, erasing all stored information. Be sure to keep copies of your documents on floppy disks or some other backup system.

Selection of software is equally important. Some firms have adapted their Word Perfect or Microsoft Word word processing software to do document control. Other firms have purchased software specifically designed for document control and related litigation management. Some of this software is expensive but effective. Some things to look for in document control software include:[8]

1. Full text capability
2. Multiple-entry fields for indexing (i.e., index all four authors in document as opposed to just the first)
3. Report writer (take data and produce attractive report)
4. Multivariable searches (i.e., all letters from D. Smith or S. Clay containing words "safety violations" for years 1988, 1989, 1990, and 1991)
5. Multivariable sorts (i.e., by author alphabetically, then by topic and author alphabetically, and then by date of writing)
6. Proximity searches (i.e., retrieving all documents within which the word "mail" or "postal" occurs within five words of "fraud")
7. *Boolean* search language (and, or, not) and root word searches (i.e., all words with root "safe")
8. On-line, on-screen, and phone line help
9. Accuracy verification of data as entered
10. Easy to learn/user friendly
11. Good user's manual, well indexed
12. Both off-line and on-line (prompt questions) data entry
13. Simultaneous multiuser (networking)
14. Simultaneous tasking (more than one task at a time)
15. Easily changed fields (no entire reformatting or reindexing of data)
16. Field and document size limits
17. Flexible security features (passwords for searching but not editing)
18. Vendor support (training and telephone support)[9]
19. Easy integration of graphics, spread sheets, and word processing
20. Search and summarize depositions on-line
21. Print lists of documents as well as full text
22. High speed
23. Utilization of all software functions by telecommunications

The Legal Technology Advisory Council (LTAC) of the American Bar Association tests lawyer software and can provide assistance in choosing a program. Some of the software companies with litigation support programs with varying features are listed next.[10]

Alexium Document Services, Inc.
2633 Eastlake Avenue, East
Seattle, WA 98102

Amicus
Baron Data
17 Marina Boulevard
San Leandro, CA 94577

Aspen Systems Corporation
1600 Research Boulevard
Rockville, MD 20850

Barrister Information Systems
45 Oak Street
Buffalo, NY 14203

Barrister Micro Systems Corporation
2000 14th Street, North
Arlington, VA 22201

Data Retrieval Corporation
8989 North Deerwood Drive
Milwaukee, WI 53223

Datapoint
9725 Datapoint Drive
San Antonio, TX 78284

DSL
One Second Street
San Francisco, CA 94105

Feld Technologies, Inc.
875 Main Street, 4th Floor
Cambridge, MA 02139

General Data Systems, Ltd.
1520 Locust Street
Philadelphia, PA 19102

Global Link Corporation
30 Tera Lane
P.O. Box 723
Pine Brook, NJ 07058

Inmagic
Inmagic, Inc.
238 Broadway
Cambridge, MA 02139

Innovative Software, Inc.
9875 Widmer Road
Lenexa, KS 66215

Lawyer's Software, Inc.
P.O. Box 48194
Seattle, WA 98148-0194

Litigation Manager II
The Institute for Paralegal Training
1926 Arch Street
Philadelphia, PA 19103

Litigation Support Program
Datalaw Company
6341 South Troy Circle, Suite E
Inglewood, CO 80111

Micro Text
Document Automation Corporation
84 West Park Place
Stamford, CT 06901

Summation
Sihero Systems
155 Sansom Street, Suite 620
San Francisco, CA 94104

ZyINDEX ZyLAB Corporation
233 East Erie Street
Chicago, IL 60611

Planning the System

Once the choice to use a computer is made, a system must be developed. The system requires attention to the issues in the case in order to classify the categories of information to be recorded. Group documents into categories by type, author, recipient, date, and so on; determine what uniform language, key words, or coding symbols should be used for those categories; what coding forms are needed; and what timetables are sought. This stage of document control is significant regardless of automation, but if automation is used, it will require extensive planning, guidance, and coordination with all persons creating and utilizing the system. The grouping and decimal numbering system described previously works well in its computer application.

Locating and Screening Documents

Once the system and its terminology are established, the same process of locating and screening documents described previously must be completed.

Entry of the Data

Documents are entered in two basic formats: indexing systems and full text systems. Indexing systems recreate the master index and all the subindices recorded for each document. The system can be searched and sorted according to key words, document number, author, and so on. Some indexing systems contain brief abstracts of the key documents.

In some cases attorneys like entire documents entered into the computer. This entry is referred to as *full text*. Searches in a full text data base are done by key words such as a certain name, a specific product, or type of injury. When documents are screened for full text entry, verify that the specific item or term is consistent throughout the document. For example, letters referring to Ann Forrester may do so in several different ways: "Ms. Forrester," "Forrester, A.," or "Ann Forrester." The computer will see each of these entries as different items, unless all key words such as names, places, dates, and so on, are standardized.[11]

The full text entry has the advantage of allowing the searcher to call up the desired documents when needed, select the particular document desired, and print it or even send it to a different location through a phone modem. Full text systems lend themselves to the entry of entire deposition and testimony transcripts, allowing key sections to be called up for review. It is worth noting here that many court reporting services (services responsible for the preparation of deposition or trial transcripts) enter the transcripts into computers. If the law firm has compatible hardware and the necessary software, such as the DISCOVERY program, the law firm can have the service's information copied on a diskette and fed directly into its own full text system. The fee is reasonable.[12] Abstracts and summaries can also be included in a full text system. Graphs, charts, and other pictorial information are generally not stored in the computer unless they have been copied or created specifically with the computer. New software is making computer storage of such material more common. Computers interfaced with new optical projectors are being used in courtrooms for large screen displays of this type of material as well as documents.

The disadvantage to full text entry is that the entry process, whether done by paralegal, data processor, or secretary, is very time-consuming, since documents must be entered through the keyboard into the computer. This makes full text capability the most expensive computerized document-control system. Multifont optical scanners permit an electronic scan of a document that automatically enters the text into the computer. Scanners are becoming less expensive (approximately $2,000) with improved quality, thus reducing full text entry problems in large cases. If documents have been placed on microfilm or microfiche, some accessories give the computer the capability of reading, storing, and printing those documents.

The most common entry system is *coding*. Coding's objective is to store significant information about a document such as source, number, type, date, author, number of pages, recipient, production request responsive to, issue, and others. Coding requires that the most significant categories of information be determined prior to the screening process and that uniform symbols (numbers, letters, or a combination of the two) be chosen to represent each specific category (or field) of information. Each symbol must be clearly defined in a glossary so that it can be recalled and used consistently through a particular case. Some software is specifically designed to aid in developing uniformity and will make format suggestions and provide guidelines. As the source document is screened, the paralegal records the information on a preprinted computer loading form. An example of such a form appears in figure 9:3.[13]

Figure 9:3   Computer Loading Form

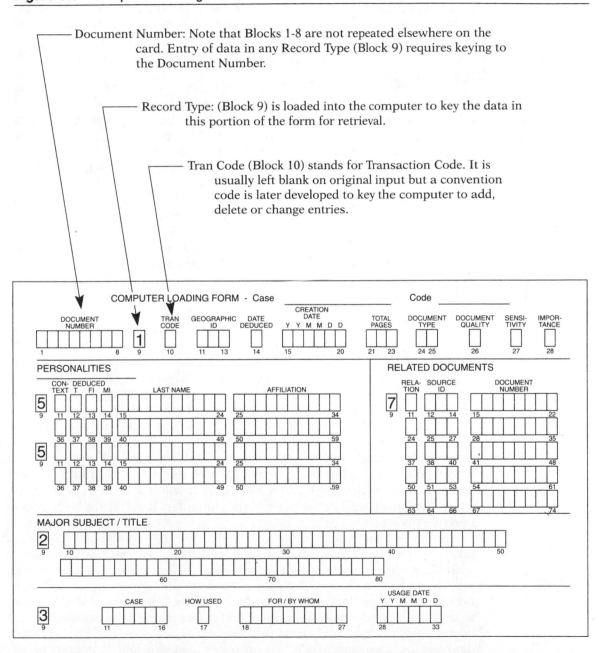

Document Number: Note that Blocks 1-8 are not repeated elsewhere on the card. Entry of data in any Record Type (Block 9) requires keying to the Document Number.

Record Type: (Block 9) is loaded into the computer to key the data in this portion of the form for retrieval.

Tran Code (Block 10) stands for Transaction Code. It is usually left blank on original input but a convention code is later developed to key the computer to add, delete or change entries.

This form can be expanded to contain checkoff entries for predefined issues such as relevant body parts for personal injury cases, pertinent key words, or even remarks or especially important quotations. Loading forms that use words instead of numbers are easier and more accurate to use.

Once recorded, the data is entered via keyboard into the computer. The software normally provides a format that reflects the computer loading form and provides directions on what information should be entered where. Although loading the coded forms can be time-consuming, the achieved ability to sort the data by unifying categories and later to locate the pertinent document numbers is amazing. Having retrieved document numbers from the computer, you can go to the original document file, pull the correct documents, and copy them for your or the attorney's use.

Retrieval

If the system has been carefully planned and implemented, retrieval of information should be relatively easy. It is more likely that you will have to employ keyboarding skills at this stage of the process rather than at the entry stage, since secretaries or other personnel are more likely to do the entry. It is important to learn the software commands needed to call up the desired data and to logically and precisely limit your search.

Keyboard commands are quite similar from one computer system to another and from one software package to another. The commonality is helpful when changing from one system to another. Differences, however, require that you consult the manual for the particular computer and software. Some companies provide keyboard command guides or small reference leaflets, which can be valuable in the early learning stages.

Formulating the query that tells the computer what you want it to do is also not difficult. If you are familiar with the entry codes or key words used for entry, it is simply a matter of entering those codes or words with a command such as "search" or "find"; the computer will do the rest. Computers possess a Boolean logic capability that can achieve various cross sortings among separate categories or fields. Therefore, for example, you can find all the "medical reports" submitted by "Dr. Smith" pertaining to a "fractured pelvis," or all "letters" mentioning both "Mr. "Wilson" and "Ms. Forrester." The computer will search and find only those documents with those particular characteristics, codes, or key words. This involves such commands as "and" and "or." When using "and" such as in the search of all letters containing "Hart *and* Forrester," note that if the computer comes across a letter with Hart but not Forrester, it will not retrieve or list that letter. "Or" means one or the other to the computer; "and" means both things must be present.

Another related skill is being able to narrow the search as precisely as possible. This involves the use of such commands as "not," as in "letters" with "Forrester and Hart," but "not Mercury Parcel." In this fashion the search can be as narrow and precise as the user's imagination and logic will permit. As long as the computer understands the command it is given, the search should go smoothly and quickly. Extremely large quantities of documents can be searched in this manner. The success of the retrieval depends on how specifically the attorney conveys which document or groupings are wanted.

Quality Control

Every system requires regular checking either by the attorney or an experienced auditor. Checks should be made to see that the uniform terminology and systems are being followed and that test retrievals produce the anticipated results.

Security

Once the data is computerized, precaution should be taken to protect it. As mentioned earlier, original documents should be placed in a room with limited access. Microfilm may be used to make a separate record in case something happens to the originals. The microfilm should be stored in a completely separate and well-protected location. Computer disks or tapes should be copied to ensure that a backup is always available. All originals and duplicates should be placed in locked cabinets so that any unauthorized use of the documents or data can be detected. Passwords programmed into the software can be instituted to prevent unauthorized access to a data base. Such passwords need to be recorded and carefully stored. Several people should know the location so the words will not be lost.

Because of the increasingly common use of computers to store data, document production requests may ask for entire data bases. It becomes difficult to protect attorney work product under such circumstances. In the process of classifying, interpreting, summarizing, and evaluating the significance of documents, it is arguable that certain items and information become attorney work product. Setting up a separate file for such material as was recommended in the manual sorting process seems equally applicable here.

Other Uses for Automated Litigation Support

The utility of automated litigation support goes beyond preparing documents for production requests. The computer can be used to store by topic countless varieties of forms, checklists, briefs, memoranda, and lists of legal authority that can be updated regularly. It can assist in reviewing and categorizing documents produced by the opponent.

The coding of all documents obtained in a case gives the computer the ability to sort out all data pertaining to a particular witness, which can be useful for preparing for a deposition or examination of a witness at trial, or for preparing a witness for trial.

The computer's sorting capability can be useful in preparing information for settlement, drafting the trial brief, keeping lists of exhibits, and for locating documents at trial to support objections to evidence or to defend against objections, and for purposes of cross-examining witnesses with inconsistent statements made at an earlier date. It can also assist in review of trial transcripts and isolation of key aspects of the record for appeal.

The extent of the use of automated litigation support depends greatly on the needs and creativity of the people using it.

ASSIGNMENT 9:2
Draft a Mini-Guide to Computer Usage based on the terminology, procedure, skills, techniques, and software covered in this section. Supplement the guide in any way you see fit. Place it in your system folder.

■ Reviewing and Interpreting Documents: Medical Records

When documents are obtained through a signed authorization, request for production of documents, subpoena duces tecum, or some other method, your task is to review those documents immediately. The procedure for reviewing different types of documents—medical, commercial, personal, industrial, and technical—is essentially the same. It consists of the following:

1. Review the case file for the facts and issues.
2. Check each document against the list of requested documents to see if all are present. If not, note any absence and explanation for the attorney.
3. Read each document to categorize it and check its completeness, legibility, and accuracy. Missing words, letters left out of an abbreviation, misused words, and any other inaccuracies should be noted to avoid misreading or inaccurate conclusions. Certain documents providing critical information should be summarized.
4. Interpret each technical document by translating it into plain English.
5. Digest each document by summarizing the most significant information.

The following section describes how this procedure is applied in the particular example of interpreting medical records.

Medical Record Interpretation

Resources

Assume that you have requested the medical records for Ann Forrester through the proper authorization. In response, the hospital has sent each record that you requested. It is now your job to read that record, verify its accuracy, and understand it so that you can summarize it in lay terms for the benefit of the attorney. The stumbling block, however, is that you cannot interpret what you do not understand. Therefore, it becomes your task to educate yourself. In the case of medical records, as is true of many other technical documents, the major obstacle is the terminology and abbreviations. To overcome this obstacle, you need specialized dictionaries and other guides. A good medical dictionary is an essential for litigation paralegals working in personal injury cases. It is a good idea to create a glossary of the obscure or technical terms raised in a particular case for quick reference for the duration of the case. Notecards are convenient for such a task and provide organizational flexibility.

Some reports use abbreviations or codes that may not be readily found in a dictionary. The people who work regularly with such documents have a code key or some other guide to abbreviations. For example, a tactful request to the medical records librarian of a hospital usually produces a list of abbreviations used by that hospital. Medical report abbreviations are somewhat standardized, but each hospital or each form may have its own peculiarities. Professional associations often have uniform abbreviations or code guides. Diagrams on human anatomy and physiology should be obtained. These are available in basic biology or nursing textbooks, as well as in appropriate sections of the medical or law library.

You should have a guide to pharmaceutical (drugs) and therapeutic terminology. The *Physician's Desk Reference* published by the Medical Economic Company is an excellent reference for medicines, their purpose, and side effects. A current guide to medical tests and procedures is also helpful. Another good source is *Paralegal Medical Records Review* by Kristyn S. Appleby and Joanne Tarver. Equipped with such resources, you should have little difficulty interpreting and summarizing hospital and physician's records. Many other technical fields have similar reference guides.

The Mini-Guide

Having acquired the necessary dictionaries and other resources, it may be worthwhile to create a mini-guide that can be used repeatedly as a quick reference when interpreting technical records. An example of such a mini-guide, A Mini-Guide for Interpreting Medical Records, is located in appendix D. Please refer to the Mini-Guide at this time.

An Example for Interpretation

Figure 9:4 is an example of a medical record from Ms. Forrester's hospital treatment.[14]

Using the Mini-Guide in Appendix D, try to interpret the medical record. Jot down your interpretation, then compare your interpretation with the translation in figure 9:5.[15]

The method for interpreting technical records that is described here is adaptable to any technical field. One paralegal describes the importance of preparation and attention to detail in document review:[16]

> In a recent case, before I began to review a set of medical records, I reviewed the file which included the attorney's narrative summary of the plaintiff's deposition testimony. In addition, I had previously summarized the plaintiff's answers to interrogatories, so I was quite familiar with the case. The lawsuit involved a motor vehicle accident in which the defendant had turned left in front of the plaintiff.
>
> The first records I reviewed were the paramedic and hospital emergency room records which noted that the plaintiff was alert and oriented with no loss of consciousness. The plaintiff was seen in the emergency department ten days later for follow-up care. The physician found no signs of trauma around the area of the plaintiff's head or face.
>
> The next sets of records I looked at were for treatment received one year after the accident, at which time the plaintiff was complaining of headaches and double vision. In these records, the plaintiff related to two different physicians (a neurologist and an ophthalmologist) that he had lost consciousness for a long period of time and had woken up in the ambulance on his way to the hospital. In addition, he stated that he was very bruised around both eyes. By pointing out these inconsistencies in my summary ("This statement is not supported by the medical record") I was able to provide information to the attorney to use as he saw fit.

Once the record is translated, it can be summarized or digested in the same manner that depositions are digested. This process is described in the next section.

Figure 9:4   Physician's Orders

INSTRUCTIONS: BEFORE PLACING IN CHART, IMPRINT PATIENT'S PLATE AS INDICATED BELOW

Reynolds+Reynolds DAYTON, OHIO LITHO IN U.S.A.   K8552 (8-84)

PHYSICIAN'S ORDERS
PATTIE A. CLAY HOSPITAL
RICHMOND, KENTUCKY 40475

IMPRINT PATIENTS PLATE HERE

ORDERED		ORDERS	NOTED BY/TIME
DATE	TIME		
2-26	0829	① admit ICU	
		② V/S & neuro checks q1h	
		③ I & O q1 / call if O < 30 cc/h	
		④ Tagamet 300 mg IV q6h	
		⑤ Keflen 1 Gm q6 IV	
		⑥ alt. Maalox & Mylanta per NG q2h & clamp × 30 min	
		⑦ NG. lo. int. wall suction	
		⑧ IV's DSRL 125 cc/h	
		DSNS c̄ 30 K meq 100 cc/h	
		⑨ O₂ 4L n/c	
		⑩ Bucks traction c̄ 20 lb wt to Ⓛ femur	
		⑪ clean lacerations q4h c̄ betadine	
		⑫ ABG's q2h tonight	
		⑬ H & H q4h & call if Hct < 36	
		⑭ a.m. lab	
		lytes	
		CBC	
		ABG's	
		repeat KUB & chest x-ray	
		⑮ When fully alert & oriented 1 codein 30 mg	
		Im q6h P.R.N. pain (after 24 hours)	
		⑯ Tylenol #3 for less pain Ī - ĪĪ tab	
		⑰ Tylenol 60 mg q6h T ↑ 101 get blood	
		cultures × 3 for T ↑ 101	
		⑱ log roll.	
		⑲ no sx	
		⑳ Halo / clean pins c̄ betadine q6h	

"Authorization is hereby given to dispense the Generic or Chemical equivalent unless otherwise indicated by the words — NO SUBSTITUTE"

Use Ball Point

AFTER DOCTOR WRITES A MEDICATION ORDER
1. Remove first yellow copy.
2. Send yellow copy to PHARMACY.
3. After last yellow sheet is used "X" out remaining unused lines.

No. must show through hole ➤ before physician writes on order

Figure 9:5 Physician's Orders (Translated)

PHYSICIAN'S ORDERS
PATTIE A. CLAY HOSPITAL
RICHMOND, KENTUCKY 40475

IMPRINT PATIENTS PLATE HERE

ORDERED DATE	TIME	ORDERS	NOTED BY	TIME
		1. admit intensive care unit		
		2. vital sign and alertness checks every hour		
		3. intake and output every hour. Call if output less than 30cc.		
		4. . . . every six hours		
		5. . . . 1 gram every six hours		
		6. Alternate . . . per naseogastric tube every two hours and clamp for 30 minutes.		
		7. . . . low intermittent		
		8. Intravenous fluids . . . 125cc per hour, 30 milequivalent potassium		
		9. Oxygen 4 liters nasal cannula		
		10. . . . with 20 pound weight . . . left		
		11. . . . every four hours		
		12. Arterial blood gases every two hours		
		13. Hemoglobin and hematocrit . . . hematocrit less than 36		
		14. Electrolytes Complete blood count Kidneys, Urine, Bladder and chest x-ray		
		15. . . . intermuscle every six hours as needed for pain		
		16. . . . one or two tablets		
		17. . . . temperature above 101		
		18. log rolling (technique for moving patients with spinal injury)		
		19. no suctioning		
		20. Halo (support for spine injury)		

"Authorization is hereby given to dispense the Generic or Chemical equivalent unless otherwise indicated by the words —
NO SUBSTITUTE"

Use Ball Point

AFTER DOCTOR WRITES A MEDICATION ORDER
1. Remove first yellow copy.
2. Send yellow copy to PHARMACY.
3. After last yellow sheet is used "X" out remaining unused lines.

No. must show through hole→ before physician writes on order

▨ Digesting Depositions and Other Documents

Introduction and Definition

Whether you are confronted with medical records, depositions, trial transcripts, a party's written statement, commercial records, expert reports, or other documents, it is critical to reduce the volume of information to a format that affords the attorney a concise and accurate summary with a handy reference for locating the complete language in the original documents. To that end, this section focuses on digesting (summarizing) documents, using depositions as the primary example. The methods used to digest depositions are applicable to most other documents. Once each deposition or each significant document is summarized, the information on each point can be organized under topical headings. This permits evidence from one or more witnesses to be compared, evaluated for evidentiary weight, and examined for inconsistencies and weaknesses.

Paralegals practice the art frequently and soon become good digesters. Digesting depositions can become tedious at times, but the task's overall importance to the success of the client's case cannot be overstressed. The attorney with good digests in hand at trial will be more organized, knowledgeable, decisive, and effective.

Purposes for Digesting Depositions

Deposition digests are used to:[17]

1. Condense large amounts of material
2. Index testimony and topics
3. End cross-examination of witness at trial
4. Lay foundation for production or admissions for discovery
5. Identify items for follow-up investigation or discovery
6. Verify key or disputed facts
7. Reveal inconsistencies in evidence or testimony
8. Review for trial or additional depositions
9. Support summary judgment and other motions
10. Include relevant facts or testimony in briefs
11. Cross-reference topics, witnesses, evidence
12. Bring new attorneys or paralegals up to speed on a case
13. Inform client
14. Prepare correspondence, settlement brochures, and material relevant to pretrial and other hearings

Techniques for Digesting Depositions

Being a good digester takes language skills, time, and experience. Doing a good digest, however, even the first time, is not difficult. Here are some techniques for a good start in this area.

1. Study the file to grasp the claim, defenses, issues, and legal theories.
2. Ask the attorney to provide the outline of the questions used at the deposition to provide an overview and suggestions for topical head-

ings, and guidance on the type of digest and indices desired, location of examples of similar summaries, desired detail, paraphrased or ellipsis format (see number 13 below), time frame, cost, need of extra assistance, key issues, key individuals, and any other special requests.

3. Skim the entire deposition first; develop a feel for its scope, importance, issues addressed, and topics for digest headings.

4. Draft a topical outline or tentative table of contents for the digest, placing topics in the order raised in the deposition, for example:
   - Personal background
   - Education
   - Prior injuries
   - Etc. (repeat headings where necessary)

5. Schedule blocks of time to do actual digesting so you will not lose sight of the continuity of the entire deposition and forget what topics have previously been addressed.

6. Handwrite, type, dictate, or better yet, compose on the word processor. The latter affords immediate editing while the deposition is fresh in mind, not always the case when written or dictated drafts take days to be typed. If your office computerizes depositions by full text, make another computer copy of the deposition and do your editing and summarizing on the computer. Through your direction, irrelevant information can be deleted by the computer, leaving only the most essential information to work with. If the depositions are not computerized, make a photocopy and delete unnecessary language and take notes on the photocopy.

7. Be as concise as possible. Eliminate unnecessary words: article adjectives such as "the," "an," "a"; previous or proper nouns if the reference is clear; exchanges between attorneys; and false starts in questioning or answering by the attorneys or deponent. Reduction quotas, such as one digest page for every ten pages of transcript, are not particularly helpful.[18]

8. Use abbreviations and short forms as much as possible, but be sure they are clear: re = regarding; ex = exhibit; 12/3/86 = December third, 1986; w/ = with; w/o = without; ∴ = therefore, ≅ = approximately, and so on.

9. Be accurate about what witnesses said. Use the witnesses' key words. Avoid distortion for the sake of obtaining a briefer phrase or having the digest coincide with your own understanding of the material. *Do not interpret!*

10. Use subheadings frequently and write in short paragraphs.

11. Use page and line number references in the margins and/or in a paragraph of summarized material, indicating where the full text of the summarized information can be found in the original transcript.

12. Utilize the "sheet" or "slip" method of recording. The sheet method condenses several pages of transcript into a single sheet of letter-size paper. Sheets are topically labeled as the topics arise in the deposition; as pertinent information is read it is summarized onto the appropriate topic sheet. The slip method employs index cards (slips) to record each new piece of information, noting the original line and page number as well as topic on the card. The individual cards pro-

vide greater flexibility, permitting the cards to be organized sequentially by page or by topic or according to some other need before typing.[19]

13. Utilize the "paraphrase" or the "ellipsis" method of summary. The paraphrase method is a concise restatement in paragraph form of what the witness said. The ellipsis method is a chronological listing of significant statements in sentence fragments preceded by ellipsis points (. . .). An example of each appears in figure 9:6, a sample deposition digest form.

14. Include, in addition to the obvious, all dates exactly as mentioned, all exhibits by name and number with attached exhibit list referring to pages where the exhibit is identified, court reporter's notes on the witness's behavior, substantive objections, admissions, stipulations, document requests, and any notes by the attorney or yourself on the effectiveness of the witness.[20]

Types of Deposition Digests and Indices

The prior techniques can then be applied to create various types of deposition digests. The three most common are the *chronological, topical,* and the *narrative* by topic.

The chronological (sequential) summary condenses the deposition of the deponent in the order matters were raised in the deposition. Each summarized fact or answer is referenced to its page and line in the transcript. Appearance of exhibits and the deponent's comments on them are also noted. The chronological digest should have a table of contents or topical index that states the topics as they arise in the deposition with appropriate page references. These can be made easily from the information on the sheets or the slips. Figure 9:6 is an example of the format for a chronological deposition digest beginning with a table of contents or topical index and ending with an exhibit index.[21]

Figure 9:6 Deposition Digest (Chronological)

DEPOSITION DIGEST

CASE: Smith v. Jones Dixon Sup Crt #234 567   Page: Contents
DEPONENT: Albert Hackston   Atty: G. Baker
DATE: 7/25/71   L/A: N. LUONO

TABLE OF CONTENTS/TOPICAL INDEX

Topic	Page	Lines
1. Personal Data	1	6–12
2. Education		
High School	2	6–8
On Job Training	2	17–20
	10	3–5
3. Employment History		
Prior to Employment w/Plaintiff	5	
Employment w/Plaintiff	6	1–4
	11	17–20
	33	12–17

DEPOSITION DIGEST (CHRONOLOGICAL)

DEPONENT: Albert Hackston   Page 1

Pg.	Ln.	Topic	Summary	Exhib/Notes
1	6–12	Personal Data	Born 6/15/30 Detroit, MI, married, 2 children, lives at 1400 North Ave., Detroit.	Speaks very softly
2	6–8	Education	Finished H.S. 47	
	17–20	"	OJT 1 year army	Most recent training
3	10	Safety training	(*Paraphrase method*) Hackston had read the instructions in detail and received 4 hours of OJT before operating the machine. In June 1969 he watched the disassembly and reassembly of the machine. It was frequently serviced and he specifically recalled preventive maintenance was performed on Sept. 8, '69.	
3	10	Safety Training	(*Ellipsis method*) . . . he had read the instructions in detail.	
	13		. . . he had 4 hours of OJT before using it.	
	18		. . . saw the apparatus disassembled and reassembled in June 1969 . . .	
4	6		. . . he was present when preventive maintenance was performed Sept. 8, '69	

DEPOSITION DIGEST

DEPONENT: Albert Hackston   Page: Exhibit Index

EXHIBIT INDEX

EXHIBIT NUMBER	DESCRIPTION
1	Ch. 3, "Safety," ST 3 Trng. Man'l dated 5/10/68
2	St 3 Operating Instructions dated 9/20/68
3	OJT Train Certificate dated 2/19/69

Figure 9:7 Page Extracts from Topical Deposition Summaries

TOPICAL DEPOSITION SUMMARY

Case: FORRESTER v. MERCURY PARCEL

Case File No. _____   Page 1

Deponent: Ann Forrester   Attorney: L. Ott

Date: 12/10/___   Paralegal: T. Salyer

TOPIC: INJURIES

Page	Line	Summary	Exhibits/ Notes
38	3	Date of accident 2/26/___ . . . she felt sharp pain at point of impact.	
	6	. . . pain was extreme in hip, lower abdomen, and upper left leg.	
39	1	. . . she felt nauseated.	
53–54	28–1	Date: 3/10/___ . . . after two weeks in hospital the leg felt numb and she could not move it. etc.	

TOPIC: EMPLOYMENT

Page	Line	Summary	Exhibits/ Notes
62	7	. . . she said she rarely missed work before the accident.	
66	12	. . . believed she would have been promoted by now to master teacher.	
71	2	. . . does not see how she can return to teaching with her current disabilities. etc.	

The topical digest is organized by topics and subtopics. Each of the deponent's answers that addresses a particular topic, regardless of where it appears in the transcript, is collected under that topical heading. These answers may then be organized as they appear in the transcript. The slip method of recording lends itself particularly well to this type of summary. An appropriate table of contents should be prepared. Sample pages from a topical deposition digest appear in figure 9:7.

The narrative digest incorporates the paraphrase method of complete sentences and is organized by topic, witness, or other categories depending on the attorney's needs. Narrative digests are particularly good to send to a client such as an insurance company so the client can get an understanding of the nature and evidence in the case.[22] An example of a page from a narrative digest arranged by topic is in figure 9:8.

Figure 9:8 Deposition Digest (Narrative)

DEPOSITION DIGEST (NARRATIVE/TOPICAL)
CASE: Johns v. Brown   No. Civ 880050   Page 1
DEPONENT: Catherine Johns

                               Atty: H. Ray
DATE: 7/16/88   Plgl: C. Borden

Background

Catherine Johns is 34 years old, residing at 1437 Oak St., Legalville, Columbia, is divorced and has one child, Edward, 10. (pages 1–2)

She has a master's in business administration from Columbia State and her high school diploma from East Legalville H.S. (3)

Employment

She worked for two years after high school for Columbia Foods as a secretary from 1980–82. She has worked for Fairmont Computers as a market analyst from 1987 to the present, earning $30,000 per year. (4–5)

The Accident

On May 3, 1987, Johns was driving to work, proceeding north on Holiday Blvd. in Legalville at 7:40 A.M. She was wearing a seat belt. She drove a 1986 Chevrolet Camero and was 200 feet from the intersection of Holiday and East Twenty-third St. when defendant, Harold Brown, suddenly backed out of his driveway at 3201 Holiday Blvd. in his 1987 Buick Le Sabre. (9, 32)

Johns "swung car to left" but the back of Brown's car hit hers in the Camero's left front. (10–11)

Johns' car "lurched" into oncoming traffic lane, crossed lane avoiding car driven by Walter Forth, went up curb and "smashed" into Roy's Hot Dog Stand and stopped. (11–12, 23)

Injuries

Johns hit her head on the steering wheel, breaking her nose and cheekbone. Ligaments in her left knee were severed, and she suffered muscle damage and internal injuries to the stomach lining causing internal bleeding. (14, 27)

Johns was rushed to Mount Sinai Hospital where she was admitted and operated on to correct fractures, stop internal bleeding, and repair ligaments in knee. Minor plastic surgery was performed on her nose by Dr. Kizar on 7/2/87. (15, 28)

One year after accident Johns still needs cane to walk. The fractures have healed satisfactorily but chewing is limited and painful, and one obvious scar remains on her nose. (16, 28–30).

Loss of Employment

(narrative continues)

Digest Aids for Complex Cases

If there are numerous deponents, you may be asked to perform several tasks to assist the attorney in trial preparation as well as at the trial. First, a master topical digest can be developed to collect the comments of all deponents on a particular topic under the respective topical heading. This facilitates a quick review of all evidence, including exhibits, from all deponents on a particular key point. This master topical digest should also include references to page, line, and deponent. The preparation of more complex cases can also be assisted by the compilation of subindexes that list all deponents, all exhibits, or are organized by topic.

ASSIGNMENT 9:3

Review the previous section on digesting the deposition. Create a List of Techniques for Digesting a Deposition and place it in your system folder.

ASSIGNMENT 9:4

Figure 9:9 contains excerpts from a deposition of Mr. Hart. Skim the deposition transcript first. Then read it and carefully draft the corresponding section of a chronological digest. Prepare a table of contents for the digest. Count lines from top of each page of deposition, since no lines are provided.

Figure 9:9   Deposition of Richard Hart

UNITED STATES DISTRICT COURT FOR THE EASTERN DISTRICT OF COLUMBIA

ANN FORRESTER
            and
WILLIAM FORRESTER,
                        Plaintiffs

            v.   Civil Action, File No. _____

RICHARD HART
            and
MERCURY PARCEL SERVICE, INC.,
                        Defendants

Cincinnati, Ohio, Wednesday, January 12, ___

Pretrial examination of Richard Hart held in the offices of Ott, Ott & Knudsen, 444 Front St., Cincinnati, Ohio, at 10:00 A.M. on the above date before Bernadette Schaffer, Certified Court Reporter and Notary of Ohio.

    APPEARANCES:
    Arthur White
White, Wilson & McDuff
Attorneys for Plaintiffs

    Lynn Ott
Ott, Ott & Knudsen
Attorneys for Defendants

                                        (signature and certification
                                        omitted)

Richard Hart, after having been duly sworn, was examined and testified as follows:

By Mr. White:

Q. Please state your full name.
A. Richard Hart
Q. Your residence?
A. 1223 Penny Lane, Cincinnati, Ohio.
Q. How long have you lived there?
A. Eight years.
Q. Where did you live prior to that?
A. 4313 East Wickland St., Columbus, Ohio.
Q. How long did you reside there?
A. Seven years.
Q. Are you married?
A. Yes.

Q. Your wife's full name?

A. Jessica Marie Hart.

Q. When were you married?

A. Seventeen years ago. June 19___.

Q. Do you have any children?

A. Yes, two boys.

Q. What are their names and ages?

A. Brett is sixteen and Jerome is fourteen.

Q. When and where were you born?

A. August 13, 19___, I am forty-one.

Q. Where?

A. Oh, ah . . . Columbus, Ohio.

Q. How far did you go in school?

A. I graduated from high school.

Q. Where did you attend high school?

A. Taft High in Columbus.

Q. What, if any, schooling have you had since high school?

A. I was trained as an ambulance driver by the army and took a truck driving course about twelve years ago.

Q. When were you in the army?

A. Twenty years ago, 19___ to 19___, for two years.

Q. How extensive was your training?

A. A few weeks each year.

Q. Where was your training?

A. Fort Oglethorp, Georgia.

Q. Did you ever have any special training for driving on ice and snow?

A. No, but I have lived in Columbus most of my life and we get plenty of winter weather.

Q. Where was the truck driving course?

A. In Cincinnati.

Q. What was the name of the school?

A. The Cincinnati Vocational Institute.

Q. How long was the course?

A. Six weeks.

Q. Did you learn how to drive vans at this school?

A. No, it was for large rigs.

Q. Did they give you any special training for winter driving?

A. They were supposed to, but we never got to it.

Q. Have you ever received any formal training for driving in wintery weather?

A. No.

Q. Not even with Mercury Parcel?

A. No.

Q. What is your current occupation?

A. Route man.

Q. Would you explain what a route man is?

A. O.K. I drive a truck—or van—and deliver parcels and things to people and stores over a certain route.

Q. What route do you cover?

A. We cover several different ones—sometimes we fill in for a guy that's sick.

Q. Are you assigned to the Legalville, Columbia route very often?

A. Oh, sure.

Q. Have you ever made deliveries on Capitol Drive outside of Legalville before?

A. No . . . possibly . . . I'm not sure.

Q. Would any records of your deliveries indicate whether you had been out there before?

A. They might. It's probably been years ago.

Q. How long ago?

A. Maybe five or six years ago . . . I don't know.

Q. What records might show that?

A. We have to fill out a record of delivery form—it has addresses on it.

Q. Do they show every delivery?

A. Yes.

Q. Does this form have a number?

A. I think so. It . . . it's a form 30.

Q. Who is your current employer?

A. Mercury.

Q. Do you mean the Mercury Parcel Service?

A. Yes.

Q. How long have you worked for them?

A. Let's see, two years in Columbus and eight years in Cincinnati. Ten years.

Q. Is this full-time employment?

A. Yes.

Q. Have you worked in any capacity other than route man for Mercury?

A. No.

Q. How much do you earn an hour?

A. $8.35 an hour.

Q. How many hours per week?

A. Usually 40 . . . unless we need to work overtime.

Q. How often do you work overtime?

A. Every so often when someone is sick or we have a lot to deliver . . . or if we volunteer to put in some extra time.

Q. Where did you work prior to working for Mercury?

A. I worked as an ambulance driver for the town of Jackson just outside Columbus. There was always trouble getting adequate funds to keep the service going, so I quit and went with Mercury.

Q. What is the address for that service?

A. If it's still there—it is Route 3, Highway 95, Jackson, Ohio.

Q. How long did you work for the ambulance service?

A. Six years.

Q. Have you had a good driving record?

A. Yes.

Q. Have you had any accidents either on or off the job?

A. Well, yes. I think most folks do.

Q. When did you have the accidents?

A. Well, I had one two years ago in Cincinnati, and . . .

Q. Were you driving for Mercury at the time of the accident?

A. Yes, I was.

Q. What happened?

A. I was trying to exit off I-75 and a guy was trying to enter I-75. They cross there. I thought he was by me and he slowed down. I ran into his left side. No one was hurt, thank goodness.

Q. Were any citations issued by the police?

A. No.

Q. Have you had any other accidents?

A. Yes, I had one about five years ago in Columbus.

Q. What happened?

A. My family and I were heading for downtown Columbus to see a Fourth of July parade. I was in a line of stopped traffic. The line began to move. I turned to say something to my wife. The car in front of me stopped and I rammed into it. An elderly lady got hurt but my insurance company paid for her doctor bills.

Q. Were any citations issued?

A. Yes, I got a ticket for inattentive driving.

Q. Any other accidents?

A. Not that I recall.

Q. Have you received any other traffic citations?

A. Well, a few over the years.
   L. Ott: Let the record reflect that I object to this question on the ground that it is not relevant to the accident in question.
   Mr. White: Counselor, if there is a pattern of reckless driving, then I believe it is relevant. Your objection is noted. May I proceed?
   L. Ott: yes.
   By Mr. White:
Q. What were those citations for?
A. Mainly for speeding.
Q. How many in the last five years?
A. Oh, not too many.
Q. More than five?
A. I guess so.
Q. Six?
A. I think about six.
Q. Where have most of these violations occurred?
A. In the Cincinnati area.
Q. How many occurred on the job?
A. Oh, about half, I'd say.
Q. Mr. Hart, do you recall the accident you had on February 26, 19___?
A. Yes, I do.
Q. Were you working for Mercury Parcel at the time of the accident?
A. Yes.
Q. When did you start work that day?
A. I was on the night shift and started at 11:00 P.M. on the twenty-fifth. I was supposed to be back in the barn by 7:00, but I was about two hours behind schedule because of the weather.
Q. So normally on night shift you work from 11:00 P.M. until 7:00 A.M.?
A. Yes.
Q. Were you driving the entire time the night of February 25 to 26?
A. Well, not constantly. We do stop and get out of the truck to deliver the packages or letters. However, because most of the deliveries were in Legalville, and due to the weather, I guess I was driving more than usual.
Q. Did you take any breaks?
A. Yes, the union says we're to get two breaks and a paid half-hour lunch break. That night, though, I only took a break at 3:00 A.M. By lunchtime and the second break I was too far behind to stop.
Q. Other than the weather, did anything else occur that was unusual that night?
A. Not that I recall.
Q. Were you having any mechanical trouble with the truck—like braking or steering problems?
A. Not really. Oh, the van pulls to the left a little when you brake hard, but I knew that and was able to allow for that when I stopped.
Q. How long had that problem existed?
A. Oh, about two weeks. I mentioned it to them about a week before the accident but told them it wasn't too serious.
Q. Who do you mean when you say "them"?
A. A couple of the mechanics at the barn—Mercury's shop.
Q. Can you name them?
A. Well, I think I told Arnie Hanson and I might have told Johnny Sloan . . . I'm not sure about Johnny.
Q. Is there a regular procedure for reporting problems with a vehicle?
A. No, not really . . . well, there is a form that we're supposed to fill out, but if it is not too serious, we just mention it to one of the mechanics.
Q. What does the mechanic do then?
A. If they can find the time, they'll look at it. If not they wait till their next regular servicing of the van.
Q. Had the problem of pulling to the left been worked on at the shop?

A. No, I don't think so.

Q. Do you always drive the same van?

A. Yes, almost always.

Q. Did you fill out a form on the braking problem?

A. No.

Q. Describe the weather conditions that night.

A. The roads were wet from melting snow at the beginning of the evening, but by mid-shift—say 3:30 A.M.—the roads began to freeze in spots. You had to be careful.

Q. Had you done any slipping that night?

A. Occasionally . . . but nothing serious.

Q. Was there a lot of ice on the roads?

A. Here and there.

Q. What was the road like just before the accident?

A. Well, it wasn't too bad. There were occasional patches of ice, but not too bad.

Q. Was there enough ice to slow you up some? In other words, did you reduce your speed?

A. Oh, maybe five or ten miles an hour . . . but not much. The road really wasn't too bad.

Q. How fast were you going just prior to the accident?

A. Well, I had just looked and I was going at about thirty-five miles per hour.

Q. What do you mean you "just looked"?

A. Well, I looked at the speedometer to check my speed.

Q. Why?

A. Well, I'm not sure . . . I think I was thinking about how late I was going to be getting back home.

Q. Were you anxious to get back to Cincinnati?

A. Yes, it had been a long night.

Q. Were you tired?

A. A little—because of the weather, I think.

Q. Couldn't you have stopped for a break?

A. I could have, but I didn't. I was late enough the way it was.

Q. Had you had any other long shifts that week?

A. The last shift had been snowy, so I was about an hour late that night.

Q. How much sleep did you get the following day, the twenty-fifth?

A. About six hours, I think. My son had a basketball game that afternoon, so I didn't get to sleep quite as much as I usually do.

Q. Are there any company rules about how much sleep you are to have before your shift?

A. No.

Q. Are there any company rules about taking a break if you become tired?

A. Oh, they tell us to pull over if we are real tired, but I felt OK.

Q. How do they tell you to pull over? Is that a rule, or do they mention it at meetings? How is this done?

A. Well, anyone who drives knows that, but I think there are some safety rules posted in the shop.

Q. Do you read those rules?

A. Not really. They're nothing most drivers don't already know.

Q. Are there any limits on how many hours you are supposed to drive at any one time?

A. I think the rule is around seven hours of actual driving time.

Q. How many hours of actual driving time did you drive that night?

A. Oh, I'd say about eight, maybe nine.

Q. And had the accident not occurred, you would have had nearly two more hours of driving?

A. Yes.

Q. Is there any penalty for driving over the limit of hours?

A. Not that I know of.

Q. On bad weather nights, or if you're late for any other reason, do you get paid overtime?

A. Only if the extra hours are unavoidable, such as for bad weather.

Q. Would you please describe the road you were driving at the time of the accident?

A. The road was quite narrow, hilly, and curvy.

Q. What was the posted speed limit on that road?

A. I'm not sure.

Q. Would you characterize the road as tricky?

A. Oh, maybe a little . . . but I have driven a lot of roads worse than that.

Q. You mentioned before that you looked at your speedometer just before the accident. What happened next?

A. Well, I looked up and suddenly there was this lady stepping out onto the road.

Q. You looked at your speedometer just before the accident occurred?

A. Yes, I glanced at it—only for a split second.

Q. Had you seen the woman before you looked at the speedometer?

A. No.

Q. Why not?

A. Well, she was hidden by a rise in the road. See, there is a dip in the road where the lady was at. I was coming over the hill just before the dip. You can't see to the bottom of the dip. And that's where the lady was.

Q. What happened then?

A. I thought she would stop, but she just kept looking ahead and kept walking into the road.

Q. What do you mean she just kept looking ahead?

A. Well, when I came over the hill she was barely onto the road. I thought she would see or hear me and stop, but her head was tucked down into her coat and she just kept walking.

Q. Did you sound your horn?

A. No.

Q. What did you do?

A. I hit the brakes.

Q. Then what?

A. The truck began to pull to the left . . . it began to fishtail back and forth. I pumped the brakes to keep control. The lady looked up then, but hesitated and then went the wrong way. I couldn't avoid her. I was trying to get control of the van and then I heard the thump. I felt sick—I knew I'd hit her.

Q. What happened then?

A. The van was crossing the middle of the road. I saw the woman fall off from my side of the van. I tried to hold the van under control, but it went into the ditch and hit a tree.

Q. How hard did the van pull to the left when you applied the brakes?

A. It started that way almost immediately. I think it might have been the same problem I described before, or it might have been the ice. I don't know.

(Assume that the examination went on to cover what happened after the accident, damages to the van, Mr. Hart's injuries, etc. The opposing counsel would have an opportunity to ask questions, and then the deposition would conclude.)

Mr. White: I have no other questions.

(Witness excused)

(Deposition concluded)

■ Organizing Files

You see yourself sitting next to your supervising attorney at counsel's table at a dramatic point in the trial. The attorney turns to you and whispers, "I need the follow-up medical report from Dr. Grimes!" Your eyes shift to a dog-eared folder swollen beyond its capacity with corners of various pages slipping toward chaotic freedom. You begin to perspire as you feverishly page through the documents. Your attorney helps by loudly whispering, "Hurry up! Hurry up!"

As you fly through the folder, it creeps toward the edge of the table and suddenly papers come flushing out like water through a broken dam as the file and its contents spread over the floor.

Then you wake up from the nightmare and swear that you will never let that happen to you. The next day you go to the office and begin organizing case files.

The Small Case File

The documents needed in most case files can be neatly organized into one manilla folder.[23] By attaching some of the documents at the top and some at the bottom of each of the two flaps of the folder, four general categories of file documents can be maintained. Four common file categories include pleadings, correspondence, factual items, and billing documents. The folder would appear as indicated in figure 9:10.

The fact section should include such things as client background sheet [see figure 3:1(a)], client interview or summary, accident reports, contracts, pertinent business records, medical reports and authorizations, witness statements, medical bills, damage estimates, and so on. The client data sheet can contain a checkoff section indicating what was done last in the case and what should be done next. This section can be a separate form (see figure 11:2) that can be standardized and computerized for ease of updating and determining the status of a case at a glance. The subcategories of the fact section may be organized into subgroups and placed in chronological or reverse chronological order and tabbed with gum labels.

The pleadings section should contain the complaint, answer, motions, affidavits, memoranda of law, proofs and acknowledgements of service, requests for admissions, and other documents filed in the case. These documents are normally filed in chronological order and may also be tabbed and color-coded for plaintiff's and defendant's pleadings.

The correspondence section consists of all letters, memos, and other correspondence. These may be divided and tabbed in subgroups and filed in reverse chronological order. Some firms use special colored carbons to allow quick identification of correspondence originating from their offices.

The billing section should include all items that will go into the client's bill: records of travel, phone calls, conferences, witness fees, filing fees,

Figure 9:10   Small Case File Folder

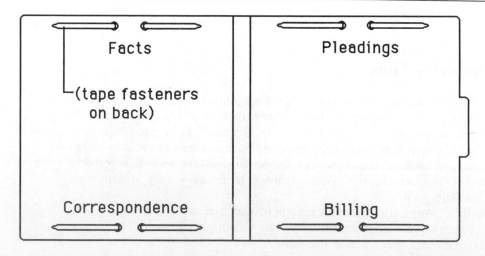

service of process expenses, time slips, and others. This facilitates the figuring of the bill and provides the basis for status reports requested by the client.

A current index of each section of the folder should be kept at the top of one leaf of the folder for quick reference.

This type of file provides some organization, allows the file to be updated in an organized way, and should reduce the amount of time needed when the supervising attorney says, "Hurry up!"

ASSIGNMENT 9:5
Collect the documents you have gathered so far in the *Forrester* case and organize a small case file for them.

The Large Case File

When the case involves lots of documents or outgrows the small case file, a more involved system is called for.[24] Many law offices have established a procedure for organizing a case file. This may be in the office procedures manual, or you may need to review other case files and their indices to see how it is done. For now, however, assume that you are the first paralegal in the office who has been assigned the task to organize several rather large files. The following method is one of several ways that it can be done.

The first step is to gather all of the documents and file folders that pertain to the case, and separate these materials into six broad divisions:

- Correspondence, bills, and miscellaneous
- Pleadings
- Transcripts
- Photographs
- Documents and exhibits
- Medical records (or other relevant category)

The second step is to take the "correspondence, bills, and miscellaneous" material and make file folders assigning the following file numbers and titles:

Correspondence, Bills, and Miscellaneous: Numbers 10–99

- 10 Correspondence
- 20 Bills
- 30 Research
- 40 Investigations
- 50 Miscellaneous memos and notes
- 60 Deposition summary and notes
- 70 Answers to interrogatories summaries
- 80 Witnesses (background, memos, statements, etc.)
- 90 Miscellaneous (as needed)

Each of the subcategories can be further broken down as needed:

10 Correspondence
    10.1 Client (to or from)
    10.2 Insured (to or from)
    10.3 Plaintiff's Counsel (to or from)

It may be useful to note that in some state courts and in some federal actions for personal injury, survival, and wrongful death, the "loss of

10.4 Co-defendant's Counsel (to or from)
10.5 Court (to or from)
10.6 Miscellaneous

If folders need to be broken down further, then use 10.1(a), (b), (c), and so on. The other categories in the division should then be broken down into logical and relevant subdivisions.

The "pleadings" division should be assigned the number 100 and subdivided accordingly. Pleadings are placed in chronological order in their subdivision and numbered in red. For example, the complaint would have a 1 in its lower right corner, the answer a 2, and so forth.

Pleadings: Numbers 100–199

110 Complaints, answers, related motions, and other related pleadings
120 Discovery pleadings to plaintiff and plaintiff's responses
121 Interrogatories to plaintiff
122 Plaintiff's response to interrogatories
123 Requests for admissions to plaintiff
124 Plaintiff's responses to admissions request
125 Requests for production and so on
130 Discovery pleadings to defendant and defendant's responses
131 Interrogatories to Defendant
132 Defendant's responses to interrogatories and so on
140 Notice of depositions and related pleadings
150 Open (to be used as specific case dictates)
160 Open
170 Pretrial/trial pleadings
180 Miscellaneous pleadings by plaintiff
190 Miscellaneous pleadings by defendant

The remaining divisions should be numbered and subdivided in like fashion. As the file folders are being created for each subdivision, a detailed index should be made of each division and the contents of each category and each subcategory. The master index should show the divisions and subdivisions with their assigned numbers. The subsequent sheets of the index would be assigned to each subfile, and as new items were placed in the subfile, a description of the item would be entered on the appropriate subfile index sheet. Figure 9:11 is an example of how the master index sheet might appear, and figure 9:12 shows the subfile index sheet.

The index can be kept and regularly updated as the first file in the case or as a three-ring binder to facilitate the rapid retrieval of needed documents. All the subfiles of the case can then be placed in one or more expandable case files in numerical order.

These index sheets kept at the top or front of a case file provide a quick overview of where everything is filed, and a more detailed log of the current holdings in each file. When kept current, such an index is a great organizer and time saver. If the case is going to be particularly voluminous, there are advantages to using the uniform decimal numbering system discussed earlier in the chapter.

ASSIGNMENT 9:6
Prepare checklists for Organizing the Small Case File and for Organizing the Large Case File. Place them in your system folder.

Figure 9:11   Master File Index Sheet

Case: Forrester v. Mercury Parcel Service Case File No. _____

File No.	Categories
0–99	Correspondence, bills, and miscellaneous
10	Correspondence
20	Bills
30	Research
100–199	Pleadings
110	Complaints, answers, motions, and other related pleadings
120	Discovery pleadings to plaintiff
200–299	Transcripts
210	Depositions of plaintiff's witnesses
220	Depositions of defendant's witnesses
230	Trial transcripts
300–399	Photographs

Figure 9:12   Subfile Index Sheet

Case: Forrester v. Mercury Parcel Service Case File No. _____

File No.	Subtitled Components
10.1	Client (to or from)
(a)	6/26/__ letter from seeking our representation
(b)	7/11/__ letter to setting up interview
(c)	7/10/__ letter to describing items to bring
(d)	7/20/__ letter to accepting case
10.2	Insured (to or from)
(a)	9/1/__ letter to requesting payment of damages
(b)	9/20/__ letter from stating not responsible for damages

Summary

Conquering the paper chase involved in most cases is a craft that requires hard work, great attention to detail, and the implementation of tried techniques. These tasks, though tedious and taken for granted at times, are absolutely critical to success in representing the client and, thus, should be learned well and performed with concentration and dedication.

Each technique discussed in this chapter, whether it is document control or digesting a deposition, requires a review of the case, an assessment of the amount of information to be dealt with, an estimate of the cost of various methods of control, a decision on whether the task should be done internally or by a vendor, and what categories should be used for organizing and summarizing data. These are attorney's decisions, but they can be facilitated by consultation with the paralegal and the rest of the litigation team.

Document control demands locating and securing the documents; screening; numbering (using the decimal system in large cases); and organizing them for retrieval, discovery requests, the file, and for trial. This can be done manually or by computer. A basic understanding of how computers can be employed in this process and other aspects of litigation support is important knowledge. You should understand how Boolean logic works to provide categorizing, sorting, reorganizing, and other searches.

Reviewing, interpreting, and digesting depositions or other documents can be enhanced if you construct appropriate mini-guides to the complex or unique language or information in medicine, areas of commerce, government, science, and other subjects.

Effective digesting of records and documents and especially depositions is one of the most important techniques addressed in this chapter. The condensing of large documents and transcripts of testimony down to concise summaries that are well indexed to the originals saves countless hours when planning strategy, negotiating, preparing for trial, and appealing a case. Deposition digests generally come in three formats: chronological, topical, and narrative. Knowing the issues in a case and what testimony is necessary to prove or refute proof of these issues is the key to good digesting.

Finally, all the paperwork in a case needs to be organized into logical, quickly accessible files. Most files are organized into five or six categories, including correspondence, pleadings, facts/investigation, medical/damages, billing, and legal research. The number of categories can be increased in complex cases with each category organized into subcategories and indexed for quick location of items.

Study Guide

1. Why is it important to plan a document production carefully?
2. What must be covered when planning and preparing for a document production?
3. Who is often the most helpful person in locating documents?
4. How does one locate the documents needed for production?
5. What steps need to be followed in pulling document files?
6. Be able to describe the objectives and each step in screening the pulled files or documents.
7. What cross files are normally kept in preparing for document production?
8. What are the steps recommended for producing documents and the key procedures for each step?
9. What is the decimal document numbering system, and how does it work? What are its advantages?
10. Why is it important to have the attorney review the tabbed documents before copying?
11. What should be done with poor or extra photocopies of documents for production?
12. What steps should be followed and indices kept at the examination stage?
13. If the documents have been identified and indexed properly, what kinds of minimum information allow you to retrieve them relatively quickly?

14. What steps are important when returning documents that have been produced to the original custodian?
15. What is the primary benefit derived from automated litigation support?
16. Is it true today that computers are valuable in only the largest discovery cases?
17. What skills must you possess to be effective in automated litigation support?
18. What functions, in addition to document production, can automated litigation assist?
19. If the office has no prior experience with automated litigation, whom should you consult?
20. What items must be considered in planning the organizational system for automation support in document production and retrieval?
21. What should one look for in document-control software?
22. What is a full text system, and how does one search it? What is an indexing or abstract system?
23. What is the benefit of a multifont optical scanning device?
24. What is a coded entry system, and how does it work? What are its advantages?
25. What should quality control in an automated production system be verifying?
26. What skills are needed for computerized document retrieval?
27. How does one form a retrieval query? How is it narrowed?
28. What is Boolean logic?
29. What security techniques should be taken to protect data stored in automated systems?
30. What are your objectives in reviewing discovery documents?
31. What techniques should be employed in reviewing discovery documents?
32. What resources are recommended for reviewing medical reports?
33. What is the purpose of digesting litigation documents?
34. What skills are needed to be a good digester?
35. What are the important uses of a deposition summary?
36. Be able to list the techniques for digesting depositions.
37. Be able to do several types of deposition digests.
38. How do you organize a small case file, and what kinds of documents go in each subsection?
39. How do you organize a large case file?

Endnotes

1. The discussion of procedure in this section is based in part on a memo from C. Bryant to James McCord (March 1986).
2. NATIONAL ASSOCIATION OF LEGAL ASSISTANTS, MANUAL FOR LEGAL ASSISTANTS 446–47 (1979) [hereinafter cited as NALA MANUAL].
3. Id., 445.
4. Id., 450.
5. The discussion of the numbering system is based on LIPSON, ART OF ADVOCACY: DOCUMENTARY EVIDENCE, § 7 [hereinafter cited as LIPSON]; and BENDER'S FORMS OF DISCOVERY, § 4.09(6)(6).

6. NALA Manual, 459.

7. Id.

8. Moses, *Using Computers in Litigation Support*, Legal Assistant Today (Nov./Dec. 1990).

9. Fawcett, *Computerized Litigation Support: When to Consider Automating a Case*, Legal Assistant Today (May/June 1990).

10. Lipson, § 14.07, 14–60, 61.

11. Mason, An Introduction to Using Computers in the Law 66 (1985).

12. Memo from J. Burton to J. McCord (March 23, 1987).

13. NALA Manual, 476, with permission of West Publishing Company.

14. Form courtesy of Pattie A. Clay Hospital, Richmond, Ky. and data on form provided by Peggy Walker, R.N.

15. Translation provided by Peggy Walker, R.N.

16. Appleby, *A Guide to Reviewing and Summarizing Medical Records*, Legal Assistant Today 26 (Sept./Oct. 1990), 27.

17. Piatz, *Organizing and Digesting Depositions*, Legal Assistant Today 45(July/Aug., 1990).

18. Hardwick, *Deposition Summaries*, Legal Assistant Today (Nov./Dec. 1986), 36–37.

19. NALA Manual, 407–8.

20. Piatz, 47–48.

21. Adapted from NALA Manual, 407, 409, with permission of West Publishing Company.

22. Piatz, 47.

23. Suggested in part by Weitzel, *Who's Coming to Dinner? The Bread and Butter of Your Files*, Texas Bar Journal 31 (May 1968).

24. This section based on Treat, ed., *Uniform Filing System*, Litigation Aids (National Association of Legal Assistants, June 1984).

10

Settlement and Other Alternative Dispute Resolutions

■ Introduction

The purpose of litigation is to resolve disputes. Going to trial is one method of resolution of the differences between the parties. Most cases, however, never go to trial. They may be negotiated and settled, or the parties may seek some alternative forum of resolution as required by contract or court process, or by choice. This chapter focuses on settlement as the primary method of resolving a case, but it also addresses other resolution procedures including arbitration, mediation, summary trials, and related processes that are growing in importance. As in other litigation processes, the role of the paralegal in organizing information and preparing it for presentation in alternative dispute resolution provides a valuable service to the client and our system of justice.

■ Settlement

Introduction

Settlement is the process of both sides reviewing strengths and weaknesses of a case and reaching a mutual agreement on how to dispose of the case.

Approximately 96 percent of all civil cases are settled or resolved without a trial. A case may be settled at nearly all stages of the litigation process, with some being disposed of before a complaint is filed, most before trial, some at trial, and a few during appeal.

Cases are settled for a variety of reasons, the most obvious being to save time, trouble, and expense. Settlement is encouraged in our system. If cases were not settled at the rate they are, our courts would overload even worse than they are, and the endless litigation that lasts over several generations as portrayed in Dickens's *Bleak House* would be a reality. Settlement removes the uncertainty of the outcome of a trial, eliminates or reduces adverse publicity, and ends the fear of the ordeal of trial.

Settlement is based on a combination of factors: amount of damages; ability of the defendant to pay; insurance coverage; ease with which liability and damages can be proven; nature of the injury (permanency, horror factor, disability); sympathy for plaintiff; whether the plaintiff needs to be paid right away or can hold out through trial; amount of verdicts in similar cases in the same area; respective ability of attorneys; attitude of the judge; desire of either party for vindication; and others. Though most of these matters are assessed by the attorney, an alert paralegal sensitive to these factors often spots things otherwise overlooked that might make a difference.

The Role of the Paralegal

The primary role of the paralegal is to gather, organize, and draft materials to help the attorney evaluate the case and present it in negotiation to the other side. If a settlement is reached, it falls to the paralegal to draft the necessary settlement documents.

Ethical Considerations

Both attorneys and paralegals must remember that the decision to accept a settlement is up to the client. New Model Rule 1.2 states, "A lawyer shall abide by a client's decision whether to accept an offer of settlement of a matter." This language incorporates the spirit of the old code, which is still the ethical standard in some states.

Regardless of confidence in the facts or fairness of a case, a paralegal may not make settlement offers, accept offers, or counsel the client on the advisability of accepting a settlement. Take caution in discussing such matters with the client and in conveying advice of the attorney. It must be crystal clear that the paralegal is not giving the advice, and the information conveyed must be accurate.

Take care when discussing matters with an adverse attorney, paralegal, or others, since a client's opportunity for settlement may be adversely affected if information is unwittingly revealed. Settlement précis and brochures (to be discussed in this chapter) or other items prepared for review by the opponent or an insurance adjuster must not reveal harmful information. Confidential information must be protected, and should be revealed only with the client's permission and approval of the attorney.

Throughout the process, you may be expected to keep the client readily informed of the progress in negotiation and any proposals. Professional ethics require the attorney to keep the client informed (Model Rule 1.4a and b).

ASSIGNMENT 10:1
Place a definition of *settlement* and a list of the factors that come to bear on the settlement process in your system folder. What factors either favoring or discouraging settlement do you see present in the *Forrester* case? Discuss.

ASSIGNMENT 10:2
Briefly outline the important ethical considerations for the settlement process. Read and list the cited sections of the Model Rules of Professional Conduct. Compare these to the rules or ethical standards in your state. Add these items to your system folder.

■ Preparing for Settlement

Introduction

The importance of the preparation needed to conduct and ultimately reach a negotiated settlement is generally underestimated. Attorneys and paralegals alike tend to focus on the trial and frequently establish all preparation timetables accordingly. Since so many cases are settled, however, timetables and preparation need to be geared to the settlement process as well. An important by-product of preparation for settlement, if done correctly, is that it becomes a significant part of the preparation for trial.

The paralegal contributes to two significant stages in settlement: the attorney's evaluation of the case and the presentation of the case for settlement. If the opponent's side is presenting the case for settlement, the paralegal's work will help prepare the attorney to evaluate the opposition's proposal.

Evaluation of the case involves a thorough look at all the elements that make up a case, such as liability, damages, ability to pay, and others.

Both sides working together toward dispute resolution can save time and money. What can you do to help your client receive the best settlement?

Presentation of the settlement involves organizing information in an economical, informative, and persuasive format to convince the opponent that the claim is a good one and worth settling.

Early Investigation and Collection of Information

A thorough early investigation is important because settlement can come early in the litigation process. To assist in the attorney's preparation for this, you need to collect and summarize the following information from the beginning of the action.

Party's Social or Business Background

Note family, education, character, occupation, income, benefits, advancement potential, life-style, activities, and interests both before and after the accident or claim. The courtroom effectiveness of witnesses should also be evaluated. For a commercial plaintiff, note: reputation, age, income, status before and after alleged injury. Comparative wealth of parties in both commercial and personal injury cases is also important.

Party's Medical Condition

Note age, race, sex, personality; prior injuries and their possible implications for injuries caused by the accident (may reduce amount of damages); details of injuries from accident; diagnosis; post-accident impediments such as shock, unconsciousness, embarrassment (these often explain statements or actions inconsistent with allegations of injuries);[1] unwillingness to admit disability; causal relationship between alleged wrong and injury; treatment required (emergency, surgery, tests, hospital care, home care, checkups, other medical consultations); progressive stages of healing; hideous nature of injury or effects; temporary injuries and disability; permanent injuries and disability; disfigurement; psychological and emotional injury; effect on personality and happiness; prognosis; need for future medical care (nursing care, prosthetic devices); pain and suffering (at time of injury, during medical treatment, permanent); change in life expectancy because of injuries; occupational implications of injuries; effect on hobbies, interests, and home life; all out-of-pocket expenses for medical bills, travel for treatment, and prosthetic devices; and projection of future medical care and related out-of-pocket expenses. Collect all the items (bills, medical reports, witness statements, etc.) necessary to prove or disprove these factors. Consider if the injured party has the three strikes: has not seen a doctor, has not lost work, has not used home remedies.[2]

Party's Commercial Condition

Note the value of land and other property involved; replacement value of property; value of property after injury; income before injury and after; loss of markets; loss of customers; loss of opportunity; loss of profits; past, present, and future losses; loss of rents; loss of business reputation; loss of the entire business; cost of any delay caused by injury; cost of finding alternatives for lost services or property; attempts to mitigate damages; and relationship of the alleged wrong to the injuries. Collect all evidence to prove these factors.

Special Areas of Investigation

You can assist by investigating other items as well. Research can be conducted on the recent verdicts rendered by juries or judges in the jurisdiction where the case will be tried. If this research is done very early in the case, it may help determine the best venue for the client. For example, rural juries are likely to produce lower awards than urban juries. Recent verdict information can be obtained from the clerk of court or from other attorneys in the vicinity. Some good sources on jury awards and amounts of damages include: the American Trial Lawyers Association's *ATLA Law Reporter*, the damages section of *West's Digests*, and sections on jury verdicts, damages, and settlements in *American Law Reports*. This information will help the attorney determine a fair settlement range in a particular jurisdiction.

Expert witnesses (including doctors) to be relied on should be researched on their reputation, background, intelligence, and courtroom abilities. Their friends, colleagues, and attorneys who have dealt with them can be helpful here.

The trial judge's attitude and previous decisions in similar cases should be researched. Other attorneys and paralegals can provide insights.

The opponent's lawyer needs to be assessed as well. If the adverse attorney is a good trial lawyer, tough minded on negotiations, and takes lowest offer to mean lowest offer, then settlement requests may differ from those of the lawyer who is inexperienced, starts high but caves in fast, and never goes to trial. Attorneys, clerks of court and assistants, and, in some cases, paralegals may be helpful in giving such information.

The track record of the insurance company in settling cases for the defendant and for how much may also be valuable.

Life expectancy statistics, vocational opportunities for the client, estimated inflation trends that may affect the cost of a child's college education, future medical care, estimated lost income and benefits, and basic cost of living (vocation experts and economists may need to be consulted) are areas that may need to be researched. Most of this kind of information can be obtained through the help of a reference librarian in most libraries.

Costs of litigation, trial, and attorney's fees should also be researched and collected if the attorney does not have a basis for this.

ASSIGNMENT 10:3
Draft a checklist of items that need to be researched and summarized in preparation for settlement. Indicate the sources for such information. Place the checklist in your system folder.

Calculating Damages

The ultimate settlement objective in most cases is a dollar amount that the plaintiff claims to deserve from the defendant. You can be of considerable assistance by recording and calculating the damages. All bills, expenses, receipts, and so on should be collected and categorized. Damages should be itemized to ensure they are clear, accurate, reviewable, and believable. Figure 10:1 is an example of a form that can be used to list and calculate damages in personal injury and other cases.[3] Read the form carefully and note each category of damages so you will know what to look for in this and future cases.

enjoyment of life" (hedonic damages) is being separated from "pain and suffering." These damages address losses in the enjoyment of recreation, family, travel, companionship, and other rewarding activities and relationships. Some courts permit separate expert evaluation on this issue. Plaintiffs try to separate the LOELs; defendants fight that separation.

A damages summary and worksheet similar to figure 10:1 can be devised for a commercial case stressing actual and anticipated damages. Pulling a file from a previous case where such damages applied can help in devising the worksheet.

When asked to review the damage claims of the other side, employ a similar process to test the thoroughness and accuracy of the opponent's proposal. In either case, all arithmetic should be double checked, and all the supporting documents should be reviewed for accuracy and applicability. Forward the damage sheet to the attorney for review and amendment.

Verify that the following items are also gathered and readied to support or contradict a settlement claim: all doctors' summaries, discovery summaries, photographs, videos, charts, diagrams, legal memoranda, witness statements, and any other material needed to help convince the other party.

ASSIGNMENT 10:4
Make a copy of the Damage Summary and Worksheet (Figure 10:1) and place it in your system folder. Make and include a special list of the formulas in the worksheet.

Figure 10:1   Damage Summary and Worksheet
_____

Plaintiff _____ Date of Accident _____

Case _____ v. _____ Case No. _____

Attorney _____ Prepared by _____

                                                    Date _____

I. Damage Totals

                                          Special Damages   _____

                                          General Damages   _____

                        Other Special and Exemplary Damages   _____

                                          _____

                                          Total Damages   _____

ITEMIZATION

II. Special Damages
        A. Special Damages (Medical)

    1. Ambulance Service: Name _____ Date _____

                              Amount _____

    2. Hospital: Name _____ Address _____

        Date _____ Service, Test, or Treatment _____

                              Amount _____

Name _____ Address _____

Date _____ Service, Test, or Treatment _____

Amount _____

(add as needed)

3. Doctor: Name _____ Address _____ Date_____

Purpose or Treatment _____ Tests _____

Amount _____

(add as needed)

4. Pharmaceutical:

Pharmacy _____ Address _____ Date_____

Medication or Prosthetic Device _____ Purpose _____

Amount _____

Pharmacy _____ Address _____ Date_____

Medication or Prosthetic Device _____ Purpose _____

Amount _____

(add as needed)

5. Travel for Medical Purposes:

Purpose _____ Date _____

Mileage _____ × _____ ¢/ mile = $_____ Lodging $_____

Meals $_____ Airfare, cabs, etc. $_____

Amount _____

(repeat as needed)

6. Home Care (Nurse or Attendant)

Purpose _____ Date(s) _____

Amount per day _____ × no. of days _____

Amount _____

(add as needed)

7. Psychologists and Physical Therapists

Name _____ Address _____

Purpose _____ Date _____

Amount _____

(add as needed)

TOTALS: _____

TOTAL PAST MEDICAL COSTS: _____

8. Future Medical Expenses
a. Special

☐ Hospitalization: no. of days _____ × cost _____ Amount _____

☐ Doctor: Purpose _____ $_____

☐ Surgery: Type _____ $_____

☐ Therapy: Type _____ no. _____ × cost _____$_____

☐ Travel: Purpose _____ miles _____ × _____¢/mi. $_____

Airfare, etc. _____ $_____

☐ Pharmacology: Nature _____ $_____

☐ Nurse: Cost/wk. _____ × no. of wks. _____ $_____

☐ Other: _____ $_____
b. Daily: Itemize current daily needs: nurse, equipment, medications, etc.

Item: _____ Purpose: _____ Daily cost $_____

Item: _____ Purpose: _____ Daily cost $_____

Total _____

(add as needed)

Total Daily Cost _____ × _____ Days/yr. × _____ Years + Special Costs

+ that figure × _____% for growth in medical costs = gross expenses × _____% for present

cash value * = $_____

TOTAL FUTURE MEDICAL EXPENSES $ _____

*Present cash value (present value discount) reduces the future gross expense to a current lump sum, which if invested will provide for the total gross expenses when needed. The percentage of reduction is usually based on projected annuity tables or average yields for savings accounts or U.S. bonds over a reasonable historical period.

B. Special Damages (Economic Loss)

1. Current Wage _____ Date returned to work _____

2. Units (hours, days, months, etc.) or percentage of annual income lost

_____ Total wages lost to date _____

3. Lost fringe benefits, bonuses, perquisites _____

_____

(list if needed) Total benefits lost to date _____

Total lost wages and benefits to date _____

4. Lost Household Services to Date:
(Market value of household chores: bookkeeper, parent [care giver, tutor, chauffeur] maid,

cook, decorator, gardener, etc.) $_____/wk. × no. of weeks _____ = $_____

5. Lost other considerations: _____

_____ $_____

Total Lost Wages, Benefits, Household Services to Date $_____

6. If the person's income is reduced by any disability, for example a need to change to a job with less pay,

then that loss should also be added. $_____

7. Future Economic Loss

a. Future Wages (if complete disability or death):

Most recent normal year's wages $_____ × years of work expectancy ** _____
(including any remaining portion of current year) + that figure × compounded annual growth rate ***

of _____% = gross wage loss $_____

Gross wage loss $_____ less _____% reduction to present cash value =

$_____

☐ If the person has partial disability, gross wage loss can be computed by applying the same formula to the percentage of current yearly wage lost because of disability. If death, reduce gross wage loss by the percentage of annual wage actually consumed by that person. See family expenses over a period of several years.

**Years to age 65 or Department of Labor Statistics for work life in specific occupations or may be set by state law.

***Based on average % raise over same number of past years as work expectancy years for that person or industry standard. Consult Department of Labor statistics but usually between 4–8%. Adjust figure upward if raises show marked increase in recent years. Note: Provide alternative set of figures if promotion, career change, or other variable is likely.

b. Future Fringe Benefits:

Annual fringe benefit $_____ × _____ years of work expectancy + that figure ×

compounded annual growth rate for benefits of _____% = gross benefits loss

$_____

Gross benefits loss $_____ less _____% reduction to present cash value =

$_____

☐ Annual growth rate for benefits is usually higher than wages. See Department of Labor statistics for occupation. Adjust if recent rise in %.

c. Future Investments (if applicable)

Amount of annual income placed in savings or other investments $_____ × compounded

annual growth rate _____% (based on average return over past years)

Total Lost Future Investment Income $_____
(reduced to present cash value if necessary)

d. Future Household Services

Annual Lost Market Value for each service (bookkeeper, cook, maid, painter, gardener,

child-care giver, etc.) _____ Annual cost × _____ yrs. life expectancy† = $_____ +

that figure × _____% annual growth rate in cost of household services‡ =

Total Future Household Services $_____

†*Life expectancy:* based on readily accessible projections (consult reference librarian or insurance sources).

‡*Annual growth rate for household services* is often tied to projections based on history of consumer price index adjusted for any recent increases. The percentage usually ranges from 3–5%.

e. Adjustments for Income Taxes: Consult with Attorney

f. Adjustments for Inflation

(Being allowed more frequently. See published reports from trustees of Federal Old Age and Survivors Insurance and Disability Insurance Trust Funds for inflation projections and what that means in real wage increases.)

Total Future Income Loss $_____ $_____

C. Special Damages (Property)

1. Personal Property:

Item _____

Destroyed: Market Value $_____ less salvage $_____ = $_____

Damaged: Cost of restoration $_____ or if cannot be restored, value before damage $_____ less value after damage $_____ plus costs to attempt to preserve or restore $_____ = $_____

Other Property:

List: Portraits, heirlooms, pets, etc., with appraiser's valuation or some other reasonable standard

$_____

Appliances, furniture, clothing, worth at time of loss $_____

2. Real Property (land, buildings)

Item _____

If permanent: value before damage $_____ less value after $_____ plus interest to date =

$_____

If temporary: reduction to rental or other profit value $_____ plus injury to crops, buildings, improvements $_____ plus restoration costs $_____ plus any applicable interest =

$_____

(consult local law)

Total Property Damages $_____ $_____

Total Special Damages $_____

III. General Damages

Pain and Suffering: fear, humiliation, inconvenience, anxiety, horror of injury, pain, discomfort; loss of companionship, status, stimulation of job, enjoyment of life's experiences; and other subjective factors caused by injury. Briefly summarize: _____

_____

_____

_____

Standard: as estimated by party or reasonable person as fair.

Value per day $_____ × no. days/yr. _____ × yrs. of life expectancy _____

× _____% inflation factor if allowed = $_____

Consortium: value per day $＿＿＿＿＿ × no. of days per year ＿＿＿＿＿ × yrs. of life expectancy

× ＿＿＿＿＿% inflation factor if allowed = $＿＿＿＿＿

Note: Review current jury verdicts for reasonable estimates. Check local statutes for any limits on awards. Most states do not require a reduction to present cash value for pain and suffering.

Total Pain and Suffering and General Damages $＿＿＿＿＿ $＿＿＿＿＿

IV. Other special and Exemplary Damages

1. Funeral Expenses $＿＿＿＿＿

2. Exemplary:

Punitive $＿＿＿＿＿

Attorney's

Fees $＿＿＿＿＿

3. Miscellaneous Damages $＿＿＿＿＿

Total of other Special and Exemplary Damages $＿＿＿＿＿ $＿＿＿＿＿

TOTAL DAMAGES $＿＿＿＿＿

Presenting the Settlement Request

Introduction

The gathered and summarized information can now be evaluated by the attorney to determine the strength of the case and a fair settlement. The settlement request usually comes from the plaintiff and is presented to convince the defense that this is a fair and reasonable settlement in their client's best interests. The actual form in which the case is presented depends to a large degree on the amount of damages. It makes little sense to prepare a settlement brochure costing $500 in a $1,200 lawsuit. There would be nothing left for the client after attorney fees and other expenses. In this kind of case, a small narrative summary sheet or letter outlining the key information may suffice. A large case may justify a more detailed version of the summary, called a **settlement précis.** In the big cases involving many thousands of dollars, a thorough settlement brochure may be prepared.

A settlement letter, précis, or brochure needs to be as convincing as possible. In marshaling the facts of the case, it must stress the obviousness of the opponent's liability; the serious and sympathetic nature of the injuries; the amount of damages that has been and will be incurred; but most of all, the presentation must stress how the accident has torn up the life of the injured person as a productive or potentially productive individual. If liability is likely to be proven, it is the human factor that will impress the jury and affect the amount of their award. A settlement presentation, therefore, can use the leverage of a potentially sympathetic jury to move the defendant to settle.

The Settlement Précis or Letter

The précis or letter must be brief and should cover the following: the identification of the plaintiff; the facts of the case that reflect the liability of the defendant; the theory of liability; the injury and past, current, and future medical consequences; all expenses; a summary of the evaluation; and a proposed figure for settlement. Figure 10:2 is an example of a settlement précis.[4]

Figure 10:2   Settlement Précis—Illustration

Social history—Sharon Williams was born July 10th, 1960, the fourth of four children born to John and Virginia Williams. The family lives at 2305 Grand Vista, Columbus, Missouri. Mr. Williams is employed as a machinist at Eagle Air Craft Co. a position he has held for six years.

Sharon is a student in the second grade of Middleton Grade School. She is a member of Girl Scout Troop 378 and is a member of the YMCA girls' swimming team.

Medical History—Sharon had a normal prenatal history and a normal birth. She has been attended by Dr. Grant Fry, a pediatrician, from birth. She has suffered from the childhood diseases of chicken pox and measles. She has never suffered any disability to her lower limbs and has never sustained any injuries to her legs, back or spine. Dr. Fry's medical report is attached.

Facts of Accident—On April 5, 1967 Sharon was enroute from her home to school. The attached police report confirms that the day was clear and warm and the streets were dry. Sharon was by herself and crossing Grand Avenue at its intersection with Washington Street moving westwardly from the southeast to the southwest corner approximately six feet south of the south curb line and within the designated crosswalk. Grand Avenue is forty feet wide with two lanes of traffic moving in each direction. It is straight and level and surfaced with asphalt. There were no cars parked within sixty feet of the intersection. A sign located one hundred feet south of the intersection on Grand has the legend "Caution Children." Police report confirming the description of the scene of the accident is attached.

Sharon was struck by the north bound automobile of defendant at a point five feet from the center line. The attached photographs show the following:

Photo 1 skid marks ten feet long, blood on street.

Photo 2 damage to left head light.

Sharon states that when she left the southeast corner of the intersection the light was in her favor. She never looked at the light again. She walked at a normal pace until she was hit. She was looking forward and never saw or heard the defendant's automobile. The accident occurred at 8:35 A.M. The school is two blocks away and convenes at 8:45 A.M.

A statement taken from the defendant, a copy of which is attached, acknowledges that he didn't see the plaintiff until she was fifteen feet from him and that his automobile came to a stop twenty feet after impact.

Theories of Recovery

The plaintiff has three theories of recovery:

1. That defendant violated a red light
2. That defendant failed to keep a lookout
3. That defendant failed to exercise the highest degree of care to bring his automobile to a stop or slacken after plaintiff came into a position of immediate danger.

The proof of the first theory is supported by plaintiff's testimony that when she left the curb the light was green for westbound traffic. By reason of the plaintiff's age the court may not permit her to testify. In that event, the defendant's failure to keep a lookout could be submitted as an alternate theory of recovery. Defendant has acknowledged that he didn't see plaintiff until he was fifteen feet away from her and she was already in his path. This would place Sharon at least twelve feet from the curb. The court will judicially notice that the pace of walk is approximately two or three miles an hour or 2.9 to 4.4 feet per second. Wofford v. St.Louis Public Service Co., Mo., 252 S.W.2d 529. Sharon was in the street and visible to defendant for almost three seconds before the accident. At defendant's acknowledged speed of twenty five miles per hour he was traveling at approximately thirty six feet per second or was approximately one hundred feet away when he should have seen Sharon. He was further alerted by the warning sign as he approached the intersection.

By reason of her age, it is questionable whether Sharon would be held responsible for her own actions. Malott v. Harvey, 199 Mo.App. 615, 204 S.W. 940; Quirk v. Metropolitan St. Ry. Co., 200 Mo.App. 585, 210 S.W. 103.

In the event Sharon could be held accountable for not maintaining a proper lookout a third theory of recovery is available: defendant's failure to stop or slacken after plaintiff came into a position of immediate danger. By defendant's admission he came to a stop twenty feet after the impact and he did not attempt evasive action until he was fifteen feet from Sharon, therefore his overall stopping distance was thirty five feet. A jury could find that by reason of Sharon's obliviousness that she was in immediate danger as she approached the path of the vehicle and when defendant's automobile was more than the thirty five feet that was available to bring his vehicle to a stop.

The skid marks indicate that no slackening took place until the defendant's vehicle was within ten feet of the impact. The damage to the automobile indicates it was the left front headlight which struck Sharon. Sharon was within two feet of safety beyond the path of the car when she was struck. Moving at 4.4 feet per second, in one half second she would have escaped injury. From this the jury could assume that a failure to slacken at an earlier time was the proximate cause of the injury.

Medical

The police report states that Sharon was "bleeding about the face and mouth" and complaining of "pain in the right hip." She was taken by police cruiser to Welfare Hospital where it was discovered that she had suffered the loss of a front upper left tooth which was permanent, a laceration of the lip necessitating six stitches, and a bruise of the right hip. Portions of the hospital record are attached. She was examined by her pediatrician Dr. Fry who referred her to Dr. William Jones a dentist for examination. He confirms the loss of the permanent tooth and outlines the dental prostheses which will be needed throughout her growth stage and into adulthood. His report is attached. The stitches were removed after six days by Dr. Fry leaving a hair line scar one-fourth inch long near the upper lip.

Expenses

Emergency room Welfare Hospital	$ 25.00
Dr. Grant Fry	$ 75.00
Dr. William Jones	
Examination	$ 35.00
Anticipated treatment	$360.00

Analysis of Evaluation

Actual out of pocket expenses total $145.00 with anticipated costs for dental prosthetic devices throughout Sharon's growth period adding $360.00 for a total of $505.00. The loss of the tooth is permanent and will necessitate special prophylactic care to maintain the prosthetic devices which must be employed. The scar above the lip is discernible and will be permanent.

It is anticipated that a jury verdict could fall within the $6,000 to $7,000 range. If the case could be settled without further legal procedure I would recommend a settlement of $4,500.

The précis can be reduced to an even more concise statement, if appropriate.

ASSIGNMENT 10:5
Using your imagination to provide missing facts, draft a settlement précis for the Ann Forrester case. Critique these in small groups with your fellow students. Place an example of the settlement précis in your system folder. Keep in mind that a well-drafted Forrester précis as part of a well-drafted system folder can be impressive when offered as a writing sample to a future employer.

The Settlement Brochure (Portfolio)

The settlement brochure is the product of a serious commitment of time and money. It is unlikely to be used unless the injuries are serious and the liability of the defendant is sufficiently clear. It does little good to "sell" the pain and suffering of a client if the opponent thinks they have a good shot at disproving liability at trial. The decision to commit the resources to a brochure rests with the attorney, but you should be prepared to give impressions and evaluations of the case if asked.

The brochure is an orderly, dramatic, and persuasive presentation of the facts, statements, reports, and exhibits in the case. When done well and prepared early in the case, it tells the other side that this is a case to be taken seriously, that the plaintiff is thorough, organized, and likely to win. In addition, the preparation of the brochure forces the attorney to evaluate the case early in the process, identify its strengths and weaknesses, and see where more investigation or evidence is needed. It also facilitates the preparation of the trial brief (see next chapter) for the pretrial conference or trial. The fact that the plaintiff has set everything out in the case can be used as evidence of the plaintiff's desire to deal openly and in good faith from the start. A juror may decide to vote for higher damages if it appears that the defendant could have avoided the time-consuming trial by settling weeks or months before.

Paralegals with good communication skills can increase their value to the law firm by being able to organize and draft an effective settlement brochure. It not only can be of tremendous assistance to the attorney, but also may be the tool that wraps up the case.

The brochure should be organized to include the following areas:

1. The facts of the case as supported by the evidence
   This section includes summaries of the cause of action; details of the accident, witnesses, and reports; photos of the accident scene, vehicle, and injured party; dramatic newspaper clippings; and other evidence to support the claim.
2. The personal history of the plaintiff
   This section introduces the client and makes a statement as to who this person is, what kind of life he or she has had, what the person has enjoyed, what joy the client has brought to others, what services he or she has provided others, employment, earnings, service and professional organizations, stature in the community, religious affiliation, education, awards, recognition, services to family, letters of citation, evidence of advancement, future prior to accident, and other "get-to-know this person" facts and evidence. One or several carefully selected before-the-accident photos can be effective here.

3. The prior medical history of the plaintiff

This section is a concise summary of the plaintiff's medical history prior to the accident. Any previous injuries or medical conditions, even if they tend to reduce the damages, should be candidly presented. This promotes credibility and makes the brochure more effective. Previous medical reports should be included if relevant and if they clearly define the extent and limits of previous problems.

4. Injury and its present and long-term effects

This section should graphically depict the fear, pain, and anguish of experiencing the accident. The injuries should be described in detail and be supported by physician's reports, hospital summary sheets, records of surgery, tests, treatment, therapy, photos, and reference to videos of healing progress. The current and future status of the client should also be described, supported by physician reports on the prognosis of the injured party. This should evoke sympathy and meaningfully portray the pathetic physical and social existence faced by the plaintiff.

5. The economic and related psychological impact of the injury

The brochure describes how the injury affects future employment and that impact on the plaintiff and the plaintiff's family. The economics of disability, reduced status, lowered self-esteem, continual problems, and the like should be thoroughly covered.

6. Damages

The special, general, and exemplary damages are summarized and explained where necessary. Copies of all bills, checks, receipts, and so on are included to substantiate the claims.

7. Evaluation of claim

The brochure ends with a summary reiterating the most significant aspects of the claim and statement of a proposed settlement figure.

Some attorneys feel that any pertinent legal memoranda and such questions as the legal issues in the case, evidentiary matters, and itemized damages should be included. Others believe that the brochure is not the place for such arguments. Some attorneys also like to include copies of the pleadings enclosing at least the complaint, summons, and answer, or go so far as to include the pertinent jury instructions. It can be effective to show that pertinent law clearly and persuasively supports your position, but be sure to discuss these items with the attorney before you draft a brochure.

The brochure should be honest and professional. It should not be overblown, simplistic, or unduly sentimental. How much it should reveal is sometimes a difficult question. A brochure should be forthright, but it can be a disadvantage if it only succeeds in better preparing the opposition to rebut creative and imaginative arguments. Supporting medical reports and witness statements should at least appear to be objective. If they show a strong bias for the plaintiff, they may simply alert the opponent to the fact that the attending physician has lost objectivity and is vulnerable to attack. These questions are addressed by the supervising attorney, but, again, an alert paralegal can point out areas that may have been overlooked and can contribute to an improved brochure.

Figure 10:3 is an example of a settlement brochure. Although it does not strictly follow the category arrangement previously proposed, most of these elements are contained in this sample.[5]

Figure 10:3 Settlement Brochure

UNITED STATES DISTRICT COURT FOR

THE _____ DISTRICT OF _____ _____ DIVISION

_____,

               Plaintiff

     v.   Civil Action, File No. _____

_____,

               Defendant

SETTLEMENT BROCHURE

_____

Plaintiff's attorney

_____

Address

_____

Phone

NOTE: (Optional)

The exhibit, statements, and reports incorporated in this brochure are submitted for settlement purposes only. They are not to be copied or reproduced in any fashion. In the event this case is tried, none of the contents of this report, neither facts, representations, nor opinions are to be used without plaintiff's permission. (Some offices place a legend on each page of the brochure so it cannot be used by the other party.)

Index (or Table of Contents)

    I. Description of Accident
          Photos of Accident
          Newspaper Reports
          Police Reports
          Witness Statements (or Summary)
          Photos: Injuries, Plaintiff Today, Others
   II. Memorandum on Admissibility of Photos (Optional)
  III. Personal History of Plaintiff
          Photos of Catherine Brown: Family, Teaching, Recreation
  IV. Medical History of Plaintiff—Summary
   V. Medical History and Physical Report by Initial Attending Physician
  VI. Operative Record of Initial Attending Physician
 VII. Consultation Report by Doctor Johnson, Orthopedic Surgeon
VIII. Operative Record of Doctor Smith, Oral Surgeon
  IX. X-Ray Interpretation
   X. Discharge Summary
  XI. Medical Report of Doctor Anderson, Orthopedic Surgeon
 XII. Medical Report of Doctor Holt, Plastic Surgeon
XIII. Medical Expenses
XIV. Effects of Injuries
 XV. Evaluation of Claims

Settlement Brochure

page 1

I. Description of Accident

Photo of Accident

News Clipping

News Clipping

News Clipping

Settlement Brochure

page 2

Police Report

(Own summary could be substituted)

Settlement Brochure

page 3

Witness Statements or Summary

Settlement Brochure

page 4

Photo of Injuries

Settlement Brochure

page 5

Photos of Plaintiff Today

(Showing scars, limitations, wheelchair, etc.)

Settlement Brochure

page 6

II. Memorandum on Admissibility of Photographic Evidence

III. Personal History of Plaintiff

Catherine Brown was born June 8, 1946 and at the time of the accident was twenty-six years of age. She was reared in Texas where she completed four years of high school at Lockhart, Texas and four years of college at Southwest Texas State College. On March 13, 1968 she was married to Fred Brown and his change of employment necessitated a move before her last semester of college could be completed.

On January 29, 1969 Catherine gave birth to her only child, Carl Robert.

Upon arrival in the Kansas City area Catherine enrolled in the Music Conservatory of the University of Missouri—Kansas City and graduated with a B.M.E. in music in 1970. She served as a substitute music teacher in the public schools of Kansas City in the Spring of 1971 and in the fall of that year was hired as Music Director of the R-7 School District in Center City, Missouri at a salary of $6,800 for the school year.

Catherine's responsibility included the directorship of three bands and two choirs. In addition she served as a sponsor for the Pep Club and Cheerleaders. Her outside activities included membership in the Mu Phi Epsilon Music Sorority and the Center City Music Club.

IV. Medical History of Plaintiff—Summary

Prior to the date of the accident, June 16, 1972, Catherine Brown was in excellent health. She had never suffered any physical disability and her only hospitalization was for the birth of her son.

The accident was unusually violent. The loaded gravel truck struck the vehicle in which plaintiff was a passenger with such force that the automobile was carried seventy-six feet and seven inches beyond the point of impact. The side on which plaintiff was sitting was literally "run over." (See attached photo from police report).

The injuries, detailed in the hospital record and medical reports which follow, consisted primarily of the following:

disfiguring lacerations of face;
multiple fractures of the jaws;
fracture of clavicle with loss of bone;
multiple fractures of the pelvis;
fracture of radius and ulna right arm;
fracture of left forearm;
severe cerebral contusion.

V. Medical History and Physical Report by Initial Attending Physician

[Date]

BROWN, Catherine.
CHIEF COMPLAINT: Auto accident.
PRESENT ILLNESS: The patient is a 26 year old Gravida I, Para I, Aborta O, white female who was involved in an auto truck accident. The patient was brought immediately to the Emergency Room of General Hospital at which time the patient was admitted through the Emergency Room by Dr. Smith. The patient was then seen by this doctor in the Intensive Care Unit at which time the patient presented with a blood pressure systolic between 80 and 90. The patient had a very rapid pulse of 120. The patient was cool and appeared to be in shock.
PHYSICAL EXAMINATION:
NEUROLOGICAL: The patient was confused as to time and place with episodes of incoherence. The pupils were dilated and extremely sluggish but were reactive. Fundoscopic examination revealed the discs to be sharp. There was no evidence of papilledema. Cranial nerves appeared to be intact. There was no evidence of motor or sensory loss of the extremities. The patient had obvious multiple fractures.
HEENT: Tympanic membranes were intact. There was no evidence of fluid or blood in the auditory canals. Posterior pharynx was clear. Oral cavity: The patient had palpable fractures of the mandible bilaterally.
NECK: Supple with no palpable masses or tenderness. No bruits. Thyroid was not palpable.
CHEST: Lungs were clear on auscultation and percussion. The patient had palpable fractures over the right chest.

ABDOMEN: No palpable masses or tenderness. Bowel sounds hypoactive. No CVA tenderness. Patient had a mild suprapubic tenderness.

EXTREMITIES: Symmetrical. The patient had marked deformity of the right forearm and wrist area with marked swelling. The patient also had deformity of the left forearm with some swelling. Pressure applied to the pelvic cage caused excruciating pain. Peripheral pulses in all extremities were grade III and equal bilaterally.

SKIN: The patient had multiple large facial lacerations that covered the entire right face, forehead and parietal area. The patient also had a laceration of the right submandibular area, and left face at the outer canthus of the mouth. The patient had multiple abrasions over the upper extremities and a large laceration over the dorsum of the left hand with no evidence of tendon involvement.

IMPRESSION: Shock syndrome secondary to blood loss and multiple fractures; fracture of the right radius and ulna; right thoracic fractures; pelvic fractures; severe cerebral contusion; multiple lacerations.

DISPOSITION: Patient will be treated for shock syndrome with intravenous fluids, plasma expanders, antibiotics, and patient will then have splinting of the extremities and lacerations closed.

DIAGNOSIS: Compound fracture right and left body of the mandible. The patient sustained the injuries in an auto accident.

RECOMMENDATIONS: Closed reduction by the application of maxillary and mandibular arch bars. Thank you for this consultation.

[*Signed*]

_____

C. A. Jones, M.D.

VI. *Operative Record of Initial Attending Physician*

[*Date*]

BROWN, Catherine.

PRE-OP DIAGNOSIS: Auto accident with shock syndrome, multiple facial lacerations, laceration of the left lower lip, laceration of left hand, open fracture of the clavicle, fracture of radius and pelvic fractures, cerebral concussion, moderate, severe.

SURGEON: C. A. Jones.

OPERATIVE PROCEDURE: The patient was placed in the supine position. Utilizing 1% Xylocaine diluted to ½% the patient had local infiltration and field blocks for closure of lacerations. The patient had multiple lacerations around the right eye, eyebrow and scalp. The patient also had a through and through laceration of the left lower lip and mouth. The patient had multiple small lacerations on the left arm and dorsum of the left hand. All the lacerations were infiltrated and thoroughly scrubbed with Betadine and Betadine solution. The patient then had excision of the margins of the lacerations. The patient had a moderate amount of skin loss on the right temporal area which required undermining of the scalp flap for primary closure. This was repaired with interrupted 4–0 chromic suture and 5–0 nylon suture. Through and through laceration of the left lower lip was repaired by first closing the subcutaneous tissue beneath the submucosa of the oral cavity with interrupted 3–0 chromic. The wound was thoroughly irrigated with Saline. The subcutaneous tissue and muscle tissue was then approximated with interrupted 4–0 chromic. The skin was closed with interrupted 5–0 nylon. The subcutaneous tissue in the lower lip and muscle tissue was then approximated with interrupted 4–0 chromic. The skin was closed with interrupted 5–0 nylon suture. The lacerations on the hand and arm were handled in a likewise manner. The patient also had an open comminuted fracture of the right clavicle with a portion of the bone sticking up through the skin and remaining attached by a piece of periosteum. The bone had apparently been ground into the dirt. It was therefore thought advisable and with consultation by Dr. Peterson that this portion of the clavicle should be excised and removed. The wound was opened and thoroughly irrigated with appproximately two liters of saline solution. The wound was then closed with interrupted 3–0 chromic and interrupted 4–0 nylon suture. All the wounds were then bandaged with Garamycin and 4 × 4 dressings. The patient also had obvious fracture of the forearm. The forearm was thus splinted due to severe edema at that time, it was felt that casting was not indicated. The arm was splinted with a posterior splint and Ace bandage.

The patient was then returned to surgical ICU for further followup. Post-operative condition was guarded.

[*Signed*]

_____

C. A. Jones, M.D., Surgeon

VII. *Consultation Report by Doctor Johnson, Orthopedic Surgeon*

[*Date*]

BROWN, Catherine.

This 26-year-old lady was seen in consultation with Dr. Jones. The initial care had been provided when the patient came into the hospital by Dr. Jones for a compound fracture of the right clavicle and thoracic fractures. The patient also had fractures of the pubis which were also treated by Dr. Jones. I saw the patient at Dr. Jones' request for treatment of a fracture of the right distal radius, and this was treated with a closed reduction on 6/18/72, and immobilized in a long arm cast.

Review of x-rays of the right clavicle revealed satisfactory position of the fracture of the clavicle and also fractures of the right pubis were in satisfactory position. The patient was treated with bed rest for the fractures of the pubis. The patient responded quite nicely to this.

Because of persistent pain in the forearm, left, x-rays were taken several weeks following the accident and these revealed a cracked fracture of the distal ulna. Although it was in good position it was felt that immobilization in a short arm cast was indicated and this was applied. At the time of discharge the patient was instructed to return to my office to be followed as an outpatient as treatment for fractures of the right radius and ulna and the left ulna.

[*Signed*]

_____

A. B. Johnson, M.D., Consultant

VIII. *Operative Record of Doctor Smith, Oral Surgeon*

[*Date*]

BROWN, Catherine.

OPERATION: Closed reduction and application of maxillary and mandibular arch bar with manual reduction.

PRE-OP DIAGNOSIS: Compound fracture of the right and left body of the mandible.

SURGEON: A. B. Smith.

OPERATIVE PROCEDURE: The patient was brought to the operating room in satisfactory physical condition. General anesthesia was induced. The patient was intubated through the right nares and draped in the usual manner for an intra-oral procedure. Mouth and throat were thoroughly cleansed. Deep throat pack was placed.

Following this a maxillary arch bar was ligated to the remaining maxillary teeth. After this had been accomplished manual reduction of the fracture sites was accomplished, circumferential wires were placed around the teeth on either side of the fracture site. After this had been accomplished a mandibular arch bar was ligated to the mandibular teeth thus holding the fracture sites in good alignment. Deep throat pack was removed. Elastids will be placed this evening or in the morning.

Dr. Johnson then continued with his part of the procedure, reduction of the right arm.

[*Signed*]

_____

A. B. Smith, D.D.S.

IX. X-ray Interpretation

[*Date*]

BROWN, Catherine.

RIGHT FOREARM EXAM including the ELBOW AND WRIST REGION with multiple views with a metal splint in place reveals recent fracture of the distal one-third of the shaft of the radius approximately 2 inches from the wrist joint. There is minimal comminution. The fragments are not widely displaced or separated. There is very slight anterior angulation.

There is also a fracture of the ulna slightly more than one cm. from the distal end with minimal displacement of these fragments.

There is no dislocation.

RIGHT SHOULDER REEXAM WITH AP VIEW shows the lateral fracture fragments of the clavicle to be displaced completely inferiorly in relation to the medial fragment. The major fragments are separated approximately one-half cm. The fracture fragments of the right 2nd rib are separated almost one-half cm. There is little callus formation in the fracture region but the fragments are not stabilized by bony union. There are also fractures of the right 5th and 6th ribs posteriorly in good position.

LEFT FOREARM EXAM reveals a fracture in the ulna about 7 cm. above the wrist joint. The fragments are in close apposition with less than ½ cm. displacement and no significant degree of angulation.

PELVIS EXAM WITH FILMS MADE AT THE BEDSIDE reveals recent fractures of the superior and inferior pelvic rami and the symphysis pubis on the right side. The fragments show only minimal displacement. There is no dislocation. There is also irregularity in the right side of the sacrum due to fracture in this region with minimal impaction of the fragments.

The sacroiliac joints are not disrupted.

RIGHT FOREARM AND ELBOW reading including with reading of the films of night before examination of the Rt Arm.

EXAMINATION OF THE SKULL AND MANDIBLE WITH MULTIPLE VIEWS reveals recent fracture of the body of the mandible on the left side. The anterior fragment is displaced medially one cm. No other definite fracture of the mandible is seen at this time. There is no apparent fracture of the skull or depression. The sella turcia is regular.

RIGHT CLAVICLE AND CHEST EXAM reveal the markedly comminuted fracture near the mid portion of the right clavicle. The major fragments are separated almost one-half inch. There is complete inferior displacement of the lateral major fragment. There is no definite rib fracture or lung injury.

RIGHT FOREARM EXAM with AP AND LATERAL VIEWS with films made at the bedside shows fracture of the radius 2 inches from the distal end with minimal comminution, and approximately 10 degrees anterior angulation of the fragments. The fragments are not widely displaced. There is also a fracture of the ulna approximately one cm. from the distal end with minimal comminution and slight impaction of these fragments. There is no dislocation.

[*Signed*]

_____

Radiologist

X. Discharge Summary

[*Date*]

BROWN, Catherine.

PRESENT ILLNESS: The patient is a 26 year old white female who was involved in an auto truck accident. The patient was apparently struck broadside by the truck and carried out through a field. The patient was brought to the Emergency Room for treatment. The patient was admitted through the Emergency Room by Dr. Smith, who initiated treatment. The patient was then seen in ICU with a blood pressure of 60 to 90 systolic. The patient was confused as to time and place. Neurological examination revealed both pupils to be extremely dilated and sluggish. Discs were sharp. The patient was able to move all extremities. The patient also had multiple facial lacerations and fractures of the extremities.

PERTINENT PHYSICAL FINDINGS: Revealed multiple facial lacerations involving the right face and right temple area. There was no palpable skull fracture. The patient had bilateral fractures of the mandible, fractures of both forearms and pelvic fracture.

The patient was also seen in consultation by Dr. Peterson, Dr. Johnson and Dr. Smith. Patient initially had closure of the facial lacerations, repair of lacerations of the lower lip and left hand. The patient had an open fracture of the right clavicle which was debrided. A small portion of bone was removed. The wound was thoroughly irrigated and closed. The patient had splinting of both forearms. The patient was treated vigorously for shock with intravenous fluids, vasopressors and blood. The patient was also started on massive doses of antibiotics. The patient became more responsive 36 hours after admission at which time the patient then had maxillary fractures and fractures of the radius and ulna bilateral corrected. The patient was then treated with bed rest for four weeks due to large pelvic fracture. The patient's hospital course following the first four days of admission was unremarkable except for slow progression of activity. The patient was ambulated on the 3rd week post-admission. At the time of discharge the patient was ambulatory without assistance, however, the patient had a wide base gait due to instability of the pelvis. The patient's forearms were in plaster splints. The patient's maxillas were still wired. The patient was on a full liquid diet. The facial lacerations had healed well with minimal amount of scar defect. The patient was given a one week return office appointment for followup examination. The patient was discharged from the hospital on Keflex 250 mgms q.i.d.

FINAL DIAGNOSIS: (1) Shock syndrome, secondary to multiple fractures and blood loss.

                          (2) Fracture of right radius and ulna.

                          (3) Fractures of left ulna.

                          (4) Fracture of right clavicle and right second rib, anteriorly.

                          (5) Multiple pelvic fractures.

                          (6) Severe cerebral contusion.

                          (7) Multiple facial and extremity lacerations.

[*Signed*]

_____

C. A. Jones, M.D.

XI. Medical Report of Orthopedic Surgeon

[*Date*]

Re: Catherine Brown

(including history, previous injuries, physical exam, summary and prognosis)

XII. Medical Report of Doctor Holt, Plastic Surgeon

James P. Holt, M.D.

Plastic and Reconstructive Surgery Maxillo-facial Surgery

[*Date*]

Mr. James W. Jeans, Attorney
U.M.K.C. Law Building
5100 Rockhill Road
Kansas City, Missouri 64110

Dear Mr. Jeans:

The following is a medical report on Catherine Brown, a 26-year-old music director, who was seen in my office on December 9, 1972, for evaluation of scars resulting from injuries in an automobile accident on June 16, 1972.

The patient states that she was hospitalized for over a month in Joplin, Missouri, with fractures of the pelvis, jaw, right forearm, left forearm, right clavicle and ribs.

She has multiple atrophic scars running from the eybrow and temple to above the ear (4–5 inches in total length), a scar at a right angle to the mandible and lower part of the ear (3–4 inches) which is also atrophic, a transverse atrophic scar of the lower lip (2 inches) with a ridge inside the labial mucosa, a scar of the dorsum of the right hand (3 inches), two scars of the radial aspect of the wrist (1 inch) and a scar of the right lower neck (1½ inches).

There is sensitivity around the right temple and clavicle and over the right wrist due to the injuries and scarring. She has some limitation of supination at the wrist and difficulty in abduction of the right fifth finger. These limitations interfere with playing the piano which is her professional activity.

My recommendation in this case would be a revision of the scars mentioned above which would require hospitalization and general anesthesia. The surgical fee for the procedures over the entire areas could be estimated at $500-$750 not to include the cost of hospitalization, anesthesia, surgical suite, laboratory fees, etc. After the initial revision, it is possible that a dermabrasion procedure might further minimize the scarring after a period of 4-6 months.

In any event, regardless of the improvement that could be obtained from the surgery, the patient would still undoubtedly have permanent, visible scarring and some cosmetic disfigurement in the areas enumerated.

[*Signed*]

James P. Holt, M.D.

XIII. Medical Expenses
The cost of the medical services necessitated by the injuries incurred in the accident are itemized as follows:

General Hospital	$2,557.98
Dr. Smith	200.00
Dr. Chess	60.00
Dr. Johnson	120.00
Dr. Jones	450.00
Misc.	52.50
Dr. Murphy	56.00
Dr. James Holt	15.00
Total	$3,511.48

In addition Dr. Holt, the plastic surgeon estimates $500-$750 for surgical fees for remedial surgery plus a like amount for hospitalization, anesthesiologist, etc. It appears fair to state that total medical will approximate five thousand dollars.

XIV. Effects of Injuries
The effects of the injuries upon Catherine Brown and her family have been pronounced. She has lost weight, has been moody and depressed and has been unable to resume her activities in music. Although rehired in 1973 at $7,000 (as evidenced by the employment contract) because of her physical and emotional effects of her injury she was unable to satisfactorily perform her duties and was not rehired. In addition her private music lessons (which accounted for approximately $30 per month) had to be discontinued.

Fred Brown, at the time of the accident, was working towards a master's degree in Counselor Education at U.M.K.C. His wife's need for constant attention and encouragement has delayed the completion of his education and has worked a real hardship on the family. Even though Catherine is no longer employed in the Bronaugh area, they continue to live there because they secure their present housing by Fred doing farm chores for the owner. He must commute over 100 miles to Kansas City for his schooling and work forty to sixty hours on the farm for house rent and living money.

XV. Evaluation of Claims
The injuries speak for themselves and anyone so victimized would be entitled to a substantial sum for the resulting pain and disability. For Catherine Brown the effects were particularly disabling. The loss of

strength, flexibility and dexterity of her right hand has seriously impaired her capacity as a musician and thus has affected her earning potential. The effects of the disfiguring facial scars on this twenty-six year old woman have been aggravated by the fact that her employment brings her before the public as well as numerous students. Although future plastic surgery may ameliorate some of the disfigurement of the skin, others will remain. The contour of the jaw and teeth have been permanently altered. The loss of bone in the clavicle has resulted in a permanent postural change.

We evaluate the damages for Catherine Brown as follows:

Medical expenses to date	$3,511.48
Medical expenses projected	1,500.00
Loss of earnings school year '73	7,200.00
Loss of earnings private lessons to date at $30 per month	450.00
	$12,661.48

Future loss of wages depends on the hirability of a physically impaired candidate suffering from permanent head injuries manifested by "nervousness, irritability, anger, fatigue, memory changes, forgetfulness, headaches, concentration difficulties." The impairment of Catherine's earning capacity is a fact—only the amount is uncertain. A strong argument could be advanced that a fair estimate could be figured at $1,000 a year or a total of $38,000 until her work expectancy of sixty five.

If permanent disability and future pain and suffering were to be evaluated on the same basis of $1,000 for each year of expectancy, one could argue an additional $43,000 for the biblical life span. A total of these sums is $93,661.48.

This computation is advanced as an example of jury argument that could be legitimately advanced with, in my opinion, a good chance of acceptance. I appreciate that for settlement purposes the sum of $93,661.48 is not a valid figure—but it does represent the degree to which each of the parties is exposed as individual or joint tort-feasor. Add to this the loss of consortium claim of the husband and the injury to the son and that exposure, again in my judgment, exceeds $100,000.

The plaintiff is assured of recovery against someone. The nature of the accident, the extensiveness of the injury and the "jury appeal" of the plaintiff lead one to conclude that a jury would be generous in evaluating the case. Our settlement demand for all claims is $72,500.

It is a common practice to include a cover letter that sets a date after which the offer will be withdrawn and a date for return of the brochure. A statement is included that the brochure is the property of plaintiff's counsel and that there are restrictions on its use. A request for the acknowledgment of receipt of the brochure and an agreement to abide by the restrictions is accompanied by a proposal to meet and reach a mutually agreed upon settlement.[6]

ASSIGNMENT 10:6
Draft an outline of the contents of a settlement brochure for the Ann Forrester case indicating what should appear and in what order. Compare your list of components and discuss the advantages of each in small groups with class members. Make a list of the typical components of a settlement brochure and place it in your system folder.

In the alternative, individual class members can accept responsibility for roughly equal parts of a Forrester settlement brochure. When finished, the students assigned to one part can meet, compare their individual work, and come up with a model section. Eventually the various model sections can be photocopied and shared to arrive at the best complete brochure.

Video: "Day in the Life"

An increasingly persuasive settlement and trial aid is a video of the injured party that tastefully and graphically demonstrates the injuries, treatment, progress, and likely future of the victim. These videos have been named "Day in the Life" videos because they focus primarily on one day in the life of the injured party. Recently, for example, a law office assigned a paralegal to videotape the progressive stages in the medical treatment of an accident victim. This videotaped record provided credible, otherwise unobtainable documentation of the pain and suffering of the client and strikingly illustrated that the healing process was going to take a long time with recovery clearly doubtful. The tapes were edited into a concise and powerful presentation by the paralegal. The cost was minimal. The "Day in the Life" video can include much of the settlement brochure including photographs, television commentary, and newspaper clippings.

Damage Calculations and Computer Software

Powerful spreadsheet programs like Lotus 1-2-3 can be used to enter and calculate damages and update them regularly. They also can be used to explore variables and make the calculation of annuities, interest, and other settlement figures much easier. A number of financial services now specialize in helping law firms develop innovative, long-term damage settlements.

■ The Role of the Defendant's or Insurance Company's Paralegal

The process of preparing for settlement on behalf of the defendant or an insurance company is in many respects the same as preparing for settlement for the plaintiff. Although the defense rarely, if ever, prepares a settlement précis or brochure, you may be asked to draft a letter proposing settlement and summarizing significant elements of the case from the defendant's perspective. Further, you will often be responsible for organizing and summarizing the information that arrives for the case. If the plaintiff submits summarized medical reports and witness statements rather than copies of the original, it may mean that there are some weaknesses in those reports. The originals should always be obtained, using discovery if more informal means have not been productive. The same process of researching jury verdicts, assessing pain and suffering, and submitting final summaries for attorney review are employed. You should inform the attorney if there appears to be a need for an independent medical exam or special surveillance of the adverse party.

■ Preparing for the Pretrial Conference

Federal Rule 16, individual state rules, local practice, and the preference of a particular judge determine what happens at the pretrial conference. In some jurisdictions the conference is mandatory, and the judge is active in trying to settle the case. In other jurisdictions the conference must be requested, and the judge may refrain from any involvement in settlment discussions.

A pretrial conference is normally conducted in the judge's chambers and is attended by the attorneys for the parties and the judge. Clients may attend but frequently do not. Traditionally the conference is a discussion by the attorneys of the facts in the case, the evidence to prove those facts, the issues remaining in the case, when and how long trial will be, and, if possible, whether settlement is in the offing. Since 1983, however, Rule 16 requires a more extensive pretrial conference process involving more than one meeting in many cases. In this context the pretrial conference takes on the important role of facilitating the overall planning and management of the progress of the case beginning at a much earlier point in the litigation (within 120 days after the filing of the complaint). Rule 16 describes the pretrial process.

Rule 16. Pretrial Conferences; Scheduling; Management

a. Pretrial Conferences; Objectives. In any action, the court may in its discretion direct the attorneys for the parties and any unrepresented parties to appear before it for a conference or conferences before trial for such purposes as

1. expediting the disposition of the action;
2. establishing early and continuing control so that the case will not be protracted because of lack of management;
3. discouraging wasteful pretrial activities;
4. improving the quality of the trial through more thorough preparation, and;
5. facilitating the settlement of the case.

b. Scheduling and Planning. Except in categories of actions exempted by district court rule as inappropriate, the judge, or a magistrate when authorized by district court rule, shall, after consulting with the attorneys for the parties and any unrepresented parties, by scheduling conference, telephone, mail, or other suitable means, enter a scheduling order that limits the time

1. to join other parties and to amend the pleadings;
2. to file and hear motions; and
3. to complete discovery.

The scheduling order also may include

4. the date or dates for conferences before trial, a final pretrial conference, and trial; and
5. any other matters appropriate in the circumstances of the case.

The order shall issue as soon as practicable but in no event more than 120 days after filing of the complaint. A schedule shall not be modified except by leave of the judge or a magistrate when authorized by district court rule upon a showing of good cause.

c. Subjects to be Discussed at Pretrial Conferences. The participants at any conference under this rule may consider and take action with respect to

1. the formulation and simplification of the issues, including the elimination of frivolous claims or defenses;
2. the necessity or desirability of amendments to the pleadings;
3. the possibility of obtaining admissions of fact and of documents which will avoid unnecessary proof, stipulations regarding the authenticity of documents, and advance rulings from the court on the admissibility of evidence;

4. the avoidance of unnecessary proof and of cumulative evidence;

5. the identification of witnesses and documents, the need and schedule for filing and exchanging pretrial briefs, and the date or dates for further conferences and for trial;

6. the advisability of referring matters to a magistrate or master;

7. the possibility of settlement or the use of extrajudicial procedures to resolve the dispute;

8. the form and substance of the pretrial order,

9. the disposition of pending motions;

10. the need for adopting special procedures for managing potentially difficult or protracted actions that may involve complex issues, multiple parties, difficult legal questions, or unusual proof problems; and

11. such other matters as may aid in the disposition of the action.

At least one of the attorneys for each party participating in any conference before trial shall have authority to enter into stipulations and to make admissions regarding all matters that the participants may reasonably anticipate may be discussed.

d. Final Pretrial Conference. Any final pretrial conference shall be held as close to the time of trial as reasonable under the circumstances. The participants at any such conference shall formulate a plan for trial, including a program for facilitating the admission of evidence. The conference shall be attended by at least one of the attorneys who will conduct the trial for each of the parties and by any unrepresented parties.

e. Pretrial Orders. After any conference held pursuant to this rule, an order shall be entered reciting the action taken. This order shall control the subsequent course of the action unless modified by a subsequent order. The order following a final pretrial conference shall be modified only to prevent manifest injustice.

f. Sanctions. If a party or party's attorney fails to obey a scheduling or pretrial order, or if no appearance is made on behalf of a party at a scheduling or pretrial conference, or if a party or party's attorney is substantially unprepared to participate in the conference, or if a party or party's attorney fails to participate in good faith, the judge, upon motion or his own initiative, may make such orders with regard thereto as are just, and among others any of the orders provided in Rule 37(b)(2)(B), (C), (D). In lieu of or in addition to any other sanction, the judge shall require the party or the attorney representing him or both to pay the reasonable expenses incurred because of any noncompliance with this rule, including attorney's fees, unless the judge finds that the noncompliance was substantially justified or that other circumstances make an award of expenses injust.

[Amended effective August 1, 1983]

Paralegal tasks in preparation for pretrial conference are to make available to the attorney all needed information and supporting documents, and to place the conference time in the docket control and reminder systems.

A pretrial preparation checklist should contain the following.

Pretrial Conference Preparation Checklist

1. Docket conference date and reminder dates for yourself and the attorney.
2. Enter reminder dates to inform the client of upcoming conferences, their significance, and whether the client should plan to be present. Check with the attorney.

3. Determine rules of pertinent jurisdiction and expectations of the assigned judge. Summarize for the attorney.
4. See that the client has signed all needed documents authorizing the attorney to enter into stipulations and to settle the case (see example following this checklist).
5. Have available for the attorney summaries of the following:

   - The facts, acts, and omissions that form the basis of the claim
   - Any specific statutes or ordinances that have been violated
   - Documents, photos, diagrams, and other tangible evidence that will be entered into evidence at trial
   - All witnesses (names, addresses, and area of testimony), including expert witnesses
   - All injuries, damages, and monetary amounts
   - All points of factual and legal contention

6. Gather and organize all documents and other evidence needed by the attorney to submit to the other side for stipulations.
7. Gather all needed records, bills, and other documents, and evidence to support claim.
8. Gather and organize all motions to be made or that are pending in the case.
9. Gather and organize any briefs, memoranda to the court, or other summaries of the law, or any points of contention.
10. Confer with the attorney to see that all that is needed is prepared.

ASSIGNMENT 10:7
Place a copy of the Pretrial Conference Preparation Checklist in your system folder.

In order for the attorney to negotiate in good conscience and to be in a position to make an offer to settle and to agree to settle at the most opportune time, the client should sign a written authorization for the attorney to negotiate and settle the lawsuit. Prior to signing, the client should be fully informed as to the likelihood of settlement negotiations, a realistic settlement figure, and what is given up when settlement is elected. If the authorization has not been obtained earlier, it should be obtained by the time of the pretrial conference. Figure 10:4 is an example of a general authorization.[7]

ASSIGNMENT 10:8
Place a copy of the attorney's authorization to settle from the client in your system folder.

Figure 10:4   Power to Settle Personal Injury Claims

For me and in my name to represent me in any negotiations with _____, or his attorney, with reference to his claim for damages against me on account of personal injuries received in a collision with my automobile on or about the _____ day of _____, 19__, hereby authorizing my said attorney either to compromise said claim for such amount as he may deem best, or to defend action thereon in the courts, if he deems that necessary to protect my interests.

Some attorneys and courts require the preparation of a pretrial statement following the pretrial conference. It includes an overall summary of the items mentioned in the previous checklist. If you have summarized the damages as previously indicated and prepared a settlement précis or brochure, the preparation of a pretrial statement should be relatively easy. The only new wrinkle is to determine the exact format preferred by the attorney or the court requiring the statement.

Some courts require the pretrial statement (memorandum) to be prepared jointly, furthering the opportunity for settlement. This may be followed by a pretrial order drafted by the judge or one or more of the parties. Because the required format varies with the jurisdiction, it is best to locate a local example of these documents. The following is an outline of one format.

[Caption]
PRETRIAL MEMORANDUM

Pretrial Conference
    Attorneys, date, location, etc.
Statement of Uncontested Facts
    Agreed times, events, damage, etc.
Contested Issues of Fact
    Disputed facts: Speed of vehicle, signature on document, intent of contract, etc.
Contested Issues of Law
    Disputed application of rules of law, defenses, and other matters for the judge to decide.
Witnesses
    A list of witnesses with their position, title, and relationship to case to be called by each party.
Exhibits
    A list and brief description of each exhibit to be presented at trial. In some jurisdictions this is added as an appendix; in others it is placed in the body of the memorandum with a column for any objections to the exhibits, i.e.,

Exhibit	Objections

Other Categories
    Other categories that may be included, depending on the jurisdiction and nature of the case, include a statement of agreed damages or special damages, attached jury instructions and any objections to them, and a statement of any agreed findings of fact and conclusions of law.

Respectfully Submitted this _____ day of _____
By:

_____
Attorney for Plaintiff

_____
Attorney for Defendant

◼ Settlement Forms

Releases and Settlement Agreements

Once the parties have agreed to settle, there are several forms that you may be asked to draft or review for accuracy. One such form is the **release.** A release is a document executed by the plaintiff or claimant that frees the defendant from any further obligations or liability stemming from the incident causing the damages in return for consideration (money). The document ends litigation on the matter between the two parties. Two common types of releases are set out in figure 10:5, an easily adapted example of a release for personal injury, and figure 10:6, a mutual release used when both sides in a lawsuit have claims against the other.[8]

Releases may be general in nature or specific, tied to a particular claim or injury. It is a good idea to consult local law on what must be included in a valid release. Some states, for instance, do not require consideration. In some circumstances a covenant not to sue is executed. This is not a release of past wrongs but simply an agreement not to sue on a claim in return for consideration. Figure 10:7 is an example of a covenant not to sue.[9]

Figure 10:5 Release and Settlement of Suit for Personal Injuries

Received of the City of _____ the sum of _____ dollars ($_____), lawful money, to me in hand paid, the receipt of which is hereby acknowledged, the same being in full payment, satisfaction and discharge of any and all claims, demands or causes of action, of whatsoever nature, which I or my heirs, executors, administrators, personal representatives, successors or assigns, may now or hereafter have against the City of _____, its officers, agents or servants, its successors and assigns, for damages for or by all reason of all personal injuries, all pain and suffering, damage to property, all losses and expenses, of whatsoever character, sustained as a result of an accident which occurred to me on or about the _____ day of _____, 19__, about _____ o'clock, ___.m., at or near _____ Avenue, on which date and at which time and place I was injured when attempting to board bus, and especially from the cause or causes of action set forth in a petition filed by me in the Court of _____, _____ County, _____, in an action entitled "_____ vs. City of _____," Case No. _____ on the docket of said Court, in which entry may be made "Settled and dismissed at defendant's costs. No record."

I hereby certify that this release is fully understood by me and is entirely satisfactory.

In Witness Whereof, *etc.*

Figure 10:6 Mutual Release of All Claims and Demands

MUTUAL RELEASE

_____, of _____ and _____, of _____, each hereby releases the other from all sums of money, accounts, actions, suits, proceedings, claims, and demands whatsoever which either of them at any time had or has up to this date against the other for or by reason of or in respect of any act, cause, matter, or thing whatsoever.

Signed and sealed on _____, 19__ at _____.

_____ [*Seal*]

_____ [*Seal*]

Figure 10:7 Covenant Not to Sue (with Reservation of Rights as to Others)

COVENANT NOT TO SUE

In consideration of _____ dollars ($_____) paid to me by _____, of _____, and _____, of _____, individually and as a partnership doing business as _____, at _____, and _____ Indemnity Company, of _____, receipt of which I hereby acknowledge, I hereby covenant not to sue _____ or _____, individually or as a partnership doing business as _____, or _____ Indemnity Company, and to refrain forever from instituting, pressing, collecting or in any way acting or proceeding upon any and all claims, judgments, debts, causes of action, suits and proceedings of any kind at law or in equity which I ever had, now have or may have against any of the aforementioned covenantees or their legal representatives, successors or assigns, arising out of the following matters: _____

_____

I have received the consideration of $_____in full payment for this covenant not to sue, notwithstanding any injuries or damages sustained, whether known or unknown.

This instrument is not intended as a release or discharge of nor as an accord or satisfaction with any person whomsoever, but only as a covenant not to sue by which each covenantee hereby purchases peace and is hereby given peace upon any and all claims and matters whatsoever which have been or may be made against covenantees by me. I acknowledge that covenantees in making payment of the consideration for this covenant have done so solely to obtain peace and do not thereby admit any liability on account of any of the above-described matters but expressly deny all of such liability whatsoever.

I hereby expressly reserve the right to proceed against or sue _____ of _____ or _____ of _____ or any other person or persons against whom I may have or assert any claim on account of damages arising out of the above-described matters. Nothing contained in this instrument shall in any way tend to release or discharge or be construed as releasing or discharging _____ or _____, or any other person or persons against whom I may have or assert any claim on account of damages arising out of the above-described matters.

Signed and sealed on _____, 19___.

_____ [*Seal*]

Witness:

_____

_____

Settlement agreements are often used in more complex cases and provide a more detailed description of the settlement than a typical release from liability. The settlement agreement is a contract between the parties that sets out all the terms, conditions, and obligations of the parties, including how the action will be dismissed. If requested to draft such an agreement, review local examples of the document and ask the attorney for specific guidelines. Figure 10:8 is an example of a settlement agreement.

Stipulation and Order for Dismissal

Once an action has been filed and settlement agreed upon, the parties generally have two options for finalizing the settlement. The first is a stipulation and order for dismissal; the second is a consent decree and order.

A stipulation and order for dismissal notifies the judge that the case has been settled and the parties want an order dismissing the action. Under

Figure 10:8   Settlement Agreement

SETTLEMENT AGREEMENT

[*Name of first party*] of [*address*], hereafter referred to as _____ and [*name of second party*] of [*address*], hereafter referred to as _____ in order to settle the controversy between them designated as _____ v. _____ civil case file number _____ filed in the [*name of court*] by the dated signatures below, HEREBY AGREE AND INTEND TO BE LEGALLY BOUND BY THE FOLLOWING TERMS:

   1. (Here state in detail each term, condition, and covenant agreed to by both parties: amount, time, and terms of payment; nature and extent of releases that will be executed and delivered; when and how the action will be dismissed; how court costs and legal fees will be handled; whether goods or documents will be exchanged or discharged; what collateral, if any, will be used to insure the agreement; and any other items suggested by the attorney.)

(Seal)   (First Party)

Attest _____   by _____
                                                               Party (or duly authorized officer)

                                                               _____
                                                               Address

                                                               Date _____

(Seal)   (Second Party)

Attest _____   by _____
                                                               Party (or duly authorized officer)

                                                               _____
                                                               Address

                                                               Date _____

Federal Rule 41(a)(1) and parallel state statutes, the plaintiff without order of the court may file a notice of dismissal at any time before the opponent has filed an answer or a motion for summary judgment, whichever occurs first. If later than this, the parties may file a stipulation for dismissal signed by all the parties that have appeared in the action. Such a dismissal is normally **without prejudice,** meaning the action may be brought again. A signed release is important in this case, since it serves as a defense to the action being brought again. If requested, however, the court may dismiss the action **with prejudice,** meaning it may not be brought again. The case is treated as an **adjudication on the merits,** as if the court had considered and decided all remaining issues. One advantage to this process is that the parties do not have to make public the terms of the settlement. If one of the parties breaches the agreement, the court may impose sanctions. Figure 10:9 is an example of a stipulation and order for dismissal. Local rules and examples should always be consulted.

Figure 10:9   Stipulation and Order for Dismissal

IN THE UNITED STATES DISTRICT COURT FOR

THE _____ DISTRICT OF _____

_____,
                                    Plaintiff
              v.   Civil Action, File No. _____

_____,
                                    Defendant

STIPULATION AND ORDER FOR DISMISSAL

On this _____ day of _____, 19___, it is stipulated between counsel for Plaintiff and counsel for Defendant that this action be dismissed [*with or without prejudice*] regarding all claims and counterclaims of the parties and without costs to the parties, and that an order consistent with this stipulation be entered without further notice to the parties.

_____
Attorney for Plaintiff

_____
Address

_____
Attorney for Defendant

_____
Address

So Ordered

____, Judge United States District

Court for the _____ District of

_____

Date _____

Consent Decree and Order

The parties may instead choose a consent decree and order. This method differs from the stipulation for dismissal by including the details of the settlement and by asking the judge to review and approve the terms of the settlement. Judgment is entered according to the terms as approved. Figure 10:10 is an example of a stipulation and consent decree and order.

Settlement Distribution Statement

The attorney or firm should give the client a settlement distribution statement that clearly itemizes the amount of the settlement and how it will be distributed. The drafting of such a statement is not difficult and can be

Figure 10:10   Stipulation and Consent Decree and Order

(Caption omitted)

STIPULATION AND CONSENT DECREE

The parties to this action, having agreed to settle this case, hereby consent to the entry of the following order.

This order and stipulation shall not be interpreted as an admission of wrongdoing by either party.

THE PARTIES, BY THEIR ATTORNEYS, STIPULATE THAT THIS CASE SHALL BE SETTLED BY CONSENT DECREE AS FOLLOWS:

1. The Defendant, _____, shall pay to the Plaintiff, _____, the agreed upon sum of $_____ for all injuries, pain and suffering, and damages, past, present, and future sustained from *[state accident or other source of claim]* on *[date]*, 19___.

2. The Defendant, _____, shall pay the sum in the following manner: _____

3. The Plaintiff, _____, shall pay to the Defendant, _____, the sum of $_____, for all damages, past, present, and future, incurred by the Defendant as a consequence of *[restate accident as source of claim]* as alleged in Defendant's counterclaim against Plaintiff.

4. The Defendant shall pay the costs of this action in the sum of $_____.

5. The parties will pay their own attorney's fees.

6. At the time of compliance with all terms of the stipulation and decree, the above captioned action shall be dismissed with prejudice.

For Plaintiff,   For Defendant,

_____   _____

Attorney for Plaintiff   Attorney for Defendant

_____   _____

Address   Address

Date _____

(Caption omitted)

ORDER

Having reviewed the above entitled case and the Stipulated Consent Decree freely entered into by both parties to this action as evidenced by the signature of their respective counsel, the Court ORDERS, ADJUDGES, and DECREES that the Stipulation is approved, and its terms, as set forth and attached hereto, so ordered this _____ day of _____, 19___.

_____

Judge, United States District

Court for the _____

District of _____

Figure 10:11   Settlement Distribution Statement

WHITE, WILSON & McDUFF

ATTORNEYS AT LAW
FEDERAL PLAZA BUILDING, SUITE 700
THIRD AND MARKET STREETS
LEGALVILLE, COLUMBIA 00000
(111) 555-0000

SETTLEMENT DISTRIBUTION STATEMENT

CASE: _____ vs. _____   CLIENT: _____

   Civil Case No. _____

   Court _____

Total Gross Settlement (recevied from _____) $_____
   Less Attorney's Expenses (Itemized)

      Travel $_____

      Printing $_____

      Doctors' Report Fees $_____

      Medical Records Fees $_____

      Phone Calls $_____

      Court Costs and Filing Fees $_____

      Photocopies $_____

      Others $_____

              Subtotal $_____ $_____

Less Attorney's Fee (figured by percentage of gross in
contingency fee case or by itemized billing entries) $_____

        Total Net settlement Due Client $_____

instrumental in avoiding unnecessary conflicts and misunderstanding with the client both now and in the future. Figure 10:11 is an example of a settlement distribution statement.

ASSIGNMENT 10:9
Make a copy of each of the previous settlement forms and the outline of the pretrial memorandum for your system folder. If time permits, draft each form at least once and adapt it to the *Forrester case.*

■ Other Alternative Dispute Resolutions: Arbitration, Mediation, and Summary Trials

Introduction

Paralegals are becoming increasingly involved in assisting attorneys and clients in preparing for alternative dispute resolution (ADR) processes. These processes include various forms of arbitration, mediation, summary trials, and others. The remaining portion of this chapter focuses on these procedures and the role of the paralegal in assisting in these processes. An excellent and concise resource book on this subject is Susan M. Leeson and Bryan M. Johnston's book *Ending It: Dispute Resolution in America,* published by Anderson Publishing Company, Cincinnati, Ohio.

The interest in and growth of alternative dispute resolution has been significant in the last decade. There are three primary reasons for greater use of these systems. Alternative dispute resolution keeps many cases out of an already overcrowded court docket. This not only relieves pressure on our courts but also allows thousands of ADR cases to be resolved more quickly than if they had been adjudicated in the courts. It is not uncommon for intense trials to go on for days, weeks, months, and some recent cases over a year. ADR hearings usually are completed in one or two days or, in complex cases, a series of one- or two-day sessions over several months.

Second, because ADR takes less time and is more informal (i.e., uses more relaxed standards of evidence, procedure, location) than a court procedure, it also saves parties a considerable amount of money. Filing fees may be as low as $25 and are even waived for indigency in some cases. A greater fee in large commercial cases is still a bargain.

Third, ADR processes are less adversarial and confrontational than a trial and substantially reduce the emotional trauma and bitterness associated with trials. Cases involving family law, business associates, employers and employees, landlords and tenants, and a host of other kinds of disputes are better served by a process that stresses reconciliation, common ground, and the mutual desire to get this matter over with as congenially as possible.

At one time ADR was reserved for the small case. Today, however, cases involving well over a million dollars have been resolved through alternative dispute resolution.

Arbitration

Arbitration is an alternative dispute resolution process consisting of the submission of a dispute to a neutral decision maker. The two most common types of arbitration are voluntary arbitration and court-annexed arbitration. In voluntary arbitration the parties agree (volunteer) to turn the dispute over to the arbitrator. This is very common in contract disputes; in fact, many contracts contain a clause requiring the parties to resolve any serious disputes arising under the contract through arbitration. The parties pay the arbitrator's fee, a filing fee, and expenses. The losing party frequently covers the prevailing party's filing fee.

Voluntary arbitration is a private (nongovernmental) process. The parties surrender decision-making power to the arbitrator. The parties, however, have considerably more control over the process than they do in litigation.

They can determine if the award will be binding or advisory, and they can select the time, place, the arbitrator who may or may not be an attorney, the conditions that invoke arbitration, the procedures, and even the standards for the arbitrator's decision.[10] Arbitrators and guidelines for arbitration are available through various arbitration associations, one of which is the American Arbitration Association.

The procedure in voluntary arbitration is initiated by a "demand for arbitration," a "statement of claim", or some similar document. This document sets out the dispute, a remedy, and the amount of the award sought. It serves the same purpose as a complaint, but is generally more informal in nature. The "demand" is usually accompanied by a "submission agreement" signed by both parties agreeing to the arbitration. Alternatively, the claim may be filed with the arbitration association, which serves the claim on the opposing party. A reply may be required.

A list of arbitrators may be sent to the parties who, generally, can cross out the names of a specified number of arbitrators. The arbitrator is then selected from the remaining names.

A form of discovery is also available: documents, information, and depositions are exchanged when deemed necessary by the arbitrator. Generally, thirty days are permitted for the response to such requests. A hearing date is set and notice given allowing approximately forty-five days for preparation.

The hearing is similar to a trial but more informal. Opening arguments are given, witnesses are heard, some cross-examination is allowed, and evidence presented. The rules of procedure and burdens of proof are more relaxed; for example, hearsay evidence is generally not objectionable. The complaining party may be given the choice on whether to go first or last in closing arguments.

Sometimes summary briefs are requested after the hearing. The decision is usually rendered within thirty days. An appeal to the courts is available, but generally the court's latitude in overturning a decision is limited to the grounds stated in the Federal Arbitration Act (9 U.S.C. § 10) and similar statutes. Generally they are:

1. The award was obtained by fraud or corruption.
2. The arbitrator was obviously partial or corrupted.
3. The arbitrator was guilty of misconduct or some obvious abuse of fairness or discretion, or otherwise exceeding delegated powers.

The standard of proof in arbitration varies depending on the type of case. It can be as indefinite as "the party whose evidence is most persuasive viewed as a whole."[11]

Here is an example of a voluntary arbitration case.[12]

Example of Voluntary Arbitration

Velda Bruno was a senior typist for Midwest Phone Systems. On December 18, 1985, she was discharged from her job. Her discharge letter said that she had proved "unable to perform the word processing job for which she was hired." Bruno protested her discharge to the Communications Workers Union that represented Midwest Phone employees. Union and management representatives were unable to resolve the dispute informally. The union argued that Bruno was fired hastily and for insufficient reasons, after being transferred to a word processing job from a typing job where she performed satisfactorily. Midwest Phone argued that Bruno's job performance had been continuously substandard, that she had been disciplined regularly, and that the discharge was a logical consequence of her failure to improve her performance.

When attempts at informal resolution failed, the union sent a demand for grievance arbitration to Midwest Phone. The collective bargaining agreement between the Communications Workers and Midwest Phone provided for arbitration of disputes arising out of employee suspension or discharge by the company. Midwest Phone's reply to the demand made it clear that the two parties would be unable to resolve the dispute themselves. Attorneys for the company and the union met and drafted an agreement to govern the arbitration. Their "submission agreement" covered the following points:

1. *Parties.* Midwest Phone Systems and Communications Workers Union.
2. *Relevant contract provision.* Article 12, section 12.1(e) on "suspensions and dismissals" provides that "the Arbitrator shall determine whether the suspension or dismissal was for just cause, but the judgment of the Arbitrator may be substituted for that of the Company only if the Arbitrator finds that the Company acted without making a reasonable investigation or that it acted upon evidence that would not have led a reasonable person to take such action."
3. *Issue.* Was Velda Bruno discharged on December 18, 1985, for just cause? If not, what is the remedy?
4. *Arbitrator.* Alfred Wong was named arbitrator.
5. *Time and place of hearing.* The hearing was to be in the conference room of the Airport Holiday Inn in Minneapolis, Minnesota, beginning at 9:30 a.m., February 10, 1986.
6. *Report of the proceedings.* The parties agreed to share the cost of a stenographic record of the hearing.
7. *Procedures.* The hearing was to be closed to the public; witnesses were to be sworn; the order of presentation of evidence was established; each side was to make an opening statement and closing argument; each side was to offer rebuttal and surrebuttal evidence; all witnesses could be cross-examined and re-examined; each side would submit a post-argument brief to the arbitrator; and each side would provide the other with copies of exhibits ten days prior to the hearing. The parties also agreed that the arbitrator would be given authority to determine any other procedural issues that might arise at the hearing.
8. *Expense of arbitration.* Each party agreed to pay one-half of the arbitrator's expenses and fee.
9. *Decision of the arbitrator.* The arbitrator was to submit a signed copy of the decision and award as soon as possible following the hearing but no later than 45 days after the hearing.

The submission agreement was signed on January 13, 1986. The parties gave themselves a relatively short time to put together their cases. Prior to the hearing, Midwest Phone moved to compel production of personal notes that Bruno previously had given to the union and to a civil rights agency. Arbitrator Wong denied the motion on the grounds that the information should be regarded as a work product of the grievant, her union and its counsel, and hence was not subject to examination by Midwest Phone. Ten days before the hearing counsel for the union and the company exchanged copies of their exhibits.

The hearing commenced at 9:30 on February 10.

Company's case   The company put on its case first. It called five witnesses: the head of the personnel department and Bruno's first and second level supervisors at the different facilities where she worked. They testified that Bruno had been hired on October 8, 1983, as a senior typist assigned to the company's word processing center in the company's main building. Bruno passed the typing test given by the company, typing between 90 and 100 words per minute with two errors on an electronic typewriter. She worked with three other employees in a separate room, away from other clerical help and clients. After about three months on the job, her first supervisor testified, Bruno suffered a broken wrist and was unable to type for about two months. During that time she answered telephones at various offices in the company's buildings. When she returned to a typing job in March 1984 she was sent to another word processing center in a satellite facility. At the second center she was trained on Vydec word processing equipment, which displayed typewritten material on a cathode-ray tube, enabling typists to edit material before storing it on a floppy disk or printing it onto paper.

In April, Bruno met with her first level supervisor at the satellite facility, who informed her that her job performance was not satisfactory. Bruno was told that she had missed 31 percent of the due dates on her jobs and that she had not advised her supervisor early enough that she would not be meeting her deadlines. Bruno was given an opportunity for additional training prior to her six-month evaluation.

In June, Bruno received her six-month evaluation. Her typing evaluation was "satisfactory," but she received an "unsatisfactory" quantity rating on work produced. Bruno's supervisor said she apparently still found it easier to retype some jobs than to make corrections on the word processing equipment. She was given two months to improve her performance.

Bruno's supervisor testified that in August she still was not producing adequate quantities of work. The first level supervisor reported Bruno's lack of progress to the second level supervisor who informed Bruno that her performance would be subject to monthly evaluations and that if she did not improve within six months, she would be discharged.

By January 1985, Bruno's supervisors testified, her work had improved considerably. The threat of discharge was lifted. In February 1985, however, one of Bruno's jobs was returned because of improper formatting on a list of telephone extension numbers. Shortly thereafter, her first level supervisor testified, she neglected to index a job to facilitate future use of stored material. A few weeks later her supervisor discovered that the second page of a job had been stored on the same track as the first page, thereby erasing the first page. The company continued to have problems with Bruno. She would make some improvement, then lapse into errors. In June, for example, she stored four pages of material on a disk but could not locate them. Her first level supervisor found that she had written the wrong information on the index sheet, which is why she could not locate the work.

By July, Bruno and her first level supervisor were having serious communications problems. Her first level supervisor at the satellite facility testified that Bruno became so defensive about her errors that she tried to hide them and would not communicate candidly. The first level supervisor again notified the second level supervisor. In August, Bruno received the first warning notice from her second level supervisor: if her work performance did not improve she would receive a second warning in late October and would be terminated before the end of the 1985 calendar year.

Bruno's first level supervisor testified that after the first warning Bruno became even more defensive. In September, the company agreed to transfer Bruno to another work unit on the assumption that she might be able to perform more adequately under a different first-level supervisor. The new unit also used Vydec equipment. Bruno's first level supervisor in the new work unit testified that Bruno had severe problems operating the printers in that unit and that because of her problems her production never came up to acceptable levels. Bruno received her second warning letter in late October.

In mid-November, according to her supervisor's testimony, Bruno missed three job deadlines and improperly stored two jobs. The improper storage made it impossible for weekend typists to find and complete the jobs. In December, Bruno was discharged.

On cross-examination, Bruno's counsel elicited testimony that Bruno's job performance on her typing job before her broken wrist was well above average and that neither her supervisors nor her clients had anything negative to say about her work. Cross-examination also revealed that although the unit to which Bruno was assigned in September 1985 did use Vydec equipment, it was an updated version of the equipment Bruno had worked on previously. The printing system was almost entirely different, and storage and retrieval processes were substantially changed. The company's testimony lasted approximately a day-and-a-half.

Union's case   The union called only one witness, Velda Bruno testified that she had been a typist for eighteen years at a local construction company before going to work for Midwest Phone. Prior to that she had been at home with her children for approximately fifteen years. During her tenure with the construction company she had consistently won merit promotions and pay increases. During that time she had worked on IBM Selectric typewriters and had learned to use electronic typewriters as well.

Bruno testified that she applied to work for Midwest Phone when the construction company went out of business. During her interview she was told that she would be required to work on the company's electronic typewriters and that she would be working in a separate typing unit with three other employees in the word processing center. Bruno also testified that in January 1984, three months after she was hired, she slipped on the ice on the way to work and broke her wrist. She was unable to type for two months. She was replaced by another typist and answered telephones until March 1984. When she was ready to resume her typing duties, Bruno testified, she was told that the company had been unable to find a temporary replacement for her while her wrist healed, that it had therefore hired a permanent replacement, and that she was being assigned to another word processing unit in a satellite building in another part of town. Bruno testified that she agreed to the transfer in order to keep her job, and that after she reviewed her contract with the company she realized that as a senior typist she was required to work on word processing equipment if asked.

When Bruno reported to her new job location she found that her hours would be 7:00 a.m. to 4:00 p.m. She received eight hours of training on the equipment. Bruno testified that her new typing duties involved primarily statistical typing, whereas her previous typing had been primarily manuscripts and letters.

Bruno admitted on both direct and cross-examination that she found the transition to her new job very difficult. Her new job required her to work in a large room with 30 other typists, on new equipment, doing very different work than she was accustomed to doing. She admitted that her production levels were lower than those of other employees and that she had trouble storing jobs on the Vydec equipment. Furthermore, she had trouble retrieving materials that had been stored by night and weekend typists. She testified that she found her first-level supervisor hard to work with and that she seemed to like to criticize Bruno's work in a loud voice in front of the other typists. Bruno said she became increasingly nervous about losing her job. When she received her first warning notice she was unable to sleep and finally requested a transfer, thinking that a different work unit might be better. She said the working conditions in the second unit were better and that she liked her new first level supervisor very much, but that it was difficult to adjust to the new Vydec equipment. Printers, for example were located in a separate room, rather than being connected to individual terminals. While that made the work place quieter, it did require typists to call up their jobs for printing and Bruno had difficulty learning the technique. As a result, her production rates dropped even further. She received no training in storage and retrieval on the new machines. She did receive a manual but could not understand it and was afraid she would be criticized if she asked too many questions.

On cross-examination Bruno was asked specifically about the jobs that had been returned to her, the material that she had lost through improper storage, and her failure to complete three jobs on time. She said that in each instance the jobs returned to her for correction had not been her original work product but that she could not prove that to her supervisor because the indexing cards on those jobs apparently had been lost. She said she felt terrible about the work she lost and that she thought it was the result of being new to the equipment and nervous about the possibility of losing her job. With respect to the jobs she failed to complete on time, Bruno explained that her work hours were 7:00 a.m. to 4:00 p.m. and that two of the jobs were called late because they were not done by her quitting time, even though she had been able to have them on her clients' desks by 8:00 a.m. the next day, their starting time. She said she received no complaints from her clients. The third late job had been marked "Rush" and on that day Bruno said she stayed late to get it done. Nonetheless, the job was called late because it was not ready at her regular quitting time.

Bruno's testimony and cross-examination took approximately three hours. Counsel for both sides then waived closing arguments, agreeing to summarize their arguments in the post-hearing briefs that were to be submitted to the arbitrator within five days of the hearing. The hearing was closed.

Arbitrator's award   Arbitrator Wong studied post-hearing briefs from each side (each approximately 25 pages long, summarizing its position based on the testimony) and reviewed some of the testimony given at the hearing. Approximately three weeks after the close of the hearing he delivered his opinion and award to the parties. The opinion addressed the issue submitted by the parties: "Was Velda Bruno discharged for just cause? If not, what is the appropriate remedy?" In a 27-page opinion Wong summarized relevant facts, including a chronological account of the events that led to Bruno's discharge, and a short statement of the positions of the parties. He included a short statement about the burden of persuasion and a statement that in his opinion, Midwest Phone had the burden of proving by a preponderance of the evidence that Bruno was discharged for just cause.

Wong concluded that although there were isolated instances of satisfactory performance on Bruno's part, her overall performance was not satisfactory and that Midwest Phone had just cause to take disciplinary action against her. Under the circumstances, however, discharge was not a reasonable penalty and should be set aside. Bruno had a good work record for eighteen years with another employer and for three months with Midwest Phone. However, Bruno did not successfully make the transition from typist on electric and electronic typewriters to the company's word processing equipment, a transition a senior typist was expected to be able to make according to the contract between the union and Midwest Phone. Hence, Wong concluded that Bruno should not be reinstated to the position of senior typist in the word processing center. Wong ordered a 30-day disciplinary suspension for Bruno without pay, and reinstatement with back pay and no interest as a typist at a reduced grade at one of the company's secretarial departments, assigned to tasks and equipment more commensurate with her former secretarial experience, training and background. In arriving at this conclusion, Wong cited as authority opinions from four other reported arbitration proceedings.

At the end of the month Arbitrator Wong submitted his bill to Midwest Phone and the union. The total included his travel and hotel expenses, stenographic assistance, research and $485 per day, his fee as an arbitrator. He spent a total of three days on the case. The company and the union each paid half of the bill, in addition to splitting the costs of renting the conference room.

Court-annexed arbitration is controlled by the court in which the action is filed and, if the arbitration is not successful, may still be tried by that court. Nearly half the states and a number of federal districts have court-annexed arbitration, and other states are seriously considering the process. Procedurally, a complaint is filed in court as it would be in any lawsuit. The defendant answers the complaint. Court personnel screen the filings and assign certain cases to the arbitration process. The assignment may be challenged by a party not wanting to go to arbitration or, if a case is not assigned to arbitration, a party or the parties may request that it be so assigned.

The arbitrator or panel of arbitrators are generally selected by the court or by the parties from a court list. Arbitrators are usually attorneys and normally paid by the court. In some jurisdictions they are expected to work hard to facilitate a settlement prior to the hearing. The hearings may be quite trial-like and formal or very informal where each side simply states its case and no witnesses testify. A decision is rendered in as little as a week in some programs. The award is entered as the court's judgment.

If a party is unsatisfied with the decision, they may request that the case be tried in a *trial de novo* (a trial as in any other case and as if no previous hearing had been held). Usually, however, such a request is discouraged by disincentives such as the requirement of a party to pay the other party's court costs and attorney's fees if it does not do significantly better at trial than it did under the arbitration award. This helps prevent abuse of arbitration as just another pretrial discovery tool, and upholds its purpose in freeing court dockets. Appeals are often limited to the grounds stated previously, such as procurement by fraud or corruption, evident partiality of the arbitrator, and others. The overall success of these programs will increase their use in the future. Cases once considered to involve too much money for arbitration are now being readily referred to arbitration—some reaching up to $150,000—and new subject matter such as family law disputes are being included.[13]

Mediation

Mediation is an alternative dispute resolution process incorporating a neutral person (the mediator) who facilitates a mutual resolution of the dispute. It differs from arbitration in that the arbitrator is asked to decide the case for the parties, while the mediator helps the parties reach their own decision as to how to resolve the dispute. Arbitration focuses on a somewhat adversarial fault-finding process of presenting evidence to decide a case and render an award; mediation focuses on common ground, how the parties can conduct themselves in the future (not how they conducted themselves in the past), and conciliatory compromise to resolve the dispute.

Generally, there are two types of mediation: voluntary and mandatory. In voluntary mediation the parties realize that they are unable to resolve a dispute on their own or, at least, realize that they need assistance. They seek assistance through mediation programs or mediation associations. Mandatory mediation is generally imposed in specific types of cases by statute or by court order. Its purpose is to require the parties to mediate their differences before exercising their right to a trial or to other procedures, such as a strike in labor disputes. In either case the agreement is strictly voluntary with few if any sanctions for going ahead with other dispute resolution processes, including litigation if mediation fails. Voluntary mediation provides more party control over the process (i.e., selection of mediator, objectives, written agreement) than does mandatory mediation.

Procedurally, the processes used in the two types of mediation are very similar. First, the parties select a mediator or are assigned one by the court or under a procedure established by the controlling statute. The parties meet with the mediator to gain an understanding of the goals of the process and how it works, and to establish some rules within which the mediation will be conducted. Where arbitration may have more formal and sometimes set rules of procedure, mediation is far more flexible with rules often created according to what will best serve the parties. For example, arbitration normally sets some standard or burden of persuasion. There is no such burden in mediation. Once the rules are formulated, then the parties or their representatives meet together or individually with the mediator in private to set out some facts and to propose solutions. When these discussions are completed, the effort focuses on the drafting of a mutually agreed plan to resolve the dispute. This agreement is to be the agreement of the parties' own work and ideas and not an agreement imposed on the parties by the mediator. Sometimes the parties will be able to agree on all issues, other times only on some—but even then progress has been made. When the parties cannot agree, the process returns to more formal remedies such as litigation. Many agreements provide for further mediation if disputes on clarifying terminology or some other matter arise later.

Mediation programs are growing, keeping numerous cases out of court, and preserving congeniality and civility in what might otherwise be far more seriously estranged relationships. Mediation is being used in contract and commercial cases, tort actions, landlord/tenant cases, property disputes, divorce and custody matters, criminal misdemeanors, and a variety of other matters. In the Dispute Resolution Program in California, for example, 63 percent of all cases undergoing mediation were successfully resolved. Forty-three percent of these cases were consumer and merchant disputes, 8 percent involved neighbors, and 7 percent involved family members.[14]

One of the most promising trends in dispute resolution is med-arb. **Med-arb** is a combination of mediation and arbitration methods where the matter is first mediated, then any unresolved issue is decided by the same or a different person who serves as an arbitrator. This approach incorporates the best features of a nonconfrontational process while still providing a decision to better ensure finality of the matter. Here is a case example of Med-Arb.[15]

Example of Med-Arb

John Cotesworth, Evan Handy and Cynthia Paul attended veterinary school together in the mid-1960s. During school they were best friends and decided to go into partnership together in a small town in the mid-west when they graduated. Because they were such close friends they decided to run their practice on a very informal basis. They each contributed money to buy equipment and supplies, rent a clinic, and advertise their services. Handy's father had been a veterinarian and gave them a lot of good advice, some equipment, and his patient list when he retired. Cotesworth, Handy and Paul agreed to share profits equally.

For almost fifteen years the practice went quite smoothly. The clinic developed an excellent reputation in the community and each of the veterinarians was highly respected and well known. Paul served three terms as mayor, Cotesworth was active in United Way, and Handy was named Citizen of the Year in 1984 for his work with senior citizens.

In May 1986, the three started to have problems. Cotesworth and his wife were divorced after several months of a child custody battle. Cotesworth's ex-wife remained Cynthia Paul's best friend. Paul found it increasingly hard to work with Cotesworth given what his former wife told her about him. Handy, who had always been a social drinker, occasionally showed up for work intoxicated or hung over and sometimes was unable to perform even routine surgeries. Cotesworth had no patience with Handy's drinking and would refuse to speak to Handy for several days after Handy had come to work intoxicated. Soon the personal problems started having professional ramifications. Cotesworth felt that because he was single Paul and Handy expected him to do most of the weekend emergency work but were unwilling to compensate him for it. Paul felt that both Cotesworth and Handy assigned the temperamental cases to her because of her diplomacy with people and her ability to calm nervous animals. By mid-year the three veterinarians could barely speak to one another and realized that they should stop trying to work together.

Every time Cotesworth, Handy and Paul tried to discuss the best way to end their partnership they got into serious arguments. None was content with a three-way split. Paul and Cotesworth felt they had contributed much more than their share of time to the practice, while Handy contended they should not be allowed to benefit from all the help they had received from his father when they were starting their practice. Neither Cotesworth nor Paul wanted to stop practicing veterinary medicine, although Handy readily admitted that he was ready for a career change. Both Cotesworth and Paul wanted the equipment and the clinic; Handy said he would rather sell his share to anybody else than Cotesworth and Paul.

Cotesworth finally consulted his lawyer about the best way to dissolve the partnership. His attorney asked to see a copy of the original partnership agreement in order to study the provisions for dissolution. Cotesworth explained that when the three had started out they were best friends and that they had operated all these years without a partnership agreement.

Cotesworth's lawyer listened to her client's explanation of the problem confronting the veterinarians and explained med-arb. The three could try to negotiate a settlement to their dispute with the aid of a neutral mediator. Lacking agreement, the mediator either could offer an opinion or could turn the dispute over to an arbitrator. Cotesworth's lawyer gave him a list of three people in the community who practiced mediation.

Cotesworth, Handy and Paul interviewed the three mediators and agreed that one would be acceptable. They agreed that they did not want everyone in the town to know about their problems and concluded that the mediator should be authorized to arbitrate the dispute if they were unable to resolve their dispute.

The mediator spent several hours with the three explaining mediation and establishing ground rules. Achieving agreement on a process was a big step. In addition to agreeing on a process, they agreed to meet twice a week for two hours until they either came to agreement or reached stalemate.

The three veterinarians stayed in mediation for almost five weeks. Sometimes they met together; sometimes the mediator met with them individually or in pairs. The mediator was able to get them to talk about what had happened to their friendship as well as the best way to dissolve the partnership. Cotesworth finally understood that Paul had been angry with him because of his divorce and comments from his ex-wife. He thought she disapproved of the way he had handled a case several months ago and was holding a grudge. Cotesworth and Paul both came to a better understanding of Handy's drinking problem, apparently precipitated by the fact that he no longer liked veterinary medicine but thought he was too old to make a career change. Cotesworth and Handy listened to Paul's resentment about being given the most difficult patients. All were able to acknowledge how important their friendship had been over the years.

Through mediation Cotesworth and Paul were able to agree that they both wanted to continue to practice veterinary medicine in the same town and that they did not want to be in competition with one another. They knew, however, that they would never be close friends as they once had been. They agreed to retain a lawyer to draw up a formal partnership agreement.

Despite their progress in mediation, the three were not able to agree how much Handy should be paid for his share of the partnership. That issue eventually was turned over to the mediator, now arbitrator, for a decision. Cotesworth and Paul then agreed on what percentage of the award each of them should pay Handy. Handy used his share of the settlement to relocate in another community to work with a group of cattle breeders.

Summary Jury Trials

Federal courts are beginning to follow a relatively new procedure called a **summary trial.** Used most often in expensive, complex trials, its purpose is to let both sides try the key points of their respective cases before a small jury in an abbreviated format. The purpose of a summary trial is to get at the results quickly, and then encourage the parties to settle the case on the basis of the additional information. Summary trials have a way of pointing out theories and evidence that will not work in fact, despite their appeal on paper. When this happens, settlement often occurs and much time and money are saved. The summary trial verdict, however, is not binding, and the case may still go to a full trial.

The Role of the Paralegal in Alternative Dispute Resolution

You may find that a case you are working on goes to arbitration, mediation, or to a summary trial. Or an attorney in the office may become the arbitrator or mediator in a case. In such circumstances your role will be similar to the role you normally play in preparing for settlement—that is, gathering facts, cooperating with the other side on a form of discovery, and drafting and filing necessary documents to start an action and present it at a hearing. You may work with witnesses in some cases, research the client's best choice of arbitrators or mediators, and research and draft summaries of evidence that can be similar to settlement packets or briefs. Most of your tasks in ADR are similar in technique to what you do in trial or settlement preparation, only abbreviated for abbreviated dispute resolution.

In some instances experienced paralegals may serve as layperson mediators. Should you become involved in assisting in a mediation or arbitration process, keep in mind that forms and procedures and names of arbitrators and mediators can be obtained from sponsoring associations such as the American Arbitration Association, Neighborhood Justice Forums, the Federal Mediation and Conciliation Service, National Academy of Arbitrators, local and federal courts, chambers of commerce, landlord/ tenant associations, and others. The entire area of alternative dispute resolution, including efforts to negotiate a settlement, can be an exciting endeavor, especially when you realize that your work has resulted in the resolution of a conflict without the cost in time, money, and emotional trauma often associated with a court trial.

ASSIGNMENT 10:10
By researching your state statutes and local federal rules, determine if there is a provision in your state for arbitration or mediation. If so, determine what types of cases and dispute amounts are considered for the program. If there is no system in your state, write a proposal to your local newspaper on why you believe there should or shouldn't be such a system.

Summary

Chapter 10 focuses on the resolution of civil cases without trial. Under the umbrella of alternative dispute resolution, this chapter addresses settlement, procedures that encourage settlement such as the pretrial conference and summary trial, and the alternative to litigation offered by arbitration and mediation. You serve the client in each procedure by gathering and organizing pertinent information and by drafting persuasive and other necessary documents.

Settlement is the traditional method of ending a case through the negotiation and agreement of the parties. It is facilitated by summarizing the collected facts and carefully totaling the damages. You may be asked to prepare a presentation of this summary in the form of a settlement request. The request can be brief in small cases or involve the preparation of a detailed settlement brochure in more complex cases. The request, regardless of size, normally includes a summary of the facts and the evidence to support those facts, background of the injured party, description of injuries or damage, impact or consequences, a summary of the actual cost in dollars of the damages, and a proposed settlement amount. It becomes the task of the defense paralegal to examine such proposals with a fine-tooth comb and to note weaknesses, inaccuracies, and inconsistencies in the settlement request.

The pretrial conference is a meeting of the opposing lawyers in the case and the judge. Its purpose is to decide what issues remain to be tried and whether the parties can reach a settlement. Again by utilizing a system and checklist approach, you can assist the attorney in preparing for the conference. If a settlement agreement is reached, the necessary releases, covenants, settlement agreement, and other documents must be drafted and filed. Some courts in complex cases where settlement has not been reached are using abbreviated summary trials to identify additional motivation for settlement.

Disputes are being resolved at an increasing rate through arbitration and mediation to keep costs down, reduce the time for ending a dispute, minimize adversarial confrontation, and keep large numbers of cases off the court trial dockets. In arbitration the parties ask a neutral third party to decide the dispute; in mediation the parties utilize a third party to help them work together to come up with a solution to their dispute. A new trend in this area is med-arb, which combines the best features of both arbitration and mediation to bring a dispute to a conclusion.

Study Guide

1. What is a settlement?
2. What percentage of civil cases are settled?
3. Why are cases settled? What factors must be taken into consideration?
4. What is your role in the settlement process?
5. What are the ethical considerations applicable to the settlement process? Why are they important?
6. What must be investigated and summarized in preparing for settlement? Why is this information necessary?
7. What kinds of information needed in preparing for settlement and in evaluating a case can be obtained from a reference librarian?
8. What formulas and processes are utilized to calculate various kinds of damages?
9. Be able to prepare a damage summary and worksheet.
10. What is included in a settlement brochure and a settlement précis? What is the difference between the two?
11. What is the definition and purpose of a pretrial conference? What Federal Rule applies? What state rule applies?
12. What things should you do to assist the attorney in preparing for the pretrial conference?
13. What is an authorization to negotiate (compromise), and why is its execution by the client important?
14. Be able to draft each of the settlement forms.
15. What are the contents and what is the purpose of a release? A settlement agreement?
16. What is ADR and its advantages and disadvantages?
17. Be able to define the following terms and explain their differences and similarities:

    Voluntary arbitration   Mandatory mediation
    Court-annexed arbitration   Summary trial
    Voluntary mediation
18. In general, explain your role in ADR processes.

Endnotes

1. JEANS, TRIAL ADVOCACY 398–403 (1975) [hereinafter cited as JEANS].
2. Id., 411.
3. Some of the formulas used in the Economic Loss section of the worksheet suggested by Stone, *Quantifying Damages in Tort Cases*, 14 TRIAL 444–49 (1978).
4. JEANS, 439—44, précis reprinted with permission of West Publishing Company.
5. Id., 444–53 and 459–62; brochure adapted and reprinted with permission of West Publishing Company.
6. WERCHICK, 4 AM. JUR. *Trials* 374.
7. WEST'S LEGAL FORMS, § 29.153 (2d ed., 1986), with permission of West Publishing Company.
8. Id., §§ 31.66 and 13.52, with permission of West Publishing Company.
9. Id., § 13.33, as adapted from a form reprinted in Hulke v. International Manufacturing Co., 14 Ill.App.2d 5, 142 N.E.2d 717 at 728–29 (1957), with permission of West Publishing Company.
10. LEESON & JOHNSTON, ENDING IT: DISPUTE RESOLUTION IN AMERICA 47 (1988) [hereinafter cited as LEESON & JOHNSTON].
11. Id., 53.
12. Id., 54–58, reprinted with permission, © 1988 by Anderson Publishing Company. All rights reserved.
13. Id., 82.
14. Foutz, *Legal Access and Consumer Redress: California Trends*, FACTS AND FINDINGS 35 (National Association of Legal Assistants, May 1991).
15. LEESON & JOHNSTON, 151–53, reprinted with permission, © 1988 by Anderson Publishing Company. All rights reserved.

11

Trial Preparation and Trial

- Introduction and Trial Preparation Checklist
- Preliminary Trial Preparation Tasks
- Subpoena Witnesses
- Jury Investigation
- Preparing Demonstrative Evidence
- The Trial Notebook
- Preparing the Client and Witness for Testifying at Trial
- Assistance at Trial

■ Introduction and Trial Preparation Checklist

Late yesterday afternoon Mr. White said that despite all our efforts, it did not appear that the *Forrester* case was going to settle, and that we should begin our final preparation for trial. The trial date, set at the pretrial conference, is two months from yesterday. It will be your job to perform much of the preparation and to assist Mr. White at trial. Good trial work is based on very thorough preparation; much of that responsibility rests in your hands.

Use the Trial Preparation Checklist (figure 11:1), which has been used for preparing several trials. Although every case has its own unique features, the checklist should be a useful guide. The remaining materials will help explain what must be done at each step on the checklist. Study the checklist, carefully noting each task.

Figure 11:1 Trial Preparation Checklist

Six Weeks Prior to Trial

☐ If a trial date has not yet been set, check with the attorney and file any request or praecipe needed to have trial date set.
☐ Calendar the trial date.
☐ Review the case status sheet and keep it updated in the file. Inform the attorney of any depositions, discovery, or other steps needing completion or updating.
☐ Review the facts of the case to determine if there is a need to amend the pleadings.
   ☐ Conduct the client interview.
   ☐ Prepare witnesses' statements or witness sheets.
   ☐ Highlight important facts both for and adverse to client.

☐ Review pretrial order to determine if the issues have been narrowed.
    ☐ List documents, exhibits, and witnesses needed on each point, including refutation of the opponent's key points and evidence.
☐ See that legal memoranda have been completed on all questions of law including any likely questions relating to the admissibility of evidence or any motions likely to be made at trial.

Three Weeks Prior to Trial

☐ Prepare a list of all witnesses needed; confirm with the attorney and have subpoenas prepared and served.
☐ Conduct the jury investigation.
☐ Conduct an investigation of the judge, the opposing attorney, and the community if not previously done.
☐ Prepare any exhibits, diagrams, audiovisual aids.

One Week Prior to Trial

☐ Verify the court date.
☐ Complete the trial notebook.
☐ Verify service of all subpoenas.
☐ Prepare client and witnesses for testimony.
☐ Make final arrangements for the following:
    ☐ Lodging of the client, witnesses, and staff as needed.
    ☐ Payment of lost wages for witnesses if committed by the attorney.
    ☐ Transportation of all files, documents, audiovisual equipment, computer terminal, and other items needed at trial.
    ☐ Petty cash needed for parking, meals, phone calls, and so on.

One Day Before Trial

☐ Meet one last time with the trial team.
☐ Meet with the client.

ASSIGNMENT 11:1
Expand the Trial Preparation Checklist in any way recommended by your instructor and file it at the beginning of the pretrial preparation section of your system folder.

■ Preliminary Trial Preparation Tasks

You should confirm the exact trial date and time if available. Some judges, however, do not set specific times. They follow a docket list for a one- or two-month period, and as cases set for trial are either settled or tried, the client's case moves up on the docket. Where such a system is used, the attorney can normally guess the approximate day of the trial, but you need to keep the attorney and all witnesses informed as the court docket progresses. The date and time must be calendared with related reminder dates for the completion of various tasks prior to the trial.

At least six weeks prior to trial check the case status sheet to verify that all necessary investigation and discovery have been completed. Figure 11:2 is an example of a Case Status Sheet.

The Case Status Sheet should be placed in the file early in the case, reviewed monthly, and possibly weekly within the last six weeks before trial. The attorney should be informed on any matters that are outstanding, such as discovery to complete, so that the necessary action can be taken.

Figure 11:2   Case Status Sheet

Trial date: Case name and no.:
Client: (plaintiff, defendant)   Defendant:
Attorney: Court:
Paralegal: Date filed:
Date client interviewed: Judge:

PLEADINGS AND MOTIONS ON PLEADINGS

Description	Date filed and served	Response date	Check if met	Hearing date
Complaint				
Motion to dismiss				
Answer and counterclaim				
Motions				
Reply				
Amended pleadings (list)/dates filed/response date				

Default: Date: Judgment for default: Date:
Jury trial demanded   ☐ yes   ☐ no

INVESTIGATION

Signify investigations to be conducted and witnesses to interview

☐ Done/date:
☐ Done/date:
☐ Done/date:

DISCOVERY

Interrogatories

Plaintiff's	Date served	Due date	Response date served	Motion to object or compel
Defendant's				

Depositions (by plaintiff)

Deponent/date	Notice/fee	Subpoena/fee	Location	Court reporter	Done
					☐
					☐
					☐

Depositions (by defendant)

☐
☐
☐

Request for Production of Documents and Things (Plaintiff's)

Describe	Served	Due	Answer/served	Objections/motions	Conducted	Copies delivered
					☐	☐

(Defendant's)

					☐	☐

Request for Mandatory Physical Examination ☐ yes ☐ no

Person examined: Date: Physician:

Request for Admissions (Plaintiff's)

Served	Due	Answer/served	Objections/motion to compel
			☐
			☐
			☐

(Defendant's)

			☐
			☐
			☐

MOTIONS

Describe	Notice	Served	Response	Argued	Result

CASE EVALUATED

Plaintiff's damages: Total:

Other notes:

PRETRIAL CONFERENCE

Date: Judge:

Preparation (describe)   Done

☐

☐

Notes on result:

SETTLEMENT

Settlement précis or brochure	☐

Date: Terms:

Releases/settlement agreement	☐
Stipulation, consent decree, order for dismissal	☐
Settlement distribution statement	☐

FINAL PRETRIAL

Witness	Address	Subpoenaed		Fees
Jury Investigation		☐		
Preparation of Exhibits and Diagrams				
		☐		
		☐		

Preparation of Trial Notebook (Proof chart, voir dire questions, witness   ☐
sheets, legal research, motions, jury instructions, etc.)

Preparation of Witnesses, Including Experts   ☐

Final Arrangements (Lodging, meals, parking, petty cash, transportation   ☐
of trial materials)

Trial Date: Verdict/Date: Judgment/Date:

Motions: Served   Reply due   Reply

☐

☐

APPEAL

Notice filed: ☐

Order transcript and preparation of record   ☐

File brief: Plaintiff/date   Defendant/date

Oral argument: Date:

Court Decision:

Motion for reconsideration: ☐

Bill of costs   ☐

Review the file, the case evaluation sheets, summaries and digests of information, witness sheets, and so on to see that all is in order and that the issues are clearly in mind. A discussion with the attorney at this point to verify the issues (possibly narrowed by the pretrial conference), and to review the evidence, exhibits, and documents needed for each issue would be helpful in better completing the tasks to follow.

The attorney should pinpoint the need for any further research on legal questions as well, in preparation for motions either before or during trial and to deal with objections or arguments that might arise at trial. These items should be researched and any memoranda or rough drafts should be completed. The writing of some of these may be assigned to you depending on the personal preference of the attorney. Memorandum preparation is good work for paralegals well versed in research skills. Offering to do this kind of work is one way to enhance your value to the law firm.

▉ Subpoena Witnesses

The client and friendly witnesses should be informed as soon as possible about the trial date and when they will be expected to testify. Client and witness preparation sessions should be calendared at this time so the client or witness can be notified of the trial and preparation session dates. The availability for trial of each witness should be determined.

The attorney should be consulted to finalize the list of witnesses to be called on behalf of the client. Some attorneys prefer to subpoena only the witnesses who are not considered friendly; however, the best practice is to subpoena all the witnesses needed for your case. Do so unless instructed otherwise. Some witnesses prefer to be subpoenaed so that it can be made clear that they have been ordered to testify. This is especially true if the witness has a business or friendly relationship with both parties of the lawsuit and wants to remain, or at least appear, neutral. It is a good idea to explain to each witness the necessity of serving them with a subpoena.

Subpoenas for trial are obtained and served in the same way they are obtained and served for depositions. The following are important points to remember:

1. Service of subpoenas is covered in Rule 45 and parallel state rules.
2. Local rules and procedures for the issuing and service of trial subpoenas should be reviewed.
3. Clerk of court issues the subpoena signed and sealed but otherwise blank.
4. In most jurisdictions any person over eighteen years of age can serve subpoenas, though they are often served by a United States marshal, sheriff, or constable. Professional process servers may be used.
5. It is best to read the subpoena to the person being served.
6. The subpoena is not valid until it is personally served on the witness, the required witness and mileage fees are tendered, and the return of service is completed and filed with the court. Normally only the first day's fee plus mileage is tendered.
7. Check with the clerk for amount of fee and mileage and check to see if the court provides an enhanced fee for an expert witness.
8. If a subpoena is issued on behalf of the United States or its officer or agency, fee and mileage need not be tendered.
9. Subpoenas reach to the boundaries of the state for state court trials and to the boundaries of the district for federal trials. Subpoenas are valid outside the federal district to within 100 miles of the place of trial or as specifically authorized by the pertinent federal statute.
10. A witness in a foreign country is subpoenaed pursuant to 28 U.S.C. § 1783.
11. A subpoena duces tecum must describe documents with reasonable certainty—that is, so they can be identified without an extensive search. Wording such as "every" or "all" is suspect.
12. If a subpoena is directed to a corporation, it is best to name the corporate official in charge of the specific documents.
13. Subpoenas are generally valid for the date or dates entered on them and for the remainder of the trial unless the person subpoenaed is dismissed by the court or the party that subpoenaed the person.
14. Subpoenas remain in effect for continuances and postponements.
15. Subpoenas need to be reissued if there is a change of venue.
16. A subpoena can be challenged as insufficient, oppressive, or unreasonable through a motion to quash, vacate, or modify.

ASSIGNMENT 11:2
Place a list of the steps in obtaining and serving subpoenas in your system folder. Having the list in both the deposition and trial preparation sections will prove useful.

At least one week prior to trial, verify that all subpoenas have been served. Occasionally a subpoena will have to be obtained at the last minute of the last working day before trial. This is when the relationship that you have nurtured with court personnel will pay off. Keep a record to show that all subpoenas have been obtained, served with amounts of fees paid, and filed with the clerk.

■ Jury Investigation

Regardless of the size of the case, if a jury has been requested, some investigation of the jury will be needed. The extent of that investigation depends on the nature and size of the case. The degree that you will be involved varies, but this is one more area where you can assume responsibility.

The purpose of the jury investigation is to gather the best possible information on each prospective juror and that juror's likely response to the issues in the case. The information will guide the attorney during **voir dire,** when the jurors are selected at trial. The overall purpose is to rid the jury of those persons biased against or not likely to be sympathetic with your client, and to shield or protect the services of those individuals who are likely to favor your client.

Figure 11:3 is a Juror Data Sheet. It can serve as a summary sheet for the attorney before and at trial, as well as your checklist in determining what information should be gathered. Check with the attorney to see if special concerns or information is needed in addition to that requested on the following form.

Figure 11:3 Juror Data Sheet

Case: File no: Court: Date:

Attorney: Paralegal:

Juror no. _____ Name: Aliases:

Overall Evaluation: Good _____ Bad _____ ? _____

Place and date of birth: Race: Ethnic group:

Address:

Previous addresses (list most recent first):

Grew up at:

Home phone: Work phone:

Employment (list most recent first):

Occupation: Employer: Address: Phone: Dates:

Present annual income:

Highest level of education completed: Date:

Health:

Marital status: single: married: divorced: widowed: remarried:

Immediate family

Parents: Age: Occupation/education:

Where lived most of life: Current address:

Spouse: Age: Occupation/education:

Children: Age: Occupation/education:

Grandchildren: Age: Occupation/education:

Juror's political affiliation: Rep (   ) Dem (   ) Ind (   )

Liberal (   ) Middle of road (   ) Conservative (   )

Juror's professional and service associations:

Veteran:

Church affiliation: Active: Inactive:

Hobbies and activities:

Friends and relatives:

Financial concerns in case:

Relationship to parties:

Prior jury service: Where: When:

Type of case: Verdict: Foreperson:

Previous or current litigation: Plaintiff: Defendant:

Where: When: Type: Outcome:

Close family or friend involved in litigation: Plaintiff: Defendant:

Where: When: Type: Outcome:

Prior experiences related to trial and issues: (for example, ever injured in an accident, ever at fault in accident, etc.)

Assessment of opinion on: Issues:

Source of information: Survey: Fellow workers: Other:

Assessment of jury leadership potential and strength of personality:

Source of information:

Record of juror on current panel:

Overall evaluation: Good: Bad: ?_____

   Explanation:

Additional comments:

ASSIGNMENT 11:3
Place the Juror Data Sheet in your system folder.

ASSIGNMENT 11:4
What special information might you want to know about jurors for the *Forrester* case?
Case II?

Sources for Juror Information

The amount of information that a paralegal is asked to gather and the money that can be spent gathering it is proportional to the size and significance of the case. The following sources are listed in approximate order from the least expensive to most expensive. Choose appropriate methods in consultation with the attorney.

1. *Jury Panel List.* A list of the names of all jurors for the upcoming term can be obtained from the clerk of court's office.
2. *Juror Information Sheets.* These are forms filled out by each juror providing a minimum of information on background, marital status, education, occupation, previous jury service, and litigation. These may be copied or reviewed in the clerk's office and are a good source of information with minimal copying cost and inconvenience.
3. *Voter Registration Lists.* Available in the county clerk's offices, these lists provide information on political party affiliation where such information is required by law.
4. *Co-workers, Friends, Others.* Sometimes your co-workers, attorneys, paralegals, relatives, friends, and others may be able to recognize the names of people on the jury list and provide valuable information. It is not uncommon in a small town for a few people to know practically everyone. Sometimes a friend of a friend can tap into that information. If attorneys or paralegals in another firm have recently had experience with this jury panel, they might also be willing to provide some insights. The client might be able to help, or have friends or relatives that can help.
5. *Clerk of Court Personnel.* If you are on particularly good terms with one or more of the local clerk's staff, that person might prove helpful.
6. *Jury Files Kept by Law Firms.* Some law firms keep extensive records on jurors. Information on particular jurors may often be purchased from these firms.
7. *Professional Jury Services.* Usually in big cities, these services compile extensive background information on prospective jurors and conduct a thorough investigation of specific jurors on request. These services can be valuable, but are expensive.

8. *Jury Surveys.* These are extensive phone surveys that are more or less scientifically based. If the law firm does not have the internal expertise, a consultant on surveying techniques should be employed to guarantee an accurate random sampling of the prospective community and to assure that questions are worded to elicit accurate and meaningful responses. Such a survey reaches only qualified jurors; their religion, occupation, and other background is recorded. The responses can then be evaluated by types or categories of persons, providing some information on how that type of person would vote as a member of the jury. Depending on how it is done and who does it, a survey like this can be quite expensive to take and to analyze, but can be useful for general guidance. If you are asked to conduct such a survey, a good source to consult is *Jurywork: Systematic Techniques*, prepared by the National Jury Project in cooperation with the National Lawyers' Guild and National Conference of Black Lawyers.

9. *Employment of Psychologists and Other Experts.* Some firms may choose to send a synopsis of the case to a psychologist or other expert to evaluate and give advice on what type of person should be chosen and avoided. This can be very helpful but expensive.

10. *Mock Juries.* Some firms employ mock juries. A scaled-down version of the trial is held and people representative of the jury's makeup or expected makeup are hired to hear the case. After their decision, the jurors are questioned at length about why they decided as they did and what impressed them the most and the least. This helps the firm make decisions on what jurors to select and how to improve their presentation.

When investigating jurors, remember that it is unethical to have any direct contact with a juror. Take every precaution to avoid having jurors become aware that they are being investigated. This awareness not only might disturb some jurors but also can cause reactions potentially damaging to the firm and the client.

All the information on a particular juror should be recorded and summarized for quick reference by the attorney. Be prepared to add your own evaluation of the juror to such a summary sheet, if requested. Summary sheets will be used at trial.

ASSIGNMENT 11:5
Make a list of the various sources and methods for conducting jury investigations and place it in your system folder.

Ancillary Investigation

The judge, opposing counsel, and the community should be researched if this has not already been done in preparation for settlement.

■ Preparing Demonstrative Evidence

When working on a case, consider what audiovisual aids might assist in conveying a significant piece of evidence or concept. There is no question that a jury will better understand the extent of an injury if they can see a photograph of it, better understand an accident if they can see a diagram of the scene, better understand the extent of lost profits in a business case through a large chart or graph, or better understand the current and future needs of a paraplegic if they can see a videotape of a day in the life of that person. People learn more and retain more when they can read something, hear about it, and see it. Therefore, be alert to these possibilities, and discuss the desirability of using such aids with the attorney. The general rule of thumb is if it does not help, do not use it. One must always be cautious about whom such evidence will help the most, plaintiff or defendant.

The maxim applies here, as well, that the bigger and more important the case, the more likely that audiovisual aids can be more fully used and the expense justified. It is equally true, however, that many fairly simple and inexpensive methods can be used to improve the presentation of even the most modest of cases.

Some evidentiary foundation is essential to the use and admission of demonstrative evidence (see earlier discussion on evidence). Diagrams for purely illustrative purpose need only be a fair representation of what is depicted. On the other hand, if a diagram or scale model is presented as evidence to be taken to the jury room, it must be accurate: drawn to scale, based on accurate measurement, and based on timely observation. Local rules may vary on what is admissible as demonstrative evidence and what is not, and should be thoroughly researched according to the type of item to be prepared (photo, videotape, diagram, document, etc.).

There are a variety of audiovisual aids that can be used at trial to help the jury understand your client's viewpoint in the case.

■ *Diagrams.* Diagrams are probably the most often used audiovisual aid. They can depict almost anything and, if kept simple, can be very inex-

Figure 11:4 Demonstrative Evidence

pensively created. The diagram of the site of an accident, for example, is frequently used in automobile injury cases.

Witnesses can use the diagram to identify streets and the location of witnesses, traffic signals, obstructions, and vehicles before, at the time of, and after the accident.

The preparation of diagrams does not require any special artistic ability. To make an effective diagram, keep it simple; strive for reasonable accuracy; make it concise and readable by using short titles and descriptions, horizontal wording, letters easily seen from the required distance, and clear lines. Keep in mind how the jury will see it.

The art department of a bookstore or school supply store should provide the necessary materials. If you tell the clerks what you are trying to do, they may have suggestions for techniques and products that can simplify your job. Some universities have an instructional media department with personnel who specialize in preparing audiovisual aids. They can provide sound, free advice on a variety of techniques and equipment.

Professional services are available that provide diagram preparation or preprinted diagrams. Several companies specialize, for example, in medical diagrams of every imaginable part of the human body.

- *Charts and Graphs.* Charts and graphs also lend themselves to simple construction by the paralegal. Follow the guidelines mentioned for diagrams to make graphs and charts that convey complex and hard-to-picture data in an easily understood manner. For example, a vertical bar graph may better dramatize the decreasing ability of an intoxicated person to react to emergencies than a simple reference to a percentage.

- *Personal Computers and Software.* The computer industry has improved the capability of the law firm to prepare professional quality diagrams, charts, and printed material. Graphics software, when combined with facility for multicolored desktop printing, produces amazing results for considerably less cost than professional art and printing services. Much of the software is easy to learn and fun to use. Mastery of these skills increases your value to the law firm. Equipment is now available to project computer screen images onto a movie screen. Seemingly endless possibilities include the ability to change or alter a diagram instantly to show a different perspective or detail.

- *Models.* Models are often used to display parts of the body, buildings, equipment, and a variety of other items. Construction of models requires great skill and should be left to the professional. Companies that construct, sell, and rent models advertise in trade journals. Costs are usually quite high for such services.

- *Photographs.* Photographs of injuries, damages, individuals, equipment, settings, and other items can be extremely helpful. The paralegal with minimal training can be the photographer, or professionals can be employed. Blown-up photographs can be particularly dramatic if allowed by the court. Sometimes the enlargement of a document or key part of a deposition statement can be very effective.

- *Slides.* Simply another form of photograph, slides have their place. They are particularly useful in portraying a sequence of events and locations, injuries, and the images created by medical tests such as x-rays and brain scans. Because slides are vivid in color and detail and can be projected onto a large screen, they are valuable and relatively inexpensive visual aids.

- *Film.* Film is rapidly becoming outmoded because it is expensive and requires technical expertise to take and develop. Film is still used, however, where the highest professional quality is needed.
- *Videotape.* Videotape is rapidly replacing film because it is relatively inexpensive and does not always require a professional technician. Video camera and editing equipment can be rented or purchased, and videotapes are inexpensive. Some firms use professional videotaping services when the case justifies it. Videotape projectors can be used to magnify the small monitor picture, making videos like a "Day in the Life" a powerful piece of evidence.
- *Overhead and Opaque Projectors.* Overhead projectors take images typed, drawn, or otherwise imprinted on letter-size sheets of clear plastic (called transparencies) and display them on a movie screen. Professionally made transparencies can be quite striking. You can learn to make transparencies of good quality. Any office supply store will have transparencies, and the staff can readily explain how to prepare them.

Opaque projectors are cumbersome and used less frequently than overheads. Their advantage is in projecting photographs, illustrations in books, and other printed material onto a movie screen. This process is particularly valuable when working with original material that should not be destroyed and cannot be adequately copied. New computer accessories can reproduce such an image without harming the original.

ASSIGNMENT 11:6
Locate the applicable state and federal rules of evidence on demonstrative evidence. Place these in your system folder.

ASSIGNMENT 11:7
Locate a number of legal periodicals such as bar journals, *Legal Assistant Today, The National Law Journal,* and others. Page through them and develop a brief bibliography or source list of companies that prepare, sell, or rent audiovisual aids. Seek information on vendors that provide such services in your area.

ASSIGNMENT 11:8
What audiovisual aids would be useful in the *Forrester* case for the plaintiff? For the defendant? Using the information that you have gathered on the scene of the accident in the *Forrester* case, prepare a courtroom diagram of the accident scene.

■ The Trial Notebook

A trial notebook (often notebooks) consists of everything that an attorney needs at the trial organized for easy and quick retrieval. The information it contains ranges from names of everyone involved in the case to a court opinion in support of admission of evidence. In some respects it is an outline of each step that must be taken to try the case, complete with indices and cross-indices. Trial notebooks, or some variation of them, are critical to successful courtroom litigation. If well prepared, they can make the difference between winning and losing, and regardless of the outcome, assist attorney and paralegal in being organized, effective, and confident.

Mr. White has asked that a trial notebook be assembled for the *Forrester* case. It is your job to put it together. The following material will help guide you in that process.

Begin organizing the sections of a trial notebook from the beginning of the case. Occasionally that is not possible and it must be done within the last few weeks before trial. In some respects, late preparation can actually save time because the issues will have been reduced by discovery and a pretrial conference. Fewer issues mean fewer witnesses, less evidence, and a smaller trial notebook. On the other hand, setting up a trial notebook early in the case has its advantages. They are: (1) organization of case materials with indices for quick retrieval of original documents, (2) paralegal control over the case materials with a checkout system for materials that have to be removed from the notebook, (3) easy reduction and editing of materials as issues narrow, and (4) immediate preparation in the form of review for settlement, pretrial conferences, and other procedures.

The trial book should consist of one or more loose-leaf three-ring binders, preferably of different colors, for standard 8½-by-11-inch paper. If some 14-inch pages must be used, they can be reduced in the copying process to the standard size. Plenty of tabbed dividers will be needed to place between major sections and their subsections.

The actual contents and order of a trial notebook vary according to the type of case and the preference of the attorney. A lot of time can be saved by asking the attorney for a detailed outline of what is wanted in the notebook, or by preparing an outline of the notebook and asking the attorney to express preferences on the outline.

Figure 11:5 is a detailed outline of the basic structure of a trial notebook. This approach has the sections arranged chronologically as they would come up at trial. Such an arrangement allows the attorney and the paralegal assisting at trial to work methodically through each section as needed.

ASSIGNMENT 11:9
Place a copy of the Outline of Trial Notebook in your system folder.

You can provide assistance in preparing the trial notebook in many areas.

Figure 11:5 Outline of Trial Notebook

Page or tab number	Divisions

Section One: Reference

    1. Table of contents (complete last)

    2. Persons and parties at trial

        a. Court, courtroom, judge, clerks, bailiff: name, phone, office.

        b. Own staff at trial: attorneys, paralegals, others: names, phone numbers, motel, etc.

            (1) Firm's office numbers for assistance

            (2) Client

(3) Witnesses   Names, addresses, phone

(4) Expert witnesses   numbers, affiliations

(5) Others

   c. Opponent's staff at trial and witnesses, experts, phone, affiliation, etc.

  3. Case summary: factual and legal issues

  4. Proof chart: elements and proof in case

EXAMPLE OF PROOF CHART

Plaintiff's elements and facts to prove	Source of proof
Negligence:	
Excessive speed	Wit: Schnabel "between 45–50 mph" Statement
	Client: "over 45" deposition p. 27 (Tab__) Photo: skidmarks, test. of Officer Timms
Inattentiveness	Hart's test.: "looking at speedometer" deposition p. 35 (Tab__)

Same for defendant's proof

Section Two: Pleadings and Pretrial

  1. Major pleadings as amended: complaint, answer, defenses (all tabbed and color coded to separate plaintiff's from defendant's with key sections highlighted)

  2. Alternative method: (Simply summarize pleadings stating allegations, admissions, and denials. Highlight remaining issues.)

  3. Any pretrial order could go here

Section Three: Last-Minute Motions

  1. Any remaining pretrial motions with supporting authorities

  2. Authority to oppose any expected last-minute motions by the opposition

Section Four: Voir Dire (Jury Selection)

  1. Jury challenge chart: (usually eighteen to twenty boxes on standard sheet of paper to enter no. and name of each juror, plus attorney's and paralegal's notes on suitability)

  2. Profiles of jurors most and least wanted (predetermined by jury investigation)

  3. Outline of voir dire questions: (if the attorney is permitted to conduct voir dire—if not, proposed questions for the judge to ask jurors with copies for the judge and opponent. Questions are usually drafted by the attorney or an experienced paralegal with attorney review. There are numerous sources on conducting voir dire.)

  4. List grounds and authority for challenges for cause (a challenge for cause is a request to remove a juror for lawful reasons such as inability to be impartial)

  5. List of authorities on any anticipated jury issues (including legality of any voir dire questions)

6. Jury panel chart (usually twelve boxes to place names and comments about jurors finally selected to hear the case)

7. Blank loose-leaf sheets to write notes on voir dire or to record any objections

Section Five: Opening Statement

1. Complete text

2. Alternative: outline (both drafted by attorney. Use large orator's type.)

Section Six: Outline of Order of Proof and of Opponent's Proof

Section Seven: Witness Examination

1. Own witnesses: direct examination (tabbed subsections for each witness in the order they will be called by the attorney). Each witness subsection should include:

   a. A synopsis of witness information, whether subpoenaed and interviewed.

   b. An outline or chronological list of the questions that will be asked on direct examination on each critical issue. Use wide margins so notes can be added.

   c. Notations of what exhibits will be introduced by the witness with inserted copies of the exhibits.

   d. Notations inserted on any references to diagrams or other audiovisual aids.

   e. Conflicting testimony of witness (references to prior statements, depositions, interrogatories, admissions)

   f. Questions to rehabilitate witness, especially if harmful cross-examination by opponent is expected

   g. Summaries of any statement, letters, memos, or depositions with key quotations highlighted. Cross-indexed to section containing copy of full statement, deposition transcript, memos, etc.

   h. Copies of subpoena with proof of service

2. Opponent's witnesses: cross-examination (Some attorneys prefer an entirely separate, different colored notebook for dramatic effect.)

   a. Similar structure to item 1 above with emphasis on conflicting and inconsistent statements, testimony, or other impeachment material

   b. Inserted copies of necessary exhibits, criminal records, etc.

Section Eight: Exhibits (sometimes kept as separate book)

1. Exhibit log

EXAMPLE OF EXHIBIT LOG

Ex. no. (as premarked or as assigned at trial)	Descript. or title of exhibit	Whether introduced, accepted or rejected. Notes.
Own ex. (in order of introduction)	Title	Introduced ( ) Accepted ( ) Rejected ( ) Notes:

P-1 (Plaintiff)

Opponent's ex.   Title   Introduced ( )   Accepted ( )   Rejected ( )
D-1 (Defendant)   Notes:

---

2. Each exhibit in expected order of introduction (may be separated by identifying tabs, including exhibit no. if premarked by clerk

3. Each exhibit section should include:

   a. Exhibit summary sheet paper-clipped to exhibit (includes brief description of exhibit and significance, case file location or code no., witness needed for introduction, foundation, brief statement of authorities on admissibility

   b. Exhibit

      (1) Marked copy for judge, opponent, one for each juror if desired, one for witness section, one for exhibit section

      (2) If oversized, specially indexed to separate container or if cannot be hole punched, place in three-hole plastic envelopes

   c. Place exhibits in box if there are too many for notebook

4. List of all audiovisual props and accessories indexed to specially numbered containers if necessary.

Section Nine: Trial Motions and Authorities

(Any motions such as for dismissal or for directed verdict. Reminders to make motions should be placed at chronologically appropriate places and cross-indexed to this section. Consult with the attorney for what and where.)

Section Ten: Jury Instructions (Charge to Jury)

1. Attorney's copy of all instructions proposed to be read to the jury. (Should contain complete language of instruction, one instruction per page, plus any legal authorities supporting its use. Each should contain a checkoff for given, modified, or refused. Have enough copies for all parties and the judge.)

2. Opponent's proposed instructions with checkoff

3. Final copy of instructions read by the judge

4. If no jury, copy of request for findings of fact and conclusions of law for the judge

Section Eleven: Proposed Plain or Special Issue

(Verdict) (Optional section depending on detail of verdict desired by attorney. Necessary copies for judge and opponent. Section for supporting authorities.)

Section Twelve: Closing Statement

1. Text or outline of closing statement (orator's size print)

2. Props or list of props

3. Notepad for recording items to add as trial progresses

Section Thirteen: Law Section

1. Trial memo or brief covering the law on all significant questions of law concerning the issues, evidence, motions, and other anticipated objections or conflicts

2. Geared to the judge's bench book (legal authority book)

3. Should include points and responses to law likely to be argued by opponent

4. May include concisely typed copy of the Rules of Evidence and pertinent Rules of Procedure with authorities

5. Cross-indexed to relevant sections in notebook

Section Fourteen: To Do, Notes, and Reminders

1. List of items to do before trial in completing notebook, serving subpoenas, gathering exhibits, etc.

2. Reminders of motions to make, whether to poll jury, and others

3. Notepad for items that come up at trial that should be commented on, argued, noted for appeal, etc.

Legal Research

You can do much of the trial brief section of the trial notebook. Initial background research on evidence, elements of a cause of action, the appropriateness of a jury instruction, and the composition of concise memoranda and lists of legal authorities for the attorney's perusal are tasks a paralegal can handle competently. These may have to be edited, expanded, or changed in other ways, but your winnowing will form a sound base for further work.

Motions

The attorney will have a good idea of what standard motions are likely to be needed just before and during trial. Many of these motions, such as a motion to dismiss or a motion for a directed verdict, require grounds that can be stated generally. The attorney will be able to fill in needed details as more specific reasons develop at trial. Authorities that generally state the legal standards necessary to grant or deny the motion can be cited. Therefore, you can prepare a skeletal or general version of the motion, along with an accompanying order. See chapter 7 on motion drafting. Figures 11:6 and 11:7 contain examples of several common trial motions to include in the trial notebook.

You might be assigned the tasks to draft a motion **in limine.** This motion asks the court for protection against prejudicial questions and statements. It is usually made when the attorney realizes that the opponent is likely to ask questions of a witness or refer to matters that will prejudice the jurors, making a fair trial difficult to achieve. An example of a motion in limine appears in figure 11:8.

ASSIGNMENT 11:10
Add copies of the trial and in limine motions to your system folder. Place an extra copy of each motion in the section on motions.

Figure 11:6   Motion for Mistrial

(Caption)

MOTION FOR MISTRIAL

_____ (Plaintiff/Defendant) respectfully moves this court for an order declaring a mistrial in this action and discharging the jury from further consideration of this case.

As grounds for said motion, _____ (Plaintiff/Defendant) states that __*[state grounds.]*__ Consequently, it is impossible for _____ to receive a fair trial by the jury.

This motion is made on the basis of all records, files, and proceedings in this case.

Date _____   Attorney for _____

                                          Address _____

Figure 11:7   Motion for Directed Verdict

At Close of All Evidence

(Caption)

MOTION FOR DIRECTED VERDICT

_____ (Plaintiff/Defendant) respectfully moves this court, at the close of all the evidence in this case, to instruct the jury to return a verdict in favor of _____.

As grounds for said motion, it is asserted that __*[state grounds.]*__

Date _____   Attorney for _____

                                          Address _____

Figure 11:8   Motion in Limine

For Order Prohibiting Reference During Trial to Insurance Payments Received by Plaintiff

(Caption)

MOTION IN LIMINE

The Plaintiff respectfully moves this Court to order counsel for the Defendant to avoid any reference during the course of trial to any compensation received or likely to be received by the Plaintiff from the Plaintiff's insurance carrier for his/her hospital and medical expenses.

Grounds for this motion are that reference to such insurance payments would be improper and prejudicial, and that such prejudice could not be corrected by any court ruling or admonition of the jury.

Date _____   Attorney for plaintiff _____

                                          Address _____

Voir Dire

You can research possible voir dire questions. A trial attorney generally has these in mind, but each case has its own peculiarities. Furthermore, new ideas and approaches are always being developed along with a current body of literature that you can review and digest into a list of questions with supporting legal authority for the attorney's consideration.

Jury Instructions

Not unlike voir dire questions, jury instructions can be researched, revealing new ideas and cases where jury instructions favorable to the client's position have been given and upheld as proper. Jury instructions or charges are read to jurors by the judge and cover a review of the evidence, burden of proof, the pertinent law, and application of the law to the facts in this case.

Figure 11:9 Jury Instructions

Jury Instruction
Instruction no. _____

Crossing between intersections, not in marked crosswalk, last clear chance
1. Although the Plaintiff had the duty to yield the right of way to vehicles on the highway, the Defendant had the duty to exercise ordinary care for pedestrians and others, including the duty of keeping a proper lookout. If you are satisfied from the evidence that immediately prior to the accident it was no longer possible for the Plaintiff, by exercise of ordinary care for his/her safety, to avoid the Defendant's vehicle, while the Defendant still had time, by the exercise of ordinary care, to discover the Plaintiff's danger and avoid the accident, you will find for the Plaintiff; otherwise you will find for the Defendant.
2. (Definition of ordinary care from other standard instructions.)
3. (Damages from other standard instructions.)

Authorities (List relevant statutes and cases.)

ALTERNATIVE JURY INSTRUCTION
1. It was the Defendant's duty while operating his/her vehicle to exercise ordinary care for others, including:
   a. keeping a lookout for others close enough to pose a danger
   b. keeping vehicle under reasonable control
   c. driving at a reasonable and prudent speed as dictated by speed limits and conditions of the road.

If you are satisfied from the evidence that the Defendant failed to comply with one or more of these duties, and that such failure was a substantial factor in causing the accident, you will find for the Plaintiff; otherwise you will find for the Defendant.

2. If you are satisfied from the evidence that the Defendant complied with all of these duties and that the Plaintiff moved into the path of the Defendant's vehicle so suddenly that the Defendant could not avoid the accident, you will find for the Defendant.
3. (Add definition of ordinary care from other standard instructions.)
4. (Add standard instruction on damages.)

Authorities

Most states have a standard jury instruction source book used by judges in the state. Many of the federal courts use standardized instructions as well. The instructions are organized by topic, so it is not difficult to find those covering each area of the case. Research into other case files, periodical literature, recent books on the topic, and recent case law may reveal instructions better suited to the client than the standard instructions. From these, you can draft a set of instructions to be reviewed by the attorney and altered or expanded where necessary. It is these special instructions, when supported by good legal authority, that can give the attorney that needed edge. Figure 11:9 is an example of how jury instructions can be worded to approach the same facts, but from slightly different viewpoints. Which instruction do you believe is preferable for Ms. Forrester?

ASSIGNMENT 11:11
Research form books for jury instructions in your jurisdiction. Place a list of the major sources in your system folder. Then make a list of each instruction that you believe will be needed in the *Forrester* case. Compare your list to those made by others in your class to see if it is inclusive. Place any samples of jury instructions in your system folder.

Noting Special Details

While working on a case, there is no question you will become very familiar with its facts and evidence. Use that familiarity to identify those special details and pieces of reality that will help sway a jury. Note these for the lawyer. If you are able to attend the trial, hearing reference to something you contributed will be very satisfying.

■ Preparing the Client and Witness for Testifying at Trial

Your role in assisting the attorney to prepare a witness for testifying can go beyond that of preparing a witness for a deposition. Trial means some new challenges for the witness, and you can be an instrumental part of the legal team preparing the witness for trial.

Most obvious is the task of communicating more frequently with the client or witness as the trial date approaches. Inform the client of the trial date, appointments at the office, and those things that the witness will need at trial. The client or witness may need to be reminded to review their deposition several weeks before the trial and again just before a final preparation session with the attorney.

You can take witnesses to the courtroom to familiarize them with the surroundings and procedures: where they should report the day of the trial, what to do when called to the stand, where the witness box is, what it is like to sit in the witness box, how important it is to address the jury and speak up, how to refer to diagrams and other props and still communicate with the jury, how to look at the attorney asking the question and turn to the jury to answer it, what it feels like to be in the jury box, and how important it is for the jury to see and hear. A brief dry-run direct examination can be conducted here. Learn how to set the stage. Such efforts will give the witness confidence and reduce a lot of unnecessary anxiety. Witnesses will greatly appreciate it.

Most attorneys try to prepare the client and most important witnesses, even in the simplest of cases. The preparation can range from a rather brief, informal discussion about the case and things to keep in mind, to a complete courtroom-like direct and cross-examination with a critique of the witness's performance. In such circumstances, most attorneys prefer to do the fine tuning with the witness, but you can still play an important role by observing, noting behavior or idiosyncracies, listening for inconsistencies, and relating any impressions to the attorney. The facilities also have to be readied and witnesses made comfortable just as in preparing for the first client interview.

Critiquing witnesses must be done tactfully because of the anxious state most witnesses are in. You can help here by saying a few words of encouragement and letting them know that they will do fine.

Videotaping the witness during mock testimony can be helpful. You can do the taping and review it with the witness. Witnesses frequently note and comment on their obvious mistakes and distracting mannerisms that need to be worked on. On the other hand, most people will be pleasantly surprised that they were more effective and confident than they thought. Videotape presentations on how to be an effective witness can also be prepared for viewing by each witness the firm works with. This could prove to be a great time saver when used repeatedly.

With the proper guidelines and authorizations from the attorney, you can help locate and enlist the expert witness. All the necessary data on the expert's qualifications should be gathered and placed in a summary format for the attorney. The expert might suggest publications, evidence, props, testing devices, and audiovisual material that need to be gathered and organized for trial or mock testimony. Summaries of the facts, theories in the case, and other relevant information may also have to be gathered and prepared for the expert. The expert can benefit from a trip to the courtroom as well. Experts need to be told not to get defensive during cross-examination, that they are there to give an opinion based on their best work and what they consider the best principles and theories of their area of expertise, despite contrary opinions of other experts and authors. Experts must also be guided tactfully to avoid appearing condescending or pompous, and cautioned against using jargon. Mock sessions with an expert can be helpful, and their time on the "stage" should be well orchestrated down to the finest detail.

The attorney may give you permission to inform some witnesses that, for their convenience, they will be called to court only at the time they will be needed, even if that is not the time listed on the subpoena. This should not be done without the express confirmation of the attorney. Witnesses should be fully informed of their place in the trial and how other witnesses are likely to testify. The client should be well informed as to the theory of the case.

ASSIGNMENT 11:12
Prepare a checklist of those things you can do to help prepare clients and other witnesses for testifying at trial. Set up a special section in the checklist on preparing expert witnesses. Place the checklist in your system folder.

Figure 11:10 Guidelines for a Witness's Trial Testimony

☐ Dress neatly in clothing that helps you feel secure.

☐ Arrive at court one half hour before the designated time.

☐ Do not discuss your testimony or the case with or in the presence of others.

☐ Look at the attorney asking the question, then look at the jury when answering.

☐ Speak up.

☐ Try to be as relaxed as possible. Remind yourself that you are not there to match wits or to out-smart someone, but you are there simply to tell the truth as best you can. Let the chips fall where they may.

☐ Do not try to memorize your testimony. If you have reviewed the facts in your own mind, and anticipated likely questions, your answers will be informed but spontaneous.

☐ Do not lose your temper, and do not argue. Your attorney will give you a chance to correct any harmful impressions or incomplete points.

☐ Listen to the opening statements of the attorneys to better understand the opposing theories and where your testimony will fit. Be prepared, however, if you are not a party, that you may be sequestered (set off in a separate room) so your testimony will not be influenced by the testimony of others.

☐ Listen to each question very carefully. Do not try to answer if you do not understand the question or a term in the question. Ask for clarification.

☐ Do not guess at an answer. If you do not know, say so, and do not be led into guessing or agreeing with the cross-examiner when you really do not know.

☐ Do not look at the attorney for help, guidance, or approval. Once on the stand, all responses should be your own.

☐ Pause if a question seems inappropriate; give your attorney a chance to object.

☐ Do not continue to answer a question if your attorney objects.

☐ Do not get trapped by the opposing attorney into a yes or no answer even if the attorney says, "Just yes or no." State what needs to be said. You have the right to fully answer a question.

☐ Avoid qualifying your answer with "maybe," "I think," "to tell you the truth," or "honestly."

☐ Your attorney will give you a chance to fully explain your side, but if the opponent gives you an opening, take it.

☐ Do not overexplain. State your point clearly and briefly and let it be.

☐ If you are a party, be prepared to be called by the opposition for cross-examination during their presentation of the case.

☐ If you are asked by the opposing attorney whether you remember saying something, agree only if you do remember it. If you do not, or are not sure, ask to see the statement. If refused, make it clear that you will have to guess.

☐ If asked, "Is that everything that occurred?" give yourself an out by saying, "That is all I recall at this time."

☐ Visit the scene prior to testimony, review photos, videotape, and diagrams; note any current changes or differences from the original scene.

☐ Review the statements or testimony of other likely witnesses.

☐ Have an understanding of the case, the theories of both sides, and the order of presentation.

☐ Bring all records and documents requested.

☐ Do not fabricate or mislead.

☐ If you have spoken with the attorney before testimony and the opponent asks, "Have you spoken with attorney so-and-so prior to testifying?" state "Yes." There is nothing improper about this as long as you have been instructed to tell the truth.

☐ If you have been reimbursed for lost wages or travel to testify or have been paid as an expert witness, acknowledge this when asked. Witnesses are frequently reimbursed and experts are paid for their time and experience. They are not paid to mislead or state something other than their well-founded, expert opinion.

☐ If an expert witness, do not readily accept other authorities as sole authority in the field.

☐ Avoid jargon and technical language.

☐ Do not get defensive if challenged by the opposition; relax and avoid a battle of egos or wits.

☐ If an expert, testimony should be extremely well prepared and planned.

☐ Be ready to show how measurements and calculations were made.

You may be asked to produce a list of suggestions for testifying. In addition, knowing the primary tips for a trial witness will help in setting-the-stage visits to the courtroom and in critiquing witnesses. Figure 11:10 is a list of common suggestions provided a witness. Such a list should not be given a witness without the direction of the attorney and should be reviewed thoroughly by the attorney for any additions or deletions.

ASSIGNMENT 11:13
Place a copy of the Guidelines for a Witness's Trial Testimony in your system folder.

An Ethics Reminder

Remember that any attempt to have a witness conceal evidence, give misleading testimony, or lie is a very serious ethical violation. It is best, therefore, to avoid even the appearance of impropriety. If any questions do arise, consult the attorney immediately. Also, keep in mind that just because an attorney tells you to do something, especially if you know it is improper, you are not relieved from exercising independent judgment based on a sound knowledge of professional ethics.

Additional Preparation

The paralegal is often charged with seeing to it that the following are arranged:

- All hotel reservations for the trial team
- All transportation to the trial site
- Parking and payment for parking, including change when necessary for parking meters
- A prearranged system for meals and payment
- A system for collecting receipts for all expenses
- Arrangements and cash for emergency copying, phone calls, etc.
- Delivery of all trial materials, diagrams, files, etc., to court

■ Assistance At Trial

Some law firms have a paralegal do much of the background preparation for the case and then make the mistake of failing to utilize the knowledge and skills of that paralegal at trial. This is a serious oversight, for the firms that utilize paralegals at trial realize the tremendous benefits that can be derived from such assistance.

Before we discuss the role of the paralegal at trial, become familiar with the key stages in trial procedure, as outlined in figure 11:11.

Jury Selection

To begin jury selection, names are drawn from the jury pool to form the potential jury panel. Those people are then questioned by the judge and attorneys for each side (voir dire), after which the attorneys are allowed to strike a certain number of people to reduce the panel to the required number. The remaining people form the trial jury.

Observing the jury and witnesses is an important task for paralegals at trial. What else can you do to assist the attorney, client, and witnesses?

As each person's name is called as a potential juror, you can quickly note on the jury selection charts the juror's name and previous assessment of that person as good, bad, or intermediate for the case. Key, relevant facts about the person should be transferred to the chart for the attorney. This is where all the jury investigation performed earlier pays off. As the attorney asks voir dire questions, significant responses should also be entered on the chart.

Paralegals are frequently asked to note their observations of both verbal and nonverbal actions of the potential juror during voir dire. Much popular literature, including quasi-scientific articles, has been written about body language and ways to tell if a person is being truthful. Some attorneys place stock in these articles and train paralegals in such techniques. The truth is, however, that most such techniques are relatively inaccurate. Only the most

Figure 11:11   Stages in Trial Procedure

1. Jury Selection (Voir Dire): Initial selection and questioning of prospective jurors by the judge and possibly the attorneys to choose an impartial jury. Attorneys exercise challenges for cause and a predetermined number of preemptory strikes to eliminate unwanted jurors.
2. Opening Statements: Introductory remarks by the opposing attorneys on the case and what they will be proving. The defendant's attorney may reserve the opening statement for later.
3. Plaintiff's Case in Chief: The attorney presents the plaintiff's case through direct examination (questioning) of the plaintiff's witnesses. Physical evidence is also presented through the appropriate witnesses. Defendant's attorney may cross-examine each of the plaintiff's witnesses.
4. Defendant's Motion for Dismissal or Directed Verdict: The defendant may move for dismissal of the action or a directed verdict requesting the judge to dismiss the case on the grounds the plaintiff has failed to sufficiently prove the allegations. If the plaintiff, in the judge's opinion, has met the requisite burden of proof, this is a **prima facie case** (sufficient to prove a claim prior to any rebuttal), and the case will continue. If the evidence is inadequate, the judge will dismiss the case.
5. Defendant's Case in Chief: Presentation of evidence through the defendant's witnesses. The plaintiff may cross-examine.
6. Plaintiff's Rebuttal: Presentation of any witnesses or evidence by the plaintiff to rebut any new items raised in the defendant's case in chief.
7. Defendant's Rejoinder: Presentation of any witnesses or evidence by the defendant to rebut evidence offered in the plaintiff's rebuttal.
8. Motions for Directed Verdict: Motion by either side stating that the other side has failed to prove or sufficiently rebut the evidence such that, as a matter of law, the verdict is clear. If granted, the judge enters the verdict and the case ends.
9. Conference to Determine Jury Instructions: Attorneys argue and judge decides what jury instructions should be given the jury. The conference takes place in chambers.
10. Closing Arguments: Attorneys review the evidence, summarize the case, and request the jurors to enter a verdict in favor of their client. In most civil cases the defendant closes first and then the plaintiff. Some jurisdictions have plaintiff, defendant, then plaintiff's rebuttal if needed.
11. Instructions or Charge to Jury: Judge reads instructions to jury on their duties and the law governing their decision.
12. Jury Decides Case: The jury adjourns to the jury room, deliberates, and reports its decision to the judge.
13. Motion for Judgment Notwithstanding the Verdict (JNOV): Either party may move the judge to enter a judgment contrary to the jury's verdict on grounds the verdict is against the great weight of the evidence.
14. Motion for New Trial: Either party may move for a new trial based on serious errors occurring at trial. If granted, the case will have to be retried.
15. Entry of Judgment: The court enters judgment consistent with the jury verdict or JNOV. It is this judgment from which the unsatisfied party may appeal.

obvious clues, requiring simply an observant eye, prove useful. A good paralegal is cautious and conservative in the use of even the very obvious. The human mind is extremely complex and often does not reveal the experience or belief system behind the behavior. Common sense should serve as a guide. For example, if the attorney asks a juror a question and the juror turns away from the attorney and starts fidgeting, it may be a better than 50 percent chance that the juror does not care much for the attorney. Or, if on questions regarding racial or ethnic prejudices a juror keeps referring to a certain group as "those people," it is probable that the person chooses to be distanced from the subject and is likely to be prejudiced. Even the most obvious clues, however, are not foolproof; do not rule out manipulation by the knowledgeable juror.

During the questioning, keep track of the voir dire questions on a copy of the voir dire outline from the trial notebook so questions overlooked can be pointed out to the attorney. The attorney can use information recorded on the jury selection chart to make challenges for cause and to strike jurors. You may be consulted. Once the final panel is selected, fill in a chart showing these jurors.

Occasionally, paralegals are asked to observe potential jurors inobtrusively where they gather and take breaks. Every so often a paralegal overhears a juror say something that provides insight as to their suitability for the case. For example, if in the rest room a prospective juror was heard to say that she had a reliable cousin who felt Ms. Forrester was akin to the wrong end of a horse, it would certainly affect the attorney's decision to strike that juror. Stranger things have happened.

Witness Control

You can help during trial by keeping track of witnesses, notifying them when to appear, meeting them, and reducing their anxiety. Sometimes it is necessary to arrange for the witness's payment, lodging, and transportation. Occasionally a witness will have to be found and subpoenaed during trial.

Documents and Exhibits

You can also serve as custodian of exhibits, diagrams, and other trial materials. In such cases you must see that everything is ready that will be needed that day at trial, and that each item is stored in a secure place at the end of the day. If others are to serve as custodians, you should have a list of who has what and where the items are stored.

Exhibit and Witness Logs

During testimony you should keep track of each exhibit that is presented by both sides. This record serves as a guide to what has been presented, objected to, and accepted. It also tells you where the attorney needs a reminder to present an exhibit.

Witness logs should also be maintained to show what witnesses have been called and whether they have deviated significantly in their testimony from previous statements, or as otherwise anticipated. Outlines of questions for each witness can be followed as a check to make sure the attorney has not forgotten important questions. It is not unusual during the course of trial for the attorney to ask the paralegal, "Have I forgotten anything?"

Trial Notes

Take notes at the trial. The attorney is frequently too busy to note or even observe some significant comment or action. These notes should be particularly detailed when your supervising attorney is cross-examining the opponent's witnesses. A good technique is to use a fresh spiral notebook with lined paper. Each page should be numbered ahead of time. A summary-outline of the proceedings can be recorded on the left page, with detailed notes on a particular witness's answer or other important notes on the right page. This provides a systematic means to take notes. Key entries at vital stages in the proceedings will be easier to locate when reviewing the notes. Notes should be kept on what the attorney specifies before trial; most commonly that includes the name of the case, judge, court reporters, and staff; all parties, attorneys, experts, and others. Indicate what witnesses have been called, by whom, and the essence of their testimony. Note exact quotations if particularly significant. Note exhibits entered through each witness. Note all objections and judge's rulings, and the times of all recesses, conferences before the bench, conferences in chambers, and times trial resumed.

Trial Day Review Meetings

Frequently the entire trial team gathers each evening to discuss the day's events and next day's strategies. Your notes of the day can be compared to the attorney's notes and recollections. You can offer suggestions when appropriate and receive instructions on what to do for the following day. This might involve last-minute subpoenas, arranging for transportation, or doing some last-minute legal research on a point expected to be argued the following day. Motions may need to be put into final form, or at least readied for the attorney's submission.

When the Paralegal Must Testify

Sometimes it becomes necessary for the paralegal to testify at trial. This is commonly done to prove that something was mailed on a specified date, that a photo is authentic, or that a chain of custody has been maintained to preserve certain evidence. The better practice is to refrain from involving the paralegal, but sometimes it is unavoidable.

When this does happen, you should review the suggestions given to any witness. It is best to have the attorney prepare you through questions, since a review of actual documents to refresh recollection will make the documents accessible to the opposing attorney for cross-examination and can result in the revelation of attorney-client privilege.

Your testimony should be kept to a minimum, advocacy should be left aside, and the testimony should be professional and truthful. Any commitment to the client or the attorney cannot and does not supersede the commitment and responsibility to the truth.

Polling the Jury

At the completion of trial, the jury may be polled to see if the verdict stated is in fact agreed to by that particular juror. This is usually done when the attorney is surprised by the verdict. The attorney may ask the jurors about what witnesses were the most significant, what evidence had the most impact, and why they decided the way they did. You can assist by taking careful notes during the polling.

ASSIGNMENT 11:14
Prepare a list of those things you can do to assist the attorney at trial. Place it in your system folder.

Figure 11:12   Findings of Fact and Conclusions of Law

(Caption)

FINDINGS OF FACT AND CONCLUSIONS OF LAW

The above entitled action, having been tried before this court without a jury on _____[*date*]_____, with _____ appearing as the attorney for _____, and _____ appearing as the attorney for _____, and having heard the evidence in this case and the arguments of counsel, this court, being fully advised herein, makes the following findings of fact and conclusions of law:

Findings of Fact

(In separately numbered paragraphs state each finding of fact.)
From the foregoing facts, the court concludes

Conclusions of Law

(In separately numbered paragraphs state each conclusion of law.)

By the Court

_____

Judge

Dated _____

Findings of Fact and Conclusions of Law

In some states, in cases when there is no jury, the prevailing party has the duty of drafting the court's **findings of fact and conclusions of law.** This document summarizes the key evidence on the necessary elements of the cause of action and the judge's conclusion that form the basis of the judgment. The paralegal is often asked to draft this document for the attorney's review. It is submitted to the court, signed by the judge, and distributed to the parties. Figure 11:12 is a form for drafting findings of fact and conclusions of law.

ASSIGNMENT 11:15
Place a copy of the form for drafting findings of fact and conclusions of law in your system folder.

■ Summary

Preparedness through organization continues to be a common thread that defines much of your responsibility as a paralegal. Preparing the litigation team for trial is not only crucial to success at trial, but also involves some of the most interesting and creative tasks that you may be asked to perform. You have learned to develop and utilize a checklist such as the Trial Preparation Checklist. You have learned the importance of and techniques for serving subpoenas, conducting jury investigations, creating demonstrative evidence, drafting motions in limine and motions to be used at trial, and preparing witnesses to testify. You have become familiar with the components and organization of an effective trial notebook.

Paralegals, as we have seen, also play an important role at trial by knowing each stage of the trial and anticipating how they can be of best use at each stage, by observing and recording information at jury selection, by coordinating witnesses and maintaining control over documents and exhibits, by taking careful notes for daily trial review, and other tasks. Although these tasks require energy and diligence, your hard work will be rewarded at the moment of victory. Here is one outstanding paralegal describing how she felt after her hard work made a significant contribution to a favorable verdict for her firm's client:[1]

> It was the most incredible feeling. . . . The last time I felt like that was when they told me it was a girl . . . I was literally shaking. . . . I've been doing this for eight years and you never get used to it; I hope I never do.

Study Guide

1. What are the tasks to be performed by the paralegal in the last six weeks before trial?
2. What is the importance of a Case Status Sheet?
3. What steps must be followed in subpoenaing witnesses?
4. How can you help in conducting a jury investigation? What information should be gathered and from what sources?
5. What purpose does the Juror Data Sheet serve?
6. What benefits are derived from diagrams and other audiovisual aids?
7. List and describe some typical audiovisual aids used in the courtroom.
8. What are the rules in your jurisdiction on the admissibility of and proper foundation for demonstrative evidence, including diagrams?
9. Whom might you consult when preparing your own diagrams and charts?
10. How might the computer be useful in preparing audiovisual aids?
11. What is a trial notebook? List and define its key components.
12. What aspects of the trial notebook can you draft?
13. What are jury instructions? What should you do to prepare a draft set of instructions for the attorney?
14. How can you assist the attorney in preparing the client or a witness for trial testimony? What ethical considerations must be kept in mind?
15. How can you assist the attorney at voir dire and other stages of the trial?

Endnote

1. Arnold, *A Once in a Lifetime Case*, NATIONAL PARALEGAL REPORTER 24 (Winter 1989) [quoting Jill Burton of Brown, Todd, and Heybrun in Louisville, Kentucky].

12

Post-Trial Practice from Motions to Appeal

- Introduction
- Post-Trial Motions
- The Judgment and Bill of Costs
- Enforcement of the Judgment
- Appeal

■ Introduction

The popular media would have us believe that the case ends with the trial verdict. The steps following the verdict, however, may modify or even reverse the apparent outcome. This chapter covers the procedures employed after the verdict is rendered to retrieve what appears to be a lost case or to confirm the results. Here you will learn the function, procedure, and forms for four post-trial processes: post-trial motions for judgment notwithstanding the verdict and a motion for a new trial, the proper filing of the judgment and bill of costs, the procedures for enforcing a judgment, and those for appealing the case.

With experience, a good paralegal should be able to perform each of these tasks. Keep in mind, however, that not all law offices will readily delegate all of these tasks to the paralegal. It falls to you to earn the confidence of the law firm and, in many situations, to *make* the opportunity and to reach out for enhanced responsibility.

This chapter should hold some excitement for another reason. On its completion you will possess the necessary fundamentals for the entire process of civil litigation. Take pride in your acquisition of knowledge in this significant area of paralegal practice.

■ Post-Trial Motions

Even if the court has entered judgment in the case, the party against whom the judgment has been entered may move to have the judgment set aside. The two most common devices to achieve this are a *motion for judgment notwithstanding the verdict* (JNOV) and a *motion for a new trial*.

Under Rule 50 of the Federal Rules of Civil Procedure and like state rules, a party who has moved for a directed verdict at the close of all the evidence may file a motion for judgment notwithstanding the verdict. The motion must be filed within ten days after judgment has been entered. The motion asks either that the judgment be set aside, combined with a motion for a new trial, or that judgment be entered in accordance with the previous motion for directed verdict. A motion for new trial may also be filed separately. Generally speaking, a motion for JNOV is granted if the weight of the evidence is contrary to the jury's verdict.

A motion for new trial must be filed within ten days of the entry of judgment (Rule 59). Typically, this motion alleges procedural errors (improperly admitted or excluded evidence, improper argument by opposing counsel, prejudicial jury instructions, etc.), a verdict contrary to law, excessive or inadequate damages, and other grounds. The motion must be supported by affidavit. The opposing party has ten days in which to file responsive affidavits.

Your role in post-trial motion practice can be significant. Immediately after trial, review with the attorney the copious notes you took at trial. From these notes the attorney develops theories on which the motion can be based.

Research the applicable rules of procedure and the legal standards and authority for the motion in the pertinent jurisdiction. After a review of the authorities with the attorney, write the rough-draft motion and any supporting affidavit. Filing dates should be entered in the deadline control system. Once in final form, the motion and supporting documents are served on the opponent and filed in court. Figures 12:1 and 12:2(a) and (b)

Figure 12:1   Motion for Judgment Notwithstanding the Verdict

IN THE UNITED STATES DISTRICT COURT FOR

THE _____ DISTRICT OF _____ _____ DIVISION

ABC		
	Plaintiff	Civil Action No. _____
v.		
XYZ		Judge _____
	Defendant	

MOTION FOR JUDGMENT NOTWITHSTANDING THE VERDICT

Plaintiff ABC moves the Court pursuant to Rule 50(b), Federal Rules of Civil Procedure, to set aside the verdict entered in the above-entitled action on _____ (and the Judgment entered thereon on _____) and to enter judgment in favor of Plaintiff ABC for the following reasons:

1. There was no substantial evidence offered by the Defendant XYZ on the issue of invalidity;
2. There was no substantial evidence offered by the Defendant XYZ on the issue of non-infringement;
3. There was no substantial evidence offered by the Defendant XYZ on the issue of damages;
4. There was no substantial evidence offered by the Defendant XYZ on the issue of reasonable royalty.

Respectfully submitted,

_____

J. Doe, Attorney for Plaintiff

[Add Proof of Service]

Figure 12:2(a)   Motion for New Trial in Non-Jury Case

IN THE UNITED STATES DISTRICT COURT

FOR THE _____ DISTRICT OF _____ _____ DIVISION

ABC

                            Plaintiff   Civil Action No. _____
          v.

XYZ   Judge _____

                            Defendant

MOTION FOR NEW TRIAL IN NON-JURY CASE

Plaintiff ABC moves the Court to set aside the Findings of Fact, Conclusions of Law and Judgment pursuant to Rule 52(b) Federal Rules of Civil Procedure, and to grant Plaintiff a new trial pursuant to Rule 59(a), Federal Rules of Civil Procedure on the grounds that:

1. The Court erred in ruling that *   *   *
2. The Court erred in admitting the following evidence offered by the Defendant over objection of Plaintiff *   *   *
3. The Court erred in excluding evidence of Plaintiff *   *   *
4. The Court erred in admitting the following exhibits over objection for the following reasons *   *   *
5. The Court erred in excluding the following exhibits *   *   *
6. The Judgment is contrary to law in that *   *   *

                                                     Respectfully submitted,

                                                     _____

                                                     J. Doe, Attorney for Plaintiff

                    [*Add Proof of Service*]

---

are examples of a motion for judgment notwithstanding the verdict and motions for new trial, respectively.[1]

ASSIGNMENT 12:1
Enter the ten-day time limit for filing the previous motions in the Motions, Pleadings, and Time Limits table. Place copies of the motions in your system folder both in a post-trial motion section and in your motion practice section. Indicate what federal and state rules govern the motions.

◼ The Judgment and Bill of Costs

Another task performed by the litigation paralegal is the preparation and filing of the bill of costs. Federal Rule 54(d) and parallel state rules provide that costs shall be awarded to the prevailing party unless otherwise directed by the court. The prevailing party files a bill of costs with the clerk of court. A copy is sent to the opposing attorney. The opposing attorney may object to all or part of the bill. If either party is dissatisfied with the clerk's determination, a motion for court review may be served within five days of the clerk's taxation of costs.

Figure 12:2(b) Motion for New Trial in Jury Case

IN THE UNITED STATES DISTRICT COURT FOR

THE ___ __ DISTRICT OF _____ _____ DIVISION

ABC

              Plaintiff | Civil Action No. _____

    v.

XYZ | Judge _____

             Defendant

MOTION FOR NEW TRIAL IN JURY CASE

Defendant XYZ moves the Court pursuant to Rule 59(a), Federal Rules of Civil Procedure, to set aside the verdict of the Jury returned herein on _____ and the Judgment entered on _____ and to grant a new trial on the grounds that:

1. The verdict is contrary to the law as follows ∗ ∗ ∗
1. The verdict is contrary to the evidence as follows ∗ ∗ ∗
3. The evidence in this case is totally insufficient to support a finding of validity, enforceability and infringement.
4. The verdict of the jury herein is excessive and appears to have been given under the influence of passion and prejudice as follows ∗ ∗ ∗
5. The Court erred in permitting the following testimony over objection of Defendant XYZ ∗ ∗ ∗
6. The Court erred in refusing to allow witnesses to answer Defendant's questions as follows:
7. The Court erred in admitting the following exhibits for the following reasons ∗ ∗ ∗
8. The Court erred in excluding the following exhibits for the following reasons:

Respectfully submitted,

_____

J. Doe, Attorney for Plaintiff

[*Add Proof of Service*]

Because costs include such things as filing fees, fees for service of pleadings, witness fees, etc., there is usually a standard fee established by the clerk of court, who can provide the necessary information. In every respect, however, the bill must be reasonable under the circumstances. What to include in the bill and what is necessary to support the charge is set out in Federal Form AO133. Some state courts provide similar forms. Figure 12:3 is the federal form for a bill of costs.

ASSIGNMENT 12:2
Place a copy of the Bill of Costs in your system folder. If your state has a similar form, include it.

■ Enforcement of the Judgment

Introduction

One of the perplexing quirks in civil procedure is that the winner of a judgment, the **judgment creditor,** often must go back into court to force

Figure 12:3   Bill of Costs

AO 133
(Rev 7/82)

BILL OF COSTS

𝔘𝔫𝔦𝔱𝔢𝔡 𝔖𝔱𝔞𝔱𝔢𝔰 𝔇𝔦𝔰𝔱𝔯𝔦𝔠𝔱 ℭ𝔬𝔲𝔯𝔱	DISTRICT
V.	DOCKET NO.
	MAGISTRATE CASE NO.

Judgment having been entered in the above entitled action on_____ against
                                                                                              date

_____ the clerk is requested to tax the following as costs:

BILL OF COSTS

Fees of the clerk . . . .$ _____

Fees for service of summons and complaint . . . . _____

Fees of the court reporter for all or any part of the transcript necessarily
    obtained for use in the case . . . . _____

Fees and disbursements for printing . . . . _____

Fees for witnesses (itemized on reverse side) . . . . _____

Fees for exemplification and copies of papers necessarily obtained
    for use in case . . . . _____

Docket fees under 28 U.S.C. § 1923 . . . . _____

Costs incident to taking of depositions . . . . _____

Costs as shown on Mandate of Court of Appeals . . . . _____

Other costs (Please itemize) . . . . _____

_____

_____

_____

TOTAL $ _____

SPECIAL NOTE: Attach to your bill an itemization and documentation for requested costs in all categories. Briefs should also be submitted
supporting the necessity of the requested costs and citing cases supporting taxation of those costs.

DECLARATION

I declare under penalty of perjury that the foregoing costs are correct and were necessarily incurred in this action and
that the services for which fees have been charged were actually and necessarily performed. A copy hereof was this day
mailed with postage fully prepaid thereon to:

SIGNATURE OF ATTORNEY _____

FOR: _____   DATE _____
          Name of claiming party

Please take notice that I will appear before the clerk who will tax said costs on the following day and time:	DATE AND TIME
Costs are hereby taxed in the following amount and included in the judgment:	AMOUNT TAXED $

CLERK OF COURT	(BY) DEPUTY CLERK	DATE

Figure 12:3   (Continued)

WITNESS FEES (computation, cf. 28 U. S. C. 1821 for statutory fees)							
NAME AND RESIDENCE	ATTENDANCE		SUBSISTENCE		MILEAGE		Total Cost Each Witness
	Days	Total Cost	Days	Total Cost	Miles	Total Cost	
						TOTAL	

NOTICE

Section 1924, Title 28, U.S. Code (effective September 1, 1948) provides:
"Sec. 1924. Verification of bill of costs."
"Before any bill of costs is taxed, the party claiming any item of cost or disbursement shall attach thereto an affidavit, made by himself or by his duly authorized attorney or agent having knowledge of the facts, that such item is correct and has been necessarily incurred in the case and that the services for which fees have been charged were actually and necessarily performed."

See also Section 1920 of Title 28 which reads in part as follows:
"A bill of costs shall be filed in the case and, upon allowance, included in the judgment or decree."

The Federal Rules of Civil Procedure contain the following provisions:
Rule 54 (d)
"Except when express provision therefor is made either in a statute of the United States or in these rules, costs shall be allowed as of course to the prevailing party unless the court otherwise directs, but costs against the United States, its officers, and agencies shall be imposed only to the extent permitted by law. Costs may be taxed by the clerk on one day's notice. On motion served within 5 days thereafter, the action of the clerk may be reviewed by the court."

Rule 6 (e)
"Whenever a party has the right or is required to do some act or take some proceedings within a prescribed period after the service of a notice or other paper upon him and the notice or paper is served upon him by mail, 3 days shall be added to the prescribed period."

Rule 58 (In Part)
"Entry of the judgment shall not be delayed for the taxing of costs."

the **judgment debtor** to comply with the judgment. Although not a difficult process, it is time-consuming and adds additional expense to the lawsuit.

More than likely, the judgment debtor will cooperate and make arrangements to pay. This may be a lump-sum payment in cash, a structured payment involving investments and annuities, installments secured by promissory notes and collateral, or some other method.

If, at the beginning of a lawsuit, the plaintiff fears that the defendant will try to hide or even transfer assets to avoid loss through judgment, the judgment creditor can seek court action to seize the property to satisfy a favorable judgment. Federal Rule 64 permits such procedure in accordance with the remedies and procedures available in the state in which the federal district court sits. Some typical prejudgment remedies include **attachment, garnishment, replevin,** and others. Some of these same remedies are available after judgment and will be discussed later in this section. Prejudgment remedies are less popular today than a few years ago, and courts are unlikely to grant them unless there is a good reason. If the action involved the title to specific property, a notice of **lis pendens** may be filed by the plaintiff. This places all other buyers of that property on notice that the plaintiff has claimed a right to that property depending on the outcome of the case. Figure 12:4 is an example of a notice of lis pendens.

The focus of this chapter, however, and the more common concern of the paralegal, is locating and obtaining the assets after the judgment has been entered and the debtor refuses to cooperate.

Locating the Assets of the Judgment Debtor

Prior to taking any action, the judgment creditor must determine if the debtor has any assets. Most likely, this was determined to some extent in the early stages of the case. Few attorneys are willing to put all that work into

Figure 12:4 Notice of Lis Pendens

STATE OF _____   CIRCUIT COURT   COUNTY _____

_____,
                            Plaintiff
        v.   Civil Case, File No. _____
_____,
                            Defendant

NOTICE OF LIS PENDENS

NOTICE IS HEREBY GIVEN that an action has been filed in the above entitled court by _____,

Plaintiff against _____, Defendant for an action *[state type of action such as "to quiet title".]*
This action affects title to real property in _____ County as described below:

(Provide legal description of property.)

Date _____   Attorney for Plaintiff _____

                                 Address _____

                                 Phone _____

a case, only to find at the end that the defendant has no assets and is, for all practical purposes, **judgment proof.** Whether at the beginning or end of the case, you need to gather the information.[2]

Your objective is to compile a list of every asset that the judgment debtor has. As you search for assets, you will want to obtain the following basic information for each asset:

A description of the asset. Be specific as to quantity, color, size or other measurements, function, component parts or any other data relevant to the kind of asset in question.
Location. Where is the asset? Give the exact addresses and names of people who have possession of the asset, including, of course, the judgment debtor.
How did the judgment debtor obtain his/her interest in the asset? If by purchase, how much was paid, when acquired, etc.?
What is the current fair market value of the asset? If the asset were sold on the open market, how much would it probably bring?
When tracking assets in an attempt to obtain the above information, it is useful to think of the various categories of assets that are possible:

1. Personal property—Real property
2. Property solely owned by the judgment debtor—Property in which others also have an interest
3. Tangible property—Intangible property
4. Property in the possession of the judgment debtor—Property in the possession of a third person
5. Property in the state where the judgment was rendered (forum state)—Property in another state (foreign state)
6. Property the judgment debtor currently has—Property that will be received in the future
7. Property the judgment debtor currently has—Property that the judgment creditor disposed of since the litigation began or just before it began
8. Property that is exempt from creditor collection—Property not protected by exemption

Any single asset may fall into a variety of categories listed above.

Personal/Real Property

Personal property would include cash, bonds, securities, uncashed checks, cars, trucks, boats, jewelry, clothing, business inventory, equipment, pension rights, insurance policies, debts owed the judgment debtor (e.g., accounts receivable), etc.

Real property: current residence, vacation home, fixtures on the land, buildings (business or personal use), etc.

Solely Owned/Others with Interest

The judgment debtor may own many assets in his/her own name without anyone else having a property interest in the asset. On the other hand, there will usually be assets in which others will also have a property interest. For example,

■ a spouse may jointly own a bank account or a home
■ a spouse may have a dower or community property interest in assets acquired during the marriage
■ an associate may have an equal partnership interest in a business

- a tenant will have a property right to remain on land owned by the judgment debtor as landlord
- the government may have a tax lien on property because of nonpayment of taxes
- a bank or some other creditor may have a security interest in property, e.g., the property was used as collateral in order to obtain a mortgage or borrow money in some other way
- a neighbor has an easement over the judgment debtor's land allowing the neighbor to use the land for a limited purpose

The following are some basic property terms with which you should be familiar. They all involve assets in which more than one person has a property interest:

Joint tenancy: individuals (called joint tenants) own the entire property together. They do not own parts of it; each individual owns all of the property. When one joint tenant dies, the property does not pass through the decedent's estate. The property passes immediately to the surviving joint tenants. This is known as the right of survivorship. (A joint tenant is not a tenant who rents an apartment; these are totally separate concepts of tenance.)

Tenancy by the entirety: this is a joint tenancy in which the joint tenants are husband and wife.

Tenancy in common: individuals (called tenants in common) own a portion or a share of the whole property. There is no right of survivorship. When one tenant in common dies, his/her interest in the property passes through his/her estate and does not go to the surviving tenants in common.

Lien: a claim against property which is usually created to secure payment of a debt. The holder of the lien can force the sale of the property when the debt is not paid. The proceeds from the forced sale are used to satisfy the debt.

Mortgage: in some states, a mortgage is simply a lien of property which is used to secure the mortgage debt.

Tangible/Intangible Property

Tangible property: having a physical form which can be seen or touched, e.g., land, car, equipment.

Intangible property: a "right" rather than a physical object, e.g., the right to receive money from an employer, the right to the exclusive use of an invention, the right to have money repaid with interest, etc. These rights may be described in documents that are tangible, e.g., a stock certificate, a promissory note, a patent, but the rights represented by these documents are intangible.

Possession of Judgment Debtor/Possession of Others

Very often the judgment debtor will have assets in the possession of other persons or institutions. Banks and employers, for example, often hold money which belongs to the judgment debtor which will be turned over upon request, or when a set date arrives. Insurance companies, unions and government agencies also hold ("possess") assets (often called benefits) which will be given to the judgment debtor at a certain time, or upon the happening of a designated condition, e.g., retirement.

A **bailment** exists when someone else's goods are being held for use, repair or storage, e.g., furniture in storage, a borrowed or rented car, a car in a repair shop. The person holding the property (called the bailee) may or may not be receiving a profit for holding the goods of the other (called the bailor).

Garnishment is the process of trying to reach the assets of the debtor (here the judgment debtor) which are in the possession of a third party in order to satisfy the debt.

Property in Forum State/Property in Foreign State

The forum state is the state that rendered the judgment for the judgment creditor against the judgment debtor. A foreign state is any other state in the United States or any other country in the world. The judgment debtor may own land or other assets in a foreign state as well as in the forum state.

Current Property/Future Property

Many of the judgment debtor's assets will already be in his/her possession. Other assets, however, may be on their way to the judgment debtor through the mail or other means of shipment. Some assets will not be received until the occurrence of a designated event or condition, e.g., a request for the asset is made by the judgment debtor, a certain age is reached, retirement, death, a designated date has arrived, etc.

Assets which the judgment debtor has a right to receive in the future can usually be *assigned* to someone else so that the latter will be entitled to receive the asset. An **assignment** is simply a transfer of rights from one person to another.

Current Property/Property Recently Disposed Of

The great fear of a judgment creditor is that the judgment debtor will voluntarily render him/herself judgment proof by giving away, destroying, or otherwise disposing of the assets before the trial is over. The judgment creditor may or may not have obtained protection against this by the kind of pre-trial attachment referred to above. Even if no such protection was obtained, the judgment creditor may be able to invalidate any transfers of assets made by the judgment debtor just before and during the trial on the ground that they were sham transfers, or were made with the intent to defraud the judgment winner.

Exempt Property/Nonexempt Property

All the assets owned by the judgment debtor are not fair game to the judgment creditor. By law, certain property is exempt, e.g., a designated percentage of the judgment debtor's salary, clothes, the tools of one's trade or profession, some furniture. Such property cannot be reached by the judgment creditor to satisfy the judgment debt.

How then does the judgment creditor go about locating the assets of the uncooperative judgment debtor that fall into one or more of the above eight categories of assets? There are some formal procedures that can be of assistance in discovering assets. Before discussing these, some thoughts will be presented on *informal* investigative techniques.

The judgment creditor has just been through a trial and perhaps an appeal with the judgment debtor. A good deal is already known about him/her. This data must be organized and evaluated at two levels. First, the data contains specific information on the possible assets and liabilities of the judgment debtor. Second, the data tells you a lot about the life style of the judgment debtor. One's life style is an excellent clue to assets and liabilities. You are interested in liabilities or other debts because the kind and extent of liabilities one assumes is often an indication of one's assets. The assumption is that someone with a lot of liabilities probably has a lot of assets to cover those liabilities. Someone who rarely gets into debt probably has very little to risk. Of course, you also want to know if the judgment debtor is over his/her head in liabilities since there may be little or nothing left for the judgment creditor to reach.

The power of the court can also be called upon to aid in locating assets of the judgment debtor. These more formal methods utilize devices designed for pre-trial discovery to gather information important to the post-trial resolution of the case.

The least expensive method is the **postjudgment interrogatory.** The paralegal draws in part on the process of informally locating assets to design a set of questions for the judgment debtor to answer. Figures 12:5 and 12:6 are forms of interrogatories for the purpose of discovering assets.[3]

Postjudgment interrogatories, however have disadvantages. The debtor can draft answers carefully to provide as little information as possible. If the debtor refuses to answer, the court must be asked to compel an answer, causing further delay.

Figure 12:5   Informal Investigative Techniques to Discover the Assets and Liabilities of the Judgment Debtor

I. Data that you already have about the judgment debtor from the trial and appeal.
  A. Data in the Office Case File
    1. Notes on the reasons why the attorney for the judgment creditor agreed to take the case initially. What led the attorney to believe that the defendant was not judgment proof?
    2. Notes on the intake interview of the client. What did the client say or imply about the status of the defendant?
    3. Notes on preliminary investigations done by the law firm.
    4. Notes on early negotiations with opposing counsel to settle the case. What was said about the defendant? Did you learn about liability insurance limits?
    5. Pleadings, e.g., the responses given in the answer to the complaint.
    6. Correspondence in the file.
    7. Data obtained through pre-trial discovery
      ■ answers to interrogatories
      ■ deposition transcripts of the defendant and other witnesses
      ■ the contents of documents obtained through a motion to produce
      ■ the answers to requests for admissions
      ■ the results of ordered physical or mental examinations
    8. Transcripts of direct and cross and re-direct examination of the defendant and other witnesses who testified about the defendant's past.
    9. Exhibits introduced at trial whether or not they were admitted into evidence, e.g., police reports on the accident, prior convictions.
    10. Motions and briefs filed by the defendant.
  B. Other Data Based on Appearances as Clues to Life-style
    1. Did the defendant hire an expensive law firm?
    2. How well did defendant dress? What kind of car?
    3. Did the defendant appear successful and prominent in business?
    4. What educational level was demonstrated?
    5. To what kind of life-style did the defendant's family appear to be accustomed?
    6. What level of integrity and openness was demonstrated? Did the defendant appear to be secretive?
    7. Was it expensive for the defendant to defend this suit? Did the defendant use extensive resources, e.g., expert witnesses, demonstrations? Do you know who paid these expenses?

II. Leads to additional data about the judgment debtor.
- **A.** Data in Public Records
    1. Telephone directory
    2. Land records in county offices
    3. Prior litigation brought by or against the defendant as revealed in court clerks' offices, e.g., breach-of-contract actions, divorce proceedings, bankruptcy proceedings
    4. Index bureaus on prior claims made by the defendant
    5. Credit bureaus with data on the defendant or on defendant's business
    6. Motor vehicle registration
    7. Government license offices
    8. Secretary of State's office for incorporation papers, financial statements, etc.
    9. Newspaper stories on the defendant or his/her business
    10. Obituary column if defendant is deceased
    11. Government Consumer Protection agencies which might list consumer complaints against defendant's business
    12. Government offices where liens and mortgages are filed (including filings pursuant to the Uniform Commercial Code)
- **B.** Other leads
    1. Interviews with neighbors
    2. Interviews with clients or other business associates of the defendant
    3. Site visit to residences
    4. Site visit to places of business

Source: Statsky, *Torts: Personal Injury Litigation.*

Figure 12:6 Written Interrogatories to Judgment Debtor

IN THE _____ COURT OF _____

_____,
Plaintiff

v.   No. _____

_____,
Defendant

PLAINTIFF'S INTERROGATORIES TO DEFENDANT–JUDGMENT DEBTOR
IN AID OF ENFORCEMENT OF JUDGMENT

To: _____, Defendant–Judgment Debtor

[c/o _____, Attorney for Defendant]

From: _____, Plaintiff

Take Notice: Under the provisions of Rules [*69(a) and 33*] of the [*Federal*] Rules of Civil Procedure [and § _____ of the _____ Code] you must answer the attached Interrogatories in writing under oath, and you must send a copy of your Answers to the undersigned attorney, and you must file the originals of your Answers with the Clerk of the above Court, all within _____ days. If you fail to file full, complete and truthful Answers within _____ days and to send a copy to the undersigned attorney, the court may order you held in contempt of court and fined and imprisoned, and the Court may also order you to pay additional costs, including reasonable attorney's fees, of proving facts about which inquiry is made.

_____
Attorney for Plaintiff
[*Address*]

[Certificate of Service]

Interrogatories

1. What are your full, correct name and any other names, alias or nickname by which you have ever been known, and your social security number?
2. What is your age and date of birth?
3. What are your present complete addresses, both business and residence, including each telephone number, whether publicly listed or not, at which you may be reached by telephone?
4. What are the name, nature, duration and place of each employment or occupation you have had during the past two years?
5. What trade names and assumed names have you done business under during the past two years, and what is the complete address of each place where each business was conducted?
6. What is the full name and present address of each person with whom you have engaged in any partnership, business enterprise or business venture in the past two years?
7. Have you prepared or issued any financial statement within the past three years?
8. If so:
   a. What is the purpose for which each statement was prepared and issued?
   b. What is the name and addess of each person, firm, corporation, partnership, mercantile or trade agency, or other organization to whom they were issued?
   c. What is the present ownership and location of each asset shown?
9. If you will do so without a motion to produce, attach a copy of each such financial statement to your answers to these interrogatories.
10. What are the date, place and name of each person or institution to whom you have furnished or exhibited any statement of your financial condition during the past two years? Please attach to your answers to these interrogatories a copy of each such financial statement.
11. What are the full description and present location and ownership of each asset or property shown on any financial statement listed in the preceding question? If any such asset or property is not presently owned by you, state the full details concerning its disposition by you, including to whom it went, when, and for what consideration, including its sale price, if any.
12. a. Have you filed or prepared income tax returns during the past two years?
    b. If so, state the source and amount of each item of income listed on each tax return.
    c. Do you have any source of income not shown on such tax returns?
    d. If so, state full details.
13. Do you have an ownership or leasehold interest in any real property?
14. If so, for each parcel of property, state:
    a. What is the address and legal description of the property?
    b. What is the size of the property?
    c. Provide a description of each structure and other improvement on the property.
    d. What is the ownership of the property as stated in the documents of title, and the location of each such document?
    e. What is the present value of your equity interest in the property?
    f. Do you claim that the property is exempt by law from forced sale?
15. What are the cost, location and estimated present market value of each item of personal property owned by you, including but not limited to vehicles of any sort, firearms, collections (stamps, coin, etc.), tools, equipment of any sort, livestock, sporting goods, and boating equipment?
16. Is any of the real or personal property owned by you, either individually, jointly, or otherwise, encumbered by either a real estate mortgage, chattel mortgage or any other type of lien?
17. If so, for each item of property, state:
    a. A description of the property encumbered.
    b. What is the nature of each encumbrance?
    c. What is the date when the property was encumbered?
    d. What is the name and address of each person who holds the encumbrance?
    e. What consideration was received for each encumbrance?

    f. What is the name and address of each person who paid the consideration for the encumbrance?

    g. What are the date and place of recordation and sufficient description of the recording data for each encumbrance to identify it?

18. Has any item of your property been pledged to secure a debt?

19. If so, for each item of property, state:

    a. A description of the property pledged.

    b. What was the amount of the debt the property was pledged to secure?

    c. How was the debt incurred?

    d. On what date was the debt incurred?

    e. At what place was the debt incurred?

    f. What is the name and address of each pledgee?

    g. On what date was possession of the property pledged transferred to the pledgee?

20. Do you have an ownership interest in any business?

21. If so, for each business, state:

    a. What is the name of the business

    b. What is the address of the principal place of business or general office?

    c. What is the address of each place at which the business is conducted?

    d. What type of business is conducted?

    e. What is the form of business organization?

    f. What is the date you acquired your interest in the business?

    g. What is the present value of your interest in the business, and its percentage of the total value of the business?

    h. What is your office or position in the business?

    i. What is the name and address of each officer and director or partner of the business?

    j. What is the name and address of each bank at which the business maintains any type of checking or deposit account or from which the business has borrowed money?

22. Were any articles of incorporation, partnership or certificates of doing business under a fictitious name filed with any governmental agency by any of the enterprises mentioned in the preceding interrogatory?

23. If so, for each such filing, state:

    a. What is the nature of the document filed?

    b. What is the location of the office where the document was filed?

    c. What was the date of filing?

24. Do you own any stocks, bonds, or other securities of any class in any government, governmental organization, company, firm or corporation, whether foreign or domestic?

25. If so, for each organization, state:

    a. What is the name and address of the organization in which you own any proprietary or security interest of any sort?

    b. Describe each security or other evidence of ownership.

    c. What is the serial number of each bond, share, stock certificate or other evidence of ownership or security?

    d. On what date was each bond, share, stock certificate or similar interest acquired by you?

    e. How was each bond, share, stock certificate or other interest acquired by you (by purchase, gift or other means)?

    f. What is the name and address of each person, firm or corporation from whom each bond, share, stock certificate or other interest was acquired, regardless of mode of acquisition?

    g. What is the name, address and telephone number of any person, firm or corporation with whom you share, under any form of joint ownership or community interest, any degree of ownership or control of any of the above securities?

    h. Do you presently owe any money to anyone for the purchase of the securities?

    i. What is the present location and custody of each bond or other certificate?

26. Are any of the bonds, shares, stock certificates or other securities owned by you pledged, mortgaged or subject to an option to repurchase by anyone?

27. If so, state:
    a. What is the name and address of each person, firm, or corporation holding such interest in your securities?
    b. On what date was such interest acquired?
    c. Describe the interest.
28. Do you maintain any business bank accounts?
29. If so, for each account, state:
    a. Where is the account located?
    b. What is the name and address of the bank holding the account?
    c. What is the name and account number under which the account is held?
    d. What was the balance of the account as of five days before you received these interrogatories?
30. Do you maintain any personal checking or savings accounts?
31. If so, for each account, state:
    a. Where is the account located?
    b. Under what name is the account held, and what is number of the account?
    c. What is the name and address of the bank holding the account?
    d. What was the balance of the account as of five days before you received these interrogatories?
32. Do you have a joint savings or checking account with anyone?
33. If so, for each account, state:
    a. Where is the account located?
    b. What is the name and address of the bank or branch holding the account?
    c. Under what name(s) and number is the account held?
    d. What was the balance of the account as of five days before you received these interrogatories?
34. Do you have any money on deposit, either in a checking account or savings account, in any name other than your own?
35. If so, for each account, state:
    a. Where is the account maintained?
    b. Under what name and number is the account maintained?
    c. What is the name of the bank or branch where the account is located?
    d. What was the amount of the account as of five days before you received these interrogatories?
    e. What is the amount or portion of the account which belongs to you?
36. Do you have any accounts in any bank which you are holding in trust for anyone else?
37. If so, for each account, state:
    a. What is the name of the bank or branch where the account is maintained?
    b. On what date was the account opened?
    c. What were the sources of all deposits into the account?
    d. What is the name and address of each beneficiary who has an interest in the account?
    e. Is any beneficiary of the account related to you, and, if so, what is the relationship.
38. List and give full details concerning any bank account not listed above on which you have check-writing authority.
39. Do you have access to any safe deposit box or other depository for securities, cash or other valuables?
40. If so, for each depository, state:
    a. What is the name and address of each person, firm or corporation to whom the depository is rented or leased?
    b. What is the name of the bank or branch where the depository is located?
    c. What is the name and address of each person having access to the depository?
    d. Describe the property contained in the depository as of five days before you received these interrogatories.
    e. On what date did you last enter the depository?
41. Have any of the contents of the above-mentioned depositories been removed during the past twelve months?

42. If so, for each item removed:
    a. Describe the property removed.
    b. What was the exact date of the removal?
    c. Why was it removed?
    d. What is the name and address of each person who removed it?
    e. What is the name and address of each person, firm or corporation to whom the property was conveyed or transferred?
43. Do you own any interest of any kind in any patent or copyright?
44. If so, for each interest owned, state:
    a. What is the registry number of the patent or copyright?
    b. Describe the item patented or copyrighted.
    c. What is the name and address of each person, firm or corporation that shares any interest in the copyright, and what is the amount or percentage of each interest?
    d. What amount of income do you receive from the patent or copyright per year?
45. Have you, at any time during the past two years, paid or had paid for you the premiums on any life insurance policy payable to you, your estate, your wife, or her estate?
46. If so, for each policy, state:
    a. What is the name and address of the company that issued it?
    b. What is the number of the policy?
    c. What is the face of the policy on the death of the insured?
    d. What is the present cash value of the policy?
    e. On what date was the policy issued?
    f. What is the total consideration paid to the company that issued the policy between the date of issuance of the policy and the present date?
    g. What is the name and address of each person, firm or corporation that made each payment?
    h. On what date was each payment made?
    i. Where is each document or contract of insurance issued to you in connection with or as evidence of the policy of insurance?
    j. What is the name, address and telephone number of each person who has custody of a copy of the document or contract?
47. Has the name of the beneficiary of any of these insurance policies been changed in the past twelve months?
48. If so, state:
    a. On what date did the change of beneficiaries take place?
    b. What is the name of each new beneficiary?
    c. Why, in each case, was the beneficiary changed?
49. If you will do so without a motion to produce, attach a copy of each document or contract of insurance to your answers to these interrogatories.
50. Do you now own any choses in action, or do you have any claims for money against any others?
51. If so, as to each, state:
    a. What is the general nature of the claim?
    b. What is the name and address of each person who you claim is liable?
    c. Is the claim or chose in action for a liquidated amount?
    d. What is the amount you claim as damages?
    e. Has any suit or action been brought to reduce the claim to judgment? If so:
        (1) What are the title and number of the case and the court in which the action is pending?
        (2) What was the date of filing the action?
        (3) What is the current status of the case?
    f. Has any offer of settlement been made, and, if so, by whom and for what amount?
    g. Has any compromise agreement been reached, and, if so, what further acts are required to effect the settlement?
52. a. Have you, at any time in the past two years, given consideration for any property which has been conveyed or transferred and is now being held for you in the name of some person other than yourself?
    b. Does anyone hold anything for you or for your benefit?

53. If the answer to either 52(a) or 52(b) is "Yes," then state:
    a. What is the name and address of each titleholder?
    b. On what date was each conveyance or transfer made?
    c. Describe each item or piece of property conveyed.
    d. What amount of consideration was given for such property?
54. Do you hold any property as trustee of a testamentary or inter vivos trust?
55. If so:
    a. Describe the property held in trust.
    b. What is the name and address of the trustor or settlor?
    c. What is the name and address of each beneficiary of the trust?
    d. Do you have a general power of appointment over any property contained in the trust?
    e. On what date was the trust created?
56. During the past two years have you created or contributed to any trust for the benefit of others?
57. If so, state:
    a. When was the trust created?
    b. Describe the property contributed by you.
    c. What is the name and address of each trustee?
    d. What is the name and address of each beneficiary of the trust?
    e. Are any of the beneficiaries related?
58. Are you an heir-at-law or beneficiary under the terms of the will of any person now deceased?
59. If so, state:
    a. What was the name of the decedent?
    b. What is the name and address of the court in which the estate is pending or the person who has possession of a will not offered for probate?
    c. Have you received any advancements from either the testator or his personal representative, and, if so, what is the amount of each advancement received?
    d. Have you renounced any bequest or legacy, and, if so
        (1) On what date?
        (2) What is the name of each person whose interest in the estate was enhanced as a result of this renunciation?
60. According to your business records, what is the present amount of your accounts receivable?
61. List each account receivable by name, address and amount due you.
62. Within the past twelve months, have any of your accounts receivable been assigned, or otherwise disposed of, other than by collection?
63. If so, as to each such account, state:
    a. What is the name of the account?
    b. When was the account assigned or otherwise disposed of?
    c. What is the name and address of each assignee or other transferee?
    d. Did the assignment or other disposition cover only present accounts receivable?
    e. Did the assignment or other disposition also include future accounts receivable, and, if so, to what extent?
    f. What amount of consideration was received for the assignment or other disposition?
64. Have you at any time in the past two years conveyed or disposed of any property either by sale, gift or otherwise?
65. If so, for each disposition:
    a. Describe the property disposed of.
    b. What was the date of disposition?
    c. What is the name and address of each person to whom disposition was made?
    d. How was disposition made (by sale, gift or otherwise)?
    e. What consideration was received?
66. Have you made any conveyances, transfers, gifts or other dispositions of property in the past two years with any reservation of rights, benefits, or options running to you for the reacquisition of the property at some future date?
67. If so, for each disposition:
    a. Describe the property conveyed, transferred or otherwise disposed of?
    b. When was the property disposed of?

    c. What is the name and address of the transferee?

    d. What is the nature of the reservation, benefit or option reserved?

68. Have you, in the past two years, assigned any thing or chose in action?

69. If so, for each assignment:

    a. Describe the thing or chose in action assigned.

    b. When did the assignment take place?

    c. What is the name and address of each assignee?

    d. What consideration was received for the assignment?

70. Have you, at any time in the past six months, either sold, transferred, or assigned, in bulk, all or a substantial part of your stock in trade or trade fixtures?

71. If so, for each transfer, state:

    a. On what date did the transaction take place?

    b. What is the legal description of the property disposed of?

    c. What is the name and address of each transferee or assignee?

    d. What was the amount or value of consideration received as the sales price?

    e. Was any notice of the intended sale, transfer, assignment or mortgage recorded, and, if so, when and where?

    f. Was any notice of the sale, transfer or assignment published in any newspaper, and, if so, on what date(s) and in what newspaper?

72. Have you, at any time in the past four years, entered into any transaction with your wife or any other relative involving the transfer, conveyance, assignment, or other disposition of any of your real or personal property?

73. If so, for each transaction:

    a. Describe the property involved.

    b. When did the transaction take place?

    c. What consideration did you receive?

    d. What is the name and address of each member of your family or other relative involved in the transaction?

74. Have you at any time in the past four years transferred any of your property, whether real or personal, to any other person in consideration of future support?

75. If so:

    a. Describe the property transferred.

    b. When did the transfer take place?

    c. What is the name and address of each person to whom the transfer was made?

76. Have you at any time in the past two years suffered any casualty loss from fire, wind, theft, or otherwise?

77. If so, for each loss:

    a. Describe the property lost or damaged.

    b. What was the cause of the loss?

    c. What was the date of the loss?

    d. What was the amount of the loss?

    e. Was the loss covered by insurance?

    If so:

        (1) What is the name and address of the insurance carrier?

        (2) What are the policy limits and policy number?

        (3) Has a claim been filed with the insurance carrier, and, if so, when?

        (4) Has the claim been paid, and, if so, when and in what amount?

78. Have you at any time in the past two years been a party to any contract or any other agreement, whereby you granted an option to anyone to purchase any or all of your assets?

79. If so, for each contract and option, state:

    a. On what date was the agreement made?

    b. Where was the agreement made?

    c. What is the name and address of each person, firm or corporation who is a party to the agreement?

    d. What consideration was received for the agreement?

    e. What is the name and address of each person furnishing the consideration?

    f. Describe the property covered by the agreement.

    g. What are the terms of the agreement?

80. Do you at the present time have any creditors in addition to the plaintiff in this case?

81. If so, for each creditor, state:

    a. What is the name and address of the creditor?

    b. What is the amount of debt owed?

    c. On what date was the debt incurred?

    d. What consideration did you receive for the debt?

    e. Describe any security given to secure the debt.

    f. Is the creditor a relative or a general partner of yours or a corporation of which you are a director or officer or a partnership of which you are a general partner?

    g. How many days are you in arrears in making payment to the creditor?

    h. What is the total amount of arrearages?

82. List, by name, address and amount, all payments you have made to each creditor within the past year.

83. Do you claim that any of the real property owned by you is exempt from the claims of your creditors?

84. If so, for each item of property:

    a. Describe the property and its estimated value.

    b. What is your reason for claiming the property to be exempt?

85. Do you keep any books or other written memoranda of your income and business affairs?

86. If so, state:

    a. In what form are the books or memoranda kept?

    b. When were the books or memoranda first maintained?

    c. What is the name, address and telephone number of each person, firm, or corporation that prepared the books or memoranda for you?

    d. Are the books or memoranda presently maintained?

    e. Do the books or memoranda accurately reflect the income contained in your federal income tax returns for each respective year?

    f. Where are all books or memoranda for the period of the last three years presently located?

    g. What is the name, address and telephone number of each person, firm or corporation that has custody of these books?

87. If you will do so without a motion to produce, attach a copy of each of your above-mentioned books and memoranda for the period of the past three years to your answers to these interrogatories, or state a time and place when and where the books and memoranda may be inspected.

88. Have you within the past three years either destroyed or otherwise disposed of any books of account, memoranda or other records relating to your business or income?

89. If so, state:

    a. When were the books of account or records destroyed or otherwise disposed of?

    b. Why were they destroyed or disposed of?

    c. What is the name and address of the person who destroyed or disposed of the books or memoranda?

90. Have you employed, or had employed in your behalf, the services of a certified public accountant or a public accountant at any time within the past two years?

91. If so, for each accountant and firm, state:

    a. What is the name and address of the accountant employed?

    b. What are the inclusive dates on which the accountant was employed?

    c. Why was the accountant employed?

    d. Describe the services performed by each accountant.

92. Have you at any time within the past two years taken an inventory of your property, either personal or business?

93. If so, for each inventory, state:

    a. On what date was the inventory taken?

    b. What is the name and address of each person who took the inventory or supervised the taking of the inventory?

    c. What is the name and address of each person having possession of a copy of the inventory?

    d. What is the total dollar value of your property stated in the inventory?

    e. Was the inventory taken at cost, market or other valuation?

    f. Why was each inventory taken?

    g. Was the inventory of personal or business property?

    h. What items were included in such inventory?

94. If you will do so without a motion to produce, attach a copy of each inventory to your answers to these interrogatories.

95. Do you have any interest in any pension plan, retirement fund or profit-sharing plan?

96. If so, state:

    a. What is the name and address of the administrator of each such plan?

    b. What is the approximate present value of your interest?

    c. What is the nature of your interest, and under what terms may you receive money or property?

97. Have you at any time within the past four years acquired personal property or interests in personal property that you now claim is exempt by law from forced sale?

98. If so, what property did you acquire?

99. Have you at any time within the past four years paid off a mortgage or other encumbrance on personal property that you now claim as exempt by law from forced sale?

100. If so, on what property did you pay off the mortgage or other encumbrance?

101. Within the past 120 days have you made an assignment for the benefit of creditors, or has a trustee, receiver or other custodian been appointed or taken possession of all or substantially all of your property?

As is true in discovery, the interrogatories could be joined with a **post-trial request for production of documents,** or the request could be submitted independently. The request can obtain a variety of documents including copies of tax returns, financial records and reports, bank statements, insurance policies, certificates of title, deeds, loan applications, mortgages, and others.

A more expensive and time-consuming process is the use of the **post-trial deposition.** This procedure is known as a *creditor's examination.* This can be used to bring the judgment debtor or other individuals knowledgeable of the debtor's finances into a setting where they can be questioned under oath about the location of the debtor's assets. Being able to question the debtor and others directly provides the opportunity for flexibility and immediate pursuit of newly raised areas of inquiry. Draft a list of those to be deposed and have them subpoenaed as approved by the attorney. Assist in preparing post-trial depositions in the same way the discovery deposition is prepared for. These procedures are referred to as **supplementary proceedings** and may be used before any action is filed to enforce a judgment or as part of separate actions to collect on the judgment. Sanctions can be imposed for failing to comply with these devices, including the contempt powers of the court. State rules and statutes should be carefully consulted before using any of these devices.

ASSIGNMENT 12:3

Research the rules of procedure and law in your jurisdiction on the availability of formal supplementary proceedings for locating a judgment debtor's assets. Check the U.S. Code as well for any such procedures. Then list the procedures and applicable rules and statutes in your system folder. Place a copy of the notice of lis pendens and the postjudgment interrogatories in your system folder.

ASSIGNMENT 12:4
Research your state law to determine what assets of a judgment debtor are exempt from execution on the judgment. List these in your system folder.

Obtaining the Assets of the Judgment Debtor

With a detailed list of the debtor's assets and consultation with the attorney, all that remains is the selection of an appropriate procedure and the drafting of the relevant documents. The easiest and least expensive collection method is to write a letter to the debtor. Figure 12:7 is an example.[4] Figure 12:8 is an example of a follow-up letter.[5]

If the letters fail, procedures used to enforce a judgment include **execution,** garnishment, and domestication of a judgment. None of these actions may be taken, however, as long as any stay has been granted by the court on the execution of the judgment. Under Federal Rule 62 and parallel state rules, an automatic stay is imposed for the first ten days after judgment, and the court may grant longer stays in its discretion, including a stay pending the outcome of an appeal. The judgment debtor may have to post a **supersedeas bond** to secure the amount of the judgment during the stay. Absent a stay, enforcement actions may be taken.

Execution

Some judgments are self-executing. For example, a divorce decree or a quiet title action requires no further action. Some judgments require the transferring of title or a deed. When the party obligated to execute the transfer refuses to do so, the court may, on application, appoint a trustee to execute the necessary documents. In other states the court has the power to order done that which the judgment says should have been done. The court order has the effect of the deed when properly recorded.[6]

A **writ of execution** is a device used to enforce a judgment for money. Both federal courts and the individual state courts rely on the procedure set out in the rules and statutes of that state. Check the local practice for the correct procedure. Most states have a local source book on the forms and procedures for collections.

Typically, the judgment creditor has a list of the property of the defendant needed to satisfy the judgment. A writ of execution is obtained from the court specifying the property to seize and sell **(levy)**. A public officer, usually the sheriff, locates the property and physically or constructively seizes it. Only the property needed to satisfy the judgment may be seized. A procedure carefully outlined in state law is followed by which the property is sold. Some delay in the sale is common to give the debtor a chance to receive notice of the levy. The property is sold at auction or other sale and the proceeds are used to pay off the costs of execution, the judgment, and any interest accrued on the principal of the judgment since entry of the judgment. Any remaining proceeds are returned to the judgment debtor. Figure 12:9 is an example of a writ of execution. These are often available in preprinted form from the court.[7]

In some cases, such as where the judgment debtor owns business property, placing the property into **receivership** may be preferable to

Figure 12:7 First Letter to Judgment Debtor

JONES & SMITH

ATTORNEYS AT LAW
100 MAIN STREET
ANYWHERE, U.S.A. 00000
(000) 000-0000

_____, 19__

Mr. Henry I. Judgment–Debtor
110 North Sycamore Street
Anywhere, U.S.A. 00000

Dear Mr. Judgment–Debtor:

A judgment was entered against you in the _____ Court of _____ on _____, 19__, in favor of our client _____, in the amount of $_____. This amount is still owing to our client on account of the judgment.

Please call this office to make arrangements for payment of this amount. By making such arrangements now, you will avoid the inconvenience, embarrassment and expense of further legal action against you to collect the judgment.

Thank you for your anticipated cooperation.

Very truly yours,

JONES & SMITH

By _____

Attorneys for _____

cc: [*Client*]

    Clerk, _____ Court

---

selling it. In this procedure, the court appoints a receiver who sees to it that the judgment is paid out of the regular income of the business until the debt is satisfied. This allows the debtor to maintain the business beyond payment of the debt unless the court orders the sale of the property.

Figure 12:8 Follow-Up Letter to Judgment Debtor

JONES & SMITH
ATTORNEYS AT LAW
100 MAIN STREET
ANYWHERE, U.S.A. 00000
(000) 000-0000

_____, 19__

Mr. Henry I. Judgment–Debtor
110 North Sycamore Street
Anywhere, U.S.A. 00000

Dear Mr. Judgment–Debtor:

Enclosed is a certified copy of the judgment which was entered against you in the
_____ Court of _____ on _____, 19__, in the amount of $_____. We have
not yet received any response to our letter to you dated _____, 19__ asking you
to make arrangements for payment of this amount. Therefore, our client _____ has
instructed us that, unless we hear from you by _____, 19__, we are to take further
legal action against you. Such legal action may include: seizure and sale at public
auction of your nonexempt personal property, including your automobile; garnishment
of a portion of your wages from your employer; and issuance of a subpoena to compel you to testify in court concerning all your assets, in default of which you may be
arrested and punished by fine or imprisonment for contempt of court.

Please pay to our office not less than $_____ by _____, 19__. Otherwise, we
will have no choice but to take further legal action against you.

Very truly yours,

JONES & SMITH

By_____

Attorneys for _____

cc: [Client]

Figure 12:9 Writ of Execution for Specific Property (or Its Value)

IN THE _____ COURT OF _____

_____,
                              Plaintiff
               v.   No. _____

_____,
                              Defendant

WRIT OF EXECUTION

The State of _____ to the Sheriff of _____ County:

On _____, 19__ in this case plaintiff _____ recovered a judgment against defendant _____ for the title and possession of the following property with costs of suit, which to date amount to $:

Property   **Valued at**
                                                        $

Therefore, you are commanded to seize the above described property and deliver possession of it to the judgment creditor _____ and to cause to be made the sum of $_____ for payment of the costs adjudged against the judgment debtor _____ and the further costs of executing this writ from property the judgment debtor owns subject to execution.

And in case a delivery of the above described property or any part of it cannot be had, you are further commanded to cause to be made the value of such undelivered property from property the judgment debtor owns subject to execution.

Bring the money [and the property] together with this process, showing how you have executed it, before this Court at _____, within _____ days.

Witness the Honorable _____, [Chief] Judge of the _____ Court of _____, on _____, 19__.

Issued on _____, 19__.

                                        ATTEST: _____
                                                Clerk of the _____

                                                Court of _____
                                                              [*Seal*]

Garnishment

This procedure is used to obtain property of the debtor held by or owed to the debtor by a third person. Property typically garnished includes money in bank accounts or wages regularly owed the debtor. The judgment creditor generally applies for a writ of garnishment. The writ is served with a summons by the sheriff or some other public official on the third person **(garnishee)**, and directs that person to disclose the amount of money being held by the garnishee. The garnishee usually has twenty days to respond to the summons. Once the amount is determined, an order for garnishment is requested and a writ issued for seizure of the property or for a lien on the property preventing its transfer to the debtor. When wages are involved, federal law exempts 75 percent of the employee's disposable earnings. Disposable earnings are all earnings less withholding taxes, Social Security,

Figure 12:10 Application and Affidavit for Writ of Garnishment After Judgment

IN THE _____ COURT OF _____

_____,
Plaintiff and Garnishor,
v.

_____,   No. _____
Defendant and Garnishee,
and

_____,
Defendant.

APPLICATION AND AFFIDAVIT FOR WRIT OF GARNISHMENT AFTER JUDGMENT

_____, being duly sworn, deposes and says:

1. My name is _____; I am the _____ of plaintiff _____; and I am duly authorized to make this affidavit on plaintiff's behalf.
2. The applicant, _____, is plaintiff in Case Number _____, styled _____ v. _____, on the docket of the _____ Court of _____ ("the main suit"). The garnishee is _____, whose address is _____.
3. In the main suit, applicant has a valid subsisting judgment, rendered on _____, 19__, against _____ in the amount of $_____ with interest thereon at a rate of __% per year until paid. There is due on the judgment the sum of $_____ which is uncollected, unpaid and unsatisfied [*or* other factual assertion]. Within my knowledge the defendant in the main suit does not have in his possession in this state property subject to execution sufficient to satisfy the judgment.
4. This writ of garnishment is not sued out to injure either the defendant or the garnishee.
5. I have reason to and do believe that garnishee _____, who resides in _____ County, State of _____, is indebted to the defendant, _____, or has possession or custody of effects belonging to the defendant. The source of my information and belief is _____.
6. [*It may be advisable to use this clause except in unusual situations.*] Applicant requests that the defendant, _____, be given notice and an opportunity to appear at a hearing before the court for the purpose of allowing him to oppose this application and to introduce evidence why the writ of garnishment applied for should not issue.
   [*OR: Alternate, for use in unusual situations*] The following facts constitute an unusual situation that justifies issuance of the writ without prior notice to the defendant and without a prior hearing: _____. Applicant requests that defendant be given notice of the issuance of the writ and an opportunity to appear at a hearing before the court for the purpose of allowing him to oppose the issuance of the writ and to introduce evidence why the writ should be dissolved.
7. Applicant requests that [after the hearing] the court issue a writ of garnishment against the garnishee, that a copy be delivered to the defendant, and for further proceeding thereon as provided by law.
8. A copy of this application has been mailed to _____ at _____ on _____, 19__.

_____

[*Acknowledgment*]

Figure 12:11 Writ of Garnishment

IN THE _____ COURT OF _____

_____,
Plaintiff and Garnishor,
v.

_____,   No. _____
Defendant and Garnishee,
and

_____,
Defendant.

WRIT OF GARNISHMENT

To: [*Name and Address*] Garnishee:

1. _____ claims that he is plaintiff in the _____ Court of _____ in cause no. _____ on the docket of that court, styled _____ v. _____, defendant, in which he has a valid, subsisting and uncollected judgment against the defendant for the sum of $_____ with interest thereon at the rate of _____% per year _____, 19__ and costs of suit.

2. Plaintiff has applied for a writ of garnishment against you, [*Name*].

3. You are hereby commanded to appear before this court at _____, 19__ [*or:* on __ __. m. on the Monday next following the expiration of _____ days from the date of service hereof]. You must then answer upon oath what, if anything, you are then indebted to [*Defendant*] and were when this writ was served upon you; and what effects, if any, of [*Defendant*] you have in your possession, and had when this writ was served; and what other persons, if any, within your knowledge, are indebted to [*Defendant*], or have effects belonging to [*Defendant*] in their possession. Answer as the law directs.

4. The officer serving this writ is directed to serve a true copy also on _____, defendant in the main action.

Dated and issued on _____, 19__.

ATTEST: _____

Clerk of the _____

Court of _____

_____

Judge Presiding

and other lawful deductions. Figure 12:10 is an example of an application and affidavit for a writ of garnishment.[8] Figure 12:11 is the writ of garnishment.[9]

ASSIGNMENT 12:5
Research the forms and procedures for garnishment in your state. Make a checklist and place it and the appropriate forms in your system folder.

Domesticating a Judgment

When a judgment is entered and recorded, it is good for a period of ten years in most jurisdictions. The recording of the judgment notifies all other creditors and potential buyers that a lien exists on the debtor's property. Most property will not be sold until all such liens are cleared. For a nominal fee, most judgments can be renewed. This becomes particularly useful when a debtor is currently unable to pay the judgment but comes into money or property at a later date.

When the debtor has property in another jurisdiction, particularly another state, creditors can levy on that property by *domesticating the judgment.* This means that the judgment from one state may be entered in a court in another state, and all rights will attach to that judgment as if it had been initially obtained in the foreign jurisdiction. This is another area where a paralegal's investigation of assets can be valuable. The procedure involves locating the court that has jurisdiction over the debtor's property, and filing an application in the foreign court. The application includes statements that enforcement of the judgment is not barred by the statute of limitations in either state, that no stay of execution on the judgment is in effect, that the judgment remains unsatisfied, that no other action based on the judgment is pending, and that no judgment based on the original judgment has been previously entered in the foreign state. In addition the name and address of the debtor and the judgment creditor are included. An authenticated, **exemplified,** or otherwise certified copy of the original judgment should be attached.[10]

Under Article 4 § 1 of the U.S. Constitution, the foreign state must give "full faith and credit" to the judgment of a sister state. Once domesticated, the judgment can be entered with the foreign state in the same fashion as the original state.

The judgment debtor may challenge the judgment on the basis that the original court lacked jurisdiction or that the judgment has been paid. The burden of proof, however, rests with the judgment debtor. There is no retrial of the original issues. Judgment may be ordered in a similar manner in foreign countries, but in such cases the procedures may vary somewhat.

Transferring federal court judgments for enforcement is quite simple. Title 28 U.S.C. at § 1963 permits the registering of a judgment from a federal court in any other federal court. Once registered, the judgment is treated as a local judgment.

ASSIGNMENT 12:6

Make an outline of the procedure for domesticating a judgment in another state and in federal court. Place the outline in your system folder.

Keeping Track of Collections of Judgment

Each case file should have a sheet kept at the front or top of the file that indicates the case, court, judgment, attorney, and the progress in collecting the judgment. If the judgment was not paid soon after its entry, a file record sheet should indicate all types of enforcement action taken and what has been collected on each action to date.

You may also choose to keep a master list of all cases in which judgments have not been satisfied. Calendar all judgment expiration dates so that renewals of those judgments can be sought where the judgment remains unsatisfied. Review the unsatisfied judgment list with the attorney on a periodic basis to see if additional action needs to be taken.

ASSIGNMENT 12:7
Check the law library for form and procedure books on enforcement of judgments or collections for your state. Draft a step-by-step checklist for enforcing a judgment in your state. Place the checklist and any pertinent forms in your system folder.

◼ Appeal

Introduction

The purpose of an appeal is to ask a higher court to review the decisions of the trial judge that the person appealing believes are erroneous. The appellate court will review legal questions only, not questions of fact decided by the trial court judge or jury. In some issues, such as whether the verdict goes against the weight of the evidence, the appellate judge must review the evidence, but the question remains a question of law—was the verdict so erroneous that, as a matter of law, it must be reversed.

Most parties choose not to appeal because appeals are expensive, and the majority of appellants are unsuccessful. The appeal, however, is an important part of our checks and balances system that guarantees a person the right to have a lower court's decision reviewed if there is a reasonable basis for the appeal. If the party did not raise an issue by objection or motion at the trial, the issue is waived for purposes of appeal.

The person bringing the appeal is called the appellant; the person defending against the appeal is called the appellee or respondent. Appellate procedure generally involves the following stages. The appellant must file a notice of appeal that is conveyed to all the other parties. The appellant is responsible to see that a transcript of the pertinent aspects of the trial is ordered, prepared, and sent to the appellate court. Briefs are filed by both parties, stating the facts, the issues to be addressed, and the arguments and authorities on the issues. Oral arguments are presented by all parties during which the judges may ask questions. The judges meet to discuss the case, and an opinion is written. The appellate court may affirm, modify, or reverse the judgment of the trial court. Even if the appellate judges rule that the trial judge was in error, the appellate court will not alter the judgment unless the error substantially affected the verdict in the case. A lesser degree of error will be declared **harmless error.**

The study of appeals in all their complexity is beyond the scope of this text, so the following discussion is simply an overview of the fundamentals in the process.

Appellate Procedure

Appellate procedure is fairly standardized in the federal courts, but it varies among states. Research the applicable state rules and adhere to them. Following is a list of the significant procedural steps and deadlines for the Federal Rules of Appellate Procedure.

☐ Consult with the attorney for go-ahead on the appeal.

☐ Develop a case appeal log for recording compliance with all requirements of the appellate process.

☐ File a petition for leave to appeal: 28 U.S.C. § 1292(b). (Appellee has seven days after service of petition to file opposition to leave to appeal.)

☐ Draft a notice of appeal (see following form).

☐ File the notice of appeal within thirty days of judgment or order, or within sixty days if the United States or an officer or agency thereof is a party [Fed.R.App.P. 4(a)(1)].

☐ File a bond for the cost of the appeal or a supersedeas bond if the execution of judgment is stayed [Fed.R.App.P. 7 and 8].

☐ Order a transcript of the trial proceedings (pertinent parts or pertinent videotape if so recorded) from the court reporter within ten days of filing notice of appeal. File a copy of the order with the clerk of district court. [Fed.R.App.P. 10]. Unless the entire transcript is ordered, file (within ten days of notice) a statement of the issues on appeal. Notify all other parties of the issues on appeal and the parts of the transcript ordered so appellee can designate other parts of the record needed for appeal within ten days of service of the order. Parties may stipulate to omit certain parts of the record.

☐ See to it that the reporter files a transcript with the clerk of district court within thirty days of the date ordered by appellant. See that record is complete (pleadings, exhibits filed in district court, transcript or parts thereof, and certified copies of docket entries), prepared by the clerk, and submitted by the clerk of court to the court of appeals. This must be done within forty days of filing of the notice of appeal. It is up to appellant to see if the record is complete and sent by clerk.

☐ Pay docket fees (28 U.S.C. § 1413) within forty days of filing of the notice of appeal. The clerk of the court of appeals will docket the case upon receipt of the notice of appeal and the docket entries.

☐ File all papers with the clerk of the court of appeals by mail addressed to the clerk. All papers must arrive within the required time limit. Briefs are considered timely if mailed before expiration of the time limit [Fed.R.App.P. 25(a)]. Proof of service should be filed with the papers [Fed.R.App.P.25(d)].

☐ Service on the party or the party's counsel may be made by mail, in person.

☐ File a motion for extension of time if good cause can be shown.

☐ File and serve brief within forty days after the date on which the record is filed. If the brief is not filed on time, the appellee may move for dismissal of the appeal. File twenty-five copies of all briefs [Fed.R.App.P. 31].

☐ File for an extension of forty days in district court.

☐ Note the date that appellee's brief is due. (Appellee has thirty days to file and serve brief. [Fed.R.App.P. 31(a)].)

☐ Check the opponent's brief for accurate statements of fact, case holdings and citations, and accurate recitation of the record.

☐ File and serve the appellant's reply brief within fourteen days after service of the appellee's brief [Fed.R.App.P. 31(a)]. Double-check all case citations and citations of the record before filing.

☐ Be sure all time limits are on the docket deadline control calendar.

☐ Record notice from the clerk of court whether oral argument is to be heard, and if so, the time, place, and duration of each side's oral argument. Notify the attorney and see that all deadlines are calendared.

☐ Assist in the preparation of oral argument as requested by the attorney. Prepare an oral argument notebook.

☐ Arrange delivery of any exhibits to the court set up prior to oral argument, and removal immediately after argument.

☐ Attend oral argument to assist the attorney if requested.

☐ Note the receipt of opinion and judgment and convey it to the attorney.

☐ Submit an itemized and certified bill of costs to the clerk with proof of service within fourteen days after entry of the judgment. Objection to any bill of costs must be filed within ten days of service of the bill [Fed.R.App.P. 39(d)].

☐ Draft and file a petition for rehearing if so directed by the attorney. The petition must be filed within fourteen days after entry of the judgment. The petition should follow the form prescribed by Rule 32(a) and served according to Rule 31(b).

ASSIGNMENT 12:8
Place a copy of the Checklist for Federal Appellate Procedure (Appellant) in your system folder. Verify appellate time requirements in the Motions, Pleadings, and Time Limits table.

ASSIGNMENT 12:9
Research appellate procedure for your state and make a separate State Appellate Checklist for your system folder.

Figure 12:12 is a notice of appeal; figure 12:13 is a designation of record on appeal,[11] figure 12:14 is a motion for enlargement of time,[12] and figure 12:15 is a notice of filing of brief.[13]

Assisting in the Appeal

The checklist spells out the tasks you can and should perform. This section will focus on a few tasks that require some amplification.

Deadline Control and Appeal Management

The experienced paralegal can assume the role of appeals manager. To prepare for this role, study the appellate rules meticulously and record all deadlines, formats, and procedures. If you have questions, ask the appropriate clerk of court. An appeal program sheet should be kept for each case. Overall management can be achieved by using a master sheet with all pending appellate cases and points of progress for each case. Regular calendared reviews by all involved paralegals and attorneys can result in thorough and effective appellate management. With a little experience, the task will be easier and your benefit to the firm enhanced.

Figure 12:12   Notice of Appeal

UNITED STATES DISTRICT COURT FOR

THE DISTRICT OF _____

_____,
                                   Plaintiff
        v.   Civil Case, File No. _____
_____,
                                   Defendant

NOTICE OF APPEAL

Notice is hereby given that _____*[plaintiff][defendant]*_____ appeals to the United States Court of

Appeals for the _____ Circuit from the _____*[final judgment]*_____ __*[order]*__

__*[describe]*__ entered in this action on the _____ day of _____, 19__.

Date _____   Signature _____

                                                   Address _____

Figure 12:13   Designation of Record on Appeal

IN THE UNITED STATES DISTRICT COURT FOR

THE _____ DISTRICT OF _____ _____ DIVISION

ABC
                                   Plaintiff
        v.   Civil Action No. _____
XYZ
                                                   Judge _____
                                   Defendant

DESIGNATION OF RECORD ON APPEAL

Plaintiff ABC hereby designates the following docket entries, as set forth on the docket sheet of this civil action, to constitute the record on appeal.
   [*Here insert a list which includes docket numbers, date and an identification of each docket entry which is being designated*]

Respectfully submitted,

_____
J. Doe, Attorney for Plaintiff

[*Add Proof of Service*]

Figure 12:14 Motion for Enlargement of Time—Court of Appeals

IN THE UNITED STATES COURT OF APPEALS FOR THE _____ CIRCUIT

ABC

        Plaintiff–Appellant

             v.   Appeal No. _____

XYZ

        Defendant–Appellee

Appeal From the United States District Court

For the _____ District of _____,

_____ Division, Civil Action No. _____

MOTION FOR ENLARGEMENT OF TIME

Appellant ABC respectfully moves for an order extending the time for filing its Brief by an additional _____ days.

The basis for this request is that Appellant's attorney has been unable to complete the Brief within the requisite forty days because of the length of the record and because of the loss of "working days" due to legal holidays [*insert any additional reasons*].

Respectfully submitted,

_____

J. Doe, Attorney for Appellant

[*Add Proof of Service*]

Research

The paralegal is frequently assigned to research potential theories for the appeal, locate authority in support of the theory, and verify the accuracy of all citations used by all parties in their briefs and oral arguments. You can frequently turn up misuse of authority by checking whether the authority cited actually stands for the principle of law being asserted, and whether the facts are as presented. Eliminating erroneous citations from one's own brief can only strengthen it, while being able to call the court's attention to misuse of authority by the opponent can be effective in challenging the overall credibility of their argument.

Verifying the Record

Before the record is sent to the appellate court, review it to verify that the reporter has accurately portrayed what happened at the trial. If a partial transcript has been requested, verification of the accuracy of the key parts is particularly important. Further, determine whether everything needed in the record is ready to be sent by the clerk.

Figure 12:15   Appellate Brief—Notice of Filing

IN THE UNITED STATES COURT OF APPEALS FOR THE _____ CIRCUIT

ABC

Plaintiff–Appellant

v.   Appeal No. _____

XYZ

Defendant–Appellee

Appeal From the United States District Court

For the _____ District _____,

_____ Division, Civil Action No. _____

NOTICE OF FILING OF BRIEF

ABC Plaintiff–Appellant hereby files ten copies of its Brief and ten copies of the Appendix and hereby serves two copies each of its brief and the Appendix on Appellee.

Respectfully submitted

_____

J. Doe, Attorney for Plaintiff—
Appellant

[*Add Proof of Service*]

Assisting with the Appellate Brief

The appellate brief is a formal document drafted to specific standards that sets out the pertinent facts, legal questions, the legal argument addressing those questions, and legal authorities in support of that argument. The brief is often accompanied by an appendix of exhibits, relevant transcript sections, and other materials.

Each law office has a different approach to what the paralegal does here. Some firms do not use paralegals in brief preparation; others utilize experienced paralegals to prepare a full rough-draft brief that is reviewed by the attorney and then honed to a sharp edge.

If asked to research the brief, verify and Shepardize authorities on each key issue. Double-check each citation stated in the record and each citation to the record. Extract from the transcript those key lines that lie at the heart of the appeal. In addition, you may be asked to organize and write initial drafts of arguments based on the authorities. Good writing and organizational skills are needed at this stage. Observe the format and style of one or two appellate briefs previously filed in the particular court in question. If a brief of the exact same point can be found, it will substantially reduce the work (and also illustrate the value of keeping a brief bank on various topics). In reviewing these materials you will learn rules of drafting such as: State your strongest argument first and use clear subheadings that state arguments. Appellate handbooks and materials on brief writing provide more techniques and should be reviewed prior to writing the rough draft.

You should assume responsibility for organizing and indexing the brief. Old briefs are of great value here, but since court rules and specifications change, the latest edition of the appellate rules and specifications for briefs should be obtained. The Federal Rules of Appellate Procedure 28, 30, and 32 set the following specifications for briefs.

Rule 28 states that the appellant's brief shall contain a table of contents, a table of cases (alphabetically arranged), authorities cited, a statement of the issues on appeal, and a statement of the case including its nature, previous proceedings, and disposition. In addition, the brief shall have a statement of the relevant facts (with appropriate references to the record), an argument based on legal authority, and a short conclusion stating the precise relief sought.

Parties shall be referred to as "plaintiff" and "defendant" rather than as "appellant" or "appellee." References in the briefs to the record shall be to the pages of the brief's appendix at which those parts appear. Relevant statutes, rules, regulations, etc., or parts thereof shall be reproduced in the brief, in an addendum, or supplied to the court in pamphlet form.

The appellee's brief shall be the same, except that a statement of the issues or of the case need not be made unless the appellee is dissatisfied with the statement of the appellant.

Appellant's brief shall not exceed fifty pages, and the reply briefs twenty-five pages, excluding the table of contents, tables of citations, and any addendum. Rule 30 requires the appellant to prepare and file the appendix to the brief, containing: the relevant docket entries in the proceeding below; relevant portions of the pleadings, charge, findings, or opinion; the judgment, order, or decision in question; and any other parts of the record for the court.

Unless filing is to be deferred, the appellant shall serve and file the appendix with the brief. Ten copies of the appendix shall be filed with the clerk, and one copy shall be served on each party.

The parties are encouraged to agree as to the contents of the appendix. If they cannot, the appellant shall, not later than ten days after the date on which the record is filed, serve on the appellee a designation of the parts of the record that he or she intends to include in the appendix and a statement of the issues that he or she intends to present for review. The appellee may, within ten days after receipt of the designation, serve upon the appellant a designation of additional parts to be included by the appellant.

The cost of producing the appendix shall initially be paid by the appellant unless otherwise agreed. If parts of the record designated by the appellee for inclusion seem unnecessary to the appellant, the appellee shall pay for including those parts. The cost of producing the appendix shall be taxed as costs in the case. If either party shall cause matters to be included in the appendix unnecessarily, the court may impose the cost of producing such parts on the party.

The court may permit the appendix to be filed after the brief in specific cases. In such cases the appendix may be filed twenty-one days after service of the brief of the appellee.

The appendix shall include a table of its contents with page references. When transcripts are included in the appendix, the transcript page shall be indicated in brackets immediately before the matter that is set out. Omissions must be indicated by asterisks. Captions, subscriptions, acknowledgments, etc., shall be omitted.

Exhibits shall be included in a separate volume. Four copies shall be filed with the appendix and one copy served on each party.

A court of appeals may by rule or in specific cases, dispense with the appendix and permit appeals to be heard on the original record, with such copies of the record.

Rule 32 sets out the form of the brief. Briefs and appendices may be printed or clearly duplicated on opaque, unglazed, white paper. Carbons may not be submitted without permission except in behalf of parties allowed to proceed in forma pauperis. Printed briefs shall be bound in volumes having pages 6⅛ by 9¼ inches and type matter 4⅙ by 7⅙ inches. Otherwise, pages shall not exceed 8½ by 11 inches with type matter double-spaced and not exceeding 6½ by 9½ inches. Transcripts and appendices may be photocopied and informally renumbered. If covers are available, the cover of the appellant's brief should be blue, the appellee's red an intervenor's green, any reply brief gray, and the cover of the appendix, if separately printed, white. The front covers, if separately printed, shall contain the name of the court; the case number; the title of the case; the nature of the proceeding; the lower court, agency, or board; the title of the document; and the names and addresses of counsel.

Figure 12:16 is a skeletal example of the proper order and format of an appellate brief to be filed in the U.S. Court of Appeals.

Figure 12:16   Sample Appellate Brief

IN THE UNITED STATES COURT OF APPEALS
FOR THE _____ JUDICIAL CIRCUIT

Case No. _____

_____

_____,
                          Appellant
          v.

_____

_____,
          Appellee

On Appeal from the United States District Court for the _____ District of _____

BRIEF AND ARGUMENT OF APPELLANT

(Attorney) _____

(Address) _____

Attorney for_____

(Table of Contents Page)

TABLE OF CONTENTS

(Authorities Page)

TABLE OF AUTHORITIES CITED

Cases*   Page

*In alphabetical order. These cites are fictional for purposes of illustration.

STATEMENT OF THE ISSUES

The Honorable Walter F. DAVIS, Judge of the Northern District of Columbia, it is asserted made three errors at or following the trial in this case. The errors alleged are stated below:

1. _____

2. _____

3. _____

STATEMENT OF THE CASE*

*(FED.R. APP. P. 28(a)(3) states: "The statement shall first indicate briefly the nature of the case, the course of proceedings, and its disposition in the court below.")

This case is on appeal from the district court's ruling . . .

STATEMENT OF THE FACTS*

*(There shall follow a statement of the facts relevant to the issues presented for review, with appropriate references to the record [Rule 28(a)(3)].)

In February of 19___, Ann Forrester, a brilliant and creative teacher and mother of two, was . . .

SUMMARY OF ARGUMENT

ARGUMENT*

*(The argument shall contain the contentions of the appellant with respect to the issues presented, and the reasons therefor, with citations to the authorities, statutes and parts of the record relied on [FED.R. APP. P. 28(a)(4)].)

I. BECAUSE THE JURY VERDICT WAS CONTRARY TO THE GREAT WEIGHT OF THE EVIDENCE, THE TRIAL COURT ERRED IN DENYING PLAINTFF'S MOTION FOR JUDGMENT NOTWITHSTANDING THE VERDICT.

The law on when a motion for judgment notwithstanding the verdict is to be granted was reiterated in the recent Supreme Court case of *Abrams v. Pure Manufacturing, Inc.*, 500 U.S. 312, 33 L.Ed.2d 419 (1985). The court stated the rule to be:

When the evidence in a case demonstrates . . .

CONCLUSION*

*(A short conclusion stating the precise relief sought [FED.R. APP. P. 28(a)(5)].)

Under the rule of law stated in *Abrams v. Pure Manufacturing, Inc.*, The plaintiff must prove . . .

APPENDIX

Page of Transcript		Page of Appendix
T–1	Amended Complaint	1
T–3	Answer	4
T–110	Motion for Judgment Notwithstanding the Verdict	8
T–19–21	Relevant Testimony of Ms. Forrester	9–11

ASSIGNMENT 12:10

Place a copy of the skeletal appellate brief in your system folder. Be sure to include one example of each key page. Research the format of an appellate brief for your state. Include a copy in your system folder plus any rules on the required format.

Oral Argument

The paralegal assists with oral argument by preparing an oral argument notebook in close consultation with the attorney. The notebook is organized to contain major arguments with references to supporting legal authority, indices to the most significant references in the record, major case authorities, copies of important statutes, jury instructions, and other key materials for quick reference.

You should attend the oral argument if possible. Your familiarity with the case, gained through months and years of work, can assist the attorney at significant points in the argument, especially in responding to unanticipated points made by the opposition.

You have worked hard to become a professional litigation paralegal. What advantages can you now offer a law firm?

ASSIGNMENT 12:11
Complete your litigation system folder, update its table of contents, and prepare it for grading.

◼ Summary

In this chapter you have learned the function, procedure, and forms for post-trial practice. You may research and draft two post-trial motions. A motion for judgment notwithstanding the verdict (JNOV), if granted, overturns the verdict as going against the weight of the evidence. A motion for a new trial because of procedural or other errors may be combined with the motion for JNOV. A bill of costs is calculated and drafted by the prevailing party.

The paralegal for the prevailing party may have to assist the attorney in gaining the enforcement of the judgment. This process may be started in the initial stages of the case to guarantee that the property or funds will be available to cover any judgment. Notice of an expected judgment against the property is filed as a lis pendens. Enforcement procedures are more commonly employed after judgments, and involve investigating the location and amount of the debtor's assets through a variety of techniques.

WHITE, WILSON & McDUFF

ATTORNEYS AT LAW
FEDERAL PLAZA BUILDING, SUITE 700
THIRD AND MARKET STREETS
LEGALVILLE, COLUMBIA 00000
(111) 555-0000

MEMO TO: Terry Salyer
FROM: Isadora Pearlman

Your preliminary work in post-trial procedure has been successful; you are now ready to assist Mr. White in the appeal of Ms. Forrester's case.

Better than that, you have come to the end of your training period. Now you have the skills to assist our attorneys in the variety of litigation cases that will be assigned to you. You know how to research what you need on your own. Always remember to ask questions and strive to improve your knowledge.

You are ready to be a highly professional litigation paralegal. Congratulations and good luck!

Interrogatories, post-trial depositions, writ of execution, garnishment, and domestication of the judgment may be used.

Appeal is a complex process allowing the losing party to seek appellate review of the trial judge's decision. Your role in this step includes developing a thorough appellate checklist, drafting and filing necessary motions and other documents, maintaining a deadline control system, researching and drafting an appellate brief, and assisting at oral argument.

Study Guide

1. What are the two most common motions to have the judgment set aside? Define each of these motions.
2. Rule 59 requires that a motion for a new trial must be filed within how many days of the entry of judgment?
3. What role can you play in post-trial motion practice?
4. What is the bill of costs? What should you include when preparing a bill of costs? What form is used for a bill of costs?
5. What is a judgment debtor? A judgment creditor?
6. To what law does a judgment creditor in federal court look to enforce a federal judgment?
7. What is a prejudgment remedy?
8. What is a lis pendens?
9. What does it mean to be judgment-proof?
10. What are the various types of property subject to execution? What is exempt in your state?
11. What are the formal methods that can be used by a judgment creditor to determine the assets of the judgment debtor?
12. Identify and describe the common procedures for enforcing a judgment.
13. What is the step-by-step process for executing on property in your state?
14. Describe the steps in domesticating a judgment.
15. On what basis may a judgment debtor challenge an attempt to enforce a domesticated judgment?
16. What procedure is followed to have a judgment rendered in one federal jurisdiction honored in another federal jurisdiction?
17. List the various ways you can assist in the appeals process.
18. Describe the steps and time limits in the federal appellate process. In your state's appellate process.
19. What are the key components of an appellate brief?
20. What are the key components of an oral argument notebook?

Endnotes

1. WEST'S LEGAL FORMS (2d ed., 1986), §§ 16.68, 16.77, 16.78, v. 25, with permission of West Publishing Company.
2. STATSKY, TORTS: PERSONAL INJURY LITIGATION 282–86 (1982), with permission of West Publishing Company.
3. WEST'S LEGAL FORMS (2d ed., 1984), § 17.92, v. 11, with permission of West Publishing Company.

4. Id., § 17.192, with permission of West Publishing Company.

5. Id., § 17.194, with permission of West Publishing Company.

6. Blanchard, Litigation and Trial Practice for the Legal Paraprofessional 260 (1982).

7. West's Legal Forms (2d ed., 1984), § 17.17, v. 11, with permission of West Publishing Company.

8. Id., § 17.52, with permission of West Publishing Company.

9. Id., § 17.54, with permission of West Publishing Company.

10. Larbalestrier, Paralegal Training Manual 228 (1981).

11. West's Legal Forms (2d ed., 1986), § 17.19, v. 25, with permission of West Publishing Company.

12. Id. § 17.23, with permission of West Publishing Company.

13. Id., § 17.13, with permission of West Publishing Company.

A

System Folder Contents

Quick Reference Information

I. Preliminary and frequently used information
   A. Office structure and procedure
      1. Office structure chart
      2. Timekeeping forms and procedure
      3. Deadline control forms and procedure
   B. General information
      1. Court structure, names, addresses, and phone numbers for clerks of court and other persons frequently contacted
      2. Time deadline chart/rules and formula for computing time
      3. Statutes of limitations
      4. Case roadmap
      5. Ethics
      6. Professional organization information

Interview

I. Client interview
   A. Task and purpose
   B. Interview plan
      1. Interview plan checklist
      2. Steps in interview plan
         a. Steps in developing interview form: interview forms and checklists
         b. List of information for client to bring to interview
         c. Appointment confirmation letter
         d. List of ethical considerations
         e. List of interview techniques
         f. Checklist of information to be given client at initial interview
         g. Fee arrangement
         h. Release of information forms
         i. Checklist for preparing interview site

Investigation

I. Investigation
   A. Purposes of investigation
   B. Quick guide to evidence

   C. Investigative sources
   D. Sample investigation plan
   E. Medical information
      1. List of available medical records
      2. Standardized request letter
      3. Authorization to release medical information
      4. Letter to doctor requesting medical summary/follow-up letter
   F. Accident scene checklist
   G. Suggestions for locating witnesses and experts
   H. Interviewing a witness
      1. Witness information cover sheet
      2. Checklist for witness interview
      3. Description of how to create interview questions
      4. Checklist of considerations for conducting a witness interview
      5. Tips for taking and drafting an effective statement
   I. Preserving evidence

Pleadings and Service

I. Drafting the complaint
   A. State and federal captions/pertinent rules including captions for multiple parties
   B. Common causes of action and remedies
   C. Checklist for drafting a complaint
   D. Sample notice and fact complaints
   E. Other sample complaints
II. Injunctions/sample forms
III. Filing the lawsuit and service of process
   A. Outline of tasks and purposes
   B. Prefiling checklist
   C. Fee schedule for federal and state courts
   D. Forms:
      1. Federal and state summons
      2. Federal civil cover sheet
      3. Notice and acknowledgement of receipt of summons and complaint
      4. Form USM-285: process receipt and return and equivalent state form
      5. Motion for special appointment to serve process
      6. Affidavit of return of service
      7. Stipulation for trial by magistrate judge
   E. Checklist for locating defendants
   F. Checklist for service of process: federal and state
   G. Checklist for filing and service of documents subsequent to the complaint: federal and state
IV. Obtaining default judgment
   A. Task and purpose
   B. Checklist for default judgment: federal and state

  C. Forms
   1. Affidavit and request for default judgments
   2. Clerk's certificate of entry of default
   3. Request to clerk for entry of default judgment and affidavit
   4. Request to court for entry of default judgment and affidavit
   5. Affidavit of nonmilitary service
   6. Judgment of default
   7. Notice of application for default judgment
   8. Notice of motion for default judgment by court to defendant who has appeared in action
  D. Setting aside a default judgment/motion to set aside
 V. Motions
  A. Checklists for drafting, filing, and serving motions: federal and state
  B. Motion to dismiss complaint
  C. Notice of motion
  D. Demurrer
  E. Memorandum of law in support of motion to dismiss
  F. Order for dismissal of complaint
  G. Stipulation for extension of time
  H. Other motions to dismiss/Form 19 Federal Rules 12(b) motions
   1. 12(b) motions to dismiss: Form 19 Federal Rules
   2. Motion to make more definite and certain: Federal Rule 12(e)
   3. Motion to strike: Federal Rule 12(f)
   4. Motion for judgment on the pleadings
   5. Motion for summary judgment/notice/affidavit
  I. Other motions (add as they come up in text)
 VI. Removal of state action to federal court
  A. Checklist for removal of action to federal court
  B. Notice of removal
 VII. Answer, counterclaim, and cross-claim
  A. Task and purpose: answer
  B. List of style and content suggestions for answer
  C. List of suggestions for drafting successful denials in the answer
  D. Chart of forms of denial in pleadings
  E. Steps in locating affirmative defenses
  F. Sample answer, counterclaim, and cross-claim
 VIII. Third-party practice pleadings
  A. Checklist for third-part complaint
  B. Third-party summons
  C. Third-party complaint
  D. Third-party motion to implead
 IX. Amended pleadings
  A. Checklist of procedures and time limits for amended pleadings
  B. Amended complaint
  C. Motion to amend the pleadings
 X. Motions for judgment on the pleadings and summary judgment: see motions
 XI. File pleading log
 XII. Pleadings, motions, and time limit chart

Discovery

I. Discovery in general/motions to compel and for protective orders
  A. Outline of definition and purpose, applicable state and federal rules on scope, limits, and sanctions
  B. Checklist of procedure to compel discovery
    1. Motion to compel
    2. Order compelling discovery
  C. Motion for protective order
  D. Ethical considerations and authority

II. Interrogatories
  A. Outline of definitions, purpose, scope, and procedure for interrogatories
  B. Checklist for Planning and Drafting Interrogatories
  C. Form interrogatories for auto accident case
  D. Copies of any other interrogatories or types of questions
  E. List of objections to interrogatories
  F. Form letter to client to gather information for answering interrogatories
  G. Checklist for answering interrogatories

III. Depositions
  A. Outline on definition, purpose, scope, applicable rules, and procedure (including time limits)
  B. Checklist on serving subpoenas
  C. Notice to take deposition
  D. Subpoena and subpoena duces tecum
  E. Deposition outline
  F. Format for deposition outline
  G. Checklist for planning and preparing an outline for taking a deposition
  H. Checklist for preparing witness files
  I. Letter to client on preparing for deposition
  J. List on preparing witnesses for testifying
  K. Checklist for attending and reviewing the deposition

IV. Production of documents and things and entry upon land for inspection and other purposes
  A. Outline on definition, purpose, scope, and procedure for requests for production
  B. Checklist for preparing a request for production of documents and things
  C. Sample request for production and inspection of documents, things, and real property
  D. Request for production of documents—business records
  E. Response to request for production
  F. Motion to compel production
  G. Checklist of pointers for assisting at a production of documents

V. Request for physical and mental examination
  A. Outline on the definition, purpose, scope, and procedure for a request for physical and mental examination
  B. Motion for compulsory physical examination
  C. Letter to client regarding compulsory physical examination

    D. Checklist on the paralegal's role in drafting and working with requests for compulsory physical examinations

VI. Requests for admissions
    A. Outline on definition, purpose, scope, and procedures related to a request for admissions
    B. Checklist for drafting requests for admissions
    C. Form for request for admissions: federal form 25
    D. Checklist on responding to requests for admissions
    E. Form for response to a request for admissions

VII. Discovery through Freedom of Information Act
    A. Checklist for making a request pursuant to the Freedom of Information Act
    B. Form for request pursuant to Freedom of Information Act

VIII. Document production checklist

IX. Mini-guide to computer usage (terminology, procedure, skills, techniques, and software)

X. Discovery analysis
    A. Mini-guide for interpreting medical records
        1. Abbreviations for medical records
        2. Anatomy diagrams
        3. Terms referring to parts of body
        4. Medical prefixes and suffixes
        5. Sample medical records and interpretations
    B. Digesting depositions
        1. List of techniques for digesting a deposition
        2. Sample digests of deposition

XI. Organizing files
    A. Checklist for organizing the small case file
    B. Checklist for organizing the large case file
        1. Master index sheet
        2. Subfile index sheet

Settlement

I. Settlement
    A. Definition and factors bearing on settlement
    B. Outline of ethical considerations
    C. Checklist of items to be researched and summarized in preparation for settlement
    D. Damage summary and worksheet
    E. Damage calculation formulas
    F. Sample settlement précis
    G. List of components of settlement brochure
    H. Related forms
        1. General authorization for settlement
        2. Release for personal injury
        3. Mutual release
        4. Covenant not to sue
        5. Settlement agreement
        6. Stipulation and order for dismissal

      7. Stipulation consent decree and order
      8. Settlement distribution statement
  II. Alternative dispute resolution

Pretrial Conference

  I. Pretrial conference
    A. Preparation checklist
    B. Applicable federal and state rules
    C. Outline for pretrial memorandum

Trial Preparation and Trial

  I. Trial preparation
    A. Trial preparation checklist
    B. Case status sheet
    C. Steps in obtaining and serving subpoenas
    C. Juror data sheet
    D. Sources and methods for conducting jury investigations
    E. Applicable state and federal rules of evidence on demonstrative evidence
    F. List of commercial sources of demonstrative evidence
    G. Structure of a trial notebook
    H. Sample trial motions (also add to motion section)
    I. Sample motion in limine (also add to motion section)
    J. Jury instruction sources
    K. Sample jury instructions
  II. Preparing the client and witness for trial
    A. Checklist for preparing clients, witnesses, and expert witnesses for trial
    B. Guidelines for witness's trial testimony
  III. Trial
    A. List of tasks at trial
    B. Form for drafting findings of fact and conclusions of law

Post-Trial Practice

  I. Post-trial motions and pertinent rules/deadlines
    A. Motion for judgment notwithstanding the verdict
    B. Motion for new trial (place extra copies in motion section)
  II. Bill of costs/state and federal
  III. Enforcement of judgment
    A. Pertinent rules of procedure and statutes
    B. Notice of lis pendens
    C. Postjudgment interrogatories
    D. List of exempt assets under state law
    E. Checklist for enforcing judgments under state law
      1. Letter to judgment debtor
      2. Follow-up letter
      3. Writ of execution
      4. Application and affidavit for a writ of garnishment

5. Writ of garnishment
6. State garnishment forms
7. Outline of procedure for domesticating a judgment in another state and in federal court

Appeal

  I. Checklist for federal appellate procedure
    A. Notice of appeal
    B. Designation of record on appeal
    C. Motion for enlargement of time
    D. Notice of filing of brief
 II. Checklist for state appellate procedure/forms
III. Outline of federal and state appellate briefs plus rules on required format

B

The Substantive Law of Torts

- Introduction
- Sources of Tort Law
- Unintentional Torts: Negligence
- Intentional Torts
- Torts that Interfere with Economic Relationships
- Vicarious Liability
- Contribution and Indemnity
- Employer's Liability to Employees
- Strict Liability
- Product Liability
- Immunity from Suit in Tort

Introduction

The importance of learning the substantive law of torts,* or for that matter any other area of law, is that you will know the unique terminology of that area, its various causes of actions or defenses to which your client may be entitled, and its evidentiary requirements—all of which helps you to distinguish the relevant facts and information from the nonrelevant. In addition, your general knowledge of an area of law helps you to recognize issues and gives you the framework from which you can construct effective research and inquiry into issues or elements identified as relevant. The goal of this appendix is to provide you with the basic knowledge necessary to begin working effectively in the area of torts, and specifically tort litigation.

A **tort** is a civil as opposed to a criminal wrong for which the injured party can sue the wrongdoer for compensation. It is distinct from breach of contract and addresses harms to persons, property, rights, and economic and other relationships. Generally, torts have four common elements: a legal duty of one person to another, an act or omission that breaches that duty, a harm, and a finding that the harm was a direct result of the act or omission. Typical torts are driving recklessly and causing an automobile accident; manufacturing a product that is defective and causes injury,

*See "A Brief Guide to Causes of Action and Remedies" in chapter 5 for a concise statement of the elements that must be proved in several of the torts mentioned in this appendix.

maliciously telling lies about a person that damages the person's reputation, and causing toxic industrial wastes to seep into the groundwater. Some torts, such as striking a person or wrongfully taking property, may also be crimes. When torts and crimes coincide, two distinct bodies of law are invoked, resulting in a government action for violation of a criminal statute and a private (or civil) action for violation of tort law.

The basic public policies underlying tort law are *fairness*—those who cause harm should bear its costs; *compensation*—an injured party ought to have access to a remedy for an injury inflicted by another; and *prevention*—holding people responsible for their wrongs will cause them to take steps to avoid those harms. This appendix will address the various kinds of torts and applicable defenses, and who can be held responsible for a tort.

Sources of Tort Law

Although many other areas of law, including contracts, have been substantially codified—placed into statutory form—tort law is founded in and primarily exists today as common (court-made) law. Some state and federal statutes create duties and define torts, but most of tort law and the individual torts are defined by a series of judicial opinions incorporating, interpreting, and adding to the common law. Some works such as the *Restatement (Second) of Torts* and treatises such as Prosser's *The Law of Torts* provide a general sense of tort law applicable in all jurisdictions, and they should be consulted along with existing statutes.

Unintentional Torts: Negligence

Introduction

Unlike criminal law that emphasizes the intentional commission of a crime, tort law addresses unintentional, careless, or accidental harms. This substantive area of tort law is referred to as negligence law. **Negligence** is defined by *Black's Law Dictionary* as "The failure to use such care as a reasonably prudent and careful person would use under similar circumstances." All persons have a duty to conduct themselves in their activities so as not to create an *unreasonable* risk of harm to others. The basic elements of negligence are:

1. duty,
2. breach of that duty,
3. injury, and
4. proximate cause—the breach has caused the injury.

In order to recover damages, the plaintiff must prove the existence of each of these elements by a preponderance of the evidence.

Duty

A *duty* is the obligation of care exercised by one person in respect to another person as dictated by the circumstances and as imposed by common law or statute. For example, when you operate a vehicle at high speeds, you have a duty to the person in the vehicle in front of you to keep a reasonable distance between your car and the other vehicle. That distance is necessary to avoid a collision should the other vehicle have to stop quickly. The harm likely to occur under the circumstances if care is not exercised defines the duty.

In addition, some duties are not invoked until some action is taken. A person seeing another person stranded on a ledge on a tall building has no duty to try to save the person, because doing so may get two people killed instead of one or none. If the bystander, however, elects to help the stranded person, the duty to do so in a nonnegligent fashion is involved. On the other hand, a firefighter has a duty to try to rescue the stranded person the same as a lifeguard cannot ignore a drowning person.

Normally the harm must be *foreseeable*—likely and predictable. Airline baggage loaders who frequently toss luggage and packages do not have the same duty of care to those around them as they would if they were told package X contained nitroglycerin or other explosives. Therefore, the duty is defined by the circumstances which include any predictable harm resulting from the absence of due care.

Breach—Standard of Care

A *breach of an existing duty* is the failure to conform to the required standard of care. The required standard of care is that which is reasonable under the circumstances. In other words, *what would a reasonable and prudent person do under similar circumstances?* If a person's conduct conforms to that standard, there is no breach; if the person's conduct falls short, there is a breach. Driving the speed limit on a dry, sunny day may be reasonable, but doing the same thing on an ice-covered road may not be.

A physically handicapped person is held to a standard that is reasonable for a physically handicapped person. Mental illness or infirmity does not generally change the standard, however. A child is held to a standard of reasonability for children of similar age. Professionals such as physicians, engineers, lawyers, and others are held to a higher standard, i.e., that which is acceptable for a member of the profession as defined by professional competence in the community. Normally these standards are proven by expert testimony.

Businesses and other land owners must make reasonable efforts to see that their property is safe for those likely to come onto or be attracted to the property.

Injury/Damages

The third element requires that an injury actually occurs to the victim. The types of injuries that are compensated (with money) are medical bills and services related to physical injuries and disabilities, pain and suffering (distress, discomfort, emotional trauma), lost wages (only if because of some physical injury), lost enjoyment of life, and damages for injury to or destruction of land or other property.

Causation

The final element required to prove the existence of negligence is a showing that the injury was caused substantially by the negligent act or omission that comprises the breach. Cause in fact is simply the determination that the evidence shows X's negligence to be the direct cause of the injury—the factual cause.

But factual cause is not enough. The act or omission must be the legal or proximate cause as well. *Proximate cause* requires the consideration of foreseeable consequences and intervening causes. The general rule on foreseeability is that if the result is not foreseeable, then there is no liability. Liability is limited only to the harm that gave rise to the duty in the first place. The most famous case on foreseeability is *Palsgraf v. Long Island R.R.*, 248 N.Y. 339, 162 N.E. 99 (1928). Railroad employees negligently caused X to drop a package containing fireworks. It exploded and caused railroad scales to fall on Mrs. Palsgraf, resulting in injuries. The court held that liability was limited to the foreseeable, i.e., that contents in the dropped package would be damaged, which defined the original duty of care. A minority of courts rule otherwise and extend liability through to the damage caused by the last falling domino.

Persons causing an accident or other damages are also liable for the harms caused by the rescuers who attempt to undo or mitigate the damage. Since the wrongdoer *(tort feasor)* has placed the person in a state of danger or injury, the wrongdoer is also responsible for the action of those who will foreseeably come and attempt to administer to the injuries or rescue the victim from the danger. Further, the tort feasor is also liable for the full extent of the injuries even if the victim was in an unpredictably weakened or vulnerable state beforehand, i.e., the person who slips on a banana peel in a store and suffers a serious heart attack because of a previous condition can recover damages for that injury in addition to the predictable and more likely injuries.

Tortious conduct may not incur liability if the cause of the injury is an *intervening* cause. This cause can be human or an act of God such as a tornado or lightning. The key is whether the intervening cause is a *superseding* cause. A qualifying superseding cause cannot simply be the foreseeable act of another that makes the situation worse or is the catalyst that sets off the harm. For example, if A carelessly erects a large flagpole and his neighbor bumps the pole with his lawn mower, and the pole falls injuring the mail carrier, A is still liable. The lawnmower bump is not sufficient to relieve the original tort feasor from liability; the cause is not superseding. The cause would probably be superseding if the neighbor deliberately pushed the pole onto the mail carrier, or if lightning struck the pole causing it to fall on the carrier. If the intervening event was a wind not sufficient to blow over a well-secured pole, then it would not be a superseding cause.

Normally the victim must prove each of these four elements in order to prevail in an action for negligence. In a situation where negligence is the likely explanation for the injury, a high duty of care is expected, and the defendant has exclusive control over the product or activity, the doctrine of *res ipsa loquitur* ("the thing speaks for itself") comes into play. This doctrine shifts the burden to the defendant to prove there was no negligence. In cases involving airplane accidents, the airline has an enormous duty of care implying that if almost *anything* goes wrong, it is obviously the airline's fault. Also, an injured passenger would normally not have access to evidence revealing negligence, so the burden falls to the airline to prove no negligence was involved.

Wrongful Death

Common law prevented civil actions based on negligence or willful conduct that resulted in the death of the victim. Consequently, laws have been passed called *wrongful death statues* that permit suits by representatives of the deceased's estate for the benefit of the deceased's family and other beneficiaries. These statutes permit actions based on negligence as well as willful conduct.

Defenses to Negligence

The defenses to negligence include the following:

1. Contributory negligence. Although most states have abolished contributory negligence as a defense, its use should be understood. If the action of the plaintiff, the person suing for injuries, was a contributing factor in the accident, the plaintiff cannot recover her losses from the defendant, the person being sued. For example, if a jury found that plaintiff Ann Forrester had contributed to her own injuries by failing to look both ways before crossing the highway, she would be barred from any recovery, even if defendant Mr. Hart was found to be primarily responsible for the accident. The harshness of this rule explains why it has been abolished in many states. Assume that contributory negligence is not the law in Columbia unless your instructor indicates otherwise.

2. Last clear chance. This is a doctrine that permits parties to recover damages who normally could not because of their contributory negligence. In that sense it is a defense to the defense of contributory negligence. It applies when the plaintiff, through her own negligence, is placed in the defendant's path so that the defendant has the last clear chance to avoid an accident. If the defendant does not react as a reasonable person should (is negligent), causing injury to the plaintiff, the plaintiff may recover regardless of her initial contributing negligence. For example, assume Ann Forrester carelessly ran across the ice on the road, slipped and fell, leaving her directly in the path of Mr. Hart's van. Also assume that Mr. Hart had a last clear chance to avoid the accident. If he was inattentive and did not avoid the accident, Ms. Forrester could still recover damages, in spite of her own negligence.

3. Comparative negligence. This is the law in the majority of states and in Columbia (unless your instructor indicates otherwise). The doctrine of comparative negligence permits a plaintiff who is contributorily negligent to recover, but the award is reduced proportionately by the percentage of the plaintiff's negligence. For example, if Ann Forrester stepped onto the highway without looking, then slipped as she tried to retreat, a jury might find her 30 percent negligent. If Mr. Hart was driving too fast to stop, a jury might find him 70 percent negligent. If Ms. Forrester's damages came to $100,000, the award would be reduced by 30 percent to $70,000. In some states, Ms. Forrester would be barred from any recovery if her comparative negligence was found to exceed 50 percent.

4. Assumption of risk. This defense states that plaintiffs may not recover for damages if they knowingly place themselves in danger. For exam-

ple, if Ms. Forrester had decided to stay in the middle of the road and thumb her nose at any oncoming vehicle, she would be assuming the risk of injury, and Mr. Hart would have a defense to Ms. Forrester's action for negligence.

Intentional Tort

Introduction

All intentional torts have three common elements:

1. An offensive act,
2. Intent to commit the act, and
3. The infringement of a victim's lawfully protected right.

The act must be purposeful and not part of a chain caused by a third party. For example, if X pushes you into Y, your act of falling into Y is not the requisite act for liability. The requisite act must also infringe on the victim's legally protected right. For example an *assault* (threat of harm) invades one's sense of well-being and security, although no discernible physical injury occurs. Because that sense of personal well-being and security has been infringed, liability attaches absent physical damage.

The requisite *intent* is the conscious decision to commit the wrongful act knowing it has harmful consequences. Intent is proven by a person's statement of intent or by circumstantial evidence. Facts such as that the wrongdoer is a child, intends to hit A but hits B, or the harm is greater than intended makes no difference.

Intentional Torts against Persons

Assault is the intentional and immediate threat or attempt to inflict injury on the victim while apparently possessing the ability to do so. No physical injury or actual contact is necessary, but generally, the tort victim must be in fear or in apprehension of harm. Words are generally an insufficient threat, but this could depend on the circumstances.

Battery is intentional physical contact on another person to cause or result in bodily injury or offensive touching. Wrongdoer A does not have to personally touch victim B—A can throw a stone that strikes B, or A can touch B's clothing or an item being carried. If A so threatens B that it is a substantial likelihood that B will be struck—and B is struck—A is liable for battery even thought A only intended to threaten B. Even a physician may be held liable for battery if an operation goes beyond that which is contemplated and necessary, or causes harm from risks that were not adequately explained to the patient.

False imprisonment is the unlawful and deliberate restraining of the liberty of another. Generally the victim must be aware of the restraint or be injured by it, but the length of confinement is irrelevant. One may be unlawfully restrained by threats as well as by walls. One can be falsely imprisoned if one is at a place voluntarily and then is deliberately prevented from leaving, or no practical way to leave is provided when released, i.e., the failure to unlock the door knowing X is ready to leave. Once the plaintiff proves the intentional confinement, it remains for the defendant to prove any justification or lawful authority.

Since shoplifting has become such a national problem, and its in-store investigation so vulnerable to actions for false imprisonment, most states have passed laws giving shopkeepers the right to detain persons reasonably suspected of shoplifting for a reasonable investigative period.

False arrest is a component of false imprisonment. It is simply the intentional abuse of the power to arrest. It occurs when a person is arrested on knowingly trumped-up charges or is detained beyond a reasonable period for investigation and interrogation. Usually, citizens can make arrests only if they have a reasonable belief the person to be detained is the perpetrator of a felony.

Intentional infliction of emotional distress is an outrageous and extreme act that is intended to cause or recklessly causes the victim to suffer severe emotional distress. A person who secretly exhumed the body of X's husband and placed it in X's house for her to discover when she arrived home would likely be guilty of this tort. In this tort the conduct must be truly abhorrent and the distress must go well beyond normal humiliation or brief depression. There is no need to prove physical injury, but the distress should normally be manifested over a significant period of time. The need for extended psychological or psychiatric care would be such evidence.

Invasion of privacy—May a business conglomerate try to silence an effective critic by tapping the critic's phone, threatening him, and hiring women to entice him and place him in a compromising light? If it does, it is liable for the tort of intrusion. [See *Nader v. General Motors Corporation*, 298 N.Y.S.2d 137 (1969).] Intrusion is one of four torts under the umbrella phrase *invasion of privacy*.

Invasion of privacy concerns a series of rights including the right to be left alone (intrusion), the right to exclusive use of one's name and image, the right not to be placed in a false light in the public eye, and the right against unreasonable publicity of private facts [RESTATEMENT (SECOND) § 652A]. Generally the award is for mental suffering, shame, or humiliation as guaged by a person's ordinary sensibilities.

Intrusion can consist of entry of another's dwelling, an illegal series of persistent phone calls or intrusive appearances, unauthorized blood tests, and the like.

The right to exclusive use of one's name and image prevents advertisers, for example, from misappropriating an actor's name in an embarrassing or humiliating way. Under such a theory, Johnny Carson successfully sued a toilet company for using "Here's Johnny" to advertise its company and product. [*Carson v. Here's Johnny Portable Toilets*, 698 F.2d 831 (1983).]

The right not to be placed in a false, and usually humiliating, light places liability on a person for, for example, taking a photo of a public official stepping out of a thunderstorm to shelter under the entrance of a triple-X-rated peep show and publishing it with a caption that suggests the official is a frequent customer of the show.

The fourth area addresses the *intentional and unreasonable publicity of private facts* and protects persons from the unwarranted publicity of very personal or private matters. The matters could include financial concerns, revelation of embarrassing diseases, intimate relations, and similar kinds of things. The publication normally involves newspapers, television, and other media where the revelation serves little public purpose and is normally embarrassing and humiliating. Truth, which is a defense to libel and defamation (to be discussed), is not a defense to this tort.

These torts and the entire area of the right of privacy are being reinforced by law and acts that secure aspects of the right of privacy. These laws give persons the right to live together as consenting, unmarried adults, the right to an abortion, the right against tampering with mail, the right against electronic eavesdropping, and others.

Fraud is the intentional deceit of another for the purpose of depriving the person of property or some other right. The tort of fraud consists of four elements:

1. A false material statement about a past or current fact known by the perpetrator to be false or in reckless disregard of the truth,
2. With the intent of securing the victim's reliance on the statement,
3. Causing the victim to reasonably rely on the statement, and
4. Resulting in loss or harm to the victim.

Tort actions for fraud generally arise in the context of business dealings. Typical fraud is the sale of used cars whose odometers have been turned back, or other misrepresentations concerning quality of performance. Fraud does not generally encompass statements of opinion such as, "This is the best value on the market," (puffing in advertising or salesmanship) or statements made from lack of information. In one of the most celebrated fraud cases, Sears was held liable for providing false information to the inventor of quick-release socket wrenches that led the inventor to believe his invention was worth far less than it was. Sears paid $10,000 in royalties for the device that brought in close to $50 million for Sears. Eventually the inventor was awarded several million dollars. [See *Roberts v. Sears, Roebuck & Co.*, 573 F.2d 976 (1978).]

Defamation is the intentional publishing of false information about a person that injures the person's reputation, respect, or goodwill, or which holds the person out to ridicule, scorn, or contempt. Its origin may lie in the admonition "Thou shalt not bear false witness against thy neighbor," and its justification stems from the fact that good reputations take years to build but can be dashed on the rocks with one lie. Defamation has become a complex area of law, especially in the struggle of values between a person's right to his or her reputation and the belief in freedom of the press.

First, a party suing for damages must show that the information communicated is false and defamatory. Second, the plaintiff must show that the information was in fact communicated to others—in other words, published. *Publication* can occur in two basic ways. The first is by *slander*, which is the oral communication of the lie, but may include gestures in some circumstances. This involves stating the lie to a third person. The other form of publication, called *libel*, is the writing or printing of the lie in a manner that will communicate the information to at least one third party. Because of the greater permanency of something written, libel is considered the more serious of the two defamation torts. Printing can include pictures or signs. When oral statements are mechanically recorded or preserved in a way that the danger of dissemination and repetition are similar to written words, then such oral statements are treated as libel rather than as slander.

In addition to the statement being a defamatory lie and being published in some form, the perpetrator must have intended to communicate the statement and there must exist a special harm or a statement that is actionable in and of itself regardless of any special harm.

Some of the principles or rules of defamation law are:

1. There is no action in tort if the person defamed is dead.
2. Individuals, corporations, and groups may be defamed if the targets are reasonably identifiable.
3. A statement is not defamatory if said in jest or humor.
4. There is no tort if only a small segment of the community would or do find the statement to be offensive.
5. The plaintiff must be able to show that he or she is the target of the statement.
6. Bookstores and libraries are not liable for libel if they are not aware the book is defamatory.
7. When newspapers and radio stations report a defamatory statement made by another, they are held liable as the primary publisher.
8. Generally the plaintiff must be able to show damages. Special damages are monetary losses such as loss of a job, loss of a promotion, loss of a business deal, or loss of sales.
9. Damages cannot be for emotional harms such as humiliation, stress, or anger.
10. No special damages need to be shown if a slanderous statement
    a. defames a person's business, business outlook, or professional qualifications,
    b. says a person committed an immoral crime (moral turpitude),
    c. says a person has a horrible and humiliating disease (venereal disease),
    d. impugns the chastity of a woman.
11. Special damages may not have to be shown in libel cases if it is *libel on its face* (obvious). Special damages may need to be shown, however, where the statement is *libel per quod* (where other information is needed). For example, if it was published that X just married Y, that is not libelous on its face. If the community knows that X is already married to Z, however, then we have a problem.
12. To defame a public figure (movie actor, athlete, or other person of voluntary celebrity) or public official (mayor, judge), it must be shown that the publication was reckless as to the truth, malicious (with a desire to hurt the victim), or knowingly false. For ordinary persons and persons involuntarily thrust into the limelight (by being party to a lawsuit), the standard is simply negligence as to the truth.

There are several defenses that are unique and specific to defamation. They are:

1. The victim's consent to publish,
2. The statement is true (but not if incomplete and thus misleading),
3. The publisher has an absolute privilege—participants in a trial and related procedures, legislators and public officials during the course of their official duties, and spouse to spouse,
4. The publisher has a qualified privilege—news reporter reporting false statements of another made in judicial or legislative hearing, critics of the arts but not the personal life of the artist, and statements made to public officials to facilitate their duties. An example of the latter would be reporting criminal behavior to a police officer or an employee reporting suspected theft by another employee to the manager. If these reports are made with malice then the limited privilege evaporates.

Intentional Torts to Property

There are also a number of intentional torts that can be committed on property. These are trespass to land or to chattels and conversion. *Trespass to land* in common law is simply an act that encroaches upon the property right of another; in modern tort law the act must be intentional, reckless, or negligent, and if reckless or negligent it must cause damage. The intent does not have to be to commit the harm; it simply must be to enter the land. Damages encompass all harm caused by the trespass plus any consequential harm including emotional distress. There is no need to show that the damage was done negligently. Planes and boats generally have a reasonable right of passage unless the manner of the passage becomes extreme. Trespass, however, may occur above or below the surface of the land. A trespass can also occur when A sells land to B and A fails to remove A's truck.

Trespass to chattels is strictly intentional as opposed to negligent or reckless interference with the personal property of another, including damage, alteration, use, etc. The tort feasor's belief that the article was his or hers is no defense. Generally damages must be shown, but nominal damages are awarded for dispossession—taking and depriving one of use of one's property. Return of the property plus damages is a common remedy.

Conversion is intentional trespass to chattels that permanently deprives a person of the rightful use of the property, or some similar act that justifies forcing the perpetrator to pay for the property. It is viewed as a serious trespass. Theft is a typical conversion. A taking, even if by mistake, coupled with a complete destruction of the property is a conversion. Receipt of property with knowledge the property belongs to a third party, or failure to release property owned by another when required to do so, are also conversions.

Nuisance is that which causes a substantial and unreasonable annoyance, disturbance, or other offensive interference with private or public land. A *public nuisance* adversely affects an entire community and is generally prosecuted through criminal law. Obstructing a highway, storing explosives, releasing untreated sewage, unlawful dumping, and an unreasonably noisy activity are all public nuisances. Normally the remedy is the enforcement of criminal law and not damages.

Private nuisances are generally remedied by damages, injunctions, or both and include activities that affect one or a few properties as opposed to the entire community. Obnoxious odors, seeping wastewater, the vibrations from explosions, and failure to maintain a property to the deleterious effect of a neighbor may all be private nuisances. Nuisance focuses on the harm rather than on the act and, therefore, can be remedied through various intentional, negligent, or strict liability tort actions. For example, a suit in negligence may be appropriate, or a suit for intentional trespass, or a combination of theories or causes of action.

Defenses to Intentional Torts

Although there may be some defenses that are unique to the specific tort, as in the case of truth being a defense to defamation, there are some general defenses to intentional torts. The most obvious is the voluntary *consent* of the injured person. If there is consent, the act becomes privileged or authorized. Some privileges are created by law or exist because of the circumstances. Football players obviously are privileged to knock each other's blocks off (within accepted parameters) without expressly giving or receiving consent. Doctors are permitted to aid accident victims in an emergency. Otherwise, the consent must come from a person qualified to give consent.

Self-defense is the permissible use of force against others if a person reasonably believes he or she or others are threatened with immediate physical harm or improper confinement and retreat is not a viable option. The force is limited to what is reasonable under the circumstances, including retreat. Retreat is not required for someone threatened in one's own dwelling. A parallel defense is available to persons defending property; however, a warning, if feasible, is required and the minimum force that is necessary to prevent trespass or to expel the intruder or an intruding object is the legal limit. Threat of force is also permissible. Force that could lead to serious bodily harm or death is never permitted to defend property.

Reasonable force or threat thereof may be employed to recover a piece of stolen property following a request to give up the property. Normally this applies in the context of hot pursuit. Generally, one may repossess land if the repossession is peaceable.

Necessity is an emergency that excuses trespass to property or conversion. A flood, starvation, or other circumstances may leave a person with little choice.

Authority of law may protect otherwise tortious behavior. For example, a store owner can generally detain suspected shoplifters, and teachers and parents may be permitted some leeway in disciplining children.

Torts That Interfere With Economic Relationships

Some torts adversely affect business relationships. *Disparagement* is akin to defamation, but is restricted to the impact on a business relationship. It is an intentional publication of a false statement that discredits the financial status of a person, the quality of goods or services, or the saleability or title to property.

Interference with contractual relations is a general tort that permits recovery for an intentional act that interferes with the performance of a contract. In this instance, a third party such as a bank might deliberately make it difficult for a party to get the financing to finish construction on a building or other property. A potential buyer of property might harass tenants so they break leases and make a rental property less profitable, so the owner will sell the property.

Interference with an economically advantageous relationship is exemplified by the famous case of *Texaco Inc. v. Pennzoil Co.*, 728 S.W.2d 768 (Texas 1987). In this case Texaco agreed to buy Getty Oil property after Pennzoil had worked out an agreement in principle to buy the same property. Texaco was found liable for the tort of interference with an economically advantageous relationship. This tort requires a spiteful or wrongful intent.

Vicarious Liability

The doctrine of vicarious liability imposes liability on persons who, because of a relationship, are held responsible for the torts committed by others.

Thus an employer is held responsible for the torts of an employee if the employee at the time of the tort is in the course of employment or doing something on behalf of the employer. This is the doctrine of *respondeat superior.* If the job requires some use of force, such as in the case of a police officer or a private security officer, the employer is liable for excessive force. Normally, however, employers are not liable for intentional torts beyond the control of the employee. Likewise, one partner is responsible for the actions of another partner if the person was acting on behalf of the partnership. And a parent is liable for the torts of a child, but only if the child is acting on behalf of the parent. Vicarious liability has expanded in some states to include the owner of a bar for the unlawful service of minors, and for the tortious acts of patrons that have become intoxicated at a bar even if the owner was not present at the bar. The negligence of the operator of a vehicle can be applied to the owner of the vehicle if the person was driving on behalf of the owner. Vicarious liability does not extend from the independent contractor to the person employing the independent contractor.

Contribution and Indemnity

Contribution permits an injured party to sue two or more parties when the wrongdoers have indivisibly contributed to the injuries or if they have acted in agreement. The plaintiff may sue one or both for the entire amount. If one is sued for the entire amount, that defendant may in turn sue the joint tort feasor for an appropriate share of the damages.

In *indemnity* one party either has or assumes the legal obligation to pay for one or more kinds of tortious acts of the other. Contracts frequently state that one party indemnifies the other party for any damages arising from the indemnifier's actions.

Employer's Liability to Employees

Today most employers are covered by *workers' compensation* insurance. Thus, an employee's injury is compensated at legislated rates from an insurance fund to which the employer contributes. Negligence or fault is no longer an issue in such cases. If the employer intentionally or recklessly subjects an employee to an unreasonable risk, however, then the employee has an action in tort.

Strict Liability

Strict liability is an area of tort law that for reasons of public policy attaches liability to certain kinds of hazardous and other activities regardless of fault. Workers' compensation, discussed previously, is one area that has been statutorily made into a strict liability matter. Traditionally, however, it is the more dangerous activities that incur strict liability. An owner of animals is generally strictly liable for the injuries and trespasses caused by the animals. There are some exceptions for dogs and cats and livestock in certain circumstances. Owners of wild animals are strictly liable for injuries caused by them. Otherwise, any use of land or other activity that is unnatural and particularly hazardous incurs strict liability. Persons using explosives, hauling gasoline, and storing toxic waste are held to a strict liability standard. The key in strict liability is that no fault must be shown if the person engaging in the dangerous activity is aware of the risk that is being created.

Product Liability

When a person is injured by a dangerous product, there are several theories under the broad term *product liability* that may provide a remedy for the injury.

Negligence: Product liability negligence requires proof of the same basic elements required in any negligence action: duty, breach of the duty, injury, and breach being the actual and proximate cause of the injury. Negligence might occur in the design, manufacture, testing, or packaging of the product. If the product is dangerous and its danger is not obvious, the failure to place adequate warnings may provide the basis for a negligence suit. The person harmed can be anyone likely to use the product, and the manufacturer, supplier of a part in the final product, the seller, and the distributor might all be liable.

Breach of warranty: An area of commercial law (Uniform Commercial Code) stemming from the old law of torts provides a remedy for physical harms caused by defective or unfit products. *Express warranties* are promises of quality on which a buyer relies when purchasing a product. A defective product that causes injury is a breach of the promise and is actionable. Express warranties are voluntarily assumed by the manufacturer to help sell the product.

Implied warranties are warranties that are required by law and follow the goods. Manufacturers and sellers can avoid such warranties by expressly disclaiming them, but such a waiver is deemed unconscionable as applied to physical harm [U.C.C. § 2-719(3)]. The implied *warranty of merchantability* promises that the product is reasonably safe, is of a certain standard of quality, and is fit for its ordinary use. The implied *warranty of fitness* arises when the buyer relies on the seller's knowledge that the product is fit for a specific purpose. Breach of these warranties imposes strict liability unless the seller has expressly limited or disclaimed the warranty.

Strict tort liability: In most jurisdictions today, the manufacturers and sellers of goods are strictly liable for any defective or unfit product that is unusually dangerous and which causes physical harm. Automobiles must withstand certain standards of "crashworthiness" and cannot, for example, have a gas tank that is likely to explode in a typical rear end collision. Defenses include assumption of risk and improper use of the product.

Immunity From Suit in Tort

Immunity from suit exists in several circumstances. Governmental bodies and officials are generally immune from suit (sovereign immunity) when acting in their official capacities, and the government itself is normally immune from personal injury suits unless it has granted individuals the right to sue it. The federal government and many state governments have passed tort claims acts that do permit such suits under the theory that persons who are injured because of the wrongful conduct of others should not be denied a remedy, especially when the cost of the remedy can be borne by an entire population through taxes and the purchase of insurance. Government employees engaged in ministerial (administrative) tasks have less or no immunity when compared to those engaged in discretionary activity. For example, a judge is immune to suit when making judicial decisions but not when hiring or firing a court employee.

Family members are increasingly being allowed to sue each other for torts. Generally, however, the right of children to sue parents is quite limited.

C

The Substantive Law of Contracts

- Introduction
- Sources of Contract Law
- Elements of a Valid Contract
- Third-Party Contracts: Beneficiaries, Assignment, and Delegation
- Remedies for Breach of Contract
- Interpreting the Terms of a Contract: The Parole Evidence Rule and Other Considerations
- Warranties

Introduction

The purpose of this appendix is to provide you with a basic working knowledge of the terms and principles of contract law.* This knowledge will facilitate solving assignments related to the litigation material in this text and the completion of entry-level paralegal tasks concerning contract litigation. The appendix should be particularly helpful in understanding the elements that must be proven for a successful breach of contract action, organizing a related investigation, performing legal research, drafting pleadings, pursuing discovery, and completing other significant stages of the litigation process.

Black's Law Dictionary defines a **contract** as an agreement between two or more parties creating reciprocal obligations to do or not to do something. If written, it sets out the agreed terms and conditions and serves as proof of the obligations. Contracts are fundamental to doing business in our world and, thus, comprise one of the most significant areas of law practice. The hundreds of thousands of contracts entered into each day inevitably result in some disputes and litigation.

The public policy (expressed societal values important to the public good) underlying contract law is that in order to conduct business and have a vibrant economy, it is essential that persons be able to rely on the promises of others. The performance (following through on the promise) of these obligations allows houses, factories, and roads to be built; goods, land, and services to be sold; and people to be employed. Each of these things

*See "A Brief Guide to Causes of Action and Remedies" in chapter 5 for a concise statement of the elements that must be proved in several of the contract actions mentioned in this appendix.

contributes significantly to an orderly society characterized by an enjoyable standard of living. It is easy to see why contracts are crucial, and why public policy favors and requires their strict enforcement.

In addition to the policies favoring contract law, this appendix will explore the sources of contract law, the components necessary to form a binding contract, quasi-contracts, the statute of frauds, how contracts are interpreted, defenses to an action for breach of contract, remedies for a breach of contract, third-party beneficiaries, assignment of rights and delegation of duties, discharge of a contract, and contractual warranties.

Sources of Contract Law

Whether you are drafting a contract or examining one in preparation for litigation, its legality and enforceability depend on the law that governs the particular type of contract in the particular jurisdiction in question. The sources of law to consult are: the common law, the *Restatement of Contracts, Second,* state statutes on contracts including the Uniform Commercial Code (U.C.C.), and any particular provisions of federal law that apply, such as those in the Federal Consumer Protection Act of 1968 (Truth in Lending Law) or the Magnuson-Moss Warranty–Federal Trade Commission Improvement Act.

The U.C.C. has been adopted by all states in some variation and covers sales by laypersons as well as merchants. It changes some of the common law of contracts and, therefore, must be consulted if it appears to apply to the contract at hand. The most significant provisions of the U.C.C. are Article 2 (sale of goods) and the recent 2A (leasing of goods). "Goods" is defined by the U.C.C. as "all things (including specially manufactured goods) which are moveable at the time of identification (performance) to the contract." The key to whether a contract for goods is covered by the U.C.C. is that the good is moveable at the time the contract is performed and that the primary focus of the contract is this good and not a service. Therefore, the U.C.C. covers the sale of trees or crops but only if they are to be harvested. The sale of machinery, vehicles, household goods, etc., are covered. Services such as the construction of a building, repairs to equipment, and legal services are not. Mixed contracts including both goods and services will be covered by the U.C.C. if the sale of goods is the primary purpose of the contract. For example, the sale of a sofa which includes delivery, removal of the old sofa, and setup is covered even though the services of setup and removal are part of the contract. Determining what law applies to a particular contract requires some good background work. In some cases the parties state the applicable law in the contract.

Elements of a Valid Contract

A valid contract requires:

1. competent parties bargaining at arm's length,
2. mutual assent including an offer and acceptance,
3. reciprocal consideration,
4. a lawful and enforceable purpose,
5. in a form required by law, and
6. absence of fraud, duress, undue influence, or mistake of fact.

Competent Parties Bargaining at Arm's Length

First, the parties to the contract must be *legally competent*. They must be adults (usually age eighteen) and not incapacitated by insanity or intoxication. Contracts entered into by minors or insane persons are usually *void* (not binding) or *voidable* (able to be terminated). This means that the incompetent person can end the contract without meeting his or her contractual obligation. Some state laws hold a child liable for the value of any contractual benefit the child has received up to that point. The legal guardian for an incompetent person may enter into an enforceable contract on behalf of the incompetent. Children may also be held liable in quasi-contracts (a statutory obligation, not a contractual one) for the value of purchased necessities and/or food, shelter, and clothing. If a person is insane or intoxicated to the extent that they cannot appreciate the nature of the legal obligation and the other party is aware of the incapacity, the contract can be rescinded. Courts are less inclined to help a person who was voluntarily inebriated.

All contracts must be at "arm's length"—that is, two or more parties exercising free will and contracting in "good faith" (RESTATEMENT, SECOND § 205 and U.C.C. § 1-203). Good faith is essentially honesty at the time the contract is made and in the execution or modification of the contract.

Mutual Assent

There must be a *mutual assent*, a meeting of the minds. This manifested agreement to enter into the contract most often requires an offer and an acceptance.

Offer

An *offer* is a proposal to enter into a contract which, if properly accepted, binds the party to the terms stated in the offer. The party making the offer is the *offeror* and the person receiving the offer is the *offeree*. The essential terms of the desired contract must be included in the offer and stated with enough certainty that the existence of a breach can be ascertained. Generally the offer must be objectively manifested. That is to say, the subjective, internalized understanding of the party is normally not relevant. A discussion between a used car dealer and buyer about how great a new paint job *would* look on the vehicle might lead the buyer to believe that paint job *is* included in the price of the car. If such is not stated clearly in the contract, however, the dealer is not obligated to provide it. The rule is what a reasonable third person would have understood under the circumstances.

Advertisements, catalogs, and the like are usually not considered to be offers because they are unspecific as to the exact type, number to be sold, color, and other factors. They are considered invitations for the customer to make an offer. The advertising of rewards for information or the return of a lost article or pet are offers because of their specificity.

Adequate manifestation of a meeting of the minds also requires the offeree to have knowledge of the offer. It must be communicated to the offeree.

An offer can be terminated. Generally the offeror can retract (revoke) an offer any time up to acceptance. The revocation must be received by the offeree and this must occur prior to a valid acceptance. Normally the offer contains a specified time when the offer expires. The date may be specified as "at noon on the thirtieth of September" or as "ten days from the receipt of this letter." If a specific date is not given, the offer expires in a reasonable time. Depending on the circumstances, a reasonable time may be six months, twenty-four hours, or by the end of a telephone conversation. An implied option to accept exists when the offeror says, "I will pay $500 for you to paint my car." Once an offeree begins painting the car, the offeree must be given the chance to complete the job.

The offer is also terminated before acceptance if the offeree rejects it, if a party or other person who is essential to the performance of the contract dies, if the object of the contract is destroyed, if one of the parties becomes incapacitated, if the offeree makes a counteroffer, or if there is a supervening illegality. A supervening illegality would occur, for example, if you offered to sell and deliver high-tech equipment to country Y, and before acceptance the U.S. government passed an act or executive order prohibiting such sales.

An *option to purchase* is a special type of contract where the seller for a fee agrees to give a prospective buyer a specified period of time in which to accept the seller's offer. The option specifies what the terms of the sale will be should the buyer exercise the option to buy. No other offers to buy can be accepted by the seller during the option period, nor can the seller terminate the offer. If the buyer does not exercise the option to buy within the specified time period, then the sale returns to the open market.

Acceptance

An *acceptance* is the manifested consent of the offeree to enter into a contract—to accept the offer. The offer must be known to the offeree and cannot be accepted by pure happenstance or coincidence. Traditionally the manner of acceptance depends on whether the offer is for a bilateral contract or a unilateral contract. A *bilateral contract* is a two-sided contract in which the offeror promises to do or not do something in trade for a promise by the offeree to do or not do a certain thing. It is a promise for a promise. Once the offeree makes the reciprocal promise, the offer is accepted and both parties are bound by the contract.

A *unilateral contract* is more one-sided. The offeree makes a promise to do or not to do something in trade for the offeree actually doing or not doing something. These are often offers for rewards. In this case the offeree makes no reciprocal promise and, therefore, is not bound by the contract. The offeror, however, remains bound. If the offeree accepts by performing the requested act, returning the lost item, then the offeror is bound and a unilateral contract is formed. If the offeree starts and then forsakes the performance, the offeror may not sue for breach because absent a completed performance, the contract has not been formed. Unilateral contracts are less common than bilateral ones.

The differences are important in traditional contract law, because if a party mistakenly accepts an offer for a bilateral contract by an act or accepts a unilateral contract with a promise, then no contract has been formed. Both the U.C.C. and the Restatement of Contracts, Second, require the traditional avenues of acceptance where the offer clearly calls for a bilateral or a unilateral response. Where there is confusion or no specific manner of acceptance is required, however, modern law permits the offeree to choose either manner of acceptance [U.C.C. §2-206; RESTATEMENT (SECOND) OF CONTRACTS, § 30(2)].

Generally speaking, for an acceptance to form a contract, it must be communicated to the offeror. If the acceptance makes changes in terms, this *counteroffer* for all practical purposes becomes a new offer terminating the original offer. Both the common law and the U.C.C. seem to take a similar approach when new terms are proposed and do not require acceptance by the original offeror. If, however, the original offer is clearly accepted and the offeree is only suggesting some *optional* modification, the contract is formed on the basis of the original offer (U.C.C. §2-207).

There are several methods by which to accept an offer. If the method (place, time, manner, medium) is specified in the offer as the only way to respond, then the acceptance must comply. Therefore, notice of acceptance by mail rather than by the required telegram is no acceptance unless acquiesced to by the offeror. If a method is suggested but not specified as the only method, another similar method true to place and time forms the contract. Section 2-206 of the U.C.C. allows "any medium reasonable in the circumstances." This includes face-to-face acceptance and acceptance by mail, fax, or other appropriate method.

A timely acceptance is generally binding when it is mailed or otherwise dispatched. If an unauthorized or untimely method is used, the acceptance may occur when received by the offeror. The time of acceptance is important, of course, in relation to the effective time for revocation or the time of acceptance made by another party. Acceptance may also be made in very specific circumstances by silence, by exercising control over received goods, or by benefiting from receipt of services.

Consideration

Consideration is an essential element to a contract and is something of value exchanged for a promise or act. It is the essence of a contract—the very reason that the parties have a meeting of the minds. The consideration must have value and that value must be reasonably determinable. The most common considerations are:

1. a promise to give money, property or service,
2. an act,
3. the foregoing of a legal right to do something, and
4. the formation, alteration, or termination of a legal relationship, like a partnership.

The crux in determining if something is valid consideration is whether the party is incurring a *legal detriment*. A police officer cannot legally claim a $2,000 reward for capturing a wanted thief because the officer had the obligation to do so anyway. Doing something you are already obligated to do is not a legal detriment and, therefore, there is no consideration. The consideration does not have to be equal in value to the promise or act, and this is not a concern of the courts in determining the legality of a contract. Things or circumstances that fall short of being legal consideration are:

1. gifts—by nature optional, free of obligation,
2. illusory promises—"I'll *consider* painting the house if you pay $250,"
3. jokes or jests—determined by the surrounding circumstances—"Kiss me and I'll follow you anywhere,"

4. a forbearance of something illegal—"I'll stop stealing your trade secrets if you pay me $25,000,"
5. stated consideration that is nonexistent or false,
6. the modification of a contract including a different obligation but no new consideration.

Renewed promises to pay a debt or other obligation previously discharged or made unenforceable by a statute of limitations or other legality are enforceable even though there is no new consideration. Similarly, a debt may be revived by partial payment. Charitable pledges are frequently enforceable even though the charity provides no consideration.

For Lawful or Enforceable Purpose

A contract that promises payment for an illegal act is unenforceable. Therefore, if a wife contracts with X to murder her husband in exchange for $100,000 of the insurance money, there is no enforceable contract. Also if the contract is contrary to public policy, it will not be enforced. For example, in many states a surrogate mother contract is unenforceable.

In some jurisdictions with blue laws, some contracts are not enforceable if entered into on a Sunday or if they are usurious or involve types of gambling. Credit or loan transactions may be enforceable only if they comply with the provisions of the Truth in Lending Law. In jurisdictions where services require a licensed technician or plumber, for example, contracts cannot be enforced if performed by an unlicensed person. But contracts made by a business that has not obtained the license required of all businesses to operate in the city are generally enforceable.

In a Form Required by Law—The Statute of Frauds

Modern contract law provides for oral and written contracts. Both are enforceable if all the normal requirements are met. All states have a *statute of frauds* that requires certain contracts to be in writing. If they are not written and do not meet the requirements set out in the statute, the contract is generally unenforceable.

The types of contracts included in most statutes of frauds concern substantial issues of value, time, or purpose. Types of contracts covered by a statute of frauds include:

1. an assumption of debts or obligations of another,
2. a promise given in exchange for a promise to marry,
3. real estate contracts,
4. an agreement that will take more than one year to perform,
5. leases exceeding one year in length,
6. promises to pay debts discharged by bankruptcy or barred by the statute of limitations,
7. vehicle repairs, warranties, and many other consumer transactions,
8. sale of goods exceeding a $500 price,
9. sale of securities,
10. sale of personal property exceeding $5,000,
11. and others.

If the contract is required to be in writing, it can be any writing signed by the party charged that identifies the subject matter, terms of the contract, and mutual assent to a reasonable certainty.

Absence of Fraud, Duress, Undue Influence, Mistake of Fact, and Other Defenses

There are numerous defenses to a suit for breach of contract. They can be pleaded individually or in the alternative. Some have been alluded to in previous sections. The following is a list of defenses.

1. Capacity to Contract
2. Undue Influence—Prevents a party to a contract from exercising free choice because the other party knowingly takes advantage of that party's innocent or weakened state of mind. The result is an unfair contract. This may occur because one party is a child; has a mental infirmity due to advanced age, alcohol, or drugs; is isolated from relatives, friends, or a spouse; or some other circumstances. It may involve a breach of a fiduciary relationship—where one party has a special position of trust in regard to another party, e.g., guardian-ward, lawyer-client, principal-agent.
3. Duress—Coercive influence such as a threat of criminal action, physical harm, or the release of damaging information depriving a party of free choice at the time of entry into the contract.
4. Mistake of Party Known to Other—Occurs when one party realizes the other party has made a mistake as to party, price, or other important error. Even though the party aware of the mistake may act to take advantage of it, no contract has been formed. For example, Shifty Industries receives an offer to sell item X at a value so clearly under the going rate that it is obviously a mistake. Shifty licks its chops and greedily accepts. There is no contract because there was no legitimate offer.
5. Mutual Mistake—Where both parties have a different or erroneous idea about a fundamental term of the contract which has a material (important) impact on the contract. The understanding of the term "denim" in the contract between Briar Patch Dolls and Teeny Tiny Manufacturing (Case IV) by Briar Patch to be a certain heavy-gauge material and by Teeny Tiny to be any coarse cotton fabric could be considered a mutual mistake.
6. Misrepresentation—Where one party attempts to conceal important facts from another party. In a car sale, the dealer may be aware a car has been in an accident, but assigns a salesperson to the car who is not aware of this. The car is represented as having never been in an accident. This is misrepresentation and may result in rescinding the contract of sale.
7. Fraud—Essentially a lie (not an opinion) or a reckless statement made with the intent to deceive the other party and to induce that party to enter a contract. The victim must be deceived, rely on the statement in agreeing to contract, and be injured by the untruthful statement.
8. Unconscionability—A doctrine to prevent oppression and unfair surprise. It may focus on the procedure to contract, including the illiteracy of a party or the arcane language and fine print in a contract. It also may focus on the substance of a contract, such as particularly harsh features that leave one party without a benefit or remedy. Generally a contract that is so unjust as to shock the public conscience is

declared unconscionable and voidable. *Adhesion contracts* are "take it or leave it" contracts providing consumers with no chance to bargain. These one-sided contracts are frequently found to be unconscionable.

9. Statute of Limitations—If the statutory time period for suing on a breach of contract (usually four years) has expired, then the cause of action is unenforceable.

In addition to the use of these defenses, there are other factors that may lead to a contract being rescinded:

Justification—Other side has failed to produce consideration.

Involuntary Breach (impossibility or impracticability)—The contract cannot be performed because of no fault of the party or parties. If a party dies, the property to be sold is destroyed, or some supervening governmental action prohibits performance, the contract is essentially void. Higher costs or greater difficulty than was anticipated to perform the contract is not an excuse.

Release—The party has been released by the other party from any obligation.

Mutual Rescission—Both parties agree to end contract.

The following defenses to an action for breach take the position that the contract has been adequately performed:

Accord and Satisfaction—A owes B $500. B pays by painting A's house, to which A assents.

Satisfaction—Adequate performance. A delivers 999 of a contracted 1,000 items and substitutes an item of similar quality for the missing item. This is probably adequate to be considered a compliance with the terms of the contract.

Other Enforceable Agreements: Detrimental Reliance and Quasi-Contracts

Detrimental Reliance (Promissory Estoppel)

Detrimental reliance or *promissory estoppel* is a cause of action that makes a party liable for a promise when another party reasonably relies on that promise and incurs financial injuries as a result of breach. Charitable pledges fall into this category.

Quasi-Contracts (Restitution)

Quasi-contracts are not real contracts, but are sufficiently close in nature and remedy as to be a close cousin—thus the name. Quasi-contracts generally involve an unenforceable bargain in which one of the parties receives a benefit at the expense of another under conditions where the benefiting party would have or should have promised to pay for it. Aid rendered by a physician in an emergency entitles the physician to recover the actual value of the services rendered. Likewise, in this case: a landscaper improves the beauty of B's property by mistake instead of A's property—the contractual property. Because of that work, B sells his house for a value higher than B could have previously, so the landscaper can recover that added value. Volunteer efforts that are the result of no bargaining process—A paints B's house because A thinks it needs it and without B's knowledge—are not recoverable. Some quasi-contracts are created by statute.

Third-Party Contracts: Beneficiaries, Assignment, and Delegation

Beneficiaries

One or both parties entering into a contract may intend that a third party receive the benefit of the contract. A common example is a life insurance policy where the husband lists his wife as the third-party beneficiary. It is best if such contracts expressly identify the beneficiary. In many instances the court is left this task.

In addition, the court must also determine if the third-party beneficiary has the right to enforce the contract and claim the benefit. Generally two classes of beneficiaries are able to do so: donee beneficiaries and creditor beneficiaries. *Donee beneficiaries* are generally given the benefits of a contract as a gift. This is true of the life insurance contract. It is also true if A agrees to provide legal services to X in return for X placing the fee for that service in a trust account for A's child. In such circumstances, A's child is a third-party beneficiary known by both the contracting parties. The right is significant and enforceable by A's child according to the terms of the trust. A's child, however, is not liable to X for A's promise to deliver legal services.

Creditor beneficiaries are those third parties who are owed money by one of the contracting parties and will receive it from money the other contracting party owes the original debtor. For example, A buys B's store and agrees to pay off B's creditors to the amount of $10,000 as part of the sale. B's creditors become creditor beneficiaries to the contract between A and B, and they can sue A for payment of the debt under the contract.

Both types of beneficiaries are called "intended" beneficiaries under the Restatement of Contracts. The key is whether the parties intended the beneficiaries to receive the performance or a part of the performance of a contract. All other beneficiaries are called *incidental beneficiaries*. They lack the degree of direct benefit from the contract that an expressly intended beneficiary has. If an airport construction company contracts to build an airport for Miami, Florida, the airline and its employees will benefit. They are not the intended beneficiaries and cannot enforce the contract like donee and creditor beneficiaries. If most of the benefit of the contract runs to the contracting party and only a small amount runs to the beneficiary, the beneficiary is likely to be an incidental beneficiary. In this case only the original party can sue.

Assignment of Contract Rights and Delegation of Contract Duties

A party may *assign* their rights or *delegate* their duties under a contract to a third party. Normally this can be done unless (1) the parties state otherwise or (2) such action would significantly alter the duty or rights of the other party to the contract. The person who assigns his or her contract rights to another is called the *assignor;* the person receiving the assignment is the *assignee*. In delegation it is *delegator* and *delegatee*, respectively. The assignee takes all rights assigned and can sue to enforce those rights, and also assumes any existing defenses that could have been asserted against the assignor. Assignments are normally sold to the assignee.

In delegation, the delegator authorizes another party or parties to fulfill all or a part of the delegator's original duty. The delegator remains responsible for performance of the overall duty, and each delegatee becomes responsible to the delegator for performing his or her part of the duty. A typical delegation of duties occurs in construction contracts where the contractor delegates some of the construction, say the plumbing and electrical work, to subcontractors. The other party to the contract to whom the duty is owed is the *obligee*.

A party may substitute another party to the contract if all parties agree. This is called *novation* and discharges the original party obtaining the novation.

Remedies For Breach of Contract

Assuming that the contract is valid and one party breached the contract, the other party is entitled to some remedy that duplicates as closely as possible the benefits the victim would have obtained from the performance of the contract. The remedy is usually money damages. The most significant remedies follow.

Compensatory Damages—Normally money damages equal to the service provided or the lost benefit plus any costs such as those to cover having to pay a higher price for the goods than that negotiated under the breached contract. Compensatory damages are also called expectation or benefit of the bargain damages.

Reliance Damages—Damages in the amount necessary to place the injured party in a position equal to that before the contract. They cover any expenses or costs incurred for relying on the promise of the breaching party. For example, a cement company promises to be at X's construction site on a specific day. X hires a crew to be there on that day to spread and finish the cement. If the cement company breaches, it is liable for the fees X had to pay the crew for that day.

Restitution Damages—Damages awarded to the wronged party to equal any benefit the other party has received from the contract. These damages are usually sought when the nonbreaching party lawfully rescinds the original contract and the other party has already received a benefit, or when the original contract was not valid but one party has performed to the benefit of the other. Restitution seeks the value of the benefit already received by the other party.

Liquidated (Stipulated) Damages—Damages described in the language of the contract and agreed to by the parties in case one side or the other breaches the contract. The damages may be a set amount or based on some formula, and must be reasonable under the circumstances. They are frequently used where actual damages may be hard to determine.

Specific Performance—Requires the breaching party to perform the stated duty under the contract. For example, X pays Y $500,000 for a very rare and unique copy of this textbook. Y backs out. Because of the uniqueness of the item, the court orders Y to deliver the rare copy. These damages are awarded rarely and generally when money damages are not adequate.

Punitive Damages—Money damages in addition to all other damages awarded to penalize the breaching party for reprehensible conduct, e.g., fraud.

Other Remedies—Interest, rescission of contract, replacement or repair of defective goods, and assurances that a party will perform the obligation under the contract.

Interpreting the Terms of a Contract: The Parole Evidence Rule and Other Considerations

The terms of the contract do not have to be written unless the contract falls within the statute of frauds. If it is written, however, the question is whether the writing comprises all the terms of the contract or only some of its terms. If the court determines that the writing *integrates* all of the terms of the contract, no evidence of other agreements prior to or contemporaneous with the writing will be allowed to add to or modify the terms expressed in the writing. There is an exception if fraud or the like is involved. If the writing is determined by the court to be only a *partial integration* of the terms, the court can consider extrinsic evidence—both written and oral evidence—to determine the terms of the contract. Technically parole evidence is oral evidence, but in contract law it applies to both written and oral evidence.

If any contract is uncertain *(ambiguous)* as to its terms or intent, the court can consider outside evidence in the form of other writings and statements to clarify the contract. If the contract is declared unambiguous, the general rule has been not to consider outside evidence. The Restatement, Second, and some states encourage the use of extrinsic evidence to show the intent and understanding of the parties whenever a question arises.

Warranties

Sellers of goods or services warrant as part of the contract the quality, character, or title (ownership) of the object of the contract. Actions under these collateral provisions are for breach of warranty. Warranty law is defined in most states by U.C.C. § 2-312. Additional requirements that warranties be in writing and clear language in consumer transactions are set out in the Magnuson-Moss Warranty Act.

In general, merchants and casual layperson sellers are bound by several implied (enforced by law, but do not have to be written) warranties:

1. Warranty of merchantability or fitness—The goods are free of defects, fit for their ordinary purpose, adequately packaged and labeled, and conform to declarations made on the package.
2. Warranty of title—Implied promise that the seller owns the goods.
3. Warranty against encumbrances—The goods are free of liens, encumbrances, or other creditor's claims not known to the buyer.

Express warranties are written or oral statements by the seller, or samples displayed by the seller, that convey or state a fact about the character, quality, uniformity, and purpose of the goods. Opinions are not warranties. Express warranties are assumed voluntary by the seller as a marketing device.

A seller can disclaim all warranties, but such must be in clear language. The warranty of merchantability must be specifically disclaimed. Display of an expression such as "as is" serves as a disclaimer. Disclaimers in situations where the buyer has little choice may be unconscionable.

D

A Mini-Guide for Interpreting Medical Records

TERMS REFERRING TO AREAS OF THE BODY[1]

Term	Meaning	Term	Meaning
anterior	front, forward	posterior	back, behind
caudal	tail or inferior	sagittal	long axis of the body or its parallel
cephalic	head or suerior		
dorsal	back or posterior	superior	above
inferior	below	thoracic	chest
lateral	side	ventral	front or anterior
medial	middle, median plane		

MEDICAL PREFIXES AND SUFFIXES[2]

Prefix or Suffix	Meaning (pertaining to)	Prefix or Suffix	Meaning (pertaining to)
a-; an-	not, without	cerebr-	brain (cerebrum)
ab-	from, absent	cervic-	neck, neck of the womb (cervix)
acro-	extremities		
adeno-	gland	chondr-	cartilage
alg-; -algia	pain or suffering	-coccus	micro-organism
am-; ambi-; amphi-	with, together, both	coccyg-	lowest end of vertebral column, tail
angi-	blood vessel		
ante-; antero-	before or in front of	col-	part of large intestine (colon)
arteri-	artery		
arthr-	joint	crani-	skull
blast-; -blast	germ or germ cell, growth	cyst-; -cyst	bladder
		cyt-; -cyte	cell, corpuscle
bronchi-	subdivision of windpipe (bronchial tube)	dactyl-	finger, toe
		-dema	swelling
cardi-	heart	dent-	tooth
-cele	sac, cyst, tumor	derma-	skin
cephal-	head	dextro-	right

Prefix or Suffix	Meaning (pertaining to)	Prefix or Suffix	Meaning (pertaining to)
dis-	apart, free of	lip-	fat
dura-	outer membrane covering brain and spinal cord (dura mater)	lith-	stone
		lumb-	back, loin
		lymph-	fluid produced by some glands (lymph)
dys-	ill, difficult, abnormal	-lysis; -lytic	loosening, breaking down
ecto-	out or outside	mamma-; mast-	breast
-ectomy	removal by cutting	-mania	madness
-emesis	vomiting	med-; mes-	middle
-emia	condition of the blood	megalo-	large, abnormally large
encephal-	brain	mening-	membranes enfolding spinal cord (meninges)
endo-; ento-; eso-	within or inside		
entero-	intestine	meno-; mens-	menstruation
epi-	upon, beside, over	-mentia	mind
-escence; -escent	beginning, condition	meta-	along with, after
-esthesia	feeling or sensation, awareness	-morph	shape or form, body
		myelo-	marrow
exo-; extra-	out or outside	myo-	muscle
fibro-	fiber	narco-	stupor, unconsciousness, sleep
-form	shaped like		
-fugal; -fuge	expelling, fleeing	nas-	nose
gastr-	stomach, abdomen	necro-	dead body
-genesis	originating, evolving	nephr-	kidney
-genic	producing, well suited for producing	neur-	nerve
		oculo-	eye
-genous	produced, producing	-ode; -oid	like, in the form of
gloss-	tongue	odont-	tooth
gon-	semen, sex; knee	oligo-	few, deficient
-gram; -graph	recorded or written	-ology	study
gyn-	female or woman	-oma	growth, tumor, swelling
hem-	blood	ophthalmo-	eye
hemi-	half	-opia	vision
hepa-	liver	-orexia	appetite
hetero-	other, different	ortho-	straight
hist-	tissue	os-; osteo-	bone
hydro-	water	-ose; -osity; -ous	full of, like
hyper-	above, excessive	-osis	disease, effect
hyph-; hypo-	below, less than	ot-	ear
hyster-	uterus	oxy-	sharp, quick, keen
-ia; -iac; -ic	of or pertaining to	pan-	all, entire
-iasis	pathological condition	para-	beside, accessary to, abnormal, closely resembling
ileo-	last division of small intestine (ileum)		
ilio-	flank, hipbone (ilium)	patho-; -pathy	disease
inter-	between or in the midst	ped-	child
intra-; intro-	in or within	-ped; -pod	foot
iso-	alike, equal	per-	through, by means of
-itis	inflammation	peri-	around, about
laryng-	organ of voice (larynx)	phago-; -phage	eating, destroying
-lent	filled, full	pharyng-	tube that connects mouth with esophagus (pharynx)
-lepsy	violent attack		
leuco-; leuko-	white, colorless		

Prefix or Suffix	Meaning (pertaining to)	Prefix or Suffix	Meaning (pertaining to)
-phasia	speech	-stalsis	movement
phlebo-	vein	staphylo-	genus of bacteria
-phobia	fear or dread	stomat-	mouth, small opening
phono-	speech, voice	strepto-	genus of bacteria
photo-	light	sub-	under, beneath
-phyma	swelling, tumor	super-; supra-	above, excess
plasma-; -plasm	blood substance (plasma)	sym-; syn-	together, joined
-plegia	paralysis, stroke	-taxia; -taxis	movement
pleur-	membrane enfolding the lungs (pleura)	teno-	tendon
		-therapy	treatment
pneu-	lungs, air	thermo-	heat
poly-	many	thoraco-	chest (thorax)
post-	behind, after	thrombo-	clot (thrombus)
pre-; pro-	before, in front of	thyro-	thyroid gland
proct-	rectum, anus	-tomy	cutting
psych-	mind	toxi-	poison
pulmo-	lungs	tropho-; -trophy	nourishment, growth
pur-; py-	pus	-ule	small or diminutive
ren-	kidney	-ulent	abounding in
retro-	backward	ur-; uria	urine
-rhage; -rhea	flow, loss	ureter-	tube that connects kidney with bladder (ureter)
rhin-	nose		
sacr-	lower part of vertebral column (sacrum)	urethr-	tube that connects bladder with urinary outlet (urethra)
schizo-	split		
scler-	hard		
sero-	fluid, water part of blood (serum)	utero-	womb (uterus)
		vasc-; vaso-	vessel
spermat-	sperm	vesi-	bladder
spleno-	spleen	xanth-	yellow
spondylo-	vertebra	xero-	dry

Anatomical Diagrams

(The following are for illustrative purposes. You may choose to include several more in your guide.)

Figure A:1   Human Skeleton[3]

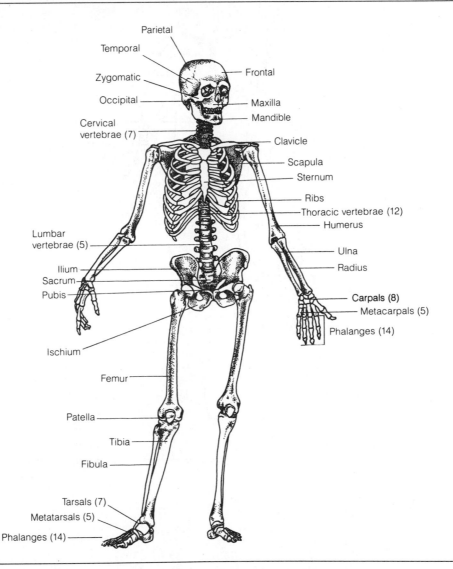

Figure A:2   Selected Muscles of the Body—Front View[4]

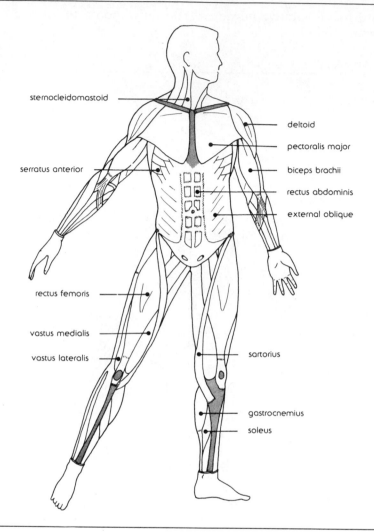

Figure A:3 Selected Muscles of the Body—Back View

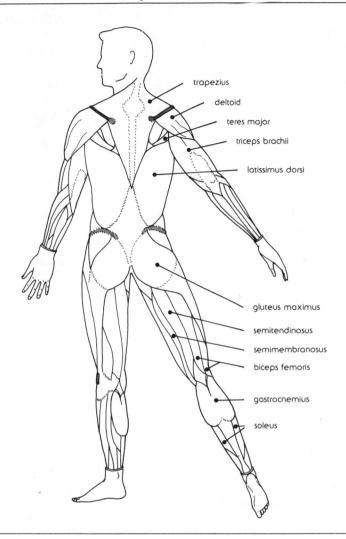

trapezius

deltoid

teres major

triceps brachii

latissimus dorsi

gluteus maximus

semitendinosus

semimembranosus

biceps femoris

gastrocnemius

soleus

Common Medical Record Abbreviations and Symbols[5]

$A + SO_4$	Atropine Sulfate	BCP	birth control pills
aa	of each	BE	barium enema
Ab	antibody (Laboratory Term)	b.i.d.	twice a day
ablib	as desired	BK	below the knee
ac	before meals	BM	bowel movement
ac & hs	before meals & bedtime	BMR	basal metabolic rate
ACTH	Adrenocorticotropic hormone	BOW	bag of water
		BP	blood pressure
AD	right ear	BPH	benign prostatic hypertrophy
ADT	Anticipate Dismissal Tomorrow	BRP	bathroom privileges
add	add or let there be added	bs	blood sugar
adv	(adverse) against	BS	bowel sounds
AFB	acid fast bacillus (Lab Term)	BSO	bilateral salpingoopherectomy
A/G ratio	albumin-globulin ration	BSP	Bromsulphalein test (Lab Term)
Ag	antigen (Laboratory Term)		
AK	above the knee	BTL	bilateral tubal ligation
alb	albumin	BUN	blood, urea, nitrogen
a.m.	before noon	bx	biopsy
AMA	against medical advice	C	carbon
ANA	antinuclear antibody	Ca	calcium
anes	anesthesia	CA	carcinoma
A.P.	anteroposterior	CAD	coronary artery disease
A & P	auscultation and percussion	caps	capsule
APAP	Acetaminophen (Pharmacy Term)	CAR	Coronary Artery Bypass
APC	Aspirin, Phenacetin, Caffeine	CBC	complete blood count
		cc	cubic centimeters
APTT	Activated Partial Thromboplastin Time (Laboratory Term)	CC	chief complaint
		CCU	coronary care unit
		CFT	complement fixation test
aq	(aqua) water	chart	powder paper (Pharmacy Term)
AS	Atropine Sulfate		
A.S.	left ear	CHD	coronary heart disease
ASA	aspirin	CHF	congestive heart failure
ASAP	as soon as possible	circ	circumcision
ASCVD	arteriosclerotic cardiovascular disease	CIS	carcinoma in situ
		CI	Chloride
ASD	atrial septal defect	cm	centimeter
ASHD	arteriosclerotic heart disease	CNS	central nervous system
AU	both ears	c/o	complaint of
AUB	abnormal uterine bleeding	CO_2	Carbon Dioxide
AV	atrioventricular	COAD	chronic obstructive airway disease
Ax	axillary		
B	bacillus	COD	Codeine (Pharmacy Term)
Ba	barium	CPD	cephalopelvic disproportion
BarB	Phenobarbital (Pharmacy Term)	CPK	creatinine phosphokinase
		C & S	culture and sensitivity
		CSF	cerebrospinal fluid
BBB	bundle branch block	cu. mm	cubic millimeters

CVA	cerebrovascular accident	FBS	fasting blood sugar (Laboratory Term)
Cx	cervix		
CXR	chest x-ray	FDP	Fibrin Degradation Products (Laboratory Term)
D5NS	Dextrose 5% normal saline (Pharmacy Term)		
		Fe	chemical symbol for Iron
D5½NS	Dextrose 5% in Sodium Chloride 0.45% (Pharmacy Term)	FFP	fresh frozen plasma (Laboratory Term)
		FH	family history
D5W	Dextrose 5% in water (Pharmacy Term)	FHT	fetal heart tone
		FS	frozen section
DC65	Darvon Compound 65 mg. (Pharmacy Term)	FSH	follicle stimulating hormone
		FUO	fever of undetermined origin
DC	discontinue		
D & C	dilatation and curettage	Fx	fracture
DAT	Diet as Tolerated	gal	gallon
decub	decubitus	GB	gallbladder
DEM	Meperidine Hydrochloride (Pharmacy Term)	GC	gonorrheal
		GI	gastrointestinal
diff	differential	gm	gram
DIP	distal interphalangeal joint	gr	grain
disc	discontinue	GSW	gunshot wound
disch	discharge	gtt	drops
DIV	divide	GTT	glucose tolerance test
DJD	degenerative joint disease	GU	genitourinary
DM	diabetes mellitus	GYN	gynecology
DOA	dead on arrival	H_2O	water
DOE	dyspnea on exertion	H_2O_2	Hydrogen Peroxide
DPT	diptheria, pertussis, tetanus	h	hour
dr	dram (Pharmacy Term)	HAA	hepatitis associated antigen (Laboratory Term)
Dt's	delerium tremens		
DTD	send of such doses (Pharmacy Term)	HBP	high blood pressure
		HCG	Human Chorionic Gonadotropin
dx	diagnosis		
ECG	electrocardiogram	HCl	Hydrochloric Acid
EDC	expected date of confinement	HCO_3	Bicarbonate
		HCT	hematocrit (Laboratory Term)
EEG	electroencephalogram		
EKG	electrocardiogram	HCVD	hypertensive cardiovascular disease
ELF	elective low forceps		
elix	elixir	HEENT	head, eyes, ears, nose, throat
ENT	ears, nose, throat		
EOM	extraocular movements	Hgb.	Hemoglobin (Laboratory Term)
EOS	eosinophils (Laboratory Term)		
		hs or HS	hour of sleep
ER	Emergency Room	Hx	history
ESR	erythrocyte sedimentation rate	i	one
		I	Iodine
et	and	ICCE	Intra Capsulary Cataract Extraction
EUA	exam under anesthesia		
Ext	extract	ICS	intercostal space
F	Farenheit	ICU	intensive care unit

I & D	incision and drainage	m	minim (Pharmacy Term)
i.e.	that is	M	mix (Pharmacy Term)
IM	intramuscular	mcg	microgram
IMP	impression	MCl	midclavicular line
in	inch	mEg	milliequivalents
inf	infection	mft	mix and make (Pharmacy Term)
INH	Isoniazid (Pharmacy Term)		
inj	injection	mg	milligram
I & O	intake & output	MGSO$_4$	Magnesium Sulfate
IOL	Intra Ocular Lens	MHFD	Modified high fiber diet
IPPB	intermittent positive pressure breathing	MI	myocardial infarction
		ml	milliliter
IQ	intelligence quotient	mm	millimeter
IUD	intrauterine device	MOM	Milk of Magnesia
IUP	intrauterine pregnancy	MS	Morphine Sulfate
IV	intravenous	MVA	motor vehicle accident
IVP	intravenous pyelogram	MVI	multivitamin infusion
JVD	jugular venous distention	Na	Sodium
K	Potassium	NaCl	Sodium Chloride
KCl	Sugar free 10% Potassium Chloride	NAD	no acute distress
		NaHCO$_3$	Sodium Bicarbonate
Kg	kilogram	NB	newborn
KMnO$_4$	Potassium Permanganate (Pharmacy Term)	neg	negative
		NG	nasogastric
KO	keep open (Pharmacy Term)	NND	No New Data
KUB	kidney, ureter, bladder	non rep	do not repeat
L or I	liter	Norm M	Normosol M
L & A	light and accommodation	NPH	type of long acting insulin
lab	laboratory	NPO	nothing by mouth
lb	pound	NPTFC	No Past Tracing For Comparison
LDH	lactohydrogenase		
LE	Lupus Erythematosis	NR BC	nucleated red blood cell (Laboratory Term)
LEVO	Levo Dromoran		
LH	Lutinizing Hormone (Laboratory Term)	NS	normal saline
		NTG	Nitroglycerin tablets (Pharmacy Term)
Li	Lithium		
LLE	left lower extremity	O	pint
LLQ	left lower quadrant	O$_2$	Oxygen
LMD	local medical doctor	OB	obstetrics
LMP	last menstrual period	occ	occasional
LNMP	last normal menstrual period	o.d.	right eye
		OD	daily
LOA	left occiput anterior	O&P	ova and parasites
LR	lactated Ringers	OR	operating room
LSF	liver function studies	ORIF	open reduction and internal fixation
LSO	left salpingoopherectomy		
LUQ	left upper quadrant	o.s.	left eye
LVH	left ventricular hypertrophy	o.u.	both eyes
lytes	electrolytes (Laboratory Term)	oz	ounce
		p	Phosphorus

PA&LAT	Chest posterior, anterior and lateral	RBC	red blood count
Pap	Papaniculaou	RHD	rheumatic heart disease
PAS	Sodium (Pharmacy Term)	RLQ	right lower quadrant
PB	Phenobarbitol	R/O	rule out
pc	after meals	ROA	right occiput anterior
PC	packed cells	ROM	range of motion
PE	physical exam	ROP	right occiput anterior
PERLA	pupils equal and react to light and accommodation	ROS	review of system
		RPCF	Reiter protein complement fixation (laboratory Term)
PETN	Peritrate (Pharmacy Term)	RR	recovery room
PI	present illness	RTC	return to clinic
PID	pelvic inflammatory disease	RUQ	right upper quadrant
pm	afternoon	Rx	treatment
PMH	past medical history	sat	saturation
PMI	point of maximum impulse	sc	subcutaneous
PND	paroxysmal nocturnal dyspnea	sed rate	sedimentation rate
		sig	let it be labeled
po	by mouth	SGOT	serum glutamic oxalo-acetic transaminase
Polio	poliomyelitis		
PORR	postoperative recovery room	SGPT	serum glutamic pyruvic transaminase
postop	postoperative		
pp	after eating	SL	sublingual
PPD	purified protein derivative	SLR	straight leg raising
preop	preoperative	SMA-7	SMA-6 Plus Creatinine
PRN	as necessary	sp. gr	specific gravity
PROM	premature rupture of membranes	S-P	Status Post
		spec	specimen
PT	physical therapy	ss	one half
PTA	prior to admission	SSE	soap suds enema
PTH	parathyroid hormone (Laboratory Term)	staph	staphylococcus
		stat	to be done immediately
PUD	peptic ulcer disease	Strep	streptococcus
pulv	powder (Pharmacy Term)	SUI	Stress Urinary Incontinence
PVC	premature ventricular contraction	sx	symptoms
		T	temperature
q	every	T & A	tonsillectomy and adenoidectomy
qd	every day		
qh	every hour	tab	tablet
qhs	every hour of sleep	tal	of such (Pharmacy Term)
q.i.d.	four times a day	TAH	total abdominal hysterectomy
qn	every night		
qns	quantity not sufficient	T.A.T.	tetanus antitoxin
qod	every other day	TB	tuberculosis
qs	sufficient quantity	TBA	To Be Admitted
qsad	to make a sufficient quantity	TBLC	term birth living child
qt	quart	Tbsp	tablespoon
R	respiration	TFS	Thyroid Function Studies
RA	rheumatoid arthritis	TIA	transient ischemic attack
RBBB	right bundle branch block	TIBC	total iron binding capacity

t.i.d.	three times a day	ua	urinalysis
tinc	tincture	UGI	upper gastrointestinal series
TL	tubal ligation	UPJ	ureteropelvic junction
TLC	tender loving care	URI	upper respiratory infection
TM	tympanic membrane	ut. dict.	as directed
TNG	Nitroglycerin tablets	UTI	urinary tract infection
TNTC	too numerous to count (Laboratory Term)	v	five
		VD	veneral disease
TP	total protein	VDRL	venereal disease research laboratory
TPR	temperature, pulse, respiration	VHD	valvular heart disease
TSH	thyroid stimulating hormone	VS	vital signs
		vs	versus
tsp	teaspoon	WB	whole blood (Laboratory Term)
TUR	transurethral resection		
TURP	transurethral resection of prostate	WBC	white blood count
		WNL	within normal limits
u	unit		

Signs and Symbols

%	percent	℥	oz.
s̄	without	℈	scruple
p̄	after	℥ⁱ	1 dram
c̄	with	m	minim
♂	male	>	greater than
♀	female	<	less than
ṫ	one	α	alpha
π̈	two	β	Beta
ℨ	dram		

Roman Numerals

V-5	C-100
X-10	D-500
L-50	

Figure A:4 Physician's Orders[6]

INSTRUCTIONS: BEFORE PLACING IN CHART, IMPRINT PATIENT'S PLATE AS INDICATED BELOW

Reynolds+Reynolds DAYTON, OHIO LITHO IN U.S.A.   K8552 (8-84)

PHYSICIAN'S ORDERS
PATTIE A. CLAY HOSPITAL
RICHMOND, KENTUCKY 40475

IMPRINT PATIENTS PLATE HERE

ORDERED		ORDERS	NOTED BY/TIME
DATE	TIME		

DATE	TIME	ORDERS	
2-26	0829	① admit ICU	
		② V/S c̄ neuro checks q1h	
		③ I & O q1 / call if O < 30 cc/h	
		④ Tagamet 300 mg IV q6h	
		⑤ Keflen 1 Gm q6 IV	
		⑥ alt. Maalox & Mylanta per NG q2h c̄ clamp x 30 min.	
		⑦ NG lo int wall suction	
		⑧ IV's DSRL 125 c.c/h	
		DSNS c̄ 30 meq K 100 cc/h	
		⑨ O₂ 4L n/c	
		⑩ Bucks traction c̄ 20 lb wt to ⓛ femur	
		⑪ clean lacerations q4h c̄ betadine	
		⑫ ABG's q2h tonight	
		⑬ H & H q4h & call if Hct < 36	
		⑭ a.m. lab	
		lytes	
		CBC	
		ABG's	
		repeat KUB c̄ chest x-ray	
		⑮ When fully alert & oriented 1 codeine 30mg	
		Im q6h P.R.N. pain (after 24 hours)	
		⑯ Tylenol #3 for less pain Ī - ĪĪ tab	
		⑰ Tylenol 60 mg q6h T↑101 get blood	
		cultures x 3 for T↑101	
		⑱ log roll.	
		⑲ no sx	
		⑳ Halo / clean pins c̄ betadine q6h	

Use Ball Point

AFTER DOCTOR WRITES A MEDICATION ORDER
1. Remove first yellow copy.
2. Send yellow copy to PHARMACY.
3. After last yellow sheet is used "X" out remaining unused lines.

No. must show through hole → before physician writes on order

Figure A:5   Physician's Orders (Translated)[7]

INSTRUCTIONS: BEFORE PLACING IN CHART, IMPRINT PATIENT'S PLATE AS INDICATED BELOW

THE REYNOLDS & REYNOLDS CO., DAYTON, OHIO   PRINTED IN U.S.A.

PHYSICIAN'S ORDERS
PATTiE A. CLAY HOSPITAL
RICHMOND, KENTUCKY 40475

IMPRINT PATIENTS PLATE HERE

ORDERED DATE	TIME	ORDERS	NOTED BY	TIME
		1. admit intensive care unit		
		2. vital sign and alertness checks every hour		
		3. intake and output every hour. Call if output less than 30cc.		
		4. . . . every six hours		
		5. . . . 1 gram every six hours		
		6. Alternate . . . per naseogastric tube every two hours and clamp for 30 minutes.		
		7. . . . low intermittent		
		8. Intravenous fluids . . . 125cc per hour, 30 milequivalent potassium		
		9. Oxygen 4 liters nasal cannula		
		10. . . . with 20 pound weight . . . left		
		11. . . . every four hours		
		12. Arterial blood gases every two hours		
		13. Hemoglobin and hematocrit . . . hematocrit less than 36		
		14. Electrolytes Complete blood count Kidneys, Urine, Bladder and chest x-ray		
		15. . . . intermuscle every six hours as needed for pain		
		16. . . . one or two tablets		
		17. . . . temperature above 101		
		18. log rolling (technique for moving patients with spinal injury)		
		19. no suctioning		
		20. Halo (support for spine injury)		

"Authorization is hereby given to dispense the Generic or Chemical equivalent unless otherwise indicated by the words — NO SUBSTITUTE"

Use Ball Point

AFTER DOCTOR WRITES A MEDICATION ORDER
1. Remove first yellow copy.
2. Send yellow copy to PHARMACY.
3. After last yellow sheet is used "X" out remaining unused lines.

No. must show through hole → before physician writes on order

Endnotes

1. CURRAN & SHAPIRO, LAW, MEDICINE, AND FORENSIC SCIENCE 37 (1982), 3d ed. Reprinted with permission of Little, Brown & Company, Inc.
2. Id., 38–40, reprinted with permission of Little, Brown & Company, Inc.
3. NELSON & JURMAIN, INTRODUCTION TO PHYSICAL ANTHROPOLOGY 527 (3d ed. 1985), with permission of West Publishing Company.
4. ROSATO, FITNESS AND WELLNESS: THE PHYSICAL CONNECTION 158–59 (1986), with permission of West Publishing Company.
5. The list of abbreviations is courtesy of Pattie A. Clay Hospital, Richmond, Kentucky.
6. Form courtesy of Pattie A. Clay Hospital, Richmond, Kentucky. Data on form provided by Peggy Walker, R.N.
7. Translation provided by Peggy Walker, R.N.

E

Model Rules of Professional Conduct

Reprinted with permission of the
American Bar Association
(Commission's comments omitted)

Client-Lawyer Relationship

Rule 1.1 Competence

A lawyer shall provide competent representation to a client. Competent representation requires the legal knowledge, skill, thoroughness and preparation reasonably necessary for the representation.

Rule 1.2 Scope of Representation

(a) A lawyer shall abide by a client's decisions concerning the objectives of representation, subject to paragraphs (c), (d) and (e), and shall consult with the client as to the means by which they are to be pursued. A lawyer shall abide by a client's decision whether to accept an offer of settlement of a matter. In a criminal case, the lawyer shall abide by the client's decision, after consultation with the lawyer, as to a plea to be entered, whether to waive jury trial and whether the client will testify.

(b) A lawyer's representation of a client, including representation by appointment, does not constitute an endorsement of the client's political, economic, social or moral views or activities.

(c) A lawyer may limit the objectives of the representation if the client consents after consultation.

(d) A lawyer shall not counsel a client to engage, or assist a client, in conduct that the lawyer knows is criminal or fraudulent, but a lawyer may discuss the legal consequences of any proposed course of conduct with a client and may counsel or assist a client to make a good faith effort to determine the validity, scope, meaning or application of the law.

(e) When a lawyer knows that a client expects assistance not permitted by the Rules of Professional Conduct or other law, the lawyer shall consult with the client regarding the relevant limitations on the lawyer's conduct.

Rule 1.3 Diligence

A lawyer shall act with reasonable diligence and promptness in representing a client.

Rule 1.4 Communication

(a) A lawyer shall keep a client reasonably informed about the status of a matter and promptly comply with reasonable requests for information.

(b) A lawyer shall explain a matter to the extent reasonably necessary to permit the client to make informed decisions regarding the representation.

Rule 1.5 Fees

(a) A lawyer's fee shall be reasonable. The factors to be considered in determining the reasonableness of a fee include the following:

    (1) the time and labor required, the novelty and difficulty of the questions involved, and the skill requisite to perform the legal service properly;

    (2) the likelihood, if apparent to the client, that the acceptance of the particular employment will preclude other employment by the lawyer;

    (3) the fee customarily charged in the locality for similar legal services;

    (4) the amount involved and the results obtained;

    (5) the time limitations imposed by the client or by the circumstances;

    (6) the nature and length of the professional relationship with the client;

    (7) the experience, reputation, and ability of the lawyer or lawyers performing the services; and

    (8) whether the fee is fixed or contingent.

(b) When the lawyer has not regularly represented the client, the basis or rate of the fee shall be communicated to the client, preferably in writing, before or within a reasonable time after commencing the representation.

(c) A fee may be contingent on the outcome of the matter for which the service is rendered, except in a matter in which a contingent fee is prohibited by paragraph (d) or other law. A contingent fee agreement shall be in writing and shall state the method by which the fee is to be determined, including the percentage or percentages that shall accrue to the lawyer in the event of settlement, trial or appeal, litigation and other expenses to be deducted from the recovery, and whether such expenses are to be deducted before or after the contingent fee is calculated. Upon conclusion of a contingent fee matter the lawyer shall provide the client with a written statement stating the outcome of the matter and, if there is a recovery, showing the remittance to the client and the method of its determination.

(d) A lawyer shall not enter into an arrangement for, charge, or collect:
  (1) any fee in a domestic relations matter, the payment or amount of which is contingent upon the securing of a divorce or upon the amount of alimony or support, or property settlement in lieu thereof; or
  (2) a contingent fee for representing a defendant in a criminal case.
(e) A division of a fee between lawyers who are not in the same firm may be made only if:
  (1) the division is in proportion to the services performed by each lawyer or, by written agreement with the client, each lawyer assumes joint responsibility for the representation;
  (2) the client is advised of and does not object to the participation of all the lawyers involved; and
  (3) the total fee is reasonable

Rule 1.6 Confidentiality of Information

(a) A lawyer shall not reveal information relating to representation of a client unless the client consents after consultation, except for disclosures that are impliedly authorized in order to carry out the representation, and except as stated in paragraph (b).
(b) A lawyer may reveal such information to the extent the lawyer reasonably believes necessary:
  (1) to prevent the client from committing a criminal act that the lawyer believes is likely to result in imminent death or substantial bodily harm; or
  (2) to establish a claim or defense on behalf of the lawyer in a controversy between the lawyer and the client, to establish a defense to a criminal charge or civil claim against the lawyer based upon conduct in which the client was involved, or to respond to allegations in any proceeding concerning the lawyer's representation of the client.

Rule 1.7 Conflict of Interest: General Rule

(a) A lawyer shall not represent a client if the representation of that client will be directly adverse to another client, unless:
  (1) the lawyer reasonably believes the representation will not adversely affect the relationship with the other client; and
  (2) each client consents after consultation.
(b) A lawyer shall not represent a client if the representation of that client may be materially limited by the lawyer's responsibilities to another client or to a third person, or by the lawyer's own interests, unless:
  (1) the lawyer reasonably believes the representation will not be adversely affected; and
  (2) the client consents after consultation. When representation of multiple clients in a single matter is undertaken, the consultation shall include explanation of the implications of the common representation and the advantages and risks involved.

Rule 1.8 Conflict of Interest: Prohibited Transactions

(a) A lawyer shall not enter into a business transaction with a client or knowingly acquire an ownership, possessory, security or other pecuniary interest adverse to a client unless:

   (1) the transaction and terms on which the lawyer acquires the interest are fair and reasonable to the client and are fully disclosed and transmitted in writing to the client in a manner which can be reasonably understood by the client;

   (2) the client is given a reasonable opportunity to seek the advice of independent counsel in the transaction; and

   (3) the client consents in writing thereto.

(b) A lawyer shall not use information relating to representation of a client to the disadvantage of the client unless the client consents after consultation, except as permitted or required by Rule 1.6 or Rule 3.3.

(c) A lawyer shall not prepare an instrument giving the lawyer or a person related to the lawyer as parent, child, sibling, or spouse any substantial gift from a client, including a testamentary gift, except where the client is related to the donee.

(d) Prior to the conclusion of representation of a client, a lawyer shall not make or negotiate an agreement giving the lawyer literary or media rights to a portrayal or account based in substantial part on information relating to the representation.

(e) A lawyer shall not provide financial assistance to a client in connection with pending or contemplated litigation, except that:

   (1) a lawyer may advance court costs and expenses of litigation, the repayment of which may be contingent on the outcome of the matter; and

   (2) a lawyer representing an indigent client may pay court costs and expenses of litigation on behalf of the client.

(f) A lawyer shall not accept compensation for representing a client from one other than the client unless:

   (1) the client consents after consultation;

   (2) there is no interference with the lawyer's independence of professional judgment or with the client-lawyer relationship; and

   (3) information relating to representation of a client is protected as required by Rule 1.6.

(g) A lawyer who represents two or more clients shall not participate in making an aggregate settlement of the claims of or against the clients, or in a criminal case an aggregated agreement as to guilty or nolo contendere pleas, unless each client consents after consultation, including disclosure of the existence and nature of all the claims or pleas involved and of the participation of each person in the settlement.

(h) A lawyer shall not make an agreement prospectively limiting the lawyer's liability to a client for malpractice unless permitted by law and the client is independently represented in making the agreement, or settle a claim for such liability with an unrepresented client or former client without first advising that person in writing that independent representation is appropriate in connection therewith.

(i) A lawyer related to another lawyer as parent, child, sibling or spouse shall not represent a client in a representation directly adverse to a person who the lawyer knows is represented by the other lawyer except upon consent by the client after consultation regarding the relationship.

(j) A lawyer shall not acquire a proprietary interest in the cause of action or subject matter of litigation the lawyer is conducting for a client, except that the lawyer may:

   (1) acquire a lien granted by law to secure the lawyer's fee or expenses; and

   (2) contract with a client for a reasonable contingent fee in a civil case.

Rule 1.9 Conflict of Interest: Former Client

(a) A lawyer who has formerly represented a client in a matter shall not thereafter represent another person in the same or a substantially related matter in which that person's interests are materially adverse to the interests of the former client unless the former client consents after consultation.

(b) A lawyer shall not knowingly represent a person in the same or a substantially related matter in which a firm with which the lawyer formerly was associated had previously represented a client,

   (1) whose interests are materially adverse to that person; and

   (2) about whom the lawyer had acquired information protected by Rules 1.6 and 1.9(c) that is material to the matter;

unless the former client consents after consultation.

(c) A lawyer who has formerly represented a client in a matter or whose present or former firm has formerly represented a client in a matter shall not thereafter:

   (1) use information relating to the representation to the disadvantage of the former client except as Rule 1.6 or Rule 3.3 would permit or require with respect to a client, or when the information has become generally known; or

   (2) reveal information relating to the representation except as Rule 1.6 or Rule 3.3 would permit or require with respect to a client.

Rule 1.10 Imputed Disqualification: General Rule

(a) While lawyers are associated in a firm, none of them shall knowingly represent a client when any one of them practicing alone would be prohibited from doing so by Rules 1.7, 1.8(c), 1.9 or 2.2.

(b) When a lawyer has terminated an association with a firm, the firm is not prohibited from thereafter representing a person with interests materially adverse to those of a client represented by the formerly associated lawyer and not currently represented by the firm, unless:

   (1) the matter is the same or substantially related to that in which the formerly associated lawyer represented the client; and

   (2) any lawyer remaining in the firm has information protected by Rules 1.6 and 1.9(c) that is material to the matter.

(c) A disqualification prescribed by this rule may be waived by the affected client under the conditions stated in Rule 1.7.

Rule 1.11 Successive Government and Private Employment

(a) Except as law may otherwise expressly permit, a lawyer shall not represent a private client in connection with a matter in which the lawyer participated personally and substantially as a public officer or employee, unless the appropriate government agency consents after consultation. No lawyer in a firm with which that lawyer is associated may knowingly undertake or continue representation in such a matter unless:

   (1) the disqualified lawyer is screened from any participation in the matter and is apportioned no part of the fee therefrom; and

   (2) written notice is promptly given to the appropriate government agency to enable it to ascertain compliance with the provisions of this rule.

(b) Except as law may otherwise expressly permit, a lawyer having information that the lawyer knows is confidential government information about a person acquired when the lawyer was a public officer or employee, may not represent a private client whose interests are adverse to that person in a matter in which the information could be used to the material disadvantage of that person. A firm with which that lawyer is associated may undertake or continue representation in the matter only if the disqualified lawyer is screened from any participation in the matter and is apportioned no part of the fee therefrom.

(c) Except as law may otherwise expressly permit, a lawyer serving as a public officer or employee shall not:

   (1) participate in a matter in which the lawyer participated personally and substantially while in private practice or nongovernmental employment, unless under applicable law no one is, or by lawful delegation may be, authorized to act in the lawyer's stead in the matter; or

   (2) negotiate for private employment with any person who is involved as a party or as attorney for a party in a matter in which the lawyer is participating personally and substantially, except that a lawyer serving as a law clerk to a judge, other adjudicative officer or arbitrator may negotiate for private employment as permitted by Rule 1.12(b) and subject to the conditions stated in Rule 1.12(b).

(d) As used in this Rule, the term "matter" includes:

   (1) any judicial or other proceeding, application, request for a ruling or other determination, contract, claim, controversy, investigation, charge, accusation, arrest or other particular matter involving a specific party or parties, and

   (2) any other matter covered by the conflict of interest rules of the appropriate government agency.

(e) As used in this Rule, the term "confidential government information" means information which has been obtained under governmental authority and which, at the time this rule is applied, the government is prohibited by law from disclosing to the public or has a legal privilege not to disclose, and which is not otherwise available to the public.

Rule 1.12 Former Judge or Arbitrator

(a) Except as stated in paragraph (d), a lawyer shall not represent anyone in connection with a matter in which the lawyer participated personally and substantially as a judge or other adjudicative officer, arbitrator or law clerk to such a person, unless all parties to the proceeding consent after consultation.

(b) A lawyer shall not negotiate for employment with any person who is involved as a party or as attorney for a party in a matter in which the lawyer is participating personally and substantially as a judge or other adjudicative officer or arbitrator. A lawyer serving as a law clerk to a judge, other adjudicative officer or arbitrator may negotiate for employment with a party or attorney involved in a matter in which the clerk is participating personally and substantially, but only after the lawyer has notified the judge, other adjudicative officer or arbitrator.

(c) If a lawyer is disqualified by paragraph (a), no lawyer in a firm with which that lawyer is associated may knowingly undertake or continue representation in the matter unless:

  (1) the disqualified lawyer is screened from any participation in the matter and is apportioned no part of the fee therefrom; and

  (2) written notice is promptly given to the appropriate tribunal to enable it to ascertain compliance with the provisions of this rule.

(d) An arbitrator selected as a partisan of a party in a multimember arbitration panel is not prohibited from subsequently representing that party.

Rule 1.13 Organization as Client

(a) A lawyer employed or retained by an organization represents the organization acting through its duly authorized constituents.

(b) If a lawyer for an organization knows that an officer, employee or other person associated with the organization is engaged in action, intends to act or refuses to act in a matter related to the representation that is a violation of a legal obligation to the organization, or a violation of law which reasonably might be imputed to the organization, and is likely to result in substantial injury to the organization, the lawyer shall proceed as is reasonably necessary in the best interest of the organization. In determining how to proceed, the lawyer shall give due consideration to the seriousness of the violation and its consequences, the scope and nature of the lawyer's representation, the responsibility in the organization and the apparent motivation of the person involved, the policies of the organization concerning such matters and any other relevant considerations. Any measures taken shall be designed to minimize disruption of the organization and the risk of revealing information relating to the representation to persons outside the organization. Such measures may include among others:

  (1) asking reconsideration of the matter;

(2) advising that a separate legal opinion on the matter be sought for presentation to appropriate authority in the organization; and

(3) referring the matter to higher authority in the organization, including, if warranted by the seriousness of the matter, referral to the highest authority that can act in behalf of the organization as determined by applicable law.

(c) If, despite the lawyer's efforts in accordance with paragraph (b), the highest authority that can act on behalf of the organization insists upon action, or a refusal to act, that is clearly a violation of law and is likely to result in substantial injury to the organization, the lawyer may resign in accordance with Rule 1.16.

(d) In dealing with an organization's directors, officers, employees, members, shareholders or other constituents, a lawyer shall explain the identity of the client when it is apparent that the organization's interests are adverse to those of the constituents with whom the lawyer is dealing.

(e) A lawyer representing an organization may also represent any of its directors, officers, employees, members, shareholders or other constituents, subject to the provisions of Rule 1.7. If the organization's consent to the dual representation is required by Rule 1.7, the consent shall be given by an appropriate official of the organization other than the individual who is to be represented or by the shareholders.

Rule 1.14 Client Under a Disability

(a) When a client's ability to make adequately considered decisions in connection with the representation is impaired, whether because of minority, mental disability or for some other reason, the lawyer shall, as far as reasonably possible, maintain a normal client-lawyer relationship with the client.

(b) A lawyer may seek the appointment of a guardian or take other protective action with respect to a client only when the lawyer reasonably believes that the client cannot adequately act in the client's own interest.

Rule 1.15 Safekeeping Property

(a) A lawyer shall hold property of clients or third persons that is in a lawyer's possession in connection with a representation separate from the lawyer's own property. Funds shall be kept in a separate account maintained in the state where the lawyer's office is situated, or elsewhere with the consent of the client or third person. Other property shall be identified as such and appropriately safeguarded. Complete records of such account funds and other property shall be kept by the lawyer and shall be preserved for a period of [five years] after termination of the representation.

(b) Upon receiving funds or other property in which a client or third person has an interest, a lawyer shall promptly notify the client or third person. Except as stated in this rule or otherwise permitted by law or by agreement with the client, a lawyer shall promptly deliver to the client or third person any funds or other property that the client or third person is entitled to receive and, upon request by the client or third person, shall promptly render a full accounting regarding such property.

(c) When in the course of representation a lawyer is in possession of property in which both the lawyer and another person claim interest, the property shall be kept separate by the lawyer until there is an accounting and severance of their interests. If a dispute arises concerning their respective interests, the portion in dispute shall be kept separate by the lawyer until the dispute is resolved.

Rule 1.16 Declining or Terminating Representation

(a) Except as stated in paragraph (c), a lawyer shall not represent a client or, where representation has commenced, shall withdraw from the representation of a client if:

(1) the representation will result in violation of the rules of professional conduct or other law;

(2) the lawyer's physical or mental condition materially impairs the lawyer's ability to represent the client; or

(3) the lawyer is discharged.

(b) Except as stated in paragraph (c), a lawyer may withdraw from representing a client if withdrawal can be accomplished without material adverse effect on the interests of the client, or if:

(1) the client persists in a course of action involving the lawyer's services that the lawyer reasonably believes is criminal or fraudulent;

(2) the client has used the lawyer's services to perpetrate a crime or fraud;

(3) the client insists upon pursuing an objective that the lawyer considers repugnant or imprudent;

(4) the client fails substantially to fulfill an obligation to the lawyer regarding the lawyer's services and has been given reasonable warning that the lawyer will withdraw unless the obligation is fulfilled;

(5) the representation will result in an unreasonable financial burden on the lawyer or has been rendered unreasonably difficult by the client; or

(6) other good cause for withdrawal exists.

(c) When ordered to do so by a tribunal, a lawyer shall continue representation notwithstanding good cause for terminating the representation.

(d) Upon termination of representation, a lawyer shall take steps to the extent reasonably practicable to protect a client's interests, such as giving reasonable notice to the client, allowing time for employment of other counsel, surrendering papers and property to which the client is entitled and refunding any advance payment of fee that has not been earned. The lawyer may retain papers relating to the client to the extent permitted by other law.

Rule 1.17 Sale of Law Practice

A lawyer or a law firm may sell or purchase a law practice, including good will, if the following conditions are satisfied:

(a) The seller ceases to engage in the private practice of law [in the geographic area] [in the jurisdiction] (a jurisdiction may elect either version) in which the practice has been conducted;

(b) The practice is sold as an entirety to another lawyer or law firm;

(c) Actual written notice is given to each of the seller's clients regarding:

    (1) the proposed sale;

    (2) the terms of any proposed change in the fee arrangement authorized by paragraph (d);

    (3) the client's right to retain other counsel or to take possession of the file; and

    (4) the fact that the client's consent to the sale will be presumed if the client does not take any action or does not otherwise object within ninety (90) days of receipt of the notice.

        If a client cannot be given notice, the representative of that client may be transferred to the purchaser only upon entry of an order so authorizing by a court having jurisdiction. The seller may disclose to the court *in camera* information relating to the representation only to the extent necessary to obtain an order authorizing the transfer of a file.

(d) The fees charged clients shall not be increased by reason of the sale. The purchaser may, however, refuse to undertake the representation unless the client consents to pay the purchaser fees at a rate not exceeding the fees charged by the purchaser for rendering substantially similar services prior to the initiation of the purchase negotiations.

Counselor

Rule 2.1 Advisor

In representing a client, a lawyer shall exercise independent professional judgment and render candid advice. In rendering advice, a lawyer may refer not only to law but to other considerations such as moral, economic, social and political factors, that may be relevant to the client's situation.

Rule 2.2 Intermediary

(a) A lawyer may act as intermediary between clients if:

    (1) the lawyer consults with each client concerning the implications of the common representation, including the advantages and risks involved, and the effect on the attorney-client privileges, and obtains each client's consent to the common representation;

    (2) the lawyer reasonably believes that the matter can be resolved on terms compatible with the clients' best interests, that each client will be able to make adequately informed decisions in the matter and that there is little risk of material prejudice to the interests of any of the clients if the contemplated resolution is unsuccessful; and

    (3) the lawyer reasonably believes that the common representation can be undertaken impartially and without improper effect on other responsibilities the lawyer has to any of the clients.

(b) While acting as intermediary, the lawyer shall consult with each client concerning the decisions to be made and the considerations relevant in making them, so that each client can make adequately informed decisions.

(c) A lawyer shall withdraw as intermediary if any of the clients so requests, or if any of the conditions stated in paragraph (a) is no longer satisfied. Upon withdrawal, the lawyer shall not continue to represent any of the clients in the matter that was the subject of the intermediation.

Rule 2.3 Evaluation for Use by Third Persons

(a) A lawyer may undertake an evaluation of a matter affecting a client for the use of someone other than the client if:

   (1) the lawyer reasonably believes that making the evaluation is compatible with other aspects of the lawyer's relationship with the client; and

   (2) the client consents after consultation.

(b) Except as disclosure is required in connection with a report of an evaluation, information relating to the evaluation is otherwise protected by Rule 1.6.

Advocate

Rule 3.1 Meritorious Claims and Contentions

A lawyer shall not bring or defend a proceeding, or assert or controvert an issue therein, unless there is a basis for doing so that is not frivolous, which includes a good faith argument for an extension, modification or reversal of existing law. A lawyer for the defendant in a criminal proceeding, or the respondent in a proceeding that could result in incarceration, may nevertheless so defend the proceeding as to require that every element of the case be established.

Rule 3.2 Expediting Litigation

A lawyer shall make reasonable efforts to expedite litigation consistent with the interests of the client.

Rule 3.3 Candor Toward the Tribunal

(a) A lawyer shall not knowingly:

   (1) make a false statement of material fact or law to a tribunal;

   (2) fail to disclose a material fact to a tribunal when disclosure is necessary to avoid assisting a criminal or fraudulent act by the client;

   (3) fail to disclose to the tribunal legal authority in the controlling jurisdiction known to the lawyer to be directly adverse to the position of the client and not disclosed by opposing counsel; or

   (4) offer evidence that the lawyer knows to be false. If a lawyer has offered material evidence and comes to know of its falsity, the lawyer shall take reasonable remedial measures.

(b) The duties stated in paragraph (a) continue to the conclusion of the proceeding, and apply even if compliance requires disclosure of information otherwise protected by Rule 1.6.

(c) A lawyer may refuse to offer evidence that the lawyer reasonably believes is false.

(d) In an *ex parte* proceeding, a lawyer shall inform the tribunal of all material facts known to the lawyer which will enable the tribunal to make an informed decision, whether or not the facts are adverse.

Rule 3.4 Fairness to Opposing Party and Counsel

A lawyer shall not:

(a) unlawfully obstruct another party's access to evidence or unlawfully alter, destroy or conceal a document or other material having potential evidentiary value. A lawyer shall not counsel or assist another person to do any such act;

(b) falsify evidence, counsel or assist a witness to testify falsely, or offer an inducement to a witness that is prohibited by law;

(c) knowingly disobey an obligation under the rules of a tribunal except for an open refusal based on an assertion that no valid obligation exists;

(d) in pretrial procedure, make a frivolous discovery request or fail to make reasonably diligent effort to comply with a legally proper discovery request by an opposing party;

(e) in trial, allude to any matter that the lawyer does not reasonably believe is relevant or that will not be supported by admissible evidence, assert personal knowledge of facts in issue except when testifying as a witness, or state a personal opinion as to the justness of a cause, the credibility of a witness, the culpability of a civil litigant or the guilt or innocence of an accused; or

(f) request a person other than a client to refrain from voluntarily giving relevant information to another party unless:

    (1) the person is a relative or an employee or other agent of a client; and

    (2) the lawyer reasonably believes that the person's interests will not be adversely affected by refraining from giving such information.

Rule 3.5 Impartiality and Decorum of the Tribunal

A lawyer shall not:

(a) seek to influence a judge, juror, prospective juror or other official by means prohibited by law;

(b) communicate *ex parte* with such a person except as permitted by law; or

(c) engage in conduct intended to disrupt a tribunal.

Rule 3.6 Trial Publicity

(a) A lawyer shall not make an extrajudicial statement that a reasonable person would expect to be disseminated by means of public communication if the lawyer knows or reasonably should know that it will have a substantial likelihood of materially prejudicing an adjudicative proceeding.

(b) A statement referred to in paragraph (a) ordinarily is likely to have such an effect when it refers to a civil matter triable to a jury, a criminal matter, or any other proceeding that could result in incarceration, and the statement relates to:

(1) the character, credibility, reputation or criminal record of a party, suspect in a criminal investigation or witness, or the identity of a witness, or the expected testimony of a party or witness;

(2) in a criminal case or proceeding that could result in incarceration, the possibility of a plea of guilty to the offense or the existence or contents of any confession, admission, or statement given by a defendant or suspect or that person's refusal or failure to make a statement;

(3) the performance or results of any examination or test or the refusal or failure of a person to submit to an examination or test, or the identity or nature of physical evidence expected to be presented;

(4) any opinion as to the guilt or innocence of a defendant or suspect in a criminal case or proceeding that could result in incarceration;

(5) information the lawyer knows or reasonably should know is likely to be inadmissible as evidence in a trial and would if disclosed create a substantial risk of prejudicing an impartial trial; or

(6) the fact that a defendant has been charged with a crime, unless there is included therein a statement explaining that the charge is merely an accusation and that the defendant is presumed innocent until and unless proven guilty.

(c) Notwithstanding paragraphs (a) and (b)(1–5), a lawyer involved in the investigation or litigation of a matter may state without elaboration:

(1) the general nature of the claim or defense;

(2) the information contained in a public record;

(3) that an investigation of the matter is in progress, including the general scope of the investigation, the offense or claim or defense involved and, except when prohibited by law, the identity of the persons involved:

(4) the scheduling or result of any step in litigation;

(5) a request for assistance in obtaining evidence and information necessary thereto;

(6) a warning of danger concerning the behavior of a person involved, when there is reason to believe that there exists the likelihood of substantial harm to an individual or to the public interest; and

(7) in a criminal case:

    (i) the identity, residence, occupation and family status of the accused;

    (ii) if the accused has not been apprehended, information necessary to aid in apprehension of that person;

    (iii) the fact, time and place of arrest; and

    (iv) the identity of investigating and arresting officers or agencies and the length of the investigation.

Rule 3.7 Lawyer as Witness

(a) A lawyer shall not act as advocate at a trial in which the lawyer is likely to be a necessary witness except where:
   (1) the testimony relates to an uncontested issue;
   (2) the testimony relates to the nature and value of legal services rendered in the case; or
   (3) disqualification of the lawyer would work substantial hardship on the client.
(b) A lawyer may act as advocate in a trial in which another lawyer in the lawyer's firm is likely to be called as a witness unless precluded from doing so by Rule 1.7 or Rule 1.9.

Rule 3.8 Special Responsibilities of a Prosecutor

The prosecutor in a criminal case shall:

(a) refrain from prosecuting a charge that the prosecutor knows is not supported by probable cause;
(b) make reasonable efforts to assure that the accused has been advised of the right to, and the procedure for obtaining, counsel and has been given reasonable opportunity to obtain counsel;
(c) not seek to obtain from an unrepresented accused a waiver of important pretrial rights, such as the right to a preliminary hearing;
(d) make timely disclosure to the defense of all evidence or information known to the prosecutor that tends to negate the guilt of the accused or mitigates the offense, and, in connection with sentencing, disclose to the defense and to the tribunal all unprivileged mitigating information known to the prosecutor, except when the prosecutor is relieved of this responsibility by a protective order of the tribunal; and
(e) exercise reasonable care to prevent investigators, law enforcement personnel, employees or other persons assisting or associated with the prosecutor in a criminal case from making an extrajudicial statement that the prosecutor would be prohibited from making under Rule 3.6.
(f) not subpoena a lawyer in a grand jury or other criminal proceeding to present evidence about a past or present client unless:
   (1) the prosecutor reasonably believes:
      (i) the information reasonably sought is not protected from disclosure by an applicable privilege;
      (ii) the evidence sought is essential to the successful completion of an ongoing investigation or prosecution;
      (iii) there is no other feasible alternative to obtain the information; and
   (2) the prosecutor obtains prior judicial approval after an opportunity for an adversarial proceeding.

Rule 3.9 Advocate in Nonadjudicative Proceedings

A lawyer representing a client before a legislative or administrative tribunal in a nonadjudicative proceeding shall disclose that the appearance is in a representative capacity and shall conform to the provisions of Rules 3.3(a) through (c), 3.4(a) through (c), and 3.5.

Transactions with Persons Other Than Clients

Rule 4.1 Truthfulness in Statements to Others

In the course of representing a client a lawyer shall not knowingly:

(a) make a false statement of material fact or law to a third person; or
(b) fail to disclose a material fact to a third person when disclosure is necessary to avoid assisting a criminal or fraudulent act by a client, unless disclosure is prohibited by Rule 1.6.

Rule 4.2 Communication with Person Represented by Counsel

In representing a client, a lawyer shall not communicate about the subject of the representation with a party the lawyer knows to be represented by another lawyer in the matter, unless the lawyer has the consent of the other lawyer or is authorized by law to do so.

Rule 4.3 Dealing with Unrepresented Person

In dealing on behalf of a client with a person who is not represented by counsel, a lawyer shall not state or imply that the lawyer is disinterested. When the lawyer knows or reasonably should know that the unrepresented person misunderstands the lawyer's role in the matter, the lawyer shall make reasonable efforts to correct the misunderstanding.

Rule 4.4 Respect for Rights of Third Persons

In representing a client, a lawyer shall not use means that have no substantial purpose other than to embarrass, delay, or burden a third person, or use methods of obtaining evidence that violate the legal rights of such a person.

Law Firms and Associations

Rule 5.1 Responsibilities of a Partner or Supervisory Lawyer

(a) A partner in a law firm shall make reasonable efforts to ensure that the firm has in effect measures giving reasonable assurance that all lawyers in the firm conform to the Rules of Professional Conduct.
(b) A lawyer having direct supervisory authority over another lawyer shall make reasonable efforts to ensure that the other lawyer conforms to the Rules of Professional Conduct.
(c) A lawyer shall be responsible for another lawyer's violation of the Rules of Professional Conduct if:
    (1) the lawyer orders or, with knowledge of the specific conduct, ratifies the conduct involved; or
    (2) the lawyer is a partner in the law firm in which the other lawyer practices, or has direct supervisory authority over the other lawyer, and knows of the conduct at a time when its consequences can be avoided or mitigated but fails to take reasonable remedial action.

Rule 5.2 Responsibilities of a Subordinate Lawyer

(a) A lawyer is bound by the Rules of Professional Conduct notwithstanding that the lawyer acted at the direction of another person.

(b) A subordinate lawyer does not violate the Rules of Professional Conduct if that lawyer acts in accordance with a supervisory lawyer's reasonable resolution of an arguable question of professional duty.

Rule 5.3 Responsibilities Regarding Nonlawyer Assistants

With respect to a nonlawyer employed or retained by or associated with a lawyer:

(a) a partner in a law firm shall make reasonable efforts to ensure that the firm has in effect measures giving reasonable assurance that the person's conduct is compatible with the professional obligations of the lawyer;

(b) a lawyer having direct supervisory authority over the nonlawyer shall make reasonable efforts to ensure that the person's conduct is compatible with the professional obligations of the lawyer; and

(c) a lawyer shall be responsible for conduct of such a person that would be a violation of the rules of Professional Conduct if engaged in by a lawyer if:

(1) the lawyer orders or, with the knowledge of the specific conduct, ratifies the conduct involved; or

(2) the lawyer is a partner in the law firm in which the person is employed, or has direct supervisory authority over the person, and knows of the conduct at a time when its consequences can be avoided or mitigated but fails to take reasonable remedial action.

Rule 5.4 Professional Independence of a Lawyer

(a) A lawyer or law firm shall not share legal fees with a nonlawyer, except that:

(1) an agreement by a lawyer with the lawyer's firm, partner, or associate may provide for the payment of money, over a reasonable period of time after the lawyer's death, to the lawyer's estate or to one or more specified persons;

(2) a lawyer who purchases the practice of a deceased, disabled, or disappeared lawyer may, pursuant to the provisions of Rule 1.17, pay to the estate or other representative of that lawyer the agreed-upon purchase price; and

(3) a lawyer or law firm may include nonlawyer employees in a compensation or retirement plan, even though the plan is based in whole or in part on a profit-sharing arrangement.

(b) A lawyer shall not form a partnership with a nonlawyer if any of the activities of the partnership consist of the practice of law.

(c) A lawyer shall not permit a person who recommends, employs, or pays the lawyer to render legal services for another to direct or regulate the lawyer's professional judgment in rendering such legal services.

(d) A lawyer shall not practice with or in the form of a professional corporation or association authorized to practice law for a profit, if:

(1) a nonlawyer owns any interest therein, except that a fiduciary representative of the estate of a lawyer may hold the stock or interest of the lawyer for a reasonable time during administration;
(2) a nonlawyer is a corporate director or officer thereof; or
(3) a nonlawyer has the right to direct or control the professional judgment of a lawyer.

Rule 5.5 Unauthorized Practice of Law

A lawyer shall not:

(a) practice law in a jurisdiction where doing so violates the regulation of the legal profession in that jurisdiction; or
(b) assist a person who is not a member of the bar in the performance of activity that constitutes the unauthorized practice of law.

Rule 5.6 Restrictions on Right to Practice

A lawyer shall not participate in offering or making:

(a) a partnership or employment agreement that restricts the right of a lawyer to practice after termination of the relationship, except an agreement concerning benefits upon retirement; or
(b) an agreement in which a restriction on the lawyer's right to practice is part of the settlement of a controversy between private parties.

Public Service

Rule 6.1 Pro Bono Publico Service

A lawyer should render public interest legal service. A lawyer may discharge this responsibility by providing professional services at no fee or a reduced fee to persons of limited means or to public service or charitable groups or organizations, by service in activities for improving the law, the legal system or the legal profession, and by financial support for organizations that provide legal services to persons of limited means.

Rule 6.2 Accepting Appointments

A lawyer shall not seek to avoid appointment by a tribunal to represent a person except for good cause, such as:

(a) representing the client is likely to result in violation of the Rules of Professional Conduct or other law;
(b) representing the client is likely to result in an unreasonable financial burden on the lawyer; or
(c) the client or the cause is so repugnant to the lawyer as to be likely to impair the client-lawyer relationship or the lawyer's ability to represent the client.

Rule 6.3 Membership in Legal Services Organization

A lawyer may serve as a director, officer or member of a legal services organization, apart from the law firm in which the lawyer practices, notwithstanding that the organization serves persons having interests adverse to a client of the lawyer. The lawyer shall not knowingly participate in a decision or action of the organization:

(a) if participating in the decision or action would be incompatible with the lawyer's obligations to a client under rule 1.7; or

(b) where the decision or action could have a material adverse effect on the representation of a client of the organization whose interests are adverse to a client of the lawyer.

Rule 6.4 Law Reform Activities Affecting Client Interests

A lawyer may serve as a director, officer or member of an organization involved in reform of the law or its administration notwithstanding that the reform may affect the interests of a client of the lawyer. When the lawyer knows that the interests of a client may be materially benefitted by a decision in which the lawyer participates, the lawyer shall disclose that fact but need not identify the client.

Information about Legal Services

Rule 7.1 Communications Concerning a Lawyer's Services

A lawyer shall not make a false or misleading communication about the lawyer or the lawyer's services. A communication is false or misleading if it:

(a) contains a material misrepresentation of fact or law, or omits a fact necessary to make the statement considered as a whole not materially misleading;

(b) is likely to create an unjustified expectation about results the lawyer can achieve, or states or implies that the lawyer can achieve results by means that violate the Rules of Professional Conduct or other law; or

(c) compares the lawyer's services with other lawyers' services, unless the comparison can be factually substantiated.

Rule 7.2 Advertising

(a) Subject to the requirements of Rules 7.1 and 7.3, a lawyer may advertise services through public media, such as a telephone directory, legal directory, newspaper or other periodical, outdoor advertising, radio or television, or through written or recorded communication.

(b) A copy or recording of an advertisement or communication shall be kept for two years after its last dissemination along with a record of when and where it was used.

(c) A lawyer shall not give anything of value to a person for recommending the lawyer's services except that a lawyer may

    (1) pay the reasonable costs of advertisements of communications permitted by this Rule;

    (2) pay the usual charges of a not-for-profit lawyer referral service or legal service organization; and

    (3) pay for a law practice in accordance with Rule 1.17.

(d) Any communication made pursuant to this rule shall include the name of at least one lawyer responsible for its content.

Rule 7.3 Direct Contact with Prospective Clients

(a) A lawyer shall not by in-person or live telephone contact solicit professional employment from a prospective client with whom the lawyer has no family or prior professional relationship when a significant motive for the lawyer's doing so is the lawyer's pecuniary gain.

(b) A lawyer shall not solicit professional employment from a prospective client by written or recorded communication or by in-person or telephone contact even when not otherwise prohibited by paragraph (a), if:

    (1) the prospective client has made known to the lawyer a desire not to be solicited by the lawyer; or

    (2) the solicitation involves coercion, duress or harassment.

(c) Every written or recorded communication from a lawyer soliciting professional employment from a prospective client known to be in need of legal services in a particular matter, and with whom the lawyer has no family or prior professional relationship, shall include the words "Advertising Material" on the outside envelope and at the beginning and ending of any recorded communication.

(d) Notwithstanding the prohibitions in paragraph (a), a lawyer may participate with a prepaid or group legal service plan operated by an organization not owned or directed by the lawyer which uses in-person or telephone contact to solicit memberships or subscriptions for the plan from persons who are not known to need legal services in a particular matter covered by the plan.

Rule 7.4 Communication of Fields of Practice

A lawyer may communicate the fact that the lawyer does or does no practice in particular fields of law. A lawyer shall not state or imply that the lawyer is a specialist except as follows:

(a) a lawyer admitted to engage in patent practice before the United States Patent and Trademark Office may use the designation "Patent Attorney" or a substantially similar designation;

(b) a lawyer engaged in Admiralty practice may use the designation "Admiralty," "Proctor in Admiralty" or a substantially similar designation; and

(c) (provisions on designation of specialization of the particular state).

Rule 7.5 Firm Names and Letterheads

(a) A lawyer shall not use a firm name, letterhead or other professional designation that violates Rule 7.1. A trade name may be used by a lawyer in private practice if it does not imply a connection with a government agency or with a public or charitable legal services organization and is not otherwise in violation of Rule 7.1.

(b) A law firm with offices in more than one jurisdiction may use the same name in each jurisdiction, but identification of the lawyers in an office of the firm shall indicate the jurisdictional limitations of those not licensed to practice in the jurisdiction where the office is located.

(c) The name of a lawyer holding a public office shall not be used in the name of a law firm, or in communications on its behalf, during any substantial period in which the lawyer is not actively and regularly practicing with the firm.

(d) Lawyers may state or imply that they practice in a partnership or other organization only when that is the fact.

Maintaining the Integrity of the Profession

Rule 8.1 Bar Admission and Disciplinary Matters

An applicant for admission to the bar, or a lawyer in connection with a bar admission application or in connection with a disciplinary matter, shall not:

(a) knowingly make a false statement of material fact; or

(b) fail to disclose a fact necessary to correct a misapprehension known by the person to have arisen in the matter, or knowingly fail to respond to a lawful demand for information from an admissions or disciplinary authority, except that this rule does not require disclosure of information otherwise protected by Rule 1.6.

Rule 8.2 Judicial and Legal Officials

(a) A lawyer shall not make a statement that the lawyer knows to be false or with reckless disregard as to its truth or falsity concerning the qualifications or integrity of a judge, adjudicatory officer or public legal officer, or of a candidate for election or appointment to judicial or legal office.

(b) A lawyer who is a candidate for judicial office shall comply with the applicable provisions of the Code of Judicial Conduct.

Rule 8.3 Reporting Professional Misconduct

(a) A lawyer having knowledge that another lawyer has committed a violation of the Rules of Professional Conduct that raises a substantial question as to that lawyer's honesty, trustworthiness or fitness as a lawyer in other respects, shall inform the appropriate professional authority.

(b) A lawyer having knowledge that a judge has committed a violation of applicable rules of judicial conduct that raises a substantial question as to the judge's fitness for office shall inform the appropriate authority.

(c) This Rule does not require disclosure of information otherwise protected by Rule 1.6.

Rule 8.4 Misconduct

It is professional misconduct for a lawyer to:

(a) violate or attempt to violate the Rules of Professional Conduct, knowingly assist or induce another to do so, or do so through the acts of another;

(b) commit a criminal act that reflects adversely on the lawyer's honesty, trustworthiness or fitness as a lawyer in other respects;

(c) engage in conduct involving dishonesty, fraud, deceit or misrepresentation;

(d) engage in conduct that is prejudicial to the administration of justice,

(e) state or imply an ability to influence improperly a government agency or official; or

(f) knowingly assist a judge or judicial officer in conduct that is a violation of applicable rules of judicial conduct or other law.

Rule 8.5 Jurisdiction

A lawyer admitted to practice in this jurisdiction is subject to the disciplinary authority of this jurisdiction although engaged in practice elsewhere.

Source

MODEL RULES OF PROFESSIONAL CONDUCT AND CODE OF JUDICIAL CONDUCT, copyright by the American Bar Association, 1989. All rights reserved. Reprinted with permission.

Glossary

Adjudication on the merits: A judgment by the court deciding the issues of an action, precluding that action from being brought again.

Admissible evidence: Evidence that may be presented in court, prescribed by the rules of evidence that it must be relevant, i.e., of consequence to the determination of the action and tending to prove or refute a fact of consequence.

Affidavit: A written statement of facts under oath; frequently supplements a motion.

Alienage jurisdiction: A diversity jurisdiction involving foreign states and their citizens or subjects.

Ancillary jurisdiction: Permits a court to add claims, counterclaims, parties, etc., that it would not have jurisdiction over to a matter it does have jurisdiction over so that all claims between the parties can be finalized at one time.

Arbitration: An alternative dispute resolution process consisting of the submission of a dispute to a neutral decision maker.

Argumentative denials: Denials that state facts suggesting a defense, but in fact are not really defenses.

Assignment: A transfer of rights from one person to another, usually of intangible property.

Attachment: The process of taking property of the defendant debtor by judicial order into the custody of the law for the purpose of satisfying a judgment.

Attorney's work product: The attorney's mental impressions, conclusions, opinions, or legal theories concerning a case; not discoverable.

Automated litigation support: The application of computers to litigation tasks, particularly document storage and retrieval.

Best evidence rule: Rule that allows only the original document or item to be admitted. Exceptions are allowed for practical reasons.

Bill of particulars: A request for the opponent to make an ambiguous pleading more definite and certain.

Billable hours: The time spent on a client's case that can be billed to the client.

Breach of contract: A failure to perform on a promise in a contract without a legal excuse.

Burden of proof: The obligation to prove the allegations; usually falls to the accuser.

Capacity: Requirements of age, competency, etc., for a party to be allowed to sue or be sued.

Cause of action: Statement of the claim upon which relief may be granted in an action.

Chain of custody: The chronological record tracing a piece of evidence to the event that has resulted in the action, proving that it is the item in question.

Circumstantial evidence: Evidence that merely suggests the existence of some other occurrence or thing.

Class action: A suit by or against an entire class (whose members are too numerous for a joinder) represented by one or a few individuals.

Clear and convincing evidence: A higher standard of proof than preponderance of evidence; requires that the matter be shown to be very probable.

Complaint: The formal document used to commence a lawsuit. It identifies the parties and states the cause of action the plaintiff alleges against the defendant.

Concurrent jurisdiction: Two courts having jurisdiction on the same type of case.

Consideration: Something of value exchanged for a promise or act.

Constructive service: Service of process other than direct service, such as through a newspaper of general circulation.

Contingent fee: A fee paid for representation based on a percentage of the award won and allowing for no fee if the plaintiff loses.

Contract: An agreement between two or more parties creating reciprocal obligations to do or not to do something.

Default judgment: Judgment rendered against defendant for the damages specified in the claim without the case going to trial, based on defendant's failure to respond to complaint within time limit.

Demurrer: Allegation by defendant that the complaint does not state a claim upon which relief can be granted; remains in use in only a few states.

Deponent: One who gives testimony under oath recorded by writing or other means.

Deposition: Discovery device where party or witness is questioned under oath by opposing attorney and testimony is recorded.

Direct evidence: Evidence that is directly observable and proves the truth asserted.

Discovery: Devices used by a party in a case to obtain information from the opponent in order to prepare for trial; to prevent trial by ambush.

Diversity of citizenship: Jurisdictional requirement for U.S. District Court requiring parties of a lawsuit to be citizens of different states.

Docket: The calendar of cases or tasks within a case; record for deadline control throughout the course of an action.

Domicile: The true, permanent home.

Due process of law: The attempt to ensure fairness in judicial proceedings where a person may be deprived of life, liberty, or property; guaranteed by the Constitution.

Duty: In tort, due care owed by one person to another.

Enforcement of judgment: The process by which the power of the court is invoked to have a judgment satisfied.

Ethics (professional): Rules of conduct that govern attorneys and serve as guidelines for those who work for them; designed to facilitate fairness and client confidentiality with the system.

Exclusive jurisdiction: Jurisdiction authorizing only one court to handle a specific type of case, e.g., juvenile court.

Execution: The process of carrying out or enforcing a judgment. Some are self-executing; for example, a divorce decree. Other judgments may require further action, either by the court or by public officers.

Exemplary damages: Damages awarded to a plaintiff beyond actual loss as punishment for conduct of defendant that is particularly aggravated. Also called punitive damages.

Exemplified: Authenticated as a true copy, as an official transcript to be used as evidence.

Fact pleading: The requirement that the body of a pleading state in detail the facts in support of each element of the rule of law or claim.

Federal question: Issue that arises directly from the U.S. Constitution or other federal laws.

Findings of fact and conclusions of law: The court's judgment summarizing the key evidence on the elements of the cause of action and the judge's conclusions that form the basis of the judgment.

Garnishee: The third party who is directed to surrender property owed to the judgment debtor to satisfy the judgment.

Garnishment: The process of trying to reach the assets of a judgment debtor which are in the possession of a third party in order to satisfy the debt.

General damages: Those damages that are a natural and direct result of the defendant's wrong, e.g., pain and suffering, humiliation, enjoyment of life.

General jurisdiction: The right to hear all types and subjects of cases rather than just a specific class.

Geographical jurisdiction: The right to hear cases that arise within a specific geographical area.

Good cause: A sufficient reason to provide a legal excuse or justification.

Guardian ad litem: Representative for a party who lacks the legal capacity to sue or be sued; serves for the duration of the action.

Habit: The semiautomatic, repeated response to a specific situation.

Harmless error: An error found to have occurred at the trial court by the appellate court, but insufficient to substantially affect the verdict of the case, and therefore, insufficient to overturn the verdict.

Impeach: In the law of evidence, to prove the testimony of a witness to be invalid.

Indemnification: Where one party insures a second party against loss or damage.

In forma pauperis: "In the manner of a pauper"; permission given to a poor person to sue without liability for costs.

In limine: A motion filed for protection against prejudicial questions and statements at trial.

In rem action: An action involving the attachment of property to resolve claims to the property.

Intangible property: A "right" rather than a physical object, e.g., the right to receive money from an employer.

Interpleader: The joining of those parties that have the same claim against a third party; done to limit the liability of the third party.

Interrogatories: A discovery device using written questions submitted to the opposing party for answers under oath.

Joinder of parties: The uniting of parties making claims or defending against an action as co-plaintiffs or co-defendants.

Joint liability: Liability potentially shared by two parties allowing one party to bring the second party into the lawsuit.

Joint tenancy: Equal ownership of an entire property by two or more individuals. They do not own parts of it, they own the whole property jointly. When one of the joint tenants dies, the property passes to the surviving tenant.

Judgment creditor: The winner in civil cases where money has been awarded.

Judgment debtor: The loser in civil cases where money has been awarded.

Judgment proof: A term describing a party who has no assets with which to pay a judgment.

Judicial notice: Admission of evidence without authentication if it is either a fact commonly known in the territorial jurisdiction of the court, or a fact readily verifiable through undisputed sources.

Jurisdiction: The power of a court to hear and decide the questions of law and/or fact presented by a lawsuit.

Jurisdictional amount: Specific dollar amounts that must be claimed in an action to meet jurisdictional minimums.

Leading question: Question phrased in such a manner as to suggest the desired answer, e.g., "It was raining that night, wasn't it?"

Levy: To seize and sell property of the judgment debtor as specified by the court to satisfy the judgment.

Lien: A claim against property to secure payment of debt.

Limited jurisdiction: Authority to hear cases dealing only with specific subjects; for example, traffic courts can hear only traffic cases.

Lis pendens: Record to notify potential buyers that the plaintiff has asserted a claim against that property in a lawsuit.

Litigation: A lawsuit; in civil law, the process whereby one person sues another, usually for compensation of injuries or other damages caused by the other person.

Long-arm statutes: Statutes designed to give a court personal jurisdiction over out-of-state residents.

Malpractice: Professional negligence or incompetence.

Mandatory injunction: Requirement that the defendant perform or refrain from conduct specified by the court.

Material: Of consequence to the determination of the action.

Med-arb: A combination of mediation and arbitration methods where the matter is first mediated, then any unresolved issue is decided by the same or a different person who serves as an arbitrator.

Mediation: An alternative dispute resolution process incorporating a neutral person (the mediator) who facilitates a mutual resolution of the dispute.

Memorandum of law: Document presenting the legal authority, statutes, and case decisions on a point of law. A formal written argument submitted to the court; often accompanies a motion.

Motion: A request for a court order granting relief to the moving party.

Negligence: "The failure to use such care as a reasonably prudent and careful person would use under similar circumstances *(Black's Law Dictionary)*.

Notice pleading: Abbreviated form of pleading authorized by the Federal Rules of Civil Procedure and parallel state rules.

Order: A directive from a judge requiring some act or restraint from some act in a lawsuit.

Original jurisdiction: The right of a specific court to hear a specific type of action first.

Pendent jurisdiction: Discretionary juristiction that permits a federal court already having jurisdiction over a matter of federal law to hear the state claim if that claim is based on essentially the same facts as the federal claim.

Personal jurisdiction: Jurisdiction over the person; authority to impose a binding judgment on a party, achieved with service of process.

Pleadings: Formal documents filed in a lawsuit that inform all parties of the basis for and defenses to the lawsuit; normally includes the complaint, answer, counterclaim and reply, answer to cross-claim, and third-party complaint and answer.

Postjudgment interrogatory: A method to discover the assets of the judgment debtor through written questions to be answered under oath.

Post-trial deposition: Device used to discover the assets of the judgment debtor through oral examination under oath.

Post-trial request for production of documents: Method to discover the assets of the judgment debtor by obtaining documents that will help in locating the assets of the debtor.

Praecipe: A request that a writ be issued in which the details of the writ are set out in the request, e.g., a praecipe for a summons.

Precedent: The published ruling of a higher court that becomes the rule of law for it and all lower courts under its jurisdiction.

Preponderance of the evidence: Evidence that is more convincing to the trier than the opposing evidence; meets the requirement for the burden of proof in civil cases.

Presumption: A mechanism that allows a jury to presume a fact is true based on indirect evidence when it might be awkward or difficult to prove by direct evidence. For example, mailing a letter creates the presumption it was received. A presumption stands unless it is rebutted.

Prima facie case: The minimum amount of proof, absent any contradictory evidence, required to prevail.

Privileged communication: Communication that is confidential and inadmissible as evidence because of its social utility; i.e., husband-wife, attorney-client, etc.

Probative value of evidence: The degree to which evidence tends to prove or actually proves something.

Pro-bono case: Case in which free legal service is provided to a person who cannot afford to pay for legal help.

Procedural law: Law that defines the rules and steps governing the course of a lawsuit.

Professional ethics: For attorneys, the rules of conduct that govern the practice of law.

Prohibitory injunction: Order that informs a defendant to refrain from a specific course of conduct.

Proof beyond a reasonable doubt: Proof that is so strong it excludes any other reasonable hypothesis or explanation—almost a certainty.

Proximate cause: In tort law, the cause and effect relationship that must be established to prove that the conduct in question was the substantial cause of the injury in question.

Quasi in rem action: A type of jurisdiction that authorizes a court to seize the defendant's property to satisfy a claim when the property is in the court's jurisdiction but the defendant is not. Some jurisdictions require the court to have at least constructive service (usually publication) on the defendant.

Real party in interest: The person who has been injured or has caused the injury. A party to a lawsuit must be a real party in interest.

Receivership: The state of having the assets of a business or an individual placed under the control of a court-appointed receiver whose job it is to protect those assets to pay a debt.

Release: A document executed by the plaintiff as claimant that frees the defendant from any further obligations or liability stemming from the incident causing damages in return for consideration.

Relevance: The quality required for evidence to be admissible in court; must be of consequence to the determination of the action and tending to prove or refute a fact of consequence.

Removal jurisdiction: The ability of federal district courts to remove cases from state courts to federal court having jurisdiction to hear the case.

Replevin: An action whereby a person having right to property can recover that property from one who wrongfully retains possession of the property.

Res gestae statements: Statements that are present-sense impressions, excited utterances, or about then-existing mental, emotional, or physical conditions.

Routine: (Custom) The equivalent of "habit" for organizations.

Sequestered: Isolated in a room apart, as witnesses not party to an action are separated from the trial to ensure their testimony will not be influenced by the testimony of others.

Service of process: Official notification to the defendant of the lawsuit and of his or her need to respond; delivery of a copy of the summons, complaint, writs, and other documents to another party.

Settlement: The process in which both sides review the strengths and weaknesses of a case and mutually agree on how to resolve the case.

Settlement agreement: A contract to resolve a lawsuit that sets out all the terms, conditions, and obligations of the parties, including how the action will be dismissed.

Settlement précis: A brief presentation of the client's case designed to persuade the opposing party to settle the case on terms satisfactory to the client.

Special damages: Damages that are incurred because of the defendant's wrong and the actual result of the injury, but not the necessary result, e.g., medical bills, lost wages, property loss. Special damages must be specifically pleaded.

Statute of limitations: Law stating the time limit in which an action must be filed. If the time limit is not met, the defendant has a defense to the action, and the case will be dismissed.

Stipulation: Formal agreement between opposing parties to a lawsuit regarding matters pertinent to the lawsuit, e.g., a stipulation to admit certain evidence without testimony.

Subject matter jurisdiction: Authority to hear cases based on the topic (subject) of those cases, e.g., diversity cases involving more that $50,000 is one area of subject matter jurisdiction of the federal district courts.

Subpoena: Document pursuant to a court order that commands a person to appear to testify.

Subpoena duces tecum: Document pursuant to a court order that commands a person to appear with certain documents or tangible things.

Substantive law: The law that defines the duties owed by one person to another; the substantive rules of law as opposed to the procedural rules.

Summary trial: A nonbinding, abbreviated trial before a summary jury to see if, in fact, either side's case merits a real trial; encourages settlement of especially large cases.

Summons: Document informing the defendant of the time to appear and defend.

Supersedeas bond: Bond filed by the judgment debtor to secure the amount of the judgment while the execution of that judgment is stayed pending posttrial motions.

Supplementary proceedings: Proceedings utilized to acquire information about the judgment debtor to enforce a judgment; for example, post-trial depositions.

Tangible property: Property having a physical form that can be seen or touched.

Tickler system: A system for regular calendaring of important deadlines and reminders.

Tort: A civil as opposed to a criminal wrong for which the injured party can sue the wrongdoer for compensation.

Venue: "Neighborhood"; the geographical area in which a court with jurisdiction can hear a case; distinct from jurisdiction.

Veracity: Truthfulness.

Voir dire: The questioning and selection of prospective jurors by judge and possibly attorneys; the process of choosing an impartial jury.

With prejudice: The dismissal of a case with the understanding that it cannot be brought again.

Without prejudice: The dismissal of a case with the understanding that it can be brought again.

Writ of certiorari: A discretionary writ that allows an appellate court to take only cases that, in its opinion, have sufficient significance to warrant its attention.

Writ of execution: A device used to enforce a judgment for money.

Index